UPON

EVERYTHING.

DISCLAIMER

This book is intended as a historical curiosity. Medical advice should be taken only under instruction from a medical practitioner. Language used within the text reflects the attitudes and usage common at the time the book was written. In no way does it reflect the attitude of the publishers.

This edition published in 2020 by Arcturus Publishing Limited
26/27 Bickels Yard, 151–153 Bermondsey Street,
London SE1 3HA

AD006865UK

Printed in the UK

CONTENTS

INTRODUCTION

'Enquire Within upon Everything' was the book that inspired the internet. Tim Berners-Lee, inventor of the World Wide Web, called his prototype ENQUIRE, noting that it was 'short for "Enquire Within upon Everything", a musty old book of Victorian advice I noticed as a child in my parents' house outside London. With its title suggestive of magic, the book served as a portal to a world of information, everything from how to remove clothing stains to tips on investing money'. And a portal to a world of information it was.

The book was a domestic bible in Victorian and post-Victorian homes. Times were changing quickly and 'Enquire Within' could be relied upon to provide insight on all manner of topics. First published in 1857, the book was continually reprinted and updated as new household gadgets and gizmos were invented and others became obsolete. It was so popular that in the preface to the 96th edition the publisher extolls its virtues with the grandest of praise and hyperbole: 'there is scarcely a spot reached by English civilization, to which this book has not found its way, receiving the most cordial welcome and winning the warmest praise'. By its 113th edition, published in 1923, it had sold 1.5 million copies and it remained in print in some form or another as late as 1994, almost 140 years after its initial publication.

To a modern reader the book is a fascinating step back in time to a bygone era with tips on topics wide and varied. Some remain practical and useful, such as how to grow and maintain a kitchen garden, while other entries may pique a reader's interest as they wonder how often such advice was needed, for instance what to do in the case of hydrophobia in dogs. Others offer fascinating insights into the everyday running of the Victorian household, with entries on the treatment of servants, the renting of property, and the rearing and 'management' of children. And others still, will induce a smile or chuckle with their quaint charm, such as entry 818 'the telephone' which guides householders in the use and function of this new technology. Either way, it is a treasure trove of historic information.

This edition is a facsimile of the 100th edition, which was first published in 1903, and contains many of the quirks of the original. Where possible all idiosyncrasies, errors and archaic spellings have been preserved with the intention of retaining as much of the charm of the original as possible. This means you may notice inconsistencies of spelling, seemingly erroneous spellings – 'dandriff' not dandruff for example – grammar that is unusual to modern eyes, and even missing articles, for example the book skips from 534 straight to 536.

One of the most fascinating quirks is perhaps the ordering of the entries within the book which is at best haphazard, and at worst bewildering: the original advert stated that 'enquirers are referred to the index' when seeking the answer to a specific query, and it is easy to see why. When reading it today the most fun can be found in delving in at a random point and enjoying whichever curious miscellany lies there as you enquire within.

EDITOR'S PREFACE

IF there be any among my Readers who, having turned over the pages of "ENQUIRE WITHIN," have hastily pronounced them to be confused and ill-arranged, let them at once refer to THE INDEX, at page 423, and for ever hold their peace.

The Index is, to the vast congregation of useful hints and recipes that fill the pages of this volume, what the DIRECTORY is to the great aggregation of houses and people in London.

No one, being a stranger to London, would run about asking for "MR. SMITH." But, remembering the Christian name and the profession of the individual wanted, he would turn to the DIRECTORY, and trace him out.

Like a house, every paragraph in "ENQUIRE WITHIN" has its number —and the INDEX is the DIRECTORY which will explain what Facts, Hints, and Instructions *inhabit* that number.

For, if it be not a misnomer, we are prompted to say that "ENQUIRE WITHIN" is *peopled* with hundreds of ladies and gentlemen, who have contributed something to its store of useful information. There they are, waiting to be questioned, and ready to reply, just as certainly as where, in the window of a dwelling, you see a paper directing you to "ENQUIRE WITHIN," some one is there to answer you.

HOUSEKEEPERS of experience live at Nos. 1, 32, 360, 1087 ; old DR. KITCHINER lives at 46 ; CAPTAIN CRAWLEY is to be found at 79 and 2183 ; the well-known MRS. WARREN lives at 2032 ; MISS ACTON at 1154 ; DR. FRANKLIN at 796 and 1577 ; MRS. HITCHING at 185 ; DR. GALEN at 1382 ; MR. BANTING at 1384 ; DR. WILSON PHILIP at 1377 ; MR. WITHERING at 1970 ; MRS. FRY at 1530 ; DR. ERASMUS WILSON at 1342 ; DR. BLAIR at 1529 ; DR. SAMUEL JOHNSON at 856 ; DEAN SWIFT at 874 ; M. SOYER at 863 ; and DR. CLARK at 512. In addition to these and many more, a DOCTOR lives at 482 ; a GARDENER at 205 ; a SCHOOL-MASTER at 184 ; HOUSE AGENTS at 236 and 1787 ; a FIREMAN at 791 ; a BUTCHER at 29 ; a DANCING-MASTER at 141 ; a NATURALIST at 1962 ; a DYER at 1282 ;

a MODELLER at 1980 ; a PROFESSED COOK at 846 ; a PHILANTHROPIST at
788 ; a LAWYER at 1759 ; a SURGEON at 687 ; a CHESS PLAYER at 75 ; a
CHEMIST at 508 ; a BREWER at 1713 ; a LAWN TENNIS PLAYER at 2204 ;
a HOMŒOPATHIC PRACTITIONER at 654 ; a WOOD-STAINER at 1273 ; CON-
FECTIONERS at 1155 and other numbers ; a POULTRY KEEPER at 1953 ; a
METEOROLOGIST at 797 ; PHILOSOPHERS at 805 and 1404 ; a PRACTICAL
ECONOMIST at 1578 ; a BAKER at 825 ; MASTERS OF THE CEREMONIES at
1455 and 1605 ; a BIRD FANCIER at 1935 ; a WASHERWOMAN at 1305 ;
an ANALYTICAL CHEMIST at 1584 ; an ACCOUNTANT at 2224 ; and so on.

Well ! there they live—always at home. Knock at their doors—
ENQUIRE WITHIN. NO FEES TO PAY ! !

Much care has been taken in selecting the information that is given,
and, as is amply shown by the above list, so many kind and competent
friends have lent a hand in the production of this volume that it is
impossible to turn to any page without at once being reminded of the
generous friend who abides there.

To some extent, though in a far less degree, assistance has been
rendered by the authors of many useful and popular works, for which
due acknowledgment must be made. Chief among these works are
Dr. Kitchiner's "COOKS' ORACLE," "THE SHOPKEEPER'S GUIDE," "THE
WIFE'S OWN COOKERY," "THE PRACTICAL HOUSEWIFE," "THE FAMILY
SAVE-ALL," and many of the volumes of the "REASON WHY" series.

Lastly, as in everyday life it is found necessary at times to make a
thorough inspection of house and home, and to carry out requisite
repairs, alterations, and additions, this has been done in the recent
issues, and more particularly in the present *enlarged edition* of "ENQUIRE
WITHIN," to which some hundreds of paragraphs have been added,
while others have been remodelled and revised in accordance with the
progress of the times in which we live. Care, however, has been taken
to alter nothing that needed no alteration, so that, practically, this
Popular Favourite is still the old "ENQUIRE WITHIN" ; improved, it is
true, but in no way so changed as to place it beyond the recognition
of those to whom it has been a BOOK OF CONSTANT REFERENCE since its
first appearance.

ENQUIRE WITHIN

UPON

EVERYTHING.

1. TO CHOOSE ARTICLES OF FOOD.—Nothing is more important in the affairs of housekeeping than the choice of wholesome food. Apropos to this is an amusing conundrum which is as follows :—"A man went to market and bought *two* fish. When he reached home he found there were *three !* How was this !" The answer is—"He had two mackerel, and one *smelt !*" Those who envy him his bargain need not care about the following rules ; but to others they will be valuable :—

2. Mackerel must be perfectly fresh, or it is a very indifferent fish ; it will neither bear carriage, nor being kept many hours out of the water. The firmness of the flesh, the clearness of the eyes, and the general brightness of its appearance, must be the criteria of fresh mackerel, as they are of all other fish. If the gills are not red the fish is stale.

3. Turbot, and all flat white fish, is rigid and firm when fresh ; the under side should be of a rich cream colour. When out of season, or too long kept, this becomes a bluish white, and the flesh soft and flaccid. A clear bright eye in any fish is also a mark of its being fresh and good.

4. Cod is known to be fresh by the rigidity of the muscles (or flesh), the redness of the gills, and clearness of the eyes. Crimping much improves

this fish. **Haddocks** are judged in the same way as cod. Dr. Kitchiner, in his *Cooks' Oracle*, considers that both cod and turbot are in better condition for eating after they have been kept for a day than when quite fresh.

5. Salmon.—The flavour and excellence of this fish depend upon its freshness and the shortness of time since it was caught ; for no method can completely preserve the delicate flavour that salmon has when just taken out of the water. When perfectly fresh there is a creamy substance between the flakes. A great deal of what is brought to London has been packed in ice, and comes from the Scotch and Irish rivers, and, though perfectly fresh, is not quite equal to salmon from English streams. **Trout** may be selected in the same way as salmon.

6. Herring and Sprats should be eaten when very fresh ; and, like mackerel, will not remain good many hours after they are caught. But they are excellent, especially for breakfast relishes, either salted, split, dried, and peppered, or pickled. **Mackerel** are very good when prepared in any of these ways.

7. Fresh-Water Fish.—The remarks as to firmness and clear fresh eyes apply to this variety of fish, of which there are carp, tench, pike, perch, &c.

8. Lobsters, recently caught, have, always some remains of muscular action in the claws, which may be excited by pressing the eyes with the finger ; when this cannot be produced, the lobster must have been too long kept. When boiled, the tail preserves its elasticity if fresh, but loses it as soon as it becomes stale. The heaviest lobsters are the best ; when light they are watery and poor. Hen lobsters may generally be known by the spawn, or by the breadth of the "flap."

9. Crab and Crayfish must be chosen by observations similar to those given above in the choice of lobsters. Crabs have an agreeable smell when fresh. When buying shell-fish, care should be taken that their weight is not due to wateriness.

10. Prawns and Shrimps, when fresh, are firm and crisp.

11. Oysters.—If fresh, the shell is firmly closed ; when the shells of oysters are open, they are dead, and unfit for food. The small-shelled oysters, the Byfleet, Colchester, and Milford, are the finest in flavour. Larger kinds, as the Torbay oysters, are generally considered only fit for stewing and sauces, and as an addition to rump-steak puddings and pies, though some persons prefer them to the smaller oysters, even when not cooked.

12. Beef.—The grain of ox beef, when good, is loose, the meat red, and the fat of a creamy white colour. When fine and well-fed, the flesh is inter-grained or marbled with fat. If the fat is yellowish, the meat is either inferior, or the beast has been fed on oil-cake. Cow beef, on the contrary, has a closer grain and whiter fat, but the meat is scarcely as red as that of ox beef. Inferior beef, which is meat obtained from ill-fed animals, or from those which have become too old for food, may be known by a hard, skinny fat, a dark red lean, and in old animals, a line of horny texture running through the meat of the ribs. When meat rises up quickly, after being pressed by the finger, it may be considered as being the flesh of an animal which was in its prime ; but when the dent made by pressure returns slowly, or remains visible, the animal had probably passed its prime, and the meat consequently must be of inferior quality.

13. Veal should be delicately white, though it is often juicy and well-flavoured when rather dark in colour. Butchers, it is said, bleed calves purposely before killing them, with a view to make the flesh white, but this also makes it dry and flavourless. On examining the loin, if the fat enveloping the kidney be white and firm-looking, the meat will probably be prime and recently killed. Veal will not keep so long as an older meat, especially in hot or damp weather : when going, the fat becomes soft and moist, the meat flabby and spotted, and somewhat porous like sponge. Large, overgrown veal is inferior to small, delicate, yet fat veal. The meat is best when the calf is from three to four months old. The fillet of a cow-calf is known by the udder attached to it, and by the softness of the skin ; it is preferable to the veal of a bull-calf.

14. Mutton.—The meat should be firm and close in grain, and red in colour, the fat white and firm. Mutton is in its prime when the sheep is between four and five years old : but at the present time it is rarely to be had above three, and is often only two years old. If too young, the flesh feels tender when pinched ; if too old, on being pinched it wrinkles up, and so remains. In young mutton, the fat readily separates ; in old, it is held together by strings of skin. In sheep diseased of the rot, the flesh is very pale-coloured, the fat inclining to yellow ; the meat appears loose from the bone, and, if squeezed, drops of water ooze out from the grains ; after cooking, the meat drops clean away from the bones. Wether mutton is preferred to that of the ewe ; it may be known by the lump of fat on the inside of the thigh. The price of New Zealand mutton averages about 4*d.* per lb. less than English.

15. Lamb.—This meat will not keep long after it is killed. The large vein in the neck is bluish in colour when the fore quarter is fresh, green when it is becoming stale. In the hind quarter, if not recently killed, the fat of the kidney will have a slight smell, and the knuckle will have lost its firmness. New Zealand lamb costs about 4*d.* per lb. less than English.

16. Pork.—When good, the rind is thin, smooth, and cool to the touch ; when changing, from being too long killed, it becomes flaccid and clammy. Enlarged glands, called kernels, in the fat, mark an ill-fed or diseased pig.

17. Bacon should have a thin rind, and the fat should be firm and tinged red by the curing ; the flesh should be of a clear red, without intermixture of yellow, and it should firmly adhere to the bone. To judge the state of a ham, plunge a knife into it to the bone ; on drawing it back, if particles of meat adhere to it, or if the smell is disagreeable, the curing has not been effectual, and the ham is not good ; it should, in such a state, be immediately cooked. In buying a ham, a short thick one is to be preferred to one long and thin. Of English hams, Yorkshire, Westmoreland, and Hampshire are most esteemed ; of foreign, the Westphalian. The bacon and "sugar cured" hams now imported in large quantities from Canada and the United States are often both cheap and good.

18. Sucking Pigs are best at about three weeks old, and they should be cooked as soon as possible after being killed.

19. Venison.—When good, the fat is clear, bright, and of considerable thickness. To know when it is necessary to cook it, a knife must be plunged into the haunch ; and from the smell the cook must determine whether to dress

it at once, or to keep it a little longer. It should be dusted with ginger and pepper, as this will keep away the flies.

20. Turkey.—In choosing poultry, the age of the bird is the chief point to be attended to. An old turkey has rough and reddish legs ; a young one smooth and black. Fresh killed, the eyes are full and clear, the feet moist, and the wattles bright red. When it has been kept too long, the parts about the vent have a greenish appearance.

21. Common Domestic Fowls, when young, have the legs and combs smooth ; when old these parts are rough, and on the breast long hairs are found when the feathers are plucked off ; these hairs must be removed by singeing. Fowls and chickens should be plump on the breast, fat on the back, and white-legged.

22. Geese.—The bills and feet are red when old, yellow when young. Fresh killed, the feet are pliable, but they get stiff when the birds are kept too long. Geese are called green when they are only two or three months old. If over a twelvemonth old they are not fit to bring to table.

23. Ducks.—Choose them with supple feet and hard plump breasts. Tame ducks have yellow feet, wild ones red.

24. Pigeons are very indifferent food when they are kept too long. Suppleness of the feet shows them to be young ; the flesh is flaccid when they are getting bad from keeping. Tame pigeons are larger than wild pigeons, but not so large as the wood-pigeon.

25. Hares and Rabbits, when old, have the haunches thick, the ears dry and tough, and the claws blunt and ragged. A young hare has claws smooth and sharp, ears that easily tear, and a narrow cleft in the lip. A leveret is distinguished from a hare by a knob or small bone near the foot.

26. Partridges, when young, have yellowish legs and dark-coloured bills.

If held up by the lower bill, it should break. Old partridges are very indifferent eating.

27. Pheasants.—Tbe spurs of old birds are long and pointed, in young birds short and round.

28. Woodcocks and Snipes, when old, have the feet thick and hard ; when these are soft and tender they are both young and fresh killed. When their bills become moist, and their throats muddy, they have been too long killed. (See FOOD IN SEASON, Pars. 32—44.)

29. NAMES AND SITUATIONS OF THE VARIOUS JOINTS.

30. MEATS.—In different parts of the kingdom the method of cutting up carcases varies. That which we describe below is the most general, and is known as the English method.

i. Beef.—*Fore Quarter.*—Fore rib (five ribs) ; middle rib (four ribs) ; chuck (three ribs, for second quality of steak). Shoulder piece (top of fore leg) ; brisket (lower or belly part of the ribs, salted, for boiling) ; clod (fore shoulder blade) ; neck ; shin (below the shoulder, used for stewing) ; cheek. *Hind Quarter.*—Sirloin ; rump (the finest part for steaks) ; aitch-bone (the boiling piece) —these are the three divisions of the upper part of the quarter ; buttock (prime boiling piece), and mouse-buttock, which divide the thigh ; veiny piece, joining the buttock ; thick flank (primest boiling piece) and thin flank (belly pieces), and leg. The sirloin and rump of both sides form a baron. *Beef is in season all the year ; best in winter.*

ii. Scottish Mode of Division.—This gives a greater variety of pieces for boiling, but is scarcely so economical as the English plan, which also affords better steaks and joints for roasting. The names of pieces in the Scotch plan, not found in the English, are the hough, or hind leg ; the nineholes, or English buttock ; the large and small runner, taken from the rib and chuck pieces of the

English plan ; the shoulder-lyer, the English shoulder, but cut differently ; the spare-rib or fore-eye, the sticking piece, &c. The Scotch also cut mutton differently.

iii. Mutton.—Shoulder ; breast (the belly) ; over which are the loin (chump, or tail end) ; loin (best end) ; neck (best end) ; neck (scrag end) ; leg ; haunch, or leg and chump end of loin ; and head. A chine is two necks ; a saddle, two loins. *Mutton is best in winter, spring, and autumn.*

iv. Lamb is cut into fore quarter and hind quarter ; saddle ; loin ; neck ; breast ; leg ; and shoulder. *Grass lamb is in season from Easter to Michaelmas : house lamb from Christmas to Lady-day.*

v. Pork is cut into leg, hand or shoulder ; hind loin ; fore loin ; belly-part ; spare-rib, or neck ; and head. *Pork is in season nearly all the year round, but is better relished in winter than in summer.*

vi. Veal is cut into neck (scrag end) ; neck (best end) ; loin (best end) ; loin (chump, or tail end) ; fillet (upper part of hind leg) ; hind knuckle, which joins the fillet ; knuckle of fore leg ; blade (bone of shoulder) ; breast (best end) ; and breast (brisket end). *Veal is always in season, but dear in winter and spring.*

vii Venison is cut into haunch ; neck ; shoulder ; and breast. *Doe venison is best in January, October, November, and December, and buck venison in June, July, August, and September.*

31. RELATIVE ECONOMY OF THE JOINTS OF BEEF.

i. The Round is, in large families, one of the most profitable parts owing to its comparative freedom from bone ; it is usually boiled, and is generally sold at a lower price than the sirloin and ribs. It is sometimes divided downwards, close to the bone ; one side being known as the *top side*, and the other as the *silver side*. Either of these parts is as good roasted as boiled.

ii. **The Brisket** is always less in price than the roasting parts. It is not so economical a part as the round, having more bone with it, and more fat. Where there are children, very fat joints are not desirable, being often disagreeable to them, and sometimes prejudicial, especially if they have a dislike to fat. This joint also requires more cooking than many others ; that is to say, it requires a double allowance of time to be given for simmering it ; it will, when served, be hard and scarcely digestible if no more time be allowed to simmer it than that which is sufficient for other joints and meats. Joints cooked in a boiler or saucepan should always be *simmered*, that is to say, boiled as slowly as possible. Meat boiled fast, or "at a gallop," as the phrase goes, is always tough and tasteless. The brisket is excellent when stewed ; and when cooked fresh (*i. e.* unsalted) an excellent stock for soup may be extracted from it, and yet the meat will serve as well for dinner.

iii. **The Edge-bone, or Aitch-bone**, is not considered to be a very economical joint, the bone being large in proportion to the meat ; but the greater part of it, at least, is as good as that of any prime part. On account of the quantity of bone in it, it is sold at a cheaper rate than the best joints. It may be roasted or boiled.

iv. **The Rump** is the part of which the butcher makes great profit, by selling it in the form of steaks, but the whole of it may be purchased as a joint, and at the price of other prime parts. It may be turned to good account in producing many excellent dishes. If salted, it is simply boiled ; if used unsalted, it is generally stewed.

v. **The Veiny Piece** is sold at a moderate price per pound ; but, if hung for a day or two, it is very good and very profitable. Where there are a number of servants and children to have an early dinner, this part of beef will be found desirable.

vi. **The Leg and Shin** afford excellent stock for soup ; and, if not reduced too much, the meat taken from the bones may be served as a stew with vegetables ; or it may be seasoned, pounded with butter, and potted ; or, chopped very fine, and seasoned with herbs, and bound together by egg and bread-crumbs, it may be fried in balls, or in the form of large eggs, and served with a gravy made with a few spoonfuls of the soup.

The proverb says, "*Of all the Fowls of the air*, commend me to the *shin of beef*, for there's marrow for the master, meat for the mistress, gristles for the servants,—and bones for the dogs."— *Kitchiner.*

vii. **The Sirloin and the Ribs** are the roasting parts of beef, and these bear in all places the highest price. The more profitable of these two joints at a family table is the ribs. The bones, if removed from the beef before it is roasted, are useful in making stock for soup. When boned, the meat of the ribs is often rolled up in the shape of a small round or fillet, tied with string, and roasted ; and this is the best way of using it, as it enables the carver to distribute equally the upper part of the meat with the fatter parts, at the lower end of the bones. The tenderest part for frying or boiling, and one most extensively used in France, is the *entrecôte*. It is the undercut of the sirloin, either cooked whole or cut into *filets*.

viii. **Ox-tail** is much esteemed for purposes of soup ; so also is the cheek. The **Tongue** is highly esteemed. The **Heart**, stuffed with veal stuffing, roasted, and served hot, with red currant jelly as an accompaniment, is a palatable dish.

ix. **Calves' Heads** are very useful for various dishes ; so also are their Knuckles, Feet, Heart, &c.

32. FOOD IN SEASON.

There is an old maxim, "A place for everything, and everything in its place." To which may be added another, "A season for everything, and everything in season."

33. IN SEASON IN JANUARY.

[Fish, Poultry, &c., whose names are distinguished by *Italics* in each month's "Food in Season," are to be had in the highest perfection during the month.]

i. Fish.—Barbel, bloaters, brill, carp, cod, crabs, cray-fish, dabs, *dace*, eels, flounders, *haddocks*, herrings, lampreys, ling, lobsters, mussels, oysters, perch, pike, plaice, prawns, Dutch salmon, shrimps, skate, smelts, soles, sprats, sturgeon, *tench*, thornback, turbot, *whiting*.

ii. Meat.—Beef, house-lamb, mutton, pork, veal, and doe venison.

iii. Poultry and Game.—Capons, chickens, ducks, wild ducks, fowls, geese, *hares*, larks, moor-game, partridges, pheasants, pigeons (tame), pullets, *rabbits*, snipes, turkeys (hen), widgeon (and wild-fowl generally), woodcocks.

iv. Vegetables.—Artichokes (globe and Jerusalem), aubergines, beet, broccoli (white and purple), Brussels sprouts, cabbage, cardoons, carrots, cauliflowers, celery, chervil, colewort, cresses, endive, garlic, herbs (dry), kale (Scotch), leeks, lettuces, mint (dry), mustard, onions, parsley, parsnips, potatoes, rape, rosemary, sage, salsify, Savoy cabbages, sea-kale, scorzonera, shalots, skirrets, sorrel, spinach (winter), tarragon, thyme, turnips, turnip-tops, tomatoes.

v. Forced Vegetables.—Asparagus, cucumbers, mushrooms, sea-kale.

vi. Fruit.—Almonds. Apples: Golden pippin, golden russet, Kentish pippin, nonpareil, winter pearmain. Pears: Bergamot d'Hollande, Bon Chrétien, Chaumontel, Colmar, winter beurré. Grapes: English and foreign. Chestnuts, medlars, oranges, walnuts, filbert nuts. Foreign preserves, dried fruits (as almonds and raisins), French plums, prunes, figs and dates.

34. IN SEASON IN FEBRUARY.

i. Fish.—Barbel, brill (inferior), carp, cockles, cod, crabs, cray-fish, daw, dace, eels, flounders, gurnets, haddocks, halibut, herrings, lampreys, ling, lobsters, mussels, oysters, perch, pike, plaice, prawns, red mullets, salmon, shrimps, skate, smelts, soles, sprats, sturgeon, tench, thornback, turbot, whiting.

ii. Meat.—Beef, house-lamb, mutton, pork, veal.

iii. Poultry and Game.—Capons, chickens, ducklings, geese, guinea-fowls, hares, partridges, pheasants (until the 15th), pigeons (tame and wild), rabbits (tame), snipes, turkeys, turkey poults, wild ducks (not in full season), woodcocks (wild birds generally).

iv. Vegetables.—Beet, broccoli (white and purple), Brussels sprouts, cabbage, cardoons, carrots, celery, chervil, colewort, cresses, endive, garlic, herbs (dry), Jerusalem artichokes, leeks, lettuces, mint (dry), mushrooms, new potatoes (Malta and Teneriffe), onions, parsnips, parsley, potatoes, radish, rape, rosemary, sage, salsify, Savoys, scorzonera, shalots, skirrets, sorrel, spinach, sprouts, tarragon, thyme, tomatoes, turnips, winter savoury.

v. Forced Vegetables.—Asparagus, cucumbers, mushrooms, sea-kale, &c.

vi. Fruit—Apples: Golden pippin, golden russet, Holland pippin, Kentish pippin, nonpareil, Wheeler's russet, winter pearmain. Bananas, chestnuts, oranges. Pears: Bergamot, winter Bon Chrétien, winter Russelet.

35. IN SEASON IN MARCH.

i. Fish.—Barbel, brill (inferior), carp (until 15th), cockles, cod, conger-eels, crabs, dabs, dory, eels, flounders, herrings, ling, lobsters, mullets, mussels, oysters, perch (till 15th), pike (till 15th), plaice, prawns, salmon, shrimps, skate, smelts, soles, sprats, sturgeon, turbot, tench (till 15th), and whiting.

ii. **Meat.**—Beef, house-lamb, mutton, pork, veal.

iii. **Poultry and Game.**—Capons, chickens, ducklings, fowls, geese, leverets, pigeons, rabbits, snipes, turkeys, woodcocks and wild-fowl (till 15th).

iv. **Vegetables.**—Artichokes (Jerusalem), beet, broccoli (white and purple), Brussels sprouts, cabbage, cardoons, carrots, celery, chervil, colewort, cresses, endive, garlic, herbs (dry), kale (sea and Scotch), lettuces, mint, mushrooms, mustard, onions, parsley, parsnips, potatoes, rape, rosemary, sage, Savoys, shalots, sorrel, spinach, tarragon, thyme, turnips, turnip-tops.

v. **Forced Vegetables.**—Asparagus, French beans, cucumbers, and rhubarb.

vi. **Fruit.**—Apples: Golden russet, Holland pippin, Kentish pippin, nonpareil, Norfolk beefing, Wheeler's russet. Chestnuts, oranges. Pears: Bergamot, Chaumontel, winter Bon Chrétien. *Forced*: Strawberries.

36. IN SEASON IN APRIL.

i. **Fish.**—Bloaters, brill (inferior), cockles, conger-eels, *crabs*, dabs, dory, eels, flounders, halibut, ling, *lobsters*, mackerel, mullets, mussels, oysters, *prawns*, plaice, *salmon* (rather scarce and dear), scallops, shrimps, *skate*, smelts, soles, sprats, sturgeon, trout, turbot, whitebait, whiting.

ii. **Meat.**—Beef, grass-lamb, house-lamb, mutton, pork, veal.

iii. **Poultry and Game.**—Capons, chickens, ducklings, fowls, goslings, leverets, pigeons, pullets, rabbits, turkey poults, wood-pigeons.

iv. **Vegetables.**—Artichokes, asparagus, broccoli, cabbages, cauliowers, carrots (new), chervil, colewort, cucumbers, endive, fennel, herbs of all sorts, lettuce, onions, parsley, parsnips, peas, potatoes (new, Malta and Teneriffe), radishes, sea-

kale, sorrel, spinach, small salad, tarragon, turnip-radishes, turnip-tops, and rhubarb.

v. **Fruit.**—Apples: Golden russet, nonpareil, Wheeler's russet. Nuts, oranges. Pears: Bergamot, Bon Chrétien, Carmelite. Bananas. *Forced:* Apricots, cherries, strawberries.

37. IN SEASON IN MAY.

i. **Fish.**—Bass, brill, bloaters, conger-eels, *crabs*, cray-fish, dabs, dace, dory, eels, flounders, gurnets, haddock, hake, halibut, ling, *lobsters*, mackerel, mullet, plaice, *prawns, salmon*, scallops, shrimps, *skate*, smelts, soles, sturgeon, trout, turbot, whitebait, whiting.

ii. **Meat.**—Beef, grass-lamb, house-lamb, mutton, pork, veal.

iii. **Poultry and Game.**—Capons, chickens, ducklings, fowls, goslings, leverets, pigeons, pullets, rabbits, wood-pigeons.

iv. **Vegetables.**—Angelica, artichokes, asparagus, balm, kidney-beans, beetroot, cabbage, carrots, cauliflowers, celeriac, chervil, cucumbers, eschalots, endive, fennel, garlic, herbs of all sorts, horseradish, leeks, lettuce, mint, mushrooms, onions, parsley, peas, new potatoes, radishes, rhubarb, salad of all sorts, sea-kale, sorrel, spinach, turnips.

v. **Fruit.**—Apples: Golden russet, winter russet. Bananas, brazils, May-duke cherries, currants, figs, gooseberries, melons, oranges, Spanish nuts. Pears: L'amozette, winter-green. *Forced:* Apricots, grapes, peaches, pines, strawberries.

38. IN SEASON IN JUNE.

i. **Fish.**—Carp (after 15th), conger-eels, crabs, cray-fish, dabs (after 15th), dory, eels, flounders, gurnets, haddocks, ling, *lobsters*, mackerel, mullet, perch (after 16th), pike (after 15th), plaice, *prawns, salmon, salmon-trout, skate*, smelts, soles, sturgeon (after 15th), trout, turbot, whitebait, whiting.

ii. **Meat.**—Beef, *grass-lamb*, house-lamb, mutton, pork, veal, buck venison.

iii. **Poultry and Game.**—Chickens, ducklings, fowls, geese, leverets, pigeons, plovers, pullets, rabbits, turkey poults, wheat-ears, wood-pigeons.

iv. **Vegetables.**—Angelica, artichokes, asparagus, beetroot, beans (French, kidney, and Windsor), white beet, cabbage, carrots, cauliflowers, celeriac, chervil, cucumbers, endive, herbs of all sorts, leeks, lettuce, mustard and cress, onions, peas, potatoes, radishes, salad of all sorts, spinach, turnips, vegetable marrow.

v. **For Drying.**—Burnet, mint, tarragon, lemon thyme.

vi. **Fruit.**—Almonds. Apples: Quarrenden, stone pippin, golden russet. Apricots, bananas. Cherries: May-duke, bigaroon, white-heart. Currants, gooseberries, melons. Pears: Winter-green. Raspberries, strawberries. *Forced:* Grapes, nectarines, peaches, pines.

39. IN SEASON IN JULY.

i. **Fish.**—Bass, bloaters, brill, carp, conger-eels, *crabs*, cray-fish, dabs, dory, eels, flounders, gurnets, haddocks, hake, herrings (end of month), ling, *lobsters*, *mackerel*, mullet, perch, pike, plaice, *prawns*, salmon, sea bream, skate, soles, tench, thornback, trout, whitebait, and whiting.

ii. **Meat.**—Beef, *grass-lamb*, mutton, veal, buck venison.

iii. **Poultry and Game.**— Capons, *chickens*, ducks, fowls, *green geese*, leverets, pigeons, plovers, quails, rabbits, turkey poults, wheat-ears, *wild pigeons*, wild ducks (flappers), wild rabbits.

iv. **Vegetables.**—Artichokes, asparagus, balm, beans (French, kidney, scarlet, and Windsor), beetroot, cabbages, carrots, cauliflowers, celery, chervil, cucumbers, endive, French beans (end of month), herbs of all sorts, lettuces, mushrooms, peas, potatoes, radishes, salads of all sorts, salsify, scarlet runners, scorzonera, sorrel, spinach, turnips.

v. **For Drying.**—Knotted marjoram, mushrooms, winter savoury.

vi. **For Pickling.**—French beans, red cabbage, cauliflowers, garlic, gherkins, nasturtiums, onions.

vii. **Fruit.**—Apples: Codlin, jennetting, Margaret, summer pearmain, summer pippin, quarrenden. Apricots, cherries (black-heart), currants, plums, greengages, gooseberries, melons, nectarines, peaches. Pears: Catherine, green-chisel, jargonelle. Pineapples, raspberries, strawberries.

40. IN SEASON IN AUGUST.

i. **Fish.**—Bass, barbel, bloaters, brill, carp, conger-eels, crabs, crayfish, dabs, *dace*, eels, flounders, gurnets, haddocks, herrings, lobsters, mullet, oysters (after 4th), *perch*, *pike*, plaice, *prawns*, salmon, skate, soles, tench, thornback, *turbot*, whiting, whitebait.

ii. **Meat.**—Beef, grass-lamb, mutton, veal, buck venison.

iii. **Poultry and Game.**—Blackcock and grey hen, capercailzie (after 20th), capons, chickens, ducks, fowls, *green geese*, grouse (from 12th), hares (after 1st), leverets, pigeons, plovers, ptarmigan (after 20th), rabbits, turkeys, turkey poults, wheat-ears, wild ducks, wild pigeons, wild rabbits.

iv. **Vegetables.**—Artichokes, beans (French, kidney scarlet, and Windsor). white beet, carrots, cauliflowers, celery, cucumbers, endive, French beans, pot herbs of all sorts, leeks, lettuces, mushrooms, onions, peas, potatoes, radishes, salad of all sorts, salsify, scorzonera, shalots, spinach, turnips.

v. **For Drying.**—Basil, sage, thyme.

vi. **For Pickling.**—Red cabbage, capsicums, chilies, tomatoes, walnuts.

vii. **Fruit.**—Apples: Codlin, summer pearmain, summer pippin. Apricots, bananas. Brazils, cherries, currants, figs, filberts, gooseberries, grapes, greengages, melons, mulberries, nectarines, peaches. Pears: Jargonelle, summer, Bon Chrétien, Windsor. Pines, plums, raspberries, Alpine strawberries, Spanish nuts.

41. IN SEASON IN SEPTEMBER.

i. **Fish.**—Barbel, bass, bloaters, brill, carp, cockles, cod, conger-eels, crabs, **dace**, eels, flounders, gurnets, haddocks, hake, herrings, lobsters, mackerel, mullet, mussels, *oysters*, *perch*, *pike*, plaice, prawns, salmon (till 7th), shrimps, soles, tench, thornback, trout (till 7th), turbot, whiting.

ii. **Meat.**—Beef, mutton, pork, veal, buck venison.

iii. **Poultry and Game.**—Black-cock, capons, chickens, ducks, fowls, *green geese, grouse, hares,* larks, leverets, *partridges* (commence on 1st), pigeons, plovers, rabbits, *teal,* turkeys, turkey poults, wheat-ears, *wild ducks,* wild pigeons, wild rabbits, and wild-fowl generally.

iv. **Vegetables.**—Artichokes, Jerusalem artichokes, beans (French and scarlet), cabbages, capsicums, carrots, cauliflowers, celery, cucumbers, endive, eschalots, herbs of all sorts, leeks, lettuces, mushrooms, onions, parsnips, peas, potatoes, radishes, salad of all sorts, turnips.

v. **Fruit.**—Apples: Golden nob, pearmain, golden rennet. Bananas, brazils, cob-nuts, cherries (Morella), damsons, figs, filberts. Grapes: Muscadine, Frontignac, red and black Hamburg, Malmsey. Hazel nuts, lemons, medlars, melons, peaches. Pears: Bergamot, brown beurré. Pineapples, plums, quinces, strawberries, walnuts.

42. IN SEASON IN OCTOBER.

i. **Fish.**—Barbel, bloaters, brill, carp, cockles, cod, conger-eels, crabs, *dace, dory,* eels, gudgeon, haddocks, *hake,* halibut, herrings, lobsters, mussels, oysters, perch, *pike,* prawns, shrimps, smelts, soles, tench, thornback, turbot, whiting.

ii. **Meat.**—Beef, mutton, pork, veal, doe venison.

iii. **Poultry and Game.**—Capons, capercailzie, chickens, dotterel, ducks, fowls, green geese, grouse, hares, larks, moor-game, partridges, *pheasants* (after 1st), pigeons, ptarmigan, rabbits, snipes, teal, turkey, wheat-ears, widgeon, wild ducks, wild pigeons, wild rabbits, woodcocks, and wild-fowl generally.

iv. **Vegetables.**—Artichokes, Jerusalem artichokes, broccoli, cabbages, carrots, cauliflowers, celery, coleworts, endive, French beans, herbs of all sorts, leeks, onions, parsnips, peas, potatoes, radishes, salad, Savoys, scarlet runners, scorzonera, skirrets, shalots, spinach (winter), tomatoes, truffles, turnips, vegetable marrows.

v. **Fruit.**—Apples: Pearmain, golden pippin, golden rennet, royal russet. Bananas, brazils, black and white bullace, cobnuts, cranberries, damsons, late figs. Almonds, filberts, hazel nuts, waluts, grapes, lemons, medlars, nectarines. Peaches: Old Newington, October. Pears: Bergamot, beurré, Chaumontel, Bon Chrétien, swan's-egg. Quinces, services, walnuts.

43. IN SEASON IN NOVEMBER.

i. **Fish.**—Barbel, bloaters, brill, turbot, carp, cockles, cod, crabs, crayfish, *dace, dory,* eels, flounders, gudgeons, gurnets, haddocks, *hake,* halibut, herrings, ling, lobsters, mackerel (scarce), mullet (red), mussels, oysters, perch, *pike,* plaice, prawns, Dutch salmon, shrimps, skate, smelts, soles, sprats (from the 9th), tench, thornback, turbot, whiting.

ii. **Meat.**—Beef, house-lamb, mutton, pork, veal, doe venison.

iii. **Poultry and Game.**—Capons, chickens, dotterel, ducks, fowls, *geese, grouse, hares,* larks, partridges, pheasants, pigeons, quails, rabbits, *snipes, teal,* turkey, wheat-ears, widgeon, wild ducks, *woodcocks,* and wild-fowl generally.

iv. **Vegetables.**—Jerusalem artichokes, beetroot, borecole, broccoli,

Brussels sprouts, cabbages, cardoons, carrots, cauliflowers, celery, chervil, coleworts, endive, herbs of all sorts, leeks, lettuces, onions, parsnips, potatoes, salad, Savoys, scorzonera, skirrets, shalots, spinach, tomatoes, turnips, turnip-tops.

v. Fruit.—Almonds. Apples: Holland pippin, golden pippin, Kentish pippin, nonpareil, winter pearmain, Wheeler's russets. Bananas, brazils, bullaces, chestnuts, filberts, hazel nuts, walnuts. Grapes, medlars, melons (water), oranges (Tangerine). Pears: Bergamot, Chaumontel, Bon Chrétien.

44. IN SEASON IN DECEMBER.

i. Fish.—Barbel, bloats, brill, turbot, carp, cockles, *cod*, crabs, dab, *dory*, eels, gudgeon, gurnets, haddocks, hake, halibut, herrings, *ling*, lobsters, mullet, mussels, oysters, perch, pike, plaice, ruff, salmon, shrimps, *skate*, smelts, soles, sprats, sturgeon, *tench*, turbot, whitings.

ii. Meat.—Beef, house-lamb, mutton, pork, veal, doe venison.

iii. Poultry and Game.—Black game and capercailzie (till 20th). Capons, chickens, ducks, fowls, geese, grouse (till 18th), guinea-fowl, hares, larks, partridges, pea-fowl, pheasants, pigeons, rabbits, snipes, teal, turkeys, wheat-ears, widgeon, wild ducks, woodcocks, wild-fowl generally.

iv. Vegetables.—Jerusalem artichokes, beetroot, borecole, white and purple broccoli, Brussels sprouts, cabbages, cardoons, carrots, celery, endive, herbs of all sorts, leeks, lettuces, onions, parsnips, potatoes, radishes, rhubarb, salad, Savoys, scorzonera, skirrets, shalots, spinach, truffles, turnips, *forced* asparagus.

v. Fruit.—Almonds. Apples: Golden pippin, nonpareil, winter pearmain, golden russet, Newtown pippins. Bananas, chestnuts, filberts, hazel nuts, walnuts. Almeria grapes, medlars, oranges. Pears: Bergeunot, beurré d'hiver.

45. DRYING HERBS.

45. DRYING HERBS.—Fresh herbs are preferable to dried ones, but as they cannot always be obtained, it is most important to dry herbs at the proper seasons :—*Basil* is in a fit state for drying about the middle of August. *Burnet* in June, July, and August, *Chervil* in May, June, and July. *Elder Flowers* in May, June, and July. *Fennel* in May, June, and July. *Knotted Marjoram* during July. *Lemon Thyme* end of July and through August. *Mint*, end of June and July. *Orange Flowers*, May, June, and July. *Parsley*, May, June, and July. *Sage*, August and September. *Summer Savoury*, end of July and August. *Tarragon*, June, July, and August. *Thyme*, end of July and August. *Winter Savoury*, end of July and August.

These herbs always at hand will be a great aid to the cook. Herbs should be gathered on a dry day ; they should be immediately well cleansed, and dried by the heat of a stove or Dutch oven. The leaves should then be picked off, pounded and sifted, put into stoppered bottles, labelled, and put away for use. Those who are unable or may not take the trouble to dry herbs, can obtain them prepared for use in bottles at the greengrocers.

46. DR. KITCHINER'S RULES FOR MARKETING.

46. DR. KITCHINER'S RULES FOR MARKETING.—The best rule for marketing is to pay ready money for everything, *and to deal with the most respectable tradesmen* in your neighbourhood. If you leave it to their integrity to supply you with a good article at the fair market price, you will be supplied with better provisions, and at as reasonable a rate as those *bargain-hunters* who trot *"around, around, around about"* a market till they are trapped to buy some *unchewable* old poultry, *tough* tup mutton, *stringy* cow beef, or *stale* fish, at a very little less than the price of prime and proper food. With *savings* like these they toddle home in triumph, cackling all the way, like a goose that has got ankle-deep into good luck. All the skill of the most accomplished cook will avail nothing unless she is furnished with prime provisions. The best way to procure these is to deal with shops of established character : you may appear to pay, perhaps, ten *per cent*. more than you would were you to deal with those who pretend to sell cheap, but you would be much more than in that proportion better served. Every trade has its tricks and deceptions ; those who follow them can deceive you if they please, and they are too apt to do so if you provoke the exercise of their over-reaching talent. Challenge them to a game at "*Catch who can*," by entirely relying on your own judgment, and you will soon find that nothing but very long experience can make you equal to the combat of marketing to the utmost advantage. If you think a tradesman has imposed upon you, never use a second word, if the first will not do, nor drop the least hint of an imposition ; the only method to induce him to make an abatement is the hope of future favours ; pay the demand, and deal with the gentleman no more ; but do not let him see that you are displeased, or as soon as you are out of sight your reputation will suffer as much as your pocket has. Before you go to market, look over your larder, and consider well what things are wanting—especially on a Saturday. No well-regulated family can suffer a disorderly caterer to be jumping in and out to make purchases on a Sunday morning. You will be enabled to manage much better if you will make out a bill-of-fare for the week on the Saturday before : for example, for a family of half-a-dozen—

Sunday—Roast beef and pudding.
Monday—Fowl, what was left of pudding fried, or warmed in the Dutch oven.
Tuesday—Calf's head, apple pie.
Wednesday—Leg of mutton.
Thursday—Ditto broiled or hashed, and pancakes
Friday—Fish, pudding.
Saturday—Fish, or eggs and bacon.

It is an excellent plan to have certain things on certain days. When your butcher or poulterer knows what you will want, he has a better chance of doing his best for you ; and never think of ordering beef for roasting except for Sunday. When you order meat, poultry, or fish, tell the tradesman when you intend to dress it : he will then have it in his power to serve you with provision that will do him credit, which the finest meat, &c., in the world will never do, unless it has been kept a proper time to be ripe and tender.—Kitchiner's *Cook's Oracle* 56th Thousand. 5*s*, Houlston & Sons.

47. SOCIAL EVENINGS.—Much enjoyment, and in some cases great benefit, might be obtained, at very little trouble or expense, if a few congenial friends arranged to meet and spend an evening together once a week for reading, discussion, music, games, or any other amusement mutually agreed on.

We suggest a few simple rules that may be useful to any one wishing to try the experiment and start a friendly social circle and thus bring about more constant, easy, intercourse amongst friends, the writer feeling convinced that society is equally beneficial and requisite—in fact, that mankind in seclusion, like the sword in the scabbard, often loses polish, and gradually rusts.

RULE I. That meetings be held weekly in rotation at each member's house.

RULE II. That such meetings commnence at eight and end before twelve.

RULE III. That only light refreshments shall be provided, such as sandwiches, sausage rolls, cakes, tea and coffee, &c.

RULE IV. That members make a point of attending each meeting unless unavoidably prevented.

48. EVENING PASTIMES.

Among the innocent recreations of the fireside, there are few more commendable and practicable than those afforded by what are severally termed Acrostics, Anagrams, Arithmorems, Charades, Conundrums, Cryptographs, Enigmas, Hidden Words, Logogriphs, Puzzles, Rebuses, Riddles, Transpositions, &c. Of these there are such a variety, that they are suited to every capacity ; and they present this additional attraction, that ingenuity may be exercised in the *invention* of them, as well as in their solution. Many persons who have become noted for their literate compositions may date the origin of their success to the time when they attempted the composition of a trifling enigma or charade.

49. ACROSTICS.—The acrostic is a short poem in which the first letters of each line, read in their order, form a name, word, or sentence. The word comes from the Greek *akron*, at the point or end, and *stichos*, order or line. The acrostic was formerly in vogue for valentine and love verses. When employed as a riddle it is called a *Rebus*, which *see*.

50. ACROSTICS (Double).— This very fashionable riddle is a double Rebus, the initial and final letters of a word or words selected making two names or two words. The usual plan is to first suggest the foundation words, and then to describe the separate words, whose initials and finals furnish the answer to the question. Thus :—

A Party to charm the young and erratic—
But likely to frighten the old and rheumatic.
1　The carriage in which the fair visitants came :
2　A very old tribe with a very old name ;
3　A brave Prince of Wales free from scandal or shame.
The answer is Picnic.

1 P	Phaeton	N
2 I	Iceni	I
3 C	Caradoc	C

Sometimes the Double Acrostic is in prose, as in this brief example : A Briton supports his wig, his grandmother, his comfort, and his country-

women. The answer is. Beef—Beer : *Bob, Eve, Ease, Fair.*

51. ACROSTICS (Triple) are formed on the same plan, three names being indicated by the initial, central, and final letters of the selected words.

52. ANAGRAMS (from *ana*, backwards, and *gramma*, a letter) are formed by the transposition of the letters of words or sentences, or names of persons, so as to produce a word, sentence, or verse, of pertinent or of widely different meaning. They are very difficult to discover, but are exceedingly striking when good. The following are some of the most remarkable :—

Words	*Transpositions*
Astronomers	No more stars.
Catalogues	Got as a clue.
Elegant	Neat leg.
Impatient	Tim in a pet.
Immediately	I met my Delia.
Masquerade	Queer as mad.
Matrimony	Into my arm.
Melodrama	Made moral
Midshipman	Mind his map.
Old England	Golden-land.
Parishioners	I hire parsons.
Parliament	Partial men.
Penitentiary	Nay I repent it
Presbyterian	Best in prayer.
Radical Reform	Rare mad frolic
Revolution	To love ruin.
Sir Robert Peel	Terrible poser.
Sweetheart	There we sat.
Telegraphs	Great helps.

53. ARITHMOREMS.—This class of riddle is of recent introduction. The Arithmorem is made by substituting figures in a part of the word indicated for Roman numerals. The nature of the riddle—from the Greek *arithmon*, number, and the Latin *remanere*, back again—will be easily seen from the following example, which also forms a double acrostic :—

H　51 and a *tub*—a fine large fish.
A　twice 50 and *gore*—a sprightly movement in music.
R　5 and *be*—a part of speech.
U　551 and *as an a*—a Spanish province.

To   201 and *ran*—a stupefying drug.
R   102 and *ni*—an acid.
OU 250 and *paa*— a Mexican town.
The   answer   is   *Havanna Tobacco*.
*Halibut, Allegro, Verb, Andalusia,
Narcotic, Nitric, Acapulco.*

54. CHARADES are compositions, poetical or otherwise, founded upon words, each syllable of which constitutes a noun, the whole of each word constituting another noun of a somewhat diiferent meaning from those supplied by its separate syllables. Words which fully answer these conditions are the best for the purposes of charades ; though many other words are employed. In writing, the first syllable is termed "*My first*," the second syllable "*My second*," and the complete word "*My whole*." The following is an example of a Poetical Charade :—

The breath of the morning is sweet ;
  The earth is bespangled with flowers,
And buds in a countless array
  Have oped at the touch of the showers.
The birds, whose glad voices are ever
  A music delightful to hear,
Seem to welcome the joy of the morning,
  As the hour of the bridal draws near.
What is that which now steals on my *first*,
  Like a sound from the dreamland of love,
And seems wand'ring the valleys among,
  That they may the nuptials approve ?
'Tis a sound which my *second* explains,
  And it comes from a sacred abode,
And it merrily trills as the villagers throng
  To greet the fair bride on her road.
How meek is her dress, how befitting a bride
  So beautiful, spotless, and pure !
When she weareth *my second*, oh, long may it be
  Ere her heart shall a sorrow endure.
See the glittering gem that shines forth from her hair—
  'Tis my *whole*, which a good father gave :
'Twas worn by her mother with honour before—
  But *she* sleeps in peace in her grave.
'Twas her earnest request, as she bade them adieu,
  That when her dear daughter the altar drew near,

She should wear the same gem that her mother had worn
  When she as a bride full of promise stood there.

The answer is *Ear-ring*. The bells *ring*, the sound steals upon the *ear*, and the bride wears an *ear-ring*. Charades may be sentimental or humorous, in poetry or prose ; they may also be *acted*, and in this way afford considerable amusement.

55.   CHARADES   (ACTED).—A drawing-room with folded doors is the best for the purpose. Various household appliances are employed to fit up something like a stage, and to supply the fitting scenes. Characters dressed in costumes made up of handkerchiefs, coats, shawls, table-covers, &c., come on and perform an extempore play, founded upon the parts of a word, and its *whole*, as indicated already. For instance, the events explained in the poem given might be *acted*—glasses might be rung for bells—something might be said in the course of the dialogues about the sound of the bells being delightful to the *ear* ; there might be a dance of the villagers, in which a *ring* might be formed ; a wedding might be performed ; and so on : but for *acting charades* there are many better words, because *Earring* could with difficulty be *represented* without at once betraying the meaning. There is a little work entitled *Philosophy and Mirth united by Pen and Pencil*, and another work, *Our Charades ; and How we Played Them*,[1] by Jean Francis, which supply a large number of these Charades. But the following is the most extensive list of words ever published upon which Charades may be founded :—

56. WORDS for Acting or Written Charades :—

Ac-cent	Aid-less	Al-tar
Acci-dent	Air-pump	Ale-house

---

1 *Philosophy and Mirth, united by Pen and Pencil*, 1s.
  Our Charades ; and How we Played Them, by Jean Francis. 1s.
  Both published by Houlston and Sons, Paternoster Square, London, E.C.

Ann-ounce	But-ton	Fire-man	Ham-let	Ill-bred	Life-guard
A-pex	Cab-in	Fire-pan	Ham-mock	Ill-nature	Like-wise
Arch-angel	Can-did	Fire-ship	Hand-cuff	Ill-usage	Live-long
Arm-let	Can-ton	Fire-work	Hang-man	Imp-lore	Load-stone
Art-less	Care-ful	Fir-kin	Hap-pen	In-action	Log-book
Ass-ail	Car-pet	Fish-hook	Hard-ship	In-born	Log-wood
Ba-boon	Car-rot	Flag-rant	Hard-ware	In-crease	Loop-hole
Back-bite	Cart-ridge	Flip-pant	Harts-horn	In-justice	Lord-ship
Back-slide	Cash-ier	Flood-gate	Head-land	Ink-ling	Love-sick
Bag-dad	Chair-man	Fond-ling	Head-less	In-land	Low-land
Bag-gage	Chamber-maid	Foot-ball	Head-long	In-mate	Luck-less
Bag-pipe	Cheer-ful	Foot-man	Head-stone	In-no-cent	Luke-warm
Bail-able	Cheer-less	Foot-pad	Head-strong	In-sane	Ma-caw
Bale-ful	Christ-mas	Foot-step	Hear-say	In-spirit	Mad-cap
Band-age	Church-yard	Foot-stool	Heart-less	In-tent	Mad-house
Band-box	Clans-men	For-age	Heart-sick	Inter-meddle	Mad-man
Bane-ful	Clerk-ship	For-bear	Heart-string	Inter-sect	Mag-pie
Bar-bed	Cob-web	For-bid	Hedge-hog	Inter-view	Main-mast
Bar-gain	Cock-pit	Found-ling	Heir-less	In-valid	Main-sail
Bar-rack	Cod-ing	Fox-glove	Heir-loom	In-vent	Main-spring
Bar-row	Coin-age	Free-hold	Hell-hound	In-vest	Mam-moth
Bat-ten	Con-fined	Free-ling	Hell-kite	In-ward	Man-age
Beard-less	Con-firm	Free-stone	Hence-forth	Ire-ful	Man-date
Bed-lam	Con-form	Fret-work	Hen-roost	Iron-mould	Marks-man
Be-head	Con-tent	Fri-day	Herb-age	I-sing-lass	Mar-row
Bid-den	Con-test	Friend-ship	Herds-man	Jac(k)o-bite	Mass-acre
Bird-lime	Con-tract	Frost-bite	Her-self	Joyful	Match-less
Birth-right	Con-verse	Fur-long	Hid-den	Joy-less	May-game
Black-guard	Cork-screw	Gain-say	High-land	Justice-ship	Meat-man
Black-smith	Count-less	Gang-way	High-way	Key-stone	Mess-mate
Blame-less	Court-ship	Glow-worm	Hind-most	Kid-nap	Mis-chance
Block-head	Crab-bed	Glut-ton	Hoar-frost	King-craft	Mis-chief
Boat-man	Cross-bow	God-child	Hob-goblin	King-fisher	Mis-count
Book-worm	Cur-tail	God-daughter	Hogs-head	Kins-man	Mis-deed
Boot-jack	Cut-lass	God-father	Home-bred	Kit-ten	Mis-judge
Bound-less	Cut-throat	God-mother	Honey-bag	Knight-hood	Mis-quote
Bow-ling	Dark-some	God-son	Honey-comb	Know-ledge	Mis-take
Brace-let	Day-break	Gold-finch	Honey-moon	Lace-man	Monks-hood
Brain-less	Death-watch	Gold-smith	Honey-suckle	Lady-bird	Moon-beam
Break-fast	Dog-ma	Goose-berry	Hood-wink	Lady-ship	Moon-light
Breath-less	Dol-phin	Grand-father	Horse-back	Lamp-black	Muf-fin
Brick-bat	Don-key	Grate-ful	Horse-shoe	Land-lady	Name-sake
Brick-dust	Drink-able	Grave-stone	Host-age	Land-lord	Nan-keen
Bride-groom	Drug-get	Green-finch	Hot-bed	Land-mark	Nap-kin
Bride-cake	Duck-ling	Grey-hound	Hot-house	Land-scape	Neck-cloth
Brim-stone	Ear-ring	Grim-ace	Hot-spur	Land-tax	Neck-lace
Broad-cloth	Earth-quake	Grind-stone	Hounds-ditch	Lap-dog	Nest-ling
Broad-side	Ear-wig	Ground-plot	Hour-glass	Lap-pet	News-paper
Broad-sword	False-hood	Ground-sell	House-hold	Laud-able	Nick-name
Brow-beat	Fan-atic	Guard-ship	House-maid	Law-giver	Night-cap
Bug-bear	Fare-well	Gun-powder	House-wife	Law-suit	Night-gown
Bull-dog	Far-thing	Had-dock	Hum-drum	Lay-man	Night-mare
Bull-rush	Fear-less	Hail-stone	Hump-back	Leap-frog	Night-watch
Bump-kin	Field-fare	Hail-storm	Hurri-cane	Leap-year	Nine-fold
Buoy-ant	Fire-lock	Half-penny	Idol	Lee-ward	Noon-tide

North-star
North-ward
Nose-gay
Not-able
Not-ice
No-where
Nut-gall
Nut-meg
Oak-apple
Oat-cake
Oat-meal
Off-end
Oil-man
O-men
On-set
O-pen
O-pinion
Out-act
Out-bid
Out-cast
Out-cry
Out-do
Out-fit
Out-grow
Out-law
Out-line
Out-live
Out-rage
Out-ride
Out-run
Out-sail
Out-shine
Out-side
Out-spread
Out-stare
Out-stretch
Out-talk
Out-ward
Out-weigh
Out-wit
Out-work
Out-worn
Over-act
Over-awe
Over-bear
Over-board
Over-boil
Over-burden
Over-cast
Over-charge
Over-cloud
Over-come
Over-do
Over-due
Over-feed

Over-flow
Over-grown
Over-head
Over-hear
Over-heard
Over-joy
Over-lay
Over-leap
Over-load
Over-look
Over-match
Over-right
Over-pass
Over-pay
Over-plus
Over-poise
Over-power
Over-press
Over-rate
Over-reach
Over-ripe
Over-rule
Over-run
Over-see
Over-seer
Over-set
Over-shadow
Over-shoe
Over-shoot
Over-sight
Over-size
Over-sleep
Over-spread
Over-stock
Over-strain
Over-sway
Over-swell
Over-take
Over-throw
Over-took
Over-value
Over-work
Our-selves
Ox-gall
Ox-lip
Pack-age
Pack-cloth
Pad-dock
Pad-lock
Pain-ful
Pain-less
Pal-ace
Pal-ate
Pal-let
Pan-cake

Pa-pa
Par-able
Pa-rent
Pa-ring
Par-snip
Par-son
Par-took
Part-ridge
Pass-able
Pass-over
Pas-time
Patch-work
Pa-tent
Path-way
Pat-ten
Peace-able
Pea-cock
Pear-led
Peer-age
Peer-less
Pen-knife
Pen-man
Pen-man-ship
Per-jury
Pert-in-a-city
Pick-lock
Pick-pocket
Pie-bald
Pike-staff
Pil-age
Pi-lot
Pin-cushion
Pine-apple
Pip-kin
Pitch-fork
Pit-men
Plain-tiff
Play-fellow
Play-house
Play-mate
Play-wright
Plough-man
Plough-share
Pole-cat
Pol-lute
Pop-gun
Pop-in-jay
Port-able
Port-hole
Post-age
Post-chaise
Post-date
Post-house
Post-man
Post-office

Pot-ash
Pot-hook
Pound-age
Prim-rose
Prior-ship
Prop-a-gate
Punch-bowl
Quad-rant
Quench-less
Quick-lime
Quick-sand
Quick-set
Quick-silver
Rain-bow
Ram-part
Ran-sack
Rap-a-city
Rasp-berry
Rattle-snake
Red-breast
Red-den
Rid-dance
Ring-leader
Ring-let
Ring-tail
Ring-worm
Rolling-pin
Rose-water
Rot-ten
Round-about
Round-house
Run-a-gate
Rush-light
Safe-guard
Sal-low
Sand-stone
Sat-in
Sat-ire
Sauce-box
Sauce-pan
Saw-dust
Saw-pit
Scare-crow
Scarf-skin
Scar-let
Scot-free
Screech-owl
Sea-born
Sea-calf
Sea-coal
Sea-faring
Sea-girt
Sea-gull
Sea-maid
Sea-man

Seam-less
Seam-stress
Sea-nymph
Sea-piece
Sea-port
Sea-sick
Sea-son
Sea-ward
Second-hand
Seed-cake
Seed-ling
Seed-pearl
Seeds-man
Seed-time
Sex-tile
Sex-ton
Shame-less
Sham-rock
Shape-less
Sharp-set
Sheep-cot
Sheep-shearing
Sheep-walk
Sheet-anchor
Shell-fish
Shift-less
Ship-board
Ship-wreck
Shirt-less
Shoe-string
Shop-board
Shop-man
Shore-less
Short-hand
Short-lived
Shot-free
Shoulder-belt
Shrove-tide
Side-board
Side-long
Side-saddle
Side-ways
Sight-less
Silk-weaver
Silk-worm
Silver-smith
Sin-less
Six-fold
Skim-milk
Skip-jack
Sky-lark
Sky-light
Slap-dash
Sleeve-less
Slip-shod

Slip-slop
Slope-wise
Slow-worm
Snip-pet
Snip-snap
Snow-ball
Snow-drop
Snuff-box
Sod-den
So-lace
So-lo
Sol-vent
Some-body
Some-how
Some-time
Some-what
Some-where
Song-stress
Son-net
Southern-wood
Spank-ing
Spare-rib
Spar-row
Speak-able
Speech-less
Spite-ful
Sports-man
Spot-less
Spring-halt
Spruce-beer
Stair-case
Star-board
Star-gazer
Star-less
Star-light
Star-like
Star-ling
States-man
Stead-fast
Steel-yard
Steer-age
Step-dame
Step-daughter
Step-father
Step-mother
Steward-ship
Stiff-neck
Still-born
Stock-jobber
Stone-fruit
Store-fruit
Store-house
Stow-age
Strata-gem
Straw-berry

Stream-let	Thought-ful	Wag-on
Strip-ling	Thought-less	Wag-tail
Sum-mary	Thread-bare	Wain-scot
Summer-house	Three-fold	Waist-coat
Summer-set	Three-score	Wake-ful
Sun-beam	Thresh-old	Wal-nut
Sun-burnt	Through-out	Wan-ton
Sun-day	Thunder-bolt	Ward-mote
Sun-dry	Thunder-	Ward-robe
Sun-flower	struck	Ward-ship
Sun-less	Till-age	Ware-house
Sup-plant	Tip-pet	War-fare
Sup-pliant	Tip-staff	War-like
Sup-port	Tire-some	War-rant
Sup-port-able	Title-page	Wash-ball
Sup-position	Toad-stool	Waste-ful
Sup-press	Toil-et	Watch-ful
Swans-down	Toil-some	Watch-man
Sweep-stake	Tom-boy	Watch-word
Sweet-bread	Tooth-ache	Water-course
Sweet-briar	Top-knot	Water-fall
Sweet-heart	Top-most	Water-fowl
Sweet-william	Top-sail	Water-man
Sweet-willow	Touch-stone	Water-mark
Swine-herd	Touch-wood	Water-mill
Swords-man	Towns-men	Water-work
Tar-get	Toy-shop	Way-lay
Tar-tar	Track-less	Way-ward
Taw-dry	Trap-door	Weather-cock
Tax-able	Tre-foil	Weather-glass
Tea-cup	Trip-let	Weather-wise
Teem-ful	Trip-thong	Web-bed
Teem-less	Trod-den	Web-foot
Tell-tale	Turn-pike	Wed-lock
Ten-able	Turn-spit	Week-day
Ten-a-city	Turn-stile	Wel-come
Ten-ant	Tutor-age	Wel-fare
Ten-dance	Twelfth-night	Well-born
Ten-don	Twelfth-tide	Well-bred
Ten-drill	Two-fold	Wheel-wright
Ten-or	Two-pence	Where-at
Thank-ful	Vain-glory	Where-by
Thank-less	Van-guard	Whet-stone
Them-selves	Vault-age	Whip-cord
Thence-forth	Up-braid	Whip-hand
There-after	Up-hill	Whirl-pool
There-at	Up-hold	Whirl-wind
There-by	Up-land	White-wash
There-fore	Up-ride	Whit-low
There-from	Up-right	Whit-sun-tide
There-in	Up-roar	Who-ever
There-on	Up-shot	Whole-sale
There-to	Up-start	Whole-some
There-with	Up-ward	Wil-low
Thick-set	Use-less	Wild-fire

Wil-ful	Wood-cock	Worm-wood
Wind-lass	Wood-land	Wrath-ful
Wind-mill	Wood-lark	Wrath-less
Wind-pipe	Wood-man	Wrist-band
Win-now	Wood-note	Writ-ten
Win-some	Wood-nymph	Year-ling
Wise-acre	Work-house	Yel-low
Wit-less	Work-man	Youth-ful
Wolf-dog	Work-shop	

57. CHRONOGRAMS OR CHRONOGRAPHS are riddles in which the letters of the Roman notation in a sentence or series of words are so arranged as to make up a date. The following is a good example :—

My Day Closed Is In Immortality.

The initials MDCIII give 1603, the year of Queen Elizabeth's death. Sometimes the Chronogram is employed to express a date on coins or medals ; but oftener it is simply used as a riddle :—A poet who in blindness wrote ; another lived in Charles's reign ; a third called the father of English verse ; a Spanish dramatist ; the scolding wife of Socrates ; and the Prince of Latin poets,— their initials give the year of the Great Plague— MDCLXV —1666 : Milton, Dryden, Chaucer, Lope-de-Vega, Xantippe, Virgil. The word comes from *Chronos*, time, and *gramma*, a letter.

58. CONUNDRUMS.—These are simple catches, in which the sense is playfully cheated, and are generally founded upon words capable of double meaning. The following are examples :—

Where did Charles the First's executioner dine, and what did he take ?
He took a chop at the King's Head.
When is a plant to be dreaded more than a mad dog ?
When it's madder.
What is majesty stripped of its externals ?
It is *a jest.* [The m and the y, externals, are taken away.]
Why is hot bread like a caterpillar ?
Because it's the grub that makes the butter fly.
Why did the accession of Victoria throw

a greater damp over England than the death of KingWilliam ?

Because the King was missed (mist) *while the Queen was reigning* (raining).

Why should a gouty man make his will ?

To have his legatees (leg at ease).

Why are bankrupts more to be pitied than idiots ?

Because bankrupts are broken, while idiots are only cracked.

Why is the treadmill like a true convert ?

Because it's turning is the result of conviction.

When may a nobleman's property be said to be all feathers ?

When his estates are all entails (hen-tails).

Why are sugar-plums like race-horses ?

Because the more you lick them the faster they go.

Why is a dog's tail like the heart of a tree ?

Because it's farthest from the bark.

Why should an alderman wear a tartan waistcoat ?

To keep a check on his stomach.

Why are journalists like chickens ?

Because they have to scratch for a living.

What was the difference between Noah's Ark and Joan of Arc ?

One was made of Gophir wood and the other Maid of Orleans.

59. CRYPTOGRAPHY, or secret writing—from the Greek *cryptos,* a secret, and *graphe,* a writing—has been largely employed in state despatches, commercial correspondence, love epistles, and riddles. The telegraphic codes employed in the transmission of news by electric wire, partake somewhat of the cryptographic character, the writer employing certain words or figures, the key to which is in the possession of his correspondent. The single-word despatch sent by Napier to the Government of India, was a sort of cryptographic conundrom—*Peccavi,* I have sinned (Scinde) ; and in the agony column of the *Times* there commonly appear paragraphs which look puzzling enough until we discover the key-letter or figure. Various and singular

have been the devices adopted—as, for instance, the writing in the perforations of a card especially prepared, so as only to allow the real words of the message to be separated from the mass of writing by means of a duplicate card with similar perforations ; the old Greek mode of writing on the edges of a strip of paper wound round a stick in a certain direction, and the substitution of figures or signs for letters or words. When one letter is always made to stand for another, the secret of a cryptograph is soon discovered, but when, as in the following example, the same letter does not invariably correspond to the letter for which it is a substitute, the difficulty of deciphering the cryptograph is manifestly increased :—

Ohs ya h sych, oayarsa rr loacys syms

Osrh srore rrhmu h smsmsmah emshyr snms.

The translation of this can be made only by the possessor of the key.

a b c d e f g h i j k l m n o p q r s t u v
h u s h m o n e y b y c h a r l e s h r o s
w z y s
　s e s q

"Hush Money, by Charles H. Ross, Esq."—twenty-six letters which, when applied to the cryptograph, will give a couplet from Parnell's "Hermit" :—

"Far in a wild, unknown to public view,
From youth to age a reverend hermit grew."

The employment of figures and signs for letters is the most usual form of the cryptograph. From the following jumble we set a portion of Hamlet's address to the Ghost :—

9 a 6 2 × ‡ 9 a 1 ‖ n 3 a 3 ‡ 2 † ‡ * 7 6 † 9 5
2 1 2 7 a 1 ; ‡
4 2 8 * ; ‡ (3 ‡ 3 , * 7 8 2 9 × , 1 * † 6 * 4
× 3 a 1 9 ‖ a 2 1

With the key—

a b c　d e f g h i j　k　l m n o　p q r　s t u v
9 4 5 1 2 7 6 8 3 + - × ‖　a *　( ) † ‡ , ; :
w x y z
. o § +

it is easy to write and not very hard to read the entire speech. The whole theory of the cryptogram is that each correspondent possesses the key to the secret. To confound an outside inquirer the key is often varied. A good plan is to take a line from any ordinary book and substitute the first twenty-six of its letters for those of the alphabet. In your next cryptogram you take the letters from another page or another book. It is not necessary to give an example. Enough will be seen from what we have written to instruct an intelligent inquirer.

60. DECAPITATIONS AND CURTAILMENTS are riddles somewhat of the nature of the Logogriph, *which see.* In the first, the omission of the successive initials produces new words, as—Prelate, Relate, Elate, Late, Ate. In the curtailment the last letter of the word is taken away with a similar result as,—Patent, Paten, Pate, Pat, Pa. Of like kind are the riddles known as variations, mutilations, reverses, and counterchanges. A good example of the last-named is this :—

> "Charge, Chester, Charge : on, Stanley, on,
> Were the last words of Marmion.
> Had I but been in Stanley's place,
> When Marmion urged him to the chase,
> A tear might come on every face."

The answer is onion—On, I on.

61. ENIGMAS are compositions of a different character, based upon *ideas* rather than upon words, and frequently constructed so as to mislead, and to surprise when the solution is made known. Enigmas may be founded upon simple catches, like Conundrums, in which form they are usually called RIDDLES such as—

> "Though you set me on foot,
> I shall be on my head."

The answer is, *A nail in a shoe.* The celebrated Enigma, on the letter H, by Miss Catherine Fanshawe, but usually attributed to Lord Byron, commencing :—

> "'Twas whispered in heaven, 'twas muttered in hell.
> And echo caught faintly the sound as it fell ;"

and given in full elsewhere in this volume, is an admirable specimen of what may be rendered in the form of an Enigma.

62. HIDDEN WORDS.—A riddle in which names of towns, persons, rivers, &c., are hidden or arranged, without transposition, in the midst of sentences which convey no suggestion of their presence. In the following sentence, for instance, there are hidden six Christian names :—Here is hid a name the people of Pisa acknowledge : work at each word, for there are worse things than to give the last shilling for bottled wine.—The names are Ida, Isaac, Kate, Seth, Ethel, Edwin. Great varieties of riddles, known as Buried Cities, Hidden Towns, &c., are formed on this principle, the words being sometimes placed so as to read backwards, or from right to left. The example given will, however, sufficiently explain the mode of operation.

63. LIPOGRAM.—from *leipo*, "I leave out," and *gramma*, a letter—is a riddle in which a name or sentence is written without its vowels, as Thprffthpddngsnthtng,—The proof of the pudding is in the eating.

> Whnhnorslst ts—rlfltd,
> Dths bt—sr rtrt ftn nfmy.

"When honour's lost 'tis a relief to die,
Death's but a sure retreat from infamy."

64. LOGOGRIPH.—This is a riddle (*logos*, a word, and *griphos*, a riddle) in which a word is made to undergo several changes. These changes are brought about by the addition, subtraction, omission, or substitution of a letter or letters. The following by the late Lord Macaulay is an excellent example :—

> "Cut off my head, how singular I act !
> Cut off my tail, and plural I appear.
> Cut off my head and tale—most curious fact,

Although my middle's left, there's
  nothing there !
What is my head out off ?—a sounding
  sea !
What is my tail cut off ?—a flowing
  river !
Amid their mingling depths I fearless
  play
Parent of softest sounds, though mute
  for ever !

The answer is *cod*. Cut off its head
and it is *od* (odd, singular) ; its tail,
and it is Co., plural, for company ;
head and tail, and it is o, nothing.
Its head is a sounding C (sea), its tail
a flowing D (river Dee), and amid
their depths the cod may fearless
play, parent of softest *sounds* yet mute
for ever.

65. METAGRAM, a riddle in
which the change of the initial
letter produces a series of words
of different meanings ; from *meta*,
implying change, and *gramma*, a letter.
Thus :—

I cover your head ; change my head, and
I set you to sleep ; change it again and again,
and with every change comee a new idea.—
Cap, Nap, Gap, Sap, Hap, Map, Lap, Pap,
Rap, Tap. This kind of riddle is also known
as word-capping.

66. PALINDROME, from the Greek
palin-dromos, running back again. This
is a word, sentence, or verse that reads
the same both forwards and backwards
—as, madam, level, reviver ; live on no
evil ; love your treasure and treasure
your love ; you provoked Harry before
Harry provoked you ; servants respect
masters when masters respect servants.
Numerous examples of Palindrome or
reciprocal word- twisting exist in Latin
and French ; but in English it is difficult
to get a sentence which will be exactly
the same when read either way. The
best example is the sentence which,
referring to the first banishment of the
Great Napoleon, makes him say, as to
his power to conquer Europe—

"Able was I ere I saw Elba."

67. PUZZLES vary much. One of
the simplest that we know is this :—

Take away half of thirteen and let eight
remain.

Write XIII on a slate, or on a piece of
paper—rub out the lower half of the figures,
and VIII will remain.

Another. From forty-five take forty-five
and let forty-five remain. To do this write
the figures 1 to 9 consecutively in a line,
above them write the same figures in reverse
order 9 to 1, subtract the bottom line from
the top line and the result as well as the
other two lines will each total 45—thus

$$987654321 = 45$$
$$\underline{123456789} = 45$$
$$864197632 = 45.$$

Upon the principle of the square-
words, riddlers form Diagonals, Diamonds, Pyramids, Crosses, Stars, &c.
These specimens will show their peculiarities :—

68. Oblique Puzzle.—Malice, eight,
a polemical meeting, a Scottish river,
what I write with, a decided negative, the
capital of Ireland. The initials downward
name a celebrated musician.

69. Diagonal Puzzle.—A direction,
a singer, a little bird, a lady's ring, a
sharp shaver. Read from left to right
and right to left, the centrals show two
favourite novelists.

The following are the answers to
these two puzzles, and afford good
examples of their construction to any
one who wishes to try his hand at their
manufacture.

OBLIQUE	DIAGONAL.
R E V E N G E	L A B E L
O C T A V E	T E N O R
S Y N O D	D I V E R
S P E Y	J E W E L
I N K	R A Z O R
N O	
I	

70. Diamond Puzzle.—The head
of a mouse, what the mouse lives in, the
county of calves, the city of porcelain, a
German town, a Transatlantic stream,
a royal county, a Yorkshire borough,
Eve's temptation, our poor relation,

myself. Centrals down and across, show a wide, wide, long river.

The constraction of the Diamond Puzzle is exhibited in the following diagram, which is, at the same time the answer to it.

DIAMOND.

```
                M
              A I R
            E S S E X
          D R E S D E N
        G O T T I N G E N
M I S S I S S I S S I P P I
        B E R K S H I R E
          H A L I F A X
            A P P L E
              A P E
                I
```

71. **REBUSES** form a class of Enigma generally formed by the first, sometimes the first and last, letters of words, or of transpositions of letters, or additions to words. Dr. Johnson, however, represents Rebus to be a word represented by a picture. And putting the Doctor's definition and our own explanation together, the reader may glean a good conception of the nature of the Rebus of which the following is an example :—

> The tether of the Grecian Jove ;
> A little boy who's blind ;
> The foremost land in all the world ;
> The mother of mankind ;
> A poet whose love-sonnets are
> Still very much admired ;—
> The *initial* letters will declare
> A blessing to the tired.

Answer—*S*aturn ; *L*ove ; *E*ngland ; *E*ve ; *P*lutarch. The initials form *sleep.*

The excellent little work mentioned on page 21, entitled *Philosophy and Mirth United by Pen and Pencil*, has this novelty, that many of the Enigmas are accompanied by enigmatical pictures, so that the eye is puzzled as well as the ear.

72. **SQUARE WORDS.**—A comparatively modern sort of riddle, in which the letters of each word selected read both across and down. With four

letters the making of the riddle is easy, but with five or six the difficulty increases. We give an example of each.

i. Inside, a thought, a liquid gem, a timid creature.

ii. To run out, odour, to boil, to loosen, unseen essence.

iii. Compensations, a court favourite, to assist, to bite slightly, Spanish money, sarcasms.

i.	ii.
P I T H	I S S U E
I D E A	S C E N T
T E A R	S E E T H
H A R E	U N T I E
	E T H E R

iii.
```
A M E N D S
M I N I O N
E N A B L E
N I B B L E
D O L L A R
S N E E R S
```

With seven or eight letters the riddle becomes exceedingly difficult, especially if the selected words are of like character and syllables.

73. **CAPPING LINES.**—In this game the company sit round the room, and one is selected as Head of the class, and reads or speaks a line of poetry. He or she then challenges the next player to give the following line, and the name of the author. If he cannot do either he pays *two* forfeits ; but if he can cap the line or give the author's name, he only pays one, goes to the top of the class, and is exempted from all forfeits for the rest of the round. He then in his turn gives a line and so on through the game.

Example :—(First player) "The way was long, the wind was cold."

(Second player) "The minstrel was infirm and old (Scott)."

74. **THE "EYES" GAME.**— The curtains having been drawn all close, the players except one go behind them. Those behind the curtains choose one of their number

who looks between the curtains, showing only his eyes. The player who is left in the room has to guess who it is. If he is wrong he has to pay a forfeit. If right, he may go behind the curtain, and the one detected has to guess.

75. CHESS, LAWS OF.—The rules given below are those which are now universally accepted by English players.[1]

i. The board is to be so placed as to leave a white square at the right hand of the player.

ii. Any mistake in placing the board or the men may be rectified before the fourth move is completed, but not after.

iii. The players draw lots for the first move, and take the move alternately.

[When odds are given, the player giving them moves first. White generally moves first. It is usual to play with the white and black men alternately.]

iv. The piece touched must be moved. When the fingers of the player have once left the piece, it cannot be again removed from the square it occupies.

[Except the move be illegal, when the opponent can insist on the piece being moved in the proper manner, or for the player's King to be moved instead.]

v. In touching a piece simply to adjust it, the player must notify to his adversary that such is his intention.

vi. If a player take one of his own men by mistake, or touch a wrong man, or one of his opponent's men, or make an illegal move, his adversary may compel him either to take the man, make the right move, move his King, or replace the piece, and make a legal move.

vii. A pawn may be played either one or two squares at a time when first moved.

[In the latter case it is liable to be taken *en passant*, i.e. with a pawn that could have taken it had it been played only one square.]

viii. A player cannot castle under any of the following circumstances :— 1. If he has moved either King or Rook. 2. If the King be in check. 3. If there be any piece between the King and the Rook. 4. If the King, in moving, pass over any square commanded by any one of his adversary's forces.

ix. If a player give a check without crying "check," the adversary need not take notice of the check. But if two moves only are made before the discovery of the mistake, the pieces may be replaced, and the game properly played.

x. If a player say check without actually attacking the King, and his adversary move his King or take the piece, the latter may elect either to let the move stand or have the pieces replaced and another move made.

xi. If, at the end of a game, the players remain, one with a superior to an inferior force, or even if they have equal forces, the defending player may call upon his adversary to mate in fifty moves on each side, or draw the game.

[If one player persist in giving perpetual check, or repeating the same move, his opponent may count the moves for the draw.]

xii. Either stalemate, or perpetual check constitute a drawn game.

xiii. Directly a pawn reaches its eighth square it must be exchanged for a piece.

[It is usual to change the pawn for a Queen, but it may be replaced by a Rook, Bishop, or Knight, without reference to the pieces already on the board. In practice it would be changed for a Queen or a Knight, seeing that the Queen's moves include those of the Book and Bishop. Thus you may have two or more Queens, three or more Rooks,

---

[1] *The Book of Chess*, by G. H. Selkirk, 5s., Houlston & Sons, London, with numerous examples and diagrams, will be found a most useful guide to the study of the game.

Bishops, or Knights on the board at the end of the game.]

76. DRAUGHTS, RULES OF THE GAME.—The accepted laws for regulating the game are as follow :—

i. The board is to be so placed as to have the black double corners at the right hand of the player.

ii. The first move is taken by agreement, and in all the subsequent games of the same sitting, the first move is taken alternately.

iii. The man touched must be moved, but the men may be properly adjusted during any part of the game. After they are so placed, if either player, when it is his turn to play, touch a man he must move it or forfeit the game.

iv. It is optional with the player either to allow his opponent to stand the huff, or to compel him to take the offered piece or let the piece remain on the board.

["Standing the huff" is when a player refuses to take an offered piece, but either intentionally or accidentally makes another move. His adversary then removes the man that should have taken the piece, and makes his own move—huff and move, as it is called.]

v. Five minutes is the longest time allowed to consider a move, which if not made within that time, forfeits the game, and where there is *only one* way of taking *one or more* pieces, one minute only is allowed, or the game is forfeited.

vi. It is compulsory upon the player to take all the pieces he can legally take by the same series of moves. On making a King, however, the latter remains on his square till a move has been made on the other side.

vii. A false move must be remedied as soon as it is discovered, or the maker of such move loses the game.

viii. When only a small number of men remain toward the end of the game, the possessor of the lesser number may call on his opponent to win in at least fifty moves, or declare the game drawn. With two Kings to one, the game must be won in at most twenty moves on each side.

77. HALMA (OR HOPPITY).—This game is played by either two or four players, upon a special board containing 256 squares, or it may be played by one person *à la solitaire*.

i. The board is so marked that in each corner there is a "goal or yard" of thirteen squares bounded by a black or coloured line. The thirteen square goals are used when four persons play. In two of the corners, however, six extra squares are marked off by a thicker line, and these nineteen square goals are used when only two persons play.

ii. Place the board in position with a nineteen-square goal at the left hand of each player. Each player selects his colour and fills his nineteen squares with his own men.

iii. The object of each player is to get all his nineteen men into his opponent's goal, and the one who does so first wins the game.

iv. Each player *steps* or *hops* one of his pieces, in turn. A *step* means shoving or pushing a piece into any adjoining square which is vacant, either forward, backward, sideways, or any way (but only one square at a time).

v. A *hop* means jumping over one or a series of men (like leapfrog), but not more than one man can be jumped over at a time, and each man jumped over must necessarily have a vacant square behind it to jump into. The move is much the same as in draughts, but there is no "taking" of pieces, and a hop may be made backwards, or in any direction the player chooses. The hop, also, may mean a series, right across the board even, until there is no piece in an adjoining square to hop over—when the jump ends.

vi. A player may hop over either his own or his opponent's pieces at his discretion, and then hop again in any direction, as often and as far as he finds opportunity : but he must not move in the same way as a knight does in Chess.

77*. HALMA FOR FOUR PLAYERS.—As we have before stated, the board in this case is placed with a thirteen-square goal on the left of each player.

i. Each player may play for himself, when the game is virtually the same as with two players.

ii. Two opposite players may be partners, in which case the object of the game is reversed, as they try to assist each other across the board, instead of blocking the way.

78. REVERSI.—This very popular game is played on an ordinary chess or draught board, with sixty-four reversible pieces or counters (usually red on one side and black on the other).

i. Each player takes thirty-two of the counters, one placing his with the red side uppermost, and the other the black side.

ii. The first player places a counter on one of the centre squares. The other player then places one of his, and so on until the four centre squares are filled up.

iii. The object of the game is to capture and keep as many of your opponent's men as you can by *reversing* them. The centre squares being filled up, the next player places a piece on one of the squares adjoining one of his opponent's pieces, thus enclosing it between two of his own colour. He is then entitled to *reverse* and claim the piece as his own. A player may capture all his opponent's pieces that happen to lie in a continuous and unbroken line (either straight or diagonally) between two of his own.

iv. At every move at least one piece must be taken, and unless this is done the player loses his turn, and his opponent proceeds to play the pieces as long as he is so situated.

v. A piece once placed on the board must not be moved from its particular square, but it can be reversed by either player as often as occasion presents itself.

vi. The player who succeeds in blocking his opponent, or who, when the whole sixty-four squares have been covered with pieces, has the greater number of his colour on the board wins the game. It may happen that the game is finished before all the squares are occupied.

vii. If a player omits to reverse all the pieces which he is entitled to reverse, he *must* correct the omission if his opponent calls his attention to it.

CARD GAMES.

79. WHIST.—(Upon the principle of Hoyle's games.)—Great silence and attention should be observed by the players. Four persons cut for partners ; the two highest are against the two lowest. The partners sit opposite to each other, and he who cuts the lowest card is entitled to the deal. The ace is the lowest in cutting.

i. **Shuffling.**—Each person has a right to shuffle the cards before the deal ; but it is usual for the elder hand only ; and the dealer after.

ii. **Dealing.**—The pack is then cut by the right-hand adversary ; and the dealer distributes the cards, one by one, to each of the players, beginning with the player on his left, until he comes to the last card, which he turns up for trump, and leaves on the table till the first trick be played.

[NOTE.— A better plan than turning up the last card and thus exposing one of the dealer's hand, is to determine the trump by cutting before commencing each deal.]

iii. **First Play.**—The eldest hand, the player on the left of the dealer, plays first. The winner of the trick plays again ; and so on till all the cards are played out

iv. **Mistakes.**—No intimations or signs are permitted between the partners. The mistake of one party is the profit of the adversary.

v. Collecting Tricks.—The tricks belonging to each player should be turned and collected by one of the partners only. All above six tricks reckon towards game.

vi. Honours.—The ace, king, queen, and knave of trumps are called honours ; and when either of the partners hold three separately, or between them, they count two points towards the game ; and in case they have four honours, they count four points.

vii. Game.—*Long Whist game consists of ten points, Short Whist of five points.*

80. TERMS USED IN WHIST.

i. *Finessing* is the attempt to gain an advantage ; thus :—If you have the best and third best card of the suit led, you put on the third best, and run the risk of your adversary having the second best ; if he has it not, which is two to one against him, you are then certain of gaining a trick.

ii. *Forcing* is playing the suit of which your partner or adversary has not any, and which in order to win he must trump.

iii. *Long Trump*, the one or more trumps in your hand when all the rest are out.

iv. *Loose Card*, a card of no value, and the most proper to throw away.

v. *Points.*—Ten make the game ; as many as are gained by tricks or honours, so many are set up to the score of the game.

vi. *Quarte*, four successive cards in suit.

vii. *Quarte Major*, a sequence of ace, king, queen, and knave.

viii. *Quint*, five successive cards in suit

ix. *Quint Major* is a sequence of ace, king, queen, knave, and ten.

x. *Ruffing.*—Trumping a suit other than trumps.

xi. *See-Saw* is when each partner trumps a suit, and when they play those suits to each other for that purpose.

xii. *Score* is the number of points set up. The following is a good method of scoring with coins or counters :—

1	2	3	4	5	6
			O	O	O
O	OO	OOO	OOO	OOO	OOO

7	8	9
OOO	OOO	OOO
O	O	O

For Short Whist there are regular markers.

xiii. *Slam* is when either side win every trick.

xiv. *Tenace* is possessing the first and third best cards, and being the last player ; you consequently catch the adversary when that suit is played : as, for instance, in case you have ace and queen of any suit, and your adversary leads that suit, you must win two tricks, by having the best and third best of the suit played, and being the last player.

xv. *Tierce*, three successive cards in suit.

xvi. *Tierce Major*, a sequence of ace, king, and queen.

81. MAXIMS FOR WHIST.

i. Lead from your strong suit, be cautious how you change suits, and keep a commanding card to bring it in again.

ii. Lead through the strong suit and up to the weak ; but not in trumps ; unless very strong in them.

iii. Lead the highest of a sequence ; but if you have a quarte or quint to a king, lead the lowest.

iv. Lead through an honour, particularly if the game is against you.

v. Lead your best trump if the adversaries be eight, and you have no honour ; but not if you have four trumps, unless you have a sequence.

vi. Lead a trump if you have four or five of a strong hand ; but not if weak.

vii. Having ace, king, and two or

three small cards, lead ace and king if weak in trumps, but a small one if strong in them.

viii. If you have the last trump, with some winning cards, and one losing card only, lead the losing card.

ix. Return your partner's lead, not the adversaries ; and if you hold only three originally, play the best ; but you need not return it immediately, when you win with a king, queen, or knave, and have only small ones, or when you hold a good sequence, a strong suit, or five trumps.

x. Do not lead from ace queen, or ace knave.

xi. Do not—as a rule—lead an ace, unless you have a king.

xii. Do not lead a thirteenth card, unless trumps be out.

xiii. Do not trump a thirteenth card, unless you be last player, or want the lead.

xiv. Keep a small card to return your partner's lead.

xv. Be cautious in trumping a card when strong in trumps, particularly if you have a strong suit.

xvi. Having only a few small trumps, make them when you can.

xvii. If your partner refuse to trump a suit, of which he knows you have not the best, lead your best trump.

xviii. When you hold all the remaining trumps, play one, and then try to put the lead in your partner's hand.

xix. Remember how many of each suit are out, and what is the best card left in each hand.

xx. Never force your partner if you are weak in trumps, unless you have a renounce, or want the odd trick.

xxi. When playing for the odd trick, be cautious of trumping out, especially if your partner be likely to trump a suit.

xxii. If you take a trick, and have a sequence, win it with the lowest

82. LAWS OF WHIST, as accepted at the best Clubs.

i. The deal is determined by cutting-in. Cutting-in and cutting-out must be by pairs.

[Less than three cards, above or below, is not a cut. Ace is lowest. Ties cut again. Lowest deals. Each player may shuffle, the dealer last. The right-hand adversary cuts to dealer.]

ii. If a card be exposed, a fresh deal may be demanded.

iii. Dealer must not look at bottom card ; and the trump-card must be left, face upwards, on the table till the first trick be turned, or opponents may call a fresh deal.

iv. Too many or too few cards is a misdeal—an exposed or face card. In either case, a fresh deal may be demanded.

[In cases of a misdeal, the deal passes to the next player.]

v. After the first round has been played, no fresh deal can be called.

[If the first player hold fewer than thirteen cards, the other hands being right, the deal stands.]

vi. If two cards be dealt to the same player, the dealer may rectify his error before dealing another card.

[The dealer must not touch the cards after they have left his hand ; but he may count those remaining in the pack if he suspect a misdeal, or he may ask the players to count their cards. One partner may not deal for another without the consent of opponents.]

vii. If the trump-card be not taken into the dealer's hand at the expiration of the first round, it may be treated as an exposed card, and called.

[After this, no one has a right to ask what was the trump-card, but he may ask "What are Trumps ?"]

viii. If the third hand play before the second, the fourth has a right to play before his partner ; or if the fourth hand play before the second, or third, the cards so played must stand, and the second be compelled to win the trick if he can.

ix. If a player lead out of his turn, or otherwise expose a card, that card may be called, if the playing of it does not cause a revoke.

[Calling a card is the insisting on its being played when the suit comes round, or when it may be played.]

x. If a player trump by mistake, he may recall his card, and play to the suit, if the card be not covered ; but he may be compelled to play the highest or lowest of the suit led, and to play the exposed trump when it is called by his adversaries.

xi If, before a trick be turned, a player discover that he has not followed suit, he may recall his card ; but the card played in error can be called when the suit is played.

xii. Before a trick is turned, the player who made it may see the preceding trick.

[Only one trick is to be shown ; not more, as is sometimes erroneously believed.]

xiii. Before he plays, a player may require his partner to "draw his card," or he may have each card in the trick claimed before the trick be turned.

xiv. When a player does not follow suit his partner is allowed to ask him whether he has any card of the suit led.

xv. The penalty for a revoke—either by wrongfully trumping the suit led, or by playing a card of another suit—is the loss of three tricks ; but no revoke can be claimed till the cards are abandoned, and the trick turned.

[Revokes forfeit three tricks from the hand or score, or opponents may add three to their score ; partner may ask and correct a trick if not turned ; the revoking side cannot score out in that deal.]

xvi. No revoke can be claimed after the tricks are gathered up, or after the cards are cut for the next deal.

[The wilful mixing up of the cards in such case loses the game.]

xvii. The proof of a revoke lies with the claimants, who may examine each trick on the completion of the round.

xviii. If a revoke occur on both sides, there must be a new deal.

xix. Honours cannot be counted unless they are claimed previous to the next deal.

[No omission to score honours can be rectified after the cards are packed ; but an overscore, if proved, must de deducted.]

xx. Honours can only be called at eight points (in Long whist), and at nine they do not count.

[In some Clubs, eight, with the deal, cannot call against nine.]

83. SHORT WHIST is the above game cut in half. Honours are not *called* at any part of the game ; but, as in Long Whist, they are counted by their holders and scored—except at the score of four. All the maxims and Rules belonging to the parent game apply to Short Whist.

84. POINTS AT SHORT WHIST.—The Game consists of Five Points. One for a Single—5 to 3 or 4 ; Two for a Double—5 to 1 or 2 ; Three for a Triple—5 to love. A Rubber—two Games successively won, or the two best Games out of three—counts for Two Points. Thus, if the first Game be won by 5 to 4, the Points are 1 to love ; the second Game won by the opposite side by 5 to 1, the Points are then 1 to 2 ; the third Game won by the side which won the first, by 5 to love. The Points are then 6 to 2—a balance of 4. This is arrived at thus : the Single in the first Game, 1 ; the Triple in the third Game, 3 ; the Rubber (two Games of three), 2 ; together, 6. From this deduct 2, for the Double gained by the opponents in the second Game, which leaves 4, as above.

85. SOLO-WHIST.—This game is played by two, three, or four persons with an ordinary pack of fifty-two cards. When five persons wish to play, the one on the right of the dealer neither joins in the current round nor pays any stakes. Pools or Kitties should not be formed when there are five players. The regular and best game is with four players.

The deal, as in Whist, is taken by the players in rotation, and is decided by the lowest of the four cards turned up. (In cutting for deal the ace is lowest, and the king is highest.) The cards are dealt *three at a time* to each player in rotation, beginning with the person at the dealer's left. When forty-eight cards have been dealt, twelve to each player, the remaining four are dealt singly, the last being turned up to indicate the trump suit.

A better plan, however, is to cut the trump suit from another pack instead of turning up and exposing the last card, and this is recommended, as it not unfrequently occurs that an exposed card spoils a Misère declarée, *e. g.* if an ace or king be exposed in an otherwise perfect Misère hand it becomes a dangerous card to the holder and may prevent a call ; if not exposed he may have a chance to discard.

86. OBJECTS IN SOLO WHIST.—Every game is played with a specific object in view, that object being declared beforehand. This is known as a "Call" or "Declaration." There are six objects or calls in Solo-Whist, each of them having a different scope and value. They are as follows—

i. *Proposition (or Proposal) and Acceptance*, where two players in partnership essay to make eight or more tricks between them against the others. The first caller, the player on the dealer's left, may accept a proposition after having originally passed, as he would otherwise be debarred the chance of accepting ; but in all other instances a player who has once passed cannot accept or make any other declaration.

ii. *Solo.* The making of not less than five tricks by a player out of his own hand, against the other three players.

iii. *Misère.* The attempt by the caller to lose all thirteen tricks, the other players trying to force him to win a trick. (There are no trumps in a misère.)

iv. *Misère ouverte.* This is the same as ordinary misère with this difference, that after the first trick has been played the caller exposes his remaining cards on the table.

v. *Abondance.* Where the player declaring endeavours to make not less than nine tricks against the other three players. The person playing the abondance selects any suit he pleases for trumps, but does not announce such selection until it appears evident that no other player can announce a superior call, the trump suit then being named. An abondance with the original turn-up suit declared as trumps, takes precedence of an abondance in another suit.

vi. *Abondance declarée.* The highest call at Solo, the caller having to make all thirteen tricks. There are no trumps, each suit being of equal value, and the caller, no matter where he sits, always leads out first ; as the leader cannot make overtricks he is not liable to pay for undertricks should he fail, but is only liable for the stakes, the game being ended directly he loses a trick.

87. SOLO-WHIST—MODE OF PLAY.—Every round at Solo is complete in itself and is played to attain one of these six objects, and there is no scoring. Honours are not counted as at ordinary Whist, and court cards in trumps are useful only for the tricks they make.

The players having examined their cards, the eldest hand (the player on the dealer's left) declares first. If he holds a superlative hand and sees a likelihood of winning all the tricks, he declares *abondance declarée*, and cannot be stopped by any player who has subsequently to declare.

If he has an exceptionally bad hand consisting almost entirely of small cards he declares *Misère ouverte*, the next highest call. Should he have a very strong hand in trumps, and thinks he can win nine tricks, he goes *Abondance*. It is rarely, however, that a player gets a sufficiently strong hand to win nine tricks, much less *thirteen*, or a sufficiently weak hand to make *Misère ouverte*. He then has four courses open to him. If he has a bad hand, he may declare a *misère*, or he may refuse to declare (saying "I pass"). If he has a pretty strong hand, he may either declare *Solo*, or he may make a *Proposition*.

The eldest hand having declared, the second makes his declaration, and then the third and fourth. A proposing hand not finding an acceptor, can alter his call to one of the superior calls, *viz.* solo, misère, or abondance ; and any caller, who has not passed, even if he be only an acceptor, if overcalled, can make any higher declaration he chooses.

If all the hands pass the deal is void, the cards are thrown in and re-dealt by the next dealer, each player contributing a certain sum (generally half or a quarter the proposed stake), and the first player who makes a successful independent call (a call other than a proposition and acceptance) takes the pool, or if unsuccessful *doubles* it.

Frequently instead of throwing up the hands, a "general" or "general misère" is played, the hand being played in the usual way and the player taking the last trick having to pay an amount agreed on (half the proposed stake, as a rule) to each of his opponents. There are no trumps in a "general."

It is usual to pay double price for overtricks (but not double for the stake) when the declaring side makes a "slam" of all thirteen tricks.

There is no penalty for a misdeal, the cards being simply re-dealt by the same player.

If, on an independent call being made, any player make a remark directly or indirectly conveying an intimation as to the state of the hands, the caller may demand that the offender pay the stakes to the side that wins, or he can throw up his hand and claim a re-deal.

A player revoking forfeits for every revoke three tricks, which are deducted from the score of his own side and added to that of his opponents : when both sides revoke, the whole deal is invalidated and neither side can win.

Stakes.—There is no scoring, and the stakes are generally agreed on beforehand and paid immediately ; but a proportionate scale should be established between the calls and overtricks. The following is an example of what is known as a one, two, three shilling, and threepenny overtrick game (the shillings for the stakes and threepences for the over or undertricks). Each adversary would have to pay to, or receive from propositions or solos, 1s. each for the stake, and 3d. each for every under or overtrick. Thus, if the proposer and accepter made eight tricks they would each receive 1s. for the stake, and 3d. for every trick they made over eight ; but if they did not make eight, they would have to pay 1s. each, and 3d. for each trick under eight ; and so with a *Solo*.

The *abondance* is on the same lines ; but in *misère*, *misère ouverte*, and *abondance declarée*, the stakes only are paid, there being no over or undertricks. The most popular arrangement is that of the sixpenny and penny game : sixpence for solos and proposals, ninepence for *abondance*, one shilling for *misères*, and penny overtricks.

88. SOLO-WHIST FOR THREE PLAYERS.

—There are two methods of playing solo with three players. The first and more preferable way is by taking out the twos, threes, and fours ; the turn-up card only being used to denote trumps. The other system is to discard one entire suit, and play the remaining three. In this case there is no odd card, the turn-up being the dealer's.

In the three players' game there are no proposals and acceptances, and the lowest call is a *solo* of six tricks. As there is very frequently a general "pass," it is usual to call solos in "flying colours" (*see* the Kimberley Game), the second solo being one of six tricks.

89. SOLO WHIST FOR TWO PLAYERS.—Here, again, the pack consists of forty cards, the twos, threes, and fours being eliminated, and the turn-up card not being used except to denote the trump suit. Deal the cards into three lots, the one to the dealer's left being used as a dummy, and not looked at until a call is decided on. It is then opened, sorted out, and exposed on the table *to the left of the caller.* The caller's opponent then plays dummy's cards with his own against the declaration. The hand to the dealer's left (whether dummy or caller) invariably having first lead.

The lowest call is a solo of *five* tricks ; the order being solo, abondance, misère, and abondance declarée.

Abondance is double the price of solo ; misère three times the price of solo ; and abondance declarée four times the price of solo.

There is necessarily no misère ouverte, the ordinary misère being more exposed than in any other variation of the game (for not only are the caller's cards known, but also those of his adversaries). This game also is played with "flying colours," solo in the second suit being of *five* tricks.

90. SOLO-WHIST. THE KIMBERLEY GAME.—This game (so called from the place whence it originated, we presume) is Solo-Whist without propositions and acceptances. A solo is therefore the lowest call, and if all the players pass, a pool is formed, the first person making a successful

call taking it, or doubling it if unsuccessful.

The Kimberley Game is played with "flying colours," that is to say, when every one passes a second chance of calling is given to them in regular rotation. This second call must be a solo of *six* tricks, the caller selecting and naming his own trump suit, but it must not be the original suit. A solo only can be called in "flying colours," and the over or undertricks are counted from *six.*

91. SCOTCH WHIST, OR CATCH THE TEN.—This may be played by any number of persons, from two to eight, with a pack of thirty-six cards (the twos, threes, fours, and fives being taken out).

i. The cards are all dealt round one at a time, the last one being turned up as the trump. Each player must have an equal number of cards ; therefore if there are five or seven players one of the sixes is also taken out ; if there are eight players the game must be played with the piquet pack of thirty-two cards (all below *seven* being taken out).

ii. If there are two, three, five, or seven players, each plays on his own account ; four play in partnership as in Whist ; six may play either in three couples, or three against three ; eight may play four against four ; or in four partnerships. The partners and their adversaries sit alternately as in Whist. If only two play, the cards are dealt so as to give three separate hands to each player, the hands being played independently. If there are three players, *two* hands are given to each of them.

iii. Should the dealer (1) omit to have the cards cut before dealing, (2) expose any of his opponent's cards (unless already exposed in the pack), or (3) give too many or too few cards to a player, it is a misdeal and the deal goes to the next player.

iv. The cards rank as in Whist, except in trumps, when the Knave is the highest card, the order then being knave, ace, king, queen, ten, nine, eight, seven, six.

v. The game is forty-one up, and the object of the play is to win tricks containing those cards which are of special value in scoring as follow :—
The Knave of trumps counts 11 points.

The Ten   „   „   10   „
The Ace   „   „   4   „
The King   „   „   8   „
The Queen   „   „   2   „

The players also score for "cards," that is to say, for all the cards obtained over their proportionate number of the pack. For example, if there were four players, their allowance would be nine cards each. If the players on one side should win seven tricks (*i. e.* twenty-eight cards) they would be ten in excess of their allowance, and would be entitled to score ten for "cards."

vi. Speaking generally, the play follows the rules of Whist ; but the special object is to "catch," or "save," the ten, as it makes a difference of twenty to one's score. The knave is even a better card, but as it is the highest trump, it of course remains with the side that received it when dealt.

92. PROGRESSIVE WHIST.—

Progressive Whist had its origin in America, and was only introduced into England in quite recent years. In playing this game three or more tables (the usual number is six tables) should be arranged, with four players at each table. The cards are dealt and played as in ordinary whist. The tables should be numbered consecutively from 1 upward, each table having in its centre a card bearing its distinctive number. After playing the first deal the two winning players "progress" to the next table— (*i. e.* from No. 1 table to No. 2 table, from No. 2 to No. 3, No. 3 to No. 4, No. 4 to No. 5, No. 5 to No. 6, No. 6 to No. 1, and so on), being careful to *change partners* at each successive table. The same method of "progressing" is

followed after each deal ; and the game may consist of any number of deals. After playing each deal, each player marks on his or her scoring card the total number of tricks *taken as partners*, and at the end of the evening the lady and gentleman having the highest totals are awarded the prizes of merit, while the lady and gentleman having the lowest totals receive the consolation or "booby" prizes. The increasing popularity of this game is largely owing to the opportunities which it affords of promoting pleasant intercourse among the players.

93. CRIBBAGE.—This game is played with the full pack of cards, often by four persons, but it is a better game for two. There are also different modes of playing—with five, six, or eight cards ; but the best games are those with five or six cards.

94. TERMS USED IN CRIBBAGE.

i. *Crib.*—The crib is composed of the cards thrown out by each player, and the dealer is entitled to score whatever points are made by them.

ii. *Pairs* are two similar cards, as two aces or two kings. Whether in hand or play they reckon for two points.

iii. *Pairs-Royal* are three similar cards, and reckon for six points, whether in hand or play.

iv. *Double Pair-Royal* are four similar cards and reckon for twelve points, whether in hand or play. The points gained by pairs, pairs-royal and double pairs-royal, in playing, are thus effected :—Your adversary having played a seven and you another, constitutes a pair, and entitles you to score two points ; your antagonist then playing a third seven, makes a pair-royal, and he marks six ; and your playing a fourth is a double pair-royal, and entitles you to twelve points.

v. *Fifteens.*—Every fifteen reckons for two points, whether in hand or play. In hand they are formed either by two or more cards. If in play, such cards as together make fifteen are played ; the player whose card completes that number, scores two points.

vi. *Sequences* are three, four or more successive cards, and reckon for an equal number of points, either in hand or play. In playing a sequence, it is of no consequence which card is thrown down first ; as thus : your adversary playing an ace, you a five, he a three, you a two, then he a four—he counts five for the sequence.

vii. *Flush.*—When the cards are all of one suit, they reckon for as many points as there are cards. For a flush in the crib, the turned up card must be of the same suit as those put out.

viii. *His Nob.*—The knave of the suit turned up reckons for one point.

ix. *His Heels.*—The knave when turned up reckons for two points, but is only once counted.

x. *The Go.*—The point scored by the last player, if he make under thirty-one ; if he make thirty-one exactly, he marks two.

xi. *Last.*—Three points taken at the commencement of the game of five-card cribbage by the non-dealer.

95. LAWS OF CRIBBAGE.

i. The players cut for deal. The ace is lowest in cutting. In case of a tie they cut again. The holder of the lowest card deals either five, six or eight cards each, as arranged.

ii. A cut must consist of not fewer than four cards.

iii. Too many or too few cards dealt constitutes a misdeal, the penalty for which is the taking of two points by the non-dealer.

iv. A faced card, or a card exposed during the act of dealing necessitates a new deal, without penalty.

v. The dealer shuffles the cards and the non-dealer cuts them for the "start."

vi. If the non-dealer touch the cards (except to cut them for the turn-up) after they have been out for the start, he forfeits two points.

vii. In cutting for the start, not fewer than three cards must be lifted from the pack or left on the table.

viii. The non-dealer throws out for the crib before the dealer. A card once laid out cannot be recalled, nor must either party touch the crib till the hand is played out. Either player confusing the crib cards with his hand is liable to a penalty of three points.

[In three and four-hand cribbage the left-hand player throws out first for the crib, then the next, the dealer last. The usual and best way is for the non-dealer to throw his crib over to the dealer's side of the board ; on these two cards the dealer places his own, and hands the pack over to be cut. The pack is then at the right side of the board for the next deal.]

ix. The player who takes more points than those to which he is entitled, either in play or in reckoning hand or crib, is liable to be "pegged ;" that is, to be put back as many points as he has overscored, and have the points added to his opponent's side.

[In pegging you must not remove your opponent's *front* peg till you have given him another. In order "to take him down," you remove your own *back peg* and place it *where his front peg ought to be* ; you then take his *wrongly placed peg* and put it *in front of your own front*, as many holes as he has forfeited by wrongly scoring.]

x. No penalty attaches to the taking of too few points in play, hand or crib.

xi. When a player has once taken his hand or crib, he cannot amend his score.

xii. When a knave is turned up, "two for his heels" must be scored before the dealer's own card can be played, or they cannot be taken.

xiii. A player cannot demand the assistance of his adversary in reckoning hand and crib.

xiv. A player may not, except to "peg him," touch his adversary's pegs, under a penalty of two points. If the foremost peg has been displaced by accident, it must be placed in the hole behind the peg standing on the board.

xv. The peg once holed cannot be removed by either player till another point or points be gained.

xvi. The player who scores a game as won when, in fact, it is not won, loses it.

xvii. A *lurch*—scoring the whole sixty-one before your adversary has scored thirty-one— is equivalent to a double game, if agreed to previous to the commencement of the game.

xviii. A card that may be legally played cannot be withdrawn after it has been once thrown face upwards on the table.

xix. If a player neglect to score his hand, crib, or any point or points of the game, he cannot score them after the cards are packed or the next card played.

xx. The player who throws up his cards and refuses to score, forfeits the game.

xxi. If a player neglect to play when he can play a card within the prescribed thirty-one, he forfeits two holes.

xxii. Each player's hand and crib must be plainly thrown down on the table and not mixed with the pack, under penalty of the forfeiture of the game.

The player who refuses to abide by the rules loses the game. Bystanders must not interfere unless requested to decide any disputed point

Five Card Cribbage is played in the same way, five cards only being dealt to each player, of which they each lay out two for crib.

96. SIX CARD CRIBBAGE.—In
this the sixty-one points or holes on the cribbage-board mark the game. The player cutting the lowest card deals ; after which, each player lays out,

face downwards, two of his six cards for the crib, which belongs to the dealer. The adversary cuts the remainder of the pack, and the dealer turns up and lays upon the crib the uppermost card, which is called the *turn-up*. If it be a knave, he marks two points. The card turned up is reckoned by both in counting their hands or crib. The eldest hand then plays a card, which the other should endeavour to pair, or find one, the pips of which, reckoned with the first, will make fifteen ; then the non-dealer plays another card, and so on alternately, until the pips on the cards played make thirty-one or the nearest possible number under that. [The Court cards count as ten each in all games of cribbage.]

97. COUNTING FOR GAME IN CRIBBAGE.—When he whose turn it is to play cannot produce a card that makes thirty-one, or under that number, he says, "Go," and his antagonist scores one, or plays any card or cards he may have that will make thirty-one, or under ; if he can make exactly thirty-one, he takes two points. Such cards as remain after this are not played, but each player then counts and scores his hand, the non-dealer first. The dealer then marks the points for his hand, and also for his crib, each reckoning the cards every way they can possibly be varied, and always including the turned-up card.

	POINTS.
For every fifteen	2
For a sequence of 3 or 4 cards . . .	3 or 4
For a pair (two of a kind)	2
For a royal pair (3 of a kind). . . .	6
For a double pair-royal (4 of a kind)	12
Knave of the suit turned up	1

For a flush in hand, that is, cards all of one suit, or for a full flush, when the cards in hand and the turn-up are of the same suit, 1 for each card.

The highest number that can be counted from five cards is 29—made from four fives and a knave ; that is, three fives and a knave of the suit turned up, and a five on the pack—for the combinations of the four fives, 16 ; for the double pair-royal, 12 ; his nob, 1=29.

98. MAXIMS FOR LAYING OUT THE CRIB CARDS.

—In laying out cards for the crib, the player should consider not only his own hand, but also to whom the crib belongs, as well as the state of the game ; for what might be right in one situation would be wrong in another. Possessing a pair-royal it is generally advisable to lay out the other cards for crib, unless it belong to the adversary. Avoid giving him two fives, a deuce and a trois, five and six, seven and eight, five and any other tenth card. When he does not thereby materially injure his hand, the player should for his own crib lay out close cards in hopes of making a sequence ; or two of a suit, in expectation of a flush ; or cards that of themselves reckoned with others will count fifteen. When the antagonist be nearly up, it may be expedient to keep such cards as may prevent him from gaining at play. The rule is to baulk your adversary's crib by laying out cards not likely to prove of advantage to him, and to lay out favourably for your own crib. This applies to a stage of the game when it may be of consequence to keep in hand cards likely to tell in play, or when the non-dealer would be either out by his hand, or has reason for thinking the crib of little moment. A king and a nine is the best baulk, as none can form a sequence beyond it ; king or queen, with an ace, six, seven, eight, or nine are good ones to put out. Low cards are generally the most likely to gain at play ; the flushes and sequences, particularly if the latter be also flushes, are eligible hands, by keeping the player will often be enabled either to assist his own crib, or baulk that of the opponent ; a knave should never be put out for his crib, if it can be retained in hand.

99. THREE OR FOUR-HAND CRIBBAGE

differs little from the preceding. The players put out but one card each to the crib, and when thirty-one, or the nearest to that has been made, the next eldest hand leads, and the players go on again in rotation, with the remaining cards, till all are played out, before they proceed to show hands and crib. For three-handed cribbage triangular boards are used.

100. ALL-FOURS

is usually played by two persons ; sometimes by four. Its name is derived from the four chances, called *High, Low, Jack, Game,* each making a point. It is played with a complete pack of cards, six of which are to be dealt to each player, one at a time ; and the next card, the thirteenth, is turned up for the trump if there are only two players, and the twenty-fifth if there are four. If the trump be a knave it belongs to the dealer, who scores one for it.

101. SCORING IN ALL-FOURS.

i. *High.*—For the highest trump out, the holder scores one point

ii. *Low.*—For the lowest trump out, the original holder scores one point, even if it be taken by the adversary.

iii. *Jack.*—For the knave of trumps the holder scores one. If it be won by the adversary, the winner scores the point.

iv. *Game,* which also counts one point, is scored by the player who can reckon the highest number in the tricks he has gained, viz.

For each *Ace*	4	For each *Knave*	1
„ *King*	3	„ *Ten*	10
„ *Queen*	2		

The other cards do not count : thus it may happen that a deal may be played without having any to reckon for *game.*

Should the eldest hand dislike his cards, he uses his privilege, and says, "*I beg ;*" in which case the dealer either allows him to score one point, saying, "*Take one,*" or gives each player three cards more from the pack, and then turns up the next card, the seventh, for trumps. If, however, the trump turned up be of the same suit as the first, the dealer must go on, giving each three cards more, and turning up the seventh, until a change of suit for trumps shall take place. The cards thus dealt are then played, winning tricks, as in Whist, except that a player may win a trick either by trumping it or by a superior card of the same suit. Each player then examines the tricks he has won, and scores as above. The player who first scores ten points wins the game.

102. LAWS OF ALL-FOURS.

i. No person can beg more than once in each hand, except by mutual agreement.

ii. Each player must trump or follow suit on penalty of the adversary scoring one point.

iii. If either player score wrongly it must be taken down, and the adversary either scores four points or one, as may have been previously agreed.

iv. When a trump is played, it is allowable to ask your adversary if it be either high or low.

v. One card may count all-fours ; for example, the eldest hand holds the knave and stands his game, the dealer has neither trump, ten, ace nor court-card ; it will follow that the knave will be both High, Low, Jack, and Game.

103. MAXIMS FOR ALL-FOURS.

i. Make your knave as soon as you can.

ii. Secure your tens by playing any small cards, by which you may throw the lead into your adversary's hand.

iii. Win your adversary's best cards when you can, either by trumping or with superior cards.

iv. If, being eldest hand, you hold either ace, king, or queen of trumps, without the knave or ten, play them immediately, as, by this means, you may chance to win the knave or ten.

104. LOO.—When this game is played for a determinate stake, as a penny for the deal and threepence for the Loo, it is called *Limited Loo*, but when each Loo must equal the amount which happens to be in the pool, it is called *Unlimited Loo*.

i. Any number of persons can play from three, but five or seven make the best game.

ii. The cards take their usual value, ace highest ; then king, queen, knave, and so on. They are cut for deal in the usual manner, the holder of the lowest card being dealer ; after which the deal goes round.

iii. The dealer then gives three cards, one at a time, face downwards, to each player, and also dealing an extra hand, called "miss." Having dealt these he turns up the next card on the pack as "trump."

iv. The stakes being settled beforehand, the dealer puts his into the pool and the game proceeds.

v. The first player on the left of the dealer looks at his hand, and declares whether he will play or take the "miss." If he decides to play, he says, "I play," or "I take the miss." Whoever takes the "miss" is compelled to play, whether it happens to be good or bad ; but he may elect to do neither ; in which case he places his cards on the pack, and has nothing further to do with that round. The next player looks at his hand, and says whether he will play or not ; and so on, till the turn comes round to the dealer, who, if only one player stand the chance of the loo, may either play or give up the stakes.

105. LOO—MODE OF PLAY.

i. When it is seen how many players stand in the round, the elder hand plays a card—his highest trump if he has two or more ; if not, any card he chooses. The next plays, and, if he can, follows suit or heads the trick with a trump. If he can do neither, he throws away any card.

ii. And so the round goes on ; the highest card of the suit, or the highest trump, winning the trick. The winner of the trick then leads another card.

iii. The game consists of three tricks, and the pool is divided equally among the players possessing them. The three tricks may of course be won by a single player, or they may be divided between two or three. Each player who fails to win a trick is looed, and pays into the next pool the amount determined on as the loo.

iv. When a club is turned up as trump card, "Club Law" comes in, when all the players must play, whether their hands are good or bad, and no one is allowed to take the "miss." By this means the pool is increased.

106. LAWS OF LOO.

i. For a misdeal the dealer is looed.

ii. For playing out of turn or looking at the "miss" without taking it, the player is looed.

iii. If the first player possess two or three trumps, he must play the highest, or be looed.

iv. With ace of trumps only, the first player must lead it, or be looed.

v. The player who looks at his own cards, or the "miss" out of his turn, is looed.

vi. The player who looks at his neighbour's hand, either during the play or when they lie on the table, is looed.

vii. The player who informs another what cards he possesses, or gives any intimation that he knows such or such cards to be in the hand or the "miss," is looed.

107. CANADIAN WHIST.—A

capital game for two players. All the cards are used, and in dealing are placed in pairs, face downwards on the table. Each player then turns over the top card of twelve of the thirteen pairs dealt to him, taking the other two cards (which are called "blinds") into his hand. The non-dealer has the choice

of trumps, after having seen all the exposed cards, and the game proceeds as at Whist ; it is optional to take a trick, but a led suit must be followed, even from the "blinds." As each exposed card is played the under card must be exposed. Counting commences after either hand has taken thirteen tricks, each trick beyond thirteen counting one. Eleven is the usual game, but any number is optional as agreed upon before starting.

108. EIGHTY.—A game for two

players. Six cards are dealt to each player, two at a time ; the trump card is then placed exposed under the remaining cards, of which one card, the top, must also be exposed. The game is to secure in one's own hand as many as possible of the tens, aces, kings, queens, knaves, these bearing respective values thus : tens 10, aces, kings 3, queens 2, knaves 1, which in the aggregate amount to eighty—hence the name. As each trick is taken, the winner takes the top card from the pack, the loser taking the next and at the same time turning over the following card on the pack. In all cases suits led must be followed when possible, if not you may throw away or trump as may appear desirable. Each hand is a game in itself, and when played out, each player counts his own cards of value as specified, the highest scorer being the winner. When stakes are played for, the difference between the two hands is reckoned and paid for at so much a point. Small stakes are recommended as the difference on each game may be considerable.

109. SPECULATION is a lively

round game, at which several may play, with a complete pack of cards, bearing the same value as at Whist. A pool is made with fish or counters, on which such value is fixed as the company may agree. The highest trump in each deal wins the pool ; and should it happen that not one trump be dealt, then the company pool again, and the event is decided by the succeeding deal. After determining the deal, &c., the dealer pools six fish, and every other player four ; then three cards are given to each, one at a time, and another turned up for trump. The cards are not to be looked at except in this manner : The eldest hand shows the uppermost card, which if a trump the company may speculate on, or bid for—the highest bidder buying and paying for it, provided the price offered be approved of by the seller. After this is settled, if the first card does not prove a trump, then the next eldest is to show the uppermost card, and so on— the company speculating as they please, till all are exposed, when the possessor of the highest trump, whether by purchase or otherwise, gains the pool. Not only may an exposed card be sold, but any card or a whole hand of cards, the purchaser not looking at them, but adding them to his own hand, and turning up one at a time as his turn comes round. The turning up of the ace of trumps of course ends the game for that round. It is sometimes made a rule that any player turning up a five or a knave shall pay into the pool. This adds fun to the game.

110. MATRIMONY.—This game is played with an entire pack of cards, by any number of persons from five to fourteen. It consists of five chances, usually marked on a board, or sheet of paper, as follows :—

Best.
The Ace of Diamonds turned up.

Confederacy.
King and Knave.

INTRIGUE ;
OR
QUEEN AND KNAVE

Matrimony.
King and Queen.

Pairs.
The Highest.

The game is generally played with counters for stakes, and the dealer puts what he pleases on each or any chance, the other players depositing each the same quantity, less one—that is, when the dealer stakes twelve, the rest of the company lay down eleven each. After this, two cards are dealt round to every one, beginning on the left ; then to each person one other card, which is turned up, and he who so happens to get the ace of diamonds sweeps all. If it be not turned up, then each player shows his hand ; and any of them having matrimony, intrigue, &c., takes the counters on that point ; and when two or more people happen to have a similar combination, the eldest hand has the preference, and, should any chance not be gained, it stands over to the next deal.—*Observe :* The ace of diamonds turned up takes the whole pool, but when in hand ranks only as any other ace ; and if not turned up, nor any ace in hand, then the king, or next superior card, wins the chance styled *best*.

111. POPE JOAN.—A game somewhat similar to Matrimony. It is played by any number, with an ordinary pack of cards, and a marking or pool board to be had of most fancy stationers. The eight of diamonds must first be taken from the pack. After settling the deal, shuffling, &c., the dealer dresses the board. This he does by putting counters into the several compartments—one counter or other stake to Ace, one each to King, Queen, Knave, and Game ; two to Matrimony, two to Intrigue, and six to the nine of diamonds, styled the Pope. This dressing is, in some companies, at the individual expense of the dealer, though the players usually contribute two stakes each towards the pool. The cards are then dealt round equally to every player, one turned up for trump, and about six or eight left in the stock to form stops. For example, if the ten of spades be turned up, the nine becomes a stop. The four kings, and the seven of diamonds, are always fixed stops, and the dealer is the only person permitted, in the course of the game, to refer occasionally to the stock for information what other cards are stops in their respective deals. If either ace, king, queen or knave happen to be the turned-up trump, the dealer may take whatever is deposited on that head ; but when Pope be turned up, the dealer is entitled both to that and the game, besides a stake for every card dealt to each player. Unless the game be determined by Pope being turned up, the eldest hand begins by playing out as many cards as possible ; first the stops, then Pope, if he have it, and afterwards the lowest card of the longest suit—particularly an ace, for that never can be led through. The other players follow, when they can, in sequence of the same suit, till a stop occurs. The player having the stop becomes eldest hand, and leads accordingly ; and so on, until some player parts with all his cards, by which he wins the pool (game), and becomes entitled besides to a stake for every card not played by the others, except from any one holding Pope, which excuses him from paying. If Pope has been played, then the player having held it is not excused. King and queen form what is called matrimony ; queen and knave, when in the same hand, make intrigue ; but neither these nor ace, king, queen, knave or pope, entitle the holder to the stakes deposited thereon unless played out ; and no claim can be allowed after the board is dressed for the succeeding deal. In all such cases the stakes remain for future determination. Pope Joan needs only a little attention to recollect what stops have been made in the course of the play. For instance, if a player begin by laying down the eight of clubs, then the seven in another hand forms a stop, whenever that suit be led from any lower card ; or the holder, when eldest, may safely lay it down, in order to clear his hand.

112. NEWMARKET.—A very similar game to Pope Joan, but requires no special board. The eight of diamonds having been taken out of the pack, the game is played with the remaining cards. The ace of spades, king of diamonds, queen of hearts, and knave of clubs from another pack are laid in the centre of the table face upwards in the form of a square. Each player stakes an agreed number of counters, the dealer staking double that number. The stakes are divided among the four exposed cards as he chooses.

The cards are dealt one at a time, an extra hand also being dealt (as at Pope Joan), in order to form a like number of "stops." There are no trumps.

The player on the dealer's left leads any suit he likes, but *must* lead the lowest (ace ranks lowest), at the same time naming the card. The player having the next highest card of the same suit plays and names it, and so on till a "stop" is reached, when the person playing the stop leads to the next round.

So the game continues till a player is "out," that is to say, has played all his cards. The winner receives from the losers one counter for each card remaining in their hands ; and when, during the game, a card corresponding with one of the pool cards is played, the person playing it receives all the counters staked on that card.

113. HEARTS is played by four persons, with a full pack of fifty-two cards. The cards rank as in Whist, to which this game has some resemblance ; there is, however, no partnership, no trump suit, and although tricks are made, the object is to avoid winning any trick which contains a card of the heart suit.

The deal having been cut for, the cards are shuffled and dealt as at whist, but the last card is not turned up. Each player is bound to follow suit if possible. If he cannot, he may play any card he chooses, getting rid of any hearts he may have. Each hand is a game.

At the finish of the hand, the tricks are turned up, and the hearts counted.

Supposing that of the 13 hearts A has 3, B 1, C 4, and D 5. Here B wins, having the smallest number, and each of the other players pays him one counter (or as agreed on) for each heart he holds. If there is a tie, as where A and B have 2 hearts each, C 4, and D 5, C and D pay 9 counters and A and B divide them ; but as this cannot be done equally the odd counter is put in the middle of the table to await the result of the next game.

Where there are three players, one of the black deuces is generally taken out ; or the complete pack may be used, leaving the last card face downward in the centre of the table at each deal.

114. COMMERCE is played with a full pack of cards, and by any number of persons. A pool is formed and then three cards are dealt, face downwards, to each player, another three being turned face upwards in the centre of the table.

The eldest hand may then exchange one of his cards for one of the three exposed ones, leaving the discarded one face upwards with the other two. The next player has the same option, and so on all round the table ; but a player who has once "passed" cannot again change a card in any subsequent round.

This goes on until two players are satisfied with their cards, which they announce by saying "Content," or by knocking on the table. Each of the other players may then make one more exchange, and having done so the cards are turned up, and the best hand takes the pool.

The object is to make (1) a Tricon, (2) Sequence, or (3) Point.

(1) A *Tricon* is three cards of like value. Tricons of higher cards prevail over those of lower.

(2) *Sequence*—Three cards of a suit in order of rank, as ace, king, queen.

(3) *The Point* means the lowest number of pips on three cards of one suit, the ace counting as eleven, tens and court cards for ten each, and the other cards according to the number of their pips.

115. CASSINO.—This game is played with an entire pack of cards, generally by four persons, in which case they take partners as in Whist, but sometimes by three, and often by two.

The deal and partners are determined by cutting, as at Whist, and the dealer gives four cards, one at a time, to each player, and either regularly as he deals, or by one, two, three, or four at a time, lays four more, face upwards, upon the board, and when each has played his four cards, four more are dealt to each person (but it is only in the first deal that any cards are to be turned up on the board) ; when these have been played the remaining sixteen cards are dealt.

Each person in turn plays one card at a time, with which he may not only take up every card of the same denomination upon the board, but likewise all that will combine therewith ; as, for instance, a ten takes not only every ten, but also nine and ace, eight and deuce, seven and three, six and four, or two fives ; and if he clear the board he scores a point ; whenever any player cannot pair or combine, then he is to put down a card.

After all the pack is dealt, the player who obtains the last trick takes all the cards then remaining unmatched upon the table. This being done, each player or pair of partners looks over the cards he has won, and scores as under : for

	Points
Great Cassino, the ten of diamond	2
Little Cassino, the two of spades	1
Cards, the player or partners who hold the majority of cards	3
Spades, the majority of this suit	1
Aces, each reckons	1

The cards are then shuffled, and again dealt out and played as described above, the deal passing to the next player.

The game is won by the player or pair of partners who first score a number of points previously agreed upon.

Building in Cassino.—An interesting variation of the game is where the player, by adding one low card from his hand to one or more cards on the table, can make a number corresponding to a higher card in his hand, in which case he places his low card on the one or two exposed ones, saying, "I build" seven, eight, or whatever the number of his higher card may be, and then leaves it till the next time round, when if not able to add to his "build" by combining another low card out of his hand with any of those on the table, he takes it with the high card he has built to. He, however, has to risk his "build" being appropriated by an opponent, as any one having a card in his hand equal to the number built may take them when it comes to his turn. Partners may help each other greatly in building—for instance, if either of the partners has in his hand an ace and eight, and on the table are ace, four, and two, the player can add the ace from his hand to those cards, saying, "I build eight." Supposing the next player puts down six, the first player's partner, if he has a two in his hand, may add that and the six to the eight already built, saying, "I add to my partner's eight," and when it comes to the first partner's turn he takes up both eights built with the eight in his hand.

Although difficult to explain it will readily be seen that the many possible combinations and changes make the game much more amusing, and give scope for considerable skill.

116. VINGT-UN.—The game of *Vingt-un*, or twenty-one, may be played by two or more persons; and, as the deal is advantageous, and often continues long with the same person, it is usual to determine it at the commencement by turning up the first ace, or knave.

Counting in Vingt-un.—Ace counts either one or eleven, court cards ten each, and the other cards according to the number of pips.

Method of Playing.—The dealer first deals one card round, each player then looks at his card, and, with the exception of the dealer, stakes what he chooses on it; a second card is then dealt round, after which the dealer asks each player in rotation, beginning with the eldest hand on the left, whether he stands or chooses another card. If he need another card, it must be given from the top of the pack, and afterwards another, or more, if desired, till the points of the additional card or cards, added to those dealt, exceed or make Vingt-un, or twenty-one exactly, or such a number less than twenty-one as the player thinks fit to stand upon. When the points on the player's cards exceed twenty-one, he throws the cards on the table, face downwards, and pays the stake. The dealer is, in turn, entitled to draw additional cards, and on making a Vingt-un, receives double stakes from all who stand the game, except such other players, likewise having twenty-one, between whom it is thereby a drawn game. When any adversary has a Vingt-un, and the dealer not, then the opponent so having twenty-one, wins double stakes from him. In other cases, except a natural Vingt-un happen, the dealer pays single stakes to all whose numbers under twenty-one are higher than his own, and receives from those who have lower numbers; but nothing is paid or received by such players as have similar numbers to the dealer. When the dealer draws more than twenty-one, he pays to all who have not thrown up. In some companies ties pay the dealer.

Natural Vingt-un.—Twenty-one, when dealt in a player's first two cards, is styled a *Natural*. It should be declared at once, and entitles the holder to double stakes from the dealer, and to the deal, except it be agreed to pass the deal round. If the dealer turns up a natural he takes double stakes from all the players and retains the deal. If there be more than one natural, all after the first receive single stakes only.

117. FRENCH VINGT-UN OR VARIATIONS.—There are eight rounds in this game, each played differently, thus—

1. As in ordinary Vingt-un.

2. (*Imaginary Tens.*) Each of the players stakes before receiving a card. Ten points are added to the value of his card, and the holder decides, according to the amount then made, to draw or otherwise.

3. (*Blind Vingt-un.*) Each of the players, having staked, receives two cards, but must not look at them. He may, if he chooses, draw one or more cards, doing so at haphazard.

4. (*Sympathy and Antipathy.*) Each of the players, having staked, is called on to elect for Sympathy or Antipathy. Having elected, he receives two cards. If they are the same colour Sympathy wins ; if different Antipathy. The player receives or pays as he has chosen correctly or not.

5. (*Rouge et noir.*) Each player, having staked, declares for either red or black, and receives a card. If he has chosen correctly he wins, or *vice versa*.

6. (*Self and Company.*) The players stake, and the dealer deals two cards, face upwards, one for himself, and the other for the company. If they are alike he wins. If not, he keeps on dealing the cards one by one, face upwards, until a card is dealt which pairs either of the two first dealt. If that for "self" is paired, the dealer wins ; and *vice versa*.

7. (*Differences.*) Two cards are dealt, face upwards, to each player, and two to the dealer. The latter pays all who are higher, and receives from all who are lower, at an agreed amount for each unit of difference. Ties cancel, and aces count *one* only.

8. (*The Clock.*) The cards being shuffled and cut, the dealer commences to deal the cards, face upwards, saying as he deals the first, "One,"—as he deals the second "Two," and so on up to king. If a card turned up agrees with the number called out, he wins the stakes. If he reaches thirteen without any card agreeing, he pays the other players.

118. THIRTY-ONE.—This game is played with a full pack of fifty-two cards ; any number of persons can play ; and the cards rank as in Whist The stakes having been placed in the pool, three cards are dealt to each player, and three more are laid in the centre of the table, face upwards.

The object of the game is to obtain three cards *of the same suit*, which together will make "thirty-one." The ace is counted as eleven, court cards ten each, and the other cards according to the number of their pips. As is evident, the "thirty-one" can only be made with an ace and two tens.

Next to the "Thirty-one" in value is a triplet, which counts thirty and a-half. The higher has the preference as between two triplets. In default of thirty-one, or a triplet, the highest total (in any one suit) wins.

The elder hand exchanges one of his cards for one of the three exposed ones, leaving his discarded one face upwards with the other two, then the other players do the same.

The players keep on discarding until one of them makes thirty-one, when he shows his cards and takes the pool ; or till one player is "content," which he announces or knocks on the table. In that case, each of the players is entitled to exchange one more card ; the hands are then shown and the highest wins.

119. QUADRILLE.—This game, formerly very popular, has been superseded by Whist. Quadrille, the game referred to by Pope in his "Rape of the Lock," is now obsolete.

120. ÉCARTÉ.—This game, which has lately revived in popularity, is played by two persons with a pack of cards from which the twos, threes, fours, fives, and sixes have been discarded. In the clubs it is usual to play with two packs, used alternately. The players cut for deal, the highest card deals. The pack is shuffled and the non-dealer cuts. The dealer then from the united pack gives five cards to each in the manner described in Rule v., beginning with his adversary. The eleventh card is turned up for trump. If the turn-up be a king, the dealer marks one point ; five points being game. The non-dealer looks at his cards, and if he be dissatisfied with them, he may propose—that is, change any or all of them for others from the *stock*, or remainder of the pack on the table. Should he propose, he says, "I propose," or "cards," and it is in the option of the dealer to give or refuse cards. When he decides to give, he says, "I accept," or "How many ?" Should he refuse to change he says, "I decline," or "Play." The dealer may, if he accept the proposal, change any or all the cards in his own hand. Sometimes a second discard is allowed, but that must be by previous agreement. Of course the non-dealer may play without discarding, in which case the dealer must play his own hand without changing any of his cards. When the hands are arranged the non-dealer plays a card, which is won or lost by the playing of a superior card of the suit led. The second must follow suit, or win the trick if he can ; otherwise he may throw any card he chooses. The order in value of the cards is—king, queen, knave, ace, ten, nine, eight, seven. Trumps win other suits. The winner of the trick leads for the next trick, and so on till the five cards on each side are played. The winner of three tricks scores one point ; if he win the whole five tricks—the *vôle*—he scores two points ; if he hold the king, he names it before playing his first card—"I mark king." Should the non-dealer play without proposing, and fail to make three tricks, his adversary marks two points ; should the dealer refuse to accept and fail to win three tricks, his opponent scores two. The game is five up ; that is, the player who first makes five points wins. The score is marked by two cards, a three and a two, or by counters. The deal is taken alternately ; but when the play is for rubbers it is usual to cut for deal at the end of each rubber. A player holding the king should not announce it till the last moment. The non-dealer should not declare the king until in the act of playing his first card ; and the dealer should not announce the king till after his opponent has led.

121. THREE-HANDED ÉCARTÉ.—If *three* persons wish to form a game they can play a *pool*, each contributing an equal amount to the pool. They all cut, the lowest being out, and the other two playing the first game. The loser puts into the pool a sum equal to that which he originally put in, and the person who was out takes his place. Should the winner of the first game lose the second, he puts a stake in the pool, stands out, and so on until one player wins two consecutive games, when he takes the pool.

122. RULES OF ÉCARTÉ.

i. Each player has the right to shuffle the cards above the table.

ii. The cut must not be fewer than two cards off the pack, and at least two cards must be left on the table.

iii. When more than one card is exposed in cutting, there must be a new deal.

iv. The highest écarté card cut secures the deal, which holds good even though the pack be imperfect.

v. The dealer most give five cards to each by three and two, or by two and three, at a time, which plan must not be changed during the game.

vi. An incorrect deal, playing out of turn, or a faced card, necessitates a new deal.

vii. The eleventh card must be turned up for trumps ; and the remaining cards placed, face downwards, on the table.

viii. The king turned up must be marked by the dealer before the trump of the next deal is turned up.

ix. A king of trumps held in hand must be announced and marked before the player lays down his first card, or he loses his right to mark it. If played in the first trick, it must be announced before it is played to.

x. A proposal or acceptance cannot be retracted or altered.

xi. Before taking cards, the player must place his discarded cards, face downwards, on the table, and neither look at nor touch them till the round be over.

xii. The player holding king marks one point ; making three tricks, one point ; five tricks, two points.

xiii. The non-dealer playing without proposing and failing to win the point, gives two tricks to his opponent.

xiv. The dealer who refuses the first proposal and fails to win the point (three tricks), gives his opponent two points.

xv. An admitted overscore or underscore may be amended without penalty before the cards are dealt for the following round.

123. EUCHRE, which is founded on Écarté, and is the national game of the United States, is played with a pack of cards from which the twos, threes, fours, fives, and sixes have been withdrawn. In the Euchre pack the cards rank as at Whist, with this exception—the knave of trumps, called the Right Bower, and the other knave of the same colour, known as the Left Bower, take precedence over the rest of the trumps. Thus, when hearts are trumps, the cards rank thus :— Knave of hearts, knave of diamonds, ace, king, queen, ten, nine, eight, and seven of hearts. When diamonds are trumps, the knave is right bower, and the knave of hearts left bower ; and in like manner the knaves of spades and clubs become right and left bower, when the black suits are trumps.—In Four-handed Euchre, two play against two, and the tricks taken by both partners count for points.

124. RULES FOR EUCHRE.

i. The players cut for deal ; the higher card cut dealing.

ii. The cards are dealt by twos and threes, each player having five.

iii. The eleventh card is turned up for trumps, but this does not become the trump card.

iv. Five points constitute game.

v. The player winning three or four tricks marks one point ; winning five tricks, two points.

vi. When the first player considers his hand strong enough to make the odd trick, he can order it up—that is, he can oblige the dealer to discard one of his cards and take up the turn-up card, which becomes confirmed as trumps, and forms part of his hand. It remains on the table however, face upwards.

vii. When the first player does not find his hand strong enough, he may pass, saying—"I pass ;" with the view of changing the suit.

viii. In case of the first player "ordering it up," the game begins by his playing a card, to which the dealer must follow suit or trump, or throw away. The winner of the trick then leads : and so on till all the five cards in each hand are played.

ix. If the player order up the trump and fail to make three tricks, he is euchred, and his opponent marks two points.

x. If the player, not being strong enough, passes, the dealer can say, "I play," and take the trump into his own hand ; but, as before, if he fail to score, he is euchred.

xi. If both players pass, the first has the privilege of altering the trump, and the dealer is compelled to play. Should the first player fail to score, he is euchred.

xii. If he pass for the second time, the dealer can alter the trump, with the same penalty if he fail to score.

xiii. When trumps are led and you cannot follow suit, you must play the left bower if you have it, to win the trick.

The score is marked, as in Écarté by each side with a two and three.

125. BÉZIQUE.—This formerly fashionable game is played with two packs of cards, from which the twos, threes, fours, fives, and sixes, have been discarded. The sixty-four cards contained in both packs, shuffled well together, are then dealt out, eight to each player, either one at a time, or by threes, twos, and threes ; the seventeenth turned up for trump, and the rest (called the "talon" or "stock") left, face downwards, on the table. If the trump card be a seven, the dealer scores ten points. An incorrect deal or an exposed card necessitates a new deal, which passes to the other player. The non-dealer has the lead. A trump card takes any card of another suit. Except trumping, the higher card, whether of the same suit or not, takes the trick—the ace ranking highest, the ten next, and then the king, queen, knave, nine, &c. When two cards of equal value are played, the first wins. *Some players require the winning card to be of the same suit as that led, unless trumped.* After each trick is taken, an additional card is drawn by each player from the top of the pack—the taker of the last trick drawing first, and so on till all the pack is exhausted, including the trump card. Players are not obliged to follow suit or trump until all the cards have been drawn from the pack. Tricks are of no value, except for the aces and tens they may contain. Tricks should not be looked at till the end of the deal, except by mutual consent. When a player plays without drawing, he must draw two cards next time, and his opponent scores ten. When a player draws out of turn, his opponent scores ten, if he has not drawn a card himself. When a player draws two cards instead of one, his opponent may decide which card is to be returned to the pack, and it should not be placed at the top, but towards the middle of the pack. A player discovering his opponent holding more than eight cards, while he only holds eight, adds 100 to his score. Should both have more than their proper number there is no penalty, but each must play without drawing.

126. Terms and counting used in Bézique.—i. A *Declaration* is the exhibition on the table of any cards or combination of cards, as follows :—

ii. Bézique is the queen of spades and knave of diamonds, for which the holder scores 40 points.

[A variation provides that when the trump is either spades or diamonds, Bézique may be queen of clubs and knave of hearts.]

iii. *Double Bézique*—Bézique having been declared, may be again used to form Double Bézique, two queens of spades and two knaves of diamonds. All four cards must be visible on the table together—500 points.

iv. *Sequence* is ace, ten, king, queen, and knave of trumps—250 points.

v. *Royal Marriage* is the king and queen of trumps—40 points.

vi. *Common Marriage* is the king and queen of any suit, except trumps—20 points.

vii. *Four aces* are the aces of any suits—100 points.

viii. *Four kings* are the kings of any suits—80 points.

ix. *Four queens* are the queens of any suits—60 points.

x. *Four knaves* are the knaves of any suits—40 points.

xi. Playing the seven of trumps—except in last eight tricks—10 ; exchanging the seven of trumps for the trump card—10 ; the last trick—10 ; each ace and ten in the tricks at the end of each deal—10.

xii. The game is 1,000, 2,000, or 4,000 up. Markers are sold with the cards.

127. Mode of Playing Bézique.

i. Play is commenced by the non-dealer, whose card is played to by the dealer. Immediately after taking a trick, and then only, a player can make a Declaration ; but he must do so before drawing another card. Only one Declaration can be made after each trick.

ii. If, in making a declaration, a player put down a wrong card or cards, either in addition to or in the place of any card or cards of that declaration, he is not allowed to score until he has taken another trick. Moreover, he must resume the cards, subject to their being called for as "faced" cards.

iii. The seven of trumps may be exchanged for the trump card, and for this exchange ten is scored. This exchange is made immediately after he has taken a trick, but he may make a declaration at the same time, the card exchanged not being used in such declaration.

iv. Whenever the seven of trumps is played, except in the last eight tricks, the player scores ten for it, no matter whether he wins the trick or not.

v. When all the cards are drawn from the pack, the players take up their eight cards. No more declarations can be made, and the play proceeds as at Whist, the ten ranking higher than the king, and the ace highest.

vi. In the last eight tricks the player is obliged to follow suit, and he must win the trick if possible, either by playing a higher card, or, if he has not a card of the same suit, by playing a trump.

vii. A player who revokes in the last eight tricks, or omits to take when he can, forfeits the eight tricks to his opponent.

viii. The last trick is the thirty-second, for which the winner scores ten.

[The game may be varied by making the last trick the twenty-fourth—the next before the last eight tricks. It is an unimportant point, but one that should be agreed upon before the game is commenced.]

ix. After the last eight tricks are played, each player examines his cards, and for each ace and ten that he holds he scores ten.

x. The non-dealer scores aces and tens first ; and in case of a tie, the player scoring the highest number of points, less the aces and tens in the last deal, wins the game. If still a tie, the taker of the last trick wins.

xi. All cards played in error are liable to be called for as "faced" cards at any period of the game, except during the last eight tricks.

xii. In counting forfeits a player may either add the points to his own score or deduct them from the score of his opponent.

Marriages, Sequences, &c.

i. The cards forming the declarations are placed on the table to show that they are properly scored, and the cards may thence be played into tricks as if in your hand.

ii. Kings and queens once married cannot be re-married, but can be used while they remain on the table, to make up four kings, four queens, or a sequence.

iii. The king and queen used in a sequence cannot afterwards be declared as a royal marriage.

iv. If four knaves have been declared, the knave of diamonds may be used again for a bézique, or to complete a sequence.

v. If four aces have been declared, the ace of trumps may be again used to perfect a sequence.

vi. If the queen of spades has been married, she may be again used to form a bézique, and *vice versa*, and again for four queens.

128. FORFEITS AT BÉZIQUE.—
The following are Forfeits :—

For drawing out of turn, 10 ; for playing out of turn, 10 ; for playing without drawing, 10 ; for overdrawing, 100 ; for a revoke in the last eight tricks, all the eight tricks.

129. CAUTIONS IN BÉZIQUE.—
In playing Bézique, it is best to keep your tens till you can make them count ; to retain your sequence cards as long as possible ; to watch your opponent's play ; to declare a royal marriage previous to declaring a sequence or double bézique ; to make sure of the last trick but one in order to prevent your opponent from declaring ; to declare as soon as you have an opportunity.

130. THREE-HANDED BÉZIQUE.

·i. The above rules hold good in the case of three-handed games—treble bézique counting 1,500. An extra pack of cards is required for the third other player ; so that, in the case of three, the trump card is the twenty-fifth.

ii. The game is always played from left to right, the first player on the left of the dealer commencing. Three-handed bézique is sometimes played with two packs of cards, suppressing an eight, thus rendering them divisible by three.

131. FOUR-HANDED BÉZIQUE.

i. Four-handed Bézique may be played by partners decided either by choice or cutting. Partners sit opposite each other, one collecting the tricks of both, and the other keeping the score, or each may keep his own score, which is preferable.

ii. A player may make a declaration immediately after his partner has taken a trick, and may inquire of his partner if he has anything to declare, before drawing.

iii. Declarations must be made by each player separately, as in two-handed bézique.

iv. The above descriptions will serve to sufficiently acquaint the reader with the rules and modes of play adopted in this excellent game. Bézique is said to be of Swedish origin, and to have been introduced to English players through the medium of some Indian officers who had learned it of a Scandinavian comrade. Variations in the play occur in different companies. These, however, having been indicated above, need not be more particularly noted.

132. NAPOLEON OR NAP.—
This popular game is played by four, five, or six persons with a full pack of cards, which take the same value as in Whist. The object of the game is to make tricks, which are paid to or received from the declarer at a fixed rate, a penny or more a trick, as previously arranged. The deal being decided in the usual way, the pack is cut and five cards are dealt one at a time to each player, beginning at the left. After every round the deal passes. Each player looks at his cards, the one to the left of the dealer being the first to declare. When he thinks he can make two or three tricks he says, "I go two," or "I go three." The next may perhaps think he can make four tricks ; and if the fourth believes he can do better he declares "Napoleon," and undertakes to win the whole five tricks. The players declare or pass in the order in which they sit ; and a declaration once made cannot be recalled. The game then proceeds. The first card played becomes the trump suit ; and to win the trick, a higher card than that led in each suit must be played. The winner of the first trick leads for the second, and so on till each of the five tricks are played out. Each player must follow suit, but he is not bound to head the trick or to trump. Each card as played remains face upwards

on the table. Supposing the stake to be a penny a trick, the declarer, if he win all the tricks he declared, receives from each of his adversaries a penny for each of the declared tricks ; but if he fail to win the required number, he pays to each of them a penny a trick. For "Napoléon" he receives double stakes from each player ; but failing to win the five tricks, he pays them single stakes. The game, though simple, requires good judgment and memory to play it well. The aim of the players is to co-operate to prevent the declarer winning the number of tricks he declared. In some companies it is varied by the introduction of a "Wellington," which is a superior call after the Napoleon, and takes triple stakes ; or "Misère," in which the player undertakes to lose all his tricks. This declaration takes precedence of all the others. Each player may Pass, or decline to make a declaration ; and when all the players pass, the deal is void. Occasionally a pool or kitty is made by each dealer paying a half stake ; or the players may purchase new cards from the pack. In either case, the pool is taken by the winner of the first Napoleon, or divided according to arrangement at the close of the play.

133. PIQUET.—A game for two players, once very fashionable in France and of some repute in England ; but now quite obsolete. Like Quadrille, it is encumbered with a vast number of rules and maxims, technical terms and calculations ; all too long and tiresome for modern card-players.

134. POKER, OR DRAW POKER, a gambling game common in the United States. An elaboration of the old English game of *Brag*, which, like *Blind Hookey* and *Baccarat*, is purely one of chance. It is generally played by two or three sharpers opposed to three or four greenhorns, and, for these reasons, is unworthy a place in this volume.

135. RANTER GO ROUND.— This game is chiefly played in the West of England, and is of a simple character. It may be played by any number, and affords plenty of fun to the youngsters. The full pack of fifty-two cards is employed, aces ranking lowest and kings highest, and each player has three counters, or "lives," of such value as may be agreed upon, their combined values making a "pool" for the winner.

The dealer gives one card to each player, and the object of the game is to avoid holding the *lowest* card. No distinction is made between the suits. When the deal is completed, each player looks at his card, and the player on the dealer's left, if he does not like his card, pushes it (face downwards) along the table towards his left-hand neighbour, at the same time saying "change."

The latter player, no matter how good his own card may be, is compelled to exchange, unless his card happens to be a king, when he retains it, saying, "King." Supposing, however, that he does not have a king and makes the exchange ; if he is also not satisfied with the card he has taken, he in his turn pushes it on to his left-hand neighbour, and thus the card goes round the table, until it gets stopped by a king, or one of the players gives a worse card for it, in which case he is content, and has no reason for making any further change. He then "stands," and the next player changes or not with *his* left-hand neighbour, as he may think fit. If a player gives an ace, two or three, in exchange, he must name it for the benefit of the other players.

If the card referred to has been given in compliance with a request for an exchange, it remains with the player who takes it, and of course the other players will be secure if they "stand" on cards of higher value, however small their own may be. For instance, should an ace be declared, a player having a deuce (and more especially a higher card) would be safe. But if the card is one offered in exchange by an elder to a younger player, it will most likely go round till it comes to the dealer, and if he also wishes to change it he cuts the pack, taking the top card of the cut, which then belongs to him. The cards are then turned up, and the player holding the *lowest* loses a life ; but if the dealer, in cutting as before mentioned, turns up a king, *he* loses a life, and this although there is an ace among the turned cards.

On a player losing all his three lives, he is "out," and the game goes on between the other players, the last out taking the pool.

136. SLOBBERHANNES.—A

pack of thirty-two cards is used (all below seven being taken out), and the cards rank in value as at whist. The game is played by four persons, but there is no partnership, each playing independently. The cut is for *lead* (not deal), the highest taking it and the player on his right deals.

There are no trumps, all suits being of the same value. Each player is obliged to follow suit where he can do so, the highest card gains the trick, and the winner leads off again.

The object, however, is *not* to make tricks, for the player who first wins ten points loses the game, and pays the other players such stake as has been previously agreed upon.

It is an advantage to have the lead, as you are pretty certain to have one losing card, and will lead accordingly.

The points are scored thus :—

For the first trick . . . . . . .1 Point
For the last do. 1   „
For the trick containing the
    queen of clubs 1   „

If, in the same hand, a player wins all three tricks above mentioned, he is said to get Slobberhannes, and must score an extra point for it.

The penalty for a revoke is one point added to the score of the player revoking.

137. SPINADO.—A variation of

Pope Joan ; but played without a board. The division of the pool is only for Matrimony, Intrigue, and Game, or "First out." The dealer pays two dozen counters, viz. one dozen to Matrimony, half-a-dozen to Intrigue, and half-a-dozen to First out. The other players pay three each, which are placed in the First out division.

The eight of diamonds and all the deuces having been taken out, the cards are dealt round (with an extra hand as at Pope Joan), but there is no "turn up." Matrimony consists of king and queen : and Intrigue, of queen and knave of diamonds. The ace of the same suit is called Spinado, or "Spin."

The player on the dealer's left leads, and those players having the next higher cards play them in rotation till a "stop" occurs, when the last player again leads.

If able to strike in, the player holding Spinado names and plays it with his own card. For instance, if the five of clubs is led, and he has the six, and Spinado, he will call "six and Spin," thus making the six of clubs a stop. He then receives three counters from each of the other players and the lead passes to him. But the holder of Spinado is not bound to play it with his first card.

The player having the king of diamonds receives two counters from each player ; and if he plays both king and queen, he takes the *Matrimony* pool. A person playing queen and knave of diamonds takes the *Intrigue* pool. If the same person holds (and plays) all three cards, he receives both pools. The player of a king (other than of diamonds) receives one counter from each player. "First out" (unless dealer) is exempt from putting into the pool next deal.

138. SOLITAIRE.—This is a game for one person, played on a board pierced with thirty-three holes ; in each one of which is placed a marble or peg. The art or motive of the game is to remove one marble and then to shift the rest about, so as to bring the last marble to the hole whence the first was removed. One marble or man takes any other over which it can leap into a vacant hole beyond ; or any number of men in succession, so long as there is a hole into which it can go.

139. BACKGAMMON.—A game of mingled chance and skill, played on a board marked with points, and generally to be found inside the box draught-board. The board has twenty-four points, coloured alternately red and blue ; the implements of play are fifteen draught-men on each side, and the movements of the men are determined by the throw of two dice ; each player being provided with a dice box and dice. It is an elaborate game to explain, and would occupy too much space to be given in detail in this work. Cheap handbooks to the game are easily procurable.

140. DOMINOES.—This game is played by two or more persons, with twenty-eight pieces of oblong ivory, plain at the back, but on the face divided by a black line in the middle, and indented with spots, from one to a double-six. Sometimes a double-set is played with, of which double-nine is the highest.

Method of Play.—At the commencement of the game the dominoes are well mixed together, with their faces upon the table. Each player draws one, and if four play, those who choose the two highest are partners against those who take the two lowest Drawing the latter also serves to determine who is to lay down the first piece—a great advantage. Afterwards each player takes seven pieces at random. The eldest hand having laid down one, the next must pair him at either end of the piece he may choose, according to the number of pips, or the blank in the compartment of the piece ; but whenever any one cannot match the part, either of the domino last put down, or of that unpaired at the other end of the row, then he says, "*Go ;*" and the next is at liberty to play. Thus they play alternately, either until one party has played all his pieces, and thereby won the game, or till the game be *blocked ;* that is, when neither party can play, by matching the pieces where unpaired at either end ; then that player wins who has the smallest number of pips on the pieces remaining in his hand. It is to the advantage of every player to dispossess himself as early as possible of the heavy pieces, such as a double-six, five, four, &c. Sometimes, when two persons play, they take each only three or five pieces, and agree to *play* or *draw*—*i. e.* when one cannot come in, or pair the pieces upon the board at the end unmatched, he draws from the pieces in stock till he finds one to suit. There are various other ways of playing dominoes, but they are all dependent on the matching of the pips.

141. DANCES.

142. QUADRILLES.—The First Set. *First Figure, Le Pantalon.* —Right and left. Balancez to partners ; turn partners. Ladies' chain. Half promenade ; half right and left (Four times.)

Second Figure, L'Été. —Leading lady and opposite gentleman advance and retire ; chassez to right and left ; cross over to each other's places ; chassez to right and left. Balancez and turn partners. (Four times.) Or *Double L'Été.*—Both couples advance and retire at the same time ; cross over ; advance and retire again ; cross to places. Balancez and turn partners. (Four times.)

Third Figure, La Poule.—Leading lady and opposite gentleman cross over, giving right hands ; recross, giving left hands, and fall in a line. Set four in a line ; half promenade. Advance two, and retire (twice). Advance four, and retire ; half right and left. (Four times.)

Fourth Figure, Trénise.—The first couple advance and retire twice, the lady remaining on the opposite side ; the two ladies go round the first gentleman, who advances up the centre ; balancez and turn partners. (Four times.) Or *La Pastorale* is sometimes danced as the *Fourth Figure.* The leading couple advance twice, leaving the lady opposite the second time. The three advance and retire twice. The leading gentleman advances and sets. Hands four half round ; half right and left to places. (Four times.)

Fifth Figure, Galop Finale.—All galopade or promenade, eight bars. Advance four, *en galopade oblique*, and retire, then half promenade, eight bars. Advance four, retire, and return to places with the half promenade, eight bars. Ladies' chain, eight bars. Repeated by the side couples, then by the top and bottom, and lastly by the side couples, finishing with grand promenade.

Instead of this figure, another one called "Flirtation" is often danced, thus : —All join hands and form a circle ; advance towards centre and retire ; loose hands and turn partners to places ; ladies advance to centre, bow, and retire ; gentlemen to centre, and each turns towards the corner lady on his left, bows, promenades round set with her, returning to his own place. Join hands in circle again and repeat as above four times, on the last occasion joining original partners. Finish with circle and turn partners.

143. LANCERS.—i. *La Rose.*—First gentleman and opposite lady advance and set—turn with both hands, retiring to places—return, leading outside—set and turn at corners.

ii. *La Lodoiska.*—First couple advance twice, leaving the lady in the centre—set in the centre—turn to places—all advance in two lines—all turn partners.

iii. *La Dorset.*—First lady advances and stops, then the opposite gentleman—both retire, turning round—ladies' hands across half round, and turn the opposite gentleman with left hands—repeat back to places, and turn partners with left hands.

iv. *L'Étoile.*—First couple set to couple at right—set to couple at left—change places with partners, and set, and pirouette to places—right and left with opposite couple.

v. *Les Lanciers.*—The grand chain. The first couple advance and turn facing the top ; then the couple at right advance behind the top couple ; then the couple at left and the opposite couple do the same, forming two lines. All change places with partners and back again. The ladies turn in a line on the right, the gentlemen in a line on the left. Each couple meet up the centre. Set in two lines, the ladies in one line, the gentlemen in the other. Turn partners to places. Finish with the grand chain.

144. THE CALEDONIANS.— *First Figure.*—The first and opposite couples hands across round the centre and back to places—set and turn partners. Ladies' chain. Half promenade—half right and left. Repeated by the side couples.

Second Figure.—The first gentleman advances and retires twice. All set at corners, each lady passing into the next lady's place on the right. Promenade by all. Repeated by the other couples.

Third Figure.—The first lady and opposite gentleman advance and retire, bending to each other. First lady and opposite gentleman pass round each other to places. First couple cross over, having hold of hands, while the opposite couple cross on the outside of them—the same reversed. All set at corners, turn, and resume partners.

All advance and retire twice, in a circle with hands joined—turn partners.

Fourth Figure.—The first lady and opposite gentleman advance and stop ; then their partners advance ; turn partners to places. The four ladies move to right, each taking the next lady's place, and stop—the four gentlemen move to left, each taking the next gentleman's place, and stop—the ladies repeat the same to the right—then the gentleman to the left. All join hands and promenade round to places, and turn partners. Repeated by the other couples.

Fifth Figure.—The first couple promenade or waltz round inside the figure. The four ladies advance, join hands round, and retire—then the gentlemen perform the same—all set and turn partners. Chain figure of eight half round, and set. All promenade to places and turn partners. All change sides, join right hands at corners, and set, back again to places. Finish with grand promenade.—These three are the most admired of the quadrilles : the First Set invariably takes precedence of every other dance.

145. SPANISH DANCE.—Danced in a circle or a line by sixteen or twenty couples. The couples stand as for a Country Dance, except that the first gentleman must stand on the ladies' side, and the first lady on the gentlemen's side. First gentleman and second lady balancez to each other, while first lady and second gentleman do the same, and change places. First gentleman and partner balancez, while second gentleman and partner do the same, and change places. First gentleman and second lady balancez, while first lady and second gentleman do the same, and change places. First gentleman and second lady balancez to partners, and change places with them. All four join hands in the centre, and then change places, in the same order as the foregoing figure, four times. All four poussette, leaving the second lady

and gentleman at the top, the same as in a Country Dance. The first lady and gentleman then go through the same figure with the third lady and gentleman, and so proceed to the end of the dance. This figure is sometimes danced in eight bars time, which not only hurries and inconveniences the dancers, but also ill accords with the music.

146. WALTZ COTILLON.—Places the same as quadrille. First couple waltz round inside ; first and second ladies advance twice and cross over, turning twice ; first and second gentlemen do the same ; third and fourth couples do the same ; first and second couples waltz to places, third and fourth do the same ; all waltz to partners, and turn half round with both hands, meeting the next lady ; perform this figure until in your places ; form two side lines, all advance twice and cross over, turning twice ; the same returning ; all waltz round ; the whole repeated four times.

147. GALOP is an extremely graceful and spirited dance, in a continual chassez. An unlimited number may join ; it is danced in couples, as waltzing.

148. MAZURKA.—This dance is of Polish origin—first introduced into England by the Duke of Devonshire, on his return from Russia. It consists of twelve movements ; and the first eight bars are played (as in quadrilles) before the first movement commences.

149. REDOWA WALTZ is composed of three parts, distinct from each other. 1st, The Pursuit. 2nd, The waltz called Redowa. 3rd, The waltz à Deux Temps, executed to a peculiar measure, and which, by a change of the rhythm, assumes a new character. The middle of the floor must be reserved for the dancers who execute the promenade, called the pursuit, while those who dance the waltz turn in a circle about the room. The position of the gentleman is the same as for the waltz. The gentleman sets out with the left foot, and the lady with the right. In the pursuit the position is different, the gentleman and his partner face, and take each other by the hand. They advance or fall back at pleasure, and balance in advance and backwards. To advance, the step of the pursuit is made by a glissade forward, without springing, *coupé* with the hind foot, and *jeté* on it. You recommence with the other foot, and so on throughout. The retiring step is made by a sliding step of the foot backwards, without spring, *jeté* with the front foot, and *coupé* with the one behind. It is necessary to advance well upon the sliding step, and to spring lightly in the two others, *sur place*, balancing equally in the *pas de poursuite*, which is executed alternately by the left in advance, and the right backwards. The lady should follow all the movements of her partner, falling back when he advances, and advancing when he falls back. Bring the shoulders a little forward at each sliding step, for they should always follow the movement of the leg as it advances or retreats ; but this should not be too marked. When the gentleman is about to waltz, he should take the lady's waist, as in the ordinary waltz. The step of the Redowa, in turning, may be thus described. For the gentleman— *jeté* of the left foot, passing before the lady. *Glissade* of the right foot behind to the fourth position aside—the left foot is brought to the third position behind—then the *pas de basque* is executed by the right foot, bringing it forward, and you recommence with the left. The *pas de basque* should be made in three very equal beats, as in the Mazurka. The lady performs the same steps as the gentleman, beginning by the *pas de basque* with the right foot. To waltz à deux temps to the measure of the Redowa, we should make each step upon each beat of the bar, and

find ourselves at every two bars, the gentleman with his left foot forwards, and the lady with her right, that is to say, we should make one whole and one half step to every bar. The music is rather slower than for the ordinary waltz.

150. VALSE CELLARIUS.—The gentleman takes the lady's left hand with his right, moving one bar to the left by *glissade*, and two hops on his left foot, while the lady does the same to the right, on her right foot ; at the second bar they repeat the same with the other foot—this is repeated for sixteen bars ; they then waltz sixteen bars, *glissade* and two hops, taking care to occupy the time of two bars to get quite round. The gentleman now takes both hands of the lady, and makes the grand square—moving three bars to his left—at the fourth bar making two beats while turning the angle ; his right foot is now moved forward to the other angle three bars—at the fourth, beat again while turning the angle ; the same repeated for sixteen bars— the lady having her right foot forward when the gentleman has his left foot forward ; the waltz is again repeated ; after which several other steps are introduced, but which must needs be seen to be understood.

151. WALTZ (the original known as the *Valse à trois temps*). This dance consists of three steps. The gentleman places his right hand on the lady's waist, taking her right hand in his left, the lady then placing her left hand on the gentleman's right shoulder. The lady begins with her right foot with a sliding step to the right, then a step forward with the left foot bringing the right foot up to it, slightly rising on the toes and turning half-round, then three similar steps commencing with the left foot complete the other half round. The gentleman takes the same steps, but commences with the left foot.

152. Valse à Deux Temps.—This waltz contains, like the common waltz, three times, but differently divided. The first time consists of a gliding step ; the second a chassez, including two times in one. A chassez is performed by bringing one leg near the other, then moving it forward, backward, right, left, and round. The gentleman begins by sliding to the left with his left foot, then performing a chassez towards the left with his right foot without turning at all during the first two times. He then slides backwards with his right leg, turning half round ; after which he puts his left leg behind, to perform a chassez forward, turning then half round for the second time. The lady waltzes in the same manner, except that the first time she slides to the right with the right foot, and also performs the chassez on the right, and continues the same as the gentleman, except that she slides backwards with her right foot when the gentleman slides with his left foot to the left ; and when the gentleman slides with his right foot backwards she slides with the left foot to the left. To perform this waltz gracefully, care must be taken to avoid jumping, but merely to slide, and keep the knees slightly bent.

153. CIRCULAR WALTZ.—The dancers form a circle, then promenade during the introduction—all waltz sixteen bars—set, holding partner's right hand, and turn—waltz thirty-two bars—rest, and turn partners slowly—face partner and chassez to the right and left—pirouette lady twice with the right hand, all waltz sixteen bars—set and turn—all form a circle, still retaining the lady by the right hand, and move round to the left, sixteen bars—waltz for finale.

154. CIRCASSIAN CIRCLE.— The company is arranged in couples round the room—the ladies being placed on the right of the gentlemen,—after which, the first and second couples lead off the dance. *Figure.* Right and left, set and turn partners—ladies' chain, waltz.—At the conclusion, the first couple with fourth, and the second with the third couple, recommence the figure,—and so on until they go completely round the circle, when the dance is concluded.

155.   POLKA.—The gentleman and lady place themselves in position as in the waltz. The lady steps to the right with the right foot, draws the left foot up to it and springs slightly on the right foot ; then steps to the left with the left foot, draws the right foot up to it and springs slightly on the left foot, at the same time turning to the right. Care should be taken to mark each *third* step as indicated by the music. The gentleman's step is exactly the same as the lady's, but of course he commences with the left foot.

156.   SCHOTTISCHE.—The gentleman holds the lady precisely as in the waltz. Beginning with the left foot, he slides it forward, then brings up the right foot to the place of the left, slides the left foot forward, and springs or hops on this foot. This movement is repeated to the right. He begins with the right foot, slides it forward, brings up the left foot to the place of the right foot, slides the right foot forward again, and hops upon it. The gentleman springs twice on the left foot, turning half round ; twice on the right foot ; twice *encore* on the left foot, turning half round ; and again twice on the right foot, taming half round. Beginning again, he proceeds as before. The lady begins with the right foot, and her step is the same in principle as the gentleman's. Vary, by a *reverse turn :* or by going in a straight line round the room. Double, if you like, each part, by giving four bars to the first part, and four bars to the second part. The *time* may be stated as pre- cisely the same as in the polka ; but let it not be forgotten that *La Schottische* ought to be danced much *slower*.

157. THE AMERICAN BARN DANCE.

—The Barn Dance can be danced to any Schottische music. The partners stand side by side, the gentleman taking his partner's left hand with his right, going straight forward in the first four bars. Start with the right foot, take three steps, extend, bring up and extend ; now swing the left foot (from behind) in front of the right, with the foot turned downwards. This finishes up the fourth beat. The left foot now being in front, the next bar is commenced with it, repeating the step, and bringing the right foot in front on the fourth beat. The next two bars are danced in the same way, finishing with four bars of hops, as in the ordinary Schottische.

158. THE IOLANTHE.

—The time is the same as in the Barn Dance. Partners give hands for the first four bars, and join as usual for the next four bars. The Iolanthe has, in addition to that used in the Barn Dance, nine other steps or figures. They are not easy to describe, and must be learned by practical experience.

159. THE NATIONAL (QUADRILLE).

—This is a very pretty and popular quadrille, and is danced thus :—

England (1st Figure). Balancez to partners—Balancez to corners—advance and retire (Four)—Advance and waltz with ladies vis-à-vis—Advance and retire once more—advance and waltz with partners to places—Hands all round, advance, retire, and turn partners—(sides repeat from the first "advance").

Wales (2nd Figure). Four ladies advance and retire—Advance, join right hands, and waltz to opposite places—Four gentlemen advance and retire—Advance, right hands across, and rejoin partners—Demi-grande chaîne to places—Grand waltz (16 bars).

Second time.—Four gentlemen advance and retire—Advance, right hands across, waltz to opposite places—Four ladies advance and retire—Advance, right hands across, rejoin their partners—Demi-grande chaîne—Grand waltz (16 bars).

Scotland (3rd Figure). Balancez to corners—Waltz with corner ladies to opposite places—Again balancez to corners—Waltz with next corner ladies to places—Repeat till all in their places—Four ladies cross right hands to opposite places while gentlemen waltz to right, and meeting partners, all waltz to places—Gentlemen cross right hands to opposite places while ladies waltz to right, and meeting partners all waltz to places—Finish with demi-grande chaîne, and all waltz to places.

Ireland (4th Figure). 1st and 2nd couples waltz round (8 bars)—Grand moulin by all the couples—Change sides—Hands all round, turn corners—Hands all round again, turn partners—Repeat, side couples beginning.

United Kingdom (5th Figure). Grand chain—1st couple promenade, sides follow, all form two lines (as in last figure of Lancers)—Ladies waltz to the right and gentlemen to left—Meet at bottom and waltz to places—Grand waltz (16 bars)—Repeat the whole four times, each couple starting to promenade in turn.

Finale. Grand chain, and finish with grand waltz (twice) and courtesy.

160. SIR ROGER DE COVERLEY.

—All form two lines, the gentlemen facing the ladies. Top lady and bottom gentleman advance to centre, present right hands and pass quickly round each other to places, top gentleman and bottom lady do the same, then top lady and bottom gentleman advance, give left hands and pass quickly round to places, top gentleman and bottom lady the same.

The beginning couple advance and give both hands, turning round to places, following couple the same. The top lady and bottom gentleman advance to centre and turn round each other back to back without touching, the other couple do the same ; first lady and bottom gentleman then advance, bow to each other and retire, first gentleman and bottom lady the same. The top gentleman then turns outwards to his right, and the lady turns outwards to her left ; each leading down to the bottom of the room, followed by the other gentlemen and ladies. The top couple meet at the bottom, join hands, holding them up as an arch for the other couples to dance through to places, but remaining themselves at the bottom. The figure is then repeated by the other couples in succession.

161. LA POLKA COUNTRY DANCE.—All form two lines, ladies on the right, gentlemen on the left. *Figure.* Top lady and second gentleman heel and toe (polka step) across to each other's place—second lady and top gentleman the same. Top lady and second gentleman retire back to places—second lady and top gentleman the same. Two couples polka step down the middle and back again—two first couples polka waltz. First couple repeat with the third couple, then with fourth, and so on to the end of dance.

162. THE HIGHLAND REEL.— This dance is performed by the company arranged in parties of three, along the room in the following manner : a lady between two gentlemen, in double rows. All advance and retire— each lady then performs the reel with the gentleman on her right hand, and retires with the opposite gentleman to places—hands three round and back again—all six advance and retire— then lead through to the next trio, and continue the figure to the end of the room. Adopt the Highland step, and music of three-four time.

163. TERMS USED IN DANCES.

Balancez.—Set to partners.

Chaîne Anglaise.—The top and bottom couples right and left.

Chaîne Anglaise double.—The right and left double.

Chaîne des Dames.—The ladies' chain.

Chaîne des Dames double.—The ladies' chain double, which is performed by all the ladies commencing at the same time.

Chassez.—Move to the right and left.

Chassez croisez.—Gentlemen change places with partners, and back again.

Demie Chaîne Anglais.—The four opposite persons half right and left.

Demie Promenade.—All eight half promenade.

Demie Moulinet.—The ladies all advance to the centre, giving hands, and return to places.

La Grande Chaîne.—All eight chassez quite round, ladies starting to their left and gentlemen to their right, giving alternately right and left hands.

La Grande Ronde.—All join hands and advance and retire twice.

Pas d'Allemande.—The gentlemen turn the partners under their arms.

Traversez.—The two opposite persons change places.

Vis-à-vis.—The opposite partner.

164. SCANDAL—LIVE IT DOWN.

Should envious tongues some malice frame.
To soil and tarnish your good name,
                Live it down !

Grow not disheartened ; 'tis the lot
Of all men, whether good or not :
                Live it down !

Rail not in answer, but be calm :
For silence yields a rapid balm :
                Live it dovn !

Go not among your friends and say,
Evil hath fallen on my way :
                Live it down !

Far better thus yourself alone
To suffer, than with friends bemoan
The trouble that is all your own :

Live it down !

What though men *evil* call your *good* !
So CHRIST Himself, misunderstood,
Was nailed unto a cross of wood !
And now shall you for lesser pain,
Your inmost soul for ever stain,
By rendering evil back again ?

Live it down !

165. ERRORS IN SPEAKING.— There are several kinds of errors in speaking. In some cases words are employed that are unsuitable to convey the meaning intended. Thus, a person wishing to express his intention of going to a given place, says, "I *propose* going," when in fact, he *purposes* going. The following affords an amus- ing illustration of this class of error :— A venerable matron was speaking of her son, who, she said, was quite stage struck. "In fact," remarked the old lady, "he is going to a *premature* performance this evening !" Consider- ing that most *amateur* performances are *premature*, it cannot be said that this word was altogether misapplied ; though, evidently, the maternal inten- tion was to convey quite another meaning.

i. Other Errors Arise from the substitution of sounds similar to the words which should be employed ; that is, spurious words instead of genuine ones. Thus, some people say "renu-merative" when they mean "remu-nerative." A nurse, recommending her mistress to have a *perambulator* for her child, advised her to purchase a *preamputator* !

ii. Errors are Occasioned by im-perfect knowledge of the English grammar : thus, many people say, "Between you and I," instead of "Between you and *me*." And there are numerous other departures from the rules of grammar, which will be pointed out hereafter.

iii. By the Misuse of the Adjective : "What *beautiful* butter !" "What a *nice* landscape !" "They should say, "What a *beautiful landscape* !" "What *nice* butter !"

iv. By the Mispronunciation of Words. Many persons say *pro*noun*cia-tion* instead of *pronunciation* ; others say pro-nun´-she-a-shun, instead of pro-nun-ce-a-shun.

v. By the Misdivision of Words and syllables. This defect makes the word *an ambassador* sound like *a nambassador*, or *an adder* like *a nadder*.

vi. To correct these errors by a systematic course of study would in-volve a closer application than most persons could afford, and require more space than we can devote to the subject. We however give numerous Rules and Hints, in a concise and simple form, which will be of great assistance to inquirers. These Rules are founded upon the authority of scholars, the usages of the bar, the pulpit, and the senate, and the authority of societies formed for the purpose of collecting and diffusing knowledge pertaining to the language of this country.

166. RULES AND HINTS FOR CORRECT SPEAKING.

1. *We* and *whom* are used in relation to persons, and *which* in relation to things. But it was once common to say "the man *which*." This should now be avoided. It is now usual to say, "Our Father *who* art in heaven," instead of "*which* art in heaven."

2. *Whose* is, however, sometimes applied to things as well as to persons. We may therefore say, "The country *whose* inhabitants are free." Gram- marians differ in opinion upon this subject, but general usage justifies the rule.

3. *Thou* is employed in solemn discourse, and *you* in common lan-guage. *Ye* (plural) is also used in serious addresses, and *you* in familiar language.

4. The uses of the word *It* are various, and very perplexing to the uneducated. It is not only used to imply persons, but things, and even ideas, and therefore, in speaking or writing, its assistance is constantly required. The perplexity respecting this word arises from the fact that in using it in the construction of a long sentence, sufficient care is not taken to ensure that when *it* is employed it really points out or refers to the object intended. For instance, "It was raining when John set out in his cart to go to the market, and he was delayed so long that it was over before he arrived." Now what is to be understood by this sentence ? Was the rain over ! or the market ? Either or both might be inferred from the construction of the sentence, which, therefore, should be written thus :— "It was raining when John set out in his cart to go to the market, and he was delayed so long that the market was over before he arrived." After writing a sentence always read it through, and see that wherever the word *It* is employed, it refers to or carries the mind back to the object which it is intended to point out.

5. The general distinction between *This* and *That* may be thus defined : *this* denotes an object present or near, in time or place, *that* something which is absent.

6. *These* refers, in the same manner, to present objects, while *those* refers to things that are remote.

7. *Who* changes, under certain conditions, into *whose and whom.* But *that* and *which* always remain the same.

8. *That* may be applied to nouns or subjects of all sorts ; as, the *girl that* went to school, the *dog that* bit me, the *ship that* went to London, the *opinion that* he entertains.

9. The misuse of these pronouns gives rise to more errors in speaking and writing than any other cause.

10. When you wish to distinguish between two or more persons, say, "*Which* is the happy man ?"—not *who*—"*Which* of those ladies do you admire ?"

11. Instead of "*Who* do you think him to be ?"—say, "*Whom* do you think him to be ?"

Whom should I see !

To *whom* do you speak ?

Who said so ?

Who gave it to you ?

Of *whom* did you procure them ?

Who was *he* ?

Who do men say that *I* am !

Whom do they represent *me* to be ?[1]

12. In many instances in which *who* is used as an interrogative, it does not become *whom* ; as "*Who* do you speak to ?" "*Who* do you expect ?" "*Who* is she married to ? " "*Who* is this reserved for ?" "*Who* was it made by ?" Such sentences are found in the writings of our best authors, and it would be presumptuous to consider them as ungrammatical. If the word *whom* should be preferred, then it would be best to say, "For *whom* is this reserved ?" &c.

13. *Self* should never be added to *his, their, mine,* or *thine.*

14. *Each* is used to denote every individual of a number.

15. *Every* denotes all the individuals of a number.

16. *Either* and *or* denote an alternative : "I will take *either* road, at your pleasure ;" "I will take this *or* that."

17. *Neither* means *not either* ; and *nor* means *not the other.*

18. *Either* is sometimes used for *each*—"Two thieves were crucified, on either *side* one."

19. "Let *each* esteem others as good as themselves," should be, "Let *each* esteem others as good as *himself.*" "

---

1 Persons who wish to become well acquainted with the principles of *English Grammar* by an easy process, are recommended to procure "The Useful Grammar," price 3*d.*, published by Houlston and Sons.

20. "There are bodies *each* of which *are* so small," should be "each of which *is* so small."

21. Do not use double superlatives, such as *most straightest, most highest, most finest.*

22. The term *worser* has gone out of use ; but *lesser* is still retained.

23. The use of such words as *chiefest, extremist,* &c., has become obsolete, because they do not give any superior force to the meanings of the primary words, *chief, extreme,* &c.

24. Such expressions as, *more impossible, more indispensable, more universal, more uncontrollable, more unlimited,* &c., are objectionable, as they really enfeeble the meaning which it is the object of the speaker or writer to strengthen. For instance, *impossible* gains no strength by rendering it *more* impossible. This class of error is common with persons who say, "A *great large* house," "A *great big* animal," "A *tiny little* hand."

25. *Here, there,* and *where,* originally denoting place, may now, by common consent, be used to denote other meanings, such as, "*There* I agree with you," "*Where* we differ," "We find pain *where* we expected pleasure," "*Here* you mistake me."

26. *Hence, whence,* and *thence,* denoting departure, &c., may be used without the word *from.* The idea of *from* is included in the word *whence*—therefore it is unnecessary to say, "*From whence.*"

27. *Hither, thither,* and *whither,* denoting to a place, have generally been superseded by *here, there,* and *where.* But there is no good reason why they should not be employed. If, however, they are used, it is unnecessary to add the word *to,* because that is implied—"*Whither* are you going ?" "*Where* are you going ?" Each of these sentences is complete. To say, "Where are you going *to* ?" is redundant.

28. Two *negatives* destroy each other, and produce an affirmative.

"*Nor* did he *not* observe them," conveys the idea that he *did* observe them.

29. But negative assertions are allowable. "His manners are not unpolite," which implies that his manners are, in some degree, marked by politeness.

30. Instead of "I *had* rather walk," say "I would rather walk."

31. Instead of "Let you and *I,*" say "Let you and me."

32. Instead of "I am not so tall as *him,*" say "I am not so tall as he."

33. When asked "Who is there ?" do not answer "*Me,*" but "*I.*"

34. Instead of "For you and *I,*" say "For you and me."

35. Instead of "*Says* I," say "I said."

36. Instead of "You are taller than *me,*" say "You are taller than I."

37. Instead of "I *ain't*" or "I *arn't,*" say "I am not."

38. Instead of "Whether I be present or *no,*" say "Whether I be present or not."

39. For "Not that I know *on,*" say "Not that I know."

40. Instead of "*Was* I to do so," say "Were I to do so."

41. Instead of "I would do the same if I *was him,*" say "I would do the same if I were he."

42. Instead of "I h*ad as lief* go myself," say "I would as soon go myself," or "I would rather."

43. It is better to say "Six weeks ago," than "Six weeks back."

44. It is better to say "Since which time," than "Since when."

45. It is better to say "I repeated it," than "I said so over again."

46. Instead of "*Less* friends," say "Fewer friends." Less refers to quantity, Fewer to numbers.

47. Instead of "A *quantity* of people," say "A number of people."

48. Instead of "*As* far as I can see," say "So far as I can see."

49. Instead of "If I am *not mistaken,*" say "If I mistake not."

50. Instead of "You *are mistaken,*" say "You mistake."

51. Instead of "What *beautiful* tea !" say "What good tea !"

52. Instead of "What a *nice* prospect !" say "What a *beautiful* prospect !"

53. Instead of "A *new pair* of gloves," say "A pair of new gloves."

54. Instead of saying "*Not no* such thing," say "Not any such thing."

55. Instead of "I hope you'll think nothing *on* it," say "I hope you'll think nothing of it."

56. Instead of "Restore it *back* to me," say "Restore it to me."

57. Instead of "I seldom *or ever* see him," say "I seldom see him."

58. Instead of "*Rather warmish*," or "A *little* warmish," say "Rather warm."

59. Instead of "I expected *to have* found him," say "I expected to find him."

60. Instead of "He is a very *rising* person," say "He is rising rapidly."

61. Instead of "Who *learns* you music ?" say "Who teaches you music ?"

62. Instead of "I *never* sing *whenever* I can help it," say "I never sing when I can help it."

63. Instead of "Before I do that I must *first* ask leave," say "Before I do that I must ask leave."

64. Instead of "To *get over* the difficulty," say "To overcome the difficulty."

65. The phrase "*get over*" is in many cases misapplied, as, to "get over a person," to "get over a week," to "get over an opposition."

66. Instead of saying "The *observation* of the rule," say "The observance of the rule."

67. Instead of "A man *of* eighty years of age," say "A man eighty years old."

68. Instead of "He died from *negligence*," say "He died through neglect," or "in consequence of neglect."

69. Instead of "Apples are plenty," say "Apples are plentiful."

70. Instead of "The *latter* end of the year," say "The end, or the close of the year."

71. Instead of "The *then* government," say "The government of that age, or century, or year or time."

72. Instead of "For *ought* I know," write "For aught I know."

73. Instead of "They are *united together* in the bonds of matrimony," say "They are united in matrimony," or "They are married."

74. Instead of "We travel *slow*," say "We travel slowly."

75. Instead of "He plunged *down* into the river," say "He plunged into the river."

76. Instead of "He jumped *from off of* the scaffolding," say "He jumped off the scaffolding."

77. Instead of "He came the last *of all*," say "He came the last."

78. Instead of "*universal*" with reference to things that have any limit, say "general" ; "generally approved," instead of "universally approved" ; "generally beloved," instead of "universally beloved."

79. Instead of "They ruined *one another*," say "They ruined each other."

80. Instead of "If *in case* I succeed," say "If I succeed."

81. Instead of "A *large enough* room," say "A room large enough."

82. Instead of "I am slight in comparison *to* you," say "I am slight in comparison with you."

83. Instead of "I went *for* to see him," say "I went to see him."

84. Instead of "The cake is all *eat up*," say "The cake is all eaten."

85. Instead of "Handsome is *as* handsome does," say "Handsome is who handsome does."

86. Instead of "As I *take* it," say "As I see," or "As I understand it."

87. Instead of "His opinions are *approved of* by all," say "His opinions are approved by all."

88. Instead of "A sad curse is war," say "War is a sad curse."

89. Instead of "He stands *six foot* high," say "He measures six feet," or "His height is six feet."

90. Instead of "I go *every now and then*," say "I go often, or frequently."

91. Instead of "Who finds him in clothes," say "Who provides him with clothes."

92. Say "The first two," and "the last two," instead of "the *two first*," "the two last ;" leave out all expletives, such as "of all," "first of all," "last of all," "best of all," &c., &c.

93. Instead of "His health was *drank with enthusiasm*," say "His health was drunk enthusiastically."

94. Instead of "*Except* I am prevented," say "Unless I am prevented."

95. Instead of "In its *primary sense*," say "In its primitive sense."

96. Instead of "Give me *them* papers," say "Give me those papers."

97. Instead of "He was a man *notorious* for his benevolence," say "He was noted for his benevolence."

98. Instead of "She was a woman *celebrated* for her crimes," say "She was notorious on account of her crimes."

99. Instead of "What may your name be ?" say "What is your name ?"

100. Instead of "By *smoking it often* becomes habitual," say "By smoking often it becomes habitual."

101. Instead of "I lifted it *up*," say "I lifted it."

102. Instead of "It is *equally of the same* value," say "It is of the same value," or "equal value."

103. Instead of "I knew it *previous* to your telling me," say "I knew it previously to your telling me."

104. Instead of "You *was* out when I called," say "You were out when I called."

105. Instead of "I thought I should *have won* this game," say "I thought I should win this game."

106. Instead of "*This* much is certain," say "So much is certain."

107. Instead of "He went away *as it may be* yesterday week," say "He went away yesterday week."

108. Instead of "Put your watch in your pocket," say "Put your watch into your pocket."

109. Instead of "He has *got* riches," say "He has riches."

110. Instead of "Will you *set* down ?" say "Will you sit down ?"

111. Instead of "The hen is *setting*," say "The hen is sitting."

112. Instead of "It is raining very *hard*," say "It is raining very fast."

113. Instead of "No *thankee*," say "No thank you."

114. Instead of "I cannot do it without *farther* means," say "I cannot do it without further means."

115. Instead of "No sooner but," or "No other *but*," say "than."

116. Instead of "*Nobody else* but her," say "Nobody but her."

117. Instead of "He fell *down* from the balloon," say "He fell from the balloon."

118. Instead of "He rose *up* from the ground," say "He rose from the ground."

119. Instead of "*These* kind of oranges *are* not good," say "This kind of oranges is not good."

120. Instead of "Somehow or *another*," say "Somehow or other."

121. Instead of "*Undeniable* references required," say "Unexceptionable references required."

122. Instead of "I cannot *rise* sufficient funds," say "I cannot raise sufficient funds."

123. Instead of "*Well*, I don't know," say "I don't know."

124. Instead of "*Will* I give you some more tea ?" say "Shall I give you some more tea ?"

125. Instead of "Oh dear, what *will* I do ?" say "Oh dear, what shall I do ?"

126. Instead of "I will send it *confirmable* to your orders," say "I will send it conformably to your orders."

127. Instead of "Give me a *few* broth," say "Give me some broth."

128. Instead of "*Her* said it was hers," say "She said it was hers."

129. Instead of "To be *given away* gratis," say "To be given away."

130. Instead of "Will you enter in ?" say "Will you enter ?"

131. Instead of "*This* three days or more," say "These three days or more."

132. Instead of "He is a bad *grammarian*," say "He is not a grammarian."

133. Instead of "We *accuse him for*," say "We accuse him of."

134. Instead of "We *acquit* him *from*," say "We acquit him of."

135. Instead of "I am adverse *from* that," say "I am adverse to that."

136. Instead of "I confide *on* you," say "I confide in you."

137. Instead of "I differ *with* you," say "I differ from you."

138. Instead of "As soon *as ever*," say "As soon as."

139. Instead of "The *very best*," or "The *very worst*," say "The best or the worst."

140. Instead of "A *winter's morning*," say "A winter morning," or "A wintry morning."

141. Instead of "Fine morning, *this* morning," say "This is a fine morning."

142. Instead of "How *do you do ?*" say "How are you ?"

143. Instead of "Not so well as I could wish," say "Not quite well."

144. Avoid such phrases as "No great shakes," "Nothing to boast of," "Down in my boots," "Suffering from the blues." All such sentences indicate vulgarity.

145. Instead of "No one *hasn't* called," say "No one has called."

146. Instead of "You have a *right* to pay me," say "It is right that you should pay me."

147. Instead of "I am going *on* a tour," say "I am about to take a tour."

148. Instead of "I am going *over* the bridge," say "I am going *across* the bridge."

149. Instead of "He lives opposite the square," say "He lives opposite to the square."

150. Instead of "He *belongs* to the Reform Club," say "He is a member of the Reform Club."

151. Avoid such phrases as "I am up to you," "I'll be down upon you," "Cut," or "Mizzle."

152. Instead of "I *should just* think I could," say "I think I can."

153. Instead of "There has been a *good deal*," say "There has been much."

154. Instead of "*Following up* a principle," say "Guided by a principle."

155. Instead of "Your *obedient, humble servant*," say "Your obedient," or, "Your humble servant."

156. Instead of saying "The effort you are making *for* meeting the bill," say "The effort you are making to meet the bill."

157. Dispense with the phrase "*Conceeal from themselves the fact* ;" it suggests a gross anomaly.

158. Never say "*Pure and unadulterated*," because the phrase embodies a repetition.

159. Instead of saying, "Adequate for," say "Adequate to.'"

160. Instead of saying "A *surplus over and above*," say "A surplus. '

161. Instead of saying "A *lasting and permanent* peace," say "A permanent peace."

162. Instead of saying "I left you *behind at* London," say "I left you behind me at London.'

163. Instead of saying "*Has been* followed by immediate dismissal," say "Was followed by immediate dismissal."

164. Instead of saying "Charlotte was met *with* Thomas," say "Charlotte was met by Thomas." But if Charlotte and Thomas were walking together, "Charlotte and Thomas were met by," &c.

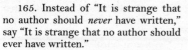

165. Instead of "It is strange that no author should *never* have written," say "It is strange that no author should ever have written."

166. Instead of "I won't never write," say "I will never write."

167. Instead of saying "They are not what nature *designed* them," say "They are not what nature designed them to be."

168. Instead of "By this *means*," say "By these means."

169. Instead of "All that was *wanting*," say "All that was wanted."

170. Instead of "The quality of the apples *were* good," say "The quality of the apples was good."

171. Instead of "The want of learning, courage, and energy *are* more visible," say "Is more visible."

172. Instead of "We are conversant about it," say "We are conversant with it."

173. Instead of "We die *for* want," say "We die of want."

174. Instead of "He died *by* fever," say "He died of fever."

175. Instead of "I *enjoy* bad health," say "My health is not good."

176. Instead of "*Either* of the three," say "Any one of the three."

177. Instead of "Better *nor* that," say "Better than that."

178. Instead of "We often think *on* you," say "We often think of you."

179. Instead of "He was *remarkable* handsome," say "He was remarkably handsome."

180. Instead of "You will *some* day be convinced," say "You will one day be convinced."

181. Instead of "Because I don't choose to," say "Because I would rather not."

182. Instead of "*Because* why ?" say "Why ?"

183. Instead of "That *there* boy," say "That boy."

184. Instead of "Direct your letter to me," say "Address your letter to me."

185. Instead of "The horse is not *much worth*," say "The horse is not worth much."

186. Instead of saying "When he *was* come back," say "When he had come back."

187. Instead of saying "His health has been *shook*," say "His health has been shaken."

188. Instead of "It was *spoke* in my presence," say "It was spoken in my presence."

189. Instead of "*Very* right," or "*Very* wrong," say "Right," or "Wrong."

190. Instead of "This town is not *as* large as we thought," say "This town is not so large as we thought."

191. Instead of "I *took you to be* another person," say "I mistook you for another person."

192. Instead of "*There's* fifty," say "There are fifty."

193. Instead of "The *best* of the two," say "The better of the two."

194. Instead of "Is Lord Lytton in ?" say "Is Lord Lytton within ?"

195. Instead of "Two *spoonsful* of physic," say "Two spoonfuls of physic."

196. Avoid such phrases as "I said, says I" "She said, says she," &c.

197. Instead of "He was in *eminent* danger," say "He was in *imminent* danger."

198. Instead of "The weather is *hot*," say "The weather is very warm."

199. Instead of "I *sweat*," say "I perspire."

200. Instead of "I *only* want two shillings," say "I want only two shillings."

201. Instead of "Whatsomever," always take care to say "Whatever," or "Whatsoever."

202. Avoid such exclamations as "God bless me !" "God deliver me !" "By God !" "By Gor' !" "My Lor !" "Upon my soul," &c., which are vulgar, and savour of impiety.

167. **PRONUNCIATION.**—To acquire a good knowledge of pronunciation, it is advisable to listen

attentively to the examples given by good speakers, and by educated persons. We learn the pronunciation of words to a great extent by *imitation*, just as birds acquire the notes of other birds which may be near them. Some valuable Rules of Pronunciation are given in paragraph 176.

168. ACCENTUATION OF WORDS is a particular stress or force of the voice upon certain syllables or words. This mark ´ in printing denotes the syllable upon which the stress or force of the voice should be placed.

i. A word may have more than one accent.—Take as an instance *aspiration*. In uttering this word we give a marked emphasis of the voice upon the first and third syllables, and therefore those syllables are said to be accented. The first of these accents is less distinguishable than the second, upon which we dwell longer, therefore the second accent in point of order is called the primary, or chief accent of the word.

ii. When the full accent falls on a vowel, that vowel should have a long sound, as in *vo´cal* ; but when it falls on or after a consonant, the preceding vowel has a short sound, as in *hab´it.*

iii. It is very important to bear in mind that there are many words having a double meaning or application, and that the difference of meaning is indicated by the difference of the accent. Among these words, *nouns* are distinguished from *verbs* by

this means : *nouns* are mostly accented on the first syllable, and *verbs* on the last.

iv. Noun signifies name ; nouns are the names of persons and things, as well as of things not material and palpable, but of which we have a conception and knowledge, such as *courage, firmness, goodness, strength* ; and *verbs* express *actions, movements,* &c. If the word used signifies that anything has been done, or is being done, or is to be done, then that word is a *verb.*

v. Thus, when we say that anything is "an in´sult," that word is a *noun,* and is accented on the first syllable ; but when we say he did it "to insult´ another person," the word insult´ implies *acting,* and becomes a *verb,* and should be accented on the last syllable. The effect is, that, in speaking, you should employ a different pronunciation in the use of the same word, when uttering such sentences as these :— "What an in´sult !" "Do you mean to insult´ me ?" In the first sentence the stress of voice must be laid upon the first syllable, *in´,* and in the latter case upon the second syllable, *sult´.*

vi. Meaning varied by accentuation.—In the following list of words that are liable to this variation it will be noticed that those in the first column, having the accent on the first syllable, are mostly nouns ; and that those in the second column, which have the accent on the second and final syllable, are mostly verbs :—

169. WORDS THE MEANING OF WHICH IS VARIED BY ACCENTUATION.

Noun, &c.	Verb, &c.	Noun, &c.	Verb, &c.	Noun, &c.	Verb, &c.
Ab´ject	abject´	Aug´ment	augment´	Com´pound	compound´
Ab´sent	absent´	Bom´bard	bombard´	Com´press	compress´
Ab´stract	abstract´	Col´league	colleague´	Con´cert	concert´
Ac´cent	accent´	Col´lect	collect´	Con´crete	concrete´
Af´fix	affix´	Com´ment	comment´	Con´duct	conduct´
As´pect	aspect´	Com´pact	compact´	Con´fine	confine´
At´tribute	attribute´	Com´plot	complot´	Con´flict	conflict´
Au´gust	august´	Com´port	comport´	Con´serve	conserve´

Noun, &c.	Verb, &c.	Noun, &c.	Verb, &c.	Noun, &c.	Verb, &c.
Con´sort	consort´	Ex´port	export´	Pre´mise	premise´
Con´test	contest´	Ex´tract	extract´	Pre´sage	presage´
Con´text	context´	Fer´ment	ferment´	Pres´ent	present´
Con´tract	contract´	Fore´cast	forecast´	Prod´uce	produce´
Con´trast	contrast´	Fore´taste	foretaste´	Proj´ect	project´
Con´verse	converse´	Fre´quent	frequent´	Prot´est	protest´
Con´vert	convert´	Im´part	impart´	Reb´el	rebel´
Con´vict	convict´	Im´port	import´	Rec´ord	record´
Con´voy	convoy´	Im´press	impress´	Ref´use	refuse´
De´crease	decrease´	Im´print	imprint´	Re´tail	retail´
Des´cant	descant´	In´cense	incense´	Sub´ject	subject´
Des´ert	desert´	In´crease	increase´	Su´pine	supine´
De´tail	detail´	In´lay	inlay´	Sur´vey	survey´
Di´gest	digest´	In´sult	insult´	Tor´ment	torment´
Dis´cord	discord´	Ob´ject	object´	Tra´ject	traject´
Dis´count	discount´	Out´leap	outleap´	Trans´fer	transfer´
Ef´flux	efflux´	Per´fect	perfect´	Trans´port	transport´
Es´cort	escort´	Per´fume	perfume´	Un´dress	undress´
Es´say	essay´	Per´mit	permit´	Up´cast	upcast´
Ex´ile	exile´	Pre´fix	prefix´	Up´start	upstart´

170. PROVINCIAL DIALECTS.—
Persons bred in many of the districts of the United Kingdom often retain methods of pronunciation and certain expressions that are peculiar to those various localities, and therefore, when they move into other districts, their peculiarities of speech often cause them to appear vulgar and uneducated, when they are not so. It is, therefore, desirable for all persons to approach the recognized standard of correctness as nearly as possible.

171. AMUSING PROVINCIALISMS.

i. **Cornish.**—An ould man found, one day, a young gentleman's portmantle, as he were a going to es dennar : he took'd et en and gived et to es wife, and said, "Mally, here's a roul of lither, look, see, I suppose some poor ould shoemaker or other have los'en ; tak'en, and put'en a top of the teaster of the bed ; he'll be glad to hab 'en agin sum day, I dear say." The ould man, Jan, that was es neame, went to es work as before. Mally then opened the portmantle, and found en et three hunderd pounds. Soon after thes, the ould man not being very well, Mally said, "Jan, I'ave saaved away a little

money) by the bye, and as thee caan't read or write, thee shu'st go to scool" (he were then nigh threescore and ten). He went but a very short time, and comed hoam one day and said, "Mally, I waint go to scool no more, 'caase the childer do be laffen at me : they can tell their letters, and I caan't tell my A, B, C, and I wud rayther go to work agen." "Do as thee wool," ses Mally. Jan had not been oat many days, afore the young gentleman came by that lost the portmantle, and said, "Well, my ould man, did'ee see or hear tell o' sich a thing as a portmantle?" "Portmantle, sar, was't that un, something like thickey ?" (pointing to one behind es saddle.) "I vound one the t'other day zackly like that." "Where es et ?" "Come along, I carr'd 'en and gov'en to my ould 'ooman, Mally ; thee sha'tav'en, never vear.—Mally, where es that roul of lither I broft en tould thee to put en a top o' the teaster of the bed, *afore I go'd to scool ?*" "Drat thee emperance," said the young gentleman ; "thee art bewattled ; *that were afore I were born.*" So he druv'd off, and left all the three hunderd pounds with Jan and Mally.

ii. **Yorkshire.**—Men an' women

is like so monny cards, played wi' be two oppoanents, Time an' Eternity : Time gets a gam' noo an' then, and hez t' pleasure o' keepin' his cards for a bit, bud Eternity's be far t' better hand, an' proves, day be day, an' hoor be hoor, 'at he's winnin' incalcalably fast.—"Hoo sweet, hoo varry sweet, is life !" as t' flee said when he wur stuck i' treacle !

iii. **West Country.**—*Tummus.* "I zay, Jim, be you a purtectionist ?" *Jim.* "E'as I be." *Tummus.* "Wall, I zay, Jim, what *be* purtection ?" *Jim.* "Loa'r, Tummus, doan't 'ee knaw ?" *Tummus.* "Naw, I doan't." *Jim.* "Wall, I doan't knaw as I can tell 'ee, Tummus, *vur I doan't ezakerly knaw mysel' !*"

172. AMUSING COCKNEYISMS.

i. **Low Cockney.**—"Seen that party lately ?" "What ! the party with the wooden leg, as come with—" "No, no—not that party. The party, you know, as—" "Oh ! ah ! I know the party you mean, now." "Well, a party told me as he can't agree with that other party, and he says that if another party can't be found to make it all square, he shall look out for a party as will."—*(And so on for half-an-hour.)*

ii. **Omnibus Driver.**—*Old acquaintance.* "'Ave a drop, Bill ?" *Driver.* "Why, yer see, Jim, this 'ere young hoss has only been in 'arness once afore, and he's such a beggar to bolt ; ten to one if I leave 'im he'll be a-runnin' hoff, and a smashin' into suthun. Howsoever—here—*(handing reins to a timid passenger)*—lay hold, sir, I'LL CHANCE IT !"

iii. **Cockney Flunkey.**—*Country Footman meekly inquires of London Footman*—"Pray, sir, what do you think of your town ? A nice place, ain't it ?" *London Footman (condescendingly).* "Well, Joseph, I likes your town well enough. It's clean : your streets are hairy ; and you have lots of rewins. But I don't like your champagne, it's all gewsberry !"

vi. **Cockney Cabby** (*with politeness*).—"Beg pardon, sir ; please don't smoke in the keb, sir ; ladies do complain o' the 'bacca uncommon. Better let me smoke it for yer outside, sir !"

v. **Juvenile Low Cockney.**—"Jack ! Whereabouts is Amstid-am !" *Jack.* "Well, I can't say exackerley, but I know it's somewhere near Ampstid-'eath !"

vi **Cockney Domestic.**—*Lady.* "Wish to leave ! why, I thought, Thompson, you were very comfortable with me !" *Thompson (who is extremely refined).* "Ho yes, mum ! I don't find no fault with you, mum—nor yet with master—but the truth *his*, mum—the other servants is so 'orrid vulgar and hignorant, and speaks so hungrammatical, tbat I reely cannot live in the same 'ouse with 'em—and I should like to go this day month, if so be has it won't illconvenience you ! "

vii. **Cockney Hairdresser.**—"They say, sir, the cholera is in the Hair, sir!" *Gent (very uneasy).* "Indeed ! Ahem ! Then I hope you're very particular about the brushes you use." *Hairdresser.* "Oh, I see you don't hunderstand me, sir ; I don't mean the 'air of the 'ed, but the *h*air *h*of the *h*atmosphere !"

173. HINTS FOR THE CORRECTION OF THE IRISH BROGUE.—

According to the directions given by Mr. B. H. Smart, an Irishman wishing to throw off the brogue of his mother country should avoid hurling out his words with a superfluous quantity of breath. It is not *broadher* and *widher* that he should say, but the *d*, and every other consonant, should be neatly delivered by the tongue, with as little riot, clattering, or breathing as possible. Next let him drop the roughness or rolling of the r in all places but the beginning of syllables ; he must not say *stor-rum* and *far-rum*, but let the word be heard in one smooth syllable. He should exercise himself until he can convert *plaze* into *please*, *plinty* into *plenty, Jasus* into *Jesus*, and so on. He should modulate his sentences, so as to avoid directing his accent all in one manner—from the acute to the grave. Keeping his ear on the alert for good examples, and exercising himself frequently upon them, he may become master of a greatly improved utterance.

174. HINTS FOR CORRECTING THE SCOTCH BROGUE.

The same authority remarks that as an Irishman uses the closing accent of the voice too much, so a Scotchman has the contrary habit, and is continually drawling his tones from the grave to the acute, with an effect which, to southern ears, is suspensive in character. The smooth guttural *r* is as little heard in Scotland as in Ireland, the trilled *r* taking its place. The substitution of the former instead of the latter must be a matter of practice. The peculiar sound of the *u*, which in the north so often borders on the French *u*, must be compared with the several sounds of the letter as they are heard in the south ; and the long quality which a Scotchman is apt to give to the vowels that ought to be essentially short, must be clipped. In fact, aural observation and lingual exercise are the best remedies for excessive brogue.

175. AMERICANISMS.

We give below a short list of words in general use in America with their English equivalents.

American.	English
Biscuit	Roll
Cracker	Biscuit
Depôt	Railway Station
Cars	Railway Carriages
Horse-Cars	Tramway Cars
Side Walk	Foot Pavement
Chore	Errand
Store	Shop
Saloon	Public House Bar
Ranch	Cattle or Sheep Farm
Lumber	Timber
Fall	Autumn

American.	English
Rooster	Cock
Sick	Ill
Boss	Master
Help	Servant
Caucus	Secret Assembly
Smart	Clever

There are also many expressions peculiar to Americans with which we are now getting quite familiar, such as—"I guess ;" "I calculate ;" "I reckon ;" "You bet ;" "fix yourself up ; " "run a store ;" "haven't a red cent ;" "to boom," &c., &c.

176. RULES FOR PRONUNCIATION.

i. C before *a, o,* and *u,* and in some other situations, is a close articulation, like *k.* Before *e, i,* and *y, c* is precisely equivalent to *s* in *same, this* ; as in *cedar, civil, cypress, capacity.*

ii. E final indicates that the preceding vowel is long ; as in hate, mete, sire, robe, lyre, abate, recede, invite, remote, intrude.

iii. E final indicates that *c* preceding has the sound of *s* ; as in *lace, lance* ; and that *g* preceding has the sound of *j*, as in *charge, page, challenge.*

iv. E final, in proper English words, never forms a syllable, and in the most-used words, in the terminating unaccented syllable it is silent. Thus, *motive, genuine, examine, granite,* are pronounced *motiv, genuin, examin, granit.*

v. E final, in a few words of foreign origin, forms a syllable ; as *syncope, simile.*

vi. E final is silent after *l* in the following terminations, —*ble, cle, dle, fle, gle, kle, ple, tle, zle* ; as in *able, manacle, cradle, ruffle, mangle, wrinkle, supple, rattle, puzzle,* which are pronounced *a ʹbl, manaʹcl, craʹdl, rufʹfl, manʹgl, wrinʹkl, supʹpl, puzzʹl.*

vii. E is usually silent in the termination en ; as in *token, broken* ; pronounced **tokn, brokn.**

viii. OUS, in the termination of adjectives and their derivatives, is pronounced *us* ; as in *gracious, pious, pompously*.

ix. CE, CI, TI, before a vowel, have the sound of *sh* ; as in *cetaceous, gracious, motion, partial, ingratitude* ; pronounced *cetashus, grashus, moshun, parshal, ingrashiate*.

x. SI, after an accented vowel, is pronounced like *zh* ; as in *Ephesian, confusion* ; pronounced *Ephezhan, confuzhon*.

xi. When CI or TI precede similar combinations, as in pronunc*i*ation, nego*ti*ation, they should be pronounced *ce* instead of *she*, to prevent a repetition of the latter syllable ; as *pronunceashun* instead of *pronunsheashon*.

xii. GH, both in the middle and at the end of words, is silent ; as in *caught, bought, fright, nigh, sigh* ; pronounced *caut, baut, frite, ni, si*. In the following exceptions, however, *gh* is pronounced as *f* :—*cough, chough, clough, enough, laugh, rough, slough, tough, trough*.

xiii. When WH begins a word, the aspirate *h* precedes *w* in pronunciation ; as in *what, whiff, whale* ; pronounced *hwat, hwiff, hwale*, w having precisely the sound of *oo*, French *ou*. In the following words *w* is silent :—*who, whom, whose, whole*.

xiv. H after *r* has no sound or use ; as in *rheum, rhyme* ; pronounced *reum, ryme*.

xv. H should be sounded in the middle of words ; as in fore*h*ead, ab*h*or, be*h*old, ex*h*aust, in*h*abit, un*h*orse.

xvi. H should always be sounded except in the following words :—heir, honest, honour, hour, humour, and all their derivatives—such as humorously, derived from humour.

xvii. K and G are silent before *n* ; as *know, gnaw* ; pronounced *no, naw*.

xviii. W before *r* is silent ; as in *wring, wreath* ; pronounced *ring, reath*.

xix. B after *m* is silent ; as in *dumb, numb* ; pronounced *dum, num*.

xx. L before k is silent ; as in *balk, walk, talk* ; pronounced *bauk, wauk, tauk*.

xxi. PH has the sound of *f* ; as in *philosophy* ; pronounced *filosofy*.

xxii. NG has two sounds, one as in *singer*, the other as *fin-ger*.

xxiii. N after *m*, and closing a syllable, is silent ; as in *hymn, condemn*.

xxiv. P before *s* and *t* is mute ; as in *psalm, pseudo, ptarmigan* ; pronounced *sarm, sudo, tarmigan*.

xxv. R has two sounds, one strong and vibrating, as at the beginning of words and syllables, such as *robber, reckon, error* ; the other as at the terminations of words, or when succeeded by a consonant, as *farmer, morn*.

xxvi. Before the letter R there is a slight sound of *e* between the vowel and the consonant. Thus, *bare, parent, apparent, mere, mire, more, pure, pyre*, are pronounced nearly *baer, paerent, appaerent, me-er, mier, moer, puer, pyer*. This pronunciation proceeds from the peculiar articulation of *r*, and it occasions a slight change of the sound of *a*, which can only be learnt by the ear.

xxvii. There are other rules of pronunciation affecting the combinations of vowels, &c. ; but as they are more difficult to describe, and as they do not relate to errors which are commonly prevalent, we shall content ourselves with giving examples ot them in the following list of words. When a syllable in any word in this list is printed in italics, the accent or stress of voice should be laid on that syllable.

177. Proper Pronunciation of Words often Wrongly Pronounced.

Ab-dōmen, not *áb´*-dŏmen

Acŭmen, not ac-ŭ-men.

Again, usually pronounced a-*gen*, not as spelt.

Alien, á-li-en not *ale-yen.*

Al-lop´-athy, not al´lo-pathy.

Antipodes, an-*tip-o*-dees.

Apostle, as *a-pos'l*, without the *t*.

Arch, *artch* in compounds of our own language, as in archbishop, archduke ; but *ark* in words derived from the Greek, as archaic, ar-*ka*-ik ; archaeology, ar-ke-*ol*-o-gy ; archangel, ark-*ain*gel ; archetype, *ar*-ke-type ; archiepiscopal, are-ke-e-*pis*-copal ; archipelago, ar-ke-*pel*-a-go ; ar-chives, *ar*-kivz, &c.

Asia, *a*-sha.

Asparagus as spelled, not asparagrass.

Aunt, ant, not *aw*nt.

Awkward, awk-*wurd*, not awk-*urd*.

Bade, bad

Because, be-*cawz*, not be-*cos*.

Beloved, as a verb, be-*luvd* ; as an adjective, be-*luv*-ed. Blessed, cursed, &c., are subject to the same rule.

Beneath, with the *th* in breath, not with the *th* in breathe.

Biog´raphy, as spelled, not beography.

Buoy, boy, not bwoy.

Cachinnation (laughter) is pronounced *kăk-in-na´shŏn.*

Calendar (an almanac), should be distinguished from *calender* (to mangle).

Canal´, as spelled, not ca-nel.

Caprice, capreece

Catch, as spelled, not k*e*tch.

Chaos, *ka*-oss.

Charlatan, *shar*-latan.

Chasm, kazm

Chasten, chasn

Chemistry, *kem´-is-tre,* not *kim*-is-tre.

Chivalry, *shiv*-alry.

Choir, kwire.

Clerk, kl*ar*k.

Cognōmen, not cog´nŏmen.

Colonel, as kernel.

Comb, kum-bat.

Conduit, kun-dit.

Corps, kor: the plural corps is pronounced korz.

Courteous, *curt*-yus.

Courtesy (politeness), *cur*-te-sey.

Courtesy (a lowering of the body), *curt*-sey.

Covetous, *cuv*-e-tus, not cuv-e-chus.

Cresses, as spelt, not *cree*-ses.

Curios´ity, cu-re-*os*-e-ty, not curio*s*ity.

Cushion, *coosh*-un, not coosh-*in.*

Daunt, d*aw*nt, not dant or darnt, as some erroneously pronounce it.

Desire should have the sound of *s.*

Despatch, de-*spatch,* not *dis*-patch.

Dew, due, not doo.

Diamond, as spelled, not *di*-mond.

Diphthong should be pronounced *dif´thong.*

Diploma, de-*plo*-ma, not *dip*-lo-ma.

Diplomacy, de-*plo*-ma-cy, not *dip*-lo-ma-cy.

Direct, de-*reckt,* not *di*-rect.

Distich (poetry) is pronounced *dis-tick.*

Divers (several), *di*-vers ; but diverse (different), *di*-verse.

Dome, as spelled, not doom.

Drought, drowt, not drawt.

Duke, as spelled, not dook.

Dynasty, *dyn*-as-te, not *dy*-nas-ty.

Edict, *e*-dickt, not *ed*-ickt.

E'en and e'er, een and air.

Egotism, *eg*-o-tizm, not *e*-go-tism.

Either, *e*-ther or *i*-ther.

Engine, *en*-jin, not *in*-jin.

Ensign, *en*-sign ; ensigncy, *en*-sine-se.

Epistle, without the *t.*

Epitome, e-*pit*-o-me.

Epoch, *e*-pock, not *ep*-ock.

Equinox, *e*-qui-nox, not *eq*-kwe-nox.

Europe, *U*-rope, not *U*-rup. Euro-*pe*-an, not Euro-pean.

Every, *ev*-er-y, not *ev*-ry.

Executor, egz-*ec*-utor, not with the sound of *x.*

Extraordinary, as spelled, not ex-*tror*-di-ner-i, or *ex*-traordinary, nor extrornarey.

Facet (of a diamond) is pronounced fas´et, not fă-set.

February, as spelled, not Februay.

Finance, fe-*nance*, not *f*nance.

Foundling, as spelled, not *fond*-ling.

Garden, *gar*-dn, not gar-den, nor gard-ing.

Gauntlet, gawnt-let, not *gant*-let.

Geography as spelled, not *jog*raphy, or gehography.

Geometry, as spelled, not *jom*-etry.

Góndōla, not gŏndōla.

Haunt, hawnt, not hant.

Height, hite, not highth.

Heinous, *hay*-nus, not *hee*-nus.

Her-ku-lēan, not her-kū-lean.

Highland, *hi*-land, not *hee*-land.

Horizon, ho-*ri*-zn, not *hor*-i-zon.

Housewife, pronounced in the ordinary way when it means the mistress of a house who is a good manager ; but *huz*-wif, when it means a small case for needles.

Hymeneal, hy-men-*e*-al, not hymenal.

Il-lus´trāted, not il-lus'-ter-ated.

Indict is pronounced in-dite, not in-dict.

Instead, in-*sted*, not instid.

Isolate, *i*-so-late, not *is*-o-late, nor *is*-olate.

Jalap, *jal*-ap, not jolup.

January, as spelled, not Jenuary.

Jū-gu-lar, not jŭg´u-lar.

Just, as spelled, not jest.

Leave, as spelled, not leaf.

Legend, *lej*-end, not *le*-gend.

Lieutenant, lef-*ten*-ant, not leu-*ten*-ant.

Lilac, not lay-lock.

Many, *men*-ney, not man-ny.

Marchioness, *mar*-shun-ness, not as spelled.

Massacre, *mas*-sa-ker, not mas-sa-cre.

Matron, *ma*-trun, not mat-ron.

Mattress, as spelled, not *mat*-trass.

Medicine, *med*-e-cin, not *med*-cin.

Minute (sixty seconds), *min*-it.

Minute (small), mi-*nute*.

Miscellany, mis-*cel*-lany, not *mis*-cellany.

Mischeivous, *mis*-chiv-us, not mis-*cheev*-ius.

Murrain is pronounced *mur'rin.*

Ne'er for never, nare.

Neighbourhood, *nay*-bur-hood.

Nephew, *nev*-u, not *nef*-u.

New, nū, not noo.

Notable (worthy of notice), *no*-ta-bl.

Oblige, as spelled, not obleege.

Oblique, ob-*leek*, not o-*blike*.

Odorous, *o*-der-us, not *od*-ur-us.

Of, ov, except when compounded with there, here, and where, which should be pronounced there-*of*, here-*of*, and where-*of.*

Often, of'n, not of-ten.

Organization, *or*-gan-i-*za*-tion, not or-ga-*ne*-za-shun.

Ostrich, *os*-trich, not *os*-tridge.

Ŏv´id, not Ō-vid.

Pageant, *paj*-ent, not *pa*-jant.

Partisan, *par*-te-zan, not par-te-*zan*, nor *par*-ti-zan.

Patent, *pa*-tent, not *pat*-ent.

Perh´aps, not praps.

Phthisis is pronounced *tis-is.*

Physiognomy, as *fis*-i-*og*-nomy, not physionnomy.

Pincers, *pin*-cerz, not pinch-erz.

Plaintiff, as spelled, not plan-tiff.

Pleb-is-cī-tum, not plē-bisci-tum.

Pneumonia, as nu-mo´-nea.

Pour, pore, not so as to rhyme with our.

Prĕb´-end-ary, not prĕ-bend-ary.

Precedent (an example), *pres*-e-dent ; pre-*ce*-dent (going before in point of time, previous, former) is the pronunciation of the adjective.

Prologue, *pro*-log, not *prol*-og.

Quadrille, ka-*dril*, not quot-ril.

Quarantine is pronounced quarantēne.

Quay, key, not as spelled.

Radish, as spelled, not red-ish.

Raillery, *rail'*-er-y, or *ral*-er-y, not as spelled.

Rather, *rar*-ther not ray-ther.

Resort, re-*sort.*

Resound, re-*sound.*

Respite, *res*-pit, not as spelled.

Rout (a party ; and to rout) should be pronounced rowt. Route (a road), root.

Saunter, *sawn*-ter, not *sarn*-ter or *san*-ter.

Sausage, *saw*-sage, not sos-sidge, nor *sus*-sage.

Sceptic is pronounced *skep'tik.*

Schedule, *shed*-ule, not shed-dle.

Seamstress is pronounced *seem*-stress ; but semp-stress, as the word is now commonly spelt, is pronounced *sem*-stress.

Sewer, *soo*-er or *su*-er, not shore, nor shure.

Shire, as spelled, when uttered as a single word, but shortened into shir in composition.

Shone, shŏn, not shun, nor as spelled.

Soldier, *sole*-jer.

Solecism, *sol*-e-cizm, not *so*-le-cizm.

Soot, as spelled, not sut.

Sovereign, *sov*-er-in, not suv-er-in.

Specious, *spe*-shus, not *spesh*-us.

Stomacher, *stum*-a-cher.

Stone (weight), as spelled, not stun.

Synod, *sin*-od, not *sy*-nod.

Tenet, *ten*-et, not *te*-net.

Tenure, *ten*-ure, not *te*-nure.

Than, as spelled, not thun.

Theatre is pronounced thĕ´atre, not the-ā´-ter.

Trait is pronounced *tray.*

Tremor, *trem*-ur, not *tre*-mor.

Twelfth should have the th sounded.

Umbrella, as spelled, not um-ber-el-la.

Vase, vaiz, or varz, not vawze.

Vi´olet not voil´et.

Was, woz, not wuz.

Weary, *weer*-i, not w*a*ry.

Were, wer, not ware.

Wont, not wunt.

Wrath, rawth, not r*a*th: as an adjective it is spelled wr*o*th, and pronounced with the vowel sound shorter, as wrăth-ful, &c.

Yacht, yot, not yat.

Yeast, as spelled, not yĕst.

Zenith, *zen*-ith, not *ze*-nith.

Zodiac, *zo*-de-ak

Zoology should have both *o*'s sounded, as zo-*ol*-o-gy, not *zoo*-lo-gy.

Note.—The tendency of all good elocutionists is to pronounce as nearly in accordance with the spelling as possible.

Pronounce—

–ace, not iss, as furn*ace*, not furn*iss*

–age, not idge, as cabbage, courage, postage, village

–ain, ane, not in, as certain, cert*ane*, not cert*in*.

–ate, not it, as moder*ate*, not moder*it*.

–ect, not ec, as asp*ect*, not asp*ec* ; subj*ect*, not subj*ec*.

–ed, not id, or ud, as wick*ed*, not wick*id*, or wick*ud*

–el, not l, as mod*el*, not mod*l* ; nov*el*, not nov*l*.

–en, not n, as sudd*en*, not sudd*n*.—Burden, burthen, garden, lengthen, seven, strengthen, often, and a few others, have the *e* silent.

–ence, not unce, as influ*ence*, not influ-*unce*.

–es, not is, as pleas*es*, not pleas*is*.

–ile should be pronounced il, as fert*il*, not fert*ile*, in all words except chamomile (*cam*), exile, gentile, infantile, reconcile, and senile, which should be prounced ile.

–in, not n, as Lat*in*, not Lat*n*.

–nd, not n, as husb*and*, not husba*n* ; thous*and*, not thousa*n*.

–ness, not niss, as careful*ness*, not careful-*niss*.

–ng, not n, as sing*ing*, not sing*in* ; speak*ing*, not speak*in*.

–ngth, not nth, as str*ength*, not strength.

–son, the *o* should be silent ; as in treason, *tre-zn*, not *tre-son*.

–tal, not tle, as capi*tal*, not capi*tle* ; metal, not met*tle*, mort*al*, not mor*tle* ; periodi*cal*, not periodi*cle*.

–xt, not x, as ne*xt*, not ne*x*.

178. PUNCTUATION.

Punctuation teaches the method of placing *Points*, or *Stops*, in written or printed matter, in such a manner as to clearly indicate the pauses which would be made by the author if he were communicating his thoughts orally instead of by written signs ; and correct punctuation is essential to convey the meaning intended, and to give due force to such passages as the author may wish to impress upon the mind of the person to whom they are being communicated.

179. THE POINTS OR STOPS

are as follows :—

Comma ,	Note of Interroga-
Semicolon ;	tion ?
Colon :	Note of Exclama-
Period, or Full Point .	tion !
Apostrophe '	Parenthesis ( )
Hyphen .-	Asterisk, or Star *

As these are all the points required in simple epistolary composition, we will confine our explanations to the rules which should govern the use of them. The Other Points, however, are the paragraph ¶ ; the section § ; the dagger † ; the double dagger ‡ ; the parallel ‖ ; the bracket or parenthesis [ ] ; and some others. These, however, are quite unnecessary, except for elaborate works, in which they are chiefly used for notes or marginal references. The rule — is sometimes used as a substitute for the bracket.

180. RELATIVE DURATION OF THE PAUSES FOR EACH POINT.

Comma	While you count			One.
Semicolon	„	„	„	Two.
Colon	„	„	„	Three.
Period	„	„	„	Four.

This, however, is not an infallible rule, because the duration of the pauses should be regulated by the degree of rapidity with which the matter is being read. In slow reading the duration of the pauses should be increased.

181. DANGER OF MISPLACING POINTS.—The misplacing of even so slight a point, or pause, as the comma, will often alter the meaning of a sentence. The contract made for lighting the town of Liverpool, during the year 1819, was made void by the misplacing of a comma in the advertisements, thus :— "The lamps at present are about 4,050, and have in general two spouts each, composed of not less than twenty threads of cotton." The contractor would have proceeded to furnish each lamp with the said twenty threads, but this being but half

the usual quantity, the commissioners discovered that the difference arose from the comma following instead of preceding the word *each*. The parties agreed to annul the contract, and a new one was ordered.

182. NECESSITY FOR USE OF POINTS.

The following sentence shows how difficult it is to read without the aid of the points used as pauses :—

Death waits not for storm nor sunshine within a dwelling in one of the upper streets respectable in appearance and furnished with such conveniences as distinguish the habitations of those who rank among the higher classes of society a man of middle age lay on his last bed momently awaiting the final summons all that the most skilful medical attendance all that love warm as the glow that fires an angel's bosom could do had been done by day and night for many long weeks had ministering spirits such as a devoted wife and loving children are done all within their power to ward off the blow but there he lay his raven hair smoothed off from his noble brow his dark eyes lifted with unnatural brightness and contrasting strongly with the pallid hue whieh marked him as an expectant of the dread messenger.

The same Sentence, properly pointed, and with capital letters placed after full-points, according to the adopted rule, may be easily read and understood :—

Death waits not for storm nor sunshine. Within a dwelling in one of the upper streets, respectable in appearance, and furnished with such conveniences as distinguish the habitations of those who rank among the higher classes of society, a man of middle age lay on his last bed, momently awaiting the final summons. All that the most skilful medical attendance—all that love, warm as the glow that fires an angel's bosom, could do, had been done ; by day and night, for many long weeks, had ministering spirits, such as a devoted wife and loving children are, done all within their power to ward off the blow. But there he lay, his raven hair smoothed off from his noble brow, his dark eyes lighted with unnatural brightness, and contrasting strongly with the pallid hue which marked him as an expectant of the dread messenger.

183. POINTS INDICATING EXPRESSION, MEANING, AND CONNECTION.—i. The Apostrophe '

is used to indicate the combining of two words in one,—as John's book, instead of John, his book ; or to show the omission of parts of words, as Glo'ster, for Gloucester—tho' for though. These abbreviations should be avoided as much as possible. Cobbet says the apostrophe "ought to be called the mark of laziness and vulgarity." The first use, however, of which we gave an example, is a necessary and proper one.

ii. The Hyphen, or conjoiner - is used to unite words which, though they are separate and distinct, have so close a connection as almost to become one word, as water-rat, wind-mill, &c. It is also used in writing and printing, at the end of a line, to show where a word is divided and continued in the next line. Look down the ends of the lines in this column, and you will notice the hyphen in several places.

iii. The Note of Interrogation ? indicates that the sentence to which it is added asks a question ; as, What is the meaning of that assertion ? What am I to do ?

iv. The Note of Exclamation or of Admiration ! indicates surprise, pleasure, or sorrow ; as Oh ! Ah ! Goodness ! Beautiful ! I am astonished ! Woe is me !

Sometimes, when an expression of strong surprise or pleasure is intended, two notes of this character are employed, thus ! !

v. The Parenthesis ( ) is used to prevent confusion by the introduction to a sentence of a passage not necessary to the sense thereof. "I am going to meet Mr. Smith (though I am not an admirer of him) on Wednesday next." It is better, however, as a rule, not to employ parenthetical sentences.

vi. **The Asterisk, or Star** * may be employed to refer from the text to a note of explanation at the foot of a column, or at the end of a letter.

₊ Three stars are sometimes used to call particular attention to a paragraph.

184. **HINTS ON SPELLING.—** The following rules will be found of great assistance in writing, because they relate to a class of words about the spelling of which doubt and hesitation are frequently felt :—

i. All words of one syllable ending in *l*, with a single vowel before it, have double *l*, at the close ; as, *mill, sell.*

ii. All words of one syllable ending in *l*, with a double vowel before it, have one *l* only at the close : as, *mail, sail.*

iii. Words of one syllable ending in *l*, when compounded, retain but one *l* each ; as, *fulfil, skilful.*

iv. Words of more than one syllable ending in *l* have one *l* only at the close ; as, delightful, faithful ; except *befall, downfall, recall, unwell*, &c.

v. All derivatives from words ending in *l* have one *l* only ; as, *equality*, from *equal* ; *fulness*, from *full* ; except they end in *er*, or *ly* ; as, *mill, miller* ; *full, fully.*

vi. All participles in ing from verbs ending in *e* lose the *e* final ; as *have, having* ; *amuse, amusing* ; unless they come from verbs ending in double *e*, and then they retain both ; as, *see, seeing* ; *agree, agreeing.*

vii. All adverbs ending in *ly* and nouns in *ment* retain the *e* final of the primitives ; as *brave, bravely* ; *refine, refinement* ; except *truly, acknowledgment*, &c.

viii. All derivatives from words ending in *er* retain the *e* before the *r* ; as *refer, reference* ; except *hindrance*, from *hinder* ; *remembrance* from *remember* ; *disastrous* from *disaster* ; *monstrous* from *monster* ; *wondrous* from *wonder* ; *cumbrous* from *cumber*, &c.

ix. Compound words, unless they both end in *l*, retain their primitive parts entire ; as, *millstone, changeable, graceless* ; except *always, also, deplorable, although, almost, admirable*, &c.

x. All words of one syllable ending in a consonant, with a single vowel before it, double that consonant in derivatives ; as, *sin, sinner* ; *ship, shipping* ; *big, bigger* ; *sad, sadder*, &c.

xi. Words of one syllable ending in a consonant, with a double vowel before it, do not double the consonant in derivatives: as, *sleep, sleepy* ; *troop, troopers.*

xii. All words of more than one syllable ending in a single consonant, preceded by a single vowel, and accented on the last syllable, double that consonant in derivatives ; as, *commit, committee* ; *compel, compelled* ; *appal, appalling* ; *distil, distiller.*

xiii. Nouns of one syllable, ending in *y* preceded by a consonant, change *y* into *ies* in the plural ; and verbs ending in *y* preceded by a consonant, change *y* into *ies* in the third person singular of the present tense, and into *ied* in the past tense and past participle, as, *fly, flies* ; *I apply, he applies* ; *we reply* ; *we replied*, or *have replied.* If the *y* be preceded by a vowel, this rule is not applicable ; as *key, keys* ; *I play, he plays* ; we have *enjoyed* ourselves.

xiv. Compound words whose primitives end in *y* change *y* into *i* ; as, *beauty, beautiful* ; *lovely, loveliness.*

185. **H OR NO H ? THAT IS THE QUESTION.—**Few things point so directly to the want of *cultivation* as the misuse of the letter H by persons in conversation. We hesitate to assert that this common defect in speaking indicates the absence of education—for, to our surprise, we have heard even educated persons frequently commit this common and vulgar error. Now, for the purpose of assisting those who desire to im-

prove their mode of speaking, we intend to tell a little story about our next-door neighbour, Mrs. Alexander Hitching,—or, as she frequently styled herself, with an air of conscious dignity, Mrs. HALEXANDER 'ITCHING.

Her husband was a post-captain of some distinction, seldom at home, and therefore Mrs. A. H. (or, as she rendered it, Mrs. *H. I.*) felt it incumbent upon herself to represent her own dignity, and the dignity of her husband also. Well, this Mrs. Hitching was a next-door neighbour of ours—a most agreeable lady in many respects, middle-aged, good-looking, uncommonly fond of talking, of active, almost fussy habits, very good-tempered and good-natured, but with a most impleasant habit of misusing the letter H to such a degree that our sensitive nerves have often been shocked when in her society. But we must beg the reader, if Mrs. H. should be an acquaintance of his, not to breathe a word of our having written this account of her—or there would be no limit to her "*h*indignation." And, as her family is very numerous, it will be necessary to keep the matter as quiet as can be, for it will scarcely be possible to mention the subject anywhere, without "'orrifying" some of her relations, and instigating them to make Mrs. H. become our "*h*enemy," instead of remaining, as we wish her to do, our intimate friend.

One morning, Mrs. H. called upon me, and asked me to take a walk, saying that it was her *h*object to look out for an 'ouse, as her lease had nearly terminated ; and as she had often heard her dear 'Itching say that he would like to settle in the neighbourhood of 'Ampstead 'Eath, she should like me to assist her by my judgment in the choice of a residence.

"I shall be most happy to accompany you," I said.

"I knew you would," said she ;

"and I am sure a *h*our or two in your society will give me pleasure. It's so long since we've 'ad a gossip. Besides which, I want a change of *h*air."

I glanced at her peruke, and for a moment laboured under the idea that she intended to call at her hairdresser's ; but I soon recollected.

"I suppose we had better take the *h*omnibus," she remarked, "and we can get out at the foot of the 'ill."

I assented, and in a few minutes we were in the street, in the line of the omnibus, and one of those vehicles soon appearing—

"Will you 'ail it !" enquired she.

So I hailed it at once, and we got in. Now Mrs. H. was so fond of talking that the presence of strangers never restrained her—a fact which I have often had occasion to regret. She was no sooner within the omnibus than she began remarking upon the *h*inconvenience of such vehicles, because of their smallness, and the *h*insolence of many of the conductors. She thought that the proprietors ought only to 'ire men upon whose civility they could depend. Then she launched out into larger topics—said she thought that the *H*emperor of *H*austria—(here I endeavoured to interrupt her by asking whether she had any idea of the part of Hampstead she would like ; but she would complete her remarks by saying)—must be as 'appy as the days are long, now that the *H*empress had presented him with a *hare* to the throne ! (Some of the passengers smiled, and turning round, looked out of the windows.)

I much wished for our arrival at the spot where we should alight, for she commenced a story about an 'andsome young nephew of hers, who was a distinguished *h*officer of the *h*army. This was suggested to her, no doubt, by the presence in the omnibus of a fine-looking young fellow, with a moustache. She said that at present her nephew was stationed in

*H*ireland ; but he expected soon to be bordered to South *H*africa.

The gentleman with the moustache seemed much amused, and smilingly asked her whether her nephew was at all *h*ambitious ? I saw that he (the gentleman with the moustache) was jesting, and I would have given anything to have been released from the unpleasant predicament I was in. But what was my annoyance when Mrs. H. proceeded to say to this youth, whose face was radiant with humour, that it was the 'ight of her nephew's *h*ambition to serve his country in the *h*our of need ; and then she proceeded to ask her fellow-traveller his opinion of the *h*upshot of the war—remarking that she 'oped it would soon be *h*over.

At this moment I felt so nervous that I pulled out my handkerchief, and endeavoured to create a diversion by making a loud nasal noise, and remarking that I thought the wind very cold, when an accident happened which took us all by surprise : one of the large wheels of the omnibus dropped off, and all the passengers were jostled down into a corner, but, fortunately, without serious injury. Mrs. H., however, happening to be under three or four persons, raised a loud cry for " 'elp ! 'elp !" She was speedily got out, when she assured us that she was not " 'urt ; but she was in such a state of *h*agitation that she wished to be taken to a chemist's shop, to get some *H*aromatic vinegar, or some *H*oe de Cologne !" The chemist was exceedingly polite to her, for which she said she could never express her *h*obligations—an assertion which seemed to me to be literally true. It was some time before she resumed her accustomed freedom of conversation ; but as we ascended the hill she explained to me that she should like to take the house as tenant from *'ear* to *'ear* !—but she thought landlords would *h*object to such an agreement, as when they got a good tenant they liked to 'old 'im as long as

they could. She expressed an opinion that 'Amstead must be very 'ealthy, because it was so 'igh *h*up.

We soon reached the summit of the hill, and turned through a lane which led towards the Heath, and in which villas and cottages were smiling on each side. "Now, there's a *h*elegant little place !" she exclaimed, "just suited to my *h*ideas—about *h*eight rooms and a *h*oriel *h*over the *h*entrance." But it was not to let—so we passed on.

Presently, she saw something likely to suit her, and as there was a bill in the window, "To be let—Enquire Within," she gave a loud rat-a-tat-tat at the door.

The servant opened it.

" I see this 'ouse is to let."

"Yes, ma'am, it is ; will you walk in !"

" 'Ow many rooms are there ?"

"Eleven, ma'am ; but if you will step in, mistress will speak to you."

A very graceful lady made her appearance at the parlour door, and invited us to step in. I felt exceedingly nervous, for I at once perceived that the lady of the house spoke with that accuracy and taste which is one of the best indications of refinement.

"The house *is* to let—and a very pleasant residence we have found it."

"'Ave you *h*occupied it long ?"

"Our family has resided here for more than nine years."

"Then, I suppose, your lease 'as run *h*out !"

"No! we have it for five years longer : but my brother, who is a clergyman, has been appointed to a living in Yorkshire, and for his sake, and for the pleasure of his society, we desire to remove."

"Well—there's nothing like keeping families together for the sake of 'appiness. Now there's my poor dear 'Itching" (here she paused, as if somewhat affected, and some young ladies who were in the room drew their heads together, and appeared to consult about their needlework ; but I saw, by dimples upon their cheeks, which they could not conceal, that they were smiling), "'e's 'itherto been *h*at 'ome so seldom, that I've 'ardly *h*ever known what 'appiness *h*is."

I somewhat abruptly broke in upon the conversation, by suggesting that she had better look through the house, and inquire the conditions of tenancy. We consequently went through the various rooms, and in every one of them she had "an *h*objection to this," or "a 'atred for that," or would give "an 'int which might be useful" to the lady when she removed. The young ladies were heard tittering very much whenever Mrs. H. broke out, in a loud voice, with her imperfect elocution, and I felt so much annoyed, that I determined to cure her of her defective speaking.

In the evening, after returning home, we were sitting by the fire, feeling comfortable and chatty, when I proposed to Mrs. Hitching the following enigma from the pen of the late Henry Mayhew :—

The Vide Vorld you may search, and my fellow not find ;
I dwells in a Wacuum, deficient in Vind ;
In the Wisage I'm seen—in the Woice I am heard.
And yet I'm inwisible, gives went to no Vurd.
I'm not much of a Vag, for I'm vanting in Vit ;
But distinguished In Werse for the Wollums I've writ.
I'm the head of all Willains, yet far from the Vurst—
I'm the foremost In Wice, though in Wirtue the first.
I'm not used to Veapons, and ne'er goes to Vor ;
Though in Walour inwincible—In Wictory sure:
The first of all Wiands and Wictuals is mine—
Rich In Wen'son and Weal, but deficient in Vine.
To Wanity given, I in Welwets abound ;
But in Woman, in Wife, and in Widder ain't found:

Yet conspicuous in Wirgins, and I'll tell you, between us.
To persons of taste I'm a bit of a Wenus ;
Yet none take me for Veal—or for Voe in its stead.
For I ranks not among the sweet Voo'd, Vun, and Ved !

Before the recital of the enigma was half completed, Mrs. Hitching laughed heartily—she saw, of course, the meaning of it—that it was a play upon the Cockney error of using the V instead of the W, and the latter instead of the V. Several times, as I proceeded, she exclaimed "*H*excellent ! *h*excellent !" and when I had finished, she remarked that it was very "*h*ingenious," and enough to "*h*open the *h*eyes" of the Cockneys to their stupid and vulgar manner of speaking.

A more difficult and delicate task lay before me. I told her that as she was so much pleased with the first enigma, I would submit another by the same author. I felt very nervous, but determined to proceed :—

I dwells in the Herth, and I breathes in the Hair ;
If you searches the Hocean, you'll find that I'm there.
The first of all Hangels, in Holympus am Hi.
Yet I'm banished from 'Eaven, expelled from on 'Igh.
But though on this Horb I am destined to grovel,
I'm ne'er seen in an 'Ouse, in an 'Ut, nor an 'Ovel ;
Not an 'Oss nor an 'Unter e'er bears me, alas!
But often I'm found on the top of a Hass.
I resides in a Hattic, and loves not to roam,
And yet I'm invariably absent from 'Ome.
Though 'ushed in the 'Urricane, of the Hatmosphere part,
I enters no 'Ed, I creeps into no 'Art.
Only look, and you'll see in the Heye I appear,
Only 'ark, and you'll 'ear me just breathe in the Hear ;
Though in sex not an 'E, I am (strange paradox!)
Not a bit of an 'Eifer, but partly a Hox.

Of Heternity Hi'm the beginning! And, mark,
Though I goes not with Noah, I am first in the Hark.
I'm never in 'Ealth, have with Fysic no power ;
I dies in a Month, but comes back in a Hour !

In reciting the above I strongly emphasised the misplaced *h*'s. After a brief pause, Mrs. Hitchings exclaimed, "Very good ; very clever." I then determined to complete my task by repeating the following enigma upon the same letter written by Miss Catherine Fanshawe and often erroneously attributed to Byron :—

'Twas whispered in heaven, 'twas muttered in hell,
And echo caught faintly the sound as it fell ;
On the confines of earth 'twas permitted to rest.
And the depths of the ocean its presence confess'd.
'Twill be found in the sphere when 'tis riven asunder,
Be seen in the lightning, and heard in the thunder.
'Twas allotted to man with his earliest breath.
Attends at his birth, and awaits him in death ;
It presides o'er his happiness, honour, and health.
Is the prop of his house, and the end of his wealth.
In the heaps of the miser 'tis hoarded with care,
But is sure to be lost on his prodigal heir.
It begins every hope, every wish it must bound.
With the husbandman toils, with the monarch is crowned.
Without it the soldier and seaman may roam.
But woe to the wretch who expels it from home.
In the whispers of conscience its voice will be found,
Nor e'en, in the whirlwind of passion be drowned.
'Twill not soften the heart, and though deaf to the ear,
'Twill make it acutely and instantly hear.

But in shade let it rest, like a delicate flower—
Oh, breathe on it softly—it dies in an hour.

She was much pleased, but seemed thoughtful, and once or twice in conversation checked herself, and corrected herself in the pronunciation of words that were difficult to her.

A few days afterwards, I called upon her, and upon being introduced to the parlour to wait for her appearance, I saw lying upon her table the following.

186. MEMORANDUM ON THE USE OF THE LETTER H.

Pronounce—	Heir,	'Eir.
„	Honesty,	'Onesty.
„	Honour,	'Onour.
„	Hour,	'Our.
„	Humour,	'Umour.

In all other cases the H is to be sounded when it begins a word.

Mem.—Be careful to sound the *H* slightly in such words as w*h*ere, w*h*en, w*h*at, w*h*y—don't say were, wen, wat, wy.

187. HINTS ON CONVERSATION.

There are many talkers, but few who know how to converse agreeably. Speak distinctly, neither too rapidly nor too slowly. Accommodate the pitch of your voice to the hearing of the person with whom you are conversing. Never speak with your mouth full. Tell your jokes, and laugh afterwards. Dispense with superfluous words—such as, "Well, I should think," etc.

The Woman who wishes her conversation to be agreeable will avoid conceit or affectation, and laughter which is not natural and spontaneous. Her language will be easy and unstudied, marked by a graceful carelessness which, at the same time, never oversteps the limits of propriety. Her lips will readily yield to a pleasant smile, she will not love to hear herself talk ; her tones will bear the impress of sincerity, and her eyes kindle with animation as she speaks. The art of pleasing is, in truth, the very soul of good breeding ; for the precise object of the latter is to render us agreeable to all with whom we associate—to make us, at the same time, esteemed and loved.

We need scarcely advert to the rudeness of interrupting any one who is speaking, or to the impropriety of pushing, to its full extent, a discussion which has become unpleasant.

Some persons have a Mania for Greek and Latin quotations : this is peculiarly to be avoided. It is like pulling up the stones from a tomb wherewith to kill the living. Nothing is more wearisome than pedantry.

If you feel your Intellectual Superiority to any one with whom you are conversing, do not seek to bear him down ; it would be an inglorious triumph, and a breach of good manners. Beware, too, of speaking lightly of subjects which bear a sacred character.

It is a Common Idea that the art of writing and the art of conversation are one ; this is a great mistake. A man of genius may be a very dull talker.

The Two Grand Modes of making your conversation interesting, are to enliven it by recitals calculated to affect and impress your hearers, and to intersperse it with anecdotes and smart things. Count Antoine Rivarol, who lived from 1767 to 1801, was a master in the latter mode.

188. HINTS ON LETTER WRITING.

i. At the head of your Letter, in the right-hand corner, put your address in full, with the day of the month underneath ; do not omit this, though you may be writing to your most intimate friend for the third or even the fourth time in the course of a day.

ii. What you have to Say in your Letter, say as plainly as possible, as if you were speaking ; this is the best rule. Do not revert three or four times to one circumstance, but finish as you go on.

iii. Do not Cross your Letters ; surely paper and postage is cheap enough now to admit of using an extra half-sheet, in case of necessity. Frequent underlining of words is another fault, and is generally unnecessary. If your letter is properly expressed, the reader will supply the emphasis.

iv. Let your Signature be written as plainly as possible (many mistakes will be avoided, especially in writing to strangers), and without any flourishes, as these do not add in any way to the harmony of your letter. We have seen signatures that have been almost impossible to decipher, being a mere mass of strokes, without any form to indicate letters. This is done chiefly by the ignorant, and would lead one to suppose that they were ashamed of signing what they had written.

v. If you are not a Good Writer it is advisable to use the best ink, paper, and pens. For although they may not alter the character of your handwriting, yet they will assist to make your writing look better. The paper on which you write should be clean, and neatly folded.

vi. If you write to a Stranger for information, or on your own business, be sure to send a stamped envelope with your address plainly written ; this will not fail to procure you an answer.

vii. Let the Direction be written very plainly ; this will save the postman trouble, and facilitate business by preventing mistakes.

viii. If the Address be in London add the letters of the postal district in which it happens to be, for this also saves trouble in the General Post Office. Thus, in writing to the publishers of "Enquire Within," whose house of business is in the East Central (E.C.) postal district, address your letter to Messrs. Houlston and Sons, Paternoster Square, London, E.C.

ix. Always put a Stamp on your envelope, at the top, in the right-hand corner.

x. **Care** must be taken in giving titled persons, to whom you write, their proper designations.

189. ADDRESSING LETTERS.—

As this branch of epistolary correspondence is one of the most important, we subjoin a few additional hints which letter writers generally would do well to attend to.

i. When writing several letters, place each in its envelope, and address it as soon as it is written, otherwise awkward mistakes may occur, your correspondents receiving letters not intended for them. If there be a town of the same name as that to which you are writing existing in another county, specify the county which you mean on the address. Thus, Richmond, *Yorkshire.*

ii. When the person to whom you are writing is visiting or residing at the house of another person, it is considered vulgar to put "at Mr. So-and-So's," but simply "Mr. So-and-So's," *at* being understood.

iii. When addressing a gentleman with the prefix "Mr.," the Christian name or initials should always follow, being more polite, as well as avoiding confusion where persons of the same surname may reside in one house.

iv. In addressing a letter to two or more unmarried ladies, write "The Misses Johnson," and not "The *Miss Johnsons* ;" and, lastly, always write an address clearly and legibly, so that it may not be delayed in delivery, nor be missent.

190. ADDRESSES OF PERSONS OF RANK AND DISTINCTION.[1]

191. **The Queen or King.**—*Superscription.*—To the Queen's (*King's*) Most Excellent Majesty.

Commencement.—"Sire" or "Madam" ; May it please your Majesty.

Conclusion.—I remain, with the profoundest veneration, Your Majesty's most faithful subject and dutiful servant.

192. **Princes of the Blood Royal.**—i. *The Sons and Daughters, Brothers and Sisters, Uncles and Aunts of the Sovereign.*—*Sup.*—To His (*Her*) Royal Highness the Prince of Wales (*Princess of Wales*).

Comm.—Your Royal Highness.

Con.—I remain, with the greatest respect (I have the honour to be), your Royal Highness's most obedient servant.

ii. *Other branches of the Royal Family.*—*Sup.*—To His Royal Highness the Duke of Cambridge.

Comm.—Your Royal Highness.

Con.—I remain, with the greatest respect, your Royal Highness's most humble and obedient servant.

193. **Nobility and Gentry.**—i. *Duke or Duchess.*—*Sup.*—To His Grace the Duke (*Her Grace the Duchess*) of Northumberland.

Comm.—My Lord Duke (Madam),

Con.—I have the honour to be, My Lord Duke (*Madam*), Your Grace's most devoted and obedient servant

ii. *Marquis or Marchioness.*—*Sup.*—To the Most Honourable the Marquis (*Marchioness*) of Salisbury.

Comm.—My Lord Marquis (*Madam*).

Con.—I have the honour to be, My Lord Marquis, Your Lordship's (Madam, Your Ladyship's) most obedient and most humble servant.

iii. *Earl or Countess.*—*Sup.*—To the Right Honourable the Earl (*Countess*) of Aberdeen.

Comm.—My Lord (*Madam*).

Con.—I have the honour to be, My Lord, Your Lordship's (*Madam, your Ladyship's*) most obedient and very humble servant.

iv. *Viscount or Viscountess.*—*Sup.*—To the Right Honourable Lord Viscount (*Lady Viscountess*) Brown.

---

[1] Adapted from the *Dictionary of Daily Wants,* published by Houlston and Sons, Paternoster Square, E.C., in one volume, half bound, at 7*s.* 6*d.*, or in three separate volumes, doth, each 2*s.* 6*d.*

Comm. and *Con.* same as Earl's.

v. *Baron or Baroness.—Sup.—*To the Right Honourable Lord (Lady) Robinson.

Comm. and *Con.* same as Earl's.

vi. *Younger Sons of Earls and all the Sons of Viscounts and Barons.— Sup.—*To the Honourable Arthur Jones.

*Comm.—*Honoured Sir.

*Con.—*I have the honour to be, Honoured Sir, Your most obedient and very humble servant.

vii. *Baronet and His Wife.—Sup.* —To Sir Stafford Smith, Bart. (*Lady Smith*).

*Comm.—*Sir (*Madam*).

*Con.—*I have the honour to be, Sir, Your most humble and obedient (*Madam, your Ladyship's most obedient and very humble*) servant.

viii. *Knight and his Wife.—Sup.—* To Sir Francis Brown (*Lady Brown*).

Comm. and *Con.* as preceding.

ix. *Maid of Honour.—*"The Hon. Miss ——"

*Begin.—*Madam.

x. *Esquire.—* This title is now accorded to every man of position and respectability, but persons entitled to superior consideration are distinguished by "&c, &c., &c.," added to their superscription.

The wives of Gentlemen, when several of the same name are married, are distinguished by the Christian name of their husbands, as Mrs. *John* Harvey, Mrs. *William* Temple.

xi. *Privy Councillors.—*These have the title of *Right Honourable*, which is prefixed to their name thus :

*Sup.—*To the Right Honourable William Jones, M.P.

*Comm.—*Sir.

*Con.—*I have the honour to be, Sir, Your most obedient very humble servant.

194. The Clergy.—i. *Archbishop.— Sup.—*To His Grace the Lord Archbishop of Canterbury.

*Comm.—*My Lord Archbishop.

*Con.—*I remain, Your Grace's most devoted obedient servant.

ii. *Bishop—Sup.—*To the Right Reverend the Lord Bishop of Winchester.

*Comm.—*My Lord Bishop.

*Con.—*I remain. My Lord Bishop, Your most obedient humble servant.

iii. *Doctor of Divinity.—Sup.—* To the Reverend James William Robinson, D.D., or, To the Reverend Dr. Robinson.

Comm.— Reverend Sir.

*Con.—*I have the honour to be, Reverend Sir, Your most obedient servant.

iv. *Dean.—Sup.—*To the Very Reverend the Dean of St Paul's ; or, To the Very Reverend Richard William Brown, M.A., D.C.L., D.D., Dean of St Paul's.

*Comm.—*Very Reverend Sir.

*Con.—*I have the honour to be, Very Reverend Sir, Your most obedient servant.

v. *Archdeacon.—Sup.—*To the Venerable Archdeacon Smith, D.C.L.

*Comm.—*Venerable Sir.

*Con.—*I have the honour to remain, Reverend Sir, Your most obedient servant.

vi. *Clergyman.—Sup.—*To the Reverend Thomas Jones.

Comm. and *Con.—*Reverend Sir.

vii. *Clergyman with Titles.—*When a Bishop or other Clergyman possesses the title of *Right Honourable* or *Honourable*, it is prefixed to his Clerical title, but Baronets and Knights have their clerical title placed first, as in the following examples :—

*Sup.—*To the Right Honourable and Right Reverend the Lord Bishop of Bath and Wells.

*Sup.—*To the Honourable and Right Reverend the Lord Bishop of Norwich.

*Sup.—*To the Right Honourable and Reverend Lord Wriothesley Brown, M.A.

*Sup.—*To the Honourable and Reverend Baptist Wriothesley Robinson, M.A.

*Sup.—*To the Reverend Sir Henry Jones, Bart, M.A.

No clerical dignity confers a title or rank on the wife of the dignitary, who is simply addressed *Mistress*, unless possessing a title in her own right, or through her husband, independently of his clerical rank.

195. Judges, &c.—i. *Lord Chancellor.*—*Sup.*—To the Right Honourable Plantagenet Smith, Lord High Chancellor of Great Britain.

ii. *Master of the Rolls.*—*Sup.*—To the Right Honourable the Master of the Rolls.

iii. *Chief Justice.*—*Sup.*—To the Right Honourable the Lord Chief Justice ; or, the Right Honourable Lord Smyth, Lord Chief Justice of England.

The Chief Justice of the Court of Common Pleas is addressed in the same form ; are all styled *My Lord.*

iv. *Lords Justices of Appeal.*—The Lords Justices of Appeal are Knights, and should be addressed thus :

Sup.— To the Right Honourable Sir Robert Brown, Knt.

v. *Puisne Judges.* "The Hon. Sir — ——" if a knight, or"The Hon. Mr. Justice ——" Begin "Sir."

vi. *Judge of County Courts.*—*Sup.*— To His Honour Judge John James Jones.

vii. *Justice of the Peace* (in England). "The Right Worshipful," referred to on the bench as "Your Worship."

106. Officers of the Navy and Army.—i. *Naval Officers.*—*Admirals* thus:—

Sup.—To Admiral the Honourable Sir Richard Smith.

If untitled they are simply styled *Sir.*

Commodores are addressed in the same way as admirals.

Captains are addressed either to "Captain William Smith, R. N. ;" or if on service, "To William Smith, Esquire, Commander of H.M.S. ——"

Lieutenants are addressed in the same way.

ii. *Military Officers.*—All officers in the army above Lieutenants, Cornets,

and Ensigns, have their military rank prefixed to their name and title.

Sup.—To *General* Sir Frederick Robinson.

Subalterns are addressed as *Esquire*, with the regiment to which they belong, if on service.

197. Governor of Colony.—"His Excellency (ordinary designation) Governor of Sydney." Begin according to rank and refer to as "Your Excellency."

108. Ambassadors.—Ambassadors have *Excellency* prefixed to their other titles, and their accredited rank added.

Sup.—To his Excellency Count Karolyi, Ambassador Extraordinary and Plenipotentiary from H.I.M. (His Imperial Majesty) The Emperor of Austria.

Sup.—To His Excellency The Right Honourable Earl of Blankshire, K.P., G.C.M.G., K.C.B., Her Britannic Majesty's Ambassador Extraordinary and Plenipotentiary to the Sublime Ottoman Porte.

Comm.—"Sir," or "My Lord," according to rank.

Con.—I have the honour to be, My Lord, Your Excellency's Most humble obedient servant.

The wives of Ambassadors have also Excellency added to their other titles.

Envoys and Chargés d'Affairee are generally styled Excellency, but by courtesy only.

Consuls have only their accredited rank added to their names or titles, if they have any, addressed thus :— "John Jones, Esq., H.B.M.'s Agent and Consul-General," "Consul," or "Vice-Consul," as it may be.

190. Municipal Officers.—i. *Lord Mayor.*—*Sup.*—To the Right Honourable the Lord Mayor (*The Lady Mayoress*) of London, York, Dublin ; The Lord Provost (*The Lady Provost*) of Edinburgh.

Comm.—My Lord (*Madam*).

Con.—I have the honour to be, my Lord, Your Lordship's (*Madam, Your Ladyship's*) most obedient humble servant.

ii. The Mayors of all Corporations, with the Sheriffs, Aldermen, and Recorder of London, are styled *Right Worshipful* ; and the Aldermen and Recorder of other Corporations, as well as Justices of the Peace, *Worshipful.*

200. Addressses of Petitions, &c.—i. *Queen in Council.*—All applications to the Queen in Council, the Houses of Lords and Commons, &c., are by *Petition*, as follows, varying only the title :

To the Queen's Most Excellent Majesty in Council,

The humble Petition of M. N., &c., showeth

That your Petitioner

. . . .

Wherefore your Petitioner humbly prays that Your Majesty will be graciously pleased to . . .

And your Petitioner, as in duty bound, will ever pray.

ii. *Lords and Commons.*—To the Right Honourable the Lords Spiritual and Temporal (To the Honourable the Commons of the United Kingdom of Great Britain and Ireland), in Parliament assembled.

The humble Petition, &c.

And your Petitioner [or Petitioners] will ever pray, &c.

201. HINTS ON WRITING FOR THE PRESS.—It would be a great service to editors and printers if all who write for the press would observe the following reasonable rules :—

i. Write with black ink, on white paper, wide ruled.

ii. Make the pages or folios small, one-fourth of a foolscap sheet is large enough.

iii. Leave the second page of each leaf blank ; or, in other words, write on one side of the paper only.

iv. Give to the written page an ample margin *all round* ; or fold down the left-hand side to the extent of one-fourth the width of the entire paper so as to leave a broad margin on the left side of the paper.

v. Number the pages in the order of their succession.

vi. Write in a plain, bold, legible hand, without regard to beauty of appearance.

vii. Use no abbreviations which are not to appear in print.

viii. Punctuate the manuscript as it should be printed.

ix. For italics underscore one line ; for small capitals, two ; capitals, three.

x. Never interline without the caret (∧) to show its place.

xi. Take special pains with every letter in proper names.

xii. Review every word, to be sure that none is illegible.

xiii. Put directions to the printer at the head of the first page.

xiv. Never write a private letter to the editor on the printer's copy, but always on a separate sheet.

202. TYPE-WRITING MACHINES.

By means of these machines we are enabled to imprint legible character and letters on paper by merely pressing a number of keys, each representing a letter or character. With a little practice type-writing may be executed more rapidly and more legibly than writing with a pen, and as, by a simple process, any number of copies of a document may be taken, much time and expense is frequently saved by the use of one of these machines, of which many varieties are to be had.

203. MANIFOLD WRITING.

The demand for a rapid and simple method of multiplying letters, circulars, &c., has led in recent years to the invention of several ingenious processes. So few copies are obtainable by the ordinary reporters' system of sheets of tissue paper, or "flimsy," interleaved with sheets of prepared black paper, that various kinds of "graphs" have been produced, by which upwards of a hundred, and in some cases many more, copies may be produced from one wnting. The "graph" process usually consists in transferring a writing made in an aniline dye on to a gelatine surface, from which, by the application of successive sheets of paper, subjected to a smoothing pressure by the hand, a number of copies may be obtained, in a manner very similar to the ordinary lithographic process. All those which may be classed as "gelatine transfer" processes are, however, open to the objection that, after a certain number of copies, the colour grows very faint. Some other methods of manifold writing, such as the Edison, the Typograph, the Cyclostyle, &c. (by which 1000 copies can be taken from one writing), do not possess this fault, being based on a principle of a fine stencil on prepared paper, and squeezing ink through the minute perforations on to a sheet of paper fixed underneath. The writing in these stencil systems, however, has a "dotty" and broken appearance, displeasing to many eyes— the Cyclostyle being, perhaps, least faulty in this respect. For those who would like to make a gelatine "graph,'" we append the following recipes ; any chemist will supply an aniline dye for the ink.

203a. RECIPES FOR GELATINE "GRAPHS."

i. Take 2 parts of Russian glue, 1½ of distilled water, and 5 of glycerine. Soak the glue in the water until soft, and then warm in the glycerine until it is dissolved ; if necessary, add 1 part of fine whitening ; pour the composition into a flat tray to cool—use when solid.

ii. Another method is to soak 3 parts of Nelson's gelatine for 10 or 12 hours in 4 parts of water. Add 3 parts of glycerine and warm it up until it is dissolved.

iii. The German *Papier Zeitung* gives the following—Soak 4 parts of best clear glue in a mixture of 5 parts pure water and 3 parts ammonia (presumably liquor ammonia) until the glue is thoroughly softened. Warm it until the glue is dissolved, and add 3 parts of granulated sugar and 8 parts of glycerine, stirring well and letting it come to the boiling point. While hot, paint it upon clean white blotting-paper, with a broad brush, until the blotting-paper is thoroughly soaked, and a thin coating remains upon the surface. Allow it to dry for 2 or 3 days and it is then ready for use. The writing or drawing to be copied is done with the usual aniline ink upon writing-paper. Before transferring to the blotting-paper, wet the latter with a sponge or brush and clean water, and allow it to stand 1 or 2 minutes. Place the document, written side down, on the blotting-paper, carefully stroking out any air bubbles, and submit the whole to gentle pressure for a few moments, remove the written paper, and a number of impressions can then be taken in the ordinary way. When the impressions begin to grow weak, wet the surface of the "graph" again. This "graph" does not require washing off, but simply laying away for 24 to 36 hours, when the surface will be ready for a new impression.

204. HINTS ABOUT PIANO-FORTES.—i. Damp is very injurious to a pianoforte ; it ought, therefore, to be placed in a dry place, and not exposed to draughts.

ii. Keep your piano free from dust, and do not allow needles, pins, or bread to be placed upon it, especially if the key-board is exposed, as such articles are apt to get inside and produce a jarring or whizzing sound.

iii. Do not load the top of a piano with books, music, &c., as the tone is thereby deadened, and the disagreeable noise alluded to in the last paragraph is often produced.

iv. Have your piano tuned about every three months ; whether it is used or not, the strain is always upon it, and if it is not kept up to concert pitch it will not stand in tune when required, which it will do if it be attended to regularly.

v. An upright instrument sounds better if placed a short distance from the wall : it is also less liable to injury from damp, and does not inflict dull and confused sounds upon your next-door neighbour.

vi. When not in use keep the piano locked.

vii. To make the polish look nice, rub it with an old silk handkerchief, being careful first of all to dust off any small particles, which otherwise are apt to scratch the surface.

viii. Should any of the notes keep down when struck, it is a sure sign that there is damp somewhere, which has caused the small joints upon which the key works to swell.

205. GARDENING OPERATIONS FOR THE YEAR.

206. JANUARY.

Indoor preparations for future operations must be made, as in this month there are only five hours a day available for out-door work, unless the season be unusually mild. Mat over tulip-beds. Begin to force roses. Place pots over seakale and surround them with manure, litter, dried leaves, &c. Plant dried roots of border flowers in mild weather. Take strawberries in pots into the greenhouse. Take cuttings of chrysanthemums and strike them under glass. Prune and plant gooseberry, currant, fruit, and deciduous trees and shrubs. Cucumbers and melons to be sown in the hot-bed. Apply manures to the soil. Make good cabbage-plots, as there may be gaps if the weather has been severe.

Flowers of the Month.—Christmas Rose, Crocus, Winter Aconite, Alyssum, Primrose, Snowdrop.

207. FEBRUARY.

Transplant pinks, carnations, sweet-williams, candy-tuft, campanulas, &c. Sow sweet and garden peas and lettuces, for succession of crops, covering the ground with straw, &c. Sow also savoys, leeks, and cabbages. Prune and nail fruit trees, and towards the end of the month plant stocks for next year's grafting ; also cuttings of poplar, elder, willow-trees, for ornamental shrubbery. Sow fruit and forest tree seeds.

Flowers of the Month.—Snowdrop, Violet, Alyssum, Primrose.

208. MARCH.

Seeds of "spring flowers" to be sown. Border flowers to be planted out. Tender annuals, ferns and geraniums, to be potted out under glasses. Mushroom beds to be made. Sow artichokes, Windsor beans, and cauliflowers for autumn ; lettuces and peas for succession of crops, onions, parsley, radishes, savoys, asparagus, red and white cabbages, and beet: turnips, early brocoli, parsnips and carrots. Plant slips and parted roots of perennial herbs. Graft trees and protect early blossoms. Force rose-tree cuttings under glasses. A hot-bed is useful for many things this month.

Flowers of the Month.—Primrose, Narcissus, Hyacinth, Wallflower, Hepatica, Daisy, Polyanthus.

209. APRIL.

Sow for succession peas, beans, and carrots ; parsnips, celery, and seakale. Sow more seeds of "spring flowers." Plant evergreens, dahlias, chrysan- themums, and the like, also potatoes, slips of thyme, parted roots, lettuces, cauliflowers, cabbages, onions. Lay down turf, remove caterpillars. Sow and graft camelias, and propagate and graft fruit and rose trees by all the various means in use. Sow cucumbers and vegetable marrows for planting out Pot tomatoes for planting out early in June, or growing on in the greenhouse. *This is the most important month in the year for gardeners.*

Flowers of the Month.—Cowslip, Anemone, Ranunculus, Tulip, Polyanthus, Auricula, Narcissus, Jonquil, Wallflower, Lilac, Laburnum.

210. MAY.

Plant out your seedling flowers as they are ready, and sow again for succession larkspur, mignonette, and other spring flowers. Pot out tender annuals. Remove auriculas to a north-east aspect. Take up bulbous roots as the leaves decay. Sow kidney beans, brocoli for spring use, rape for autumn, cauliflowers for December ; Indian corn, cress, onions to plant out as bulbs next year, radishes, aromatic herbs, turnips, cabbages, savoys, lettuces, &c. Plant celery, lettuces, and annuals ; thin spring crops ; stick peas, &c. Earth up potatoes, &c. Moisten mushroom beds.

Flowers of the Month.—Hawthorn, Gentianella, Anemone, Ranunculus, Columbine, Honeysuckle, Laburnum, Wisteria.

211. JUNE.

Sow giant stocks to flower next spring. Take slips of myrtles to strike, pipings of pinks, and make layers of carnation. Put down layers and take cuttings of roses and evergreens. Plant annuals in borders, and place auriculas in pots in shady places. Sow kidney beans, pumpkins, cucumbers for pick- ling, and (late in the month) endive and lettuces. Plant out cucumbers, marrows, leeks, celery, brocoli, cauliflowers, savoys, tomatoes, and seedlings, and plants propagated by slips. Earth up potatoes, &c. Cut herbs for drying when in flower.

Flowers of the Month.—Water-lily, Honeysuckle, Sweet-william, Pinks, Syringa, Rhododendron, Delphinium, Stock.

212. JULY.

Part auricula and polyanthus roots. Take up summer bulbs as they go out of flower, and plant saffron crocus and autumn bulbs. Gather seeds. Clip evergreen borders and edges, strike myrtle slips under glasses. Net fruit trees. Finish budding by the end of the

month. Head down espaliers. Sow early dwarf cabbages to plant out in October for spring ; also endive, onions, kidney beans for late crop, and turnips. Plant celery, endive, lettuces, cabbages, leeks, strawberries, and cauliflowers. Tie up lettuces. Earth celery. Take up onions, &c., for drying.

Flowers of the Month.—Rose, Carnation, Picotee, Asters, Balsams.

213. AUGUST.

Sow annuals to bloom indoors in winter, and pot all young stocks raised in the greenhouse. Sow early red cabbages, cauliflowers for spring and summer use, cos and cabbage lettuce for winter crop. Plant out winter crops. Dry herbs and mushroom spawn. Plant out strawberry roots, and net currant trees, to preserve the fruit through the winter.

Flowers of the Month.—Geranium, Verbena, Calceolaria, Hollyhock.

214. SEPTEMBER.

Plant crocuses, scaly bulbs, and evergreen shrubs. Place chrysan-themums under cover towards the end of the month, or before, if frosts appear. Propagate by layers and cuttings of all the herbaceous plants, currant, gooseberry, and other fruit trees. Plant out seedling pinks. Sow onions for spring plantation, carrots, spinach, and Spanish radishes in warm spots. Earth up celery. House potatoes and edible bulbs. Gather pickling cucumbers. Make tulip and mushroom beds.

Flowers of the Month.—Clematis, or Traveller's Joy, Jasmine, Passion Flower, Arbutus.

215. OCTOBER.

Sow fruit stones for stocks for future grafting, also larkspurs and the hardier annuals to stand the winter, and hyacinths and smooth bulbs in pots and glasses. Plant young trees, cuttings of jasmine, honeysuckle, and evergreens. Sow mignonette for pots in winter. Plant cabbages, &c., for spring. Gather potatoes, ripe or not ; and earth up celery. Cut down asparagus, separate roots of daisies, irises, &c. Trench, drain, and manure.

Flowers of the Month.—Asters, Indian Pink, Chrysanthemum, Stock.

216. NOVEMBER.

Sow sweet peas and garden peas for early flowers and crops. Take up dahlia roots. Complete beds for asparagus and artichokes. Plant dried roots of border flowers, daisies, &c. Take potted mignonette indoors. Make new plantations of strawberries, though it is better to do this in October. Sow peas, leeks, beans, and radishes. Plant Rhubarb in rows. Prune hardy trees, and plant stocks of fruit trees. Store carrots, &c. Shelter from frost where it may be required. Plant shrubs for forcing. Continue to trench and manure vacant ground.

Flowers of the Month.—Laurustinus, Michaelmas Daisy, Chrysanthemum.

217. DECEMBER.

Continue in open weather to prepare vacant ground for spring, and to protect plants from frost. Cover bulbous roots with matting. Dress flower borders. Prepare forcing ground for cucumbers, and force asparagus and seakale. Plant gooseberry, currant, apple, and pear trees. Roll grass-plots if the season be mild and not too wet. Prepare poles, stakes, pea-sticks, &c., for spring. Finish all pruning.

Flowers of the Month.—Cyclamen and Winter Aconite. Holly berries are now available for floral decoration.

218. THE KITCHEN GARDEN.

This is one of the most important parts of general domestic economy, whenever the situation of a house, and the size of the garden, will permit the members of a family to avail themselves of the advantages it offers.

It is, indeed, much to be regretted that small plots of ground, in the immediate vicinity of the metropolis more especially, are too often converted into flower gardens and shrubberies, or used as mere playgrounds for children, when they might more usefully be employed in raising vegetables for the family. With a little care and attention, a kitchen garden, though small, might be rendered not only useful, but, in fact, as ornamental as a modern grass lawn ; and the same expense incurred to make the ground a laboratory of sweets, might suffice to render it agreeable to the palate as well as to the olfactory nerves, and that, even without offending the most delicate optics. It is only in accordance with our plan to give the hint, and to put before the reader such novel points as may facilitate the proposed arrangement. One objection to the formation of a kitchen garden in front of the dwelling, or in sight of the drawing-room and parlour is, that its very nature makes it rather an eyesore than otherwise at all seasons. This, however, may be readily got over by a little attention to neatness and good order, for the vegetables themselves, if properly attended to, may be made really ornamental ; but then, in cutting the plants for use, the business must be done neatly—all useless leaves cleared from the ground, the roots no longer wanted taken up, and the ravages of insects guarded against by sedulous extirpation. It will also be found a great improvement, where space will admit of it, to surround the larger plots of ground, in which the vegetables are grown, with flower borders stocked with herbaceous plants and others, such as annuals and bulbs in due order of succession, or with neat espaliers, with fruit trees, or even gooseberry and currant bushes, trained along them, instead of being suffered to grow in a state of ragged wildness, as is too often the case.

219. TOMATO, OR LOVE APPLE.—This plant is a native of South America ; its fruit has of late years become a very favourite article of food, and may be prepared in a great many ways. It is equally applicable for soups, ketchups, and sauces, and the unripe fruit may also be pickled. It can be easily cultivated in a greenhouse or a small garden, and with care yields a plentiful crop of fruit. For pot culture, in cold greenhouse (temperature 65˚), sow the seeds in March in a compost formed of two parts decayed turfy loam, and one part of well decomposed manure, transferring the seedlings singly into two-inch pots as soon as three or four leaves have formed, and afterwards, when the plants are six inches high, into six-inch pots, and again into ten-inch pots when twelve inches high. Drain the pots well. Only let one stem grow, rubbing off all side shoots. Water sparingly until the fruit is set, then apply liquid or artificial manures.

In outdoor culture—plant in June, against south or west walls, twelve inches apart, or in the open, placing stout stakes to support the plants.

220. ARTIFICIAL MUSHROOM BEDS.—Mushrooms may be grown in pots, boxes, or hampers. Each box may be about three feet long, one and a half broad, and seven inches in depth, and should be half filled with manure in the form of fresh horse-dung from the stables, the fresher the better, but if wet, it should be allowed to dry for three or four days before it is put into the boxes. When the manure has been placed in the box it should be well beaten down. After the second or third day, if the manure has begun to generate heat, break each brick of mushroom spawn (which may be obtained from any seedsman) into pieces about three inches square, then lay the pieces about four inches apart upon the surface of the manure in the box ; here they are to lie for

six days, when it will probably be found that the side of the spawn next to the manure has begun to run in the manure below ; then add one and a half inch more of fresh manure on the top of the spawn in the box, and beat it down as formerly. In the course of a fortnight, when you find that the spawn has run through the manure, the box will be ready to receive the mould on the top ; this mould must be two and a half inches deep, well beaten down, and the surface made quite even. In the space of five or six weeks the mushrooms will begin to come up ; if the mould then seems dry, give it a gentle watering with lukewarm water. The box will continue to produce from six weeks to two months, if duly attended to by giving a little water when dry, for the mushrooms need neither *light* nor *free air*. If cut as button mushrooms each box will yield from twenty-four to forty-eight pints, according to the season and other circumstances. They may be kept in dry dark cellars, or any other places where the frost will not reach them. By preparing a succession of boxes, mushrooms may be had all the year through. They may be grown without the manure, and be of a finer flavour. Take a little straw, and lay it carefully in the bottom of the mushroom box, about an inch thick, or rather more. Then take some of the spawn bricks and break them down—each brick into about ten pieces, and lay the fragments on the straw, as close to each other as they will lie. Cover them up with mould three and a half inches deep, and well pressed down. When the surface appears dry give a little tepid water, as directed for the mode of raising them described above ; but this method needs about double the quantity of water that the former does, owing to having no moisture in the bottom, while the other has the manure. The mushrooms will begin to start in a month or five weeks, sometimes sooner, sometimes later, according to the heat of the place where the boxes are situated.

221. DWARF PLANTS.—The following method of producing miniature trees is taken from an article on this subject in *Gardening Illustrated.* "Take an orange, and having cut a hole in the peel about the size of a shilling, take out the juice and pulp. Fill the skin thus emptied with some cocoanut fibre, fine moss, and charcoal, just stiffened with a little loam, and then put an acorn or a date stone, or the seed or kernel of any tree that it is proposed to obtain in a dwarfed form in this mixture, just about the centre of the hollow orange peel. Place the orange peel in a tumbler or vase in a window, and occasionally moisten the contents with a little water through the hole in the peel, and sprinkle the surface apparent through the hole with some fine woodashes. In due time the tree will push up its stem through the compost and the roots will push through the orange peel. The roots must then be cut off flush with the peel, and this process must be repeated at frequent intervals for about two years and a half. The stem of the tree will attain the height of four or five inches and then assume a stunted gnarled appearance, giving it the appearance of an old tree. When the ends of the roots are cut for the last time, the orange peel, which, curiously enough, does not rot, must be painted black and varnished." The writer of the article saw this process carried out by a Chinaman that he had in his service, and the trees thrived and presented a healthy appearance for eight years, when the Chinaman left his employ and took the trees with him. He tried the plan which has been described but failed, but he was successful with an acorn and a datestone which were planted each in a thumb-pot in a mixture of peat and loam. The dwarfing was effected by turning the plants out of the pots at

intervals of six weeks and pinching off the ends of the roots that showed themselves behind the compost. This shows that the production of dwarf plants is chiefly due to a constant and systematic checking of the root growth.

222. TO CLEAR ROSE TRESS FROM BLIGHT.—Mix equal quantities of sulphur and tobacco dust, and strew the mixture over the trees in the morning when the dew is on them. The insects will disappear in a few days. The trees should then be syringed with a decoction of elder leaves.

223. TO PREVENT MILDEW IN TREES.—The best preventive against mildew is to keep the plant subject to it occasionally syringed with a decoction of elder leaves, which will prevent the growth of fungus.

224. TOADS are among the best friends the gardener has ; for they live almost exclusively on the most destructive kinds of vermin. Unsightly, therefore, though they may be, they should on all accounts be encouraged ; they should never be touched nor molested in any way ; on the contrary, places of shelter should be made for them, to which they may retire from the burning heat of the sun. If you have no toads in your garden, it will be quite worth your while to search for them in your walks, and bring them home, taking care to handle them tenderly, for although they have neither the will nor the power to injure you, a very little rough treatment will injure them. No cucumber or melon frame should be without one or two.

225. SLUGS AND SNAILS are great enemies to every kind of garden plant, whether flower or vegetable ; they wander in the night to feed, and return at daylight to their haunts. In order to catch them lay cabbage leaves about the ground, especially on the beds which they frequent. Every morning examine these leaves, and you will find a great many taking refuge beneath, and these may be killed by sprinkling them with a little lime or salt. These minerals are very annoying to snails and sings ; a pinch of salt kills them, and they will not touch fresh lime. It is a common practice to sprinkle lime over young crops, and along the edges of beds, about rows of peas and beans, lettuces and other vegetables ; but when it has been on the ground some days, or has been moistened by rain, it loses its strength.

226. TRAPS FOR SNAILS.— Snails are particularly fond of bran ; if a little is spread on the ground, and covered over with a few cabbage-leaves or tiles, they will congregate under them in great numbers, and may be readily caught and destroyed.

227. GRUBS on orchard trees, and gooseberry and currant bushes, will sometimes be sufficiently numerous to spoil a crop ; but if a bonfire be made with dry sticks and weeds on the windward side of the orchard, so that the smoke may blow among the trees, you will destroy thousands ; for the grubs have such an objection to smoke, that very little of it makes them roll themselves up and fall off : they must then be swept up and destroyed.

228. CATERPILLARS AND APHIDES.—A garden syringe or engine, with a cap on the pipe full of very minute holes, will wash away these disagreeable visitors very quickly. You must bring the pipe close to the plant, and pump hard, so as to have considerable force on, and the plant, however badly infested, will soon be cleared, without receiving any injury. Afterwards rake the earth under the trees, and kill the insects that have been dislodged, or many will recover and climb up the stems of the plants. Aphides may also be cleared by means of tobacco smoke, but after this has been applied, the plant should be well syringed.

229. BUTTERFLIES AND MOTHS, however pretty, are the worst enemies one can have in a garden ; a single insect of this kind may deposit eggs enough to overrun a tree with caterpillars, therefore they should be destroyed at any cost of trouble.

230. TO PROTECT FRUIT BUDS FROM BIRDS.—Just before the buds are ready to burst, and again when they have begun to expand, give them a plentiful dusting with chimney soot. The soot is unpalatable to the birds, and they will attack no bush that is thus sprinkled. It in no way injures the nascent blossom or leaf, and is washed off in due course of time by the rain.

231. WASPS destroy a good deal of fruit, but every pair of wasps killed in spring saves the trouble and annoyance of a swarm in autumn. Later in the season, it is customary to hang vessels of beer, or water and sugar, in the fruit-trees, to entice them to drown themselves. A wasp in a window may be killed almost instantaneously by the application of a little sweet oil on the tip of a feather. It is necessary, however, to be very careful in any attempt upon a wasp, for its sting, like that of the bee, causes much pain and frequently induces considerable swelling.

232. CURES FOR THE STING OF WASP OR BEE.—In case of being stung, get the blue-bag from the laundry, and rub it well into the wound as soon as possible. A little ammonia applied to the puncture will speedily relieve the pain, and so will the juice of an onion obtained by cutting an onion in half and rubbing the cut part over the part affected.

233 TO PROTECT DAHLIAS FROM EARWIGS.—Dip a piece of

wool or cotton in oil, and tie it lightly round the stalk, about a foot from the earth. The stakes which you will put into the ground to support your plants must also be surrounded by the oiled cotton or wool, or the insects will climb up them to the blossoms and tender tops of the stems. Insects may be prevented from climbing up stakes, trees, &c., by encircling them with a broad ring of tar, which may be renewed as often as necessary. Small pots containing a little hay, dried grass, or cotton wool inverted and placed on the top of stakes form a useful trap for slugs, snails, earwigs, &c., which crawl into them for shelter in the early rooming, and may thus be caught and destroyed.

234. TO FREE PLANTS FROM LEAF-LICE.

The following is recommended as a cheap and easy mode of getting rid of this pest :—Mix one ounce of flowers of sulphur with one bushel of sawdust ; scatter this over the plants infected with these insects, and they will soon be freed, though a second application may possibly be necessary.

235. A GARDENING MORAL.

I HAD a little Spot of ground,
    Where blade nor blossom grew,
Though the bright sunshine all around
    Life-giving radiance threw.
I mourned to see a spot so bare
    Of leaves of healthful green,
And thought of bowers, and blossoms fair
    I frequently had seen.

Some seeds of varions kinds lay by—
    I knew not what they were—
But, rudely taming o'er the soil,
    I strewed them thickly there ;
And day by day I watched them spring
    From out the fertile earth,
And hoped for many a loving thing
    Of beauty and of worth.

But as I marked their leaves unfold
    As weeds before my view,
And saw how stubbornly and bold
    The thorns and nettles grew—

I sighed to think that I had done.
    Unwittingly, a thing
That, where a beauteous bower should thrive.
    But worthless weeds did spring.

And thus I mused : the things we do.
    With little heed or ken,
May prove of worthless growth, and strew
    With thorns the paths of men ;
For little deeds, like little seeds,
    May flowers prove, or noxious weeds !

236. HINTS ON TAKING A HOUSE.

i. **Rent.**—Before taking a house, be careful to calculate that the rent is not too high in proportion to your means ; for remember that the rent is a claim that must be paid with but little delay, and that the landlord has greater power over your property than any other creditor. It is difficult to assign any fixed proportion between income and rental to suit all cases, but a reasonable basis for the settlement of this point may be found in the assertion that while not less than one-tenth of a man's entire income need be set apart for rent, not more than a sixth, or at the very utmost a fifth should be devoted to this purpose, and this amount ought to include parochial rates and taxes. Having determined the amount of rent which you can afford to pay, be careful to select the best and most convenient house which can be obtained for that sum. And in making that selection let the following matters be carefully considered :

ii. **Healthy Situation.**—Find out the nature of the sub-soil on which the house stands—for example, a gravel on chalk subsoil, is better than a subsoil of clay, because the former admits of a speedy escape of the surplus water in time of heavy and continuous rain, while the latter does not. Avoid the neighbourhood of graveyards, and of factories giving forth unhealthy vapours. Avoid low and damp districts, the course of canals, the localities of reservoirs of water, gas works, &c. Make inquiries as to the drainage of the neighbourhood, and inspect the drainage and water supply of the premises. A house standing on an incline is likely to be better drained than one standing upon the summit of a hill, or on a level below a hill. Endeavour to obtain a position where the direct sunlight falls upon the house, for this is absolutely essential to health ; and give preference to a house the openings of which are sheltered from the north and east winds. Consider the distance of the house from your place of occupation : and its relation to provision markets, and shops in the neighbourhood.

iii. **Sanitary Condition and State of Repair.**—Having considered these material and leading features, examine the house in detail, carefully looking into its state of repair. When a furnished house is let, the law implies that it shall be fit for habitation ; but this is not the case with regard to an unfurnished house. In the latter case the tenant is presumed to have satisfied himself beforehand as to its condition, and therefore a person who intends taking an unfurnished house should have it surveyed, and should have an undertaking from the landlord that the drainage is in perfect order. Ascertain if possible that the foundations are air-tight and water-tight ; whether the cellars are dry or danp ; state of the water supply and sources of supply ; water-closet apparatus ; bathroom ; bell-pulls ; ventilation ; gas supply ; electric lighting or bells. Also notice the windows that are broken ; whether the chimneys smoke ; whether they have been recently swept ; whether the paper on the walls is damaged, especially in the lower parts, and the corners, by the skirtings ; whether the locks, bolts, handles of doors, and window fastenings are in proper condition ; make a list of the fixtures ; ascertain whether all rates and taxes have been paid by the previous tenant, and whether the person

from whom you take the house is the original landlord, or his agent or tenant. Do not commit yourself by the signing of any agreement until you are satisfied upon all these points, *and see that all has been done which the landlord may have undertaken to do, before you take possession of the house.*

237. HINTS ON FURNISHING A HOUSE.—It is only by experience that you can tell what will be the wants of your family, so at first buy merely enough to get along with, and add other things by degrees. If you spend all your money, you will find you have purchased many things you do not actually want, and have no means left to get many things which you do want. If you have enough, and more than enough, to get everything suitable to your situation, do not think you must spend all you may be able to lay out in furniture, merely because you happen to have it. Begin humbly. As riches increase, it is easy and pleasant to increase in comforts ; but it is always painful and inconvenient to decrease. Neatness, tastefulness, and good sense may be shown in the management of a small household, and the arrangement of a little furniture, as well as upon a larger scale. The consideration which many purchase by living beyond their income, and, of course, living upon others, is not worth the trouble it costs. It does not, in fact, procure a man valuable friends, or extensive influence.

238. CHOOSING CARPETS.—In buying carpets, as in everything else, those of the best quality are cheapest in the end. One need only compare a good Brussels with a Tapestry half the price. Kidderminster wears well and can be turned. As it is extremely desirable that it should look as clean as possible, avoid buying carpeting that has any white in it. Even a very small portion of of white interspersed through the pattern will in a short time give a dirty appearance to the whole.

A Carpet in which all the Colours are Light never has a clean, bright effect, from the want of dark tints to contrast and set off the light ones. For a similar reason, carpets whose colours are all of what artists call middle tint (neither dark nor light) cannot fail to look dull and dingy, even when quite new.

For a Carpet to be really Beautiful and in good taste, there should be, as in the picture, a judicious disposal of light and shadow, with a gradation of very bright and of very dark tints ; some almost white, and others almost or quite black.

The most truly chaste, rich, and elegant carpets are those which are of one colour only, the pattern, if pattern it may be called, being formed by a judicious arrangement of every variety of shade of this colour. For instance, a Brussels carpet entirely red ; the pattern formed by shades or tints varying from the deepest crimson (almost a black), to the palest pink (almost a white). Also one of green only, shaded from the darkest bottle-green, in some parts of the pattern, to the lightest pea-green in others. Or one in which there is no colour but brown, in all its various gradations, some of the shades being nearly black, others of a light buff.

239. HEARTHRUGS.—If you cannot obtain one that exactly corresponds with the carpet, get one entirely different ; for a decided contrast looks better than a bad match. The hearthrug, however, should reflect the colour or colours of the carpet if possible.

Large Rugs of Sheepskin, in white, crimson, or black, form comfortable and effective hearthrugs for a drawing-room or dining-room. In the winter these may be removed and an ordinary woollen rug laid down as long as fires are kept up.

240. CURTAINS AND UPHOLSTERY of Furniture, and the wall papers and paint should also harmonize with the colours of the carpets, that the effect of the whole may be satisfactory to the eye.

241. LINOLEUM, KAMPTULICON, &c., are now very generally used as floor coverings for halls, kitchens, &c., on account of their cleanliness and warmth ; and with proper care they may be made to last a long while, but the tile or inlaid linoleum, though more expensive, will be found best suited for hard wear, as the pattern, instead of being merely on the surface, goes through the material. They are, as a rule, made of canvas painted over.

The best way to clean these floor coverings is to wash them with soap and luke-warm water, and then rub them over with a cloth and a little oil. Do not use too much water, or it will get underneath and rot the material. In buying linoleum or kamptulicon, test it by its weight, for the heavier it is the better it is.

Some excellent floor coverings are now made of a material largely consisting of *cork.* It is very cleanly, and is an excellent floor cover for nurseries, bedrooms, and bathrooms, being very warm to the feet, and easily cleaned.

242. HOUSEHOLD TOOL CHESTS.—Much inconvenience and considerable expense might be saved if it were the general custom to keep in every house certain tools for the purpose of performing at home what are called small jobs, instead of being always obliged to send for a mechanic and pay him for executing little things that, in most cases, could be sufficiently well done by a man or boy belonging to the family, if the proper instruments were at hand. The cost of these articles is very moderate, and the advantages of having them always in the house are far beyond the expense.

243. LIST OF USEFUL TOOLS.

There should be an axe, a hatchet, a saw, a hammer, a tack-hammer, a mallet, three or four gimlets and bradawls of different sizes, two screw-drivers, two chisels, a small plane, one or two jack-knives, a pair of large scissors or shears, and a carpet fork or stretcher. Also an assortment of screws and nails of various sizes, from large spikes down to small tacks, not forgetting some large and small brass-headed nails, together with hooks of various sizes upon which to hang things.

The nails and screws should be kept in a wooden box, made with divisions to separate the various sorts and sizes, for it is very troublesome to have them mixed. Care should also be taken to keep up the supply, lest it should run out unexpectedly, and the deficiency cause delay and inconvenience at a time when some are wanted.

244. TOOL CLOSET.—It is well to have somewhere, in the lower part of the house, a roomy light closet, appropriated entirely to tools, and things of equal utility, for executing promptly such little repairs as may be required from time to time, without the delay or expense of procuring an artisan. This closet should have at least one large shelf, and that about three feet from the floor. Beneath this shelf may be a deep drawer, divided into two compartments. This drawer may contain cakes of glue, pieces of chalk, and balls of twine of different sizes and quality. There may be shelves at the sides of the closet for glue-pots, paste-pots and brushes, pots for black, white, green, and red paint, cans of oil and varnish, paint-brushes, &c.

245. THE TOOLS SHOULD BE SUSPENDED against the wall, above the large shelf, or laid across nails or hooks of proper size to support them. This is much better than keeping them in a box, where they are apt to be injured by rubbing against each other, and the hand may be hurt in feeling amongst them to find the thing that is wanted. But when hung up against the back wall of the closet, each tool can be seen at a glance.

An excellent and simple contrivance for designating the exact places allotted to all these articles is to draw on the closet wall with paint or ink a representation in outline of the tool belonging to that particular place. For instance, under each saw is sketched the outline of that saw, under each gimlet a sketch of that gimlet, under the screw-drivers are slight drawings of screw-drivers. So that when any tool that has been taken away for use is brought back, the exact spot to which it belongs can be found in a moment ; and the confusion which is occasioned in putting tools away in a box and looking for them again when they are wanted, is thus prevented.

246. TO LOOSEN SCREWS AND NAILS which have become *rusted* into wood. These may be moved by dropping a small quantity of kerosene over them. Allow this to soak in, and after a short time the screws, &c., may be taken out.

247. WRAPPING PAPER.—This may be piled on the floor under the large shelf in the tool closet. It can be bought at a low price by the ream, at the large paper warehouses ; and every house should keep a supply of it in several varieties.

i. **Coarse brown paper** for common purposes, which is strong, thick, and in large sheets, is useful for packing heavy articles ; and equally so for keeping silks, ribbons, blondes, &c., as it preserves their colours.

ii. **Printed Papers** are unfit for wrapping anything, as the printing ink rubs off on the articles enclosed in them, and also soils the gloves of the person who carries the parcel.

iii. **Waste Newspapers** had best

be used for lighting fires and singeing poultry. If you have accumulated more than you can use, your butcher or grocer will generally buy them of you if they are clean.

iv. **Waste Paper** that has been written on, cut into slips, and creased and folded, makes very good allumettes or lamp-lighters. These matters may appear of trifling importance, but order and regularity are necessary to happiness.

248. BEDS FOR THE POOR.—Beech-tree leaves are recommended for filling the beds of poor persons. They should be gathered on a dry day in the autumn, and perfectly dried. It is said that the smell of them is pleasant and that they will not harbour vermin. They are also very springy.

249. TO PRESERVE GILT FRAMES.—These may be protected from flies and dust by pinning tarlatan over them. Tarlatan fit for the purpose may be purchased at the draper's. It is an excellent material for keeping dust from books, vases, wool work, and every description of household ornament.

250. TO RESTORE GILT FRAMES.—Rub them lightly with a sponge moistened with turpentine.

251. REMEDIES FOR DAMP WALLS.

The following method is recommended to prevent the effect of damp walls on paper in rooms :—Line the damp part of the wall with sheet lead, rolled very thin, and fastened up with small copper nails. It may be immediately covered with paper. The lead is not to be thicker than that which is used to line tea-chests.

Another mode of preventing the ill effects of damp in walls on wall-paper is to cover the damp part with a varnish formed of naphtha and shellac, in the proportion of ¼ lb. of the latter to a quart of the former. The smell of the mixture is unpleasant, but it wears off in a short time, and the wall is covered with a hard coating utterly impervious to damp, and to which the wall paper can be attached in the usual way.

252. HINTS ON SCOURING BEDROOMS.

They should not be scoured in the winter time, as colds and sickness may be produced thereby. Dry scouring upon the French plan, which consists of scrubbing the floors with dry brushes, may be resorted to, and will be found more effective than can at first be imagined. If a bedroom is wet scoured, a dry day should be chosen, the windows should be opened, the linen removed, and a fire should be lit when the operation is finished.

253. TO GET RID OF A BAD SMELL IN A ROOM.—Place a vessel full of lighted charcoal in the middle of the room, and throw on it two or three handfuls of juniper berries, shut the windows, the chimney, and the door close ; twenty-four hours afterwards, the room may be opened, when it will be found that the sickly, unwholesome smell will be entirely gone. The smoke of the juniper berry possesses this advantage, that should anything be left in the room, such as tapestry, &c., none of it will be spoiled.

254. TO REMOVE SMELL OF PAINT.—To get rid of the smell of oil paint, place a handful of hay in a pailful of water and let it stand in the room newly painted.

255. TO KEEP BEDS AIRED. When not being used, they should be put under other beds which are in use ; or they may now and then be placed in front of a good fire and turned over occasionally.

256. TO ASCERTAIN WHETHER A BED CAN BE AIRED.—Introduce a drinking glass between the sheets for a minute or two, just when the warming-pan is taken out ; if the bed be dry, there will only be a slight cloudy appearance on the glass, but if not, the damp of the bed will collect in and on the glass and assume the form of drops—a warning of danger.

257. DRINKING WATER.

To test its purity Heisch gives a simple method. Put half-a-pint of water in a clear glass-stoppered bottle ; add a few grams of the best white lump sugar. Let the bottle be exposed in a warm room to the daylight. If the water is pure, the liquid should not become turbid, even if it has been exposed for a week or ten days.

258. TO TEST IF WATER IS HARD OR SOFT.

Dissolve some good soap in alcohol, and put a few drops into a glass of the water. If it turns milky it is hard ; if not, it is soft.

259. TO SOFTEN HARD WATER,

or purify river water, simply boil it, and then leave it exposed to the atmosphere for some little time.

260. TO PREVENT WATER ENCRUSTING THE INSIDE OF KETTLES.

Water of every kind, except rain water, will speedily cover the inside of a tea-kettle with an unpleasant crust ; this may easily be guarded against by placing a clean oyster shell or piece of stone or marble in the tea-kettle. The shell or stone will always keep the interior of the kettle in good order by attracting the particles of earth or stone.

261. CABBAGE WATER, or any

water in which green vegetables have been boiled, should be thrown away out of doors (not down the sink) immediately it is done with, and the vessel rinsed with clean water or it will cause unpleasant smells.

262. DISINFECTANTS FOR SINKS, DRAINS, &c.

A little charcoal mixed with clean water thrown into a sink will disinfect and deodorize it. Chloride of lime and carbolic acid considerably diluted, if applied in a liquid form, are good disinfectants, and carbolic powder—a pink powder with a smell resembling tar, and sold at about 2d. per lb.—is both useful and effective. The air of a bedroom may be pleasantly sweetened by throwing some ground coffee on a fire shovel previously heated.

263. CHIMNEY SMOKING.—

When this occurs only when the fire is first lighted, it may be guarded against by allowing the fire to kindle gradually, or by heating the chimney by burning straw or paper in the grate previous to laying in the fire.

264. TO PREVENT A LAMP SMOKING.—Soak the wick in strong

vinegar, and dry it well before you use it ; the flame will then burn clear and bright.

265. GROUND GLASS IMITATED. The frosted appearance

of ground glass may be very nearly imitated by gently dabbing the glass over with a paint brush dipped in white paint or any other oil colour. The paint should be thin, and but very little colour taken up at one time on the end of the bristles. When applied with a light and even touch the resemblance is considerable.

266. TO OIL CLOCKS use only

the very purest oil, purified by a quart of lime water to a gallon of oil in which it has been well shaken, and suffered to stand for three or four days, when it may be drawn off.

267. NEAT MODE OF SOLDERING.—Cut out a piece of tinfoil the

size of the surfaces to be soldered. Then dip a feather in a solution of sal ammoniac, and wet over the surfaces of the metal, then place them in their proper position with the tinfoil between. Put the metals thus arranged on a piece of iron hot enough to melt the foil. When cold the surfaces will be found firmly soldered together.

268. TO WATERPROOF MAPS, CHARTS, &c.

—Maps, charts, or engravings may be effectually varnished by brushing a very delicate coating of gutta-percha solution over their surface. It is perfectly transparent, and is said to improve the appearance of pictures. By coating both sides of important documents they can be kept waterproof and preserved perfectly.

269. PAPER FIRE SCREENS

should be sized and coated with transparent varnish, otherwise they will soon become soiled and discoloured.

270. PASTILLES FOR BURNING.

—Cascarilla bark, 'eight drachms ; gum benzoin, four drachms ; yellow sanders, two drachms ; styrax, two drachms ; olibanum, two drachms ; charcoal, six ounces ; nitre, one drachm and a half ; mucilage of tragacanth, sufficient quantity. Reduce the substances to a powder, and form into a paste with the mucilage, and divide into small cones ; then dry them in an oven.

271. EASY METHOD OF BREAKING GLASS TO ANY REQUIRED SHAPE.

—Make a small notch by means of a file on the edge of a piece of glass, then make the end of a tobacco-pipe, or of a rod of iron of the same size, red hot in the fire ; apply the hot iron to the notch, and draw it slowly along the surface of the glass in any direction you please ; a crack will follow the direction of the iron.

272. TO REMOVE BROKEN WINDOW-PANES.

—If you have not a glazier's knife, you can melt the putty in a few hours by putting soft soap

upon it ; then you can cut it away easily with a knife, without risk of breaking the glass.

273. BOTTLING AND FINING.

—Corks should be sound, clean, and sweet. Beer and porter should be allowed to stand in the bottles a day or two before being corked. If for speedy use wiring is not necessary. Laying the bottles on their sides will assist the ripening for use. Those that are to be kept should be wired, and put to stand upright in sawdust. Wines should be bottled in spring. If not fine enough, draw off a jugful and dissolve isinglass in it, in the proportion of half-an-ounce to ten gallons, and then pour back through the bung-hole. Let it stand a few weeks. Tap the cask above the lees. When the isinglass is put into the cask, stir it round with a stick, taking great care not to touch the lees at the bottom. For white wine only, mix with the isinglass a quarter of a pint of milk to each gallon of wine, some whites of eggs, beaten with some of the wine. One white of an egg to four gallons makes a good fining.

274. TO SWEETEN CASKS.

Mix half-a-pint of vitriol with a quart of water, pour it into the barrel, and roll it about ; next day add one pound of chalk, and roll again. Bung down for three or four days, then rinse well with hot water.

276. TO LOOSEN GLASS STOPPERS OF BOTTLES.

With a feather rub a drop or two of salad oil round the stopper, close to the mouth of the bottle or decanter, which must then be placed before the fire, at the distance of about eighteen inches ; the heat will cause the oil to insinuate itself between the stopper and the neck. When the bottle has grown warm, gently strike the stopper on one side, and then on the other, with any light wooden instrument ; then try it with the hand ; if it will not yet move, place it again before the fire, adding another drop of oil. After a while strike again as before ; and, by persevering in this process, however tightly it may be fastened in, you will at length succeed in loosening it.

Another Method.—Dip one end of a cloth in boiling water, and then wrap it round the neck of the bottle ; the heat causes the neck to expand, and the stopper can generally be moved with ease ; or put a piece of string twice round the neck and fix one end to a ring or hook, draw the bottle backwards and forwards sharply. The heat caused by the friction expands the neck as in the preceding case.

276. CHINA TEAPOTS are the safest, and, in many respects, the most pleasant. Wedgwood ware is very apt, after a time, to acquire a disagreeable taste.

277. CARE OF LINEN.—When linen is well dried and laid by for use, nothing more is necessary than to secure it from damp and insects. It may be kept free from the latter by a judicious mixture of aromatic shrubs and flowers, cut up and sewed in silken bags, which must be interspersed among the drawers and shelves. The ingredients used may consist of lavender, thyme, roses, cedar-shavings, powdered sassafras, cassia, &c., into which a few drops of otto of roses, or other strong-scented perfume may be thrown.

278. REPAIRING LINEN.—in all cases it will be found more consistent with economy to examine and repair all washable articles, more especially linen, that may stand in need of it, previous to sending them to the laundry. It will also be prudent to have every article carefully numbered, and so arranged, after washing, as to have their regular turn and term in domestic use.

279. MENDING.—When you make a new article always save the pieces until "mending day," which may come sooner than expected. It will be well even to buy a little extra quantity for repairs. Read over the paragraphs 360—368 in this volume headed GOLDEN HINTS FOR HOUSEWIVES AND HOME COMFORTS. These contain most valuable suggestions, that will be constantly useful if well remembered. They should be read frequently that their full value may be secured. Let your servants also read them, for nothing conduces more to good housekeeping than for the servant to understand the "system" which her mistress approves of.

280. TO POLISH FURNITURE.

This forms an important part of domestic economy, not only in regard to neatness, but also in point of expense. The readiest mode consists in good manual rubbing, or the application of a little elbow-grease, as it is whimsically termed ; but our finest cabinet work requires something more, where brilliancy of polish is of importance.

Italian Cabinet-Work in this respect excels that of any other country. The workmen first saturate the surface with olive oil, and then apply a solution of gum arabic dissolved in boiling alcohol. This mode of varnishing is equally brilliant, if not superior, to that employed by the French in their most elaborate works.

281. A GOOD POLISH FOR FURNITURE, which has less the appearance of a hard varnish, and may always be applied so as to restore the pristine beauty of the furniture by a little manual labour. Heat a gallon of water, in which dissolve one pound and a half of potash ; and a pound of virgin wax, boiling the whole for half-an-hour, then suffer it to cool, when the wax will float on the surface. Put the wax into a mortar, and triturate it with a marble pestle, adding soft water to it until it forms a soft paste, which, laid neatly on furniture, or even on paintings, and carefully rubbed when dry with a woollen rag, gives a polish of great brilliancy, without the harshness of the drier varnishes.

282. TO POLISH MARBLE CHIMNEY-PIECES.

After cleaning the marble with diluted muriatic acid, or warm soap and vinegar, they may be rubbed with the above polish, but the iron or brass work connected with them requires other processes.

283. TO REMOVE THE STAINS OF IRON FROM MARBLE.

Carefully rub the *spot only* with strong hydrochloric acid. If the polish is taken off, it may be restored with emery paper and putty powder.

284. POLISHED IRON WORK

may be preserved from rust by an inexpensive mixture, consisting of copal varnish intimately mixed with as much olive oil as will give it a degree of greasiness, adding thereto nearly as much spirit of turpentine as of varnish.

285. CAST IRON WORK

is best preserved by the common method of rubbing with black-lead.

286. TO REMOVE RUST FROM FIRE-IRONS, &c.

Apply a mixture of two parts of rotten-stone to one of sulphur, intimately mingled on a marble slab, and laid on with a piece of soft leather. Or emery and oil may be applied with excellent effect ; not laid on in the usual slovenly way, but with a spongy piece of fig-wood fully saturated with the mixture. This will not only clean but impart a polish to the metal as well.

287. TO CLEAN BRASS ORNAMENTS.

These, when not gilt or lacquered, may be cleaned in the same way, and a fine colour given to them, by two simple processes.

i. Beat sal ammoniac into a fine powder, then moisten it with soft water, rubbing it on the ornaments, which must be heated over charcoal, and rubbed dry with bran and whitening.

ii. Wash the brasswork with roche alum boiled in strong ley, in proportion of an ounce to a pint ; when dry, rub it with fine rotten-stone. Either of these processes will give to brass the brilliancy of gold.

288 LOOSE CARPETS.

If the corner of a carpet becomes loose and prevents the door opening, or trips every one up that enters the room, nail it down at once. A dog's-eared carpet marks the sloven as well as the dog's-eared book. An English gentleman, travelling some years ago in Ireland, took a hammer and tacks with him, because he found dog's-eared carpets at all the inns where he rested. At one of these inns he tacked down the carpet, which, as usual, was loose near the door, and soon afterwards rang for his dinner. While the carpet was loose the door could not be opened without a hard push ; so when the waiter came up he just unlatched the door, and then going back a couple of yards, he rushed against it, as his habit was, with a sudden spring, to force it open. But the wrinkles of the carpet were no longer there to stop it, and not meeting with the expected resistance, the unfortunate waiter fell full length into the room. It had never entered his head that so much trouble might be saved by means of a hammer and half-a-dozen tacks, until his fall taught him that makeshift is a very unprofitable kind of shift. There are a good many houses in England where a similar practical lesson might be of service.

289. CLEANING CARPETS.

Take a pail of cold water, and add to it three gills of ox-gall. Rub it into the carpet with a soft brush. It will raise a lather, which must be washed off with clear cold water. Rub dry with a clean cloth. Before nailing down a carpet after the floor has been washed, be certain that the floor is quite dry, or the nails will rust and injure the carpet. Fuller's earth is used for cleaning carpets, and weak solutions of alum or soda are used for reviving the colours. The crumb of a hot wheaten loaf rubbed over a carpet has been found effective.

290. TO TAKE GREASE OR OIL OUT OF A CARPET.—As soon as possible, put plenty of flour or whitening on the spot, to prevent the grease spreading. If the oil is near a seam, you can rip it, and put the whitening on the floor under the carpet. Next day sweep up the flour and put on some fresh whitening, then rub the spots with a flannel dipped in spirits of turpentine.

291. BEATING CARPETS.—Always beat on the wrong side first ; and then more gently on the right side. Beware of using sticks with sharp points, which may tear the carpet

292. SWEEPING CARPETS.—Persons who are accustomed to use tea-leaves for sweeping their carpets, and find that they leave stains, will do well to employ fresh-cut grass instead. It is better than tea-leaves for preventing dust, and gives the carpets a very bright fresh look.

293. SWEEPING TURKEY CARPETS.—In the case of heavy-piled Turkey or Axminster carpets, they should always be brushed in the direction the pile goes. By doing this the carpet will last twice as long : but if swept the other way the dust will be driven into the carpet. Small sweeping machines, with boxes to collect the dust, are now extensively used for sweeping carpets.

294. SWEEPING STAIR CARPETS.—These should never be swept down with a long broom, but always with a short-handled brush, a dust-pan being held closely under each step of the stairs during the operation of sweeping.

295. TO CLEAN OIL-CLOTH.—This should never be scrubbed with a brush, but, after being first swept, it should be cleansed by washing with a large soft cloth and lukewarm or cold water. On no account use soap or hot water, as either will injure the paint, and in time remove it.

296. TO CLEAN STRAW MATTING.—Use a large coarse cloth dipped in salt and water, then wipe it dry. The salt prevents the matting from turning yellow.

297. TO CLEAN PAPER HANGINGS.—Cut into eight half-quarters a quartern loaf, two days old ; it must be neither newer nor staler. With one of these pieces, after having blown off all the dust from the paper to be cleaned, by means of a good pair of bellows, begin at the top of the room and, holding the crust in the hand, wipe lightly downward with the crumb, about half-a-yard at each stroke, till the upper part of the paper is completely cleaned all round. Then go round again, with the like sweeping stroke downwards, always commencing each successive course a little higher than the upper stroke had extended, till the bottom be finished. This operation, if carefully performed, will frequently make very old paper look almost equal to new. Great care must be taken not to rub the paper hard, nor to attempt cleaning it the cross or horizontal way. The surface of the bread, too, must be always cut away as soon as it becomes dirty, and the pieces renewed as often as may be necessary.

Another Method is to make a stiff dough with flour and water. Take a handful, knead it into a ball and carefully rub the paper as directed above, turning in the soiled portions of the dough from time to time and taking fresh pieces as required.

298. OTTOMANS AND SOFAS, covered with cloth, damask, or chintz, will look better for being cleaned occasionally with bran and flannel.

299. MAHOGANY FRAMES of Sofas, Chairs, &c., should be first well dusted, and then cleaned with a flannel dipped in sweet oil or linseed oil.

300. ROSEWOOD FURNITURE should be rubbed gently every day with a clean soft cloth to keep it in order.

301. DINING TABLES may be polished by rubbing them for some time with a soft cloth and a little linseed oil.

302. TO PRESERVE THE POLISH OF TABLES.—A piece of oil-cloth (about twenty inches long) is a useful appendage to a sitting-room. Kept in the closet, it can be available at any time, in order to place upon it jars, lamps, &c., whose contents are likely to soil your table during the process of emptying or filling them. A wing and duster are harmonious accompaniments to the oil-cloth.

303. TO CLEAN CANE-BOTTOM CHAIRS.—Turn the chair bottom upwards, and with hot water and a sponge wash the cane-work well, so that it may become completely soaked. Should it be very dirty you must add soap. Let it dry in the open air, or in a place where there is a thorough draught, and it will become as tight and firm as when new, provided none of the strips are broken.

304. TO POLISH ALABASTER.—Rub first with pumice-stone, and then with a paste made up of whitening, soap and milk (or water), and finish off with dry flannel.

Another Method is to first rub with dried shave-grass, and then with finely-powdered slacked lime made into a paste with water. Then rub with French chalk, powder, or putty powder, until the required polish is produced.

305. Calcareous Alabaster is cleaned with a brush and warm water and soap, or with warm water with a small quantity of ammonia, or soda ; being afterwards rinsed in clean water. If it is much stained cover the article for twenty-four hours in a paste of slacked lime and water, and then wash with soap and water.

306. TO CLEAN MARBLE.

Take two parts of common soda, one part of pumice-stone, and one part of finely-powdered chalk ; sift it through a fine sieve, and mix it with water. Rub the marble well all over with the mixture, and the stains will be removed ; then wash the marble with soap and water, and it will be as clean as it was at first.

307. GLASS should be washed in cold water, which gives it a brighter and clearer look than when cleansed with warm water ; or, what is better, wash in warm water and rinse in cold water.

308. GLASS VESSELS, and other utensils, may be purified and cleaned by rinsing them out with powdered charcoal.

309. TO CLEAN BOTTLES.—There is no easier method of cleaning glass bottles than putting into them fine coal-ashes, and well shaking, either with water or not, hot or cold, according to the substance that fouls the bottle. Charcoal left in a bottle or jar for a little time will take away disagreeable smells.

Caution. If bottles are cleaned with shot it should be seen that none are left sticking to the sides or corners of the bottles, as should these be refilled with vinegar, wine, cider, &c., the shot will impregnate the liquid with lead. Small pebbles are preferable.

310. TO CLEAN JAPANNED WAITERS, URNS, &c.

Rub on with a sponge a little white soap and some lukewarm water, and wash the waiter or urn quite clean. Never use hot water, as it will cause the japan to scale off. Having wiped it dry, sprinkle a little flour over it ; let it remain untouched for a short time, and then rub it with a soft dry cloth, and finish with a silk handkerchief. White heat marks on the waiters are difficult to remove ; but rubbing them with a flannel dipped in sweet oil, and afterwards in spirits of wine may be tried.

311. Papier Mâché articles of all kinds should be washed with a sponge and cold water, without soap, dredged with flour while damp, and, when dry, polished with a flannel or a silk handkerchief.

312. BRUNSWICK BLACK for Varnishing Grates.—Melt four pounds of common asphaltum, and add two pints of linseed oil, and one gallon of oil of turpentine. This is usually put up in stoneware bottles for sale, and is used with a paint brush. If too thick, more turpentine may be added.

313. BLACKING FOR STOVES may be made with half-a-pound of black-lead finely powdered, and (to make it stick) mix with it the whites of three eggs well beaten ; then dilute it with sour beer or porter till it becomes as thin as shoe-blacking ; after stirring it, set it over hot coals to simmer for twenty minutes ; when cold it may be kept for use.

314. TO CLEAN KNIVES AND FORKS.—Wash the blades in warm (but not hot) water, and afterwards rub them lightly over with powdered rotten-stone mixed to a paste with a little cold water ; then polish them with a clean cloth.

315. To take Stains out of Knives.—Take some potato parings and some finely-powdered brick-dust. Dip the white portion of the potato paring in the brick-dust and rub the knife with it, when the stains will disappear ; or a rag dipped in strong potash, or soda may be used (with the brick-dust also).

316. TO CLEAN PAINTED WAINSCOT or other woodwork, fuller's earth will be found cheap and useful: on wood not painted it forms an excellent substitute for soap.

317. TO CLEAN VARNISHED PAINT.—If soap or soda be used the varnish will come off. Take the tea-leaves which are left in the teapot, pour some hot water on them, and let them stand for some ten minutes. Then pour the tea into a basin, wash the paint with a clean flannel and dry with a clean cloth.

318. TO SCOUR BOARDS.—Use lime, one part ; sand, three parts ; soft soap, two parts. Lay a little on the boards with the scrubbing brush, and rub thoroughly. Rinse with clean water, and rub dry. This will keep the boards of a good colour, and keep away vermin.

319. CHARCOAL AS A PURIFIER.

All sorts of glass vessels and other utensils may be purified from long-retained smells of every kind, in the easiest and most perfect manner, by rinsing them out well with charcoal powder, after the grosser impurities have been scoured off with sand and potash. Rubbing the teeth and washing out the mouth with fine charcoal powder, will render the teeth beautifully white, and the breath perfectly sweet, when an offensive breath has been owing to a scorbutic disposition of the gums. Putrid water is immediately deprived of its bad smell by charcoal. When meat, fish, &c., from intense heat, or long keeping, are likely to become tainted, a simple mode of keeping them sound and healthful is to put a few pieces of charcoal, each about the size of an egg, into the pot or saucepan wherein the fish or flesh is to be boiled. Among others, an experiment of this kind was tried upon a turbot, which appeared to be too far gone to be eatable ; the cook, as advised, put three or four pieces of charcoal under the strainer in the fish-kettle ; after boiling the proper time, the turbot came to the table sweet and firm.

320. TO TAKE STAINS OUT OF MAHOGANY.—Stains and spots may be taken out of mahogany with a little aquafortis or oxalic acid and water, rubbing the part with a cork dipped in the liquid till the colour is restored. Then wash the wood well with water, and dry and polish as usual.

321. TO TAKE INK-STAINS OUT OF MAHOGANY.—Put a few drops of spirits of nitre in a teaspoonful of water ; touch the spot with a feather dipped in the mixture, and as soon as the ink disappears, rub it over with a rag wetted in cold water, or there will be a white mark, which will not be easily effaced.

322. SCRATCHES ON VARNISH may be removed by placing over them a coarse cloth well soaked in linseed oil.

323. TO TAKE INK-STAINS OUT OF A COLOURED TABLE-COVER.—Dissolve a teaspoonful of oxalic acid in a teacup of hot water ; rub the stained part well with a flannel or linen rag dipped in the solution. Very frequently, however, when log-wood has been used in manufacturing ink, a reddish stain still remains, after the use of oxalic acid, as in the former directions. To remove it, procure a solution of the chloride of lime, and apply it in the same manner as directed for the oxalic acid.

324. TO REMOVE INK-STAINS FROM LINENS, CALICOES, &c.—A very simple but effectual method is to squeeze some lemon juice on to the stains, which will disappear when the article is washed.

325. TO TAKE INK OUT OF BOARDS.—Apply strong muriatic acid or spirits of salts, with a piece of cloth ; afterwards wash well with water.

326. OIL OR GREASE SPILT ON THE HEARTH may be removed by covering it immediately with hot ashes, or with burning coals.

327. TO CLEAN SILVER AND PLATED WARE.—The following is taken from *Spon's Workshop Receipts.*—"Take an ounce each of cream of tartar, common salt, and alum, and boil in a gallon or more of water. Plate washed in this solution when rubbed dry, puts on a beautiful silvery whiteness. Powdered magnesia may be used dry for articles slightly tarnished, but if very dirty it must be used first wet and then dry."

This ware should be washed with a sponge and warm soapsuds every day after using, and wiped dry with a clean soft towel.

328. BRONZED CHANDELIERS, LAMPS, &c. should be merely dusted with a feather-brush, or with a soft cloth, as washing them will take off the bronzing.

329. TO CLEAN BRASSES, BRITANNIA METAL, TINS, COPPERS. &c., use rotten-stone, soft soap, and oil of turpentine, mixed to the consistency of stiff putty. The stone should be powdered very fine and sifted. The articles should first be washed with hot water, to remove grease ; then a little of the above mixture, with a little water, should be applied to the metal, and then rubbed off briskly with dry, clean rag or leather, and a beautiful polish will be obtained.

330. Brasses attached to Furniture should be cleaned with either powdered whitening or scraped rotten-stone, mixed with sweet oil and rubbed on with chamois leather.

331. TO CLEAN DISH COVERS.—Silver and plated ones should be polished with plate powder and a leather ; those made of block tin should be first rubbed with sweet oil, and then dusted over the oil with fine powdered whitening, finally polishing with a soft rag. If the handles are movable, take them off whilst cleaning.

332. TO PRESERVE BRIGHT STEEL FROM RUST.—After bright grates have been thoroughly cleaned, they should be dusted over with unslacked lime, and thus left until wanted. Coils of piano wires, thus sprinkled, will keep from rust for many years. Table-knives which are not in constant use ought to be put in a case in which sifted quicklime is placed, about eight inches deep. They should be plunged to the top of the blades, but the lime should not touch the handles.

333. TO KEEP IRON AND STEEL GOODS FROM RUST.— Dissolve half-an-ounce of camphor in one pound of hog's lard ; take off the scum: mix as much black-lead as will give the mixtnre an iron colour. Iron and steel goods, rubbed over with this mixture, and left with it on twenty-four hours, and then dried with a linen cloth, will keep clean for months. Valuable articles of cutlery should be wrapped in zinc foil, or be kept in boxes lined with zinc. This is at once an easy and most effective method.

334. TO REMOVE RUST FROM POLISHED IRON.—Use emery paper or powdered bath-brick mixed with oil. Steel fire-irons and fenders, when put away for the summer, should be thinly smeared over with vaseline. Old soft towels, or pieces of old sheets or table-cloths, make excellent wipers for iron and steel goods.

335. TO CLEAN LOOKING-GLASSES.—First wash the glass all over with lukewarm soapsuds and a sponge. When dry, rub it bright with a chamois leather on which a little prepared chalk, finely powdered, has been sprinkled.

336. TO CLEAN MIRRORS, &c.—Take a piece of soft sponge, well washed, and cleaned from everything gritty, dip it into water and squeeze it almost dry, dip it into some spirit of wine, and then rub it over the glass. Next, dust the glass over with some powder blue or whitening sifted through muslin ; wipe the powder lightly and quickly off again with a cloth ; then take a clean cloth, and rub the glass well once more, and finish by rubbing it with a silk handkerchief. If the glass be very large, clean one-half at a time, as otherwise the spirit of wine will dry before it can be rubbed off. If the frames are not varnished, the greatest care must be taken not to touch them with the sponge, as this will discolour or take off the gilding. To clean the frames, take a little cotton wool, and rub the frames with it ; this will take off all the dust and dirt without injuring the gilding. If the frames are well varnished, rub them with spirit of wine, which will take out all spots, and give them a fine polish. Varnished doors may be done in the same manner. Never use any cloth to *frames* or *drawings*, or oil paintings, when cleaning and dusting them.

337. TO CLEAN WINDOWS.

First brush the dust off the window-frames, then take an ounce of rock ammonia and dissolve it in a pint of cold water. Pour half a tumblerful of the liquid into a basin, with the same quantity of cold water. Then the windows should be wiped over with a piece of cotton rag dipped in the ammonia water, care being taken not to touch the window-frames. Dry and polish with another rag.

338. TO CLEAN GAS GLOBES. These should be scrubbed with a nail brush, curd soap, soda, and water. Rinse them in warm water, and let them drain *without wiping them.* They should not be touched till quite dry on the outside. Then lift them with a soft towel and wipe the insides dry. If the outsides are wiped, they will be smeared.

339. TO CLEAN LAMP CHIMNEYS.—When you fill the lamp, drop a little kerosene on a piece of newspaper and rub the glass with it.

340. CLEANING CHINA AND GLASS ORNAMENTS.—The best material for cleansing either porcelain or glass, is fuller's earth: but it must be beaten into a fine powder, and carefully cleared from all rough or hard particles, which might endanger the polish of the surface. As articles intended solely for ornament are not so highly annealed as others, they should never be washed in water beyond a tepid temperature.

341. A Simple Mode of Annealing Glass has been some time in use by chemists. It consists in immersing the vessel in cold water, gradually heated to the boiling point, and suffered to remain till cold, when it will be fit for use. Should the glass be exposed to a higher temperature than that of boiling water, it will be necessary to immerse it in oil.

342. TO TAKE MARKING-INK OUT OF LINEN.—Use a solution of cyanide of potassium applied with a camel-hair brush. After the marking-ink disappears, the linen should be well washed in cold water.

343. TO TAKE STAINS OF WINE OUT OF LINEN.—Hold the article in milk while it is boiling on the fire, and the stains will soon disappear.

344. FRUIT STAINS IN LINEN.—To remove them, rub the part on each side with yellow soap, then tie up a piece of pearlash in the cloth, &c., and soak well in hot water or boil ; afterwards expose the stained part to the sun and air until the stain is removed.

345. TO TAKE IRONMOULD OUT OF LINEN.—Soak the spots with a solution of one drop of sulphuric acid and one grain of ferrocyanide of potassium. Wash with soft water, and then take out the spots (which will have turned blue) with a solution of potash.

345a. MILDEWED LINEN may be restored by soaping the spots while wet, covering them with fine chalk scraped to powder, and rubbing it well in.

346. TO KEEP MOTHS, &c., FROM CLOTHES.—Put a piece of camphor in a linen bag, or some aromatic herbs in the drawers, among linen or woollen clothes, and no insects will come near them.

346a. Clothes Closets that have become infested with moths, should be well rubbed with a strong decoction of tobacco, and repeatedly sprinkled with spirits of camphor.

347. TO REMOVE COFFEE STAINS FBOM LINEN.—Apply a mixture of egg yolk and glycerine, wash out with warm water, and iron whilst damp on the reverse side with a fairly hot iron.

348. TO REMOVE STAINS FROM FLOORS.—For removing spots of grease from boards, take fuller's earth and pearlash, of each a quarter of a pound, and boil in a quart of soft water. While hot lay the mixture on the greased parts, allowing it to remain on them from ten to twelve hours ; after which it may be scoured off with sand and water. A floor much spotted with grease should be completely washed over with this mixture the day before it is scoured. Fuller's earth and ox-gall, boiled together, form a very powerful cleansing mixture for floors and carpets. Stains of ink are removed by the application of strong vinegar or salts of lemon.

349. SCOURING DROPS FOR REMOVING GREASE.—There are several preparations of this name ; one of the best is made as follows:— Camphine, or spirit of turpentine, three ounces ; essence of lemon, one ounce ; mix and put in a small phial for use when required.

350. TO TAKE GREASE OUT OF VELVET OR CLOTH.—Pour some turpentine over the part that is greasy ; rub it till quite dry with a piece of clean flannel ; if the grease be not quite removed, repeat the application, and when done brush the part well, and hang up the garment in the open air to take away the smell.

351. TO EXTRACT GREASE SPOTS FROM BOOKS OR PAPER. —Gently warm the greased or spotted part of the book or paper, and then press upon it pieces of blotting paper, one after another, so as to absorb as much of the grease as possible. Have ready some fine clear essential oil of turpentine heated almost to a boiling state, warm the greased leaf a little, and then, with a soft clean brush, apply the heated turpentine to both sides of the spotted part. By repeating this application, the grease will be extracted. Lastly, with another brush dipped in rectified spirit of wine, go over the place, and the grease will no longer appear, neither will the paper be discoloured.

352. STAINS AND MARKS FROM BOOKS.—A solution of oxalic acid, citric acid, or tartaric acid, is attended with the least risk, and may be applied to paper and prints without fear of damage. These acids, which take out writing ink, and do not touch the printing, can be used for restoring books where the margins have been written upon.

353. TO TAKE WRITING INK OUT OF PAPER.—Solution of muriate of tin, two drachms; water, four drachms. To be applied with a camel-hair brush. After the writing has disappeared, the paper should be passed through water, and dried.

354. MEDICINE STAINS ON SILVER SPOONS may be removed by rubbing them with a rag dipped in sulphuric acid, and washing it off with soapsuds.

355. BLACKING FOR LEATHER SEATS, &c.—Beat well the yolks of two eggs and the white of one : mix a tablespoonful of gin and a teaspoonful of sugar, thicken it with ivory black, add it to the eggs and use as common blacking ; the seats or cushions being left a day or two to harden. This is good for dress boots and shoes.

356. REVIVER FOR BLACK CLOTH.—Bruised galls, one pound ; logwood, two pounds ; green vitriol, half-a-pound; water five quarts. Boil for two hours and strain.

357. ENAMEL PAINT.—Special preparations of paint, styled "enamel," are now made, suitable for both useful and decorative purposes—garden stands, indoor furniture or ornaments, baths, &c. They are ready mixed in a variety of shades, can be easily applied, and dry with a hard glossy surface.

357a. WORM-EATEN WOOD may be treated by fumigating it with benzoin, or soaking it with a solution of corrosive sublimate.

358. A HINT ON HOUSEHOLD MANAGEMENT.—Have you ever observed what a dislike servants have to anything cheap ? They hate saving their master's money. I tried this experiment with great success the other day. Finding we consumed a vast deal of soap, I sat down in my thinking chair, and took the soap question into consideration, and I found reason to suspect we were using a very expensive article, where a much cheaper one would serve the purpose better. I ordered half-a-dozen pounds of both sorts, but took the precaution of changing the papers on which the prices were marked before giving them into the hands of Betty. "Well, Betty, which soap do you find washes best ?" "Oh, please, sir, the dearest, in the blue paper ; it makes a lather as well again as the other." "Well, Betty, you shall always have it then ;" and thus the unsuspecting Betty saved me some pounds a year, and washed the clothes much better—*Rev. Sydney Smith.*

359. DOMESTIC RULES.— Mrs. Hamilton, in her *Cottagers of Glenburnie*, gives three simple rules for the regulation of domestic affairs, which would, if carried into practice, be the means of saving time, labour, and patience, and of making every house a "well-ordered" one. They are:

i. Do everything in its proper time.

ii. Keep everything to its proper use.

iii. Put everything in its proper place.

360. GOLDEN HINTS FOR HOUSE-WIVES AND HOME COMFORTS.

361. Household Management.

i. Between husband and wife little attentions beget much love.

ii. Always lay your table neatly, whether you have company or not.

iii. Whatever you may choose to give away, always be sure to *keep your temper*.

iv. Late at breakfast—hurried for dinner—cross at tea.

v. Breakfast should always be served regularly, as it is the starting point of the day's duties and engagements; if it is late it upsets the whole day's programme.

vi. In winter, get the work forward by daylight, to prevent running about at night with candles. Thus you escape grease spots, and risks of fire.

vii. Matches should be kept in every bedroom, well out of the reach of children. They are cheap enough.

viii. A wire fire-guard, for each fire-place in a house, costs little, and greatly

diminishes the risk to life and property. Fix them before going to bed.

ix. Allowing children to talk incessantly is a mistake. We do not mean to say that they should be restricted from talking in proper seasons, but they should be taught to know when it is proper for them to cease.

x. A leather strap, with a buckle to fasten, is much more commodious than a cord for a box in general use for travelling ; cording and uncording is a tedious job.

362. Economy.

i. Much knowledge may be obtained by the good housewife observing how things are managed in well-regulated families.

ii. Regularity in the payment of accounts is essential to housekeeping. All tradesmen's bills should be paid weekly, for then any errors can be detected whilst the transactions are fresh in the memory.

iii. It is better to accomplish perfectly a very small amount of work than to half do ten times as much.

iv. See that nothing is thrown away which might have served to nourish your own family or a poorer one.

v. If you have children who are learning to write, buy coarse white paper by the quantity, and make it up into writing-books. This does not cost half so much as it does to buy them ready made at the stationer's.

vi. All linen rags should be saved, for they are useful in sickness. If they have become dirty and worn by cleaning silver, &c., wash them and scrape them into lint.

vii. New iron should be very gradually heated at first. After it has become inured to the heat, it is not so likely to crack.

363. Cleanliness.

i. There is not anything gained in economy by having very young and inexperienced servants at low wages; the cost of what they break, waste, and destroy, is more than an equivalent for higher wages, setting aside comfort and respectability.

ii. An ever-dirty hearth, and a grate always choked with cinders and ashes, are infallible evidences of bad housekeeping.

iii. Dirty windows speak to the passer-by of the negligence of the inmates.

iv. Shaking Carpets.—The oftener carpets are shaken the longer they wear ; the dirt that collects under them grinds out the threads.

v. Never put away plate, knives and forks, &c., uncleaned, or great inconvenience will arise when the articles are wanted.

vi. Never allow your servants to put wiped knives on your table, for, generally speaking, you may see that they have been wiped with a dirty cloth. If a knife is brightly cleaned, they are compelled to use a clean cloth.

vii. Do not let knives be dropped into hot dish-water. It is a good plan to have a large tin pot to wash them in, just high enough to wash the blades *without wetting* the handles.

viii. Charcoal powder will be found a very good thing to give knives a first-rate polish.

ix. Scald your wooden-ware often, and keep your tin-ware dry.

x. New wooden utensils should be first well soaked in cold, and then in scalding water. Wooden bowls very frequently split when hot water is put into them ; they should be well greased, inside and out, and laid by for a day or two, then scour them well for several days till clean and free from grease.

xi. Clean a brass kettle with salt and vinegar before using it for cooking.

xii. A warming-pan full of coals, or a shovel of coals, held over varnished furniture, will take out white spots. Care should be taken not to hold the pan near enough to scorch ; the place to which heat has thus been applied, should be rubbed with a flannel while warm.

xiii. Sal-volatile or hartshorn will restore colours taken out by acid. It may be dropped upon any garment without doing harm.

364. Health.

i. Eat slowly and you will not over-eat.

ii. Persons very commonly complain of indigestion ; how can it be wondered at, when they seem, by their habit of swallowing their food wholesale, to forget for what purpose they are provided with teeth ?

iii. Keeping the feet warm will tend to prevent headaches.

iv. Take pains to keep your children's feet dry and warm. Don't bury their bodies in heavy flannels and wools, and leave their arms and legs naked.

v. People in general are not aware how very essential to the health of the inmates, is the free admission of light into their houses.

vi. For ventilation open your windows both at top and bottom. The fresh air rushes in at the bottom, while the foul escapes at the top. This is letting in your friend and expelling your enemy.

vii. Thick curtains, closely drawn round the bed, are very injurious, because they not only confine the exhalations thrown off from our bodies whilst in bed, but interrupt the current of pure air.

viii. Feather beds should be opened every third year, the ticking well dusted, soaped, and waxed, the feathers dressed and returned.

ix. Blankets when not in use should be neatly folded and placed under a bed that is being slept on. If they are placed in drawers or cupboards, they should be looked at every now and then to free them from moths, which may be done by shaking them in the open air.

x. There is much more injury done by admitting visitors to invalids than is generally supposed.

xi. When reading by candle-light, place the candle behind you, that the rays may pass over your shoulder on to the book. This will relieve the eyes.

xii. As accidents and sudden ill-nesses unfortunately cannot always be prevented, every house should be provided with a set of ENQUIRE WITHIN UPON EVERYTHING EMERGENCY CARDS, see par. 688.

365. Food.

i. When you are particular in wishing to have precisely what you want from a butcher, go and buy it yourself.

ii. In cold weather a leg of mutton improves by being hung three or four weeks.

iii. When meat is hanging, change its position frequently, to equally dis-tribute the juices.

iv. "Wilful waste makes woful want."—Do not cook a fresh joint whilst any of the last remains uneaten—hash it up, and with gravy and a little management, eke out another day's dinner.

v. The shanks of mutton make a good stock for nearly any kind of gravy, and they are very cheap—enough may be had for a penny to make a quart of delicious soup.

vi. As far as possible, have pieces of bread eaten up before they become hard: spread those that are not eaten, and let them dry, to be pounded for puddings, or soaked for brewis. Do not let crusts accumulate in such quantities that they cannot be used. With proper care, there is no need of losing a particle of bread.

vii. Brewis is made of crusts and dry pieces of bread, soaked a good while in hot milk, mashed up, and eaten with salt.

viii. Apples intended for dumplings should not have the core taken out of them, as the pips impart a delicious flavour to the dumpling.

ix. Apple and suet dumplings are lighter when boiled in a net than in a cloth. Skim the pot well.

x. Apples and pears, cut into quarters and stripped of the rind, baked with a little water and sugar, and eaten with boiled rice, are capital food for children.

xi. A rice pudding is excellent without either eggs or sugar, if baked gently ; it keeps better without eggs.

xii. When you dry salt for the table, do not place it in the salt cellars until it is cold, otherwise it will harden into a lump.

366. Washing.

i. If you have difficulty in getting soft water for washing, fill a tub or barrel half full of wood ashes, and fill it up with water, so that you may have ley whenever you want it. A gallon of strong ley, put into a copper of hard water, will make it as soft as rain water. Some people use pearlash, or potash ; but this costs something, and is very apt to injure the texture of the cloth.

ii. Woollen clothes should be washed in very hot suds, and not rinsed. Lukewarm water shrinks them.

iii. Soapsuds form a good manure for bushes and young plants, therefore do not throw them all down the sink or drains.

367. Mending.

i. All the mending in the house should be done once a week if possible.

ii. Never put out sewing. If it be not possible to do it in your own family, hire some one to come to the house and work with them.

iii. After washing, overlook linen and stitch on buttons, hooks and eyes, &c. ; for this purpose keep a "house-wife's friend," full of miscellaneous threads, cottons, buttons, hooks, &c.

iv. A short needle makes the most expedition in plain sewing.

v. Put your balls or reels of cotton into little bags, leaving the ends out.

vi. When sheets or chamber towels get thin in the middle, cut them in two, sew the selvedges together and hem the sides.

vii. In mending sheets and shirts, put in pieces sufficiently large, or in the first washing, the thin parts give way, and the work done is of no avail.

viii. A flannel petticoat will wear nearly as long again, if turned hind part before when the front begins to wear thin.

ix. Persons of defective sight, when threading a needle, should hold it over something white, by which the sight will be assisted.

x. Sitting to sew by candle-light at a table with a dark cloth on it is injurious to the eyesight. When no other remedy presents itself, put a sheet of white paper before you.

368. Clothes.

i. There is not any real economy in purchasing cheap calico for night-shirts. Cheap calico soon wears into holes, and becomes discoloured in washing.

ii. A bonnet and trimmings may be worn a much longer time, if the dust be brushed well off after use before putting them away.

iii. No article of dress tarnishes so readily as black crape trimmings, and few things injure them more than damp ; ladies should therefore be careful to protect them as much as possible.

369. DOMESTIC PHARMACOPŒIA.

In compiling this part of our hints, we have endeavoured to supply that kind of information which is so often wanted in the time of need, and cannot be obtained when a medical man or a druggist is not near. *The doses are all fixed for adults, unless otherwise specified.* The various remedies are arranged in sections, according to their uses, as being more easy for reference.

370. COLLYRIA OR EYE WASHES.

371. Alum.—Dissolve half-a-drachm of alum in eight ounces (half-a-pint) of water. *Use* as astringent wash. When twice as much alum and only half the quantity of water are used, it acts as a discutient, but not as an eye-water. *Note* that this and the following washes are for *outward application* only.

372. Compound Alum.—Dissolve alum and white vitriol, of each one drachm, in one pint of water, and filter through paper. *Use* as astringent wash.

373. Ordinary.—Add half-an-ounce of diluted acetic acid to three ounces of decoction of poppy heads. *Use* as anodyne wash.

374. Zinc and Lead.—Dissolve white vitriol and acetate of lead, of each seven grains, in four ounces of elder-flower water ; add one drachm of laudanum (tincture of opium), and the same quantity of spirit of camphor ; then strain. *Use* as detergent wash.

375. Acetate of Zinc.—Dissolve half-a-drachm of white vitriol in five ounces of water. Dissolve two scruples of acetate of lead in five ounces of water. Mix these solutions, then set aside for a short time, and afterwards filter. *Use* as astringent wash ; this forms a most valuable collyrium.

376. Sulphate of Zinc.—Dissolve twenty grains of white vitriol in a pint of water or rose water. *Use* for weak eyes.

377. Zinc and Camphor.—Dissolve a scruple of white vitriol in ten ounces of water ; add one drachm of spirit of camphor, and strain. *Use* as a stimulant.

378. Compound Zinc.—Dissolve fifteen grains of white vitriol in eight ounces of camphor water (*Mistura camphora*), and the same quantity of decoction of poppy heads. *Use* as anodyne and detergent wash ; it is useful for weak eyes.

379. CONFECTIONS AND ELECTUARIES.

Confections are used as vehicles for the administration of more active medicines, and **Electuaries** are made for the purpose of rendering some remedies palatable. Both should be kept in closely covered jars.

380. Almond Confection.—Remove the outer coat from an ounce of sweet almonds, and pound them well in a mortar with one drachm of powdered gum arabic, and half-an-ounce of white sugar. *Use* to make a demulcent mixture known as "almond emulsion."

381. Alum Confection.—Mix two scruples of powdered alum with four scruples of treacle. *Dose*, half-a-drachm. *Use* as astringent in sore throat, relaxed uvula, and ulcerations of mouth.

382. Orange Confection.—Take one ounce of the freshly-rasped rind of orange, and mix it with three ounces of white sugar, and beat till perfectly incorporated. *Dose*, from one drachm to an ounce. *Use* as a gentle stomachic and tonic, and as a vehicle for administering tonic powders.

383. Black Pepper Confection.—Take of black pepper and elecampane root, each one ounce ; fennel seeds, three ounces ; honey and sugar, of each two ounces. Rub the dry ingredients to a fine powder, and when the confection is wanted, add the honey, and mix well. *Dose*, from one to two drachms. *Use* in hæmorrhoids, or piles.

384. Cowhage.—Mix in treacle as much of the fine hairs or spiculæ of cowhage as the treacle will take up. *Dose*, a teaspoonful every morning and evening. *Use* as an anthelmintic.

385. Senna Confection. No. 1.—Take of senna, powdered, four ounces ; figs, half-a-pound, cassia pulp, tamarind pulp, and the pulp of prunes, each four ounces ; coriander seeds, powdered, two ounces ; liquorice root, one ounce and a half ; sugar, one pound and a quarter ; water, one pint and a half. Rub the senna with the coriander and separate, by sifting, five ounces of the mixture. Boil the water, with the figs and liquorice added, until it is reduced to one half ; then press out and strain the liquor. Evaporate the strained liquor in a jar by boiling until twelve fluid ounces remain ; then add the sugar, and make a syrup. Now mix the pulps with the syrup, add the sifted powder, and mix well. *Use* as a purgative. *Dose*, one to two teaspoonfuls, most useful in constipation.

386. Senna Confection. No. 2.—A more simple confection, but equally efficacious, may be made in the following manner. Infuse an ounce of senna leaves in a pint of boiling water, pouring the water on the leaves in a covered mug or jug, or even an old earthenware teapot. Let the infusion stand till it is cold, then strain off the liquor, and place it in a saucepan or stewpan, adding to it one pound of prunes. Let the prunes stew gently by the side of the fire till the liquor is entirely absorbed. *Use* as a purgative or laxative, giving half-a-teaspoonful to little children, and a teaspoonful to children over ten years of age, and from two to four teaspoonfuls to adults.

387. Castor Oil and Senna Confection.—Take one drachm of powdered gum arabic, and two ounces of confection of senna, and mix, by gradually rubbing together in a mortar, with half an-ounce of castor oil. *Dose*, from half-a-tablespoon to two tablespoonfuls. *Use* as a purgative.

388. Sulphur and Senna Confection.—Take of sulphur and sulphate

---

☞ *The above doses are for adults, unless otherwise specified.*

of potash, each half-an-ounce ; confection of senna, two tablespoonfuls ; oil of aniseed, twenty minims ; mix well. *Dose*, from one to two teaspoonfuls. *Use* as a purgative.

389. Cream of Tartar Confection.—Take one ounce of cream of tartar, one drachm of jalap, and half-a-drachm of powdered ginger ; mix into a thick paste with treacle. *Dose*, two teaspoonfuls. *Use* as a strong purgative.

390. Antispasmodic Electuary.—Take six drachms of powdered valerian and orange leaves, mixed and made into an electuary, with a sufficient quantity of syrup of wormwood. *Dose*, from one to two teaspoonfuls, to be taken two or three times a day.

391. DECOCTIONS.

These should only be made as they are wanted ; pipkins or tin saucepans should be used for the purpose ; and no decoction should be boiled longer than ten minutes.

392. Chimaphila.—Take one ounce of pyrola (chimaphila, or wintergreen), and boil it in a pint and a half of water until the water is reduced to one pint ; then strain. *Dose*, from one to two tablespoonfuls, four times a day. *Use* in dropsies, as a diuretic.

393. Logwood.—Boil one ounce and a half of bruised logwood in two pints of water until the water is reduced to one pint : then add one drachm of bruised cassia, and strain. *Dose*, from one to two tablespoonfuls. *Use* as an astringent.

394. Dandelion.—Take two ounces of the freshly-sliced root, and boil in a quart of water until it comes to a pint. *Dose*, from two to four tablespoonfuls, that is to say, from an eighth of a pint to a quarter of a pint. *Use* for sluggish state of the liver.

395. EMBROCATIONS AND LINIMENTS.

These remedies are used externally as local stimulants, to relieve deep-seated inflammations when other means cannot be employed, as they are more easily applied locally.

396. Anodyne and Discutient.—Take two drachms of scraped white soap, half-a-drachm of extract of henbane, and dissolve them by a gentle heat in six ounces of olive oil. *Use* for bruises and sprains but not glandular enlargements, which should never be rubbed.

397. Strong Ammoniated.—Add one ounce of strong liquid ammonia to two ounces of olive oil ; shake well together until properly mixed. *Use* as a stimulant in rheumatic pains, paralytic numbnesses, chronic glandular enlargements, lumbago, sciatica, and in bronchitis, &c. *Note* that this embrocation must be used with care, and only employed in very obstinate cases.

398. Compound Ammoniated.—Add six drachms of oil of turpentine to the strong ammoniated liniment above. *Use* for the diseases mentioned in the preceding paragraph, and chronic affections of the knee and ankle joints.

399. Lime and Oil.—Take equal parts of common linseed oil and lime water and shake well. *Use* when soaked on lint, for burns, scalds, sun peelings, &c.

400. Camphorated.—Take half-an-ounce of camphor and dissolve it in two ounces of olive oil. *Use* as a stimulant and soothing application for stubborn breasts, dropsy of the belly, and rheumatic pains.

401. Soap Liniment with Spanish Flies.—Take three ounces and a half of soap liniment and half-an-ounce of tincture of Spanish flies ; mix and shake well. *Use* as a stimulant to chronic bruises, sprains, rheumatic pains, and indolent swellings.

401a. For Rheumatism, Lumbago, Pains, Bruises, and Bites of Insects.—One raw egg well beaten, half-a-pint of vinegar, one ounce of spirits of turpentine, a quarter of an ounce of spirits of wine, a quarter of an ounce of camphor. These ingredients to be beaten well together, then put in a bottle and shaken for ten minutes, after which, to be corked down tightly to exclude the air. In half-an-hour it is fit for use. *Directions.*—To be well rubbed in, two, three, or four times a day. For rheumatism in the head, to be rubbed at the back of the neck and behind the ears.

402.   Turpentine.—Take two ounces and a half of resin cerate, and melt it by standing the vessel in hot water ; then add one ounce and a half of oil of turpentine, and mix. *Use* as stimulant to ulcers, burns, scalds, &c.

402a. Roche's Embrocation for Hooping Cough.—Olive oil, two ounces ; oil of amber, one ounce ; oil of cloves, one drachm. Mix : to be rubbed on the chest at bedtime.

403. ENEMAS.

These are a peculiar kind of medicine, administered by injecting them into the rectum or outlet of the body. The intention is either to empty the bowels, kill worms, protect the lining membrane of the intestines from injury, restrain copious discharges, allay spasms in the bowels, or to nourish the body. These clysters, or glysters, are administered by means of an enema syringe.

404.   Laxative.—Take two ounces of Epsom salts, and dissolve in three-quarters of a pint of gruel, or thin broth, with an ounce of olive oil.

405.   Nutritive.—Take eight tablespoonfuls of strong beef-tea and add the yolk of one egg beaten well up.

May be given every six hours, the bowel being well washed out first with one pint of warm water given as an enema.

406.   Turpentine.—Take half-an-ounce of oil of turpentine, the yolk of one egg, and half-a-pint of gruel. Mix the turpentine and egg, and then add the gruel. *Use* as an anthelmintic.

407.   Ordinary.—Dissolve two tablespoonfuls of salt in twelve ounces of gruel.

408. Castor Oil.—Mix two ounces of castor oil with one drachm of starch, then rub them together, and add fourteen ounces of thin gruel. *Use* as a purgative.

409. Opium.—Rub three grains of opium with two ounces of starch, then add two ounces of warm water. Use as an anodyne in colic, spasms, and in bleeding from the bowel, &c.

410. Oil.—Mix four ounces of olive oil with half-an-ounce of mucilage, and half-a-pint of warm water. *Use* as a demulcent.

411. Assafœtida.—Mix one drachm of the tincture of assafoetida in a pint of barley water. *Use* as an anthelmintic, or in convulsions from teething.

412. GARGLES.

These are remedies used to stimulate chronic sore throats, or a relaxed state of the swallow, or uvula.

413.   Acidulated.—Mix one part of white vinegar with three parts of honey of roses, and twenty-four of barley water. *Use* in chronic inflammation of the throat, malignant sore throat, &c.

414.   Astringent.—Take two drachms of roses and mix with eight ounces of boiling water, infuse for one hour, strain, and add one drachm of alum and one ounce of honey of roses. Use for severe sore throat, relaxed uvula, &c.

415. For Salivation.—Mix from one to four drachms of braised gall-nuts with a pint of boiling water, and infuse for two hours, then strain and sweeten.

416. Tonic and Stimulant.—Mix six ounces of decoction of bark with two ounces of tincture of myrrh, and half-a-drachm of diluted sulphuric acid. *Use* for chronic sore throats.

417. Alum.—Dissolve one drachm of alum in fifteen ounces of water, then add half-an-ounce of treacle, and one drachm of diluted sulphuric acid. *Use* as an astringent

418. Myrrh.—Add six drachms of tincture of myrrh to seven ounces of infusion of linseed, and then add one drachm of diluted sulphuric acid. *Use* as a detergent.

419. For Slight Inflammation of the Throat.—Add one drachm of sulphuric ether to half-an-ounce of syrup of marsh-mallow, and six ounces of barley water. This may be used frequently.

420. LOTIONS.

Lotions are usually applied to the parts required by means of a piece of linen rag or piline, wetted with them, or by wetting the bandage itself. They are for *outward application only.*

421. Emollient.—Use decoction of marsh-mallow or linseed.

422. Elder Flowers.—Add two drachms and a half of elder flowers to one quart of boiling water, infuse for one hour, and strain. *Use* as a discutient.

423. Sedative.—Dissolve one drachm of extract of henbane in twenty-four drachms of water.

424 Opium.—Mix two drachms of bruised opium with half-a-pint of boiling water. *Use*, when cold, for painful ulcers, bruises, &c.

425. Stimulant.—Dissolve one drachm of caustic potash in one pint of water, and then gradually pour it upon twenty-four grains of camphor and one drachm of sugar, previously bruised together in a mortar. *Use* for fungoid and flabby ulcers.

426. Ordinary.—Mix one drachm of salt with eight ounces of water. *Use* for foul ulcers and flabby wounds.

427. Cold Evaporating.—Add two drachms of Goulard's extract and the same quantity of sulphuric ether to a pint of cold water. *Use* as a lotion for contusions, sprains, inflamed parts, &c.

428. Hydrochlorate of Ammonia.—Dissolve two drachms of sal ammoniac in six ounces of water, then add an ounce of distilled vinegar and the same quantity of rectified spirit. *Use* as a refrigerant.

429. Yellow Lotion.—Dissolve one grain of corrosive sublimate in an ounce of lime water, taking care to bruise the crystals of the salt in order to assist its solution. *Use* as a detergent. *Note*, that corrosive sublimate is a *violent and deadly poison.*

430. Black Wash.—Add half-a-drachm of calomel to four ounces of lime water, or eight grains to an ounce of lime water ; shake well. *Use* as a detergent, and in bad ulcers.

431. Acetate of Lead with Opium.—Take twenty grains of acetate of lead, and a drachm of powdered opium, mix, and add an ounce of vinegar and four ounces of warm water, set aside for an hour, then filter. *Use* as an astringent.

432 Creosote.— Add a drachm of creosote to a pint of water, and mix by shaking. *Use* as an application in cutaneous disease.

433. Galls.—Boil one drachm of bruised galls in twelve ounces of water until only half-a-pint remains, then strain, and add one ounce of laudanum. *Use* as an astringent and sedative.

434. OINTMENTS AND CERATES.

These remedies are used as local applications to parts, generally ulcers. They are usually spread upon linen or other materials.

435. Camphorated.—Mix half-an-ounce of camphor with one ounce of lard, having, of course, previously powdered the camphor, by adding a few drops of spirits of wine. *Use* as a discutient and stimulant in indolent tumours.

436. Chalk.—Mix as much prepared chalk as you can into some lard, so as to form a thick ointment. *Use* as an application to burns and scalds.

437. For Itch.—Mix four drachms of sublimed sulphur, two ounces of lard, and half-a-drachm of diluted sulphuric acid together. *Use* as an ointment to be rubbed into the body.

438. For Scrofulous Ulcerations.— Mix one drachm of oxide of zinc and one ounce of lard together. *Use* twice a day to the ulcerations.

439. Catechu.—Mix one ounce of powdered catechu, two drachms and a half of powdered alum, one ounce of powdered white resin, and two ounces and a half of olive oil, together. *Use* for flabby and indolent ulcerations.

440. Tartar Emetic.—Mix twenty grains of tartar emetic and ten grains of white sugar with one drachm and a half of lard. *Use* as a counter-irritant in white swellings, &c.

440a. Rose Lipsalve.—i. Oil of almonds, three ounces ; alkanet, half-an-ounce. Let them stand together in a warm place, then strain. Melt one ounce and a half of white wax and half -an-ounce of spermaceti with the oil ; stir it till it begins to thicken, and add twelve drops of otto of roses. —ii. White wax, one ounce ; almond

oil, two ounces ; alkanet, one drachm ; digest in a warm place, stir till sufficiently coloured, strain and stir in six drops of otto of roses.

441. PILLS.

442. Strong Purgative.—Take of powdered aloes, scammony, and gamboge, each fifteen grains, mix, and add sufficient Venice turpentine to make into a mass, then divide into twelve pills. *Dose*, one or two occasionally.

443. Milder Purgative.—Take four grains of powdered scammony and the same quantity of compound extract of colocynth, and two grains of calomel ; mix well, and add two drops of oil of cloves, or thin gum-water, to enable the ingredients to combine properly, and divide into two pills. *Dose*, one or two when necessary.

444. Common Purgative.—Take of powdered jalap and compound extract of colocynth each four grains, of calomel two grains, mix as usual, and divide into two pills. *Dose*, one or two occasionally.

445. Tonic.—Mix twenty-four grains of extract of gentian and the same of purified green vitriol (*sulphate of iron*) together, and divide into twelve pills. *Dose*, one or two when necessary. *Use* in debility.

446. Cough.—Mix one drachm of compound powder of ipecacuanha with one scruple of gum ammoniacum and one of dried squill bulb in powder. Make into a mass with mucilage, and divide into twenty pills. *Dose*, one three times a day.

447. Astringent.—Mix sixteen grains of acetate of lead (*sugar of lead*) with four grains of opium, and make into a mass with extract of dandelion, so as to make eight pills. *Dose*, from one to two. *Use* as an astringent in obstinate diarrhœa, dysentery, and spitting of blood.

☞ The above doses are for adults, unless otherwise specified.

447a. Gout and Rheumatism.—Acetic extract of colchicum, two grains; powdered ipecacuanha, four grains; compound extract of colocynth, half-a-drachm; blue pill, four grains. Divide into twelve pills; one to be taken night and morning.

448. MIXTURES.

448a. Acute Rheumatism, or for Rheumatic Gout.—Half-an-ounce of nitre (saltpetre), half-an-ounce of sulphur, half-an-ounce of flour of mustard, half-an-ounce of Turkey rhubarb, quarter of an ounce of powdered gum guaiacum. A teaspoonful to be taken in a wineglassful of cold water, every other night for three nights, and omit three nights. The water should have been well boiled.

449. Fever, Simple.—Add three ounces of spirit of mindererus (*Liquor ammoniæ acetatis*), three drachms of spirits of sweet nitre, four drachms of antimonial wine, and a drachm of syrup of saffron, to four ounces of water, or medicated water, such as cinnamon, aniseed, &c. *Dose*, for an adult, one or two tablespoonfuls every three hours. *Use* as a diaphoretic.

450. Aromatic.—Mix two drachms of aromatic confection with two drachms of compound tincture of cardamoms, and eight ounces of peppermint water. *Dose*, from one ounce to one ounce and a half. *Use* in flatulent colic and spasms of the bowels.

451. Cathartic.—Dissolve two ounces of Epsom salts in six ounces of compound infusion of senna, then add two ounces of peppermint water. *Dose*, from one and a half to two ounces. *Use* as a warm and active cathartic.

452. Diuretic.—Dissolve one drachm of powdered nitre in three ounces of camphor mixture; add five ounces of the decoction of broom, with six drachms of sweet spirits of nitre, and three drachms of tincture of squills; mix. *Dose*, one teaspoonful every two hours, or two tablespoonfuls every two hours. *Use*, excellent in dropsies.

453. Cough.—Dissolve three grains of tartar emetic and fifteen grains of opium in one pint of boiling water, then add four ounces of treacle, two ounces of vinegar, and one pint more of boiling water. *Dose*, from two teaspoonfuls to two tablespoonfuls, according to circumstances, every three hours, or three times a day. *Use* in common catarrh, bronchitis, and irritable cough.

453a. Bad Cold and Cough.—Solution of acetate of ammonia, two ounces; ipecacuanha wine, two drachms; antimony wine, two drachms; solution of muriate of morphine, half-a-drachm; treacle, four drachms; water, add eight ounces. Two tablespoonfuls to be taken three times a day.

454. Cough (for Children).—Mix three drachms of ipecacuanha wine with half-an-ounce of oxymel of squills, the same quantity of balsam of tolu, one ounce of mucilage, and two ounces of water. *Dose*, one teaspoonful for children under one year, two teaspoonfuls from one to five years, and a tablespoonful from five years, every time the cough is troublesome.

455. Antispasmodic.—Dissolve fifty grains of camphor in two drachms of chloroform, and then add two drachms of compound tincture of lavender, six drachms of mucilage of gum arabic, eight ounces of aniseed, cinnamon, or some other aromatic water, and two ounces of distilled water; mix well. *Dose*, one tablespoonful every half-hour if necessary. *Use* in cholera in the cold stage, when cramps are severe, or exhaustion very great; and as a general anti-spasmodic in doses of one dessertspoonful when the spasms are severe.

☞ *The above doses are for adults, unless otherwise specified.*

456. Tonic and Stimulant.—Dissolve one drachm of extract of bark and half-a-drachm of powdered gum arabic, in six ounces of water, and then add one ounce of syrup of marsh-mallow, and the same quantity of syrup of tolu. *Dose,* one tablespoonful every three hours. *Use* after fevers and catarrhs.

457. Stomachic.—Take twenty grains of powdered rhubarb, and rub it down in three ounces and a half of peppermint water, then add sal volatile and compound tincture of gentian each one drachm and a half ; mix. *Dose,* from one to one ounce and a half. *Use* this mixture as a tonic, stimulant, and stomachic.

457a. Indigestion.—Infusion of calumba, six ounces ; carbonate of potass, one drachm ; compound tincture of gentian, three drachms. *Dose,* two or three tablespoonfuls daily at noon.

458. DRINKS.

459. Tamarind No. 1.—Boil two ounces of the pulp of tamarinds in two pints of milk, then strain. *Use* as cooling drink.

460. Tamarind No. 2.—Boil two ounces of the pulp in two pints of warm water, and allow it to get cold, then strain. *Use* as cooling drink.

461 POWDERS.

462. Compound Soda.—Mix twenty-four grains of calomel, thirty-six grains of sesquicarbonate of soda, and one drachm of compound chalk powder, together. Divide into twelve powders. One of the powders to be given for a dose when required. *Use* as a mild purgative for children during teething.

463. Tonic.—Mix one drachm of powdered rhubarb with the same quantity of dried carbonate of soda, then add two drachms of powdered calumba root. *Dose,* from ten to twenty grains as a tonic after fevers, in all cases of debility and dyspepsia attended with acidity.

464. Rhubarb and Magnesia.—Mix one drachm of powdered rhubarb with two drachms of carbonate of magnesia, and half-a-drachm of ginger. *Dose,* from fifteen grains to one drachm. *Use* as a purgative for children.

465. Sulphur and Potash.—Mix one drachm of sulphur with four scruples of bicarbonate of potash, and two scruples of nitre. *Dose,* from half-a-drachm to one drachm. *Use* as a purgative, diuretic, and refrigerant

466. Anti-Diarrhœal.—Mix one grain of powdered ipecacuanha, and one grain of powdered opium, with the same quantity of camphor. *Dose,* one of these powders to be given in jam, treacle, &c., once or twice a day ; but to adults only.

467. Antispasmodic.—Mix four grains of subnitrate of bismuth, forty-eight grains of carbonate of magnesia, and the same quantity of white sugar, and then divide into four equal parts. *Dose,* one-fourth part. *Use* in obstinate pain in the stomach with cramps, unattended by inflammation.

468. Antipertussal, or against Hooping-Cough.—Mix one drachm of powdered belladonna root and two ounces of white sugar together. *Dose,* six grains morning and evening for children under one year ; nine grains for those under two and three years of age ; fifteen grains for those between five and ten ; and thirty grains for adults. *Caution*—This should be prepared by a chemist, as the belladonna is a poison, and occasional doses of castor oil should be given while it is being taken.

469. Purgative (Common).—Mix ten grains of calomel with one drachm of powdered jalap and twenty grains of sugar. *Dose,* one half of the whole for adults.

☞ *The above doses are for adults, unless otherwise specified.*

470. Sudorific.—Mix six grains of compound antimonial powder, two grains of ipecacuanha, and two grains of sugar together. *Dose*, as mixed, to be taken at bedtime. *Use* in catarrh and fever.

471. MISCELLANEOUS REMEDIES.

472. Anthelmintic, or Vermifuge. —For ridding the bowels of all forms of worms, an excellent medicine exists in the male fern—*Aspidium felix mas.* A decoction may be made of the fresh roots, or the root may be dried and powdered. *Dose*, of the powdered root, from ten to thirty grains ; of the decoction, from a tablespoonful to a wineglassful, according to age, the bowels being cleared out afterwards by a purgative, such as one tablespoonful of castor oil. *Use* to kill tape worm.

478. Another Anthelmintic.—For thread-worms, which infest the rectum and especially the lower portion, near the orifice of the body, an injection of salt and water, in the proportion of one ounce and a half of salt to a pint, or twenty ounces of water, or of quassia chips, will generally prove effectual, and obviate the necessity of administering medicine.

474. Emulsion, Laxative.—Rub down an ounce of castor oil in two drachms of mucilage of gum arabic, add three ounces of dill water, and a drachm of tincture of jalap, gradually. *Dose*, as prepared, the whole to be taken while fasting in the morning.

475. Emulsion, Purgative.—Rub down six grains of scammony with six drachms of white sugar in a mortar, and gradually add four ounces of almond emulsion, and two drops of oil of cloves. *Dose*, as prepared, early in the morning.

476. To prevent Pitting after Small-pox.—Spread a sheet of thin leather with the ointment of ammonia-cum with mercury, and cut out a place for the mouth, eyes and nostrils. This forms what is called a mask, and, after anointing the eyelids with a little blue ointment, it should be applied to the face, and allowed to remain for three days for the distinct kind, and four days for the running variety. *Apply before* the spots fill with matter, although it will answer sometimes even after they have become pustulous. It may be applied to any part in the same way.

477. Another Method, and one more reliable, is that of touching every pustule, or poc, on the face or bosom, with a camel-hair pencil dipped in a weak solution of lunar caustic (*nitrate of silver*), made in the proportion of two grains of nitrate of silver to one ounce of distilled water. The time for application is about the seventh day, while each pustule is filled with a limpid fluid, or before suppuration takes place, the lotion arresting that action, and by preventing the formation of matter, saving the skin from being pitted ; a result that follows from the conversion of the adipose tissue into pus.

478. A Third Method is to paint the face with ordinary collodion, which as it dries shrinks, and if used early, will effectually prevent all pitting.

479. A Fourth Method is to lightly touch every part of the face with a feather dipped in sweet oil. Having the patient's room darkened with blinds giving a yellow tinge of colour also tends to prevent this disfigurement.

480. Mucilage of Gum Arabic.—Rub one ounce of gum arabic in a mortar, with four ounces of warm water. *Use* for coughs, &c.

481. Mucilage of Starch.—Rub one drachm of starch with a little water, and gradually add five ounces of water, then boil until it forms a mucilage. *Use* for enemas, topical applications, and demulcents.

482. DISEASES.

☞ *For the proper Remedies and their Doses see "Prescriptions" (par. 568).*

It should be clearly understood, that in all cases of disease, the advice of a skilful physician is of the first importance. It is not, therefore, intended by the following information to supersede the important and necessary practice of the medical man ; but rather, by exhibiting the treatment required, to show in what degree his aid is imperative. In cases, however, where the disorder may be simple and transient, or in which remote residence, or other circumstances, may deny the privilege of medical attendance, the following particulars will be found of the utmost value. Moreover, the hints given upon what should be AVOIDED will be of great service to the patient, since the *physiological* is no less important than the *medical* treatment of disease.

483. Asthma.—The following is recommended as a relief:— Two ounces of the best honey, and one ounce of castor oil, mixed. A teaspoonful to be taken night and morning.

484. Apoplexy.—Immediate and large bleeding from the arm, cupping at the back of the neck, leeches to the temples, aperients Nos. 1 and 7, one or two drops, *not more*, of croton oil rubbed or dropped on the tongue, or six grains of calomel. Avoid excesses, intemperance, animal food.

485. Baldness.—The decoction of boxwood, which has been found successful in some cases of baldness, is thus made :—Take of the common box, which grows in garden borders, stems and leaves four large handfuls ; boil in three pints of water, in a closely covered vessel, for a quarter of an hour, and let it stand in a covered earthenware jar for ten hours or more ; strain, and add an ounce and a half

of eau de Cologne or lavender water, to make it keep. The head should be well washed with this solution every morning.

486. Baldness when Caused by Ill-health or Age.—Rub onions frequently on the part requiring it. The stimulating powers of this vegetable are of service in restoring the tone of the skin, and assisting the capillary vessels in sending forth new hair ; but it is not infallible. Should it succeed, however, the growth of these new hairs may be assisted by the oil of myrtle-berries, the repute of which, perhaps, is greater than its real efficacy. Even if they do no good, these applications are harmless.

487. Bile, Bilious, or Liver Complaints.—Abstinence from malt liquors, cool homœopathic cocoa for drink, no tea or coffee, few vegetables, no broths or soups ; lean juicy meat not over cooked for dinner, with stale bread and occasionally a slice of toasted bacon for breakfast. Nos. 44 and 45.

488. Boils should be brought to a head by warm poultices of camomile flowers, or boiled white lily root, or onion root ; by fermentation with hot water, or by stimulating plasters. When perfectly ripe and ready to break, they may be discharged by a needle or the lancet. *Constitutional treatment :*— Peruvian bark, port wine, and sea-bathing are desirable.

489. Chapped Hands may be prevented by the use of camphor balls made as follows:—Melt three drachms of spermaceti, four drachms of white wax, with one ounce of almond oil, and stir in three drachms of camphor (previously powdered by moistening it with a little spirits of wine) ; pour small quantities into small gallipots, so as to turn out in the form of cakes.

490. Chicken Pox.—Mild aperients, No. 4, succeeded by No. 7,

☞ *For the Remedies and Doses see "Prescriptions," page 131.*

and No. 8, if much fever accompany the eruption.

491. Chilblains.—Warm, dry, woollen clothing to exposed parts in cold weather, as a preventive. In the first stage, friction with No. 48, used cold. When ulcers form they should be poulticed with bread and water for a day or two, and then dressed with calamine cerate. Or, chilblains in every stage, whether of simple inflammation or open ulcer, may always be successfully treated by Goulard's extract, used pure or applied on lint twice a day.

492. Chilblains, Broken, or Chapped Hands, &c. —Sweet oil, one pint ; Venice turpentine, three ounces ; hog's-lard, half-a-pound ; bees-wax, three ounces. Put all into a pipkin over a slow fire, and stir it with a wooden spoon till the bees-wax is all melted, and the ingredients simmer. It is fit for use as soon as cold, but the longer it is kept the better it will be. It must be spread very thin on soft rag, or (for chaps or cracks) rubbed on the hands when you go to bed.

493. Common Continued Fever.—Aperients in the commencement, No. 1, followed by No. 7, then diaphoretics. No. 8, and afterwards tonics. No. 13, in the stage of weakness. Avoid all excesses.

494. Common Cough.—The linctus, No. 42, or No. 43, abstinence from malt liquor, and protection from cold damp air. Avoid cold, damp, and draughts.

495. Cough, Another Remedy.—Syrup of poppies, oxymel of squills, simple oxymel, in equal parts, mixed, and a teaspoonful taken when the cough is troublesome. It is best to have it made up by a chemist. The cost is trifling.

496. Constipation.—The observance of a regular period of evacuating the bowels, which is most proper in the morning after breakfast. The use of mild aperients, No. 47, also porridge for breakfast, and brown bread instead of white. There should be an entire change in the dietary for a few days while taking opening medicine.

497. Consumption.—The disease may be complicated with various morbid conditions of the lungs and heart ; which require appropriate treatment. To allay the cough, No. 42 is an admirable remedy. Avoid cold, damp, excitement, and over-exertion.

498. Convulsions (Children).—If during teething, free lancing of the gums, the warm bath, cold applications to the head, leeches to the temples, an emetic, and a laxative clyster, No. 20.

499. Convulsions.—The following remarkable case, in which a surgeon saved the life of an infant in convulsions, by the use of chloroform, will be read with interest. He commenced the use of it at nine o'clock one evening, at which period the child was rapidly sinking, numerous remedies having been already tried without effect He dropped half-a-drachm of chloroform into a thin muslin handkerchief, and held it about an inch from the infant's face. In about two minutes the convulsions gave way, and the child fell into a sleep. By slightly releasing the child from the influence of the chloroform, he was able to administer food, by which the child was nourished and strengthened. The chloroform was continually administered, in the manner described, from Friday evening at nine o'clock until Monday morning at nine. This treatment lasted sixty hours, and sixteen ounces of chloroform were used, and no injurious effects, however trivial, followed.

500. Cramp in the Legs.—Stretch out the heel of the leg as far as

☞ For the Remedies and Doses see "Prescriptions," page 131.

possible, at the same time drawing up the toes as far as possible. This will often stop a fit of cramp after it has commenced.

501. Croup.—Leeches to the throat, with hot fomentations as long as the attack lasts ; the emetic. No. 16, afterwards the aperient, No. 5. Avoid cold and damp.

502. Deafness.—It is now considered injurious to use water for the ear in cases of ear complaint. A solution of Sodium Bicarbonate has been found to act most beneficially as a solvent. In some forms of ear complaint powdered borax, as a constituent of the "drops" to be used, has been found useful, and tannic acid in other forms. Carbolic acid mixed with glycerine is used when a disinfectant is necessary. So delicate, however, is the structure of the internal ear that in all cases it is desirable to consult a medical practitioner.

503. Dropsy.—Evacuate the water by means of No. 10, but if possible call in a medical man, as dropsy may be due to either heart or kidney complaint, and each needs different treatment.

504. Epilepsy.—During fit put something between the teeth to prevent biting the tongue, and see patient is lying in a safe place. Loosen all tight clothing. If accompanied or produced by fulness of the vessels of the head, leeches to the temples, blisters, and No. 1 and No. 7. If from debility or confirmed epilepsy, the mixture, No. 18. Avoid drinking and excitement.

505. Eruptions on the Face.—The powder, No. 30, internally, sponging the face with the lotion, No. 31. Avoid excesses in diet.

506. Erysipelas.—Aperients, if the patient be strong, No. 1, followed by No. 7, then tonics, No. 27. No. 27 may be used from the commence-

ment for weak subjects. Smear the affected part with vaseline to keep the air away.

507. Weak and Sore Eyes.—Sulphate of zinc, three grains ; tincture of opium, ten drops ; water, two ounces. To be applied three or four times a day.

508. Faintness.—Effusion of cold water on the face, stimulants to the nostrils, pure air, and the recumbent position ; afterwards, avoidance of the exciting cause. Avoid excitement

509. Frost-Bite and Frozen Limbs.—No heating or stimulating liquors must be given. Rub the parts affected with ice, cold, or snow water, and lay the patient on a cold bed.

510. Gout.—The aperients No. 1, followed by No. 24, bathing the parts with very weak gin-and-water ; give for drink, weak tea or coffee. Warmth by flannels. Abstain from wines, spirits, and animal food.

511. Gravel.—No. 5, followed by No. 7, the free use of magnesia as an aperient. The pill No. 22. Abstain from fermented drinks and hard water. Another form of gravel must be treated by mineral acids, given three times a day.

512. Dr. Clark's Pills for Nervous Headache.—Socotrine aloes, powdered rhubarb, of each one drachm ; compound powder of cinnamon, one scruple ; hard soap, half-a-drachm ; syrup enough to form the mass. To be divided into fifty pills, of which two will be sufficient for a dose ; to be taken occasionally.

513. Hooping Cough. —Dissolve a scruple of salt of tartar in a quarter pint of water ; add to it ten grains of cochineal ; sweeten it with sugar. Give to an infant a fourth part of a tablespoonful four times a day ; two years old, half-a-spoonful ; from four years, a tablespoonful. Great care

☞ *For the Remedies and Doses see "Prescriptions," page 131.*

is required in the administration of medicines to infants. This disease may be complicated with congestion or inflammation of the lungs, or convulsions, and then becomes a serious disease. If uncomplicated, No. 43.

514. Hysterics.—The fit may be prevented by the administration of thirty drops of ether. When it has taken place, open the windows, loosen the tight parts of the dress, sprinkle cold water on the face, &c. A glass of wine or cold water when the patient can swallow. Avoid excitement and tight lacing.

515. Indigestion.—The pills No. 2, with the mixture No. 18, or the mixture par. 457a, at the same time abstinence from veal, pork, mackerel, salmon, pastry, and beer ; for drink, homœopathic cocoa, a glass of cold spring water the first thing every morning. Avoid excesses.

516. Hiccough or Hiccup.—This is a spasm of the diaphragm, caused by flatulency, indigestion, or acidity. It may be relieved by the sudden application of cold, also by two or three mouthfuls of cold water, by eating a small piece of ice, taking a pinch of snuff ; or anything that excites counteraction.

517. Inflammation of the Bladder.—Bleeding, aperients No. 5 and No. 7, the warm hip-bath, afterwards opium ; the pill No. 11, three times a day till relieved. Avoid fermented liquors, &c.

518. Inflammation of the Bowels.—Leeches, blisters, fomentations, hot baths, iced drinks, the pills No. 19 ; move the bowels with clysters, if necessary, No. 20. Avoid cold, indigestible food, &c.

519. Inflammation of the Brain. Application of cold to the head, bleeding from the temples or back of the neck by leeches or cupping ; aperients No. 1, followed by No. 7 ; mercury to salivation, No. 15. Avoid excitement, study, and intemperance.

520. Inflammation of the Kidneys.—Apply leeches over the seat of pain, aperient No. 3, the warm bath. Avoid violent exercise, rich living. Adopt mainly a milk diet.

521. Inflammation of the Liver.—Leeches over the right side, the seat of pain, blisters, aperients No. 1, followed by No. 7, afterwards the pills No. 19, till the gums are slightly tender. Avoid cold, damp, intemperance, and anxiety.

522. Inflammation of the Lungs.—Over painful part of chest use linseed meal poultices in which a dessertspoonful of mustard is added, to be changed every four hours ; the demulcent mixture, No. 14, to allay the cough, with the powders No. 15. Avoid cold, damp, and draughts.

523. Inflammation of the Stomach.—Leeches to the pit of the stomach, followed by fomentations, cold iced water for drink, bowels to be evacuated by clysters ; abstinence from all food except cold gruel, milk and water, or tea made with milk. Avoid excesses and condiments.

524. Sore Throat—Those subject to sore throat will find the following preparation simple, cheap, and highly efficacious when used in the early stage. Pour a pint of boiling water upon twenty-five or thirty leaves of common sage ; let the infusion stand for half-an-hour. Add vinegar sufficient to make it moderately acid, and honey according to the taste. This combination of the astringent and the emollient principle seldom fails to produce the desired effect. The infusion must be used as a gargle several times a day. It is pleasant to the taste, and if swallowed contains nothing to render it dangerous in any way.

525. Inflammatory Sore Throat.—Leeches and blisters externally,

☞ *For the Remedies and Doses see "Prescriptions," page 131.*

aperients No. 1, followed by No. 7, gargle to clear the throat, No. 17. Avoid cold, damp, and draughts.

526. Inflamed Eyes.—The bowels to be regulated by No. 5, a small blister behind the ear or on the nape of the neck—the eye to be bathed with No. 35.

527. Influenza (Symptoms).—This infectious disease is characterized by general catarrh of the mucous membranes and accompanied by great prostration. Initial symptoms are headache, pains in the body and limbs, with usually fever and a small, quick, irregular pulse. Affections of the lungs are very prone to occur, especially pneumonia ; nausea, vomiting and diarrhœa may be present. Persistent neuralgia and great depression of spirits are often experienced in the convalescent stage.

528. Influenza (Treatment).—Keep in bed, if fever is present give aperient No. 4. In early stage give a hot bath and afterwards a hot drink, and see that the bed is well warmed. Antifebrin in ten-grain doses every four hours for an adult may be given during the fever. With weak pulse give brandy. Lung complications should receive their appropriate treatment. In convalescence, a nutritious diet, fresh air, and take No. 27 as a tonic.

529. Intermittent Fever, or Ague.—Take No. 13 during the intermission of the paroxysm of the fever ; keeping the bowels free with a wine-glass of No. 7. Avoid bad air, stagnant pools, &c.

530. Itch.—The ointment of No. 28, or lotion No. 29.

531. Jaundice.—One pennyworth of allspice, ditto of flowers of brimstone, ditto of turmeric ; these to be well pounded together, and afterwards to be mixed with half-a-pound of treacle. Two tablespoonfuls to be taken every day. Or the pills No. 1, afterwards the mixture No. 7, drinking freely of dandelion tea.

532. Looseness of the Bowels (English Cholera).—One pill No. 19, repeated if necessary ; afterwards the mixture No. 21. Avoid unripe fruits, acid drinks, ginger-beer ; wrap flannel round the abdomen.

533. Measles.—A well-ventilated room, aperient No. 4, with No. 14 to allay the cough and fever.

534. Menstruation (Excessive).—No. 40 during the attack, with rest in the recumbent position ; in the intervals, No. 39.

536. Menstruation (Scanty).—In strong patients, cupping the loins, exercise in the open air, No. 40, the feet in warm water before the expected period, the pills No. 38 ; in weak subjects, No. 89. Gentle and regular exercise. Avoid hot rooms, and too much sleep. In cases of this description it is desirable to apply to a medical man for advice. It may be useful to many to point out that pennyroyal tea is a simple and useful medicine for inducing the desired result.

537. Menstruation (Painful).—No. 41 during the attack ; in the intervals, No. 38 twice a week, with No. 39. Avoid cold, mental excitement, &c.

538. Mumps.—Fomentation with a decoction of camomiles and poppy heads ; No. 4, as an aperient, and No. 9 during the stage of fever. Avoid cold and attend to the regularity of the bowels.

539. Nervousness.—Cheerful society, early rising, exercise in the open air, particularly on horseback, and No. 12. Avoid excitement, study, and late meals.

540. Palpitation of the Heart.—The pills No. 2, with the mixture No. 12.

☞ *For the Remedies and Doses see "Prescriptions," page 131.*

541. Piles.—The paste No. 34, at the same time a regulated diet. When the piles are external, or can be reached, one or two applications of Goulard's extract, with an occasional dose of lenitive electuary, will generally succeed in curing them. Bathe frequently with cold water.

542. Quinsey.—Hot fomentations applied all round the throat ; an emetic, No. 16, commonly succeeds in breaking the abscess ; afterwards the gargle No. 17. Avoid cold and damp.

543. Rheumatism.—Bathe the affected parts with No. 23, and take internally No. 24, with No. 25 at bedtime, to ease pain, &c. Avoid damp and cold, wear flannel. Take no malt liquors, sugar or pastry, &c.

544. Rickets.—The powder No. 33, a dry, pure atmosphere, a nourishing diet. Give cod-liver oil.

545. Ringworm.—It is best for the part affected, if in the hair, to be shaved and then apply by rubbing a solution of one pint of strong vinegar to four pints of water, and atterwards painting on a solution of iodine ; this should be done night and morning. The patient should take a little sulphur and treacle, or some other gentle aperient, every morning. Brushes and combs should be washed every day. The lotion No. 32, with the occasional use of the powder No. 5. Fresh air and cleanliness.

546. Scarlet Fever.—Well-ventilated room, sponging the body when hot with cold or tepid vinegar, or spirit and water ; aperients. No. 4 ; diaphoretics, No. 8. If dropsy succeed the disappearance of the eruption, frequent purging with No. 5, succeeded by No. 7. If sore throat use gargle No. 17.

547. Scrofula.—Pure air, light but warm clothing, diet of fresh animal food, bowels to be regulated by No. 6 and No. 26, taken regularly for a considerable time, and cod-liver oil.

548. Sourf in the Head.—Into a pint of water drop a lump of fresh quicklime, the size of a walnut ; let it stand all night, then pour the water off clear from the sediment or deposit, add a quarter of a pint of the best vinegar, and wash the head with the mixture, which is perfectly harmless, and forms a simple and effective remedy.

549. Scurvy.—Fresh animal and vegetable food, and the free use of ripe fruits and lemon juice. Avoid cold and damp.

550. Small-pox.—A well-ventilated apartment, mild aperients ; if fever be present, No. 7, succeeded by diaphoretics No. 8, and tonics No. 13 in the stage of debility, or decline of the eruption.

551. Cutaneous Eruptions.—The following mixture is very useful in all cutaneous eruptions : Ipecacuanha wine, four drachms ; flowers of sulphur, two drachms ; tincture of cardamoms, one ounce. Mix : one teaspoonful to be taken three times a day, in a wine-glassful of water.

552. Wash for a Blotched Face.—Rose water, three ounces : sulphate of zinc, one drachm. Mix : wet the face with it, gently dry it, and then touch it over with cold cream, which also dry gently off.

553. Freckles.—To disperse them, take one ounce of lemon juice, a quarter of a drachm of powdered borax, and half-a-drachm of sugar ; mix, and let them stand a few days in a glass bottle till the liquor is fit for use, then rub it on the hands and face occasionally.

554. To Remove Sun Freckles.—Dissolve, in half-an-ounce of lemon juice, one ounce of Venice soap, and add a quarter of an ounce each of oil of bitter almonds, and deliquated oil

☞ *For the Remedies and Doses see "Prescriptions," page 131.*

of tartar. Place this mixture in the sun till it acquires the consistency of ointment. When in this state add three drops of the oil of rhodium and keep it for use. Apply it to the face and hands in the manner following :—Wash the parts at night with elderflower water, then anoint with the ointment. In the morning cleanse the skin by washing it copiously in rose water.

555. Wash for Sunburn.—Take two drachms of borax, one drachm of Roman alum, one drachm of camphor, half-an-ounce of sugar-candy, and a pound of ox-gall. Mix and stir well for ten minutes or so, and repeat this, stirring three or four times a day for a fortnight, till it appears clear and transparent. Strain through blotting-paper, and bottle up for use.

556. Ointment for Sore Nipples.—Take of tincture of tolu, two drachms ; spermaceti ointment, half-an-ounce ; powdered gum, two drachms. Mix these materials well together to make an ointment. The white of an egg mixed with brandy is the best application for sore nipples ; the person should at the same time use a nipple shield.

557. St Vitus's Dance.—The occasional use, in the commencement, of No. 5, followed by No. 7, afterwards No. 46.

558. Thrush.—One of the powders No. 6 every other night ; in the intervals a dessertspoonful of the mixture No. 18 three times a day ; white spots to be dressed with the honey of borax.

559. Tic-Douloureux.—Regulate the bowels with No. 3, and take in the intervals of pain, No. 27. Avoid cold, damp, and mental anxiety. A severe attack of tic-douloureux is said to have been cured by the following simple remedy :—take half-a-pint of rose water, add two teaspoonfuls of white vinegar, to form a lotion. Apply it to the part affected three or four times a day. It requires fresh linen and lotion at each application ; this will, in two or three days, gradually take the pain away.

560. Teething.—Young children, whilst cutting their first set of teeth, often suffer severe constitutional disturbance. At first there is restlessness and peevishness, with slight fever, but not unfrequently these are followed by convulsive fits, as they are commonly called, which are caused by the brain becoming irritated ; and sometimes under this condition the child is either cut off suddenly, or the foundation of serious mischief to the brain is laid. The remedy, or rather the safeguard, against these frightful consequences, is trifling, safe, and almost certain, and consists merely in lancing the gum.

561. Toothache.—Use No. 3 for a few alternate days. Apply liquor ammoniæ to reduce the pain, and when that is accomplished, fill the decayed spots with silver succedaneum without delay, or the pain will return. A drop of creosote, or a few drops of chloroform on cotton, applied to the tooth, or a few grains of camphor placed in the decayed opening, or camphor moistened with turpentine, will often afford instant relief.

562. Another Remedy for Tooth-ache.—Two or three drops of essential oil of cloves put upon a small piece of lint or cotton wool, and placed in the hollow of the tooth, will be found to have the active power of curing the toothache without destroying the tooth or injuring the gums.

563. Succedaneum.—Take an old silver thimble, an old silver coin, or other silver article, and with a very fine file convert it into filings. Sift through gauze, to separate the coarse from the fine particles. Take the finer portion, and mix with sufficient quicksilver to form a stiff amalgam, and

☞ *For the Remedies and Doses see "Prescriptions," page 131.*

while in this state, fill the cavities of decayed teeth. This is precisely the same as the metallic amalgam, used by all dentists. *Caution.*—As it turns black under the action of the acids of the mouth, it should be used sparingly for *front* teeth. A tooth should never be filled while it is aching.

564. Typhus Fever.—Sponging the body with cold or tepid water, a well-ventilated apartment, cold applications to the head and temples. Aperients No. 4, with refrigerants No. 9, tonics No. 13 in the stage of debility.

565. Water on the Brain.—Local bleeding by means of leeches, blisters, aperients No. 5, and mercurial medicines, No. 15.

566. Whites.—The mixture No. 36, with the injection No. 37. Clothing light but warm, moderate exercise in the open air, country residence.

567. Worms in the Intestines.—The aperient No. 5, followed by No. 7, afterwards the free use of lime water and milk in equal parts, a pint daily. Avoid unwholesome food. (See also pars. 472 and 473.)

568. PRESCRIPTIONS.

To be Used in the Cases enumerated under the head "Diseases" (page 124).

The following prescriptions, originally derived from various prescribers' Pharmacopœias, embody the favourite remedies employed by the most eminent physicians :—

NB.— 1 drachm = 1 teaspoonful.

   1 ounce = 2 tablespoonfuls.

1. Take of powdered aloes, nine grains ; extract of colocynth, compound, eighteen grains ; calomel, nine grains ; tartrate of antimony, two grains ; mucilage, sufficient to make a mass, which is to be divided into six pills ; two to be taken every twenty-four hours, till they act thoroughly on the bowels : in case of inflammation, apoplexy, &c.

2. Powdered rhubarb, Socotrine aloes, and gum mastic, each one scruple ; make into twelve pills : one before and one after dinner.

3. Compound extract of colocynth, extract of jalap, and Castile soap, of each one scruple ; make into twelve pills.

4. James's powder, five grains ; calomel, three grains : in fevers, for adults. For children, the following : —Powdered camphor one scruple ; calomel and powdered scammony, of each nine grains ; James's powder, six grains ; mix and divide into six powders. Half of one powder twice a day for an infant a year old ; a whole powder for two years : and for four years, the same three times a day.

5. James's powder, six grains ; powdered jalap, ten grains ; mix and divide into three or four powders, according to the child's age ; in one powder if for an adult.

6. Powdered rhubarb, four grains ; mercury and chalk, three grains ; ginger in powder, one grain ; an alterative aperient for children.

7. Dried sulphate of magnesia, six drachms ; sulphate of soda, three drachms ; infusion of senna, seven ounces ; tincture of jalap, and compound tincture of cardamoms, each half-an-ounce: in acute diseases generally ; take two tablespoonfuls every four hours till it operates freely.

8. Nitrate of potass, one drachm and a half ; spirits of nitric ether, half-an-ounce ; camphor mixture, and the spirit of mindererus, each four ounces: in fevers, &c. ; two tablespoonfuls, three times a day, and for children a dessertspoonful every four hours.

9. Spirit of nitric ether, three drachms ; dilute nitric acid, two drachms ; syrup, three drachms ; camphor mixture, seven ounces ; in fevers, &c., with debility ; dose as in preceding prescription.

10. Decoction of broom, half-a-pint ; cream of tartar one ounce, tincture of

squills, two drachms : in dropsies ; a third part three times a day.

11. Pills of soap and opium five grains for a dose as directed.

12. Ammoniated tincture of valerian six drachms ; camphor mixture, seven ounces ; a fourth part three times a day ; in spasmodic and hysterical disorders.

13. Disulphate of quina, half-a-drachm ; dilute sulphuric acid, twenty drops ; compound infusion of roses, eight ounces ; two tablespoonfuls every four hours, in intermittent and other fevers, during the absence of the paroxysm.

14. Almond mixture seven ounces and a half ; wine of antimony and ipecacuanha, of each one drachm and a half : a tablespoonful every four hours ; in cough with fever, &c.

15. Calomel, one grain ; powdered white sugar, two grains ; to make a powder to be placed on the tongue every two or three hours. Should the calomel act on the bowels, powdered kino is to be substituted for the sugar.

16. Antimony and ipecacuanha wines, of each an ounce ; a teaspoonful every ten minutes for a child till vomiting is produced ; but for an adult a large tablespoonful should be taken.

17. Compound infusion of roses, seven ounces ; tincture of myrrh, one ounce.

18. Infusion of orange peel, seven ounces ; tincture of hops, half-an-ounce ; and a drachm of carbonate of soda ; two tablespoonfuls twice a day. Or, infusion of valerian, seven ounces ;carbonate of ammonia, two scruples ;compound tincture of bark, six drachms ;spirits of ether, two drachms: one tablespoonful every twenty-four hours.

19. Blue pill, four grains ; opium, half-a-grain : to be taken three times a day.

20. For a Clyster.—A pint and a half of gruel or fat broth, a tablespoonful of castor oil, one of common salt, and a lump of butter ; mix, to be injected slowly. A third of this quantity is enough for an infant.

21. Chalk mixture, seven ounces ; aromatic and opiate confection, of each one drachm ; tincture of catechu, six drachms ; two tablespoonfuls every two hours.

22. Carbonate of soda, powdered rhubarb, and Castile soap, each one drachm ; make thirty-six pills ; three twice a day.

23. Lotion.—Common salt, one ounce ; distilled water, seven ounces ; spirits of wine, one ounce : mix.

24. Dried sulphate of magnesia, six drachms ; heavy carbonate of magnesia, two drachms ; wine of colchicum, two drachms ; water eight ounces: take two tablespoonfuls every four hours.

25. Compound powder of ipecacuanha, ten grains ; powdered guaiacum, four grains: in a powder at bedtime.

26. Brandish's solution of potash ; thirty drops twice a day in a wineglass of beer.

27. Disulphate of quina, half-a-drachm ; dilute sulphuric acid, ten drops ; compound infusion of roses, eight ounces : two tablespoonfuls every four hours, and as a tonic in the stage of weakness succeeding fever.

28. Flowers of sulphur, two ounces ; hog's lard, four ounces ; white hellebore powder, half-an-ounce ; oil of lavender sixty drops.

29. Hydriodate of potass, two drachms ; distilled water, eight ounces.

30. Flowers of sulphur, half-a-drachm ; carbonate of soda, a scruple ; tartarized antimony, one-eighth of a grain : one powder, night and morning, in eruptions of the skin or face.

31. Milk of bitter almonds, seven ounces ; bichloride of mercury, four grains ; spirits of rosemary, one ounce : bathe the eruption with this lotion three times a day.

32. Sulphate of zinc, two scruples ; sugar of lead, fifteen grains ; distilled

water, six ounces : the parts to be washed with the lotion two or three times a day.

33. Carbonate of iron, six grains ; powdered rhubarb, four grains ; one powder night and morning.

34. Elecampane powder, two ounces ; sweet fennel-seed powder, three ounces ; black pepper powder, one ounce ; purified honey, and brown sugar, of each two ounces ; the size of a nutmeg, two or three times a day.

35. Sulphate of zinc, twelve grains ; wine of opium, one drachm ; rose water, six ounces.

36. Sulphate of magnesia, six drachms ; sulphate of iron, ten grains ; diluted sulphuric acid, forty drops ; tincture of cardamoms (compound), half-an-ounce ; water, seven ounces ; a fourth part night and morning.

37. Decoction of oak bark, a pint ; dried alum, half-an-ounce: or liquor plumbi subacetatis one teaspoonful to a pint of water, for an injection, a syringeful to be used night and morning.

38. Compound gamboge pill, and a pill of assafœtida and aloes, of each half-a-drachm : make twelve pills ; two twice or three times a week.

39. Griffiths' mixture—one table-spoonful three times a day.

40. Ergot of rye, five grains ; in a powder, to be taken every four hours. This should only be taken under medical advice and sanction.

41. Powdered opium, half-a-grain ; camphor, two grains in a pill ; to be taken every three or four hours whilst in pain.

42. Syrup of balsam of tolu, two ounces ; the muriate of morphia, two grains ; muriatic acid, twenty drops : a teaspoonful twice a day.

43. Salts of tartar, two scruples, twenty grains of powdered cochineal ; ¼ lb of honey ; water, half-a-pint ; boil, and give a tablespoonful three times a day.

44. Calomel, ten grains ; Castile soap, extract of jalap, extract of colocynth, of each one scruple ; oil of juniper, five drops : make into fifteen pills ; one three times a day.

45. Infusion of orange peel, eight ounces ; carbonate of soda, one drachm ; and compound tincture of cardamoms, half-an-ounce ; take a tablespoonful three times a day, succeeding the pills.

46. Carbonate of iron, three ounces ; syrup of ginger, sufficient to make an electuary: a teaspoonful three times a day.

47. Take of Castile soap, compound extract of colocynth, compound rhubarb pill, and the extract of jalap, each one scruple ; oil of caraway, ten drops ; make into twenty pills, and take one after dinner every day whilst necessary.

48. Spirit of rosemary, five parts ; spirit of wine, or spirit of turpentine, one part.

49. Take of thick mucilage, one ounce ; castor oil, twelve drachms ; make into an emulsion : add mint water, four ounces ; spirit of nitre, three drachms ; laudanum, one drachm ; mixture of squills, one drachm ; and syrup, seven drachms ; mix ; two tablespoonfuls every six hours.

569. USEFUL APERIENTS.—In the spring time of the year, the judicious use of aperient medicines is much to be commended.

570. Spring Aperients for Children.

i. An excellent medicine is brimstone and treacle, prepared by mixing an ounce and a half of sulphur, and half-an-ounce of cream of tartar, with eight ounces of treacle ; and, according to the age of the child, giving from a small teaspoonful to a dessertspoonful, early in the morning, two or three times a week.

As this sometimes produces sickness, the following may be used :—

ii. Take of powdered Rochelle salts one drachm and a half, powdered jalap and powdered rhubarb each fifteen grains, ginger two grains ; mix.

Dose for a child above five years, one *small* teaspoonful ; above ten years, a *large* teaspoonful ; above fifteen, half the whole, or two teaspoonfuls : and for a person above twenty, three teaspoonfuls, or the whole, as may be required by the habit of the person.

This medicine may be dissolved in warm water, mint, or common tea. The powder can be kept for use in a wide-mouthed bottle, and be in readiness for any emergency. The druggist may be directed to treble or quadruple the quantities, as convenient.

571. Aperient Pills.—To some adults all liquid medicines produce such nausea that pills are the only form in which aperients can be exhibited ; the following is a useful formula :

i. Take of compound rhubarb pill a drachm and one scruple, of powdered ipecacuanha ten grains, and of extract of hyoscyamus one scruple ; mix, and beat into a mass, and divide into twenty-four pills ; take one or two, or if of a very costive habit, *three* at bedtime.

ii. For persons requiring a more powerful aperient, the same formula, with twenty grains of compound extract of colocynth, will form a good purgative pill. The mass receiving this addition must be divided into thirty, instead of twenty-four pills.

572. Black Draught.—The common aperient medicine known as black draught is made in the following manner :—

i. Take of senna leaves six drachms, bruised ginger half-a-drachm, sliced liquorice root four drachms, Epsom salts two and a half ounces, boiling water half an imperial pint. Keep this standing on the hob or near the fire for three hours, then strain, and after allowing it to grow cool, add of sal volatile one drachm and a half, of tincture of senna, and of tincture of cardamoms, each half-an-ounce. This mixture will keep a long time in a cool place. *Dose*, a wineglassful for an adult ; and two tablespoonfuls for young persons about fifteen years of age. It is not a suitable medicine for children.

573. Tonic Aperient. —The following will be found a useful medicine for persons of all ages. Epsom salts one ounce, diluted sulphuric acid one drachm, infusion of quassia chips half an *imperial* pint, compound tincture of rhubarb two drachms. *Dose*, half a wineglassful twice a day.

574. Infants' Aperients.—The following may be used with safety for young children.

i. Take of rhubarb five grains, magnesia three grains, white sugar a scruple, grey powder five grains ; mix. *Dose*, for an infant from twelve to eighteen months of age, from one-third to one-half of the whole.

ii. A useful laxative for children is composed of calomel five grains, and sugar a scruple, made into five powders. *Dose*, half of one of these for a child from birth to one year, and a whole one from that age to three years.

575. Flour of Brimstone is a mild aperient in doses of about a quarter of an ounce ; it is best taken in milk. Flour of brimstone, which is also called sublimed sulphur, is generally put up in ounce packets at 7*d.* ; its wholesale price is 4*d.*, per pound.

576. PREPARATION OF MEDI-CINES.

The following directions are of the utmost value in connection with the DOMESTIC PHARMACOPŒIA, DISEASES, AND PRESCRIPTIONS. *They will be found most important to emigrants, attendants upon the sick, and persons who reside out of the reach of medical aid, sailors, &c., &c. They contain instructions not only for the compounding of medicines but most useful hints and cautions upon the application of leeches, blisters, poultices, &c.*

577. Articles required for Mixing Medicines.—*Three glass measures,* one to measure ounces, another to measure drachms, and a measure for minims, drops, or small doses. *A pestle and mortar,* both of glass and Wedgwood-ware, a glass funnel, and glass stirring rods. A *spatula,* or flexible knife for spreading ointments, making pills, &c. *A set of scales and weights. A small slab of marble,* or porcelain, for making pills upon, mixing ointments, &c.

578. Medicine Weights.—Medicines are made up by troy weight, although drugs are bought by avoir-dupois weight. In the box containing the scales and weights, there are several square pieces of brass, of different sizes and thicknesses, and stamped with a variety of characters. These are the weights, which may now be explained. There are twelve ounces to the pound troy, which is marked lb. ; the ounce, which contains eight drachms, is marked ℥i ; the drachm, containing three scruples, is marked ℈i ; and the scruple of twenty grains is marked ℈i. The grain weights are marked by little circles, thus :—

Five ☐ Grains.

Each of the grain weights, in addition to the circles denoting their several weights, bears also the stamp of a crown. Care must be taken not to mistake this for one of the numerals. Besides these weights there are others marked ℈ss, which means half-a-scruple ; ʒss, meaning half-a-drachm ; and ℥ss, meaning half-an-ounce. When there are ounces, drachms, or scruples, the number of them is shown by Roman figures, thus :—i. ii. iii. iv. v., &c., and prescriptions are written in this style.

579. Medicine Measures.—Liquid medicines are always measured by the following table;—

60 minims . . .			1 fluid drachm.
8 fluid drachms	are con-		1 fluid ounce.
20 fluid ounces .	tained in		1 pint.
8 pints.			1 gallon.

And the signs which distinguish each are as follows :—Q means a gallon ; *o* a pint ; *fl* ℥, a fluid ounce ; *fl* ʒ, a fluid drachm ; and m, a minim, or drop. Formerly drops used to be ordered, but as the size of a drop must necessarily vary, minims are always directed to be employed now for any particular medicine, although for such medicines as oil of cloves, essence of ginger, &c., drops are frequently ordered. When proper glass measures (*see* par. 577) are not at hand, it is necessary to adopt some other method of determining the quantities required, and therefore the following table has been drawn up for that purpose :—

A tumbler . . .			10 ounces.
A teacup			6 ,,
A wineglass. . .	usually		2 ,,
2 tablespoons. .	contains		1 ,,
A tablespoon . .	about		4 drachms.
A dessertspoon .			2 ,,
A teaspoon . . .			1 ,,

These quantities refer to ordinary sized spoons and vessels. Some cups hold half as much more, and some tablespoons contain six drachms. A medicine glass, which is graduated so as to show the number of spoonfuls it contains, should be kept in every family.

580. PROCESS OF MAKING MEDICINES.

581. To Powder Substances.—Place the substance in the mortar, and strike it *gently* with direct perpendicular blows of the pestle, until it separates into several pieces, then remove all but a small portion, which bruise gently at first, and rub the pestle round and round the mortar, observing that the circles described by the pestle should gradually decrease in diameter, and then increase again, because by this means every part of the powder is subjected to the process of pulverization.

Some substances require to be prepared in a particlar manner before they can be powdered, or to be assisted by adding some other body. For example, camphor powders more easily when a few drops of spirits of wine are added to it ; mace, nutmegs, and such oily aromatic substances are better for the addition of a little white sugar ; resins and gum-resins should be powdered in a cold place, and if they are intended to be dissolved, a little fine well-washed white sand mixed with them assists the process of powdering. Tough roots, like gentian and calumba, should be cut into thin slices ; and fibrous roots like ginger, cut slanting, otherwise the powder will be full of small fibres. Vegetable matter, such as peppermint, loosestrife, senna, &c., requires to be dried before it is powdered.

Be careful not to pound too hard in glass, porcelain, or Wedgwood-ware mortars ; they are intended only for substances that pulverize easily, and for the purpose of mixing or incorporating medicines. Never use acids in a marble mortar, and be sure that you do not powder galls or any other astringent substance in any but a brass mortar.

582. Sifting is frequently required for powdered substances, and this is usually done by employing a fine sieve, or tying the powder up in a piece of muslin, and striking it against the left hand over a piece of paper.

583. Filtering is frequently required for the purpose of obtaining clear fluids, such as infusions, eye-washes, and other medicines ; and it is, therefore, highly important to know how to perform this simple operation. First of all take a square piece of white blotting paper, and double it over so as to form an angular cup. Open out this filter paper very carefully, and having placed it in a funnel, moisten it with a little water. Then place the funnel in the neck of the bottle, and pour the liquid gently down the side of the paper, otherwise the fluid is apt to burst the paper.

584. Maceration is another process that is frequently required to be performed in making up medicines, and consists simply in immersing the medicines *in cold water* or spirits for a certain time.

585. Digestion resembles maceration, except that the process is assisted by a gentle heat. The ingredients are placed in a flask, such as salad oil is sold in, which should be fitted with a plug of tow or wood, and have a piece of wire twisted round the neck. The flask is held by means of the wire over the flame of a spirit lamp, or else placed in some sand warmed in an old iron saucepan over the fire, care being taken not to place more of the flask below the sand than the portion occupied by the ingredients.

586. Infusion is one of the most frequent operations required in making up medicines, its object being to extract the aromatic and volatile principles of substances, that would be lost by decoction or digestion ; and to extract the soluble from the insoluble parts of bodies. Infusions as calumba and quassia may be made with cold water, in which case they are weaker, but more pleasant. The general method employed consists in slicing, bruising, or rasping the ingredients first, then placing them in a common jug (which should be as globular as possible), and pouring boiling water over them. Cover the jug with a cloth folded six or eight times, but if there be a lid to the jug so much the better. When the infusion has stood the time directed, hold a piece of *very coarse* linen over the spout, and pour the liquid through it into another jug.

587. Decoction, or boiling, is employed to extract the mucilaginous or gummy parts of substances, their bitter, astringent, or other qualities, and is nothing more than boiling the ingredients in a saucepan with the lid slightly raised. Be sure never to use an iron saucepan for astringent decoctions, such as oak-bark, galls, &c., as they will turn the saucepan black, and spoil the decoction. The enamelled saucepans are very useful for decoctions, but an excellent plan is to put the ingredients into a jar and boil the jar, thus preparing it by a water bath, as it is technically termed ; or by using a common pipkin, which answers still better. No decoction should be allowed to boil for more than ten minutes.

588. Extracts are made by evaporating the liquors obtained by infusion in decoction, but these can be bought much cheaper and better of chemists and druggists, and so can tinctures, confections, cerates and plasters, and syrups : but as every one is not always in the neighbourhood of druggists, we shall give recipes for those most generally useful, and the method of making them.

589. PRECAUTIONS TO BE OBSERVED IN GIVING MEDICINES.

590. Sex.—Medicines for females should not be so strong as those for males, therefore it is advisable to reduce the doses about one-third. This, however, varies greatly.

591. Temperament.—Persons of a phlegmatic temperament bear stimulants and purgatives better than those of a sanguine temperament, therefore the latter require smaller doses.

592. Habits.—Purgatives never act so well upon persons accustomed to take them as upon those who are not, therefore it is better to change the form of purgative from pill to potion, powder to draught, or aromatic to saline. Purgatives should never be given when there is an irritable state of the bowels.

593. Stimulants and Narcotics never act so quickly upon persons accustomed to use spirits freely as upon those who live abstemiously.

594. Climate.—The action of medicines is modified by climate and seasons. In summer, certain medicines act more powerfully than in winter, and the same person cannot bear the dose in July that he could in December.

595. General Health.—Persons whose general health is good bear stronger doses than the debilitated and those who have suffered for a long time.

596. Idiosyncracy.—By this is meant a peculiar temperament or disposition not common to people generally. For example, some persons cannot take calomel in the smallest dose without being salivated, or rhubarb without having convulsions ; others cannot take squills, opium, senna, &c. ; and this peculiarity is called the patient's idiosyncrasy, therefore it is wrong to *insist* upon their taking these medicines.

597. Doses of Medicine for Different Ages.—It must be plain to every one that children do not require such powerful medicine as adults or old people, and therefore it is desirable to have some fixed method of determining or regulating the administration of doses of medicine. Now let it be supposed that the dose for a full-grown person is one drachm, then the following proportions will be suitable for the various ages given, keeping in view other circumstances, such as sex, temperament, habits, climate, state of *general health*, and idiosyncrasy. All forms of opium should be avoided for a child under five years unless ordered by a medical man.

Age.	Proportion.	Proportionate Dose.
7 weeks	one-fifteenth	or grains 4
7 months	one-twelfth	or grains 5
Under 2 years	one-eighth	or grains 7½
„ 3 „	one-sixth	or grains 10
„ 4 „	one-fourth	or grains 15
„ 7 „	one-third	or scruple 1
„ 14 „	one-half	or drachm ½
„ 20 „	two-fifths	or scruples 2
Above 21 „	the full dose	or drachm 1
„ 65 „	The inverse	gradation

598. Intervals between Doses.—
Medicines should be given in such a manner that the effect of the first dose shall not have ceased when the next dose is given, therefore the intervals between the doses should be regulated accordingly. Fluids act quicker than solids, and powders sooner than pills.

599. TO PREVENT THE NAUSEOUS TASTE OF MEDICINES.

Castor oil may be taken in milk, coffee, or spirit, such as brandy ; but the best method of covering the nauseous flavour is to put a tablespoonful of strained orange juice in a wineglass, pour the castor oil into the centre of the juice, and then squeeze a few drops of lemon juice upon the top of the oil. The wineglass should first be dipped, rim downwards, into water, so that the interior may be wetted. Cod-liver oil may be taken, like castor oil, in orange juice. Peppermint water neutralizes, to a great extent, the nauseous taste of Epsom salts ; a strong solution of extract of liquorice, that of aloes ; milk, that of cinchona bark ; and cloves, that of senna.

600. Another Method is to have the medicine in a glass, as usual, and a tumbler of water by the side of it ; take the medicine, and retain it in the mouth, which should be kept closed, and if drinking the water be then commenced, the taste of the medicine is washed away. Even the bitterness of quinine and aloes may be prevented by this means. If the nostrils are firmly compressed by the thumb and finger of the left hand, while taking a nauseous draught, and so retained till the mouth has been washed out with water, the disagreeable taste of the medicine will be almost imperceptible.

601. DRUGS, THEIR DOSES AND PROPERTIES.

The various drugs are here arranged according to their properties, and the doses of each *for adults* are given. Many, however, have been necessarily omitted from each class, because they should not be employed except by a medical man.

They are divided into four grand classes—1. **General Stimulants ;** 2. **Local Stimulants;** 3. **Chemical Remedies ;** 4. **Mechanical Remedies.**

602. GENERAL STIMULANTS.

General stimulants are subdivided into two classes, diffusible and permanent stimulants : the first comprising *Narcotics and Antispasmodics*, and the second *Tonics and Astringents*.

603. NARCOTICS.

Narcotics are medicines which stupefy and diminish the activity of the nervous system. Given in small doses, they generally act as stimulants, but an increased dose produces a sedative effect. Under this head are included alcohol, camphor, ether, the hop, and opium.

1. **Alcohol,** or rectified spirit, is a very powerful stimulant, and is never used as a remedy without being diluted to the degree called proof spirit ; and even then it is seldom used internally. It is *used externally* in restraining bleeding, when there is not any vessel of importance wounded, and also for all bruises and sprains when diluted to one in three parts of water. It is also used as a lotion to burns, and is applied by dipping a piece of lint into the spirit, and laying it over the part. Freely diluted

(one part to eighteen) with water, it forms a useful eye-wash in the last stage of ophthalmia. *Used internally*, it acts as a very useful stimulant when diluted and taken moderately, increasing the general excitement, and giving energy to the muscular fibres ; hence it becomes very useful in certain cases of debility, epecially in habits disposed to create acidity ; and in the low stage of all fevers. *Dose.*—It is impossible to fix anything like a dose for this remedy, as much will depend upon the individual ; but diluted with water and sweetened with sugar, from half-an-ounce to two ounces may be given three or four times a day. In cases of extreme debility, however, much will depend upon the disease. *Caution.*—Remember that alcohol is an irritant *poison,* and that daily indulgence in its use originates dyspepsia, or indigestion, and many other serious complaints. Of all kinds of spirits the best as a tonic and stomachic is *brandy.*

2. Camphor is not a very steady stimulant, as its effect is transitory ; but in large doses it acts as a narcotic, abating pain and inducing sleep. In moderate doses it operates as a diaphoretic, diuretic, antispasmodic, increasing the heat of the body, allaying irritation and spasm. It is *used externally* as a liniment when dissolved in oil, alcohol or acetic acid, being employed to allay rheumatic pains ; and it is also useful as an embrocation in sprains, bruises, chilblains, and, when combined with opium, it has been advantageously employed in flatulent colic, and severe diarrhœa, being rubbed over the bowels. *When reduced to fine powder,* by the addition of a little spirit of wine and friction, it is very useful as a local stimulant to indolent ulcers, especially when they discharge a foul kind of matter ; a pinch is taken between the finger and thumb, and sprinkled into the ulcer, which is then dressed as usual. *When dissolved in oil of turpentine,*

a few drops placed in a hollow tooth and covered with jeweller's wool, or scraped lint, give almost instant relief to toothache. *Used internally*, it is apt to excite nausea, and even vomiting, especially when given in the solid form. *As a stimulant* it is of great service in all low fevers, malignant measles, malignant sore throat, and confluent small-pox ; and when combined with opium and bark, it is extremely useful in checking the progress of malignant ulcers, and gangrene. As a narcotic, it is dangerous, as it may produce rapid depression referable to the heart. *When powdered and sprinkled* upon the surface of a blister, it prevents the cantharides acting in a peculiar and painful manner upon the bladder. *Combined with senna,* it increases its purgative properties ; and it is also used to correct the nausea produced by squills, and the irritating effects of drastic purgatives and mezereon. *Dose,* from four grains to half-a-scruple, repeated at short intervals when used in small doses, and long intervals when employed in large doses. *Doses of the various preparations.*—Camphor mixture, from half-an-ounce to three ounces ; compound tincture of camphor (*paregoric elixir*) from fifteen minims to two drachms. *Caution.*—When given in an overdose it acts as a poison, producing vomiting, giddiness, delirium, convulsions, and sometimes death. Opium is the best antidote for camphor, whether in excess or taken as a poison. *Mode of exhibition.*—It may be rubbed up with almond emulsion, or mucilage, or the yolk of eggs, and by this means suspended in water, or combined with chloroform as a mixture, in which form it is a valuable stimulant in cholera and other diseases. (*See* MIXTURES, pars. 448—457*a*.)

3. Ether is a diffusible stimulant, narcotic and antispasmodic.

4. Sulphuric Ether is used *externally* both as a stimulant and a refrigerant. In the former case its evaporation is prevented by covering a rag moistened with it with oiled silk, in order to relieve headache , and in the latter case it is allowed to evaporate, and thus produce coldness ; hence it is applied over scalded surfaces by means of rags dipped in it. *As a local application*, it has been found to afford almost instant relief in ear-ache, when combined with almond oil, and dropped into the ear. It is used *internally* as a stimulant and narcotic in low fevers and cases of great exhaustion. *Dose* from fifteen minims to half-a-drachm, repeated at short intervals, as its effects soon pass off. Give in a little camphor julep, or water.

5. **Nitric Ether** is a refrigerant, diuretic, and antispasmodic, well known as "*sweet spirit of nitre.*" Used externally, its evaporation relieves headache, and it is sometimes applied to burns. It is used *internally* to relieve nausea, flatulence, and thirst in fevers ; also as a diuretic. *Dose*, from ten minims to one drachm. The smaller dose taken in a little warm water or gruel is useful as a sudorific in cases of cold and chill, to induce and promote the proper action of the skin which has been checked. If a larger dose be taken, it acts as a diuretic and not as a sudorific, and so fails to produce the desired effect.

6. **Compound Spirit of Sulphuric Ether** is a very useful stimulant, narcotic, and antispasmodic. *Used internally* in cases of great exhaustion, attended with irritability. *Dose*, from half-a-drachm to two drachms, in camphor julep. When combined with laudanum, it prevents the nauseating effects of the opium, and acts more beneficially as a narcotic.

7. **The Hop** is a narcotic, tonic, and diuretic ; it reduces the frequency of the pulse, and does not affect the head, like most anodynes. *Used externally*, it acts as an anodyne and discutient, and is useful as a foment-ation for painful tumours, rheumatic pains in the joints, and severe contu-sions. A pillow stuffed with hops acts as a narcotic. When the powder is mixed with lard, it acts as an anodyne dressing in painful ulcers. *Dose*, of the *extract*, from five grains to one scruple ; of the *tincture*, from half-a-drachm to two drachms ; of the *powder*, from three grains to one scruple ; of the *infusion, half-an-ounce to one and a half ounces.*

8. **Opium** is a stimulant, narcotic, and anodyne. *Used externally* it acts almost as well as when taken into the stomach, and without affecting the head or causing nausea. Applied to irritable ulcers in the form of tincture, it promotes their cure, and allays pain. Cloths dipped in a strong solution, and applied over painful bruises, tumours, or inflamed joints, allay pain. A small piece of solid opium stuffed into a hollow tooth relieves toothache. A weak solution of opium forms a valuable collyrium in ophthalmia. Two drops of the wine of opium dropped into the eye acts as an excellent sedative in blood- shot eye ; or after long-continued inflammation, it is useful in strengthen- ing the eye. Applied as a liniment, in combination with ammonia and oil, or with camphorated spirit, it relieves muscular pain. When com-bined with oil of turpentine, it is useful as a liniment in spasmodic colic. *Used internally*, it acts as a very powerful stimulant ; then as a sedative, and finally as an anodyne and narcotic, allaying pain in the most extraordinary manner, by acting directly upon the nervous system. In acute rheumatism it is a most excel-lent medicine when combined with calomel and tartrate of antimony ; but its exhibition requires the judicious care of a medical man. *Doses of the various preparations.—Confection of opium*, from five grains to half-a-drachm ; *extract of opium*, from one to five grains (this is a valuable form, as it does not produce so much after derangement of the nervous system as solid opium) ; *pills of soap and opium*, from five to ten grains ; *compound*

ipecacuanha powder ("Dover's Powder"), from ten to fifteen grains ; *compound kino powder*, from five to fifteen grains ; *wine of opium*, from ten minims to one drachm. *Caution.* —Opium is a powerful *poison* when taken in too large a quantity (*see* POISONS, pars. 760—782), and thus should be used with extreme caution. It is on this account that we have omitted some of its preparations. The best antidote for opium is camphor or strong coffee, and generally stimulating the patient. Potassium permanganate in half-grain doses acts as a powerful antidote.

604. ANTISPASMODICS.

Antispasmodics are medicines which possess the power of overcoming the spasms of the muscles, or allaying any severe pain which is not attended by inflammation. The class includes a great many, but the most safe and serviceable are ammonia, assafœtida, galbanum, valerian, bark, ether, camphor, opium, and chloroform ; with the minerals, oxide of zinc and calomel.

1. Ammonia, or Sal Volatile, is an antispasmodic, antacid, stimulant, and diaphoretic. *Used externally*, combined with oil, it forms a cheap and useful liniment, but it should be dissolved in *proof* spirit before the oil is added. One part of this salt, and three parts of extract of belladonna, mixed and spread upon leather, makes an excellent plaster for relieving rheumatic pains. As a local stimulant it is well known, as regards its effects in hysterics, faintness, and lassitude, when applied to the nose, as common smelling salts. It is used *internally* as an adjunct to infusion of gentian in dyspepsia or indigestion, and in moderate doses in gout. *Dose*, from five to fifteen grains. *Caution.*—Overdoses act as a narcotic and irritant poison.

2. Bicarbonate of Ammonia is used internally the same as *sal volatile*. *Dose*, from six to twelve grains. It

is frequently combined with Epsom salts.

3. Solution of Sesquicarbonate of Ammonia, used the same as *sal volatile. Dose*, from half-a-drachm to one drachm, combined with some milky fluid, like almond emulsion.

4. Assafœtida is an antispasmodic, expectorant, excitant, and anthelmintic. *Used internally*, it is extremely useful in dyspepsia, flatulent colic, hysteria, and nervous diseases ; and where there are no inflammatory symptoms, it is an excellent remedy in hooping cough and asthma. *Used locally* as an enema, it is useful in flatulent colic, and convulsions that come on through teething. *Doses of various preparations.—Solid gum,* from five to ten grains as pills ; *mixture,* from half-an-ounce to one ounce ; *tincture,* from fifteen minims to one drachm ; *ammoniated tincture,* from twenty minims to one drachm. *Caution.*—Never give this drug when inflammation exists.

5. Galbanum is stimulant, antispasmodic, expectorant, and deobstruent. *Used externally*, when spread upon leather as a plaster, it assists in dispelling indolent tumours and is useful in weakness of the legs from rickets, being applied as a plaster to the loins. *Employed internally*, it is useful in chronic or old-standing rheumatism and hysteria. *Doses of preparations.*—Of the *gum*, from ten to fifteen grains as pills ; *tincture*, from fifteen minims to one drachm. It may be made into an emulsion with mucilage and water.

6. Valerian is a powerful antispasmodic, tonic, and excitant, acting chiefly on the nervous centres. *Used internally*, it is employed in hysteria, nervous languors, and spasmodic complaints generally. It is useful in low fevers. *Doses of various preparations.—* *Powder*, from ten grains to half-a-drachm, three or four times a day ; *tincture*, from two to four drachms ; *ammoniated tincture*, from one to two drachms ; *infusion*, from two to three ounces or more.

7. Bark, or, as it is commonly called, Peruvian bark, is an antispasmodic, tonic, astringent, and stomachic. *Used externally*, it is an excellent detergent for foul ulcers, and those that heal slowly. *Used internally*, it is particularly valuable in intermittent fever or ague, malignant measles, dysentery, diarrhœa, intermittent rheumatism, St. Vitus's dance, indigestion, nervous affections, malignant sore throat, and erysipelas ; its use being indicated in all cases of debility. *Doses of its preparations*—*Powder*, from five grams to two drachms, mixed in wine, water, milk, syrup, or solution of liquorice ; *infusion*, from one to three ounces ; *decoction*, from one to three ounces ; tincture and compound tincture, each from one to three drachms. *Caution.*— If it causes oppression at the stomach, combine it with an aromatic ; if it causes vomiting, give it in wine or soda water ; if it purges, give opium ; and if it constipates, give rhubarb.

8. Sulphuric Ether is given internally as an antispasmodic in difficult breathing and spasmodic asthma ; also in hysteria, cramp of the stomach, hiccough, locked jaw, and cholera. It is useful in checking sea-sickness. *Dose*, from twenty minims to one drachm. *Caution.*—An overdose produces apoplectic symptoms.

9. Camphor is given internally as an antispasmodic in hysteria, cramp in the stomach, flatulent colic, and St Vitus's dance. *Dose*, from two to twenty grains.

10. Opium is employed internally in spasmodic affections, such as cholera, spasmodic asthma, hooping cough, flatulent colic, and St. Vitus's dance. *Dose*, from one-sixth of a grain to two grains of the solid opium, according to the disease.

11. Oxide of Zinc is an antispasmodic, astringent, and tonic. *Used externally*, as an ointment, it forms an excellent astringent in affections of the eyelids, arising from relaxation ; or as a powder, it is an excellent detergent for unhealthy ulcers. *Used internally*, it has proved efficacious in St. Vitus's dance, and some other spasmodic affections. *Dose*, from one to six grains twice a day.

12. Calomel is an antispasmodic, alterative, purgative, and errhine. *Used internally*, combined with opium, it acts as an antispasmodic in locked jaw, cholera, and many other spasmodic affections. As an alterative it has been found useful in leprosy and itch, when combined with antimonials and guaiacum, in enlargement of the liver and glandular affections. It acts beneficially in dropsies, by producing watery motions. In typhus it is of great benefit when combined with antimonials ; and it may be given as a purgative in almost any disease, provided there is not any inflammation of the bowels, irritability of the system, disease of kidneys, or great debility. *Dose*, as an alterative, from one to five grains, daily ; as a cathartic, from five to fifteen grains ; to produce ptyalism, or salivation, from one to two grains, in a pill, with a quarter of a grain of opium, night and morning. *Caution.*—When taking calomel, exposure to cold or dampness should be guarded against, as such an imprudence would bring out an eruption of the skin, attended with fever. When this does occur, leave off the calomel, and give bark, wine, and purgatives ; take a warm bath twice a day, and powder the surface of the body with powdered starch.

605. TONICS.

Tonics are given to improve the tone of the system, and restore the natural energies and general strength of the body. They consist of quassia, gentian, camomile, wormwood, and angostura bark.

1. Quassia is a simple tonic, and can be used with safety by any one, as it does not increase the animal heat, or quicken the circulation. *Used internally*, in the form of infusion, it has been found of great benefit in indigestion and nervous irritability, and is useful after bilious fevers and diarrhœa. *Dose*, of the *infusion*, from one and a half to two ounces, three times a day.

2. Gentian is an excellent tonic and stomachic ; but when given in large doses, it acts as an aperient. It is *used internally* in all cases of general debility, and when combined with bark is used in intermittent fevers. It has also been employed in indigestion, and it is sometimes used, combined with sal volatile, in that disease ; but at other times alone, in the form of infusion. After diarrhœa, it proves a useful tonic. Its infusion is sometimes applied *externally* to foul ulcers. *Dose*, of the *infusion*, one and a half to two ounces ; of the *tincture*, one to four drachms ; of the *extract*, from ten to thirty grains.

3. Camomile.—The flowers of the camomile are tonic, slightly anodyne, antispasmodic, and emetic. They are *used externally* as fomentations, in colic, face-ache, and tumours, and to unhealthy ulcers. They are *used internally* in the form of infusion, with carbonate of soda, ginger, and other stomachic remedies, in dyspepsia, flatulent colic, debility following dysentery and gout. Warm infusion of the flowers acts as an emetic ; and the powdered flowers are sometimes combined with opium or kino, and given in intermittent fevers. *Dose*, of the *powdered* flowers, from ten grains to one drachm, twice or thrice a day ; of the *infusion*, from one to two ounces, as a tonic, three times a day : and from six ounces to one pint as an emetic ; of the *extract*, from five to twenty grains.

4. Wormwood is a tonic and anthelmintic. It is *used externally* as a discutient and antiseptic. It is *used internally* in long-standing cases of dyspepsia, in the form of infusion, with or without aromatics. It has also been used in intermittents. *Dose*, of the

infusion, from one to two ounces, three times a day ; of the *powder*, from one to two scruples.

5. Angostura Bark, or Cusparia, is a tonic and stimulant. It expels flatulence, increases the appetite, and produces a grateful warmth in the stomach. It is *used internally* in intermittent fevers, dyspepsia, hysteria, and all cases of debility, where a stimulating tonic is desirable, particularly after bilious diarrhœa. *Dose*, of the *powder*, from ten to fifteen grains, combined with cinnamon powder, magnesia, or rhubarb ; of the *extract*, from three to ten grains ; of the *infusion*, from one to two ounces. *Caution.*— This drug should never be given in inflammatory diseases or hectic fever.

606. ASTRINGENTS.

Astringents are medicines given for the purpose of diminishing excessive discharges, and to act indirectly as tonics. This class includes catechu, kino, oak bark, logwood, rose leaves, chalk, and white vitriol.

1. Catechu is a most valuable astringent. It is *used externally*, when powdered, to promote the contraction of flabby ulcers. As a local astringent it is useful in relaxed uvula, a small piece being dissolved in the mouth ; small, spotty ulcerations of the mouth and throat, and bleeding gums, and for these two affections it is used in the form of infusion to wash the parts. It is *given internally* in diarrhœa, dysentery, and hæmorrhage from the bowels. *Dose*, of the *infusion*, from one to three ounces ; of the *tincture*, from one to four drachms ; of the *powder*, from ten to thirty grains. *Caution.*—It must not be given with soda or any alkali ; nor metallic salts, albumen, or gelatine, as its property is destroyed by this combination.

2. Kino is a powerful astringent. It is *used externally* to ulcers, to give tone to them when flabby, and discharging foul and thin matter. It is *used internally* in the same diseases as catechu. *Dose,* of the powder, from ten to fifteen grains ; of the *tincture,* from one to two drachms ; of the *compound powder,* from ten to twenty grains ; of the *infusion,* from a half to one and a half ounces. *Caution.*—Kino is used in combination with calomel, when salivation is intended, to prevent, by its astringency, the action of the calomel on the bowels, and thereby insure its affecting the constitution.

3. **Oak Bark** is an astringent and tonic. It is *used externally* in the form of decoction, to restrain bleeding from lacerated surfaces. As a local astringent, it is used in the form of decoction, as a gargle in sore throat and relaxed uvula. It is *used internally* in the same diseases as catechu, and when combined with aromatics and bitters, in intermittent fevers. *Dose* of the *powder,* from fifteen to thirty grains ; of the *decoction,* from two to eight drachms.

4. **Logwood** is not a very satisfactory astringent It is *used internally* in diarrhœa, the last stage of dysentery, and a lax state of the intestines. *Dose,* of the extract, from ten grains to one drachm ; of the *decoction* from one to three ounces, three or four times a day.

5. **Rose Leaves** are astringent and tonic. They are *used internally* in spitting of blood, hemorrhage from the stomach, intestines, &c., as a gargle for sore throat, and for the night sweats of consumption. The infusion is frequently used as a tonic with diluted sulphuric acid (oil of vitriol), after low fevers, or in combination with Epsom salts and sulphuric acid in certain states of the bowels. *Dose* of *infusion,* from two to four ounces.

6. **Chalk,** when prepared by washing, becomes an astringent as well as antacid. It is *used internally* in diarrhœa, in the form of mixture, and *externally* as an application to burns, scalds, and excoriations. *Dose* of the *mixture,* fom one to two ounces.

7. **White Vitriol,** or Sulphate of Zinc, is an astringent, tonic, and emetic. It is *used externally* as a collyrium for ophthalmia (*See* EYE WASHES, par. 376) ; it is also very efficacious as a detergent for scrofulous ulcers, in the proportion of three grains of the salt to one ounce of water. It is *used internally* in indigestion, and many other diseases ; *but it should not be given unless ordered by a medical man, as it is a poison.*

607. LOCAL STIMULANTS.

Local stimulants comprise **Emetics, Laxatives** and **Purgatives, Diuretics, Diaphoretics, Expectorants, Sialogogues, Epispastics** and **Rubefacients**.

608. EMETICS.

Emetics are medicines given for the purpose of causing vomiting, as in cases of poisoning. They consist of ipecacuanha, camomile, antimony, copper, zinc, and several others.

1. **Ipecacuanha** is an emetic, diaphoretic, and expectorant. It is *used internally* to excite vomiting, in doses of from ten to twenty grains of the powder, or one to one and a half ounces of the infusion, every half-hour until vomiting takes place. To make it act well and easily, the patient should drink half pints of warm water after each dose of the infusion. As a diaphoretic, it should be given in doses of three grains, mixed with some soft substance, such as crumbs of bread, and repeated every four hours. In dysentery it acts like a charm, but must be given in doses of twenty to thirty grains repeated every three or four hours. *Dose* of the *wine,* from twenty minims to one drachm as a diaphoretic, and from one drachm to one and a half ounces as an emetic. *Caution.*—Do not give more than the doses named above, because, although a safe emetic, yet it is an acrid narcotic poison.

2. Mustard is too well known to require describing. It is an emetic, diuretic, stimulant, and rubefacient. It is *used externally* as a poultice, in cases where a stimulant is required, such as sore throats, rheumatic pains in the joints, cholera, cramps in the extremities, diarrhœa, and many other diseases. Mustard poultices are made of the powder, bread crumbs, and water ; or of one part of mustard to two of flour ; or, especially for children, of linseed meal, mixed with a little of the powder, or having some of the powder slightly sprinkled on the surface. Sometimes a little vinegar is added under the idea that it increases the strength of the poultice, but this is not necessary. When applied it should not be left on too long, as it is apt to cause ulceration of the part. From ten to thirty minutes is quite long enough. When *used internally* as an emetic, a large teaspoonful mixed with a tumbler of warm water generally operates quickly and safely, frequently when other emetics have failed. In dropsy it is sometimes given in the form of whey, which is made by boiling half-an-ounce of the bruised seeds in a pint of milk, and straining off the curd. From three to four ounces of this is to be taken for a dose three times a day.

609. LAXATIVES AND PURGATIVES.

Manna, tamarinds, castor oil, sulphur, and magnesia are *laxatives* ; senna, rhubarb, jalap, colocynth, buckthorn, aloes, cream of tartar, scammony, calomel, Epsom salts, Glauber's salts, sulphate of potash, and Venice turpentine are *purgatives*.

1. Manna is a very gentle laxative, and therefore used for children and delicate persons. *Dose* for *children*, from one to two drachms ; and for *adults*, from one to two ounces, combined with rhubarb and cinnamon water.

2. Tamarinds are generally laxative and refrigerant. As it is agreeable, this medicine will generally be eaten by children when they will not take other medicines. *Dose*, from half to one ounce. As a refrigerant beverage in fevers it is extremely grateful.

3. Castor Oil is a most valuable medicine, as it generally operates quickly and mildly. It is *used externally* combined with citron ointment, as a topical application in common leprosy. It is *used internally* as an ordinary purgative for infants, as a laxative for adults, and in diarrhœa and dysentery. In colic it is very useful and safe ; and also after delivery. *Dose* for *infants*, from forty drops to two drachms ; for *adults*, from half-an-ounce to one and a half ounces.

4. Sulphur.—Sublimed sulphur is laxative and diaphoretic. It is *used externally* in skin diseases, especially itch, both in the form of ointment and as a vapour bath. It is used internally in hemorrhoids, combined with magnesia, as a laxative for children, and as a diaphoretic in rheumatism. *Dose*, from one scruple to two drachms, mixed in milk or with treacle. When combined with an equal proportion of cream of tartar, it acts as a purgative.

5. Magnesia.—*Calcined magnesia* possesses the same properties as the carbonate. *Dose*, from ten to thirty grains, in milk or water. *Carbonate of magnesia* is an antacid and laxative, and is very useful for children when teething, and for heartburn in adults. *Dose*, from a half to two drachms, in water or milk. *Fluid Magnesia* is a useful preparation by whose use is avoided the grittiness that is inseparable from magnesia when taken in the form of powder.

6. Senna is a purgative, but is apt to gripe when given alone ; therefore it is combined with some aromatic, such as cloves or ginger, and the infusion should be made with *cold* instead of hot water. It usually acts in about four hours, but its action should be assisted by drinking warm fluids. *Dose*, of the *confection*, commonly called *"lenitive electuary,"* from one to three or four drachms at bedtime ; of the *infusion*, from one to two ounces ; of the *tincture* from one to two drachms ; of the *syrup* (used for children), from one drachm to one ounce. *Caution.*—Do not give senna, in any form except confection, in hemorrhoids, and never in irritability of the intestines.

7. **Rhubarb** is a purgative, astringent and stomachic. It is *used externally* in the form of powder to ulcers, to promote a healthy action. It is given *internally* in diarrhœa, dyspepsia, and a debilitated state of the bowels. Combined with a mild preparation of calomel, it forms an excellent purgative for children. *Dose*, of the *infusion*, from one to two ounces ; of the *powder*, from one scruple to half-a-drachm as a purgative, and from six to ten grains as a stomachic ; of the *tincture* and *compound tincture*, from one to four drachms ; of the *compound pill*, from ten to twenty grains.

8. **Jalap** is a powerful cathartic and hydrogogue, and is therefore apt to gripe. *Dose*, of the *powder*, from ten to thirty grains, combined with a drop or two or aromatic oil ; of the *compound powder*, from fifteen to forty grains ; of the *tincture*, from one to three drachms ; of the *extract*, from ten to twenty grains. The watery extract is better than the alcoholic.

9. **Colocynth** is a powerful drastic cathartic, and should never be given alone, unless ordered by a medical man, as its action is too violent for some constitutions. *Dose*, of the extract, from five to fifteen grains ; of the compound *extract*, from five to fifteen grains ; of the *compound colocynth pill*, the best of all its preparations, from ten to twenty grains.

10. **Buckthorn** is a brisk purgative for children in the form of syrup.

Dose of the *syrup*, from one to six drachms.

11. **Aloes** is a purgative and cathartic in large, and tonic in smaller doses. *Dose*, of *powder*, from two to ten grains, combined with soap, bitter extracts or other purgative medicines, and given in the form of pills ; of the *compound pill*, from five to twenty grains ; of the *pill of aloes* and *myrrh*, from five to twenty grains ; of the *tincture* from four drachms to one ounce ; of the *compound tincture*, from one to four drachms ; of the *extract*, from six to ten grains ; of the *compound decoction*, from four drachms to two ounces.

12. **Cream of Tartar** is a purgative and refrigerant. It is *used internally* in dropsy, especially of the belly, in doses of from one scruple to one drachm. As a refrigerant drink it is dissolved in hot water, and sweetened with sugar, and is used in febrile diseases, care being taken not to allow it to rest too much upon the bowels. *Dose*, as a *purgative*, from two to four drachms, as a *hydrogogue*, from four to six drachms, mixed with honey or treacle. *Caution.*—Its use should be followed by tonics, especially gentian and angostura.

13. **Scammony** is a drastic purgative, generally acting quickly and powerfully ; sometimes producing nausea, and even vomiting, and being very apt to gripe. It is *used internally*, to produce watery evacuations in dropsy, to remove intestinal worms and correct the slimy motions of children. *Dose*, of the *powder*, from five to sixteen grains, given in liquorice water, treacle, or honey ; of the *confection*, from twenty to thirty grains. *Caution.*—Do not give it in an irritable or inflamed state of the bowels.

14. **Epsom Salts** is a purgative and diuretic. This medicine generally operates quickly, and therefore is extremely useful in acute diseases. It is found to be beneficial in dyspepsia when combined with infusion of

gentian and a little ginger. It forms an excellent enema with olive oil. *Dose*, from a half to two ounces, dissolved in warm tea or water. Infusion of roses partially covers its taste and assists its action. *Note* that with regard to Epsom salts, the *larger in reason* is the amount of water in which they are taken, the *smaller* the dose of salts required : thus, half-an-ounce properly dissolved may be made a strong dose. The action and efficacy of Epsom salts may be greatly increased by adding one grain of tartar emetic to a dose of salts.

15. **Glauber's Salt** is a very good purgative. *Dose*, from a half to two ounces, dissolved in warm water.

16. **Sulphate of Potash** is a cathartic and deobstruent It is *used internally*, combined with aloes or rhubarb, in obstructions of the bowels, and is an excellent saline purgative in dyspepsia and jaundice. *Dose*, from ten grains to one drachm.

17. **Venice Turpentine** is cathartic, diuretic, stimulant, and anthelmintic. It is *used externally* as a rubefacient, and is given *internally* in flatulent colic, in tapeworm, rheumatism, and other diseases. *Dose*, as a *diuretic*, from ten grains to one drachm ; as a *cathartic*, from ten to twelve drachms ; as an *anthelmintic*, from one to two ounces every eight hours, till the worm be ejected.

610. DIURETICS.

Diuretics are medicines which promote an increased secretion of urine. They consist of nitre, acetate of potassa, squills, juniper, oil of turpentine, and others, vegetable and mineral

1. **Nitre** is a diuretic and refrigerant. It is *used externally* as a detergent when dissolved in water, and as a lotion to inflamed and painful rheumatic joints. It is given *internally* in doses of from ten grains to half-a-drachm, or even one drachm ; in spitting blood it is given, in one drachm doses with great benefit. It is beneficial in sore throat, a

few grains being allowed to dissolve in the mouth.

2. **Acetate of Potassa** is diuretic and cathartic It is given *internally* as a diuretic, in combination with infusion of quassia ; in dropsy, in doses of from one scruple to one drachm, every three or four hours. *Dose*, as a *cathartic*, from two to three drachms.

3. **Squills** is diuretic and expectorant when given in small doses ; and emetic and purgative when given in large doses. It is *used internally* in dropsy, in combination with calomel and opium ; in asthma, with ammoniacum ; in catarrh, in the form of oxymel. *Dose*, of the *dried bulb powdered*, from one to two grains every six hours ; of the *compound pill*, from ten to fifteen grains ; of the *tincture*, from ten minims to half-a-drachm ; of the *oxymel*, from a half to two drachms ; of the *vinegar*, from twenty minims to two drachms.

4. **Juniper** is diuretic and stomachic. It is given *internally* in dropsy. *Dose*, of the *infusion*, from two to three ounces every four hours ; of the *oil*, from one to five minims.

5. **Oil of Turpentine** is a diuretic, anthelmintic, and rubefacient. It is *used externally* in flatulent colic, sprinkled over flannels dipped in hot water and wrung out dry. It is *used internally* in the same disease as Venice turpentine. *Dose*, from five minims to two drachms.

611. DIAPHORETICS.

Diaphoretics are medicines given to increase the secretion from the skin by sweating. They comprise acetate of ammonia, calomel, antimony, opium, camphor, sarsaparilla.

1. **Solution of Acetate of Ammonia** is a most useful diaphoretic. It is *used externally* as a discutient, as a lotion to inflamed milk-breasts, as an eye-wash, and a lotion in scald head. It is given *internally* to promote perspiration in febrile diseases, which it does most effectually, especially when

combined with camphor mixture. This is the article so frequently met with in prescriptions, and called spirits of mindererus. *Dose*, from a half to one and a half ounces every three or four hours.

2. Antimony in the form of Tartar Emetic is diaphoretic, emetic, expectorant, alterative, and rubefacient. It is *used externally* as an irritant in white swellings and deep-seated inflammations, in the form of an ointment. It is given *internally* in pleurisy, bilious fevers, and many other diseases, but its exhibition requires the skill of a medical man, to watch its effects. *Dose*, from one-sixth of a grain to four grains. *Caution.*—It is a *poison*, and therefore requires great care in its administration.

3. Antimonial Powder is a diaphoretic, emetic, and alterative. It is given *internally* in febrile diseases, to produce determination to the skin, and is useful in rheumatism, when combined with opium or calomel. *Dose*, from three to ten grains every four hours, taking plenty of warm fluids between each dose.

4. Sarsaparilla is diaphoretic, alterative, diuretic, and tonic. It is given *internally* in cutaneous diseases, old-standing rheumatism, scrofula, and debility. *Dose*, of the *decoction*, from four to eight ounces ; of the *compound decoction*, from four to eight ounces ; of the *extract*, from five grains to one drachm.

612. EXPECTORANTS.

Expectorants are medicines given to promote the secretion from the windpipe, &c. They consist of antimony, ipecacuanha, squills, ammoniacum, and tolu.

1. Ammoniacum is an expectorant, antispasmodic, diuretic, and deobstruent. It is *used externally* as a discutient, and is given internally, with great benefit in asthma, hysteria, and chronic catarrh. *Dose*, from ten to twenty grains.

2. Tolu is an excellent expectorant, when there are no inflammatory symptoms. It is given *internally* in asthma and chronic catarrh. *Dose*, of the *balsam*, from five to thirty grains, combined with mucilage and suspended in water ; of the *tincture,* from a half to one drachm ; of the *syrup*, from a half to four drachms.

613. SIALOGOGUES.

These are given to increase the flow of saliva or spittle. They consist of ginger and calomel, pelletory of Spain, tobacco, the acids, and some others.

Ginger is a sialogogue, carminative, and stimulant. It is *used internally* in flatulent colic, dyspepsia, and to prevent the griping of medicines. When chewed, it acts as a sialogogue, and is therefore useful in relaxed uvula. *Dose*, from ten to twenty grains of the powder ; of the *tincture*, from ten minims to one drachm.

614. EPISPASTICS AND RUBEFACIENTS.

These are remedies which are applied to blister and cause redness of the surface. They consist of cantharides, ammonia, Burgundy pitch, and mustard.

1. Cantharides, or Spanish Flies, when used internally, are diuretic and stimulant ; and epispastic and rubefacient when applied externally. *Mode of application.*—A portion of the blistering plaster is spread with the thumb upon brown paper, linen, or leather, to the size required ; its surface then *slightly* moistened with olive oil and sprinkled with camphor, and the plaster applied by a *light* bandage : or it is spread on adhesive plaster, and attached to the skin by the adhesive margin of the plaster. *Caution.*—If a blister is to be applied to the head, shave it at least ten hours before it is put on ; it is better to place a thin piece of gauze wetted with vinegar between the skin and the blister. If a distressing feeling be

experienced about the bladder, give warm and copious draughts of linseed tea, milk, or decoction of quince seeds, and apply warm fomentations of milk and water to the blistered surface. The *period required* for a *blister* to remain on varies from eight to ten hours for adults, and from twenty minutes to two hours for children : as soon as it is removed, if the blister is not raised, apply a "spongio-piline" poultice, and it will then rise properly. When it is required to act as a rubefacient, the blister should remain on from one to three hours for adults, and from fifteen to forty minutes for children. *To dress a blister.*—Cut the bag of cuticle containing the serum at the lowest part, by snipping it with the scissors, so as to form an opening like this— V ; and then apply a piece of calico, spread with spermaceti or some other dressing. Such is the ordinary method ; but a much better and more expeditious plan, and one that prevents all pain and inconvenience in the healing, is, after cutting the blister as directed above, to immediately cover it with a warm bread and water poultice for about an hour and a half, and on the removal of the poultice to dust the raw surface with violet powder ; apply a handkerchief to retain the powder, and lastly dust the part every two hours. It will be healed in twelve hours. *Caution.*—Never attempt to take cantharides internally, except under the advice of a medical man, as it is a poison, and requires extreme caution in its use.

2. **Burgundy Pitch** is warmed and spread upon linen or leather and applied over the chest in cases of catarrh, difficult breathing, and hooping cough ; over the loins in debility or lumbago ; and over any part that it is desirable to excite a mild degree of inflammation in.

615. CHEMICAL REMEDIES.

These comprise **Refrigerants, Antacids, Antalkalies,** and **Escharotics.**

616. REFRIGERANTS.

These are medicines given for the purpose of suppressing an unnatural heat of the body. They are Seville oranges, lemons, tamarinds, nitre, and cream of tartar.

1. **Seville Oranges** and sweet oranges are formed into a refrigerant beverage, which is extremely grateful in febrile diseases. The *rind* is an agreeable mild tonic, carminative, and stomachic. *Dose*, of the *tincture*, from one to four drachms ; of the *infusion*, from one to two ounces.

2. **Lemons** are used to form a refrigerant beverage, which is given to quench thirst in febrile and inflammatory diseases. Lemon *juice* given with carbonate of potash (half-an-ounce of the juice to twenty grains of the salt), and taken while effervescing, allays vomiting ; a tablespoonful, taken occasionally, allays hysterical palpitations of the heart. It is useful in scurvy caused by eating too much salt food, but requires to be taken with sugar. The rind forms a nice mild tonic and stomachic in certain forms of dyspepsia. *Dose* of the *infusion* (made the same as from orange peel), from one to two ounces.

617. ANTACIDS.

These are given to correct acidity in the system. They are soda, ammonia, chalk and magnesia.

Soda, Carbonate of, and **Sesqui-carbonate of Soda,** are antacids and deobstruents. They are *used internally* in acidity of the stomach and dyspepsia. *Dose* of both preparations, from 10 grains to half-a-drachm.

618. ANTALKALIES.

These are given to neutralize an alkaline state of the system. They are citric acid, lemon juice, and tartaric acid.

1. **Citric Acid** is used to check profuse sweating, and as a substitute for lemon juice when it cannot be procured. *Dose*, from ten to thirty grains.

2. Tartaric Acid, when largely dilated, forms an excellent refrigerant beverage and antalkali. It enters into the composition of extemporaneous soda and Seidlitz waters. *Dose,* from ten to thirty grains.

619. ESCHAROTICS.

These are remedies used to destroy the vitality of a part. They comprise bluestone, lunar caustic, and solution of chloride of zinc.

1. Bluestone, or Sulphate of Copper, is used in a solution of from four to fifteen grains to the ounce of water, and applied to foul and indolent ulcers, by means of rag dipped in it. It is rubbed in substance on fungous growths, warts, &c, to destroy them. *Caution.*—It is a poison.

2. Lunar Caustic, or Nitrate of Silver, is an excellent remedy in erysipelas when applied in solution (one drachm of the salt to one ounce of water), which should be brushed all over the inflamed part, and for an inch beyond it. This blackens the skin, but it soon peels off. To destroy warts, proud flesh, and unhealthy edges of ulcers, &c., it is invaluable ; and as an application to bed sores, pencilled over with a solution of the same strength, and in the same manner as for erysipelas. *Caution.*—It is a poison.

3. Solution of Chloride of Zinc, more commonly known as Sir William Burnett's "Disinfecting Fluid," is a valuable escharotic in destroying the parts of poisoned wounds, such as the bite of a mad dog. It is also very useful in restoring the hair after the scalp has been attacked with ring-worm ; but its use requires extreme caution, as it is a powerful escharotic. In itch, diluted (one part to thirty-two) with water, it appears to answer very well. *Caution.*—It is a most powerful poison.

620. MECHANICAL REMEDIES.

These comprise **Anthelmintics, Demulcents, Diluents,** and **Emollients.**

621. ANTHELMINTICS.

These are medicines given for the purpose of expelling or destroying worms. They are cowhage, scammony, male fern root, calomel, gamboge, santonin, and turpentine.

1. Cowhage is used to expel the round worm, which it does by wounding it with the fine prickles. *Dose* of the *confection,* for a child three or four years old, a teaspoonful early, for three mornings, followed by a dose of castor oil. (*See* par. 491.) The mechanical anthelmintics are strictly confined to those agents which kill the worm in the body by piercing its cuticle with the sharp darts or spiculæ of the cowhage hairs, or the fine metallic points of powdered tin (*pulvis stanni*). When these drops are employed, they should be given in honey or treacle for ten or fifteen days, and an aperient powder every fourth morning, to expel the killed worms. This remedy should only be adopted under the advice of a medical man, as it is liable to cause some inflammation of the bowel if given in excess.

2. Male Fern Root is a powerful anthelmintic, and an astringent. It is used to kill tapeworm. *Dose,* three drachms of the powdered root mixed in a teacupful of water, to be taken in the morning while in bed, and followed by a brisk purgative two hours afterwards ; or from a tablespoonful to a wineglassful, according to age, to be taken early in the morning. (*See* par. 472.)

3. Gamboge is a powerful drastic and anthelmintic. It is *used internally* in dropsy, and for the expulsion of tapeworm ; but its use requires caution, as it is an irritant poison. *Dose,* from two to six grains, in the form of pills, combined with colocynth, soap, rhubarb, or bread-crumbs.

4. Santonin in doses of one to two grains for a child, and two to six grains for an adult. If given over-night and followed by castor oil in the morning, is fatal to the round worm.

622. DEMULCENTS.

These are used to diminish irritation and soften parts by protecting them with a viscid matter. They are tragacanth, linseed, marsh-mallow, mallow, liquorice, arrowroot, isinglass, suet, wax, and almonds.

1. Tragacanth is used to allay tickling cough, and lubricate abraded parts. It is usually given in the form of mucilage. *Dose*, from ten grains to one drachm, or more.

2. Linseed is emollient and demulcent. It is *used externally*, in the form of powder or "meal," as a poultice ; and the oil, combined with lime water, is applied to burns and scalds. It is *used internally* as an infusion in diarrhœa, dysentery, and irritation of the intestines after certain poisons, and in catarrh. The best form of linseed meal is that which is obtained from seed from which the oil has not been extracted. *Dose*, of the *infusion*, as much as the patient pleases.

3. Marsh-Mallow *used internally* in the same diseases as linseed. The leaves are *used externally* as a fomentation, and the boiled roots are bruised and applied as an emollient poultice. *Dose*, the same as for linseed.

4. Mallow is *used externally* as a fomentation and poultice in inflammation, and the infusion is *used inlemally* in dysentery, diseases of the kidneys, and the same diseases as marsh-mallow and linseed. It is also used as an enema. *Dose*, same as for linseed and marsh-mallow.

5. Liquorice is an agreeable demulcent, and is given in the form of decoction in catarrh, and some forms of dyspepsia, and the extract is used in catarrh. *Dose*, of the *extract*, from ten grains to one drachm ; of the *decoction*, from two to four ounces.

6. Arrowroot, isinglass, almonds, suet, and wax, are too well-known to require descriptions. (*See* par. 380,

for "Almond Confection" for preparations.)

623. DILUENTS.

These are chiefly watery compounds, such as weak tea, water, thin broth, gruel, weak infusions of balm, horehound, pennyroyal, ground-ivy, mint, and sage.

624. EMOLLIENTS.

These consist of unctuous remedies, such as cerates and ointments, and any materials that combine heat with moisture—poultices of bread, bran, linseed meal, carrots, and turnips. (*See* par. 701.)

625. TERMS USED TO EXPRESS THE PROPERTIES OF MEDICINES.

1. Absorbents are medicines which destroy acidity in the stomach and bowels, such as magnesia, prepared chalk, &c.

2. Alteratives are medicines which restore health to the constitution, without producing any sensible effect, such as sarsaparilla, sulphur, &c.

3. Analeptics are medicines that restore the strength which has been lost by sickness, such as gentian, bark, &c.

4. Anodynes are medicines which relieve pain, and they are divided into three kinds, *sedatives*, *hypnotics*, and *narcotics* (*See* these terms) ; camphor is anodyne as well as narcotic.

5. Antacids are medicines which destroy acidity, such as lime, magnesia, soda, &c.

6. Antalkalies are medicines given to neutralize alkalies in the system, such as citric, nitric, and sulphuric acids, &c.

7. Anthelmintics are medicines used to expel and destroy worms from the stomach and intestines, such as turpentine, cowhage, male fern, &c.

8. Antibilious are medicines which are useful in bilious affections, such as calomel, &c.

9. Antirheumatics are medicines

used for the care of rheumatism, such as colchicum, iodine of potash, &c.

10. Antiscorbutics are medicines against scurvy, such as citric acid, &.

11. Antiseptics are substances used to correct putrefaction, such as bark, camphor, charcoal, vinegar, and creosote.

12. Antispasmodics are medicines which possess the power of overcoming spasms of the muscles, or allaying severe pain from any cause unconnected with inflammation, such as valerian, ammonia, opium, and camphor.

13. Aperients are medicines which move the bowels gently, such as rhubarb, manna, and grey powder.

14. Aromatics are cordial, spicy, and agreeably-flavoured medicines, such as cardamoms, cinnamon, &c.

15. Astringents are medicines which contract the fibres of the body, diminish excessive discharges, and act indirectly as tonics, such as oak bark, galls, &c.

16. Attenuants are medicines which are supposed to thin the blood, such as ammoniated iron, &c.

17. Balsamics are medicines of a soothing kind, such as tolu, Peruvian balsam, &c.

18. Carminatives are medicines which allay pain in the stomach and bowels, and expel flatulence, such as aniseed water, &c.

19. Cathartics are strong purgative medicines, such as jalap, &c.

20. Cordials are exhilarating and warming medicines, such as aromatic confection, &c.

21. Corroborants are medicines and food which increase the strength, such as iron, gentian, meat, and wine.

22. Demulcents correct acrimony, diminish irritation, and soften parts by covering their surfaces with a mild and viscid matter, such as linseed-tea, gum, mucilage, honey, and marsh-mallow.

23. Deobstruents are medicines which remove obstructions, such as iodide of potash, &c.

24. Detergents clean the surfaces over which they pass, such as soap, &c.

25. Diaphoretics produce perspiration, such as tartrate of antimony, James's powder, and camphor.

26. Digestives are remedies applied to ulcers or wounds, to promote the formation of matter, such as resin, ointments, warm poultices, &c.

27. Discutients possess the power of repelling or resolving tumours, such as galbanum, mercury, and iodine.

28. Diuretics act upon the kidneys and bladder, and increase the flow of urine, such as nitre, squills, cantharides, camphor, antimony, and juniper.

29. Drastics are violent purgatives, such as gamboge, &c.

30. Emetics produce vomiting, or the discharge of the contents of the stomach, such as mustard and hot water, tartar-emetic, ipecacuanha, sulphate of zinc, and sulphate of copper.

31. Emmenagogues are medicines which exercise a direct action on the uterus or womb, provoking the natural periodical secretion, such as castor, assafœtida, galbanum, iron, mercury, aloes, hellebore, savine, ergot of rye, juniper, and pennyroyal.

32. Emollients are remedies used externally to soften the parts they are applied to, such as spermaceti, palm oil, &c.

33. Epispastics are medicines which blister or cause effusion of serum under the cuticle, such as Spanish flies, Burgundy pitch, rosin, and galbanum.

34. Errhines are medicines which produce sneezing, such as tobacco, &c.

35. Escharotics are medicines which corrode or destroy the vitality of the part to which they are applied, such as lunar caustic, &c.

36. Expectorants are medicines which increase expectoration, or the discharge from the bronchial tubes, such as ipecacuanha, squills, opium, ammonicum.

37. Febrifuges are remedies used in fevers, such as all the antimonials, bark, quinine, mineral acids, arsenic.

38. Hydragogues are medicines which have the effect of removing the fluid of dropsy, by producing watery evacuations, such as gamboge, calomel, &c.

39. Hypnotics are medicines that relieve pain by procuring sleep, such as hops, henbane, morphia, poppy.

40. Laxatives are medicines which cause the bowels to act rather more than is natural, such as manna, &c.

41. Narcotics are medicines which cause sleep or stupor, and allay pain, such as opium, &c.

42. Nutrients are remedies that nourish the body, such as sugar, sago, &c.

43. Paregorics are medicines which actually assuage pain, such as compound tincture of camphor, henbane, hops, opium.

44. Prophylactics are remedies employed to prevent the attack of any particular disease, such as quinine, &c.

45. Purgatives are medicines that promote the evacuation of the bowels, such as senna, aloes, jalap, salts.

46. Refrigerants are medicines which suppress an unusual heat of the body, such as wood-sorrel, tamarind, &c.

47. Rubefacients are medicaments which cause redness of the skin, such as mustard, &c.

48. Sedatives are medicines which depress the nervous energy, and destroy sensation, so as to compose, such as foxglove. (*See* PAREGORICS.)

49. Sialogogues are medicines which promote the flow of saliva, or spittle, such as salt, calomel, &c.

50. Soporifics are medicines which induce sleep, such as hops, &c.

51. Stimulants are remedies which increase the action of the heart and arteries, or the energy of the part to which they are applied, such as food, wine, spirits, ether, sassafra, which is an internal stimulant, and savine, which is an external one.

52. Stomachics restore the tone of the stomach, such as gentian, &c.

53. Styptics are medicines which constrict the surface of a part, and prevent the effusion of blood, such as kino, Friar's balsam, extract of lead, and ice.

54. Sudorifics promote profuse perspiration or sweating, such as ipecacuanha, antimony, James's powder, ammonia.

55. Tonics give general strength to the constitution, restore the natural energies, and improve the tone of the system, such as all the vegetable bitters, most of the minerals, also some kinds of food, wine, and beer.

56. Vesicants are medicines which blister, such as strong liquid ammonia, &c.

626. RULES FOR THE PRESERVATION OF HEALTH.

627. Pure Atmospheric Air is composed of nitrogen, oxygen, and a *very* small proportion of carbonic acid gas. Air once breathed has lost the chief part of its oxygen, and acquired a proportionate increase of carbonic acid gas. *Therefore*, health requires that we breathe the same air once only.

628. Food.—The solid part of our bodies is continually wasting, and requires to be repaired by fresh substances. *Therefore* food which is to repair the loss, should be taken with due regard to the exercise and waste of the body.

629. Pure Water.—The fluid part of our bodies also wastes constantly ; there is but one fluid in animals, which is water. *Therefore*, water only is necessary, and no artifice can produce a better drink.

630. Proportion of Fluid Required.—The fluid of our bodies is to the solid in proportion as nine to one. *Therefore*, a like proportion should prevail in the total amount of food taken.

631. Light exercises an important influence upon the growth and vigour of animals and plants. *Therefore*, our dwellings should freely admit the solar rays.

632. Noxious Gases.—Decomposing animal and vegetable substances yield various noxious gases which enter the lungs and corrupt the blood. *Therefore*, all impurities should be kept away from our abodes, and every precaution be observed to secure a pure atmosphere.

633. Warmth is essential to all the bodily functions. *Therefore*, an equal bodily temperature should be maintained by exercise, by clothing, or by fire.

634. Exercise warms, invigorates, and purifies the body ; clothing preserves the warmth the body generates ; fire imparts warmth externally. *Therefore*, to obtain and preserve warmth, exercise and clothing are preferable to fire.

635. Ventilation.—Fire consumes the oxygen of the air, and produces noxious gases. Therefore, the air is less pure in the presence of candles, gas, or coal fire, than otherwise, and the deterioration should be repaired by increased ventilation.

636. The Skin is a highly-organized membrane, full of minute pores, cells, bloodvessels, and nerves ; it imbibes moisture or throws it off, according to the state of the atmosphere and the temperature of the body. It also "breathes," as do the lungs (though less actively). All the internal organs sympathize with the skin. *Therefore*, it should be repeatedly cleansed.

637. Rest.—Late hours and anxious pursuits exhaust the nervous system, and produce disease and premature death. *Therefore*, the hours of labour and study should be short.

638. Mental and Bodily Exercise are equally essential to the general health and happiness. Therefore, labour and study should succeed each other.

639. Sudden Changes of Temperature.—Sudden alternations of heat and cold are dangerous (especially to the young and the aged). *Therefore*, clothing, in quantity and quality, should be adapted to the alternations of night and day, and of the seasons ; and drinking cold water when the body is hot, and hot tea and soups when cold, are productive of many evils.

640. Indulgences.—Man will live most healthily upon simple solids and fluids, of which a sufficient but temperate quantity should be taken. *Therefore*, over indulgence in strong drink, tobacco, snuff, opium, and all mere indulgences, should be avoided.

641. Moderation in eating and drinking, short hours of labour and study, regularity in exercise, recreation, and rest, cleanliness, equanimity of temper and equality of temperature,— these are the great essentials to that which surpasses all wealth, *health of mind and body.*

642. SPECIAL RULES FOR THE PREVENTION OF CHOLERA.

i. It is impossible to urge too strongly the necessity, in all cases of cholera, of instant recourse to medical aid, and also in every form and variety of indisposition ; for all disorders are found to merge in the dominant disease.

ii. Let immediate relief be sought under disorder of the bowels especially, however slight. The invasion of cholera may thus be readily prevented.

iii. Let every impurity, animal and vegetable, be quickly removed to a distance from the habitation, such as slaughterhouses, pig-sties, cesspools, necessaries, and all other domestic nuisances.

iv. Let all uncovered drains be carefully and frequently cleansed.

v. Let the grounds in and around the habitation be drained, so as effectually to carry off moisture of every kind.

vi. Let all partitions be removed from within and without habitations, which unnecessarily impede ventilation.

vii. Let every room be daily thrown open for the admission of fresh air ; this should be done about noon, when the atmosphere is most likely to be dry.

viii. Let dry scrubbing be used in domestic cleansing in place of water cleansing.

ix. Let excessive fatigue, and exposure to damp and cold, especially during the night, be avoided.

x. Let the use of cold drinks and acid liquors, especially under fatigue, be avoided, or when the body is heated.

xi. Let the use of cold acid fruits and vegetables be avoided.

xii. Let excess in the use of ardent and fermented liquors and tobacco be avoided.

xiii. Let a poor diet, and the use of impure water in cooking, or for drinking, be avoided.

xiv. Let the wearing of wet and insufficient clothes be avoided.

xv. Let a flannel or woollen belt be worn round the belly.

xvi. Let personal cleanliness be carefully observed.

xvii. Let every cause tending to depress the moral and physical energies be carefully avoided. Let exposure to extremes of heat and cold be avoided.

xviii. Let crowding of persons within houses and apartments be avoided.

xix. Let sleeping in low or damp rooms be avoided.

xx. Let fires be kept up during the night in sleeping or adjoining apartments, the night being the period of most danger from attack, especially under exposure to cold or damp.

xxi. Let all bedding and clothing be daily exposed during winter and spring to the fire, and in summer to the heat of the sun.

xxii. Let the dead be buried in places remote from the habitations of the living. By the timely adoption of simple means such as these, cholera, or other epidemic, will be made to lose its venom.

643. LAWS WITH REGARD TO INFECTIOUS DISEASES.

i. **Notification of Infectious Diseases.**—By a recent enactment (52 and 53 Vic. c. 72) it is made compulsory that notice of infectious disense shall in all cases be given to the local authority. By section 3 this duty is imposed on the head of the family, or, failing him, the nearest relative of the patient. The notice must be in writing or print, in an approved form, and must be sent to the medical officer of health of the district. In addition to this, the medical man attending the patient must send a certificate, with all particulars, to the same official. Omitting to send either the notice or the certificate, renders the legally responsible person liable to a fine not exceeding £2. Each local authority should publish a list of the diseases to which the act applies in its district.

ii. **Cleansing of Infected Premises.**—The Infectious Diseases (Prevention) Act, 1890, is supplemental to the Act of 1889. By its provisions *Local Authorities* may inspect dairies in cases of infection ascribed to milk ; may require the cleansing and disinfecting of infected premises, bedding, &c. Penalties are imposed on persons ceasing to occupy infected houses without previous disinfection, or giving notice to owner ; and the retention for more than forty-eight hours, except in a mortuary or other suitable place, of the body of a person who has died from an infectious disease, is prohibited except under medical sanction.

644. DISINFECTANTS.

645. FOR SICK ROOMS.

1. **Disinfecting Liquid.**—In a wine bottle of cold water, dissolve two ounces acetate of lead (sugar of lead), and then add two (fluid) ounces of strong nitric acid (aquafortis). Shake the mixture, and it will be ready for use.—A very small quantity of the liquid, in its strongest form, should be used for cleansing all kinds of chamber utensils. In order to remove offensive odours, clean cloths thoroughly moistened with the liquid, diluted with eight or ten parts of water, should be suspended in various parts of the room.—In this case the offensive and deleterious gases are neutralized by chemical action. Fumigation in the usual way is only the substitution of one odour for another. In using the above, or any other disinfectant, let it never be forgotten that *fresh* air, and plenty of it, is cheaper and more effective than any other material.

2. **Charcoal.**—Any room, however offensive it may be, can be perfectively deodorized by means of a few trays filled with a thin layer of freshly-heated wood charcoal. The efficiency of the charcoal may be greatly increased by making it red-hot before using it. This can easily be done by heating it in an iron saucepan covered with an iron lid. When the charcoal is to be applied to inflammable substances, such as wooden floors, &c., of course it must be allowed to cool in close vessels before being used.

3. **Chloride of Lime.**—This substance, which is well known for its bleaching properties, is a useful disinfectant. It will neutralize the foul smell arising from drains, closets, &c., when mixed with water and thrown down the pipes whence the smell proceeds. A little dissolved in a bucket of water, when used in scrubbing rooms and passages, will purify them and render them wholesome, and also whiten the boards. It is sold by oil-men, &c., at 3*d.* or 4*d.* per lb.—a much lower rate than that at which it is sold by chemists.

4. **Carbolic Powder and Fluid.**—Carbolic acid in a fluid state is a highly concentrated disinfectant, and a strong irritant poison. Care should be taken in its use and storage, as many lives have been lost through taking carbolic acid under the impression that it was some medicine or beverage. It is far safer when in the form of powder which has been impregnated with the acid. The powder has a pink colour, and is sold at the rate of 2*d.* per pound by oilmen, &c.

5. **Coffee a Disinfectant.**—Numerous experiments with roasted coffee prove that it is the most powerful means, not only of rendering animal and vegetable effluvia innocuous, but of actually destroying them. A room in which meat in an advanced degree of decomposition had been kept for some time, was instantly deprived of all smell on an open coffee-roaster being carried through it, containing a pound of coffee newly roasted. In another room, exposed to the effluvium occasioned by the clearing out of the dung-pit, so that sulphuretted hydrogen and ammonia in great quantities could be chemically detected, the stench was completely removed in half-a-minute, on the employment of three ounces of fresh-roasted coffee, whilst the other parts of the house were permanently cleared of the same smell by being simply traversed with the coffee-roaster, although the cleansing of the dung-pit continued for several hours after. The best mode of using the coffee as a disinfectant is to dry the raw bean, pound it in a mortar, and then roast the powder on a moderately-heated iron plate, until it assumes a dark brown tint, when it is fit for use. Then sprinkle it on sinks or cess-pools, or lay it on a plate in the room which you wish to have purified. Coffee acid or

coffee oil acts more readily in minute quantities.

6. Sanitas in its various forms is highly esteemed by many persons as a valuable disinfectant.

646. FOR DRAINS.

1. Flush them frequently and wash down with chloride of lime, half pound to a gallon of water, or carbolic powder in same proportion ; or Condy's fluid, two tablespoonfuls to a gallon of water.

2. Borax.—Alone or dissolved in water, and used freely to pour down closets, sinks, &c., it removes all noisome smells, acting as a purifier, and rendering even impure water wholesome. It should be used frequently where sewer gas is suspected.

3. Permanganate of Potash is a most convenient and useful disinfectant. It is cheap, and a small bottle of the crystals should always be kept in the house. For general purposes, one teaspoonful of the crystals dissolved in a gallon of water is the best strength.

647. TO DISINFECT ROOMS AFTER CASES OF FEVER, &c.

All articles of furniture, floors, &c., should be washed well with a solution of carbolic add of a strength of two teaspoonfuls to a quart of water. Afterwards effectually close all openings in rooms by pasting paper over windows, &c. Place in centre of room on a large iron tray, half-a-pound of ordinary sulphur, for every 500 cubic feet of space in room, set fire to the sulphur and leave to burn for two hours. Then open all windows for twenty-four hours. The walls should be stripped and re-papered, ceilings whitewashed, and all woodwork freshly painted.

648. TO DISINFECT CLOTHING.—All old things should be burnt ; soak all linen, &c, in cold water for one hour, and afterwards in boiling water for ten minutes. Articles which cannot be boiled should be exposed to the sun's rays, or to a dry heat of a temp. of 212°.

649. TO DISINFECT PERSONS AFTER INFECTIOUS DISEASES.—Give frequent warm baths and afterwards rub the body all over with ordinary sweet oil or carbolic oil, strength of one in forty. Or give bath of sanitas, eight tablespoonfuls to gallon of water, after well soaping with soft soap. In cases of death, the corpse may be kept perfectly sweet by dusting powdered borax into ears, nose, mouth, under arm-pits, feet, &c., or when any moisture exudes. It will preserve features and skin fresh as in life, and the corpse free from decomposition for a considerable time.

650. HOMŒOPATHY AND ALLOPATHY.

651. Homœopathy is now practised so widely and, indeed, in many families, preferred to the older system, that the Domestic Pharmacopœia could scarcely be considered complete without a brief mention of the principal remedies used and reommended by homœopathic practitioners, and the disorders for which these remedies are specially applicable. The principle of homœopathy is set forth in the Latin words *"similia similibus curantur,"* the meaning of which is "likes are cured by likes." The meaning of this is simply that the homœopathist in order to cure a disease administers a medicine which would produce in a perfectly healthy subject, symptoms *like*, but not *identical* with or the *same* as, the symptoms to counteract which the medicine is given. The homœopathic practitioner therefore, first makes himself thoroughly acquainted with the symptoms that are exhibited by the sufferer ; having ascertained these, in order to neutralize them and restore the state of the patient's health to a state of equilibrium, so to speak, he administers preparations that would produce symptons of a like character in persons in good health. It is not said, be it remembered, that the drug can produce in a healthy person the disease from which the patient is suffering : it is only advanced by homœopathists that the drug given has the power of producing in a person in health, symptoms similar to those of the disease under which the patient is languishing, and that the correct mode of treatment is to counteract the disease symptoms by the artificial production of similar symptoms by medicinal means.

652. Allopathy is the name given to the older treatment of disorders, and the name is obtained from the fact that the drugs given do not produce symptoms corresponding to those of the disease for whose relief they are administered as in homœopathy. The introduction of the term is contemporary with homœopathy itself. It was merely given to define briefly the distinction that exists between the rival modes of treatment, and it has been accepted and adopted by all medical men who have no faith in homœopathy, and the treatment that its followers prescribe.

653. The Treatments Contrasted.—Allopathic treatment is said to be experimental, while Homœopathic treatment is based on certainty, resulting from experience. The allopathist tries various drugs, and if one medicine or one combination of drugs fails, tries another ; but the homœopathist administers only such medicaments as may be indicated by the symptoms of the patient. If two drugs are given, as is frequently, and perhaps generally, the case, it is because the symptoms exhibited are of such a character that they cannot be produced in a healthy person by the action of one and the same drug, and consequently, cannot be counteracted or neuralized by the action of a single drug.

654. HOMŒOPATHIC TREATMENT OF AILMENTS.—Great stress is laid by homœopathists on attention to diet, but not so much so in the present day as when the system was first introduced. The reader will find a list of articles of food that may and may not be taken in par. 686. For complete direction on this point, and on diseases and their treatment and remedies, he must be referred to various standard works on this subject. All that can be done here is to give briefly a few of the more common ailments "that flesh is heir to," with the symptoms by which they are indicated, and the medicines by which they may be alleviated and eventually cured.

655. Asthma, an ailment which should be referred in all cases to the medical practitioner. *Symptoms.* Difficulty of breathing, with cough, either spasmodic and without expectoration, or accompanied with much expectoration. *Medicines.* Aconitum napellus, especially with congestion or slight spitting of blood ; Antimonium tartaricum for wheezing and rattling in the chest ; Arsenicum for chronic asthma ; ipecacuanha ; Nux vomica ; Lobelia, or Stramonium.

656. Bilious Attacks if attended with diarrhœa and copious evacuations of a bright yellow colour. *Medicines.* Bryonia, if arising from sedentary occupations, or from eating and drinking too freely ; or Nux vomica and Mercurius in alternation, the former correcting constipation and the latter nausea, fulness at the pit of the stomach, and a foul tongue.

657. Bronchitis.—*Symptoms.* Catarrh accompanied with fever, expectoration dark, thick and sometimes streaked with blood ; urine dark, thick, and scanty. *Medicines.* Aconitum napellus, especially in earlier stages ; Bryonia for pain in coughing and difficulty of breathing ; Antimonium tartaricum, loose cough with much expectoration and a feeling of, and tendency to, suffocation ; Ipecacuanha, accumulation of phlegm in bronchial tubes, and also for children.

658. Bruises and Wounds.—For all bruises, black eyes, &c., apply Arnica lotion, or Spirit lotion, viz. one of spirit to three of water ; for slight wounds, after washing well with cold water, apply Arnica plaster ; when ordinary means fail to stop bleeding, and for larger wounds, apply concentrated tincture of Calendula.

659. Cold in the Head or Catarrh.—*Symptoms.* Feverish feeling generally, and especially about the head, eyes, and nose, running from, and obstruction of, nose ; soreness and irritation of the throat and bronchial tubes. *Medicines.* Aconitum napellus for feverish symptoms ; Belladonna for sore throat and headache with inclination to cough ; Mercurius for running from nose and sneezing ; Nux vomica for stoppage of nostrils ; Chamomilla for children and women, for whom Pulsatilla is also useful in such cases.

660. Chilblains. —*Symptoms.* Irritation and itching of the skin, which assumes a bluish red colour. *Medicines.* Arnica montana, taken internally or used as outward application, unless the chilblain be broken, when arsenicum should be used. If the swelling and irritation do not yield to these remedies use Belladonna and Rhus toxicodendron.

661. Cholera.—i. Bilious or English Cholera. *Symptoms.* Nausea, proceeding to vomiting, griping of the bowels, watery and offensive evacuations, in which much bile is present, accompanied with weakness and depression. *Medicines.* Bryonia, with ipecacuanha at commencement of attack.

ii. Malignant or Asiatic Cholera. *Symptoms* as in English cholera, but in a more aggravated form, followed by what is called the "cold stage," marked by great severity of griping pain in the stomach, accompanied with frequent

and copious watery evacuations, and presently with cramps in all parts of the body ; after which the extremities become chilled, the pulse scarcely discernible, the result of which is stupor and ultimately death. *Medicines.* Camphor, in the form of tincture, in frequent doses, until the sufferer begins to feel warmth returning to the body, and perspiration ensues. (*See* par. 662.) in the later stages. Cuprum and Veratrum ; give brandy hourly.

662. Tincture of Camphor is one of the most useful of the homœopathic remedies in all cases of colic, diarrhœa, &c. In ordinary cases fifteen drops on sugar may be taken every quarter of an hour until the pain is allayed. In more aggravated cases, and in cases of cholera, a few drops may be taken at intervals of from two to five minutes. A dose of fifteen drops of camphor on sugar tends to counteract a chill if taken soon after premonitory symptoms show themselves, and act as a prophylactic against cold.

663. Colic or Stomach-Ache.—This disorder is indicated by griping pains in the bowels, which sometimes extend upwards into and over the region of the chest. Sometimes the pain is attended with vomiting and cold perspiration. A warm bath is useful, and hot flannels, or a jar or bottle filled with hot water should be applied to the abdomen. *Medicines.* Aconitum napellus, especially when the abdomen is tender to the touch, and the patient is feverish ; Belladonna for severe griping and spasmodic pains ; Bryonia for bilious colic and diarrhœa ; Chamomilla for children.

664. Constipation.—Women are more subject than men to this confined state of the bowels, which will, in many cases, yield to exercise, plain nutritious diet, with vegetables and cooked fruit, and but little bread, and an enema of milk and water, or thin gruel if it is some time since there has been any action of the bowels. *Medicines.* Bryonia, especially for rheumatic patients, and disturbed state of the stomach ; Nux vomica, for persons of sedentary habits, especially males ; Pulsatilla, for women ; Sulphur, or Cascara Sagrada are most useful for constipation that is habitual or of long continuance.

665. Convulsions.—Arising from whatever cause, a warm bath is desirable, and a milk and water enema, if the child's bowels are confined. *Medicines.* Belladonna, Chamomilla, and Potassium bromide, if the convulsions are caused by teething, with Aconitum napellus, if the little patient is feverish ; Aconitum napellus, Cina, and Belladonna, for convulsions caused by worms ; Aconite and Coffœa, when they arise from fright ; Ipecacuanha and Nux vomica, when they have been caused by repletion, or food that is difficult of digestion.

666. Cough.—For this disorder, a light farinaceous diet is desirable, with plenty of out-door exercise and constant use of the sponging-bath. *Medicines.* Aconitum napellus, for a hard, dry, hacking cough, and a combination of ammonium carbonate and ipecacuanha wine. Antimonium, for cough with wheezing and difficulty of expectoration; Belladonna, for spasmodic cough, with tickling in the throat, or sore throat ; Bryonia, for hard, dry cough, with expectorations streaked with blood ; ipecacuanha, for children.

667. Croup.—As this disorder frequently and quickly terminates fatally recourse should be had to a duly qualified practitioner as soon as possible. The disease lies chiefly in the larynx and bronchial tubes, and is easily recognisable by the sharp, barking sound of the cough. A warm bath and mustard poultice will often tend to give relief. *Medicines.* Aconitum napellus, in the earlier stages of the disorder, and spongia and Hepar sulphuris, in the more advanced stages, the latter medicine being desirable when the cough is not so violent and the breathing easier.

668. Diarrhœa.—The *medicines* to be used in this disorder are those which are mentioned under colic and bilious attacks.

669. Dysentery is somewhat similar to diarrhœa, but the symptoms are more aggravated in character, and the evacuations are chiefly mucus streaked with blood. As a local remedy hot flannels or a stone jar filled with hot water and wrapped in flannel, should be applied to the abdomen. *Medicines.* Colocynth and Mercurius in alternation. Ipecacuanha in thirty to forty grain powders acts like a charm.

670. Dyspepsia or Indigestion arises from weakness of the digestive organs. *Symptoms.* Chief among these are habitual costiveness, heartburn and nausea, disinclination to eat, listlessness and weakness, accompanied with fatigue after walking, &c., restlessness and disturbed sleep at night, bad taste in the mouth, with white tongue, especially in the morning, accompanied at times with fulness in the region of the stomach, and flatulence which causes disturbance of the heart. The causes of indigestion are too numerous to be mentioned here, but they may be inferred when it is said that scrupulous attention must be paid to diet (*see* par. 686) ; that meals should be taken at regular and not too long intervals ; that warm drinks, stimulants, and tobacco should be avoided ; that early and regular hours should be kept, with a cold or chilled sponge bath every morning ; and that measures should be taken to obtain a fair amount of exercise, and to provide suitable occupation for both body and mind during the day. *Medicines.* Arnica montana for persons who are nervous and irritable, and suffer much from headache ; Bryonia for persons who are bilious and subject to rheumatism, and those who are listless, disinclined to eat, and have an unpleasant bitter taste in the mouth ; Hepar sulphuris for chronic indigestion and costiveness, attended with tendency to vomit in the morning ; Mecurius in cases of flatulence, combined with costiveness ; Nux vomica for indigestion that makes itself felt from 2 a.m. to 4 a.m., or thereabouts, with loss of appetite and nausea in the morning, and for persons with a tendency to piles, and those who are engaged in sedentary occupations ; Pulsatilla for women generally, and Chamomilla for children.

671. Fevers.—For all fevers of a serious character, such as scarlet fever, typhus fever, typhoid fever, gastric fever, intermittent fever, or ague, &c., it is better to send at once for a medical man. In cases of ordinary fever, indicated by alternate flushes and shivering, a hot dry skin, rapid pulse, and dry foul tongue, the patient should have a warm bath, take but little nourishment, and drink cold water. *Medicine.* Aconitum napellus.

672. Flatulency.—This disorder, which arises from, and is a symptom of, indigestion, frequently affects respiration, and causes disturbance and quickened action of the heart. The patient should pay attention to diet, as for dyspepsia. *Medicines.* China ; Nux vomica ; Charcoal ; Pulsatilla for women, and Chamomilla for children. (*See* DYSPEPSIA, par. 670.)

673. Headache.—This disorder proceeds from so many various causes, which require different treatment, that it is wiser to apply at once to a regular homœopathic practitioner, and especially in headache of frequent occurrence. *Medicines.* Nux vomica when headache is caused by indigestion ; Pulsatilla being useful for women ; Belladonna and Ignatia, for sick headache ; Aconitum napellus and Arsenicum for nervous headache.

674. Heartburn.—For this unpleasant sensation of heat, arising from the stomach, accompanied by a bitter taste, and sometimes by nausea, Nux vomica is a good medicine. Pulsatilla may be taken by women.

675. Indigestion.—(*See* DYSPEPSIA, par. 670.)

676. Measles.—This complaint, which seldom attacks adults, is indicated in its early stage by the usual accompaniments and signs of a severe cold in the head—namely, sneezing, running from the nose and eyelids, which are swollen. The sufferer also coughs, does not care to eat, and feels sick and restless. About four days after the first appearance of these premonitory symptoms, a red rash comes out over the face, neck, and body, which dies away, and finally disappears in about five days. The patient should be kept warm, and remain in one room during the continuance of the disorder, and especially while the rash is out, lest, through exposure to cold in any way, the rash may be checked and driven inwards. *Medicine.* Aconitum napellus, and Pulsatilla, which are sufficient for all ordinary cases. If there be much fever, Belladonna ; and if the rash be driven in by a chill, Bryonia.

677. Mumps.—This disorder is sometimes consequent on measles. It is indicated by the swelling of the of glands under the ears and lower jaw. It is far more painful than dangerous. Fomenting with warm water is useful. *Medicines.* Mercurius generally ; Belladonna may be used when mumps follow an attack of measles.

678. Nettlerash.—This rash, so called because in appearance it resembles the swelling and redness caused by the sting of a nettle, is generally produced by a disordered state of the stomach. *Medicines.* Aconitum napellus, Nux vomica, or Pulsatilla, in ordinary cases ; Arsenicum is useful if there be much fever ; Belladonna if the rash is accompanied with headache. Tar lotions at once stop the irritation of skin.

679. Piles.—The ordinary homœopathic remedies for this painful complaint are Nux vomica and Sulphur.

680. Sprains.—Apply to the part affected a lotion formed of one part of tincture of Arnica to two of water. For persons who cannot use Arnica, in consequence of the irritation produced by it, a lotion of tincture of Calendula may be used in the proportion of one part of the tincture to four of water.

681. Teething.—Infants and very young children frequently experience much pain in the mouth during dentition, and especially when the tooth is making its way through the gum. The child is often feverish, the mouth and gums hot and tender, and the face flushed. There is also much running from the mouth, and the bowels are disturbed, being in some cases confined, and in others relaxed, approaching to diarrhœa. *Medicines.* These are Aconitum napellus, in ordinary cases ; Nux vomica, when the bowels are confined ; Chamomilla, when the bowels are relaxed ; Mercurius, if the relaxed state of the bowels has deepened into diarrhœa ; Belladonna, if there be symptoms of disturbance of the brain.

682. Whooping-Cough.—This disease is sometimes of long duration, for if it shows itself in the autumn or winter months, the little patient will frequently retain the cough until May or even June, when it disappears with the return of warmer weather. Change of air when practicable is desirable, especially when the cough has been of long continuance. In this cough there are three stages. In the first the symptoms are those of an ordinary cold in the head and cough. In the second the cough becomes hard, dry and rapid, and the inhalation of the air, after or during the paroxysm of coughing, produces the peculiar sound from which the disease is named. In the final stage the cough occurs at longer intervals, and the paroxysms are less

violent and ultimately disappear. In this stage the disease is subject to fluctuation, the cough again increasing in frequency of occurrence and intensity if the patient has been unduly exposed to cold or damp, or if the weather is very changeable. Children suffering from whooping-cough should have a light nourishing diet and only go out when the weather is mild and warm. *Medicines.* Aconitum napellus in the very commencement of the disorder, followed by Ipecacuanha and Nux vomica when the second stage is just approaching and during its continuance. These medicines may be continued if necessary during the third stage.

683. Worms.—The presence of worms is indicated by irritation of the membrane of the nose, causing the child to thrust its finger into the nostrils ; by irritation of the lower part of the body ; by thinness, excessive appetite and restlessness in sleep. Children suffering from worms should eat meat freely and not take so much bread, vegetables, and farinaceous food as children generally do. They should have as much exercise as possible in the open air, and be sponged with cold water every morning. The worms that mostly trouble children are the thread worms, which are present chiefly in the lower portions of the intestines, and the round worm. *Medicines, &c.* Administer an injection of weak salt-and-water, and give Aconitum napellus, to be followed by Ignatia and Sulphur in the order in which they are here given. These are the usual remedies for thread worms. For round worms, whose presence in the stomach is indicated by great thinness, sickness and discomfort, and pain in the stomach, Aconitum napellus, Cina, Ignatia and Sulphur are given.

684. HOMŒOPATHIC MEDICINES.

These are given in the form of globules, pilules or tinctures, the latter being generally preferred by homœopathic practitioners. When contrasted with the dose of drugs given by allopathists, the small doses administered by homœopathists must at first sight appear wholly inadequate to the purpose for which they are given; but homœopathists, whose dilution and trituration diffuse the drug given throughout the vehicle in which it is administered, argue that by this *extension of its surface* the active power of the drug is greatly increased ; and that there is reason in this argument is shown by the fact that large doses of certain drugs administered for certain purposes will pass through the system without in any way affecting those organs, which will be acted on most powerfully by the very same drugs when administered in much smaller doses. Thus a small dose of sweet spirit of nitre will act on the skin and promote perspiration, but a large dose will act as a diuretic only, and exert no influence on the skin. Small cases of the principal medicines used in homœopathy can be procured from most chemists, and with each case a little book showing the symptoms and treatment of all ordinary complaints is usually given.

685. Doses in Homœopathy.

The proper quantity for a dose is always given in books and manuals for the homœopathic treatment of disease, but the average doses for adults are from half a drop to one drop of the tincture given in a tablespoonful of water, from two to four pilules, or from three to six globules. In using the tincture it is usual to measure out a few tablespoonfuls of water and to add to it a certain number of drops regulated by the quantity of water that is used. For children medicine is mixed at the same strength, but a less quantity is given.

686. Diet in Homœopathy.

The articles of food that are chiefly recommended when attention to diet is necessary are stale bread, beef, mutton, poultry, fresh game, fish, chiefly cod and flat fish (avoiding mackerel), &c., eggs and oysters. Rice, sago, tapioca, and arrowroot are permitted, as are also potatoes, carrots, turnips, broccoli, cauliflower, asparagus, French beans, and broad beans. Water, milk, cocoa, and chocolate may be drunk. It is desirable to avoid all things that are not specified in the foregoing list. Ripe fruit may be eaten, but unripe fruit, unless cooked, should be scrupulously avoided.

687. DOMESTIC SURGERY.

This will comprise such hints and advice as will enable any one to act on an emergency, or in ordinary trivial accidents requiring simple treatment : and also to distinguish between serious and simple accidents, and the best means to adopt in all cases that are likely to fall under a person's notice. These hints will be of the utmost value to heads of families, to emigrants, and to persons who are frequently called upon to attend the sick. We strongly recommend the Parent, Emigrant, and Nurse, *to read over these directions occasionally,— to regard it as a duty to do so at least three or four times a year,* so as to be prepared for emergencies whenever they may arise. When accidents occur, people are too excited to acquire immediately a knowledge of what they should do ; and many lives have been lost for want of this knowledge. Study, therefore, at moderate intervals, the *Domestic Surgery, Treatment of Poisons, Rules for the Prevention of Accidents, How to Escape from Fires, the Domestic Pharmacopœia, &c.,* which will be found in various pages of *Enquire Within.* And let it be impressed upon your mind that THE INDEX will enable you to refer to *anything* you may require IN A MOMENT. Don't trouble to hunt through the pages ; but when you wish to ENQUIRE WITHIN, remember that the INDEX is the knocker, by which the door of knowledge may be opened.

688. EMERGENCY CARDS.

Messrs. Houlston and Sons, the publishers of this volume, have issued under the title of ENQUIRE WITHIN UPON EVERYTHING EMERGENCY CARDS a series of cards containing in clear bold type concise and lucid instructions as to the best course to pursue in cases of the sudden accidents which will occur even in the best-regulated families. Instructions are given for immediate treatment of Poisonings, Bleedings in various parts of the body, Swallowing Pins, &c., Bites of Dog or Snake, Matters in the Eye, Choking, Suffocation, Convulsions or Fits, Whooping Cough, Teething, Croup, Fainting, Lamp Upsetting, Burns, Scalds, Falls, Broken Bones, Dislocations, Person on Fire, House on Fire, Drowning, &c., also List of Requisites to be kept at hand. The cards are contained in a pretty ornamental case (10 in. × 6½ in.) intended for hanging permanently on the wall of room so as to be *always at hand.* A book is apt to be mislaid, and in sudden accidents people are so frightened, that, even if they know what should be done, they cannot remember. As the set of cards costs but *One Shilling* they should be purchased by every one, for probably they might be the means of saving life and alleviating suffering in many instances.

689. SURGICAL DRESSINGS.

These are substances usually applied to parts for the purpose of soothing, promoting their reunion when divided, protecting them from external injuries, absorbing discharges, protecting the surrounding parts, insuring cleanliness, and as a means of applying various medicines.

690. INSTRUMENTS REQUIRED.

Scissors, a pair of tweezers or simple forceps, a knife, needles and thread, a razor, a lancet, a piece of lunar caustic in a quill, and a sponge.

691. MATERIALS FOR SURGICAL DRESSINGS.

These consist of lint, scraped linen, carded cotton, tow, ointment spread on calico, adhesive plaster, compresses, pads, bandages, poultices, old rags of linen or calico, and water.

692. RULES IN APPLYING DRESSINGS.

i. Always prepare the new dressing before removing the old one.

ii. Always have hot and cold water at hand, and a vessel to place the foul dressing in.

iii. Have one or more persons at hand ready to assist, and, to prevent confusion, tell each person what they are to do before you commence ; thus, one is to wash out and hand the sponges, another to heat the adhesive plaster, or hand the bandages and dressings, and if requisite, a third to support the limb, &c.

iv. Always stand on the outside of a limb to dress it.

v. Place the patient in as easy a position as possible, so as not to fatigue him.

vi. Arrange the bed *after* changing the dressings ; but in some cases you will have to do so before the patient is placed on it.

vii. Never be in a hurry when applying dressings, do it quietly.

viii. When a patient requires moving from one bed to another, the best way is for one person to stand on each *side* of the patient, and each to place an arm behind his back, while he passes his arms over their necks, then let their other arms be passed under his thighs, and by holding each other's hands, the patient can be raised with ease, and removed to another bed. If the leg is injured, a third person should steady it ; and if the arm, the same precaution should be adopted. Sometimes a stout sheet is passed under the patient, and by several people holding the sides, he is lifted without any fatigue or much disturbance.

693. LINT, HOW MADE.

This may be quickly made by nailing a piece of old linen on a board, and scraping its surface with a knife. It is used either alone or spread with ointment. Scraped lint is the fine filaments from ordinary lint, and is used to stimulate ulcers and absorb discharges ; it is what the French call *charpie.*

694. USES OF SCRAPED LINT.

This is made into various shapes for particular purposes. When it is screwed up into a conical or wedge-like shape, it is called a *tent*, and is used to dilate fistulous openings, so as to allow the matter to escape freely, and to plug wounds so as to promote the formation of a clot of blood, and thus arrest bleeding. When rolled into little balls, called *boulettes*, it is used for absorbing matter in cavities, or blood in wounds. Another useful form is made by rolling a mass of scraped lint into a long roll, and then tying it in the middle with a piece of thread ; the middle is then doubled and pushed into a deep-seated wound, so as to press upon the bleeding vessel, while the ends remain loose and assist in forming a clot ; or it is used in deep-seated ulcers to absorb the matter and keep the edges apart. This form is called the *bourdonnet.* Another form is called the *pelote*, which is merely a ball of scraped lint tied up in a piece of linen rag, commonly called a dabber. This is used in the treatment of protrusion of the navel in children.

695. CARDED COTTON is used

as a dressing for superficial burns, and care should be taken to free it from specks, as flies are apt to lay their eggs there, and generate maggots.

696. TOW is chiefly employed as

a padding for splints, as a compress, and also as an outer dressing where there is much discharge from a surface.

697. OINTMENTS are spread on

calicoes, lint, or even thin layers of tow, by means of a knife ; they should not be spread too thick. Sometimes ointment is applied to discharging surfaces on a piece of linen, folded over on itself several times, and then cut at the corners with scissors, in order to make small holes in it The matter discharged passes through these holes, and is received in a layer of tow spread over the linen.

698. ADHESIVE PLASTER is cut

into strips, ranging in width, according to the nature of the wound, &c., but the usual width is about three-quarters of an inch. Isinglass plaster is not so irritating as diachylon, and is more easily removed.

699. COMPRESSES are made

of pieces of linen, calico, lint, or tow, doubled or cut into various shapes, according to the purposes for which they are required. They are used to confine dressings in their places, and to apply an equal pressure on parts. They should be free from darns, hems and knots. Ordinary compresses are square, oblong, and triangular. Compresses are also graduated by placing square pieces of folded cloth on one another, so arranged that they decrease in size each time. They are used for keeping up pressure upon certain parts.

700. PADS are made by sewing tow

inside pieces of linen, or folding linen and sewing the pieces together. They are used to keep off pressure from parts such as that caused by splints in fractures.

701. POULTICES are usually

made of linseed meal, oatmeal, or bread, either combined with water or other fluids ; sometimes they are made of carrots, charcoal, potatoes, yeast, and linseed meal, mustard, &c., but the best and most economical method of preparing them is with a fabric called *"Spongio Piline."*

702. Spongio Piline for poultices. —This material is made of sponge and wool felted together, and backed by India rubber. The method of using is as follows :—A piece of the material of the required form and size is cut off and the edges are pared or bevelled off with a pair of scissors, so that the caoutchouc may come in contact with the surrounding skin, in order to prevent evaporation of the fluid used ; for, as it only forms the vehicle, the various poultices generally used can be employed with much less expenditure of time and money, and increased cleanliness. For example,—a *vinegar* poultice is made by moistening the fabric with distilled vinegar ; an *alum* poultice, by using a strong solution of alum ; a *charcoal* poultice, by sprinkling powdered charcoal on the moistened surface of the material ; a *yeast* poultice, by using warmed yeast, and moistening the fabric with hot water, which is to be well squeezed out previous to the absorption of the yeast ; a *beer* poultice, by employing warm porter-dregs or strong beer as the fluid ; and a *carrot* poultice, by using the expressed and evaporated liquor of boiled carrots. Spongio puline costs about one farthing a square inch and may be obtained of the chemist. As a fomentation it is most invaluable, and by moistening the material with compound camphor liniment or hartshorn, it acts the same as a mustard poultice.

703. Mustard Poultices.—These may be made of the mustard powder alone, or in combination with bread crumbs, or linseed meal. When mustard only is used, the powder should be moistened with water, and the paste thus produced spread on a piece of linen, and covered with muslin to intervene between the mustard and the skin. When mixed with linseed the powder and the meal may be incorporated before water is added, or the meal may be moistened and spread on linen for application and the

mustard be then strewn on the surface, more or less thickly according to the age of the patient. Rigollot's Mustard leaves, which can be procured from any chemist, are now much used in the place of mustard poultices. They only require wetting before application, and they are both clean and economical.

704. BANDAGES.

Bandages are strips of calico, linen, flannel, muslin, elastic webbing, bunting, or some other substance, of various lengths, and from one to six inches wide, free from hems or darns, soft and unglazed. They are better after they have been washed. Their uses are to retain dressings, apparatus, or parts of the body in their proper positions, support the soft parts, and maintain equal pressure.

705. Bandages, Simple and Compound.—The former are single slips rolled up tightly like a roll of ribbon. Sometimes it is rolled from both ends and is called a double-headed bandage. The compound bandages are formed of many pieces.

706. Sizes of Bandages.—Those for the Head should be two inches wide and five yards long ; for the Neck, two inches wide and three yards long ; for the Arm, two inches wide and seven yards long ; for the Leg, two inches and a half wide and seven yards long ; for the Thigh, three inches wide and eight yards long ; and for the Body, four or six inches wide and ten or twelve yards long.

707. To Apply a Single-Headed Bandage, lay the *outside of the end* near to the part to be bandaged, and hold the roll between the little, ring, and middle fingers and the palm of the left hand, using the thumb and forefinger of the same hand to guide it, and the right hand to keep it firm, and pass the bandage partly round the leg towards the left hand. It is sometimes necessary to reverse this order, and therefore it is well to be able to use both hands. Particular parts require a different method of applying bandages, and therefore it is necessary to describe the most useful separately ; and there are different ways of putting on the same bandage, which consist in the manner the folds or turns are made. For example, the *circular* bandage is formed by horizontal turns, each of which overlaps the one made before it ; the *spiral* consists of spiral turns ; the *oblique* follows a course oblique or slanting to the centre of the limb ; and the *recurrent* folds back again to the part whence it started.

708. Circular Bandages are used for the *neck*, to retain dressings on any part of it, or for blisters, setons, &c. ; for the *head*, to keep dressings on the forehead or any part contained within a circle passing round the head ; for the *arm*, previous to bleeding ; for the *leg*, above the knee ; and for the *fingers*, &c.

709. To Confine the Ends of Bandages some persons use pins, others slit two strips into a knot, and some use a strip of adhesive plaster. Always place the point of a pin in such a position that it cannot prick the patient, or the person dressing the limb, or be liable to be drawn out by using the limb ; therefore, as a general rule, turn the head of the pin from the free end of the bandage, or towards the upper part of the limb. The best mode is to *sew* the bandage on. A few stitches will hold it more securely than pins can.

710. The Oblique Bandage is generally used for arms and legs, to retain dressings.

711. The Spiral Bandage is generally applied to the trunk and extremities, but is apt to fall off even when very carefully applied ; therefore the recurrent bandage, which folds back again, is generally used.

712. The Reversing of Recurrent Bandage is the best kind of bandage that we can employ for general purposes. The method of putting it on the leg is as follows :—Apply the end of the bandage that is free, with the outside of it next the skin, and hold this end with the finger and thumb of the left hand, while some one supports the heel of the patient ; then with the right hand pass the bandage over the piece you are holding, and keep it crossed thus, until you can place your right forefinger upon the spot where it crosses the other bandage, where it must be kept firm. Now hold the roll of the bandage in your left hand, with the palm turned upwards, and *taking care to keep that part of the bandage between your right forefinger and the roll in your left hand quite slack* ; turn your left hand over, and bring the bandage down upon the leg ; then pass the roll under the leg towards your right hand, and repeat this until the leg is bandaged up to the knee, taking care *not to drag* the bandage at any time during the process of bandaging. When you arrive at the knee, pass the bandage round the leg in circles just below the knee, and pin it as usual. Bandaging is very easy, and if you once see any one apply a bandage properly, and attend to these rules, there will not be any difficulty ; but bear one thing in mind, without which you will never put on a bandage even decently : and that is, *never to drag* or pull at a bandage, but make the turns while it is slack, and you have your right forefinger placed upon the point where it is to be folded down. When a limb is properly bandaged, the folds should run in a line corresponding to the shin-bone. *Use*, to retain dressings, and for varicose veins.

713. A Bandage for the Chest is always placed upon the patient in a sitting posture ; and it may be put on in circles, or spirally. *Use*, in fractures of the ribs, to retain dressings, and after severe contusions.

714. A Bandage for the Belly is placed on the patient as directed for the chest, carrying it spirally from above downwards. *Use*, to compress belly after dropsy, or retain dressings.

715. The Hand is Bandaged by crossing the bandage over the back of the hand. *Use*, to retain dressings.

716. A Bandage for the Head may be circular, or spiral, or both ; in the latter case, commence by placing one circular turn just over the ears ; then bring down from left to right, and round the head again, so as to alternate a spiral with a circular turn. *Use*, to retain dressings on the head or over the eye ; but this form soon gets slack. The circular bandage is the best, crossing it over both eyes.

717. Bandage for the Foot.— Place the end just above the outer ankle, and make two circular turns, to prevent its slipping ; then bring it down from the inside of the foot over the instep towards the outer part ; pass it under the sole of the foot, and upwards and inwards over the instep towards the inner ankle, then round the ankle and repeat again. *Use*, to retain dressings to the instep, heel, or ankle.

718. Bandage for Leg and Foot. —Commence and proceed as directed in the preceding paragraph ; then continue it up the leg as ordered in the *Recurrent Bandage* (par. 712).

719. HANDKERCHIEFS AS BANDAGES.

As it sometimes happens that it is necessary to apply a bandage at once, and the materials are not at hand, it is desirable to know how to substitute something else *that any one may apply with ease.* This can be readily done with handkerchiefs. Any ordinary handkerchief will do ; but a square of linen folded into various shapes answers better. The shapes generally required are as follows :—The Tri-angle, the Long Square, the Cravat, and the Cord.

1. **The Triangular Handkerchief** is made by folding it from corner to corner. *Use*, as a bandage for the head. *Application*,—Place the base round the head, and the short part hanging down behind, then tie the long ends over it

2. **The Long Square** is made by folding the handkerchief in three. *Use*, as a bandage to the ribs, belly, &c. If one handkerchief is not long enough, sew two together.

3. **The Cravat** is folded as usual with cravats. *Use*, as a bandage for the head, arms, legs, feet, neck, &c.

4. **The Cord** is used to compress vessels, when a knot is made in it, and placed over the vessel to be compressed. It is merely a handkerchief twisted in its diagonal.

720. Two or more Handkerchiefs must sometimes be applied, as in a broken collar-bone, or when it is necessary to keep dressings under the arm. The bandage is applied by knotting the opposite corners of one handkerchief together, and passing the left arm through it, then passing another handkerchief under the right arm, and tying it. By this means we can brace the shoulders well back, and the handkerchief will press firmly over the broken collar-bone : besides, this form of bandage does not readily slip or get slack, but it requires to be combined with the sling, in order to keep the arm steady.

721. For an Inflamed Breast that requires support, or dressings to be kept to it, pass one corner over the shoulder, bring the body of it over the breast, and pass it upwards and backwards under the arm of that side, and tie the opposite corners together.

722. An Excellent Sling is formed by placing one handkerchief around the neck, and knotting opposite corners over the breast bone, then placing the other in triangle under the arm to be supported, with the base near to the hand ; tie the ends over the handkerchief, and pin the top to the other part, after passing it around the elbow.

723. APPARATUS TO RELIEVE PRESSURE OF BED-CLOTHES.

When a person receives a severe contusion of the leg or foot, or breaks his leg, or has painful ulcers over the leg, or is unable from some cause to bear the pressure of the bed-clothes, it is advisable to know how to keep them from hurting the leg. This may be done by bending up a fire-guard, or placing a chair, resting upon the edge of its back and front of the seat, over the leg, or putting a box on each side of it, and placing a plank over them, or using a band-box minus its lid and bottom ; but the best way is to make a *cradle* as it is called. This is done by getting three pieces of wood and three pieces of iron wire, and passing the wire or hoop through the wood. This can be placed to any height, and is very useful in all cases where pressure cannot be borne. Wooden hoops cut in halves answer better than the wire.

724. EXTEMPORIZED SPLINTS.

When a person breaks his leg or arm and *splints* cannot be had directly, get bunches of straw or twigs, roll them up in handkerchiefs, and placing one on each side of the leg or arm, bind another handkerchief firmly around them ; or make a long bag about three inches in diameter, or even more, of coarse linen duck, or carpet, and stuff this full of bran, sawdust, or sand, sew up the ends, and use this the same as the twigs. It forms an excellent extemporaneous splint Another good plan is to get a hat-box made of chip, and cut it into suitable lengths ; or for want of all these, take some bones out of a pair of stays, and run them through a stout piece of rug, protecting the leg with a fold of rug, linen, &c.

A still better splint or set of splints can be extemporized by cutting a sheet of thick pasteboard into proper sized slips, then passing each piece through a basin of hot water to soften it. It is then applied to the fractured limb like an ordinary splint, when it hardens as it dries, taking the exact shape of the part to which it is applied.

725. TO APPLY DRY WARMTH

to any part of the body. Warm some sand or bran and place in the patient's socks, and lay it to the part ; salt put into a paper bag does as well ; or warm water put into a stone jar, and rolled up in flannel.

726. BLEEDING is sometimes

necessary at once in certain accidents, such as concussion, and therefore it is well to know how to do this. First of all, bind up the arm above the elbow with a piece of bandage or a handkerchief pretty firmly, then place your finger over one of the veins at the bend of the arm, and feel if there is any pulsation ; if there is try another vein, and if it does not pulsate or beat, choose that one. Now rub the arm from the wrist towards the elbow, place the left thumb upon the vein, and hold the lancet as you would a pen, and nearly at right angles to the vein, taking care to prevent its going in too far, by keeping the thumb near to the point, and resting the hand upon the little finger. Now place the point of the lancet on the vein, push it suddenly inwards, depress the elbow, and raise the hand upwards and outwards, so as to *cut obliquely across* the vein. When sufficient blood is drawn off, which is known by feeling the pulse at the wrist and near the thumb, bandage the arm. If the pulse feel like a piece of cord, more blood should be taken away, but if it is soft and can be easily pressed, the bleeding should be stopped. When you bandage the arm, place a piece of lint over the opening made by the lancet, and pass a bandage lightly but firmly around the arm, so as to cross it over the bend of the elbow, in form of a figure 8.

727. DRY CUPPING is performed by throwing a piece of paper dipped into spirit of wine, and ignited, into a wine-glass, and inverting it over the part, such as the neck, temples, &c. It thus draws the flesh into the glass, and causes a determination of blood to the part, which is useful in headache, and many other complaints. This is an excellent method of extracting the poison from wounds made by adders, mad dogs, fish, &c.

728. ORDINARY CUPPING is performed the same as dry cupping, with this exception, that the part is scarified or scratched with a lancet, so as to cause the blood to flow ; or by the application of a scarificator, which makes by one action from seven to twenty-one light superficial cuts. Then the glass, with the lighted paper in it, is placed over it, and when sufficient blood has been taken away, the parts are sponged, and a piece of sticking-plaster placed over them.

729. LEECHES AND THEIR APPLICATION.

The leech used for medical purposes is called the *hirudo medicinalis*, to distinguish it from other varieties, such as the horse-leech and the Lisbon leech. It varies from two to four inches in length, and is of a blackish brown colour, marked on the back with six yellow spots, and edged with a yellow line on each side. Formerly leeches were supplied by Lincolnshire, Yorkshire, and other fenny countries, but latterly most of the leeches are procured from France.

730. To Apply Leeches hold them over the part with a piece of linen cloth, or by means or an inverted glass, under which they must be placed. The part should first be thoroughly freed from down or hair by shaving, and all liniments, &c., carefully and effectually cleaned away by washing. If the leech is hungry it will soon bite, but sometimes great difficulty is experienced in getting them to fasten. When this is the case, roll the leech into a little porter, or moisten the surface with a little blood, or milk, or sugar and water.

When applied to the gums, care should be taken to use a leech glass, as they are apt to creep down the patient's throat : a large swan's quill will answer the purpose of a leech glass.

731. Amount of Blood Drawn by a Leech.

Each leech is supposed to abstract about two drachms of blood, or six leeches draw about an ounce ; but this is independent of the bleeding after they have come off, and more blood generally flows then than during the time they are sucking. The total amount of blood drawn and subsequently lost by each leech-bite, is nearly half-an-ounce.

732. To Remove Leeches.—When leeches are gorged they will drop off themselves ; never *tear* them off from a person, but just dip the point of a moistened finger into some salt and touch them with it. After leeches come away, encourage the bleeding by flannels dipped in hot water and wrung out dry, and then apply a warm spongio-piline poultice. If the bleeding is not to be encouraged, cover the bites with a rag dipped in olive oil, or spread with spermaceti ointment, having previously sponged the parts clean.

733. To Stop Continued Bleeding from Leech-Bites apply pressure with the fingers over the part, or dip a rag in strong solution of alum and lay over them, or use the tincture of sesquichloride of iron, or apply a leaf of matico to them, placing the under surface of the leaf next to the skin, or touch each bite with a finely-pointed piece of lunar caustic, or lay a piece of lint soaked in the extract of lead over the bites ; and if all these tried in succession fail, pass a fine needle through a fold of the skin so as to include the bite, and twist a piece of thread round it. Be sure never to allow any one to go to sleep with leech-bites bleeding, without watching them carefully.

734. Treatment of Leeches after Use.

Place them in water containing sixteen per cent of salt, which facilitates the removal of the blood they contain ; and they should afterwards be placed one by one in warm water, and the blood forced out by *gentle* pressure. The leeches should then be thrown into fresh water, which is to be renewed every twenty-four hours : they may then be re-applied after an interval of eight or ten days, and be disgorged a second time. The best plan, however, is to empty the leech by drawing the thumb and forefinger of the right hand along its body from the tail to the mouth, the leech being firmly held at the sucking extremity by the fingers of the left hand. By this means, with a few minutes' rest between each application, the same leech may be useld four or five times in succession.

735. If a Leech be accidentally swallowed, or by any means should get into the body, employ an emetic, or enema of salt and water.

736. SCARIFICATION is useful in severe contusions and inflammation of parts. It is performed by scratching or slightly cutting through the skin with a lancet, holding the lancet as you would a pen when you are ruling lines on paper.

737. ACCIDENTS.

Always send for a Surgeon immediately an accident occurs, but treat as directed until he arrives. Every householder should have a set of the ENQUIRE WITHIN EMERGENCY CARDS *(See* par. 688) *hanging permanently on a wall in his house. The instructions in the following pages are there given in a greally condensed form.*

738. Useful Articles to have always at hand, kept in a dry place and renewed when stale—

Sticking Plaster.
Bandages (old linen).
Safety Pins.
Whitening (in a tin).
Carbonate of Soda (in a tin).
Carron Oil (a pint bottle made of equal parts linseed Oil and Lime Water ; shake when using).
Lime Water (made of unslacked lime, a piece the size of an egg, in wine bottle of cold water).
Ipecacuanha Wine (well corked) or Ipecacuanha Powder.
Salad Oil.

739. SCALDS AND BURNS.

We cannot too firmly impress on the mind of the reader, that in either of these accidents the *first, best,* and *often the only remedies required,* are sheets of wadding, or cotton wool, and in default of these, violet powder, flour, magnesia, chalk, *pure* lard, or oil. The reason these several articles are employed is the same in each instance ; namely, to exclude the air from the injured part ; for if the air can be effectually shut out from the raw surface, and care is taken not to expose the tender part till the new cuticle is formed, the cure may be safely left to nature. The moment a person is called to a case of scald or burn, he should cover the part with a sheet, or a portion of a sheet, of wadding, taking care not to break any blister that may have formed, or stay to remove any burnt clothes that may adhere to the surface, but as quickly as possible envelope every part of the injury from all access of the air, laying one or two more pieces of wadding on the first, so as effectually to guard the burn or scald from the irritation of the atmosphere ; and if the article used is wool or cotton, the same precaution, of adding more material where the surface is thinly covered, must be adopted ; a light bandage finally securing all in their places. Any of the popular remedies recommended below may be employed when neither wool, cotton, nor wadding are to be procured, it being always remembered that that article which will best exclude the air from a burn or scold is the best, quickest, and least painful mode of treatment. And in this respect nothing has surpassed cotton wool, or wadding.

1. If the skin is much injured in burns, spread some linen pretty thickly with chalk ointment, and lay over the part, and give the patient some brandy and water if much exhausted ; then send for a medical man. If not much injured, and very painful, use the same ointment, or apply carded cotton dipped in carron oil, or you may lay cloths dipped in ether over the parts, or cold lotions. Treat scalds in the same manner, or cover with scraped raw potato ; but the chalk ointment is the best. In the absence of all these, cover the injured part with treacle, and dust it thickly over with flour. Lime water beaten up with sweet oil is also an excellent application for burns.

2. **Another Remedy.**—Take chalk and linseed, or common olive oil, and mix them in such proportions as will produce a compound as thick as thin honey ; then add vinegar so as to reduce it to the thickness of treacle ; apply with a soft brush or feather, and renew the application from time to time. Each renewal brings fresh relief, and a most grateful coolness. If the injury is severe, especially if it involve the chest, give ten drops of laudanum to an adult, and repeat it in an hour, and again a third time. To a child of ten years give, in like manner, only three drops, but beware of giving any to an infant. This plan with an internal stimulant,

according to age, as brandy, or sal volatile, or both, should be at once adopted, until the arrival of the doctor.

740. DIRT IN THE EYE.

Place your forefinger upon the cheek-bone, having the patient before you ; then slightly bend the finger, this will draw down the lower lid of the eye, and you will probably be able to remove the dirt ; but if this will not enable you to get at it, repeat this operation while you have a netting-needle or bodkin placed over the upper lid, ask patient to look down, and then turn the lid upwards over the bodkin, this will turn it inside out, and enable you to remove the sand, or eyelash, &c., with the corner of a fine silk handkerchief. As soon as the substance is removed, bathe the eye with cold water, drop in one drop of castor oil, and exclude the light for a day. If the inflammation is severe, let the patient take a purgative, and use a refrigerant lotion.

741. LIME IN THE EYE.

Syringe it well with warm vinegar and water in the proportion of one ounce of vinegar to eight ounces of water, and afterwards drop in castor oil, take a purgative, and exclude light.

742. IRON OR STEEL SPICULÆ IN THE EYE.

These occur while turning iron or steel in a lathe, and are best remedied by doubling back the upper or lower eyelid, according to the situation of the substance, and with the flat edge of a silver probe, taking up the metallic particle, using a lotion made by dissolving six grains of sugar of lead, and the same of white vitriol, in six ounces of water, and bathing the eye three times a day till the inflammation subsides. Another plan is —Drop a solution of sulphate of copper (from one to three grains of the salt to one ounce of water) into the eye, or keep the eye open in a wineglassful of the solution. Take a purgative, bathe with cold lotion, and exclude light to keep down inflammation.

743. DISLOCATED THUMB.

This is frequently produced by a fall. Make a clove hitch, by passing two loops of cord over the thumb, placing a piece of rag under the cord to prevent it cutting the thumb ; then pull in the same line as the thumb. Afterwards apply a cold lotion of one part spirit to three parts water.

744. CUTS AND WOUNDS.

Clean-cut wounds, whether deep or superficial, and likely to heal by the first intention, should never be washed or cleaned, but at once evenly and smoothly closed by bringing both edges close together, and securing them in that position by adhesive plaster. Cut thin strips of sticking-plaster, and bring the parts together ; or if large and deep, cut two broad pieces, so as to look like the teeth of a comb, and place one on each side of the wound, which must be cleaned previously. These pieces must be arranged so that they shall interlace one another ; then, by laying hold of the pieces on the right side with one hand, and those on the other side with the other hand, and pulling them from one another, the edges of the wound are brought together without any difficulty.

Ordinary Cuts are dressed by thin strips, applied by pressing down the plaster on one side of the wound, and keeping it there and pulling in the opposite direction ; then suddenly depressing the hand when the edges of the wound are brought together.

745. CONTUSIONS.

These are best healed by laying a piece of folded lint, well wetted with extract of lead, on the part, and, if there is much pain, placing a hot bran poultice over the dressing, repeating both, if necessary, every two hours. When the injuries are very severe, lay a cloth over the part, and suspend a basin over it filled with cold lotion. Put a piece of cotton into the basin, so that it shall act as a syphon and allow the lotion to drop on the cloth, and thus keep it always wet.

746. HÆMORRHAGE OR BLEEDING.

When caused by an artery being divided or torn, may be known by the blood issuing out of the wound in leaps or jerks, and being of a bright scarlet colour. If a vein is injured, the blood is darker and flows continuously. To arrest the latter, apply pressure by means of a compress and bandage. To arrest arterial bleeding, get a piece of wood (part of a broom handle will do), and tie a piece of tape to one end of it ; then tie a piece of tape loosely over the arm, and pass the other end of the wood under it ; twist the stick round and round until the tape compresses the arm sufficiently to arrest the bleeding, and then confine the other end by tying the string round the arm. A compress made by enfolding a penny piece in several folds of lint or linen should, however, be first placed under the tape and over the artery. If the bleeding is very obstinate, and it occurs in the *arm*, place a cork underneath the string, on the inside of the fleshy part, where the artery may be felt beating by any one ; if in the *leg*, place the cork in the direction of a line drawn from the inner part of the knee towards the outer part of the groin. It is an excellent thing to accustom yourself to find out the position of these arteries, or, indeed, any that are superficial, and to explain to every person in your house where they are, and how to stop bleeding. If a stick cannot be got, take a handkerchief, make a cord bandage of it, and tie a knot in the middle ; the knot acts as a compress, and should be placed over the artery, while the two ends are to be tied around the thumb. *Observe always to place the ligature between the wound and the heart.* Putting your finger into a bleeding wound, and making pressure until a surgeon arrives, will generally stop violent bleeding.

747. BLEEDING FROM THE NOSE.

This may generally be stopped by putting a plug of lint into the nostrils. If this does not do, apply a cold lotion to the forehead, raise the head, and place over it both arms, so that it will rest on the hands ; dip the lint plug, *slightly moistened,* into some powdered gum arabic, and plug the nostrils again ; or dip the plug into equal parts of powdered gum arabic and alum, and plug the nose. Or the plug may be dipped in Friar's balsam, or tincture of kino. Heat should be applied to the feet ; and, in obstinate cases, the sudden shock of a cold key, or cold water poured down the spine, will often instantly stop the bleeding. If the bowels are confined, take a purgative.

748. VIOLENT SHOCKS.

These will sometimes stun a person, and he will remain unconscious. Untie strings, collars, &c. ; loosen anything that is tight, and interferes with the breathing ; raise the head ; see if there is bleeding from any part : apply smelling-salts to the nose, and hot bottles to the feet.

749. CONCUSSION.

The surface of the body is cold and pale, and the pulse weak and small, the breathing slow and *gentle,* and the pupil of the eye generally contracted or small. You can get an answer by speaking loud, so as to arouse the patient. Give a little brandy and water, keep the place quiet, apply warmth, and do not raise the head too high. If you tickle the feet, the patient feels it.

750. COMPRESSION OF THE BRAIN.

This from any cause, such as apoplexy, or a piece of fractured bone pressing on it, involves loss of sensation. If you tickle the feet of the injured person he does not feel it. You cannot arouse him so as to get an answer. The pulse is slow and laboured ; the breathing deep, laboured, and *snorting,* the pupils enlarged or unequal. Raise the head, loosen strings or tight things, and send for a surgeon. If one cannot be got at once, apply mustard poultices to the feet and thighs, leeches to the temples, and hot water to the feet, and purge the bowels.

751. CHOKING FROM FISH BONE.

When a person has a fish bone in the throat, insert the forefinger, press upon the root of the tongue, so as to induce vomiting ; if this does not do, let him swallow a *large piece* of potato or soft bread ; and if these fail give a mustard emetic.

752. FAINTING, HYSTERICS, &c.

Lay patient down or bend head between knees while seated. Loosen the garments, bathe the temples with water or eau-de-Cologne ; open the window, admit plenty of fresh air, dash cold water on the face, apply hot bricks to the feet, and avoid bustle and excessive sympathy.

753. DROWNING.

Attend to the following *essential rules :*—

i. Lose no time.

ii. Handle the body gently.

iii. Carry the body face downwards, with the head gently raised, and never hold it up by the feet.

iv. Send for medical assistance immediately, and in the meantime act as follows :—

v. Strip the body, rub it dry ; then wrap it in hot blankets, and place it in a warm bed in a warm room.

vi. Cleanse away the froth and mucus from the nose and mouth.

vii. Apply warm bricks, bottles, bags of sand, &c., to the armpits, between the thighs, and to the soles of the feet.

viii. Rub the surface of the body with the hands enclosed in warm dry worsted socks.

ix. If possible, put the body into a warm bath.

x. To restore breathing, lay patient on his back, raising head and shoulders by placing a folded coat or other garment under him, put the pipe of a common bellows into one nostril, carefully closing the other, and the mouth ; at the same time drawing downwards, and pushing gently backwards, the upper part of the windpipe, to allow a more free admission of air ; blow the bellows gently, in order to inflate the lungs, till the breast be raised a little ; then set the mouth and nostrils free, and press gently on the chest : repeat this until signs of life appear.

xi. Or induce artificial respiration by SILVESTER's METHOD, viz., stand at head of patient, grasp both arms above elbows and raise them slowly above the patient's head, keeping them there for two seconds (this expands the chest and air is admitted to the lungs), the feet being held ; then quickly lower arms and press into sides of chest and repeat this movement about every five seconds until the patient shows signs of returning respiration. This is usually denoted by a flush of colour in the face.

The body should be covered the moment it is placed on the table, except the face, and all the rubbing carried on under the sheet or blanket. When they can be obtained, a number of tiles or bricks should be made tolerably hot in the fire, laid in a row on the table, covered with a blanket, and the body placed in such a manner on them, that their heat may enter the spine. When the patient revives, apply smelling salts to the nose, give warm wine or brandy and water. *Cautions.*—Never rub the body with salt or spirits. Never roll the body on casks. Continue the remedies for twelve hours without ceasing.

754. HANGING.

Loosen the cord, or whatever it may be by which the person has been suspended. Open the temporal artery or jugular vein, or bleed from the arm ; employ electricity, if at hand, and proceed as for drowning, taking the additional precaution to apply eight or ten leeches to the temples.

755. APPARENT DEATH FROM DRUNKENNESS.

Raise the head, loosen the clothes, maintain warmth of surface, and give a mustard emetic as soon as the person can swallow, or if possible use stomach-pump.

756. APOPLEXY AND FITS GENERALLY.

Raise the head ; loosen all tight clothes, strings, &c ; put a cork or roll of paper between teeth to prevent tongue being bitten ; apply cold lotions to the head, which should be shaved ; apply leeches to the temples, bleed, and send for a surgeon. No stimulants should be given in cases of apoplexy or sun-stroke.

757. SUFFOCATION FROM NOX-IOUS GASES, &c.

Remove to the fresh air ; dash cold vinegar and water in the face, neck, and breast ; keep up the warmth of the body ; if necessary, apply mustard poultice to the soles of the feet and spine, and try artificial respirations as in drowning, with electricity.

758. LIGHTNING AND SUN-STROKE.

Treat the same as apoplexy.

759. POISONING.

*The abbreviations used are as follows :
—E., Effects or Symptoms. T., Treatment.*

A., Antidotes or Counter Poisons. D.A., Dangerous Antidotes.

760. EFFECTS OF POISONS.

A poison is a substance which is capable of altering or destroying some or all of the functions necessary to life. When a person is in good health, and is suddenly attacked, after having taken some food or drink, with violent pain, cramp in the stomach, feeling of sickness or nausea, vomiting, convulsive twitchings, and a sense of suffocation ; or if he be seized, under the same circumstances, with giddiness, delirium, or unusual sleepiness, it may be supposed that he has been poisoned.

761. POISONS CLASSIFIED.

Poisons have been divided into four classes:—

i. Those causing local symptoms.

ii. Those producing spasmodic symptoms.

iii. Narcotic or sleepy symptoms ; and

iv. Paralytic symptoms. Poisons may be mineral, animal, or vegetable.

762. HINTS IN CASES OF POISONING.

i. Always send immediately for a medical man.

ii. Save all fluids vomited, and articles of food, cups, glasses, &c., used by the patient before being taken ill, and lock them up.

iii. Examine the cups to guide you in your treatment : that is, smell them, and look at them.

iv. As a rule give emetics after poisons that cause sleepiness and raving ;—give chalk, milk, eggs, butter, and warm water, or oil, after poisons that cause vomiting and pain in the stomach and bowels, with purging ; and when there is no inflammation about the throat, tickle it with a feather to excite vomiting.

v. Do not give emetics in cases of poisoning by violent acids.

763. ARSENIC. *(White arsenic ; orpiment, or yellow arsenic ; realgar, red arsenic ; Scheele's green, or arsenic of copper ; King's yellow ; ague drops ; and arsenical paste.)* E. Little or no taste. Within an hour, heat and pain in the stomach, followed by vomiting of green, yellow, and bloody matter, burning, and violent thirst ; purging and twisting about the navel ; pulse small, quick, and irregular, breathing laboured, voice hoarse, speaking painful ; skin cold and clammy. Sometimes there are cramps and convulsions, followed by death.—*T.* Give plenty of warm water, *new milk* in large quantities, lime water, white of egg, mixed with gruel or honey, gruel, linseed tea ; apply leeches to the bowels, foment, and give starch or gruel enemas. Scrape the iron rust off anything you can get at, mix it with plenty of water, and give in large draughts frequently, and give an emetic of mustard or ipecacuanha. The chief dependence, however, must be placed on the use of the stomach-pump. *Caution.*—Never give large draughts of fluid until those given before have been vomited, because the stomach will not contract properly if filled with fluid, and the object is to get rid of the poison as speedily as possible.

764. COPPER. *(Blue vitriol, or bluestone ; verdigris ; verditer ; verdigris crystals.)*—E. An acid, rough, disagreeable taste in the mouth ; a dry, parched tongue, with sense of strangling in the throat ; coppery eructations ; frequent spitting ; nausea ; frequent desire and effort to vomit or copious vomiting ; severe darting pains in the stomach ; griping ; frequent purging ; belly swollen and painful ; skin hot, and violent burning thirst ; breathing difficult ; intense headache and giddiness, followed by cold sweats, cramps in the legs, convulsions, and death.—*A.* White of eggs mixed with water (twelve to one pint), to be given in wineglassfuls every two minutes ; iron filings mixed with water, or very strong coffee, accompanied by small and repeated doses of castor oil.—*D. A.* Vinegar, bark, alkalies, gall nuts.—*T.* If there is much pain in the belly or stomach, apply leeches. Give large draughts of milk and water, to encourage vomiting.

765. MERCURY. (*Corrosive sublimate ; calomel ; red precipitate ; vermilion : turbeth mineral ; prussiate of mercury.*)—*E.* Acid metallic taste ; tightness and burning in the throat ; pain in the back part of the mouth, stomach, and bowels ; anxiety of countenance ; nausea ; and vomiting of bloody and bilious fluids ; profuse purging and difficulty of making water ; pulse small, hard, and quick ; skin clammy, icy coldness of the hands and feet ; and death in 24 or 36 hours.—*A.* White of eggs mixed with water, given as above ; milk ; flour and water, mixed pretty thick ; linseed tea ; and barley water.—*T.* Give large draughts of warm water, if you cannot get anything else ; strong emetic of ipecacuanha, the stomach-pump, a dose of castor oil and laudanum. Apply poppy-head fomentations to bowels, and leeches if the belly is very tender.

766. ANTIMONY. (*Tartar emetic ; butter of ; Kermes' mineral.*)—*E.* A rough metallic taste in the mouth, nausea, copious vomiting, sudden hiccough, purging of bilious and bloody stools, pains resembling those caused by colic, frequent and violent cramps, sense of choking, severe heartburn, pain at the pit of the stomach, difficult breathing, wildness of speech, cramp in the legs, and death.—*A.* Decoction or tincture of galls ; strong tea ; decoction or powder of Peruvian bark. *D.A.* White vitriol, ipecacuanha, as emetics.—*T.* Give large draughts of water, or sugar and water, to promote vomiting ; apply leeches to the throat and stomach if painful ; and give one grain of extract of opium dissolved in a wine-glassful of sugar and water, as soon

as the vomiting ceases, and repeat three times at intervals of a quarter of an hour ; and finally, one grain, in a little castor oil emulsion, every six hours.

767. TIN. (*Butter of tin ; putty powder.*)—*E.* Colic and purging.—*A.* Milk.—*T.* Give warm or cold water to promote vomiting, or tickle the throat with a feather.

768. ZINC. (*White vitriol ; flowers of ; chloride of.*)—*E.* An astringent taste, sensation of choking, nausea, vomiting, purging, pain and burning in the throat and stomach, difficult breathing, pallor and coldness of the surface, pinched face, cramps of the extremities, but, with the exception of the chloride, seldom death.—*A.* For the first two give copious draughts of milk, and white of eggs and water, mucilage, and olive oil; for the third, carbonate of soda, and warm water in frequent draughts, with the same as for the other compounds.—*T.* Relieve urgent symptoms by leeching and fomentations, and after the vomiting give castor oil. For the chloride, use friction and warmth.

769. SILVER. (*Lunar caustic ; flowers of silver*) ; **Gold** (*Chloride of*) ; and **Bismuth** (*Nitrate ; flowers of ; pearl white*), are not frequently met with as poisons.—*E.* Burning pain in the throat, mouth, accompanied with the usual symptoms, of corrosive poisons.—*A.* For silver, common salt and water ; for gold and bismuth, no antidotes are known.—*T.* Give milk and mucilaginous fluids, and castor oil.

770. ACIDS. (*Hydrochloric*, or *spirit of salt* ; *nitric*, or *aquafortis* ; *sulphuric*, or *oil of vitriol.*)—*E.* Acid burning taste acute pain in the gullet and throat, vomiting of bloody fluid, which effervesces when chalk is added to it ; hiccough, tenderness of the belly, cold sweats, pinched face, convulsions, and death.—*A.* Give *calcined* magnesia, chalk, soap and water. Administer frequent draughts of water to weaken the acid, with carbonate of soda, potass, or magnesia, to neutralize it ; thick soap-suds made with common soap ; chalk, or in default of the alkalies and chalk, break down the plaster of the wall or ceiling, mix in water, and give the sufferer. Then a quarter of a pint of salad oil, white of eggs in water, barley water or linseed tea.

771. CHLORINE (*gas*).—*E.* Violent coughing, tightness of the chest, debility, inability to stand.—*A.* The vapour of caustic ammonia to be inhaled, or ten drops of liquid ammonia to one ounce of water to be taken.—*T.* Dash cold water over the face, and relieve urgent symptoms.

772. LEAD (*Sugar of ; red lead ; wine sweetened by ; and water impregnated with.*)—*E.* Sugary astringent metallic taste, tightness of the throat, pains as if caused by colic, violent vomiting, hiccough, convulsions, and death.—*A.* Epsom or Glauber's salt ; plaster of Paris ; or phosphate of soda.—*T.* An emetic of sulphate of zinc (twenty-four grains to half-a-pint of water) ; leeches to belly ; fomentations if necessary ; and a dose of castor oil mixed with laudanum.

773. PHOSPHORUS.—*E.* Intense burning and pain in the throat and stomach.—*A.* Magnesia and carbonate of soda.—*T.* Large draughts of chalk and water, and tickle the throat with a feather. *Caution.* Do not give oil.

774. LIME.—*E.* Burning in the throat and stomach, cramps in the belly, hiccough, vomiting, and paralysis of limbs.—*A.* Vinegar or lemon juice.—*T.* Thin starch water to be drunk frequently.

775. ALKALIES. (*Caustic potash ; soda ; ammonia.*)—*E.* Acrid, hot, disagreeable taste ; burning in the throat, nausea, and vomiting bloody matter ; profuse purging, pain in the stomach, colic, convulsions, and death.—*A.* Vinegar and vegetable acids.—*T.* Give

linseed tea, milk, almond or olive oil, and excite vomiting.

776. BARYTA (*Carbonate, pure, and muriate.*) (*See* LIME, par. 774.)

777. NITRE.—*E.* Heartburn, nausea, violent vomiting, purging, convulsions, difficult breathing, violent pain in the bowels, kidneys, and bladder, with bloody urine.—*T.* Emetics, frequent draughts of barley water, with castor oil and laudanum.

778. NARCOTIC POISONS. (*Bane berries ; fool's parsley ; deadly nightshade ; water hemlock ; thorn apple ; opium,* or *laudanum ; camphor, &c.*)— *E.* Giddiness, faintness, nausea, vomiting, stupor, delirium, and death.— *T.* Give emetics, large draughts of fluids, tickle the throat, apply smelling salts to the nose, dash cold water over the face and chest, apply mustard poultices, and, above all, endeavour to rouse the patient by forced walking about between two persons ; and, if possible, by electricity ; and give forty drops of sal volatile in strong coffee every half-hour.

779. VEGETABLE IRRITATING POISONS. (*Mezereon ; monk's-hood ; bitter apple ; gamboge ; white hellebore, &c.*)—*E.* Acrid, biting, bitter taste, choking sensation, dryness of the throat, retching, vomiting, purging, pains in the stomach and bowels, breathing difficult, and death.— *T.* Give emetics of camomile, mustard, or sulphate of zinc ; large draughts of warm milk, or other bland fluids ; foment and leech the belly if necessary, and give strong *infusion* of coffee.

780. OXALIC ACID.—*E.* Vomiting and acute pain in the stomach, general debility, cramps, and death.— *A.* Chalk.—*T.* Give large draughts of lime water or magnesia.

781. SPANISH FLIES.—*E.* Acrid taste, burning heat in the throat, stomach, and belly, bloody vomitings, colic, purging, retention of urine, convulsions, death.—*T.* Large draughts of olive oil ; thin gruel, milk, starch enemas, linseed tea, laudanum, and camphorated water.

782. POISONOUS FISH. (*Old-wife* ; *sea-lobster* ; *mussel* ; *tunny* ; *blower*; *rock-fish, &c.*)—*E.* Intense pain in the stomach after swallowing the fish, vomiting, purging, and sometimes cramps.—*T.* Give an emetic ; excite vomiting by tickling the throat, and plenty of warm water. Follow emetics by active purgatives, particularly of castor oil and laudanum, or opium and calomel, and abate inflammation by the usual remedies.

783. POISONOUS BITES AND STINGS.

784. SNAKE BITES. (*Viper* ; *black viper* ; *Indian serpents* ; *rattle-snake.*)—*E.* Violent and quick inflammation of the part, extending towards the body, soon becoming livid ; nausea, vomiting, convulsions, difficult breathing, mortification, cold sweats, and death.—*T.* Suppose that the wrist has been bitten ; immediately tie a tape between the wound and the heart, scarify the parts with a penknife, razor, or lancet, and apply a cupping-glass over the bite, frequently removing it and bathing the wound with volatile alkali, or heat a poker and burn the wound well, or drop some disinfecting fluid into the wound, or cauterize the bite freely with lunar caustic, but not till the part has been well sucked with the mouth, or frequently washed and cupped. The strength is to be supported by brandy, ammonia, ether, and opium. Give plenty of warm drinks, and cover up in bed.

785. BITES OF MAD ANIMALS.—*E.* Hydrophobia, or a fear of fluids.—*T.* Tie a string tightly over the part, cut out the bite, and cauterize the wound with a red-hot poker, lunar caustic, or disinfecting fluid. Then apply a piece of "spongio piline," give a purgative, and plenty of warm drink. Whenever chloro-

form can be procured, sprinkle a few drops upon a handkerchief, and apply to the nose and mouth of the patient before cauterizing the wound. When the breathing appears difficult, cease the application of the chloroform. A physician, writing in the *Times*, strongly urged this course, and stated, many years ago, that there is no danger, with ordinary care, in the application of the chloroform, while the cauterization may be more effectively performed.

786. INSECT STINGS. (*Wasp, bee, gnat, hornet, gadfly, scorpion.*)—*E.* Swelling, nausea, and fever.—*T.* Press the barrel of a watch-key over the part, so as to expose the sting, which must be removed. Give fifteen drops of hartshorn or sal volatile in half a wine-glassful of camomile tea, and cover the part stung with a piece of lint soaked in extract of lead.

The sting of a bee is generally more virulent than that of a wasp, and with some people attended with very violent effects. The sting of a bee is barbed at the end, and is consequently always left in the wound ; that of a wasp is pointed only, so that the latter insect can sting more than once, which a bee cannot do. When stung by a bee, let the sting be instantly pulled out ; for the longer it remains in the wound, the deeper it will pierce, owing to its peculiar form, and emit more of the poison, which is the sole cause of the pain and inflammation. The pulling out of the sting should be done carefully, and with a steady hand, to avoid breaking it. When the sting is extracted, suck the wounded part, if possible, and very little inflammation, if any, will ensue. If hartshorn drops are immediately afterwards rubbed on the part, the cure will be more complete. Among other simple remedies for this purpose, rubbing the part affected with sweet oil, the juice of onion, or the blue-bag used in washing, slightly moistened, will be found efficacious.

787. THE STING OF A NETTLE may be cared by rubbing the part with rosemary, mint, or sage leaves. Dock leaves are also said to supply an effectual remedy.

788. CAUTIONS FOR THE PREVENTION OF ACCIDENTS.

The following regulations should be engraved on the memory of all :—

i. Look closely after children, whether they are up or in bed ; and particularly when they are near the fire, an element with which they are very apt to amuse themselves.

ii. Leave nothing poisonous open or accessible ; and never omit to write the word "Poison" in large letters upon it, wherever it may be placed.

iii. Never point a gun or pistol at any one in jest, whether it is loaded or unloaded. A loaded gun should never be brought into the home.

iv. Never meddle with gunpowder by candle-light.

v. In trimming a lamp with naphtha, never fill it. Leave space for the spirit to expand with warmth.

vi. Keep lucifer matches in their cases, and never let them be strewed about.

vii. Never quit a room leaving the poker in the fire.

viii. Do not rake out fires at bed-time, as hot cinders are apt to be scattered about ; it is better to let the fire burn itself out.

ix. Never sleep near charcoal ; if drowsy at any work where charcoal fires are used, take the fresh air.

x. Avoid reading in bed at night, as besides the danger of an accident, the practice is very injurious to the eyes.

xi. Beware of damp clothes.

xii. When benumbed with cold beware of sleeping out of doors ; rub yourself, if you have it in your power, with snow, and do not hastily approach the fire.

xiii. Always air vaults, and damp, confined places, by letting them remain open some time before you enter

or scattering powdered lime in them. Where a lighted candle will not burn, animal life cannot exist ; it is therefore an excellent caution to use this simple test before entering.

xiv. Do not stand near a tree, or any leaden spout, iron gate, or palisade, in times of lightning.

xv. In walking in the streets, keep out of the line of the cellars, and never look one way and walk another.

xvi. Never throw pieces of orange-peel, or broken glass bottles, into the streets, but kick into the gutter any that you may see on the pavement or the roadway. By so doing you may save many from meeting with dangerous accidents.

xvii. Quit your house with care on a frosty morning.

xviii. Have your horses' shoes roughed directly there are indications of frost.

xix. Never leave saddle or draught horses, while in use, by themselves ; nor go immediately behind a led horse, as he is apt to kick. When crossing a roadway always go behind a cart or carnage, never in front of if.

xx. Do not ride on footways.

xxi. When the brass rod of the stair-carpet becomes loose, fasten it immediately.

xxii. Never allow your servants to leave brooms, brushes, slop-pails, water-cans, &c., in outside doorways, or at the head of a flight of stairs when engaged in housework.

xxiii. Should an infant lay hold of a knife or razor, do not try to pull it away, or to force open the hand ; but, holding the child's hand that is empty, offer to its other hand anything nice or pretty, and it will immediately open the hand, and let the dangerous instrument fall

789. CARRIAGE ACCIDENTS.— It is safer, as a general rule, to keep your place than to jump out. Getting out of a gig over the back, provided you can hold on a little while, and run, is safer than springing from the side. But it is best to keep your place, and hold fast. In accidents people act not so much from reason as from excitement : but good rules, firmly impressed upon the mind, generally rise uppermost, even in the midst of fear.

790. CAUTIONS IN VISITING THE SICK.—Do not visit the sick when you are fatigued, or when in a state of perspiration, or with the stomach empty—for in such conditions you are liable to take the infection. When the disease is very contagious, place yourself at the side of the patient which is nearest the window. Do not enter the room the first thing in the morning, before it has been aired ; and when you come away, take some food, change your clothing immediately, and expose the latter to the air for some days. Tobacco smoke is a preventive of malaria.

791. PRECAUTIONS IN CASES OF FIRE.

The following precautions should be impressed upon the memory of all our readers :—

i. Should a Fire break out, send off to the nearest engine or police station.

ii. Fill Buckets with Water, carry them as near the fire as possible, and throw the water in showers on the fire with a garden syringe or a mop until assistance arrives.

iii. If a Fire is violent, wet a blanket, and throw it on the part which is in flames.

iv. Should the Bed or Window Curtains catch fire, lay hold of any woollen garment, and beat it on the flames until extinguished.

v. Do not leave the Window or Door open in the room where the fire has broken out, as the current of air increases the force of the fire.

vi. Should the Staircase be burning, so as to cut off all communication, endeavour to escape by means of a trap-door in the roof, a ladder leading to which should always be at hand.

vii. Avoid Hurry and Confusion ; no person except a fireman, friend, or neighbour, should be admitted.

viii. If a Lady's Dress takes Fire, she should endeavour to roll herself in a rug, carpet, or the first woollen garment she meets with.

ix. It is a Good Precaution to have always at hand a large piece of baize, to throw over a female whose dress is burning, or to be w etted and thrown over a fire that has recently broken out.

x. A Solution of Pearlash in Water, thrown upon a fire, extinguishes it instantly. The proportion is a quarter of a pound, dissolved in some hot water, and then poured into a bucket of common water.

xi. All Householders, but particularly hotel, tavern, and inn-keepers, should exercise a wise precaution by directing that the last person up should look over the premises previous to going to rest, to ascertain that all fires are safe and lights extinguished.

xii. In Escaping from a Fire, creep or crawl along the room with your face close to the ground. Children should be early taught how to press out a spark when it happens to reach any part of their dress, and also that running into the air will cause it to blaze immediately.

792. TO RENDER CHILDREN'S DRESSES UNINFLAMMABLE.

The following simple suggestions are worthy of observation :—Add one ounce of alum to the last water used to rinse children's dresses, and they will be rendered uninflammable, or so slightly combustible that in event of coming into contact with fire, they would only smoulder away very slowly, and not burst into flame. This is a simple precaution, which should be adopted in families. Bed curtains, and linen in general, may also be treated in the same way. Tungstate of soda and chloride of zinc have been recommended for the purpose of rendering any article of female dress incombustible. Any chemist will intimate to the purchaser the manner in which the tungstate of soda should be employed.

793. TO EXTINGUISH A FIRE IN A CHIMNEY.

So many serious fires have been caused by chimneys catching fire, and not being quickly extinguished, that the following method of doing this should be made generally known. Throw some salt or powdered brimstone on the fire in the grate, or ignite some on the hob, and then put a board or something in the front of the fire-place, to prevent the fumes descending into the room. The vapour of the brimstone, ascending the chimney, will then effectually extinguish the fire. Keep all the doors and windows tightly shut, and hold before the fireplace a wetted blanket, or some woollen article, to exclude the air.

794. SWIMMING.

Every person should endeavour to acquire the power of swimming. The fact that the exercise is a healthful accompaniment of bathing, and that lives may be saved by it, even when least expected, is a sufficient argument for the recommendation. The art of swimming is, in reality, very easy. The first consideration is not to attempt to learn to swim too hastily. That is to say, you must not expect to succeed in your efforts to swim, until you have become accustomed to the water, and have overcome your repugnance to the coldness and novelty of bathing. Every attempt will fail until you have acquired a certain confidence in the water, and then the difficulty will soon vanish. It should be kept in mind that the human body only weighs one pound in the water, and a chair, a small stool, or a box will suffice to keep a man's head out of water !

Those who prefer the aid of belts will find it very easy and safe to make belts upon the plan explained in the next two paragraphs ; and by gradually reducing the floating power of the belts from day to day, they will gain confidence, and speedily acquire the art of swimming.

795. TO MAKE LIFE BELTS.

An excellent and cheap life belt, for persons proceeding to sea, bathing in dangerous places, or learning to swim, may be thus made :—Take a yard and three-quarters of strong jean, double, and divide into nine compartments. Let there be a space of two inches after each third compartment. Fill the compartments with very fine cutting of cork, which may be made by cutting up old corks, or (still better) purchased at the cork- cutter's. Work eyelet-holes at the bottom of each compartment, to let the water drain out. Attach a neckband and waist-strings of stout bootweb, and sew them on strongly.

Another Method.—Cut open an old boa, or victorine, and line it with fine cork-cuttings instead of wool. For ladies going to sea these are excellent, as they may be worn in stormy weather, without giving appearance of alarm in danger. They may be fastened to the body by ribands or tapes, of the colour of the fur. Gentlemen's waistcoats may be lined the same way.

796. **DR. FRANKLIN'S ADVICE TO SWIMMERS.**—"The only obstacle to improvement in this necessary and life-preserving art is fear : and it is only by overcoming this timidity that you can expect to become a master of the following acquirements. It is very common for novices in the art of swimming to make use of cork or bladders to assist in keeping the body above water ; some have utterly condemned the use of them ; however, they may be of service for supporting the body while one is learning what is called the stroke, or that manner of drawing in and striking out the hands and feet that is necessary to produce progressive motion. But you will be no swimmer till you can place confidence in the power of the

water to support you ; I would, therefore, advise the acquiring that confidence in the first place ; especially as I have known several who, by a little practice, necessary for that purpose, have insensibly acquired the stroke, taught, as it were, by nature. The practice I mean is this : choosing a place where the water deepens gradually, walk coolly into it till it is up to your breast ; then turn round your face to the shore, and throw an egg into the water between you and the shore ; it will sink to the bottom and be easily seen there if the water be clear. It must lie in the water so deep that you cannot reach to take it up but by diving for it. To encourage yourself in order to do this, reflect that your progress will be from deep to shallow water, and that at any time you may, by bringing your legs under you, and standing on the bottom, raise your head far above the water ; then plunge under it with your eyes open, which must be kept open on going under, as you cannot open the eyelids for the weight of water above you ; throwing yourself toward the egg, and endeavouring by the action of your hands and feet against the water to get forward, till within reach of it. In this attempt you will find that the water buoys you up against your inclination ; that it is not so easy to sink as you imagine, and that you cannot, but by active force, get down to the egg. Thus you feel the power of water to support you, and learn to confide in that power, while your endeavours to overcome it, and reach the egg, teach you the manner of acting on the water with your feet and hands, which action is afterwards used in swimming to support your head higher above the water, or to go forward through it.

"I would the more earnestly press you to the trial of this method, because I think I shall satisfy you that your body is lighter than water, and that you might float in it a long time with your mouth free for breathing, if you would put yourself into a proper posture, and would be still, and forbear struggling ; yet, till you have obtained this experimental confidence in the water, I cannot depend upon your having the necessary presence of mind to recollect the posture, and the directions I give you relating to it. The surprise may put all out of your mind.

"THOUGH THE LEGS, ARMS, AND HEAD of a human body, being solid parts, are specifically somewhat heavier than fresh water, as the trunk, particularly the upper part, from its hollowness, is so much lighter than water, so the whole of the body, taken altogether. is too light to sink wholly under water, but some part will remain above until the lungs become filled with water, which happens when a person, in the fright, attempts breathing while the mouth and nostrils are under water.

"THE LEGS AND ARMS ARE SPECIFICALLY LIGHTER than salt water, and will be supported by it, so that a human body cannot sink in salt water, though the lungs were filled as above, but from the greater specific gravity of the head. Therefore a person throwing himself on his back in salt water, and extending his arms, may easily lie so as to keep his mouth and nostrils free for breathing ; and, by a slight motion of his hand, may prevent turning if he should perceive any tendency to it.

"IN FRESH WATER IF A MAN THROW HIM-SELF ON HIS BACK near the surface, he cannot long continue in that situation, but by proper action of his hands on the water ; if he use no such action, the legs and lower part of the body will gradually sink till he come into an upright position, in which he will continue suspended, the hollow of his breast keeping the head uppermost.

"BUT IF IN THIS ERECT POSITION the head be kept upright above the shoulders, as when we stand on the ground, the immersion will, by the weight of that part of the head that is out of the water, reach above the mouth and nostrils, perhaps a little above the eyes, so that a man cannot long remain suspended in water with his head in that position.

"THE BODY CONTINUING SUSPENDED as before, and upright, if the head be leaned quite back, so that the face look upward, all the back part of the head being under water, and its weight consequently in a great measure supported by it, the face will remain above water quite free for breathing, will rise an inch higher every inspiration, and sink as much every expiration, but never so low as that the water may come over the mouth.

"IF THEREFORE A PERSON UNACQUAINTED

with Swimming and falling accidentally into the water, could have presence of mind sufficient to avoid struggling and plunging, and to let the body take this natural position he might continue long safe from drowning, till, perhaps, help should come ; for, as to the clothes, their additional weight when immersed is very inconsiderable, the water supporting it ; though when he comes out of the water, he will find them very heavy indeed.

"But I would not advise any one to depend on having this Presence of Mind on such an occasion, but learn fairly to swim, as I wish all men were taught to do in their youth ; they would on many occasions be the safer for having that skill ; and on many more, the happier, as free from painful apprehensions of danger, to say nothing of the enjoyment in so delightful and wholesome an exercise. Soldiers particularly should, methinks, all be taught to swim ; it might be of frequent use, either in surprising an enemy or saving themselves ; and if I had now boys to educate, I should prefer those schools (other things being equal) where an opportunity was afforded for acquiring so advantageous an art, which, once learned, is never forgotten.

"I know by experience that it is a great comfort to a swimmer, who has a considerable distance to go, to turn himself sometimes on his back, and to vary, in other respects, the means of procuring a progressive motion.

"When he is seized with the Cramp in the leg, the method of driving it away is to give the parts affected a sudden, vigorous, and violent shock ; which he may do in the air as he swims on his back.

"During the Great Heats in Summer there is no danger in bathing, however warm we may be, in rivers which have been thoroughly warmed by the sun. But to throw one's self into cold spring water, when the body has been heated by exercise in the sun, is an imprudence which may prove fatal. I once knew an instance of four young men who, having worked at harvest in the heat of the day, with a view of refreshing themselves, plunged into a spring of cold water ; two died upon the spot, a third next morning, and the fourth recovered with great difficulty.

A copious draught of cold water, in similar circumstances, is frequently attended with the same effect in North America.

"The exercise of Swimming is one of the most healthy and agreeable in the world. After having swum for an hour or two in the evening one sleeps coolly the whole night, even during the most ardent heat of summer. Perhaps the pores being cleansed, the insensible perspiration increases, and occasions this coolness. It is certain that much swimming is the means of stopping diarrhœa and even of producing a constipation. With respect to those who do not know how to swim, or who are affected with diarrhœa at a season which does not permit them to use that exercise, a warm bath, by cleansing and purifying the skin, is found very salutary, and often effects a radical cure. I speak from my own experience, frequently repeated, and that of others, to whom I have recommended this.

"When I was a boy I amused myself one day with flying a paper kite ; and approaching the banks of the lake, which was nearly a mile broad, I tied the string to a stake, and the kite ascended to a very considerable height above the pond, while I was swimming. In a little time, being desirous of amusing myself with my kite, and enjoying at the same time the pleasure of swimming, I returned, and loosening from the stake the string, with the little stick which was fastened to it, went again into the water, where I found that lying on my back, and holding the stick in my hand, I was drawn along the surface of the water in a very agreeable manner. Having then engaged another boy to carry my clothes round the pond to a place which I pointed out to him on the other side, I began to cross the pond with my kite, which carried me quite over without the least fatigue, and with the greatest pleasure imaginable. I was only obliged occasionally to halt a little in my course, and resist its progress, when it appeared that by following too quickly, I lowered the kite too much ; by doing which occasionally I made it rise again. I have never since that time practised this singular mode of swimming, and I think it not impossible to cross, in this manner, from Dover to Calais."

797. SIGNS OF THE WEATHER.

i. Dew.—If the dew lies plentifully on the grass after a fair day, it is a sign of another fair day. If not, and there is no wind, rain must follow. A red evening portends fine weather ; but if the redness spread too far upwards from the horizon in the evening, and especially in the morning, it foretells wind or rain, or both.

ii. Colour of Sky.—When the sky, in rainy weather, is tinged with sea green, the rain will increase ; if with deep blue, it will be showery.

iii. Clouds.—If you wish to know what sort of weather you may expect, go out and choose the smallest cloud you can see. Watch it, and if it grows smaller and finally disappears you may be pretty sure of fine weather ; or the opposite, if the cloud grows larger. The reason is that when the air is becoming charged with electricity each cloud attracts smaller ones, until it passes off in rain ; but if rain is diffusing itself, a large cloud breaks up and dissolves. Previous to much rain falling, the clouds grow bigger, and increase very fast, especially before thunder. When the clouds are formed like fleeces, but dense in the middle and bright towards the edges, with the sky bright, they are signs of a frost, with hail, snow, or rain. If clouds form high in the air, in thin white trains like locks of wool, they portend wind, and probably rain. When a general cloudiness covers the sky, and small black fragments of clouds fly underneath, they are a sure sign of rain, and probably will be lasting. Two currents of clouds always portend rain, and, in summer, thunder.

iv. Heavenly Bodies.—A haziness in the air, which dims the sun's light, and makes the orb appear whitish, or ill-defined—or at night, if the moon and stars grow dim, and a ring encircles the former, rain will follow. If the sun's rays appear like Moses' horns—if white at setting or shorn of his rays, or if he goes down into a bank of clouds in the horizon, bad weather is to be expected. If the moon looks pale and dim, we expect rain ; if red, wind ; and if of her natural colour, with a clear sky, fair weather. If the moon is rainy throughout, it will clear at the change, and, perhaps, the rain return a few days after. If fair throughout, and rain at the change, the fair weather will probably return on the fourth or fifth day.

798. A RAINY DAY.

The day is cold, and dark, and dreary ;
It rains, and the wind is never weary ;
The vine still clings to the mouldering wall.
But at every gust the dead leaves fall,
    And the day is dark and dreary.

My life is cold, and dark, and dreary ;
It rains, and the wind is never weary ;
My thoughts still cling to the mouldering Post,
But the hopes of youth fall thick in the blast,
    And the days are dark and dreary.

Be still, sad heart, and cease repining;
Behind the clouds is the sun still shining ;
Thy fate is the common fate of all.
Into each life some rain must fall,
Some days must be dark and dreary.

LONGFELLOW.

799. BAROMETERS.

These instruments are most useful for indicating appproaching changes in the weather, according to variations in the pressure of the atmosphere. There are several kinds, the mercurial is generally considered the best.

800. MERCURIAL BAROMETER.

This consists of a narrow glass tube upwards of thirty inches in length, open at one end and closed at the other. This tube contains quicksilver which rises and falls as the pressure of air on the open surface increases or decreases ; the variations being shown by an index hand on a dial plate engraved with the words "Fair, Change, Rain," &c. Fair weather is usually indicated by a rise in the mercury, and bad weather by a fall.

These barometers should be hung securely on the wall where they are neither exposed to draughts nor varying heat ; a sheltered nook in a passage is the best position.

801. ANEROID BAROMETER.

This, if well made, is an excellent weather glass, and has the advantage of being extremely portable, as it is made in a compact circular form in sizes varying from one inch in diameter. Excellent instruments are made about the size of a watch admirably adapted for tourists, and enabling them to measure the heights of mountains, buildings, &c.

In these instruments the variations of the atmosphere cause the expansion and contraction of two discs of corrupted metal, soldered together, forming a vacuum chamber, the action of these discs being indicated on the dial plates by a needle very similar to the hand of a watch.

802. LEECH BAROMETER.

Take a two-ounce phial three-parts filled with pure water, and place in it a healthy leech, cover the mouth of the bottle with a piece of muslin, and it will most accurately prognosticate the weather. If the weather is to be fine, the leech lies motionless at the bottom of the glass, and coiled together in a spiral form ; if rain may be expected, it will creep up to the top of its lodgings, and remain there till the weather is settled ; if we are to have wind, it will move through its habitation with amazing swiftness, and seldom goes to rest till it begins to blow hard ; if a remarkable storm of thunder and rain is to succeed, it will lodge for some days before almost continually out of the water, and discover great uneasiness in violent throes and convulsive-like motions ; in frost as in clear summer-like weather it lies constantly at the bottom ; and in snow as in rainy weather it pitches its dwelling in the very mouth of the

phial. The water should be changed weekly in summer and fortnightly in winter.

803. CHEMICAL BAROMETER.

Take a long narrow bottle, such as an old-fashioned Eau-de-Cologne bottle, and put into it two and a half drachms of camphor and eleven drachms of spirit of wine ; when the camphor is dissolved, which it will readily do by slight agitation, add the following mixture :—Take water, nine drachms ; nitrate of potash (saltpetre), thirty-eight grains ; and muriate of ammonia (sal ammoniac), thirty-eight grains. Dissolve these salts in the water prior to mixing with the camphorated spirit ; then shake the whole well together. Cork the bottle well, and wax the top, but afterwards make a very small aperture in the cork with a red-hot needle. The bottle may then be hung up, or placed in any stationary position. By observing the different appearances which the materials assume, as the weather changes, it becomes an excellent prognosticator of a coming storm or of fine weather. In fine weather the solid part will collect at the bottom and the liquid be quite clear ; at the approach of rain the solid matter will gradually rise, and small crystalline stars will float about. Wind is indicated by flakes of the composition, in the form of leaves or feathers, appearing on the surface, and the whole seeming thick and in a state of fermentation. The quarter from which the wind blows is shown by the particles lying more closely to the glass on the opposite side from which the tempest is coming.

804. PHIAL BAROMETER.

Cut off with a file the rim and part of the neck of an ordinary glass phial. Then fill it three parts full of water, pure or coloured as may be desired, place a finger over the mouth of the phial and turn it upside down ; hang it up by means of wire or string, and take your finger away. In fair weather the water remains level with the neck of the phial ; but in damp weather a drop forms at the mouth and enlarges until it falls, to be followed by others.

805. NOTES ON THE BAROMETER.[1]

i. Why is a Barometer called also a "Weather Glass" ?

Because changes in the weather are generally preceded by alterations in the atmospheric pressure. But we cannot perceive those changes as they gradually occur ; the alteration in the eight of the column of mercury, therefore, enables us to know that atmospheric changes are taking place, and by observation we are enabled to determine certain rules by which the state of the weather may be foretold with considerable probability.

ii. Why does the Hand of the Weather Dial change its position when the Column of Mercury rises or falls ?

Because a weight which floats upon the open surface of the mercury is attached to a string, having a nearly equal weight at the other extremity ; the string is laid over a revolving pivot, to which the hand is fixed, and the friction of the string turns the hand as the mercury rises or falls.

iii. Why does Tapping the Face of the Barometer sometimes cause the Hand to Move ?

Because the weight on the surface of the mercury frequently leans against the side of the tube, and does not move freely. And, also, the mercury clings to the sides of the tube by capillary attraction ; therefore, tapping on the face of the barometer sets the weight free, and overcomes the attraction which impedes the rise or fall of the mercury.

iv. Why does the Fall of the Barometer denote the Approach of Rain ?

Because it shows that as the air cannot support the full weight of the column of mercury, the atmosphere must be thin with watery vapours.

v. Why does the Rise of the Barometer denote the Approach of Fine Weather ?

Because the external air, becoming dense, and free from highly elastic vapours, presses with increased force upon the mercury upon which the weight floats ; that weight, therefore, sinks in the short tube as the mercury rises in the long one, and in sinking, turns the hand to Change, Fair, &c.

vi. When does the Barometer stand highest ?

When there is a duration of frost, or when north-easterly winds prevail.

vii. Why does the Barometer stand highest at these times ?

Because the atmosphere is exceedingly dry and dense, and fully balances the weight of the column of mercury.

viii. When does the Barometer stand lowest ?

When a thaw follows a long frost, or when south-west winds prevail.

ix. Why does the Barometer stand lowest at these times ?

Because much moisture exists in the air, by which it is rendered less dense and heavy.

806. SIGNIFICATION OF CHRISTIAN NAMES OF MEN.

Aaron, *Hebrew*, a mountain, or lofty.
Abel, *Hebrew*, vanity.
Abraham, *Hebrew*, the father of many.
Adam, *Hebrew*, red earth.
Adolphus, *Saxon*, happiness and help.
Adrian, *Latin*, one who helps.
Alan, *Celtic*, harmony ; or *Slavonic*, a hound.
Alaric, *Saxon*, king or ruler.
Albert, *Saxon*, all bright.
Alexander, *Greek*, a helper of men.
Alfred, *Saxon*, all peace.
Algernon, *French*, bearded.
Alonzo, form of Alphonso, *q.v.*
Alphonso, *German*, ready or willing.
Ambrose, *Greek*, immortal.

---

1 Taken from "*The Reason Why—General Science,*" containing 1,400 Reasons for things generally believed but imperfectly understood. London : Houlston and Sons.

Amos, *Hebrew*, a burden.
Andrew, *Greek*, outrageous.
Anselm, *Saxon*, safeguard of God.
Anthony, *Latin*, flourishing.
Archibald, *German*, a bold observer.
Arnold, *German*, a maintainer of honour.
Arthur, *British*, a strong man.
Augustus, } *Latin*, venerable, grand.
Augustin, }
Baldwin, *German*, a bold winner.
Bardulph, *German*, a famous helper.
Barnaby, *Hebrew*, a prophet's son.
Bartholomew, *Hebrew*, the son of him who made the waters to rise.
Basil, *Greek*, kingly.
Beaumont, *French*, a pretty mount.
Bede, *Saxon*, prayer.
Benedict, *Latin*, blessed.
Benjamin, *Hebrew*, the son of a right hand.
Bennet, *Latin*, blessed.
Bernard, *German*, bear's heart.
Bertram, *German*, fair, illustrious.
Bertrand, *German*, bright raven.
Boniface, *Latin*, a well-doer.
Brian, *French*, having a thundering voice.
Cadwaller, *British*, valiant in war.
Caesar, *Latin*, adorned with hair.
Caleb, *Hebrew*, a dog.
Cecil, *Latin*, dim-sighted.
Charles, *German*, noble-spirited.
Christopher, *Greek*, bearing Christ.
Clarence, *Latin*, illustrious.
Claude, *Latin*, lame.
Clement, *Latin*, mild-tempered.
Conrad, *German*, able-counsel.
Constantine, *Latin*, resolute.
Cornelius, *Latin*, meaning uncertain.
Crispin, *Latin*, having curled locks.
Cuthbert, *Saxon*, known famously.
Cyril, *Greek*, commanding.
Dan, *Hebrew*, judgment.
Daniel, *Hebrew*, well-beloved.
Dennis, *Greek*, belonging to the god of wine.
Donald, *Celtic*, proud.
Douglas, *Gaelic*, dark grey.
Duncan, *Saxon*, brown chief.
Dunstan, *Saxon*, most high.
Edgar, *Saxon*, happy honour.
Edmund, *Saxon*, happy peace.
Edward, *Saxon*, happy keeper.
Edwin, *Saxon*, happy conqueror.
Egbert, *Saxon*, ever bright.
Elijah, *Hebrew*, God the Lord.

Elisha, *Hebrew*, the salvation of God.
Emmanuel, *Hebrew*, God with us.
Enoch, *Hebrew*, dedicated.
Ephraim, *Hebrew*, fruitful.
Erasmus, *Greek*, lovely, worthy to be loved.
Eric, *Anglo-Saxon*, kingly.
Ernest, *Greek*, earnest, serious.
Esau, *Hebrew*, hairy.
Eugene, *Greek*, nobly descended.
Evan, or Ivan, *British*, the same as John.
Everard, *German*, well reported.
Ezekiel, *Hebrew*, the strength of God.
Felix, *Latin*, happy.
Ferdinand, *German*, pure peace.
Fergus, *Saxon*, manly strength.
Francis, *German*, free.
Frederic, *German*, rich peace.
Gabriel, *Hebrew*, the strength of God.
Geoffrey, *German*, joyful.
George, *Greek*, a husbandman.
Gerard, *Saxon*, all towardliness.
Gideon, *Hebrew*, a breaker.
Gilbert, *Saxon*, bright as gold.
Giles, *Greek*, a little goat.
Godard, *German*, a godly disposition.
Godfrey, *German*, God's peace.
Godwin, *German*, victorious in God.
Gregory, *German*, watchful.
Griffith, *British*, having great faith.
Gustavus, *Swedish*, a warrior.
Guy, *French*, a leader.
Hannibal, *Punic*, a gracious lord.
Harold, *Saxon*, a champion.
Hector, *Greek*, a stout defender.
Henry, *German*, a rich lord.
Herbert, *German*, a bright lord.
Hercules, *Greek*, the glory of Hera, or Juno.
Herman, *Saxon*, a valiant soldier.
Hezekiah, *Hebrew*, cleaving to the Lord.
Horace, *Latin*.
Horatio, *Italian*, worthy to be beheld.
Howel, *British*, sound or whole.
Hubert, *German*, a bright colour.
Hugh, *Dutch*, high, lofty.
Humphrey, *German*, domestic peace.
Ignatius, *Latin*, fiery.
Ingram, *German*, of angelic purity.
Isaac, *Hebrew*, laughter.
Ivan, Russian, for *John*.
Jabez, *Hebrew*, one who causes pain.
Jacob, *Hebrew*, a supplanter.
James or Jacques, beguiling.
Jasper, *Persian*, radiant.

Jerome, *Greek*, holy name.
Joab, *Hebrew*, fatherhood.
Job, *Hebrew*, sorrowing.
Joel, *Hebrew*, acquiescing.
John, *Hebrew*, the grace of the Lord.
Jonah, *Hebrew*, a dove.
Jonathan, *Hebrew*, the gift of the Lord.
Joscelin, *German*, just.
Joseph, *Hebrew*, addition.
Joshua, *Hebrew*, a Saviour.
Josiah or Josias, *Hebrew*, the fire of the Lord.
Julian and Julius, *Latin*, soft-haired.
Kenneth, *Gaelic*, leader of men.
Lambert, *Saxon*, a fair lamb.
Lancelot, *Spanish*, a little lance.
Laurence, *Latin*, crowned with laurels.
Lazarus, *Hebrew*, destitute of help.
Leonard, *German*, like a lion.
Leopold, *German*, defending the people.
Lewis or Louis, *French*, the defender of the people.
Lionel, *Latin*, a little lion.
Llewellin, *British*, like a lion.
Llewellyn, *Celtic*, lightning.
Lubin, *Anglo-Saxon*, friend.
Lucius, *Latin*, shining.
Luke, *Greek*, a wood or grove.
Manfred, *German*, great peace.
Mark, *Latin*, a hammer.
Marmaduke, *Saxon*, noble and powerful.
Martin, *Latin*, a hammer.
Matthew, *Hebrew*, a gift or present.
Maurice, *Latin*, sprung of a Moor.
Meredith, *British*, the roaring of the sea.
Michael, *Hebrew*, who is like God ?
Morgan, *British*, a mariner.
Moses, *Hebrew*, drawn out.
Nathaniel, *Hebrew*, the gift of God.
Neal, *French*, somewhat black.
Nicholas, *Greek*, victorious over the people.
Noah, *Hebrew*, consolation.
Noel, *French*, belonging to one's nativity.
Norman, *French*, one born in Normandy.
Obadiah, *Hebrew*, the servant of the Lord.
Octavius, *Latin*, eighth born.
Oliver, *Latin*, an olive.
Orlando, *Italian*, counsel for the land.
Orson, *Latin*, a bear.
Oscar, *Celtic*, eager to fight.
Osmund, *Saxon*, house peace.
Oswald, *Saxon*, ruler of a house.
Owen, *British*, well-descended.
Patrick, *Latin*, a nobleman.
Paul, *Latin*, small, little.

Paulinus, *Latin*, little Paul.
Percival, *French*, a place in France.
Percy, *English*, adaptation of "pierce eye."
Peregrine, *Latin*, outlandish.
Peter, *Greek*, a rock or stone.
Philip, *Greek*, a lover of horses.
Phineas, *Hebrew*, of bold countenance.
Ralph, contracted from Randolph, or Randal, or Ranulph, *Saxon*, pure help.
Raymond, *German*, quiet peace.
Reginald, *Saxon*, ruler.
Reuben, *Hebrew*, the son of vision.
Reynold, *German*, a lover of purity.
Richard, *Saxon*, powerful.
Robert, *German*, famous in counsel.
Roderick, *German*, rich in fame.
Roger, *German*, strong counsel.
Roland or Rowland, *German*, counsel for the land.
Rollo, form of Roland, *q. v.*
Rufus, *Latin*, reddish.
Rupert, form of Robert.
Samson, *Hebrew*, a little son.
Samuel, *Hebrew*, heard by God.
Saul, *Hebrew*, desired.
Sebastian, *Greek*, to be reverenced.
Seth, *Hebrew*, appointed.
Sigismund, *Saxon*, one who conquers.
Silas, *Latin*, sylvan or living in the woods.
Silvester, *Latin*, born in the woods.
Simeon, *Hebrew*, hearing.
Simon, *Hebrew*, obedient.
Solomon, *Hebrew* peaceable.
Stephen, *Greek*, a crown or garland.
Swithin, *Saxon*, very high.
Thaddeus, *Syrian*, wise and prudent.
Theobald, *Saxon*, bold over the people.
Theodore, *Greek*, the gift of God.
Theodosius, *Greek*, the given of God.
Theophilus, *Greek*, a lover of God.
Thomas, *Hebrew*, a twin.
Timothy, *Greek*, a fearer of God.
Titus, *Greek*, meaning uncertain.
Tobias, *Hebrew*, the goodness of the Lord.
Tristram, *Latin*, grave, sad.
Uriah, *Latin*, light of God.
Valentine, *Latin*, powerful.
Victor, *Latin*, conqueror.
Vincent, *Latin*, conquering.
Vivian, *Latin*, living.
Walter, *German*, a conqueror.
Walwin, *German*, a conqueror.
Wilfred, *Saxon*, bold and peaceful.
William, *German*, defending many.

Zaccheus, *Syriac*, innocent.

Zachary, *Hebrew*, remembering the Lord.

Zebedee, *Syriac*, having an inheritance.

Zecharaiah, *Hebrew*, remembered of the Lord.

Zedekiah, *Hebrew*, the justice of the Lord.

807. SIGNIFICATION OF CHRISTIAN NAMES OF WOMEN

Abigail, *Hebrew*, father's delight.

Ada, *German*, same as Edith, *q. v.*

Adela, *German*, same as Adeline, *q. v.*

Adelaide, *German*, same as Adeline, *q.v.*

Adeline, *German*, a princess.

Agatha, *Greek*, good.

Agnes, *German*, chaste.

Alberta, *Saxon*, illustrious.

Alethea, *Greek*, the truth.

Alexandra, *Greek*, defender of men.

Alice, Alicia, *German*, noble.

Alma, *Latin*, benignant.

Althea, *Greek*, hunting.

Amabel, *Latin*, loveable.

Amanda, *Latin*, worthy of love.

Amelia, *Saxon*, industrious.

Amy, Amelia, *French*, a beloved.

Angelina, *Greek*, lovely, angelic.

Anna, or Anne, *Hebrew*, gracious.

Antoinette, *Latin*, invaluable.

Arabella, *Latin*, a fair altar.

Aurelia and Aureola, *Latin*, like gold.

Aurora, *Latin*, morning brightness.

Barbara, *Latin*, foreign or strange.

Beatrice, *Latin*, making happy.

Belinda, *Latin*, useful.

Bella, *Italian*, beautiful.

Benedicta, *Latin*, blessed.

Bernice, *Greek*, bringing victory.

Bertha, *Greek*, bright or famous.

Bessie, *short form of* Elizabeth, *q. v.*

Blanche, *French*, fair.

Bona, *Latin*, good.

Bridget, *Irish*, shining bright.

Camilla, *Latin*, attendant at a sacrifice.

Carlotta, *Italian*, same as Charlotte, *q. v.*

Caroline, *feminine of* Carolus, *the Latin of* Charles, noble-spirited.

Cassandra, *Greek*, a reformer of men.

Catherine, *Greek*, pure or clean.

Cecilia, *Latin*, from Cecil.

Celestine, *Latin*, heavenly.

Charity, *Greek*, love, bounty.

Charlotte, *French*, all noble.

Chloe, *Greek*, a green herb.

Christine and Christiana, *Greek*, belonging to Christ.

Cicely, *a corruption of* Cecilia, *q. v.*

Clara, *Latin*, clear or bright.

Claudia, *Latin*, lame.

Constance, *Latin*, constant.

Cora, *Greek*, a girl

Cornelia, *Latin*, steadfast.

Dagmar, *German*, joy of the Danes.

Deborah, *Hebrew*, a bee.

Diana, *Greek*, Jupiter's daughter.

Dinah, *Hebrew*, judged.

Dorcas, *Greek*, a wild rose.

Dorothea or Dora, Dorothy, *Greek*, the gift of God.

Edith, *Saxon*, happiness.

Edna, *Hebrew*, pleasure.

Eleanor, *Saxon*, all fruitful.

Eliza, Elizabeth, *Hebrew*, the oath of God.

Ellen, *another form of* Helen, *q. v.*

Elvira, *Arabic*, white.

Emily, *corrupted from* Amelia.

Emma, *German*, a nurse.

Esther, Hesther, *Hebrew*, secret.

Ethel, *Saxon*, of noble birth.

Eudoia, *Greek*, prospering in the way.

Eudora, *Greek*, good gift.

Eudosia, *Greek*, good gift or well-given.

Eugenia, *French*, well-born.

Eunice, *Greek*, fair victory.

Euphemia, *Greek*, of good report.

Eva or Eve, *Hebrew*, causing life.

Evangeline, *Greek*, bearer of good tidings.

Fanny *diminutive of* Frances, *q.v.*

Felicia, *Latin*, happiness.

Fenella, *Greek*, bright to look on.

Flora, *Latin*, flowers.

Florence, *Latin*, blooming, flourishing.

Frances, *German*, free.

Frederica, *Saxon*, abounding in peace.

Georgina, *Greek*, a tiller of the ground.

Geraldine, *Saxon*, strong.

Gertrude, *German*, all truth.

Gladys, *Welsh*, a fair maiden.

Grace, *Latin*, favour.

Griselda, *Teutonic*, patient and firm.

Hadassah, *Hebrew, form of* Esther, *q.v.*

Hagar, *Hebrew*, a stranger.

Hannah, *Hebrew*, gracious.

Harriet, *German*, head of the house.

Helen or Helena, *Greek*, alluring.

Henrietta, *fem. and dim. of* Henry, *q. v.*

Hephzibah, *Hebrew*, my delight is in her.

Hilda, *German*, warrior maiden.

Honora or Honoria, *Latin*, honourable.
Hortensia, *Latin*, a lover of a garden.
Huldah, *Hebrew*, a weazel.
Ida, *Saxon*, like a goddess.
Irene, *Greek*, peaceful.
Isabella, *Spanish*, fair Eliza.
Jane or Jeanne, *feminine of* John. *q.v.*
Janet, Jeanette, little Jane.
Jemima, *Hebrew*, a dove.
Joan, *Hebrew, fem. of* John, *q.v.*
Joanna or Johanna, *form of* Joan, *q.v.*
Josepha, *Hebrew*, addition.
Joyce, *French*, pleasant.
Judith, *Hebrew*, praising.
Julia, Juliana, *feminine* of Julius, *q.v.*
Justina, *Latin*, honourable.
Katharine, *form of* Catherine, *q.v.*
Keturah, *Hebrew*, incense.
Kexiah, *Hebrew*, cassia.
Laura, *Latin*, a laurel.
Lavinia, *Latin*, of Latium.
Letitia, *Latin*, joy of gladness.
Lilian, Lily, *Latin*, a lily.
Lois, *Greek*, better.
Louisa, *German, fem. of* Louis, *q.v.*
Lucretia, *Latin*, a chaste Roman lady.
Lucy, *Latin, feminine of* Lucius.
Lydia, *Greek*, descended from Lud.
Mabel, *Latin*, lovely or loveable.
Madeline, *form of* Magdalen, *q.v.*
Magdalen, *Syriac*, magnificent.
Margaret, *Greek*, a pearl.
Maria, Marie, *forms of* Mary, *q.v.*
Martha, *Hebrew*, bitterness.
Mary, *Hebrew*, bitter.
Matilda, *German*, a lady of honour.
Maud, *German, form of* Matilda, *q.v.*
May, *Latin*, month of May, or *dim. of* Mary, *q.v.*
Melissa, *Greek*, a honey bee.
Mercy, *English*, compassion.
Mildred, *Saxon*, speaking mild.
Millicent, *Latin*, a sweet singer.
Minnie, *dim of* Margaret, *q.v.*
Miranda, *Latin*, admirable.
Miriam, *Hebrew*, exalted.
Myra, *Greek*, grieving.
Nancy, a form of Anne.
Naomi, *Hebrew*, bitterness.
Nest, *British, the same as* Agnes.
Nicola, *Greek, feminine of* Nicolas.
Olive, Olivia, *Latin*, an olive.
Olympic, *Greek*, heavenly.
Ophelia, *Greek*, a serpent.

Parnell, or Petronilla, little Peter.
Patience, *Latin*, bearing patiently.
Paulina, *Latin, feminine of* Paulinus.
Penelope, *Greek*, destroying.
Philadelphia, *Greek*, brotherly love.
Philippa, *Greek, feminine of* Philip.
Phoebe, *Greek*, the light of life.
Phyllis, *Greek*, a green bough.
Polly, *variation of* Molly, *dim. of* Mary, *q.v.*
Priscilla, *Latin*, somewhat old.
Prudence, *Latin*, discretion.
Psyche, *Greek*, the soul.
Rachel, *Hebrew*, a lamb.
Rebecca, *Hebrew*, fat or plump.
Rhoda, *Greek*, a rose.
Rosa or Rose, *Latin*, a rose.
Rosalie or Rosaline, *Latin*, little rose.
Rosalind, *Latin*, beautiful as a rose.
Rosabella, *Italian*, a fair rose.
Rosamond, *Saxon*, rose of peace.
Roxana, *Persian*, dawn of day.
Ruth, *Hebrew*, trembling or beauty.
Sabina, *Latin*, sprung from the Sabines.
Salome, *Hebrew*, perfect.
Sapphira, *Greek*, like a saphhire stone.
Sarah, *Hebrew*, a princess.
Selina, *Greek*, the moon.
Sibylla, *Greek*, a prophetess.
Sophia, *Greek*, wisdom.
Sophronia, *Greek*, of a sound mind.
Stella, *Latin*, a star.
Susan, Susanna, *Hebrew*, a lily.
Tabitha, *Syriac*, a roe.
Temperance, *Latin*, moderation.
Teresa, *Greek*, a gleaner.
Theodora or Theodosia, *Greek*, given by God.
Thomasine, *Hebrew*, a twin.
Tryphena, *Greek*, delicate.
Tryphosa, *Greek*, delicious.
Ulrica, *Saxon*, very rich.
Ursula, *Latin*, a she bear.
Valeria, *Latin*, strong and powerful.
Victoria, *Latin*, all conquering.
Vida, *Hebrew*, beloved.
Viola, *Latin*, a violet.
Virginia, *Latin*, chaste.
Vivien, *Latin*, lively.
Walburga, *Saxon*, gracious.
Wilhelmina, *Saxon*, helmet of defence.
Winifred, *Saxon*, winning peace.
Zenobia, *Greek*, the life of Jupiter.
Zoe, *Greek*, lively.

Precious Stones and their Language.

Among the ancients, precious stones were symbolical of certain qualities, and they were also sacred to certain months of the year.

The *Garnet*, signifying his faithfulness, was sacred to January.

Amethyst, peace-making, to February.

Bloodstone, courage and wisdom, to March.

Sapphire, repentance, to April.

Emerald, true love, to May.

Agate, health and longevity, to June.

Ruby, true friendship, to July.

Sardonyx, conjugal happiness, to August.

Chrysolite, freedom from evil, September.

Opal, hope, October.

Topaz, friendship, November.

Turqoise, happiness in love, December.

808. ECONOMY OF FUEL.

There is no part of domestic economy which every body professes to understand better than the management of a fire, and yet there is no branch in the household arrangement where there is a greater proportional and unnecessary waste than arises from ignorance and mismanagement in this article.

i. **To Light a Fire.**—Before lighting the fire in the morning, thoroughly clean out the grate ; lay a piece of thick paper, cut to the form and size of the grate, at the bottom ; *pile up fresh* coal, *nearly as high as the level of the top bar* ; the pieces should be about the size of small potatoes or walnuts, but this is not absolutely necessary ; the larger lumps should he laid in front, the smaller ones behind ; then put a liberal supply of paper, or shavings, and sticks, on the top, and cover the whole with yesterday's cinders, adding a very little coal. Thus, it will be seen, the fire is to be lighted *at the top*. The results will be not only satisfactory, but astonishing. The fire lights up at once, without further trouble. The centre of the fuel soon catches, and the inferior strata of coal ignite. The fire spreads downwards, and the smoke is forced

to pass through the upper layers of burning coal ; the consequence is, there is perfect combustion, the great volume of gas and smoke usually sent off from fires, and which consists of the most combustible part of coal, being thoroughly consumed, and yielding heat. A fire so made will go on burning for six, eight, or even ten hours, without poking, without adding fresh coal, or any attention whatever. There is little or no smoke, and the fire gives out a pleasant and uniform glow. One fair trial of this system will satisfy every body ; and the servant will soon find that it will not only save her master an incredible quantity of coals, but that it will also save her a vast amount of trouble ; the coal-scuttle will require filling less frequently, the hearth will not require sweeping so often ; and the services of the sweep will seldom be needed. It will sometimes be necessary to loosen, or stir slightly the upper part of the fire, if it begins to cake ; but the lower part must not be touched, otherwise it will burn away too soon. The above method is best adapted for rooms, and offices, where the fires are not required for cookery, immediately after being lit, as the heat is developed more gradually than in the old method of under-lighting. Deep grates are best suited for the new system.

ii. **Regulation of Fires.**—Fires upon this plan may be regulated to the temperature of the weather, and to the number of hours they are required to burn. For instance :— When the weather is very cold, and the fire requires to be lit early, and kept up until late, put a much deeper layer of coal in the bottom—quite up to the *top* bar ; when the weather is mild, &c., then lay the coals only up to the *second* bar from the top, and so on. When you have tried this experiment a few times, and are fully satisfied with it, have pieces of *Sheet Iron*, cut to fit the bottom of your grates, instead of the paper. This will save the trouble of cutting the papers daily, and the sheet iron will last an indefinite time.

iii. **Clear Fires for Cooking.**— After making your fire as directed in par. i, replenish it with bits of coke and you will save half the cost of coal fires.

iv. **The Use of the Poker** should be confined to two particular points—the opening of a dying fire, so as to admit the free passage of the air into it, and sometimes, but not always through it ; or else, drawing together the remains of a half-burned fire, so as to concentrate the heat, whilst the parts still ignited are opened to the atmosphere.

v. **When using a pair of Bellows** to a fire only partially ignited, or partially extinguished, blow, at first, not into the part that is still alight, but into the dead coals close to it, so that the air may partly extend to the burning coal. After a few blasts blow into the burning fuel, directing the stream partly towards the dead coal, when it will be found that the ignition will extend much more rapidly than under the common method of blowing furiously into the flame at random.

vi. **Preserve the Coal Ashes** which are usually thrown away as worthless. When you have a sufficient quantity, add to them an equal amount of small coal from your cellar, and then pour on a little water, and mix with a shovel. Use this compost for placing on the *top* or the back of the fire. It will burn brightly and pleasantly and only a little dust will remain unconsumed.

vii. **Fill up your Coal Cellars in the middle of Summer** when coal is cheapest, instead of waiting for the winter, when it gets dearer.

viii. **Slow Combustion Fire Grates.** Many of the modern grates constructed on this principle will be found to effect a great saving in the consumption of fuel, and at the same time throw out greater heat into the room than the old-fashioned varieties.

809. A CHEAP FUEL.

One bushel of small coal or sawdust, or both mixed together, two bushels of sand, one bushel and a half of clay. Let these be mixed together with common water, like ordinary mortar ; the more they are stirred and mixed together the better ; then make them into balls, or, with a small mould, in the shape of bricks, pile them in a dry place, and use when hard and sufficiently dry. A fire cannot be lighted with them, but when the fire is lighted, put two or three on behind with some coals in front, and the fire will be found to last longer than if made up in the ordinary way.

810. GAS STOVES.

These are very useful, and the simpler the stove the better. They are cleanly and very little trouble. With even a cheap stove, costing only a few shillings, one can bake, fry, and boil. With the terra-cotta circles sometimes supplied with the stove, one can warm a bed, or by wrapping them in flannel, make foot-warmers.

Some stoves cook by hidden gas, in others the food is exposed to the jets. In the case of the circles of jets used in boiling, care must be exercised in selecting a stove in which the top plate does not come down too close on the jets, as then a sufficient quantity of gas cannot be turned on without causing a flattening of the flame by the bottom of the saucepan, and thus spread an unpleasant smell in the house.

If the stove is properly regulated, and the gas turned off when not in use, it will be quite as cheap as using coal, and much dirt and trouble will be avoided.

811. GAS LIGHTS.

Gas, as every one is aware, is the most general source of artificial light. It has its advantages, and, computed with the electric light, its disadvantages. It makes a room hot, it occasionally declines to produce a good light, and it certainly makes ceilings, &c., dirty.

The following are some of the best methods of preserving the parity of the air in a room while using light supplied by ordinary gas :—

i. The incandescent gas-burners.

ii. The globe light, by which the elements arising from combustion are removed without coming into contact with the air in the room.

iii. The sun burner, which has the same object.

812. HINTS ON THE USE OF GAS.

i. When gas is laid on to a house, it is very important to have all the pipes tested, in order to see if there is any leakage.

ii. Before turning off the gas at the main at night, it should be seen that each light has previously been turned off, as otherwise when the gas is again turned on at the main, it will escape from the unturned taps, often to a dangerous extent.

iii. Don't look for an escape of gas with a light ! Go without a light, and open the doors and windows for a quarter of an hour before bringing a flame near.

iv. Sometimes a small leak makes itself evident, and there may not be a gas-fitter available. Get a piece of yellow soap and rub it on the place of escape. This will do until you can replace the soap with some white lead and oil.

v. Some gasaliers have a sliding tube, and where this is the case the gas sometimes escapes. This is remedied by slowly pouring a small quantity of water down the tube.

vi. If the gas in burning makes a hissing sound, it shows that it is turned on too fully at the main, and means so much unconsumed gas to be paid for.

813. HOW TO READ YOUR GAS METER.

It is remarkable how few house-holders know how to read their gas

meters. You will see that there are three dials, about the size of a half-crown, and over these is sometimes a fourth, which is only an indicator of any gas entering the meter.

The figures on the right-hand dial show the number of *hundreds* of feet consumed, up to 1000. The centre dial shows the number of *thousands* up to 10,000 ; and the left-hand dial the number of *ten-thousands* up to 100,000.

The quantity of gas which has passed through the meter since the last date is ascertained by reading from the dials the total amount registered, and deducting from that total the quantity shown by the dial at the former observation, thus :—

The total registered by the 3 dials is		59,000
Amount at previous observation	=	52,500
Amount since last observation	=	6,500

814. ELECTIC LIGHT.

This illuminant is fast coming into general use, and is in many respects superior to gas-lighting. It is cooler, cleaner, and in every respect handier. If we come home late at night from the theatre or elsewhere, and have an electric light in the hall, we have merely to press the button and there is a light at once.

The same thing in the dining-room, wine (or coal) cellar, and the bedrooms. What a saving of matches struck with frozen fingers on a cold winter's night, and avoidance of bad temper consequent on the matches going out.

815. The Incandescent Lamps are the most suitable for lighting interiors of houses and other buildings, and are made in a variety of sizes and degrees of power, and combined with innumerable styles and designs of fittings, from quite plain to extremely ornamental and artistic.

Sometimes the lamps fail in light-giving power, by reason of having an imperfect vacuum (the globes of the incandescent light are exhausted of air). This may be detected by feeling the globe. If the vacuum is faulty it gets quite hot.

816. Great Care is required in fitting up Electric Lights to avoid danger from fire—none but the best insulated wire should be used, and only thoroughly skilled workmen should be entrusted with the work.

817. ELECTRIC BELLS.

No house of any pretensions is now considered complete without being fitted with electric bells, the wires of which are carried in tubes concealed by the skirtings, &c., of the walls. The ordinary electric bell is a vibrating contact breaker carrying a tiny hammer on its spring which strikes a bell ; the force being supplied by a galvanic battery. The old-fashioned troublesome system of crank bells is rapidly becoming supplanted by its electric rival

How convenient it is to have an electric bell in one's study ; one has no need to get up and interrupt one's work. Again, how useful at the dinner table to summon a servant without leaving one's seat. In fact, it is a most useful addition, in a thousand ways, to the comforts of life.

818. THE TELEPHONE.

The object of this instrument is to make sounds audible at a distance by means of electricity. It is very largely used for business and other public purposes, and is also extensively fitted to modern private houses. The master can from his study give verbal instructions to his servants in the stables, or other offices, although they may be some considerable distance from the house.

The limit of the capabilities of this wonderful instrument cannot yet be gauged, vast strides having of late years been made in its adaptation. At the present time most of the principal cities in Europe are connected by telephone wires, and merchants and others are thus enabled to carry on audible conversations with persons in distant mercantile centres. It is even possible for friends situate in London and Paris respectively, to indulge in a chat.

819. THE MICROPHONE.

This instrument was invented by Professor Hughes in 1878. By its means the very faintest sounds, such as the fall of a feather, or a very delicate piece of paper or tissue, may be distinctly heard.

820. THE PHONOGRAPH.

This marvellous contrivance was invented by Mr. Edison of America about the year 1877. By this instrument the human voice, singing, and other sounds are mechanically recorded and reproduced. It is about the same size as an ordinary sewing machine.

When sounds pass into the receiver, a very fine steel or jewel point, influenced by the pressure of the sound waves, produces almost invisible cuts on a cylinder of wax, which can be removed and preserved. Having thus established the record, when the point again passes over the cylinder, the diaphragm on the instrument naturally produces the same vibrations as before, and reproduces the same sounds.

The instrument is extensively used by musicians, reciters, actors, clergymen, &c., to improve their powers of singing or elocution. There are now many places where it can be heard for a few pence.

821. THE CINEMATOGRAPH, AND THE KINETOSCOPE.

These wonderful instruments reproduce actual scenes of life and motion. Thus a railway train travelling at express speed is photographed on a succession of films, whilst they rotate very rapidly. The pictures are then developed, and are thrown, by means of an optical or other lantern, on to the screen, when the train is again presented to us rushing along at full speed, and apparently actually in motion.

822. OIL FOR LIGHTING.

Whenever oil, whether animal, vegetable or mineral, is used for the purpose of artificial light, it should be kept free from all exposure to atmospheric air ; as it is apt to absorb considerable (quantities of oxygen. If animal oil is very coarse or tenacious, a very small quantity of oil of turpentine may be added.

823. CANDLES.

These improve by keeping a few months. If wax candles become discoloured or soiled, they may be restored by rubbing them over with a clean flannel slightly dipped in spirits of wine. In lighting candles always hold the match to the side of the wick, and not over the top of it, as is generally done.

824. NIGHT LIGHTS.

In cases where the manufactured articles are not easily obtainable, the waste of candles may be thus applied. Make a *fine* cotton, and wax it with white wax. Then cut into the requisite lengths. Melt the grease and pour into pill boxes, previously either fixing the cotton in the centre, or dropping it in just before the grease sets. If a little white wax be melted with the grease, all the better. In this manner, the ends and drippings of candles may be used up. When set to burn, place in a saucer, with sufficient water to rise to the extent of the 16th of an inch around the base of the night light

825. BREAD MAKING.

826. TO MAKE PLAIN BREAD.

To one quartern of flour (three pounds and a half), add a dessertspoonful of salt, and mix them well ; mix about two tablespoonfuls of good fresh yeast with half-a-pint of water a little warm, but not hot ; make a hole with your hand in the middle of the flour, but not quite touching the bottom of the pan ; pour the water and yeast into this hole, and stir it with a spoon till you have made a thin batter ; sprinkle this over with flour, cover the pan over with a dry cloth, and let it stand in a warm room for an hour ; not near the fire, except in cold weather, and then not too close ; then add a pint of water a little warm, and knead the whole well together, till the dough comes clean through the hand (some flour will require a little more water ; but in this, experience must be your guide) ; make it into loaves, then let it stand again for about a quarter of an hour, and bake in a hot oven for about one and a half hours ; small loaves take less time ; when sufficiently baked they sound hollow.

827. TO MAKE BREAD WITH GERMAN YEAST.

To one quartern of flour add a dessertspoonful of salt as before ; dissolve one ounce of dried German yeast in about three tablespoonfuls of cold water ; add to this one pint and a half of water a little warm, and pour the whole into the flour ; knead it well immediately, and let it stand as before directed for one hour ; then bake at pleasure. It will not hurt if you make up a pack of flour at once and bake three or four loaves in succession, provided you do not keep the dough too warm. German yeast may be obtained at almost any corn-chandler's. In winter it will keep good for a week in a dry place, and in summer it should be kept in cold water, and the water changed every day. Wheat meal requires a little more yeast than fine flour, or a longer time to stand in the dough for rising.

828. UNFERMENTED BREAD.

Three pounds wheat meal, or four pounds of white flour, two heaped tablespoonfuls of baking powder, a tablespoonful of salt, and about two and a half pints of lukewarm water, or just sufficient to bring the flour to a proper consistency for bread-making ; the way to make it is as follows :— First mix the baking powder, salt, and about three-fourths of the flour well together by rubbing in a pan ; then pour the water over the flour, and mix well by stirring. Then add most of the remainder of the flour, and work up the dough with the hand to the required consistency, which is indicated by the smoothness of the dough, and its not sticking to the hands or the sides of the pan when kneaded. The rest of the flour must then be added to stiffen the dough, which may then be placed in tins or formed by the hand into any shape that may be preferred and placed on flat tins for baking. The tins should be well floured. Put the loaves at once in a well-heated oven. After they have been in the oven about a quarter of an hour open the ventilator to slacken the heat and allow the steam to escape. In an hour the process of baking will be completed. Bread made in this way keeps moist longer than bread made with yeast, and is far more sweet and digestible. This is especially recommended to persons who suffer from indigestion, who will find the brown bread invaluable.

829. PURE AND CHEAP BREAD.

Whole-meal bread may be made by any one who possesses a small hand-mill that will grind about twenty pounds of wheat at a time. This bread is far more nutritious than ordinary bread made from flour from which the bran has been entirely separated. The meal thus obtained may be used for puddings, &c. There are mills which grind and dress the wheat at one operation. Such mills may be obtained at any ironmonger's. The saving in the cost of bread amounts to nearly one-third, which would soon cover the cost of the mill, and effect a most important saving, besides promoting health by avoiding the evil effects of adulterated flour.

830. BREAD MADE WITH LIME WATER.

It has been found that water saturated with lime produces in bread the same whiteness, softness, and capacity of retaining moisture, as results from the use of alum ; while the former removes all acidity from the dough, and supplies an ingredient needed in the structure of the bones, but which is deficient in corn. The best proportion to use is, five pounds of water saturated with lime, to every nineteen pounds of flour. No change is required in the process of baking. The lime most effectually coagulates the gluten, and the bread weighs well ; bakers must therefore approve of its introduction, which is not injurious to the system, like alum, &c.

831. BREAD MADE WITH BRAN WATER.

A great increase on home-made bread, even equal to one-fifth, may be produced by using bran water for kneading the dough. The proportion is three pounds of bran for every twenty-eight pounds of flour, to be boiled for an hour, and then strained through a hair sieve.

832. INDIAN CORN FLOUR AND WHEATEN BREAD.

The peculiarity of this bread consists in its being composed in part of Indian corn flour, which may be seen by the following analysis to be much richer in gluten and fatty matter than the flour of wheat, to which circumstance it owes its highly nutritive character:—

	English Fine Wheaten Flour		Indian Corn Flour.
Water	.	16 .	14
Gluten	.	10 .	12
Fat	.	2 .	8
Starch, &c.	.	72	66
		100	100

Take of Indian corn flour seven pounds, pour upon it four quarts of boiling water, stirring it all the time ; let it stand till about new-milk warm, then mix it with fourteen pounds of fine wheaten flour, to which a quarter of a pound of salt has been previously added. Make a depression on the surface of this mixture, and pour into it two quarts of yeast, which should be thickened to the consistence of cream with some of the flour ; let it stand all night ; on the following morning the whole should be well kneaded, and allowed to stand for three hours ; then divide it into loaves, which are better baked in tins, in which they should stand for half-an-hour, then bake. It is of importance that the flour of Indian corn should be procured, as Indian corn meal is that which is commonly met with at the shops, and the coarseness of the husk in the meal might to some persons be prejudicial.

833. RYE AND WHEAT FLOUR, in equal quantities, make an excellent and economical bread.

834. RICE IN BREAD.

Take one pound and a half of rice, and boil it gently over a slow fire in three quarts of water about five hours, stirring it, and afterwards beating it up into a smooth paste. Mix this, while warm, into two gallons or four pounds of flour, adding at the same time the usual quantity of yeast. Allow the dough to work a certain time near the fire, after which divide it into loaves. When baked it is excellent white bread.

835. POTATOES IN BREAD.— Place in a dish three pounds of flour near the fire to warm ; take one pound of good potatoes, those of a mealy kind being preferable, peel and boil them as if for the table, mash them fine, and then mix with them as much cold water as will allow all except small lumps to pass through a coarse sieve into the flour, which will now be ready to receive them ; add yeast, &c., and mix for bread in the usual way. This plan

will be found economical, particularly when flour is dear.

836. APPLES IN BREAD.

A very light, pleasant bread is made in France by a mixture of apples and flour, in the proportion of one of the former to two of the latter. The usual quantity of yeast is employed, as in making common bread, and is beaten with flour and warm pulp of the apples after they have boiled, and the dough is then considered as set ; it is then put in a proper vessel, and allowed to rise for eight or twelve hours, and then baked in long loaves. Very little water is requisite.

837. PULLED BREAD.

Take from the oven an ordinary loaf when it is about half baked, and with the fingers, while the bread is yet hot, dexterously pull the half-set dough into pieces of irregular shape, about the size of an egg. Don't attempt to smooth or flatten them—the rougher their shapes the better. Set upon tins, place in a very slow oven, and bake to a rich brown. This forms a deliciously crisp crust for eating with cheese, and is also very nice with wine instead of biscuits. If you do not bake at home, your baker will prepare it for you, if ordered.

838. FRENCH BREAD AND ROLLS.

Take a pint and a half of milk ; make it quite warm ; half-a-pint of small-beer yeast ; add sufficient flour to make it as thick as batter ; put it into a pan ; cover it over, and keep it warm ; when it has risen as high as it will, add a quarter of a pint of warm water and half-an-ounce of salt,— mix them well together,—rub into a little flour two ounces of butter ; then make your dough, not quite so stiff as for your bread ; let it stand for three-quarters of an hour, and it will be ready to make into rolls, &c. :—let them stand till they have risen, and bake them in a quick oven.

839. FANCY ROLLS.

With one pound of flour rub in two ounces of butter. Add one teaspoonful of salt and two teaspoonfuls of baking powder ; then make into a light dough with half-a-pint of milk. Divide into small portions and form into crescents, rings, or any other fancy shape. Glaze by washing over with milk, and bake for fifteen or twenty minutes in a quick oven.

840. SALLY LUNN TEA CAKES.

Take one pint of milk quite warm, a quarter of a pint of thick small beer yeast ; put them into a pan with flour sufficient to make it as thick as batter,—cover it over, and let it stand till it has risen as high as it will, *i.e.* about two hours ; add two ounces of lump sugar, dissolved in a quarter of a pint of warm milk, a quarter of a pound of butter rubbed into the flour very fine—then make the dough the same as for French rolls, &c. ; let it stand half-an-hour ; then make up the cakes, and put them on tins :—when they have stood to rise, bake them in a quick oven. Care should be taken never to mix the yeast with water or milk too hot or too cold, as either extreme will destroy the fermentation. In summer it should be lukewarm,—in winter a little warmer,—and in very cold weather, warmer still. When it has first risen, if you are not prepared, it will not harm if it stand an hour.

841. "As Hot as an Oven" —A

gentleman having occasion to call on a solicitor found him in his office, which was very hot. He remarked the great heat, and said the room "was as hot as an oven."—"So it ought to be," replied the lawyer, "for it is here *I make my bread.*"

842. TO MAKE YEAST.

Boil, say on Monday morning, two ounces of the best hops in four quarts of water for half-an-hour ; strain the liquor, and let it cool to new-milk warmth ; then put in a small handful of salt, and half-a-pound of sugar ; beat up one pound of the best flour with some of the liquor, and then mix well all together in a bowl. On Wednesday add three pounds of potatoes, boiled, and then mashed, to stand till Thursday ; then strain it and put into bottles, and it is ready for use. *It must be stirred frequently while it is making, and kept near the fire.* Before using, shake the bottle up well. It will keep in a cool place for two months, and is best at the latter part of the time. This yeast ferments spontaneously, not requiring the aid of other yeast ; and if care be taken to let it ferment well in the earthen bowl in which it is made, you may cork it up tight when bottled. The quantity above given will fill four seltzer-water bottles.

843. USE OF BAKING POWDERS.

These useful preparations are now much used in making bread and pastry of all kinds, and have the merit of being both cheap and wholesome. By the action of these substances, carbonic acid is generated in the dough, which causes it to rise in the same manner as the so-called "aerated bread" made on Dr. Dauglish's system, by which carbonic acid is forced into the dough before baking.

844. RECIPE FOR A BAKING POWDER.

Tartaric acid, eight ounces ; rice flour, twelve ounces ; bi-carbonate of sodium, ten ounces.

845. HOW TO USE BAKING POWDER.

This may be used instead of yeast in making all kinds of bread, cake, tea-cakes, &c., and for biscuits and pastry, either without or in combination with butter, suet, &c. Bread, &c., made with baking powder is never placed before the fire to rise, as when made with yeast, but the dough may be shaped and put into the ovens as soon as it is made. The chief points to bear in remembrance are that in making bread two teaspoonfuls of baking powder should be used to every pound of floor, but for pastry, cakes, buns, &c., three teaspoonfuls should be used. The ingredients should always be thoroughly incorporated by mixing ; the tins on which or in which the dough is placed to bake should be well floured, and not greased ; and the oven should always be very hot, so that the baking may be effected as rapidly as possible.

846. COOKING INSTRUMENTS.

847. THE SAUCEPAN AND STEWPAN.

When we come to speak of the Saucepan, we have to consider the claims of a very large, ancient, and useful family. There are large saucepans, dignified with the name of Boilers, and small saucepans, which come under the denomination of Stew pans. There are few kinds of meat or fish which the Saucepan will not receive, and dispose of in a satisfactory manner ; and few vegetables for which it is not adapted. When rightly used, it is a very economical servant, allowing nothing to be lost ; that which escapes from the meat while in its charge forms broth, or may be made the basis of soups. Fat rises upon the surface of the water, and may be skimmed off ; while in various stews it combines, in an eminent degree, what we may term the *fragrance* of cookery, and the *piquancy* of taste. The French are perfect masters of the use of the Stewpan. And we shall find that, as all cookery is but an aid to digestion, the operations of the Stewpan resemble the action of the stomach very closely. The stomach is a close sac, in which solids and fluids are mixed together, macerated in the gastric juice, and dissolved by the aid of heat and motion, occasioned by the continual contractions and re-laxations of the coats of the stomach during the action of digestion. This is more closely resembled by the process of stewing than by any other of our culinary methods.

848. THE GRIDIRON.

This, although the simplest of cooking instruments, is by no means to be despised. In common with all cooking utensils, the Gridiron should be kept scrupulously clean ; and when it is used, the bars should be allowed to get warm before the meat is placed upon it, otherwise the parts crossed by the bars will be insufficiently dressed. The fire should be sharp, clear, and free from smoke. The heat soon forms a film upon the surface of the meat, by which the juices are retained. There is a description of gridiron in which the bars are grooved to catch the juice of the meat, but a much better invention is the upright gridiron, which is attached to the front of the grate, and has a pan at the bottom to catch the gravy. Kidneys, rashers, &c., dressed in this manner will be found delicious.

849. THE FRYING-PAN.

This noisy and greasy servant requires much watchfulness. Like the Gridiron, the Frying-pan requires a clear but not a large fire, and the pan should be allowed to get thoroughly hot, and be well covered with fat, before meat is put into it. The excellence of frying very much depends upon the sweetness of the oil, butter, lard, or fat that may be employed. The Frying-pan is very useful for warming up cold vegetables and other kinds of food, and in this respect may be considered a real friend of economy. All know the relish afforded by a pancake, eggs, and various kinds of fried fish for which, as they require that which is the essence of frying, *boiling and browning in fat*, both the Saucepan and Gridiron are quite unsuited.

850. THE SPIT.

A very ancient and useful implement for the process of roasting, it has, however, been superseded in most middle class families by the Meat Hook and Roasting Jack.

851. THE HEAT HOOK AND JACK.

These have taken the place of the Spit for roasting. The joint or article to be cooked is suspended before the fire. For roasting in this manner the lintel of the mantelpiece is furnished with a brass or iron arm, turning on pivots in a plate fastened to the lintel, and notched along its upper edge. From this arm, which is turned back against the lintel when not in use, the meat is hung and turned by means of a Jack, an instrument containing a spring, which when wound up keeps the joint revolving, or a skein of worsted, knotted in three or four places, which answers the same purpose, and may be replaced by a new one when required, at a merely nominal cost. Meat roasted in this manner should be turned occasionally, the hook being inserted first at one end and then at the other.

852. THE OVEN.

The old-fashioned kitchen range was usually furnished with an oven at the side of the fire grate, and was suitable for baking purposes only. The ovens attached to the modern kitchen ranges, or kitcheners as they are called, whether heated by coal fires or gas, are constructed in such a manner that a current of air may be allowed to circulate through them, in this way enabling a joint to be roasted in the oven almost as satisfactorily as before the fire.

853. THE DUTCH OVEN.

A miniature roasting and toasting apparatus designed for cooking small things, which could not well be cooked by means of the Spit, or the ordinary oven ; they are suspended to the bars of the grate, and the hooks with which they are furnished are movable, so that what is being cooked may be readily turned.

854. UTILITY OF THE KITCHEN.

"In the hands of an expert cook," says Majendie, "alimentary substances are made almost entirely to change their nature, their form, consistence, odour, savour, colour, chemical composition, &c ; everything is so modified, that it is often impossible for the most exquisite sense of taste to recognize the substance that makes up the basis of certain dishes. The greatest utility of the kitchen consists in making the food agreeable to the senses, and rendering it easy of digestion."

"Hey—what !" said a gay Marquess to Descartes, "do you Philosophers eat dainties ?" The latter replied, "Do you think that God made good things only for Fools !"— (*Dr. Kitchiner.*)

855. SEVEN NEEDS FOR A WELL-COOKED JOINT.

1. The meat must be *good.*
2. Must have been kept a *good* time.
3. Must be roasted at a *good* fire.
4. By a *good* cook.
5. Who must be in a *good* temper.
6. With all this felicitous combination, you must have *good* luck, and
7. *Good* appetite.—(*Dr. Kitchiner.*)

856. DR. SAMUEL JOHNSON ON FOOD.

"Some people have a foolish way of not minding, or pretending not to mind, what they eat ; for my part I mind my belly very studiously and very carefully, and I look upon it, that he who does not mind his belly, will hardly mind anything else."

857. THEORY OF COOKING.

To some extent the claims of either process of cooking depend upon the taste of the individual. Some persons may esteem the peculiar flavour of fried meats, while others will prefer broils or stews. It is important, however, to understand the *theory* of each method of cooking, so that whichever may be adopted may be done well. Bad cooking, though by a good method, is far inferior to good cooking by a bad method.

858. **Roasting,** by causing the contraction of the cellular substance which contains the fat, expels more fat than boiling. The free escape of watery particles in the form of vapour so necessary to produce flavour, must be regulated by frequent basting with the fat which has exuded from the meat, combined with a little salt and water—otherwise the meat would burn, and become hard and tasteless.

859. **Boiling** extracts a portion of the juice of the meat, which mixes with the water, and also dissolves some of its solids ; the more fusible parts of the fat melt out, combine with the water, and form soup or broth. The meat loses its red colour, becomes more savoury in taste and smell, and more firm and digestible. If the process is continued too long, the meat becomes indigestible, less succulent, and tough.

860. **The Loss by Roasting** is said to vary from 14$\frac{3}{5}$ths to nearly double that rate per cent. The average loss on roasting butcher's meat is 22 per cent ; and on domestic poultry, is 20½.

861. **The Loss by Boiling** varies from 6¼ to 16 per cent The average loss on boiling butcher's meat, pork, hams, and bacon, is 12 ; and on domestic poultry, is 14¾.

So that it will be seen by comparison with the percentage given of the loss by boiling, that roasting is not so economical ; especially when we take into account that the loss of weight by boiling is not actual loss of economic materials, for we then possess the principal ingredients for soups, whereas, after roasting, the fat only remains.

862. PROCESSES OF COOKING.

863. ROASTING.

The success of every branch of cookery depends upon the good management of the kitchen fire ; roasting especially, requires a brisk, clear, and steady fire. In stirring the fire, be careful to remove the dripping-pan, else dust and ashes may fall into it ; on no account let the fire get dull and low, as a strong heat is requisite to brown the meat. Paper should be placed round meat that is not very fat, to prevent it from being scorched. When steam rises from the meat it is done.

N.B.—Soyer recommends that all dark meats, such as beef and mutton, should be put down to a sharp fire for at least fifteen minutes, until the outside has acquired a coating of condensed gravy, and then put back, and allowed to cook gently. Lamb, veal, and pork, if young and tender, should be cooked with a moderate fire.

863a. **Sirloin of Beef** of about fifteen pounds will require to be before the fire about three and a half or four hours. Take care to spit it evenly, that it may not be heavier on one side than the other ; tie a sheet of paper over the fat to preserve it, and having put a little clean dripping into the dripping-pan, baste it well as soon as it is put down, and every quarter of an hour all the time it is roasting, till the last half-hour ; then take off the paper and make some gravy for it, stir the fire and make it clear ; to brown and froth it, sprinkle a little salt over it, baste it with butter, and dredge it with flour ; let it go a few minutes longer, till the froth rises, take it up, put it on the dish, &c. Garnish it with horseradish, scraped as fine as possible with a very sharp knife.

864. Ribs of Beef.—The first three ribs, of fifteen or twenty pounds, will take three hours, or three and a half ; the fourth and fifth ribs will take as long, managed in the same way as the sirloin. Paper the fat and the thin part, or it will be done too much, before the thick part is done enough. As a rule, beef, mutton, and veal take about a quarter of an hour per lb. to roast. Lamb and poultry only take twelve to thirteen minutes per lb., but veal takes quite fifteen minutes, and pork twenty minutes, to cook.

865. Ribs of Beef boned and rolled.—Keep two or three ribs of beef till quite tender, take out the bones, and skewer the meat as round as possible, like a fillet of veal. Some cooks egg it, and sprinkle it with veal stuffing before rolling it. As the meat is in a solid mass, it will require more time at the fire than ribs of beef with the bones : a piece of ten or twelve pounds weight will not be well and thoroughly roasted in less than four and a half or five hours. For the first half-hour it should not be less than twelve inches from the fire, that it may get gradually warm to the centre, the last half-hour before it is finished, sprinkle a little salt over it, and, if you like, flour it, to froth it.

866. Roasting Mutton.—As beef requires a large sound fire, mutton must have a brisk and sharp one. If you wish to have mutton tender it should be hung as long as it will keep, and then good eight-tooth (*i. e.* four years old) mutton is as good eating as venison.

867. The Leg of eight pounds will take a little over two hours ; let it be well basted.

868. A Chine or Saddle—*i. e.* the two loins, of ten or eleven pounds—two hours and a half. It is the business of the butcher to take off the skin and skewer it on again, to defend the meat from extreme heat, and preserve its succulence. If this is neglected, tie a sheet of paper over it ; baste the strings you tie it on with directly, or they will burn. About a quarter of an hour before you think it will be done, take off the skin or paper, that it may get a pale brown colour, and then baste it, and flour it lightly to froth it.

869. A Shoulder, of seven pounds, an hour and three-quarters. If a spit is used, put it in close to the shank-bone, and run it along the blade-bone.

870. A Loin of Mutton, of six pounds, from an hour and a half to an hour and three-quarters. A choice way of carving this is to cut it lengthwise, as you do a saddle. A neck takes about the same time as a loin. It must be carefully jointed to prevent any difficulty in carving.

871. The Neck and Breast are, in small families, commonly roasted together. The cook should crack the bones across the middle before they are put down to roast. If this is not done carefully, the joint is very troublesome to carve. Time for a breast, an hour and a quarter. The breast, when eaten by itself, is better stewed. It may be boned, rolled, and then roasted.

872. A Haunch—*i. e.* the leg and part of the loin of mutton, generally weighs about fifteen pounds, and requires about three hours and a half to roast it. Send up two sauce-boats with it ; one of rich-drawn mutton gravy, made without spice or herbs, and the other of sweet sauce.

873. Mutton as Mock Venison.—Take a neck of good four or five-year-old Southdown wether mutton, cut long in the bones ; let it hang in mild weather, at least a week. Two days before you dress it, take allspice and black pepper, ground and pounded fine, a quarter of an ounce each, rub them together and then rub your mutton well with this mixture twice a day. When you dress it, wash off the spice with warm water, and roast it in paste.

374. DEAN SWIFT'S RECIPE FOR ROASTING MUTTON.

"Gently stir and blow the fire.
Lay the mutton down to roast,
Dress it *quickly* I desire,
In the dripping put a toast.
That I hunger may remove,
Mutton is the meat I love.

"On the dresser see it lie ;
Oh ! the charming white and red ;
Finer meat ne'er met the eye,
On the sweetest grass it fed.
Let the jack go swiftly round,
Let me have it nicely brown'd,

"On the table spread the cloth,
Let the knives be sharp and clean ;
Pickles get and salad both.
Let them each be fresh and green ;
With small beer, good ale, and wine,
O ye gods ! how I shall dine."

875. Roasting Veal.—This meat requires particular care to roast it a nice brown. Let the fire be the same as for beef ; a sound large fire for a large joint, and a brisker for a smaller ; put it at some distance from the fire to soak thoroughly, and then draw it nearer to finish it brown. When first laid down it is to be basted ; baste it again occasionally. When the veal is on the dish, pour over it half-a-pint of melted butter ; if you have a little brown gravy by you, add that to the butter. With those joints which are not stuffed, send up forcemeat in balls, as garnish to the dish, or fried pork sausages. Bacon is always eaten with veal.

876. Fillet of Veal, of from twelve to sixteen pounds, will require from four to five hours at a good fire : make some stuffing or forcemeat, and put it under the flap, that there may be some left to eat cold, or to season a hash : brown it, and pour good melted butter over it. Garnish with thin slices of lemon, and cakes or balls of stuffing, or duck stuffing, or fried pork sausages, curry sauce, bacon, &c.

877. Loin of Veal is the best part of the calf, and will take about three hours' roasting. Paper the kidney fat, and the back : some cooks send the fat up on a toast, to be eaten with the kidney ; it is more delicate than any marrow. If there is more of it than you think will be eaten with the veal, cut it out before roasting, it will make an excellent suet pudding.

878. Shoulder of Veal takes from three hours to three hours and a half : stuff it with the forcemeat ordered for the fillet of veal, in the under side.

879. Neck of Veal, best end, will take two hours. The scrag part is best made into a pie or broth.

880. Breast of Veal requires from an hour and a half to two hours. Let the caul remain till it is almost done, then take it off to brown the meat ; baste, flour, and froth it.

881. Veal Sweetbread.—Trim a fine sweetbread — it cannot be too fresh ; parboil it for five minutes, and throw it into a basin of cold water; roast it plain, or beat up the yolk of an egg, and prepare some fine bread-crumbs. Or when the sweetbread is cold, dry it thoroughly in a cloth, run a lark spit or a skewer through it, and tie it on the ordinary spit; egg it with a paste brush, powder it well with bread-crumbs, and roast it For sauce, put fried bread-crumbs round it, and melted butter with a little mushroom ketchup and lemon juice, or serve on buttered toast, garnished with egg sauce, or with gravy.

882. Roasting Lamb.—This is a delicate, and commonly considered tender meat ; but those who talk of tender lamb, while they are thinking of the age of the animal, forget that even a chicken must be kept a proper time after it has been killed, or it will be tough eating. Grass-lamb is in season from Easter to Michaelmas. House-lamb from Christmas to Lady-day. To the usual accompaniments of roast meat, green mint sauce or a salad is commonly added : and some cooks, about five minutes before it is done, sprinkle it with a little minced parsley. When green mint cannot be got, mint vinegar is an acceptable snbstitute for it.

883. Hind-quarter of eight pounds will take from an hour and three-quarters to two hours ; baste and froth it.

884. Fore-quarter of ten pounds, about two hours. It is usual, when you take off the shoulder from the ribs, to rub them with a lump of butter, and then to squeeze a lemon or Seville orange over them, and sprinkle them with a little pepper and salt.

885. Leg of Lamb of five pounds takes from an hour to an hour and a half to roast.

886. Shoulder of Lamb requires, with a quick fire, an hour to an hour and ten minutes.

887. Ribs of Lamb, about an hour to an hour and a quarter; joint it nicely; crack the ribs across, and bend them up to make it easy for the carver.

888. Loin of Lamb of five pounds, an hour and a quarter. Neck, an hour. Breast, three-quarters of an hour.

889. Roasting; Leg of Pork. This requires about twenty minutes for each pound. When partly cooked score the rind with a sharp knife at distances of half-an-inch. Sage and onions and apple sauce are served with it.

890. Loin of Pork.—Score the rind and have it well jointed before cooking, then roast in the usual way. Sprinkle with dried sage and serve with sage and onions and apple sauce.

891. Spare-rib of Pork.—Joint it nicely before roasting, and crack the ribs across as lamb. Take care not to have the fire too fierce. The joint should be basted with very little butter and flour and may be sprinkled with fine dried sage. It takes from two to three hours. Apple sauce, mashed potatoes, and greens are the proper accompaniments.

892. Roasting Turkey.—After the sinews have been drawn from the legs and thighs, and the bird carefully trussed, stuff with sausage meat and veal stuffing. Pin a well-greased paper over the breast to prevent it burning. Baste well, and be careful to keep up a good fire. A good-sized turkey will take from two to three hours. Serve with gravy and bread sauce.

893. Roasting Goose.—When a goose is well picked, singed, and cleaned, make the stuffing, with about two ounces of onion—if you think the flavour of raw onions too strong, cut them in slices, and lay them in cold water for a couple of hours, add as much apple or potato as you have of onion, and half as much green sage, chop them very fine, adding four ounces, *i. e.* about a large breakfast-cupful, of stale bread-crumbs, a bit of butter about as big as a walnut, and a very little pepper and salt, the yolk of an egg or two, and incorporating the whole well together, stuff the goose ; do not quite fill it, but leave a little room for the stuffing to swell. From an hour and a half to an hour and three-quarters will roast a fine full-grown goose. Send up gravy and apple sauce with it.

894. Roasting Fowls.—Singe, dust with flour, put down before a good fire, and baste well. Make a gravy of the necks and gizzards, froth them, and send to table garnished with bacon or sausage meat balls.

895. Roast Duck.—Put into the body of the bird a seasoning of parboiled onions mixed with finely-chopped sage, salt, pepper, and a slice of butter. Place it before a brisk fire, but not sufficiently near to be scorched ; baste it constantly, and when the breast is well plumped, and the steam from it draws towards the fire, dish and serve it quickly, with a little good brown gravy poured round it, and also some in a gravy tureen. Young ducks will take about half-an-hour to roast ; full-sized ones from three-quarters of an hour to an hour.

896. Roast Partridge.—Let the bird hang as long as it can be kept without being offensive. Pick it carefully, and singe it ; wipe the inside thoroughly with a clean cloth, truss it with the head turned under the wing, and the legs drawn close together, but not crossed. Flour partridges prepared in this manner when first laid to the fire, and baste them plentifully with butter. Serve them with bread sauce.

897. To Truss and Roast a Pheasant.—The following—which applies equally to partridges, grouse, &c., and to fowls, guinea-fowls, &c.—is prescribed by Francatelli in his *Cook's Guide* :—"Rub the scaly cuticle off the legs with a cloth ; trim away the claws and spurs ; cut off the neck close up to the back, leaving the skin of the breast entire ; wipe the pheasant clean and truss it in the following manner, viz. :— Place the pheasant upon its breast, run a trussing needle and string through the left pinion (the wings being removed) ; then turn the bird over on its back, and place the thumb and forefinger of the left hand across the breast, holding the legs erect ; thrust the needle through the middle joint of both thighs, draw it out and then pass it through the other pinion, and fasten the strings at the back ; next pass the needle through the hollow of the back, just below the thighs, thrust it again through the legs and body, and tie the strings tightly ; this will give it an appearance of plumpness." Roast and send to table in the same manner and with the same accompaniments as directed for ROAST PARTRIDGE (*see* par. 896).

898. Roast Grouse.—Truss the birds in the same manner as pheasants, and set down before a brisk fire. When nearly ready—they will be done in from twenty to twenty-five minutes— baste well with butter and sprinkle with

flour in order to froth them, and send to table with some good brown gravy and some fried bread-crumbs and bread sauce. These accompaniments should be served in different sauce tureens.

899. Roast Ptarmigan.—The ptarmigan (which is either a variety of grouse or grouse in its winter plumage) and black game, when roasted, are cooked in precisely the same manner as grouse.

900. Roast Quails.—Pluck, draw, and truss, cover the breast with a vine leaf, and over that a thin slice of fat bacon. Put the birds on a long skewer and roast for ten to fifteen minutes.

901. Roast Woodcook.—Take out the gizzard, truss the bird and tie a piece of bacon round it. Roast in front of a brisk fire and baste unceasingly with butter. A piece of toast should be placed under the bird to catch the trail, and the bird is served up on this toast. Ten to fifteen minutes will suffice to roast the bird, and it should be served up with plain white sauce. (Of course the bird is not drawn.)

902. Roast Snipe.—The birds are treated in the same way as woodcocks. Time, ten to fifteen minutes.

903. TABLE OF TIMES FOR ROASTING.

	H.	M.
A small capon, fowl, or chicken requires	0	25
A large fowl	0	45
A capon, full size	0	35
A goose	1	0
Wild ducks, and grouse	0	15
Pheasants, and turkey poults	0	20
A moderate-sized turkey, stuffed	1	15
Partridges	0	25
Quail	0	10
A hare, or rabbit	about 1	0
Leg of pork, ¼ hour for each pound, and above that allowance	0	20
Chine of pork, as for leg, and	0	20
A neck of mutton	1	30
A haunch of venison	about 3	30

904. TIME-TABLE FOR HANGING GAME, POULTRY, &c.

The average times are as follows :—

	Mild Weather	Cold Weather
Capon	3 days	6 days
Chickens	2 ,,	4 ,,
Duck, goose	2 ,,	6 ,,
Hare	3 ,,	6 ,,
Partridge	2 ,,	6 to 8 days
Pheasant	4 ,,	10 days
Pigeons, young	2 ,,	4 ,,
Pullet, do.	4 ,,	10 ,,
Rabbit	2 ,,	4 ,,
Turkey	2 ,,	6 ,,
Venison	7 ,,	10 to 15 days
Wild duck	3 ,,	7 ,, 8 ,,

905. HOW TO COOK FROZEN MEAT.

In the first instance it is necessary to thaw the joint, in order that it may be cooked right through. If the meat were boiled or roasted before being perfectly thawed, it would be raw in the middle. The proper way to *roast* a shoulder of New Zealand mutton is as follows :—First cut two or three ounces of fat off the joint and throw it on the fire, but take care that the fire does not become smoky. Then, with the tongs, hold the lean side of the meat in the flame till the meat becomes seared and the fibre closed up. Or the joint may be placed on a gridiron and treated as described.

In roasting a leg of frozen mutton the above process should be applied to the thick end.

If it is required to *boil* the leg, the water must boil very quickly, and the thick end just laid in the water so as to be immersed for about an inch or so, and no more, for ten minutes or a quarter of an hour. If the whole leg were placed in the water, it would stop boiling, and the flesh would not be sealed up. To boil a neck of mutton, hang the lean end in the water, while it is quickly boiling, and afterwards put the whole joint in, the water being kept at the boiling point.

906. BOILING.

This most simple of culinary processes is not often performed in perfection ; it does not require quite so much nicety and attendance as roasting ; to skim your pot well, and keep it boiling, or rather simmering, all the while, to know how long is required for doing the joint, &c., and to take it up at the critical moment when it is done enough, comprehends almost the whole art and mystery. This, however, demands a patient and perpetual vigilance, of which, unhappily, few persons are capable. The cook must take especial care that the water boils gently *all the while* she is cooking, or she will be deceived in the time. A sufficient fire should be made up at first, to last all the time, without much mending or stirring, and thereby save much trouble. When the pot is coming to a boil, there will always, from the cleanest meat and clearest water, rise a scum to the top of it ; proceeding partly from the foulness of the meat, and partly from the water : this must be carefully taken off, as soon as it rises. When you have skimmed well, put in some cold water, which will throw up the rest of the scum. The oftener it is skimmed, and the clearer the surface of the water is kept, the cleaner will be the meat. If let alone, it soon boils down and sticks to the meat, which, instead of looking delicately white and nice, will have that coarse appearance we have too often to complain of. Others wrap it up in a cloth ; but these are needless precautions ; if the scum be attentively removed, meat will have a much more delicate colour and finer flavour than it has when muffled up. This may give rather more trouble—but those who wish to excel in their art must only consider how the processes of it can be most perfectly performed : a cook who has a proper pride and pleasure in her business will make this her maxim and rule on all occasions.—Put your meat into cold water, in the proportion of about a quart of water to a pound of meat ; it should be covered with water during the whole of the process of boiling, but not drowned in it ; the less water, provided the meat be covered with it, the more savoury will be the meat, and the better will be the broth in every respect. The water should be heated gradually, according to the thickness, &c., of the article boiled ; for instance, a leg of mutton of ten pounds weight should be placed over a moderate fire, which will gradually make the water hot without causing it to boil, for about forty minutes ; if the water boils much sooner, the meat will be hardened, and shrink up as if it was scorched, but by keeping the water a certain time heating without boiling, its fibres are dilated, and it yields a quantity of scum, which must be taken off as soon as it rises, for the reasons already mentioned. "If a vessel containing water be placed over a steady fire, the water will grow continually hotter, till it reaches the limit of boiling ; after which, the regular accessions of heat are wholly spent in converting it into steam ; the water remains at the same pitch of temperature, however fiercely it boils. The only difference is, that with a strong fire it sooner comes to boil, and more quickly boils away, and is converted into steam." Such are the opinions stated by Buchanan in his *Economy of Fuel.* A thermometer was placed in water in that state which cooks call gentle simmering—the heat was 212°, *i. e.* the same degree as the strongest boiling. Two mutton chops were covered with cold water, and one boiled fiercely, and the other simmered gently, for three-quarters of an hour ; the flavour of the chop which was simmered was decidedly superior to that which was boiled ; the liquor which boiled fast was in like proportion more savoury, and, when cold, had much more fat on its surface ; this explains why quick boiling renders meat hard,

&c.—because its juices are extracted in a greater degree.

i. **Reckon the Time** from the water first coming to a boil. The old rule, of fifteen minutes to a pound of meat, is, perhaps, rather too little ; the slower the meat boils, the tenderer, the plumper, and whiter it will be. For those who like their food thoroughly cooked (which all will who have any regard for their stomachs), twenty minutes to a pound will not be found too much for gentle simmering by the side of the fire ; allowing more or less time, according to the thickness of the joint and the coldness of the weather. Without some practice it is difficult to teach any art ; and cooks seem to suppose they must be right, if they put meat into a pot, and set it over the fire for a certain time—making no allowance whether it simmers, or boils at a gallop.

ii. **Fresh-killed Meat** will take much longer time boiling than that which has been kept till it is what the butchers call ripe, and longer in cold than in warm weather. If it be frozen it must be thawed before boiling as before roasting. In cold weather, the night before you dress it, bring it into a place of which the temperature is not less than forty-five degrees Fahrenheit.

iii. **The size of the boiling-pots** should be adapted to what they are to contain ; the larger the saucepan the more room it takes upon the fire ; and a larger quantity of water requires a proportionate increase of fire to boil it. In small families block tin saucepans are best, as being lightest and safest : moreover, if proper care is taken of them, and they are well dried after they are cleansed, they are by far the cheapest ; the purchase of a new tin saucepan being little more than the expense of tinning a copper one. Take care that the covers of your boiling-pots fit close, not only to prevent unnecessary evaporation of the water, but that the smoke may not insinuate itself under the edge of the lid, and give the meat a bad taste.

907. Boiling Round of Salt Beef.—Skewer it tight and round, and tie a fillet of broad tape about it. Put it into plenty of cold water, and carefully remove the scum ; let it boil till all the scum is removed, and then put the boiler on one side of the fire, to continue simmering slowly till it is done. Half a round may be boiled for a small family. When you take it up, wash the scum off with a paste-brush—garnish with carrots and turnips.

908. Aitchbone of Beef.—Manage in the same way as the round. The soft, marrow-like fat which lies on the back is best when hot, and the hard fat of the upper corner is best cold.

909. Boiling Leg of Mutton.—Soak the joint previously for an hour or so in cold water, then place in pot with just sufficient boiling water to cover it—follow the instructions given for boiling. When done serve with caper sauce, mashed turnips, &c.

910. Neck of Mutton.—This is boiled in a similar way, but special care must be taken to cook it slowly.

911. Boiling Ham.—Soak the ham in cold water the night before, scrape it clean, put it in water just warm, skim the liquor while boiling, do not let it boil fast, but simmer only, and add a little cold occasionally to check it. When done peel the skin off carefully and dust with bread raspings—set before the fire for a few minutes—dress the knuckle bone with a frill of white paper.

912. Boiling Turkey.—Make a stuffing with grated bread, lemon peel, chopped oysters, pepper, salt, nutmeg, about four ounces of butter or chopped suet, a little cream and yolk or egg to make it bind ; fill the craw—if there is any left make it into balls. Boil the turkey in a floured cloth ; put it into cold water and let it boil gently ; serve with oyster or white sauce.

913. Boiling Fowls.—These should be trussed especially for boiling, and may have an onion and a little butter placed inside them. Boil slowly for about an hour with carrots, parsley, celery or other flavouring vegetable—serve with parsley and butter, or onion sauce.

914. Boiling Bacon.—Dr. Kitchiner very justly says :—"The boiling of bacon is a very simple subject to comment upon ; but our main object is to teach common cooks the art of dressing common food in the best manner. Cover a pound of nice streaked bacon with cold water, let it boil gently for three-quarters of an hour ; take it up, scrape the under side well, and cut off the rind : grate a crust of bread not only on the top, but all over it, as you would ham, put it before the fire for a few minutes, not too long, or it will dry and spoil it. Bacon is sometimes as salt as salt can make it, therefore before it is boiled it must be soaked in warm water for an hour or two, changing the water once ; then pare off the rusty and smoked part, trim it nicely on the under side, and scrape the rind as clean as possible."

915. TABLE OF TIMES FOR BOILING.

	H.	M.
A ham, 20 lbs. weight, requires	6	30
A tongue (if dry), after soaking	4	0
A tongue out of pickle	2½ to 3	0
A neck of mutton	1	30
A chicken	0	20
A large fowl	0	45
A capon	0	35
A pigeon	0	15

916. HINTS ABOUT BOILING.

i. If you let meat or poultry remain in the water after it is done enough, it will become sodden and lose its flavour.

ii. Beef and mutton is preferred by some people a little underdone. Very large joints if slightly underdone will make the better hash or broil. Lamb, pork, and veal are uneatable if not thoroughly boiled—but these meats should not be overdone.

iii. A trivet, a fish-drainer, or an American contrivance called a "spider"—which is nothing more than a wire dish raised on three or four short legs—put on the bottom of a boiling-pot, raising the contents about an inch and a half from the bottom, will prevent that side of the meat which comes next the bottom being done too much ; and the lower part will be as delicately done as the upper ; and this will enable you to take out the meat without inserting a fork, &c., into it. If you have not a trivet, a drainer, or a "spider," use a soup-plate laid the wrong side upwards.

iv. Take care of the liquor you have boiled poultry or meat in, as it is useful for making soup. The good housewife never boils a joint without converting the broth into some sort of soup.

v. If the liquor be too salt, use only half the quantity, and add some water ; wash salted meat well with cold water before you put it into the boiler.

917. BAKING.

By this process articles of food are cooked entirely in the oven. The old close oven was the least advantageous mode of cookery for meat, as it lost about one-third of its weight, but owing to the many improvements now made in kitchen ranges, the heat and ventilation can be so regulated that an endless variety of articles may thus be cooked.

918. Baking Meat and Poultry—

For these it is best to use a double tin, one fitting into the other, the bottom one being filled with hot water to prevent the gravy from drying up ; the upper one should be fitted with a low grid to stand the joint on. Baste the joint with dripping occasionally as in roasting.

Baked pigs, geese, and ducks eat almost equal to roasted ones, as does a hare also, when well basted with raw milk and butter. Many persons prefer a baked ham to a boiled one.

919. Baking Pies, Cakes, &c.—

These require a hot oven. Custards or any egg puddings cook better in a cooler one, but experience will prove the best guide in these matters.

920. STEWING.

This is a most economical, convenient, and wholesome mode of cookery, as nothing is wasted, the cheaper kinds of meat can be utilized, and less fire is required to sustain the gentle degree of ebullition necessary. The articles to be cooked are placed with gravy or water, vegetables, &c., if desired, and flavouring, in a stewpan, saucepan, or even a covered jar set in a saucepan of water ; covered down *tightly*, and cooked slowly either in the oven or over the fire.

It is advisable to put a small grid or an inverted plate under the meat to prevent it sticking to the bottom of the vessel.

Vegetables, if old, should be parboiled before being added to the stew.

921. How to Stew Fresh Beef, Pork, Mutton, and Veal.—

Cut or chop two pounds of fresh beef into ten or twelve pieces ; put these into a saucepan, with one and a half teaspoonfuls of salt, one teaspoonful of sugar, half a teaspoonful of pepper, two middle-sized onions sliced, half-a-pint of water. Set on the fire for ten minutes until forming a thick gravy. Add a good teaspoonful of flour, stir on the fire a few minutes ; add a quart and a half of water ; let the whole simmer until the meat is tender. Beef will take from two hours and a half to three hours ; mutton and pork about two hours ; veal, one hour and a quarter to one hour and a half. Onions, if not to be had, may be omitted ; it will even then make a good dish ; half-a-pound of sliced potatoes, or two ounces of preserved potatoes ; either fresh or preserved vegetables may be added if they can be obtained, also a small dumpling.

922. Stewed Brisket of Beef.— Stew in sufficient water to cover the meat ; when tender, take out the bones, and skim off the fat ; add to the gravy, when strained, a glass of wine, and a little spice tied up in a muslin bag. (This can be omitted if preferred.) Have ready either mushrooms, truffles, or vegetables boiled, and cut into shapes. Lay them on and around the beef ; reduce part of the gravy to glaze, lay it on the top, and pour the remainder into the dish.

923. Stewed Ox-Cheek.— Prepare the day before it is to be eaten ; clean the cheek and put it into soft water, just warm ; let it lie for three or four hours, then put it into cold water, to soak all night ; next day wipe it clean, put it into a stewpan, and just cover it with water ; skim it well when it is coming to the boil, then add two whole onions with two or three cloves stuck into each, three turnips quartered, a couple of carrots sliced, two bay-leaves, and twenty-four corns of allspice, a head of celery, and a bundle of sweet herbs, pepper, and salt ; lastly, add a little cayenne and garlic, if liked. Let it stew gently till perfectly tender, about three hours ; then take out the cheek, divide into pieces fit to help at table ; skim and strain the gravy ; melt an ounce and a half of butter in a stew-pan ; stir into it as much flour as it will take up ; mix with it by degrees a pint and a half of the gravy ; add a teaspoonful of mushroom or walnut ketchup, or port wine, and boil a short time. Serve up in a soup or ragout dish, or make it into barley broth. This is a very economical, nourishing, and savoury meal.

924. Irish Stew.— Take two pounds of potatoes ; peel and slice them ; cut rather more than two pounds of mutton chops, either from the loin or neck ; part of the fat should be taken off ; beef, two pounds, six large onions sliced, a slice of ham, or lean bacon, a spoonful of pepper, and two of salt. First put a layer of potatoes, then a layer of meat and onions ; sprinkle the seasoning, then a layer of potatoes and again the meat and onions and seasoning ; the top layer should be potatoes, and the vessel should be quite full. Then put in half-a-pint of good gravy, and a spoonful of mushroom ketchup. Let the whole stew for an hour and a half ; be very careful it does not burn.

925. Palatable Stew.— Cut pieces of salt beef and pork into dice, put them into a stewpan with six whole peppercorns, two blades of mace, a few cloves, a teaspoonful of celery seeds, and a faggot of dried sweet herbs ; cover with water, and stew gently for an hour ; then add fragments of carrots, turnips, parsley, or any other vegetables at hand, with two sliced onions, and some vinegar to flavour ; thicken with flour or rice, remove the herbs, and pour into the dish with toasted bread, or freshly baked biscuit, broken small, and serve hot. When they can be procured, a few potatoes improve it very much.

926. Stewed Hare.— Prepare the hare as for jugging ; put it into the stewpan with a few sweet herbs, half-a-dozen cloves, the same of allspice and black pepper, two large onions, and a roll of lemon peel ; cover it with water : when it boils, skim it clean, and let it simmer gently till tender (about two hours) ; then take the meat up with a slice, set it by a fire to keep hot while you thicken the gravy ; take three ounces of butter and some flour, rub together, put in the gravy, stir it well, and let it boil for about ten minutes ; strain it through a sieve over the meat, and it is ready.

927. BROILING OR GRILLING.

This process is to small joints, &c., what roasting is to large ; all the apparatus required is a gridiron placed over the fire, or one with channelled bars leading to a trough beneath, placed before the fire. Broiling requires a brisk bright fire, the surface being modified by the sprinkling of salt. The rapid heat produces a greater degree of change in the affinities of the raw meat than roasting, and thus generates a higher flavour, so that broiled meat is more savoury than roast. The surface becomes charred, a dark-coloured crust is formed, which retards the evaporation of the juices ; and, therefore, if properly done, broiled meat may be as tender and juicy as roasted meat. As the great art in broiling is to keep the juice in the meat, it should always be turned with tongs. If, however, there are no tongs to turn the meat over, stick the fork into the fat, and avoid making holes in the meat.

928. How to Broil a Steak or Chop.—A steak must be cooked very quickly. Put the gridiron on the fire, and when it is hot rub it first with paper and then with a clean dish-cloth. Put it on the fire again, and rub the bars with a small piece of suet in order to prevent the meat sticking to them. Put the dish in which the steak is to be served in front of the fire. Put the steak on the gridiron, and let it grill for two minutes. Then turn it, and keep on turning it every two minutes till half-cooked, then put it on the dish, press it on both sides with a knife, smear a little butter over it, add a little pepper, and again place it on the gridiron, turning it only once. When done, add a little more butter and serve *at once*. It is excellent served up with onion sauce (*see* par. 999).

929. Macbeth's recipe for cooking a steak is the best—

"When 'tis done, *then* 'twere well
It were done quickly." (*Kitchiner.*)

930. Grilled Fowl.—Take the remains of cold fowls, and skin them or not, at choice ; pepper and salt them, and sprinkle over them a little lemon juice, and let them stand an hour ; wipe them dry, dip them in clarified butter, and then into fine bread-crumbs, and broil gently over a clear fire. A little finely-minced lean of ham or grated lemon peel, with a seasoning of cayenne, salt, and mace, mixed with the crumbs, will vary this dish agreeably. When fried instead of broiled, the fowls may be dipped into yolk of egg instead of butter.

931. Broiled Goose.—*The legs of geese*, &c., broiled, and laid on a bed of apple sauce, form an appetizing dish for luncheon or supper.

932. FRYING.

This is of all methods the most objectionable, because food is less digestible when thus prepared, as the fat employed undergoes chemical changes. An iron frying-pan, and not a tin one, should be used for frying ; and a panful of oil can be used several times. Lard is the worst fat for frying, as it imparts an unpleasant taste to the food. Olive oil is the best. The crackling noise which accompanies the process of frying meat in a pan is occasioned by the explosions of steam formed in fat, the temperature of which is much above 212 degrees. If the meat is very juicy it will not fry well, because it becomes sodden before the water is evaporated ; and it will not brown, because the temperature is too low to scorch it.

933. To fry fish well the fat should be boiling hot (600 degrees)—when the fat boils it ceases to hiss—and the fish *well dried* in a cloth ; otherwise, owing to the generation of steam, the temperature will fall so low that it will be boiled in its own steam, and not be browned. Meat, or indeed any article, should be frequently turned and agitated during frying to promote the evaporation of the watery particles. To make fried things look well, they should be done over *twice* with egg and stale bread-crumbs.

934. TO ECONOMIZE FAT.

In most families many members are not fond of fat—servants seldom like it : consequently there is frequently much wasted ; to avoid which, take off bits of suet fat from beefsteaks, &c., previous to cooking ; they can be used for puddings. With good management there need be no waste in any shape or form.

935. BASTINGS.

i. Fresh butter.

ii. Clarified suet.

iii. Minced sweet herbs, butter, and claret, especially for mutton and lamb.

iv. Water and salt.

v. Cream and melted butter, especially for a flayed pig.

vi. Yolks of eggs, grated biscuit and juice of oranges.

936. DREDGINGS.

i. Flour mixed with grated bread.

ii. Sweet herbs dried and powdered, and mixed with grated bread.

iii. Lemon peel dried and pounded, or orange peel mixed with flour.

iv. Sugar finely powdered, and mixed with pounded cinnamon, and flour or grated bread.

v. Fennel seeds, corianders, cinnamon, and sugar, finely beaten and mixed with grated bread or flour.

vi. For young pigs, grated bread or flour, mixed with beaten nutmeg, ginger, pepper, sugar, and yolks of eggs.

vii. Sugar, bread, and salt mixed.

937. CHARCOAL IN COOKING.

Cooks should be cautioned against the use of charcoal in any quantity, except where there is a free current of air ; for charcoal is highly prejudicial in a state of ignition, although it may be rendered even actively beneficial when boiled, as a small quantity of it, if boiled with meat on the turn, will effectually cure the unpleasant taint.

938. HINTS ABOUT VEGE-TABLES.

There is nothing in which the difference between an elegant and an ordinary table is more seen than in the dressing of vegetables, more especially of greens : they may be equally as fine, at first, at one place as at another, but their look and taste are afterwards very different, resulting from the way in which they have been cooked. They are in greatest perfection when in greatest plenty, *i. e.* when in full season. By season, we do not mean those early days, when luxurious tastes induce the growers to force the various vegetables, but the time of the year in which, by nature and common culture, and the mere operation of the sun and climate, they are most plenteous and in perfection.

i. New potatoes and green peas, unless sent to us from warmer latitudes than our own, are seldom worth eating before Whitsuntide.

ii. Unripe vegetables are as insipid and unwholesome as unripe fruits.

iii. If vegetables are a minute or two too long over the fire, they lose all their beauty and flavour, but if not thoroughly boiled tender, they are very indigestible, and much more troublesome during their residence in the stomach than underdone meats.

iv. Quality of vegetables. The middle size are preferable to the largest or the smallest ; they are more tender, juicy, and full of flavour just before they are quite full-grown : freshness is their chief value and excellence. The eye easily discovers if they have been kept too long ; they soon lose their beauty in all respects.

v. Take care to wash and cleanse vegetables thoroughly from dust, dirt, and insect,—this requires great attention. Pick off the outside leaves, trim them nicely, and if they are not quite fresh-gathered and have become flaccid, it is absolutely necessary to restore their crispness before cooking them, or they will be tough and unpleasant. To do this, lay them in a pan of clean water, with a handful of salt in it, for an hour before you dress them. Most vegetables being more or less succulent, it is necessary that they possess their full proportion of fluids in order to retain that state of crispness and plumpness which they have when growing.

vi. On being cut or gathered, the exhalation from their surface continues, while from the open vessels of the cut surface there is often great exudation or evaporation, and thus their natural moisture is diminished ; the tender leaves become flaccid, and the thicker masses or roots lose their plumpness. This is not only less pleasant to the eye, but is a serious injury to the nutritious powers of the vegetable ; for in this flaccid and shrivelled state its fibres are less easily divided in chewing, and the water which exists in the form of their respective natural juices is less directly nutritious.

vii. Roots, greens, salads, &c., and the various productions of the garden, when first gathered, are plump and firm, and have a fragrant freshness no art can give them again ; though it will refresh them a little to put them into cold spring water for some time before they are dressed.

939. TO BOIL VEGETABLES.

Soft water will best preserve the colour of such as are green ; if you have only hard water, put to it a teaspoonful of carbonate of potash. They should always be boiled in a saucepan by themselves, and have plenty of water : if meat is boiled with them in the same pot, the one will spoil the look and taste of the other.

940. To Preserve the Colour of Green Vegetables.—Put on your pot, make it boil, put a little salt in, and skim it perfectly clean before you put in the greens, &c., which should not be put in till the water boils briskly ; the quicker they boil the greener they will be. When the vegetables sink, they are generally done enough, if the water has been kept constantly boiling. Take them up immediately, or they will lose their colour and goodness. Be careful to *thoroughly* drain the water from them before you send them to table.

941. To Prepare a Cabbage for Boiling.—Take off all the outside leaves, which are thick and useless. Cut the leaves into shreds across the fibres, in the same way as a red cabbage is prepared for pickling. Wash the pieces first in hot water and then in cold, and then leave them in cold water for ten minutes or so ; and before cooking let them drain for half-an-hour.

942. TO BOIL CARROTS.

Some people place carrots into cold water, but this takes all the flavour out of them. They should be put into boiling water, with a little salt, and a piece of fat or dripping, and boiled for two hours. Young carrots should not be pared or scraped, but merely washed and put into boiling water with a little salt.

943. CARDOONS, TO BOIL.

Cut the stalks into lengths as required, taking off the prickles, and parboil them in salted water for a quarter of an hour ; then drain them and scrape off the outer skin, and put them in cold water ; cook them as artichokes.

944. CELERY, TO BOIL.

Peel, and cut into slices or quarters, throw them into boiling water with a little salt in it, boil till done, drain, and serve with white sauce.

Salsify, boiled.—Scrape and cut into lengths, and put into vinegar and water. Boil in salted water until tender, drain, and put in a saucepan with a little butter, lemon juice, minced parsley, and salt.

945. POTATOES.

Most people esteem potatoes beyond any other vegetable, yet few persons know how to cook them. The following will be found to be excellent methods of cooking this delicious esculent.

946. To Boil Potatoes.—Having washed them put them into a saucepan with scarcely sufficient cold water to cover them. Boil them slowly, and directly the skins begin to break, lift them from the fire, and as rapidly as possible pour off *every drop* of the water. Then place a coarse (we need not say clean) towel over them, and return them to the fire again until they are thoroughly done, and quite dry. A little salt, to flavour, should be added to the water before boiling.

947. To Peel Potatoes.—The above recipe is for boiling potatoes in their jackets, as the phrase goes. When potatoes are to be peeled prior to cooking, they should first be well washed and put in a bowl of clean water. As each potato is taken out of this receptacle and peeled, it should be thrown into another bowl of cold water, close at hand to receive them. This prevents undue discolouration of the potatoes.

948. To Boil Peeled Potatoes.—Having pared and washed them, put them into a saucepan. Pour in sufficient boiling water to just cover them, and add about an ounce of salt. Put the lid on the saucepan, and let the potatoes boil slowly for twenty minutes. At the end of that time drain off nearly all the water, put the saucepan down by the side of the fire with just a little water in it, and let the potatoes remain in the steam until they become soft and floury. Then drain *all* the water off, turn the potatoes into the cover of the

saucepan, then back into the pan, and again on to the lid, and they are ready to dish up.

949. Reason for Boiling Slowly— If the potatoes were boiled fast the outsides would be broken before the insides were done, and the potatoes would be watery outside and lumpy inside. When done they should *not be covered over*, as the steam would then be pressed down into them again.

950. To Steam Potatoes.—Some kinds of potatoes are better steamed than boiled. Whether dressed with the skins on or off, a careful eye must be kept on them, and when they are nearly done the steamer should be removed, the water in the saucepan thrown off, and the steamer then replaced, in order to allow the process of cooking to be completed. Some people shake the steamer when potatoes are somewhat close and heavy, under the idea that it renders them floury, and in many cases the shaking has this effect.

951. Potatoes Roasted under Meat.—Half boil large, peeled potatoes ; drain them and put them into an earthen dish, or small tin pan, under meat roasting before the fire ; baste them with the dripping. Turn them to brown on all sides ; send up in a separate dish.

952. Potatoes Fried with Fish.—Take cold fish and cold potatoes. Pick all the bones from the former and mash the fish and the potatoes together : form into rolls, and fry with lard until the outsides are brown and crisp. For this purpose, the drier kinds of fish, such as cod, hake, &c., are preferable ; turbot, soles, eels, &c., are not so good. This is an economical and excellent relish.

953. Potatoes Mashed with Onions.—Prepare some boiled onions, by putting them through a sieve, and mix them with potatoes. Regulate the proportions according to taste.

954. Potato Cheesecakes.—One pound of mashed potatoes, quarter of a pound of currants, quarter of a pound of sugar and butter, and four eggs, to be well mixed together ; bake them in patty-pans, having first lined them with puff paste.

955. Potato Colcanon.—Boil potatoes and greens (or spinach) separately ; mash the potatoes ; squeeze the greens dry ; chop them quite fine, and mix them with the potatoes with a little butter, pepper, and salt. Put into a mould, buttering it well first ; let it stand in a hot oven for ten minutes.

956. Potato Balls Ragout.—Add to a pound of potatoes a quarter of a pound of grated ham, or some sweet herbs, or chopped parsley, an onion or shallot, salt, pepper, and a little grated nutmeg, and other spice, with the yolk of a couple of eggs ; then dress as POTATOES ESCALLOPED (*see* par. 960).

957. Potato Snow.—Pick out the whitest potatoes, put them on in cold water ; when they begin to crack, strain, and put them in a clean stewpan before the fire until they are quite dry, and fall to pieces ; rub them through a wire sieve upon the dish they are to be sent up on, and do not disturb them afterwards.

958. Potatoes Fried Whole.—When nearly boiled enough, put them into a stewpan with a bit of butter, or some clean beef dripping ; shake them about often, to prevent burning, till they are brown and crisp ; drain them from the fat. It will be an improvement if they are floured and dipped into the yolk of an egg, and then rolled in finely-sifted bread-crumbs.

959. Potatoes Fried in Slices.—Peel large potatoes, slice them about a quarter of an inch thick, or cut them into shavings, as you would peel a lemon ; dry them well in a clean cloth, and fry them in lard or dripping. Take care that the fat and frying-pan are quite clean ; put it on a quick fire, and as soon as the lard boils, and is still, put in the slices of potato, and keep moving them until they are crisp ; take them up, and lay them to drain on a sieve. Send to table with a little salt sprinkled over them.

960. Potatoes Escalloped.—Mash potatoes in the usual way ; then butter some nice clean scallop-shells, patty-pans, or tea-cups or saucers ; put in your potatoes ; make them smooth at the top ; cross a knife over them ; strew a few fine bread-crumbs on them ; sprinkle them with a paste-brush with a few drops of melted butter, and set them in a Dutch oven. When nicely browned on the top, take them carefully out of the shells, and brown on the other side. Cold potatoes may be warmed up this way.

961. Potato Scones.—Mash boiled pototoes till they are quite smooth, adding a little salt ; then knead out the flour, or barley-meal, to the thickness required ; toast on the griddle, pricking them with a fork to prevent them blistering. When eaten with fresh or salt butter they are equal to crumpets—even superior, and very nutritious.

962. Potato Pie.—Peel and slice your potatoes very thinly into a pie-dish ; between each layer of potatoes put a little chopped onion, and sprinkle a little pepper and salt ; put in a little water, and cut about two ounces of fresh butter into bits and lay them on the top ; cover it close with paste. The yolks of four eggs may be added ; and when baked, a tablespoonful of good mushroom ketchup poured in through a funnel. Another method is to put between the layers small bits of mutton, beef, or pork. In Cornwall, turnips are added, constituting a cheap and satisfactory dish for families.

963. Mashed Potatoes and Spinach or Cabbage.—Moisten cold mashed potatoes with a little white sauce : take cold cabbage or spinach, and chop it very finely. Moisten with a brown gravy. Fill a tin mould with layers of potatoes and cabbage ; cover the top, and put it into a stewpan of boiling water. Let it remain long enough to warm the vegetables ; then turn the vegetables out and serve them. Prepare by boiling the vegetables separately, and put them into the mould in layers, to be turned out when wanted. It forms a very pretty dish for an entrée.

964. To Utilize Cold Potatoes.—There are few articles in families more subject to waste, whether in paring, boiling, or being actually wasted, than potatoes ; and there are few cooks who do not boil twice as many potatoes every day as are wanted, and fewer still who do not throw the residue away as being totally unfit in any shape for the next day's meal ; yet if they would take the trouble to beat up the despised cold potatoes with an equal quantity of flour, they would find them produce a much lighter dumpling or pudding than they can make with flour alone : and by the aid of a few spoonfuls of good gravy, they will provide a cheap and agreeable appendage to the dinner-table.

965. Cold Carrots and Turnips.—These may be added to soups, if they have not been mixed with gravies : or if warmed up separately, and put into moulds in layers, they may be turned out, and served the same as the potatoes and cabbage described above.

966. To Boil French Beans.—Cut away the stalk-end, and strip off the strings, then cut them into shreds. If not quite fresh, have a basin of spring water, with a little salt dissolved in it, and as the beans are cleaned and stringed throw them in ; put them on the fire in boiling water, with some salt in it ; after they have boiled fifteen or twenty minutes, take one out and taste it ; as soon as they are tender take them up, throw them into a colander or sieve to drain. Send up the beans whole when they are very young. A piece of butter mixed with the beans when placed in the dish is a great improvement to them.

967. Boiled Turnip Radishes.—Boil in plenty of salted water, and in about twenty-five minutes they will be tender ; drain well, and send them to table with melted butter. Common radishes, when young, tied in bunches, boiled for twenty minutes and served on a toast are excellent.

968. Haricot Beans, to boil.—Wash the beans, put them into a calico bag, and throw them into a saucepan filled with quite boiling water, with half-a-teaspoonful of salt and some dripping. Boil quickly for three and a half hours, drain them, and turn into a basin full of nice gravy.

969. Asparagus (often miscalled "*asparagrass*").—Scrape the stalks till they are clean ; throw them into a van of cold water, tie them up in bundles of about a quarter of a hundred each ; cut off the stalks at the bottom to a uniform length, leaving enough to serve as a handle for the green part ; put them into a stewpan of boiling water, with a handful of salt in it. Let it boil, and skim it. When they are tender at the stalk, which will be in from twenty to thirty minutes, they are done enough. Watch the exact time of their becoming tender ; take them up that instant. While the asparagus is boiling, toast a round of a quartern loaf, about half-an-inch thick ; brown it delicately on both sides ; dip it lightly in the liquor the asparagus was boiled in, and lay it in the middle of a dish ; melt some butter, do not put it over them, but serve in a butter-boat.

970. Artichokes.—Soak them in cold water, wash them well ; put them into plenty of boiling water, with a handful of salt, and let them boil gently for an hour and a half or two hours : trim them and drain on a sieve ; send up melted butter with them, which some put into small cups, one for each guest.

971. Stewed Water-cress.—Lay the cress in strong salt and water, to clear it from insects. Pick and wash nicely, and stew it in water for about ten minutes ; drain and chop, season with pepper and salt, add a little butter, and return it to the stewpan until well heated. Add a little vinegar previously to serving ; put round it sippets of toast or fried bread. The above, made thin, as a substitute for parsley and butter, will be found an excellent sauce for a boiled fowl. There should be considerably more of the cress than of the parsley, as the flavour is much milder.

972. Stewed Mushrooms.—Cut off the ends of the stalks, and pare neatly some middle-sized or button mushrooms, and put them into a basin of water with the juice of a lemon as they are done. When all are prepared, take them from the water with the hands to avoid the sediment, and put them into a stewpan with a little fresh butter, white pepper, salt, and a little lemon juice ; cover the pan close, and let them stew gently for twenty minutes or half-an-hour ; then thicken the butter with a spoonful of flour, and add gradually sufficient cream, or cream and milk, to make the same about the thickness of good cream. Season the sauce to palate, adding a little pounded mace or grated nutmeg. Let the whole stew gently until the mushrooms are tender. Remove every particle of butter which may be floating on the top, before serving.

973. Indications of Wholesome Mushrooms.—Whenever a fungus is pleasant in flavour and odour, it may be considered wholesome. If, on the contrary, it have an offensive smell, a bitter, astringent, or styptic taste, or even if it leave an unpleasant flavour in the mouth, it should not be considered fit for food. The colour, figure, and texture of these vegetables do not afford any characters on which we can safely rely ; yet it may be remarked that in colour the pure yellow,

gold colour, bluish pale, dark or lustre brown, wine red, or the violet, belong to many that are eatable ; whilst the pale or sulphur yellow, bright or blood-red, and the greenish belong to few but the poisonous. The safe kinds have most frequently a compact, brittle texture ; the flesh is white ; they grow more readily in open places, such as dry pastures and waste lands, than in places humid or shaded by wood. In general, those should be suspected which grow in caverns and subterranean passages, on animal matter undergoing putrefaction, as well as those whose flesh is soft or watery.

974. To Distinguish Mushrooms from Poisonous Fungi.

i. Sprinkle a little salt on the spongy parts or gills of the sample to be tried. If they turn yellow, they are poisonous,— if black, they are wholesome. Allow the salt to act before you decide on the question.

ii. False mushrooms have a warty cap, or else fragments of membrane, adhering to the upper surface, are heavy, and emerge from a vulva or bag ; they grow in tufts or clusters in woods, on the stumps of trees, &c., whereas the pure mushrooms grow in pastures.

iii. False mushrooms have an astringent, styptic, and disagreeable taste. When cut they turn blue. They are moist on the surface, and generally of a rose or orange colour.

iv. The gills of the true mushroom are of a pinky rod, changing to a liver colour. The flesh is white. The stem is white, solid, and cylindrical.

975. COOKERY FOR SOLDIERS, SAILORS, TRAVELLERS, AND EMIGRANTS.

The following recipes are due to the inventive genius of the late Alexis Soyer, who at one time was chief cook of the Reform Club :—

976. Stewed Salt Beef and Pork. —Put into a saucepan about two pounds of well-soaked beef, cut in eight pieces ; half-a-pound of salt pork, divided in two, and also soaked ; half-a-pound of rice, or six tablespoonfuls ; a quarter of a pound of onions, or four middle-sized ones, peeled and sliced ; two ounces of brown sugar, or a large tablespoonful ; a quarter of an ounce of pepper, and five pints of water ; simmer gently for three hours, remove the fat from the top, and serve. This dish is enough for six people, and it cannot fail to be excellent if the recipe be closely followed. Butchers' salt meat will require only four hours' soaking, having been but lightly pickled.

977. Mutton Soup.—Put into a pan—half-a-pound of mutton will make a pint of good family soup—six pounds of mutton, cut in four or six pieces ; three-quarters of a pound of mixed vegetables, or three ounces of preserved, three and a half teaspoonfuls of salt, one teaspoonful of sugar, and half a teaspoonful of pepper, if handy ; five tablespoonfuls of barley or rice ; eight pints of water ; let it simmer gently for three hours and a half, remove the fat, and serve. Bread and biscuit may be added in small quantities.

978. Plain Pea Soup.—Put in a pan six pounds of pork, well soaked and cut into eight pieces ; pour six quarts of water over ; one pound of split peas ; one teaspoonful of sugar ; half a teaspoonful of pepper ; four ounces of fresh vegetables, or two ounces of preserved, if handy ; let it boil gently for two hours, or until the peas are tender. When the pork is rather fat, as is generally the case, wash it only. A quarter of a pound of broken biscuit may be used for the soup. Salt beef, when rather fat and well soaked, may be used for pea soup.

979. French Beef Soup, or Pot au Feu (Camp Fashion).—Put into the kettle six pounds of beef, cut into two or three pieces, bones included ; one pound of mixed green vegetables, or half-a-pound of preserved, in cakes ; four teaspoonfuls of salt ; if handy, one teaspoonful of pepper, one of sugar, and three cloves ; and eight pints of water. Let it boil gently three hours ; remove some of the fat, and serve. The addition of a pound and a half of bread, cut into slices, or one pound of broken biscuits, well soaked, will make a very nutritious soup. Skimming is not required.

980. Plain Boiled Beef.—Put in a saucepan six pounds of well-soaked beef, cut in two, with three quarts of cold water ; simmer gently three hours, and serve. About a pound of either carrots, turnips, parsnips, greens, or cabbage, as well as dumplings, may be boiled with it.

981. Cossack's Plum Pudding.—Put into a basin one pound of flour, three-quarters of a pound of raisins (stoned, if time be allowed), three-quarters of a pound of the fat of salt pork (well washed, cut into small squares, or chopped), two tablespoonfuls of sugar or treacle ; and half-a-pint of water ; mix all together : put into a cloth tied lightly ; boil for four hours, and serve. If time will not admit, boil only two hours, though four are preferable. How to spoil the above :— Add anything to it.

982. MISCELLANEOUS COOKERY.

983. Beef Minced.—Cut into small dice remains of cold beef : the gravy preserved from it on the first day of it being served should be put in the stewpan, with the addition of warm water, some mace, sliced shallot, salt, and black pepper. Let the whole simmer gently for an hour. A few minutes before it is served, take out the meat and dish it ; add to the gravy some walnut ketchup, and a little lemon juice or walnut pickle. Boil up the gravy once more, and when hot, pour it over the meat. Serve it with bread sippets.

984. Beef with Mashed Potatoes.—Mash some potatoes with hot milk, the yolk of an egg, some butter and salt. Slice the cold beef and lay it at the bottom of a pie-dish, adding to it some sliced shallot, pepper, salt, and a little beef gravy ; cover the whole with a thick paste of potatoes, making the crust to rise in the centre above the edges of the dish. Score the potato crust with the point of a knife in squares of equal sizes. Put the dish before a fire in a Dutch oven, and brown it on all sides ; by the time it is coloured, the meat and potatoes will be sufficiently done.

985. Beef Bubble and Squeak.— Cut into pieces convenient for frying, cold roasted or broiled beef ; pepper, salt, and fry them ; when done, lay them on a hot drainer, and while the meat is draining from the fat used in frying them, have in readiness a cabbage already boiled in two waters ; chop it small, and put it in the frying-pan with some butter, add a little pepper and keep stirring it, that all of it may be equally done. When taken from the fire, sprinkle over the cabbage a very little vinegar, only enough to give it a slightly acid taste. Place the cabbage in the centre of the dish, and arrange the slices of meat neatly round it.

986. Beef or Mutton Lobscouse.— Mince, not too finely, some cold roasted beef or mutton. Chop the bones, and put them in a saucepan with six potatoes peeled and sliced, one onion, also sliced, some pepper and salt ; of these make a gravy. When the potatoes are completely incorporated with the gravy, take out the bones and put in the meat ; stew the whole together for an hour before it is to be served.

987. Beef Rissoles.— Mince and season cold beef, and flavour it with mushroom or walnut ketchup. Make of beef dripping a very thin paste, roll it out in thin pieces, about four inches square ; enclose in each piece some of the mince, in the same way as for puffs, cutting each neatly all round ; fry them in dripping to a very light brown. The

paste can scarcely be rolled out too thin.

988. Veal Minced.— Cut veal from the fillet or shoulder into very small dice ; put into veal or mutton broth with a little mace, white pepper, salt, some lemon peel grated, and a table-spoonful of mushroom ketchup, or mushroom powder rubbed smooth into the gravy. Take out some of the gravy when nearly done, and when cool enough thicken it with flour, cream, and a little butter ; boil it up with the rest of the gravy, and pour it over the meat when done. Garnish with bread sippets. A little lemon juice added to the gravy improves its flavour.

989. Veal dressed with White Sauce.— Boil milk or cream with a thickening of flour and butter ; put into it thin slices of cold veal, and simmer it in the gravy till it is made hot without boiling. When nearly done, beat up the yolk of an egg, with a little anchovy and white sauce ; pour it gently to the rest, stirring it all the time ; simmer again the whole together, and serve it with sippets of bread and curled bacon alternately.

990. Veal Rissoles.— Mince and pound veal extremely fine ; grate into it some remains of cooked ham. Mix these well together with white sauce, flavoured with mushrooms : form this mixture into balls, and enclose each in pastry. Fry them in butter to a light brown. The same mince may be fried in balls without pastry, being first cemented together with egg and breadcrumbs.

991. Hashed Mutton or Beef.— Slice the meat small, trim off the brown edges, and stew down the trimmings with the bones, well broken, an onion, a bunch of thyme and parsley, a carrot cut into slices, a few peppercorns, cloves, salt, and a pint and a half of water or stock. When this is reduced to little more than three-quarters of a pint, strain it, clear it from the fat, thicken it with a large dessertspoonful of flour or arrowroot, add salt and pepper, boil the whole for a few minutes, then lay in the meat and heat it well. Boiled potatoes are sometimes sliced hot into the hash.

992. Haricot Mutton.—Cut *small* pieces from the neck, or loin, put them into boiling gravy (previously skimming the fat off), and boil gently for an hour and a half, adding some sliced fried onions, a few carrots, and some salt and pepper to taste.

993. Lamb Cutlets.—Fry slices or chops of lamb in butter till they are slightly browned. Serve them on a purée of cucumbers, or on a dish of spinach ; or dip the slices in bread-crumbs, chopped parsley, and yolk of an egg ; some grated lemon and a little nutmeg may be added. Fry them, and pour a little nice gravy over them when served.

994. Pork Rissoles.—Cold boiled pork minced very fine and seasoned judiciously may be made into rissoles with egg and bread-crumbs and fried. Slices of cold pork fried and laid on apple sauce also form an excellent side or corner dish.

995. Baked Brisket of Beef.—The bones being removed, fill the holes with oysters, fat bacon, parsley, or all three in separate holes ; these stuffings being chopped and seasoned to taste. Dredge it well with flour, pour upon it half-a-pint of broth, bake for three hours, skim off the fat, strain the gravy over the meat, and garnish with cut pickles.

996. Lamb Stove or Lamb Stew.—Take a lamb's head and lights, open the jaws of the head, and wash them thoroughly ; put them in a pot with some beef stock, made with three quarts of water and two pounds of shin of beef, strained ; boil very slowly for an hour ; wash and string two or three good handfuls of spinach ; put it in twenty minutes before serving ; add a little parsley, and one or two onions, a short time before it comes off the fire ; season with pepper and salt, and serve all together in a tureen.

997. Roast Beef Bones furnish a very relishing luncheon or supper, prepared with poached or fried eggs and mashed potatoes as accompaniments. Divide the bones, having good pickings of meat on each ; score them in squares, pour a little melted butter over, and sprinkle with pepper and salt ; put them on a dish ; set in a Dutch oven for half or three-quarters of an hour, according to the thickness of the meat ; keep turning till they are quite hot and brown : or broil them on the gridiron. Brown but do not burn them. Serve with piquant sauce.

998. Marrow Bones.—Saw the bones evenly, so that they will stand steadily ; put a piece of paste into the ends ; set them upright in a saucepan, and boil till they are done enough—a beef marrow bone will require from an hour and a half to two hours ; serve fresh-toasted bread with them.

999. Rump Steak and Onion Sauce.—Peel and slice two large onions, put them into a quart stewpan, with two tablespoonfuls of water ; cover the pan close, and set on a slow fire till the water has boiled away, and the onions have become a little browned ; then add half-a-pint of good broth, and boil the onions till they are tender ; strain the broth, and chop very fine ; season with mushroom ketchup, pepper, and salt ; put in the onions then, and let them boil gently for five minutes, pour into the dish, and lay over it a broiled rump steak. If instead of broth you use good beef gravy, it will be delicious.

1000. Beef or Veal Alamode.—Take about eleven pounds of the mouse buttock,—or clod of beef,—or blade bone,—or the sticking-piece, or the like weight of the breast of veal ;—cut it into pieces of three or four ounces each ; put in three or four ounces of beef dripping, and mince a couple of large onions, and lay them into a large deep stewpan. As soon as it is quite hot, flour the meat, put it into the stewpan, continue stirring with a wooden spoon ; when it has been on about ten minutes, dredge with flour, and keep doing so till you have stirred in as much as you think will thicken it ; then add by degrees about a gallon of boiling water ; keep stirring it together ; skim it when it boils, and then put in one drachm of ground black pepper, two of allspice, and two bay-leaves ; set the pan by the side of the fire, or at a distance over it, and let it stew *very slowly* for about three hours ; when you find the meat sufficiently tender, put it into a tureen, and it is ready for table.

1001. Ragout of Cold Veal.— Either a neck, loin, or fillet of veal will furnish this excellent ragout with a very little expense or trouble. Cut the veal into handsome cutlets ; put a piece of butter, or clean dripping, into a frying-pan ; as soon as it is hot, flour and fry the veal of a light brown ; take it out, and if you have no gravy ready, put a pint of boiling water into the frying-pan, give it a boil-up for a minute, and strain it in a basin while you make some thickening in the following manner :— Put an ounce of butter into a stewpan ; as soon as it melts, mix as much flour as will dry it up ; stir it over the fire for a few minutes, and gradually add the gravy you made in the frying-pan : let them simmer together for ten minutes ; season with pepper, salt, a little mace, and a wineglassful of mushroom ketchup or wine ; strain it through a tammy, or fine sieve, over the meat, and stew very gently till the meat is thoroughly warmed. If you have any ready-boiled bacon, cut it in slices, and put it to warm with the meat.

1002. Mock Goose (being a leg of pork skinned, roasted, and stuffed goose fashion).—Parboil the leg ; take off the skin, and then put it down to roast ; baste it with butter, and make a *savoury powder* of finely-minced or dried or powdered sage, ground black pepper, salt, and some bread-crumbs, rubbed together through a colander ; add to this a little very finely minced onion ; sprinkle it with this when it is almost roasted ; put half-a-pint of made gravy into the dish, and goose stuffing under the knuckle skin ; or garnish the dish with balls of it fried or boiled.

1003. Jugged Hare.—Wash it very nicely, cut it up in pieces proper to help at table, and put them into a jugging-pot, or into a stone jar, just sufficiently large to hold it well ; put in some sweet herbs, a roll or two of rind of a lemon, and a fine large onion with five cloves stuck in it ; and, if you wish to preserve the flavour of the hare, a quarter of a pint of water ; but if you wish to make a ragout, a quarter of a pint of claret or port wine, and the juice of a lemon. Tie the jar down closely with a bladder, so that no steam can escape ; put a little hay in the bottom of the saucepan, in which place the jar ; let the water boil for about three hours, according to the age and size of the hare, keeping it boiling all the time, and fill up the pot as it boils away. Care, however, must be taken that it is not overdone, which is the general fault in all made dishes. When quite tender, strain off the gravy from the fat, thicken it with flour, and give it a boil-up ; lay the pieces of hare in a hash dish, and pour the gravy over it. You may make a pudding the same as for roast hare, and boil it in a cloth, and when you dish up your hare, cut it in slices, or make forcemeat balls of it for garnish. For sauce, red currant jelly (*see also* STEWED HARE, par. 926).

1004. Curried Beef, Madras Way. —Take about two ounces of butter, and place it in a saucepan, with two small onions cut up into slices, and let them fry until they are a light brown ; then add a tablespoonful and a half of curry powder, and mix it up well. Now put in the beef, cut into pieces about an inch square ; pour in from a quarter to a third of a pint of milk, and let it simmer for thirty minutes ; then take it off, and place it in a dish, with a little lemon juice. Whilst cooking stir constantly, to prevent it burning. Send to table with a wall of mashed potatoes or boiled rice round it. It greatly improves any curry to add with the milk a quarter of a cocoa-nut, scraped very small, and squeezed through muslin with a little water ; this softens the taste of the curry, and, indeed, no curry should be made without it.

1005. Collared Beef.—The ribs or thinnest piece of the flank is the best for this purpose. Rub the beef with some coarse sugar and put it away for two or three days : then slightly salt it, and let it rest for eight or ten days. Next take off the bones and skin, and sprinkle the underside with savoury herbs and parsley, and roll it up tightly in a cloth, binding it round with a wide piece of tape. When cooking boil slowly.

1006. Ragout of Duck, or any kind of Poultry or Game.—Partly roast, then divide into joints, or pieces of a suitable size for helping at table. Set it on in a stewpan, with a pint and a half of broth, or, if you have no broth, water, with any little trimmings of meat to enrich it ; a large onion stuck with cloves, a dozen berries of allspice, the same quantity of black pepper, and the rind of half a lemon shaved thin. When it boils, skim it very clean, and then let it simmer gently, with the lid close, for an hour and a half. Then strain off the liquor, and take out the pieces, which keep hot in a basin or deep dish. Rinse the stewpan, or use a clean one, in which put two ounces of butter, and as much flour or other thickening as will bring it to a stiff paste ; add to it the gravy by degrees. Let it boil up, then add a glass of port wine, a little lemon juice, and a teaspoonful of salt ; simmer a few minutes. Put the meat in a deep dish, strain the gravy over, and garnish with sippets of toasted bread. The flavour may be varied at pleasure by adding ketchup, curry powder, or vinegar. "There should be two," said

the Abbé Morellet, "to eat a turkey stuffed with truffles. I am going to have one to-day. We shall be *two*, the turkey and myself !"

1007. To Dress Cold Poultry, or Rabbit.—Cut the cold bird or rabbit in quarters, beat up an egg or two (according to the quantity to be dressed) with a little grated nutmeg, and pepper and salt, some parsley minced fine, and a few crumbs of bread ; mix these well together, and cover the pieces with this batter : broil them, or put them in a Dutch oven, or have ready some dripping hot in a pan, in which fry them a light brown colour ; thicken a little gravy with some flour, put a large spoonful of ketchup to it, lay the fry in a dish, and pour the sauce round it ; garnish with slices of lemon and toasted bread.

1009. Pulled Turkey, Fowl, or Chicken.—Skin a cold chicken, fowl, or turkey ; take off the fillets from the breasts, and put them into a stewpan with the rest of the white meat and wings, side-bones, and merry-thought, with a pint of broth, a large blade of mace pounded, a shallot minced fine, the juice of half a lemon, and a strip of the peel, some salt, and a few grains of cayenne ; thicken it with flour and butter, and let it simmer for two or three minutes, till the meat is warm. In the meantime score the legs and rump, powder them with pepper and salt, broil them in a dish, and lay the pulled chicken round them. Three tablespoonfuls of good cream, or the yolks of as many eggs, will be a great improvement to it.

1010. Hashed Poultry, Game, or Rabbit.—Cut them into joints, put the trimmings into a stewpan with a quart of the broth in which they were boiled, and a large onion cut in four ; let the whole boil half-an-hour : strain it through a sieve ; then put two table-spoonfuls of flour in a basin, and mix it well by degrees with the hot broth ; set it on the fire to boil up, then strain it through a sieve : wash out the stewpan, lay the poultry in it, and pour the gravy on it (through a sieve) ; set it by the side of the fire to simmer very gently (it must not *boil*) for fifteen minutes ; five minutes before you serve it up, cut the stuffing in slices, and put it in to warm, then take it out, and lay it round the edge of the dish, and put the poultry in the middle ; skim the fat off the gravy, then shake it round well in the stewpan, and pour it over the hash. Garnish the dish with toasted sippets.

1011. Hashed Ducks or Geese.— Cut an onion into small dice ; put it into a stewpan with a bit of butter ; fry it, but do not let it get any colour ; put as much boiling water into the stewpan as will make sauce for the hash ; thicken it with a little flour ; cut up the duck, and put it into the sauce to warm ; do not let it boil ; season it with pepper and salt and ketchup.

1012. Country Captain.—Cut a chicken up small, melt some butter in a frying-pan, in which there is an onion cut into fine slices. Fry the chicken, sprinkling it plentifully with good curry powder, add a little salt, and fry till cooked. Turn the pieces frequently and serve very hot, placing some fried onions over them.

1013. A Nice Way of Cooking Cold Fowl.—Beat the whites of two eggs to a thick froth ; add a small bit of butter, or some salad oil, flour, a little lukewarm water, and two tablespoonfuls of beer, beaten altogether till it is of the consistency of very thick cream. Cut up the fowl into small pieces, strew over it some chopped parsley and shallot, pepper, salt, and a little vinegar, and let it lie till dinner-time ; dip the fowl in the batter, and fry it in boiling lard, of a nice light brown. Veal that has been cooked may be dressed in the same way.

1014. To Curry Meat, Poultry, &c.—Cut up a good fowl ; skin it or not, as you please ; fry it nicely brown : slice two or three onions, and fry them ;

put the fried fowl and onions into a stewpan with a tablespoonful of curry powder, and one clove of garlic : cover it with water or veal gravy : let it stew slowly for one hour, or till very tender ; have ready, mixed in two or three spoonfuls of good cream, one teaspoonful of flour, two ounces of butter, juice of a lemon, some salt ; after the cream is in, it must only have one boil up, not to stew. Any spice may be added if the curry powder is not highly seasoned. With chicken, rabbit, or fish, observe the same rule. Curry is made also with sweetbreads, breast of veal, veal cutlets, lamb, mutton or pork chops, lobster, turbot, soles, eels, oysters, &c. Any kind of white meat is fit for a curry.

1015. Curried Eggs.—Slice two onions and fry them in butter, add a tablespoonful of curry powder ; let the onions and curry powder stew in a pint of good broth till the former are quite tender ; mix a cup of cream, and thicken with arrowroot, or rice flour. Simmer a few minutes, then add six or eight hard-boiled eggs cut in slices ; heat them thoroughly, but do not let them boil.

1016. Curried Oysters.—This recipe may be greatly modified, both in quantity and ingredients. Let a hundred of large oysters be opened into a basin without losing one drop of their liquor. Put a lump of fresh butter into a good-sized saucepan, and when it boils, add a large onion, cut into thin slices, and let it fry in the uncovered stewpan until it is of a rich brown : now add a bit more butter, and two or three tablespoonfuls of curry powder. When those ingredients are well mixed over the fire with a wooden spoon, add gradually either hot water, or broth from the stock-pot ; cover the stewpan, and let the whole boil up. Meanwhile, have ready the meat of a cocoa-nut, grated or rasped fine, put this into the stewpan with an unripe apple, chopped. Let the whole simmer over the fire until the apple is dissolved, and the cocoanut very tender ; then add a cupful of strong thickening made of flour and water, and sufficient salt, as a curry will not bear being salted at table. Let this boil up for five minutes. Have ready also a vegetable marrow, or part of one, cut into bits, and sufficiently boiled to require little or no further cooking. Put this in with a tomato or two. These vegetables improve the flavour of the dish, but either or both of them may be omitted. Now put into the stewpan the oysters with their liquor, and the milk of the cocoa-nut, if it be perfectly sweet ; stir them well with the former ingredients ; let the curry stew gently for a few minutes, then throw in the strained juice of half a lemon. Stir the curry from time to time with a wooden spoon, and as soon as the oysters are done enough, serve it up with a corresponding dish of rice on the opposite side of the table. This dish is considered at Madras the *ne plus ultra* of Indian cookery.

1017. Fried Oysters.—Large oysters are the best. Simmer for a minute or two in their own liquor ; drain perfectly dry ; dip in yolk of egg, and then in bread-crumbs, seasoned with nutmeg, cayenne, and salt ; fry them of a light brown. They are chiefly used as garnish for fish, or for rump steaks ; but if intended to be eaten alone, make a little thick melted butter, moistened with the liquor of the oysters, and serve as sauce.

1018. Stewed Oysters.—The beard or fringe is generally taken off. When this is done, set on the beards with the liquor of the oysters, and a little white gravy, rich, but unseasoned ; having boiled for a few minutes, strain off the beards, put in the oysters, and thicken the gravy with flour and butter (an ounce of butter to half-a-pint of stew), a little salt, pepper, and nutmeg, or mace, a spoonful of ketchup, and three of cream ; some

prefer a little essence of anchovy to ketchup, others the juice of a lemon, others a glass of white wine ; the flavour may be varied according to taste. Simmer till the stew is thick, and the oysters warmed through, but avoid letting them boil. Lay toasted sippets at the bottom of the dish and round the edges.

1019. Cold Meat Broiled with Poached Eggs.—The inside of a sirloin of beef or a leg of mutton is the best for this dish. Cut the slices of equal thickness, and broil and brown them carefully and slightly over a clear smart fire, or in a Dutch oven ; give those slices most fire that are least done ; lay them in a dish before the fire to keep hot, while you poach the eggs and mash the potatoes. This makes a savoury luncheon or supper. The meat should be *underdone* the first time.

1020. Pork Sausages.—Take some pig's meat, and cut out all the skin and nerves. Chop fine, and put it in a pan with some parsley, mint, garlic, thyme, burnet, and marjoram (minced up fine), some powdered pepper and cloves, and a little salt. Well mix these with a wooden spoon, then put in a tumblerful of white wine for each two pounds of meat—and again mix with the spoon. Have some nice clean skins, which should be well rubbed with lemon juice and put them in clean water in which there is plenty of lemon juice. After a short time take them out, fill with the meat, and tie up in lengths of three or three and a half inches. They should then be hung up to dry for a few days.

1021. Oxford Sausages.—To each pound of lean pork allow one pound of lean veal, one pound of fat, part pork and part veal. Chop and beat well with a lard-beater. Allow one pound of bread-crumbs, thyme, a little parsley ; an ounce of sage leaves, chopped very small ; two heads of leeks, or a little garlic, or shallot, chopped very fine ; salt, pepper, and nutmeg. To each pound allow one egg, the yolks and whites separately ; beat both well, mix in the yolks, and as much of the whites as is necessary to moisten the bread. Then make the sausages in the usual way.

1022. Worcester Sausages are made of beef, &c. ; add allspice, and any other spices and herbs you may choose.

1023. Mutton Sausages.—The lean of the leg is the best. Add half as much of beef suet ; that is, a pound of lean and half-a-pound of suet (this proportion is good for all sausages). Add oysters, anchovies chopped very fine, and flavour with seasoning. No herbs. These will require a little fat in the pan to fry.

1024. Veal Sausages. are made exactly as Oxford sausages, except that you add ham fat, or fat bacon ; and, instead of sage, use marjoram, thyme, and parsley.

1025. Bologna Sausages.—Take equal quantities of bacon, fat and lean, beef, veal, pork, and beef suet ; chop them small, season with pepper, salt, &c., sweet herbs, and sage rubbed fine. Have a well-washed intestine, fill, and prick it ; boil gently for an hour, and lay on straw to dry. They may be smoked the same as hams.

1026. Saveloys are made of salt pork, fat and lean, with bread-crumbs, pepper, and sage ; they are always put in skins ; boil half-an-hour slowly. These are eaten cold.

1027. To Prepare Sausage Skins.—Turn them inside out, and stretch them on a stick ; wash and scrape them in several waters. When thoroughly cleansed, take them off the sticks, and soak in salt and water two or three hours before filling.

1028. Black Hog Pudding.—Catch the blood of a hog ; to each quart of blood put a large teaspoonful of salt, and stir it without ceasing till it is cold. Simmer half-a-pint or a pint of Embden groats in a small quantity of water till tender ; there must be no gruel. The best way of doing it is in a double saucepan, so that you need not put more water than will moisten them. Chop up (for one quart of blood) one pound of the inside fat of the hog, and a quarter of a pint of bread-crumbs, a tablespoonful of sage, chopped fine, a teaspoonful of thyme, three drachms each of allspice, salt and pepper, and a teacupful of cream. When the blood is cold, strain it through a sieve, and add to it the fat, then the groats, and then the seasoning. When well mixed, put it into the skin of the largest gut, well cleansed ; tie it in lengths of about nine inches, and boil gently for twenty minutes. Take them out and prick them when they have boiled a few minutes.

1029. Sweetbread.—Trim a fine sweetbread (it cannot be too *fresh*) ; parboil it for five minutes, and throw it it into a basin of cold water. Then roast it plain—or beat up the yolk of an egg, and prepare some fine bread-crumbs ; or when the sweetbread is cold, dry it thoroughly in a cloth ; run a lark-spit skewer through it ; egg it with a paste-brush ; powder it well with bread-crumbs, and roast it. For sauce, fried bread-crumbs, melted butter, with a little mushroom ketchup, and lemon juice, or serve on buttered toast, garnished with egg sauce, or with gravy. It may also be cooked in a tin Dutch oven, or fried.

1030. Sweetbreads Plain.—Parboil and slice them as before, dry them in a clean cloth, flour them, and fry them a delicate brown ; take care to drain the fat well, and garnish with slices of lemon, and sprigs of chervil or parsley, or crisp parsley. Serve with sauce, and slices of ham or bacon, or forcemeat balls.

1031. Broiled Kidneys.—Cut them through the long way, score them, sprinkle a little pepper and salt on them, and run a wire skewer through to keep them from curling on the gridiron, so that they may be evenly broiled. Broil over a clear fire, taking care not to prick the kidney with the fork, and turning them often till they are done ; they will take about ten or twelve minutes, if the fire is brisk.

1032. Fried Kidneys.—Another mode is to fry them in butter, and make gravy for them in the pan (after you have taken out the kidneys), by putting in a teaspoonful of flour ; as soon as it looks brown, put in as much water as will make gravy. Kidneys will take five minutes more to fry than to broil.

1033. Sauté Kidneys.—Take the skins off the kidneys, and cut away the piece of cartilage by which they are held ; *but do not cut the kidneys into halves.* Place some rashers of bacon along the bottom of an iron saucepan, and when they are cooked take them out. Then put the kidneys into the saucepan, with just sufficient fat to cover them, having previously floured them. Leave the cover off the saucepan, after they have been in for five minutes, turn them over (but not with a fork, or you may prick them and let the gravy out). Put a dish, with a little butter, salt, and pepper in it, in the oven or in front of the fire to warm ; and in another five minutes the kidneys will be cooked. Take them out and put them all in the dish ; then cut them in half, placing a piece of the bacon between each piece of kidney. They cannot be cooked in a frying-pan, as it is not deep enough to hold sufficient fat to cover them.

1034. Devilled Turkey, &c.—The gizzard and rump, or legs, &c., of a dressed turkey, capon, or goose, or mutton or veal kidney, scored, peppered, salted, and broiled, sent up for a relish, being made very hot with cayenne pepper.

1035. Scotch Woodcock.—Three or four slices of bread ; toast and butter well on both sides,—nine or ten anchovies washed, scraped and chopped fine ; put them between the slices of toast,—have ready the yolks of four eggs well beaten, and half-a-pint of cream—which set over the fire to thicken, but not boil,—then pour it over the toast, and serve it to table as hot as possible.

1036. Anchovy Toast—Toast a thin round of bread, cut the crusts off, and butter it. Mix a little melted butter with a tablespoonful of anchovy sauce and a teaspoonful of flour, mixed with cold and set with boiling water. Slightly soften the toast by drips of boiling water on it, then spread the anchovy on the toast, make it hot in the oven, and serve on a hot dish, the toast being cut into sippets, each with half a hard-boiled egg upon it.

1037. Broiled Ham or Bacon.—The slices should not be less than one-eighth or more than a quarter of an inch thick, and, for delicate persons, should be soaked in hot water for a quarter of an hour, and then well wiped and dried before broiling. If you wish to curl a slice, roll it up, and put a wooden skewer through it ; then it may be dressed in a cheese-toaster or a Dutch oven.

1038. Relishing Rashers of Cold Bacon.—If you have any *cold bacon*, you may make a very nice dish of it by cutting it into slices about a quarter of an inch thick. Then grate some crust of bread as directed for ham, and powder the slices well with it on both sides ; lay the rashers in a cheese-toaster,—they will be browned on one side in about three minutes :— turn them and do the other. These are a delicious accompaniment to poached or fried eggs :—the bacon, having been boiled first, is tender and mellow.—They are an excellent garnish round veal cutlets, sweetbreads, calf's-head hash, green peas, or beans, &c.

1039. Liver and Bacon.—Wash the liver (but do not soak it), wipe, and cut into slices, flouring each piece. Cut off the rind from the bacon, and fry the latter in rashers. Place them in a dish in front of the fire while the liver is being fried in the bacon fat. Mix a little flour into a paste with water, add pepper and salt, and place in frying-pan. Let boil gently, and strain it over the liver and bacon. Serve nice and hot.

1040. SCOTCH PORRIDGE.—For Four Persons.—Boil three pints of water in a clean saucepan, add a teaspoonful of salt ; mix very gradually, while the water is boiling, one pound of fine oatmeal, stirring constantly, while you put in the meal, with a round stick about eighteen inches long, called a "spirtle." Continue stirring for fifteen minutes ; then pour into soup plates, allow it to cool a little, and serve with sweet milk. Scotch porridge is one of the most nutritive diets that can be given, especially for young persons, on account of the bone-producing elements contained in oatmeal. It is sometimes boiled with milk instead of water, but the mixture is then rather rich for delicate stomachs.

1041. SCOTCH BROSE.—This favourite Scotch dish is generally made with the liquor in which meat has been boiled. Put half-a-pint of oatmeal into a porringer with a little salt, add as much broth as will mix it to the consistence of hasty pudding or a little thicker,—lastly, take a little of the fat that swims on the broth and put it on the porridge, and eat it in the same way as hasty pudding.

1042. SCOTCH BARLEY BROTH.—Dr. Kitchiner, from whose *Cook's Oracle*[1] we take this recipe, after

testing it, says :—"This is a most frugal, agreeable, and nutritive meal. It will neither lighten the purse nor lie heavy on the stomach. It will furnish you with a pleasant soup, AND MEAT for eight persons. Wash three-quarters of a pound of Scotch barley in a little cold water ; put it in a soup-pot with a shin or leg of beef, of about ten pounds weight, sawn into four pieces (tell the butcher to do this for you) ; cover it well with cold water ; set it on the fire ; when it boils, skim it very clean, and put in two onions, of about three ounces weight each ; set it by the side of the fire to simmer very gently for about two hours ; then skim all the fat clean off, and put in two heads of celery and a large turnip cut into small squares ; season it with salt, and let it boil for an hour and a half longer, and it will be ready : take out the meat carefully with a slice (cover it up, and set it by the fire to keep warm), and skim the broth well before you put it in the tureen. Put a quart of the soup into a basin, and about an ounce of flour into a stewpan, and pour the broth to it by degrees, stirring it well together ; set it on the fire, and stir it till it boils, then let it boil up, and it is ready. Put the meat in a ragout dish, and strain the sauce through a sieve over the meat ; you may put to it some capers, or minced gherkins, or walnuts, &c. If the beef has been stewed with proper care, in a very gentle manner, and taken up at 'the critical moment when it is just tender,' you will obtain an excellent and savoury meal."

1043. HOTCH-POTCH FOR SUMMER.—Make a stock from the neck or ribs of lamb or mutton, reserving some chops, which cook for a shorter time and serve in the tureen. Chop small four turnips, four carrots, a few young onions, a little parsley, and one lettuce ; boil for one hour. Twenty minutes before they are done, put in a cauliflower cut small, one quart of shelled peas, and a pint of young beans.

1044. HOTCH-POTCH FOR WINTER.—This can be made of beef or mutton, or, for those who are partial to Scotch cookery, a sheep's head and feet, one pound of old green peas, steeped all the night previously, one large turnip, three carrots, four leeks, a little parsley, all cut small, with the exception of one carrot, which should be grated ; add a small bunch of sweet herbs, pepper, and salt. The peas take two hours and a half to cook ; the other vegetables two hours ; the head three hours ; and the feet four hours.

1045. BEEF BROTH may be made by adding vegetables to essence of beef—or you may wash a leg or shin of beef, the bone of which has been well cracked by the butcher ; add any trimmings of meat, game, or poultry, heads, necks, gizzards, feet, &c. ; cover them with cold water ; stir the whole up well from the bottom, and the moment it begins to simmer, skim it carefully. Your broth must be perfectly clear and limpid ; on this depends the goodness of the soups, sauces, and gravies of which it is the basis. Add some cold water to make the remaining scum rise, and skim it again. When the scum has done rising, and the surface of the broth is quite clear, put in one moderate-sized carrot, a head of celery, two turnips, and two onions,—it should not have any taste of sweet herbs, spice, or garlic, &c. ; either of these flavours can easily be added, if desired,—cover it close, set it by the side of the fire, and let it simmer very gently (so as not to waste the broth) for four or five hours, or more, according to the weight of the meat. Strain it through a sieve into a clean and dry stone pan, and set it in the coldest place you have, if for after use.

1046. CLEAR GRAVY SOUP.—This may be made from shin of beef, which should not be large or coarse.

The meat will be found serviceable for the table. From ten pounds of the meat let the butcher cut off five or six from the thick fleshy part, and again divide the knuckle, that the whole may lie compactly in the vessel in which it is to be stewed. Pour in three quarts of cold water, and when it has been brought slowly to boil, and been well skimmed, throw in an ounce and a half of salt, half a large teaspoonful of peppercorns, eight cloves, two blades of mace, a faggot of savoury herbs, a couple of small carrots, and the heart of a root of celery ; to these add a mild onion or not, at choice. When the whole has stewed very softly for four hours, probe the large bit of beef, and, if quite tender, lift it out for table ; let the soup be simmered from two to three hours longer, and then strain it through a fine sieve, into a clean pan. When it is perfectly cold, clear off every particle of fat : heat a couple of quarts ; stir in, when it boils, half-an-ounce of sugar, a small tablespoonful of good soy, and twice as much of Harvey's sauce, or, instead of this, of clear and fine mushroom ketchup. If carefully made, the soup will be perfectly transparent, and of good colour and flavour. A thick slice of ham will improve it, and a pound or so of the neck of beef, with an additional pint of water, will likewise enrich its quality. A small quantity of good broth may be made of the fragments of the whole, boiled down with a few firesh vegetables.

1047. JULIENNE SOUP.—Take three carrots, three turnips, one onion, a leek, a few celery leaves, half a lettuce, some chervil, one ounce of butter, and two quarts of stock. Cut the vegetables into thin strips : fry the carrots in the butter, boil the stock and pour over them ; add the other vegetables and stew for an hour.

1048. MOCK TURTLE SOUP.—Take three pounds of knuckle of veal. one cow-heel, a large onion stuck with cloves, some sweet herbs, two blades of mace, six peppercorns, eighteen forcemeat balls, a little lemon juice, and a glass of sherry. Put everything, except the forcemeat balls and the lemon juice, into an earthen jar and stew for six hours; when cold skim off the fat and strain the liquor. Add the forcemeat balls and lemon juice, cut up the meat into small squares and warm the soup up.

1049. MULLIGATAWNY SOUP. —Three onions, one carrot, one turnip, one stick of rhubarb, one ounce of bacon, one ounce of butter, two ounces of flour, one tablespoonful of curry powder, some cayenne, salt, lemon juice, and one quart of stock. Melt the butter and fry the bacon in it for five minutes, then fry the vegetables and rhubarb. Add the flour and curry powder, and fry all. Then add the stock and boil, skim, pass through a sieve, and add the lemon juice.

1050. OXTAIL SOUP.—One ox-tail, two carrots, one turnip, one onion stuck with cloves, half head of celery, three ounces of butter, two ounces of flour, a bunch of herbs, twelve pepper-corns, two quarts of water, and some salt. Blanch and joint the tail and dry the pieces. Melt half the butter in a stewpan, put in the pieces of tail and the vegetables (cut small) and fry for eight or ten minutes. Add salt and water and let simmer for two hours. In another pan fry the butter till brown and add the stock. Stir till it comes to the boil, skim, and season to taste. Then strain it off into the tureen, with the tail, carrots and turnips.

1051.   COCK-A-LEEKIE.—Boil from four to six pounds of good shin of beef well broken, until the liquor is very good. Strain it and add a good-sized fowl, with two or three leeks cut in pieces about an inch long, put in pepper and salt to taste, boil slowly about an hour, then put in as many more leeks, and give it three-quarters of an hour longer. A somewhat similar soup may be made of good beef stock,

and leeks cut up and put in without a fowl, though this cannot be called Cock-a-Leekie with propriety.

1052. ASPARAGUS SOUP.—Two quarts of good beef or veal stock, four onions, two or three turnips, some sweet herbs, and the white parts of a hundred young asparagus,—if old, half that quantity,—and let them simmer till fit to be rubbed through a hair sieve; strain and season it; have ready the boiled green tops of the asparagus, and add them to the soup.

1053. CARROT SOUP.—Scrape and wash half-a-dozen large carrots; peel off the red outside (which is the only part used for this soup); put it into a gallon stewpan, with one heart of celery, and an onion cut into thin pieces; take two quarts of beef, veal, or mutton broth, or liquor in which mutton or beef has been boiled, as the foundation for this soup. Stock that is equally good may be made by boiling down some cold roast mutton or beef bones. When you have put the broth to the roots, cover the stewpan close, and set it on a slow stove for two hours and a half, when the carrots will be soft enough. At this stage some cooks put in a teacupful of bread-crumbs. Next boil the soup for two or three minutes; rub it through a hair sieve, with a wooden spoon, and add as much broth as will make it a proper thickness, *i.e.* almost as thick as pea-soup; put it into a clean stewpan, make it hot and serve.

1054. VEGETABLE SOUP.—Peel and cut into very small pieces three onions, three turnips, one carrot, and four potatoes, put them into a stewpan with a quarter of a pound of butter, the same of lean ham, and a bunch of parsley, pass them ten minutes over a sharp fire; then add a large spoonful of flour, mix well in, moisten with two quarts of broth, and a pint of boiling milk; boil up, keeping it stirred; season with a little salt and sugar, and run it through a hair sieve; put it into another stewpan, boil again, skim, and serve with fried bread in it.

1055. VERMICELLI SOUP.—To three quarts of gravy soup, or stock, add six ounces of vermicelli. Simmer for half-an-hour ; stir frequently.

1056. BEEF EXTRACT.—Take a pound of good juicy beef from which all the skin and fat has been cut away, chop it up like sausage meat ; mix it thoroughly with a pint of cold water, place it on the side of the stove to heat *very slowly*, and give it an occasional stir. It may stand two or three hours before it is allowed to simmer, and will then require but fifteen minutes of gentle boiling. Salt should be added when the boiling commences, and this for invalids in general, is the only seasoning required. When the extract is thus far prepared, it may be poured from the meat into a basin, and allowed to stand until any particle of fat on the surface can be skimmed off, and the sediment has subsided and left the soup quite clear, when it may be poured off gently, heated in a clean saucepan, and served. The scum should be well cleared as it accumulates.

1057. BEEF TEA.—Beef extract, by adding water, forms the best beef tea or broth for invalids. A dessert-spoonful of sago put into a pint of *cold* beef tea, and boiled until the sago is dissolved, will be found most nourishing. You may use tapioca or rice instead ; those will have to be put into cold beef tea, and boiled, or they will not dissolve.

1058. ESSENCE OF BEEF may be prepared as follows :—Take one pound of lean beef, chopped very small, and a half-pint of water. Put these into a bottle and agitate them for half-an-hour ; then run them through a sieve into a jug. Boil the undissolved part for twenty minutes in one pint of water. Strain and mix with the other portion, adding spice, salt, &c., and pour the essence whilst hot into a bottle, or

can, which must be tightly closed up at once. There are many kinds of essences of meat now on the market, chief among which are Bovril, Brand's essence, Liebig's and Lipton's extracts, &c. They are all of great service in the sick-room, and are not very expensive.

1059. BEEF GLAZE, OR PORTABLE SOUP, is simply the essence of beef condensed by evaporation. It may be put into pots, like potted meats, or into skins, as sausages, and will keep for many months. If further dried in cakes or lozenges, by being laid on pans or dishes, and frequently turned, it will keep for years, and supply soup at any moment.

1060. BROWN STOCK.—Put five pounds of shin of beef, three pounds of knuckle of veal, and some sheep's trotters or cow-heel into a closely-covered stewpan, to draw out the gravy very gently, and allow it to become nearly brown. Then pour in sufficient boiling water to entirely cover the meat, and let it boil up, skimming it frequently ; seasoning it with whole peppers, salt, and roots, herbs, and vegetables or any kind. That being done, let it boil gently five or six hours, pour the broth off from the meat, and let it stand during the night to cool. The following morning take off the scum and fat, and put it away in a stone jar for further use. It may be made from all sorts of meat, bones, remnants of poultry, game, &c.

1061. BROWN GRAVY.—Three onions sliced, and fried in butter to a nice brown ; toast a large thin slice of bread until quite hard and of a deep brown. Take these with any pieces of meat, bone, &c., and some herbs, and set them on the fire, with water according to judgment, and stew down until a rich and thick gravy is produced. Season, strain, and keep cool.

1062. The use of little or much gravy with one's food is, of course, a matter of taste ; but Sydney Smith, in describing a dinner at which he was present, says—"I heard a lady who sat next to me say in a low, sweet voice, 'No gravy, sir.' I had never seen her before, but I turned suddenly round and said, 'Madam, I have been looking for a person who disliked gravy all my life ; let us swear eternal friendship !' She looked astonished, but took the oath, and what is better—kept it.'

1063. POTTED BEEF.—Take three or four pounds, or any smaller quantity, of lean beef, free from sinews, and rub it well with a mixture made of a handful of salt, one ounce of saltpetre, and one ounce of coarse sugar ; let the meat lie in the salt for two days, turning and rubbing it twice a day. Put it into a stone jar with a little beef gravy, and cover it with a paste to keep it close. Bake it for several hours in a very slow oven till the meat is tender ; then pour off the gravy, which should be in a very small quantity, or the juice of the meat will be lost ; pound the meat, when cold, in a marble mortar till it is reduced to a smooth paste, adding by degrees a little fresh butter melted. Season it as you proceed with pepper, allspice, nutmeg, pounded mace, and cloves, or such of these spices as are thought agreeable. Some flavour with anchovy, ham, shallots, mustard, wine, flavoured vinegar, ragout powder, curry powder, &c., according to taste. When it is thoroughly beaten and mingled together, press it closely into small shallow pots, nearly full, and fill them up with a layer a quarter of an inch thick of clarified butter, and tie them up with a bladder, or sheet of Indian rubber. They should be kept in a cool place.

1064. STRASBURG POTTED MEAT.—Take a pound and a half of rump of beef, cut into dice, and put it in an earthen jar, with a quarter of a pound of butter at the bottom ; tie the jar close up with paper, and set over a pot to boil ; when nearly done, add cloves, mace, allspice, nutmeg, salt,

and cayenne pepper to taste ; then boil till tender, and let it get cold. Pound the meat, with four anchovies washed and boned ; add a quarter of a pound of oiled butter, work it well together with the gravy, warm a little, and add cochineal to colour. Then press into small pots, and pour melted mutton suet over the top of each.

1065. POTTED MEATS AND PASTES.—A great variety of these useful relishes may be purchased ready prepared, such as anchovy paste, beef, bloater paste, cod's roe, game, ham, ham and chicken, shrimps, Strasburg meat, tongue, turkey and tongue, and various kinds of game. They are most convenient and tasty articles for breakfast, luncheon, or supper. Be careful to buy those made by reliable firms.

1066. FORCEMEAT BALLS (for turtle, mock turtle, or made dishes).—Pound some veal in a marble mortar, rub it through a sieve with as much of the udder as you have veal, or about a third of the quantity of butter : put some bread-crumbs into a stewpan, moisten them with milk, add a little chopped parsley and shallot, rub them well together in a mortar, till they form a smooth paste ; put it through a sieve, and when cold, pound, and mix all together, with the yolks of three eggs boiled hard ; season the mixture with salt, pepper, and curry powder, or cayenne ; add to it the yolks of two raw eggs, rub it well together, and make it into small balls, which should be put into the soup or hash, as the case may be, ten minutes before it is ready.

1067. GOOSE OR DUCK STUFFING.—Chop very fine about two ounces of onion, of *green* sage leaves about an ounce (both unboiled), four ounces of bread-crumbs, a bit of butter about as big as a walnut, &c., the yolk and white of an egg, and a little pepper and salt ; some add to this a minced apple.

1068. WILD DUCK, TO DRESS
—The birds are roasted like common ducks, but without stuffing, and with a rather less allowance of time for cooking. For example, a full-sized duck will take from three-quarters of an hour to an hour in roasting, but a wild duck will take from forty to fifty minutes. Before carving the knife should be drawn longitutudinally along the breast, and upon these a little cayenne pepper must be sprinkled, and a lemon squeezed. They require a good made gravy, as described below. They are excellent half roasted and hashed in a good gravy made as follows :—

1069. SAUCE FOR WILD DUCK.
—Simmer a teacupful of port wine, the same quantity of good gravy, a small shallot, with pepper, nutmeg, mace, and salt to taste, for about ten minutes ; put in a bit of butter and flour ; give it all one boil, and pour it over the birds, or serve in a sauce tureen.

1070. WIDGEON AND TEAL, TO DRESS.—These birds may be roasted or half roasted and hashed, according to the directions given for wild duck, and served up with a sauce or gravy made in precisely the same way. A widgeon will take as long to roast as a wild duck, but a teal, being a smaller bird, will take only from twenty to thirty minutes.

1071. SALMI OF COLD GROUSE.
—A very tasty dish is made by cutting the bird up and placing the pieces in a stewpan. The bones, &c., should be broken up and put into another stewpan with some gravy, small pieces of cooked ham, some lemon peel, half-a-dozen shallots, some parsley, bay-leaves, pepper, salt, and two glasses of white wine. Boil for one hour, and strain it over the grouse in the other pan. Simmer, but don't let it boil, and serve very hot with sippets.

1072. MEAT AND GAME PIES AND PUDDINGS.

1073. RAISED PIES.—Put two pounds and a half of flour on the pasteboard,—and set on the fire, in a saucepan, three-quarters of a pint of water, and half-a-pound of good lard. When the water boils, make a hole in the middle of the flour, pour in the water and lard by degrees, gently incorporating the flour with a spoon, and when it is well mixed, knead it with your hands till it becomes stiff ; dredge a little flour to prevent it sticking to the board, or you cannot make it look smooth. Roll the dough with your hands—the rolling-pin must not be used—to about the thickness of a quart pot ; leave a little for the covers, and cut the remainder into six circular discs. Take each of these pieces in succession ; put one hand in the middle, and keep the other close on the outside till you have worked it either into an oval or a round shape. Have your meat ready cut, and seasoned with pepper and salt ; if pork, cut it in small slices—the griskin is the best for pasties : if you use mutton, cut it in very neat cutlets, and put them in the pies as you make them ; roll out the covers with the rolling-pin, and cut them to the size of the pies, wet them round the edge, put them on the pie. Then press the paste of each pie and its cover together with the thumb and finger, and lastly, nick the edge all round with the back of a knife, and bake them an hour and a half.

1074. COLD PARTRIDGE OR GAME PIES.—Bone as many partridges as the size of pie to be made may require. Put a whole raw truffle, peeled, into each partridge, and fill up the remaining space in each bird with good forcemeat. Make a raised crust ; lay a few slices of veal in the bottom, and a thick layer of forcemeat ; then the partridges, and four truffles to each partridge ; then cover the partridges and truffles over with sheets of bacon, cover the pie in, and finish it. It will take four hours' baking. Cut two pounds of lean ham (if eight partridges are in the pie) into very thin slices, put it in a stewpan along with the bones and giblets of the partridges, and any other loose giblets that are at hand, an old fowl, a faggot of thyme and parsley, a little mace, and about twenty-four shallots : add about a pint of stock. Set the stewpan on a stove to simmer for half-an-hour, then put in three quarts of good stock ; let it boil for two hours, then strain it off, and reduce the liquid to one pint ; add sherry wine to it, and put aside till the pie is baked. When the pie has been out of the oven for half-an-hour, boil the residue strained from the bones, &c., of the partridges, and put it into the pie. Let it stand for twenty-four hours before it is eaten.—*Do not take any of the fat from the pie, as that is what preserves it.* A pie made in this manner will be eatable for three months after it is cut ; in short, it cannot spoil in any reasonable time. All cold pies are made in this manner. Either poultry or game, when put into a raised crust and intended not to be eaten until cold, should be boned, and the liquor that is to fill up the pie made from the bones, &c.

1075. PARTRIDGE PUDDING. —Skin a brace of well-kept partridges, and cut them into pieces ; line a deep basin with suet crust, and lay in the pieces, which should be rather highly seasoned with white pepper and cayenne, and moderately with salt. Pour in water for the gravy, close the pudding carefully, and boil it for three hours or three hours and a half. When mushrooms are plentiful, put a layer of buttons or small mushrooms, cleaned as for pickling, alternately with a layer of partridge in filling the pudding. When carving, the crust may be left untouched and merely emptied of its contents, where it is objected to, or a richer crust made with butter may be used instead of the ordinary suet crust.

1076. CALF's HEAD PIE.—Boil the head an hour and a half, or rather more. After dining from it, cut the remaining meat off in slices. Boil the bones in a little of the liquor for three hours ; then strain it off, let it remain till next day, and then take off the fat. *To make the Pie*—Boil two eggs fof five minutes ; let them get cold, then lay them in slices at the bottom of a pie dish, and put alternate layers of meat and jelly, with pepper and chopped lemon also alternately, till the dish is full ; cover with a crust and bake it. Next day turn the pie out upside down.

1077. SEA PIE.—Make a thick pudding crust, line a dish with it, or what is better, a cake-tin ; put a layer of sliced onions, then a layer of salt beef cut in slices, a layer of sliced potatoes, a layer of pork, and another of onions ; strew pepper over all, cover with a crust, and tie down tightly with a cloth previously dipped in boiling water and floured. Boil for two hours, and serve hot in a dish.

1078. RUMP-STEAK PIE—Cut three pounds of rump-steak (that has been kept till tender) into pieces half as big as your hand, trim off all the skin, sinews, and every part which has not indisputable pretensions to be eaten, and beat them with a chopper. Chop very fine half-a-dozen shallots, and add to them half-an-ounce of pepper and salt mixed ; strew some of the seasoning at the bottom of the dish, then a layer of steak, then some more of the seasoning, and so on till the dish is full ; add half-a-gill of mushroom ketchup, and the same quantity of gravy, or red wine ; cover it as in the preceding recipe, and bake it two hours. Large oysters, parboiled, bearded, and laid alternately with the steaks—their liquor reduced and substituted instead of the ketchup and wine, will impart a delicious flavour to the pie.

1079. BEEFSTEAK PUDDING. —Line the basin with thin suet crust. Cut some rump-steak into slices (first removing the fat and gristle) ; mix a little pepper and salt together, and dip the slices into it, then place it round the basin in layers until nearly full. Fill the puddle with oysters or mushrooms, tie it up tightly and boil for three hours, but do not let the water in the saucepan reach the top of the basin. Have a little extra hot gravy to pour into the pudding when carving.

1080. LARK PIE.—Take a dozen larks, pluck, singe, and draw them (except the trails). Chop small, and mix with some scraped bacon, a few mushrooms, some parsley and sweet herbs, pepper, salt, nutmeg, and mace ; stuff the larks with it. Place some bacon over the bottom of a pie-dish, with some pepper, salt, and sweet herbs. Put in the birds, with some more seasoning over them, and cover them over with fat bacon. Make a rich top crust, egg it over, and bake. When sufficiently done, take up the crust, remove the bacon, pour in some good gravy, place the crust down again, warm up, and serve.

1081. ROOK PIE.—Skin and draw six rooks, cut out the backbones and put them on one side. Be careful not to break the galls. Season the birds with pepper and salt, and place them in a deep pie-dish. Pour over them half-a-pint of water, and place a piece of butter on them. Make a light crust, cover it with a sheet of buttered paper, and bake for two and a half to three hours.

1081a. VEAL PIE.—Take some of the middle or scrag of a small neck ; season it with pepper and salt, and put to it a few pieces of lean bacon or ham. If a high seasoning is required, add mace, cayenne, and nutmeg to the salt and pepper ; and forcemeat and egg balls, truffles, morels, mushrooms, sweetbreads cut into small bits, and cocks' combs blanched, can form part of the materials, if liked, but the pie will be very good without them. Have a rich gravy to pour in after baking.

1082. MUTTON PIE.—The following is a capital family dish.—Cut mutton into pieces about two inches square, and half-an-inch thick ; mix pepper, pounded allspice, and salt together, dip the pieces in this ; sprinkle stale bread-crumbs at the bottom of the dish ; lay in the pieces, strewing the crumbs over each layer ; put a piece of butter the size of a hen's egg at the top ; add a wineglassful of water, and cover in, and bake in a moderate oven rather better than an hour. Take an onion, chopped fine ; a faggot of herbs ; half an anchovy ; and add to it a little beef stock or gravy ; simmer for a quarter of an hour ; raise the crust at one end, and pour in the liquor— not the thick part.

1083. SEVEN-BELL PASTY.—Shred a pound of suet fine, cut salt pork into dice, potatoes and onions small, rub a sprig of dried sage up fine ; mix with some pepper, and place in the corner of a square piece of paste ; turn over the other corner, pinch up the sides, and bake in a quick oven. If any bones, &c., remain from the meat, season with pepper and sage, place them with a gill of water in a pan, and bake with the pasty ; when done, strain and pour the gravy into the centre of the pasty.

1084. POTATO AND MEAT PIE.—Boil some mealy potatoes, peel and mash them with a little milk. Grease a baking dish ; put a layer of potatoes, then a layer of meat cut in bits, and seasoned with pepper, salt, a little all-spice, either with or without chopped onions ; a little gravy of roast meat is a great improvement : then put another layer of potatoes, then meat, and cover with potatoes. Put a buttered paper over the top, to prevent it from being burnt, and bake it from an hour to an hour and a half.

1085. PEAS PUDDING.—Dry a pint or quart of split peas thoroughly before the fire ; then tie them up loosely in a cloth, put them into warm water, boil them a couple of hours, or more, until quite tender ; take them up, beat them well in a dish, with a little salt, the yolk of an egg, and a bit of butter. Make it quite smooth, tie it up again in a cloth, and boil it an hour longer. This is highly nourishing.

1086. CULINARY ECONOMY.

The English, generally speaking, are very deficient in the practice of culinary economy ; a French family would live well on what is often wasted in an English kitchen. The bones, dripping, pot-liquor, remains of fish, vegetables, &c., which are too often consigned to the grease pot, or the dust-heap, especially where pigs or fowls are not kept, might, by a very trifling degree of management on the part of the cook, or mistress of a family, be converted into sources of daily support and comfort, at least to some poor pensioner or other, at an expense that even a miser could scarcely grudge. Housekeepers who wish to know how to economize all kinds of nutritious fragments, will find valuable hints and information on the subject in *The Family Save-all*,[1] which supplies a complete course of Secondary Cookery, and also in *The Practical Housewife*.[1]

1087. MY WIFE'S LITTLE SUPPERS.

1088. MEAT CAKES.—Take any cold meat, game, or poultry (if underdone, all the better), mince it fine, with a little fat bacon or ham, or an anchovy ; season it with pepper and salt ; mix well, and make it into small cakes three inches long, an inch and a half wide, and half-an-inch thick ; fry these a light brown, and serve them with good gravy, or put into a mould, and boil or bake it. Bread-crumbs, hard yolks of eggs, onions, sweet herbs, savoury spices, zest, curry-powder, or

any kind of forcemeat may be added to these meat cakes.

1089. FISH CAKES.—Take the meat from the bones of any kind of cold fish, and put the bones with the head and fins into a stewpan with a pint of water, a little salt, pepper, an onion, and a faggot of sweet herbs, to stew for gravy. Mince the meat, and mix it well with crumbs of bread and cold potatoes, equal parts, a little parsley and seasoning. Make into a cake, with the white of an egg, or a little butter or milk ; egg it over, and cover with bread crumbs, then fry a light brown. Pour the gravy over, and stew gently for fifteen minutes, stirring it carefully twice or thrice. Serve hot, and garnish with slices of lemon, or parsley. These cakes afford a capital relish from scraps of cold fish.

1090. OYSTER PATTIES.—Roll out puff paste a quarter of an inch thick, cut it into squares with a knife, sheet eight or ten pattypans, put upon each a bit of bread the size of half a walnut ; roll out another layer of paste of the same thickness, cut it as above, wet the edge of the bottom paste, and put on the top ; pare them round to the pan, and notch them about a dozen times with the back of the knife, rub them lightly with yolk of egg, bake them in a hot oven about a quarter of an hour : when done, take a thin slice off the top, then with a small knife, or spoon, take out the bread and the inside paste, leaving the outside quite entire ; then parboil two dozen of large oysters, strain them from their liquor, wash, beard, and cut them into four ; put them into a stewpan with an ounce of butter rolled in flour, half-a-gill of good cream, a little grated lemon-peel, the oyster liquor, free from sediment, reduced by boiling to one-half, some cayenne pepper, salt, and a teaspoonful of lemon juice ; stir it over a fire five minutes, and fill the patties.

1091. LOBSTER PATTIES.—Prepare the patties as in the last recipe. Take a hen lobster already boiled ; pick the meat from the tail and claws, and chop it fine ; put it into a stewpan with a little of the inside spawn pounded in a mortar till quite smooth, an ounce of fresh butter, half-a-gill of cream, and half-a-gill of veal consommé, cayenne pepper, and salt, a teaspoonful of essence of anchovy, the same of lemon juice, and a tablespoonful of flour and water : stew for five minutes.

1092. EGG AND HAM PATTIES. —Cut a slice of bread two inches thick, from the most solid part of a stale quartern loaf : have ready a tin round cutter, two inches in diameter ; cut out four or five pieces, then take a cutter two sizes smaller, press it nearly through the larger pieces, then remove with a small knife the bread from the inner circle : have ready a large stewpan full of boiling lard ; fry the discs of bread of a light brown colour, drain them dry with a clean cloth, and set them by till wanted ; then take half-a-pound of lean ham, mince it small, add to it a gill of good brown sauce ; stir it over the fire a few minutes, and put to it a small quantity of cayenne pepper and lemon juice : fill the shapes with the mixture, and lay a poached egg upon each.

1093. VEAL AND HAM PATTIES. —Chop about six ounces of ready-dressed lean veal, and three ounces of ham, very small ; put it into a stewpan with an ounce of butter rolled in flour, half-a-gill of cream, half-a-gill of veal stock, a little grated nutmeg and lemon peel, some cayenne pepper and salt, a spoonful of essence of ham, and lemon juice, and stir it over the fire some time, taking care it does not burn.

1094. CHICKEN AND HAM PAT-TIES.—Use the white meat from the breast of the chickens or fowls, and proceed as for veal and ham patties.

1095. MINCED COLLOPS.— Two pounds of good rump steak, chopped very fine ; six good-sized onions, also chopped small ; put both into a stewpan, with as much water or gravy as will cover the meat ; stir it without ceasing till the water begins to boil ; then set the stewpan aside, where the collops can simmer, not boil, for three-quarters of an hour. Just before serving, stir in a tablespoonful of flour, a little pepper and salt, and boil it up once. Serve with mashed potatoes round the dish. The above quantity will be enough for four persons.

1096. ECONOMICAL DISH.—Cut some rather fat ham or bacon into slices, and fry to a nice brown ; lay them aside to keep warm ; then mix equal quantities of potatoes and cabbage, bruised well together, and fry them in the fat left from the ham. Place the mixture at the bottom, and lay the slices of bacon on the top. Cauliflower, or broccoli, substituted for cabbage, is excellent. The dish must be well seasoned with pepper.

1097. FRIED EGGS AND MINCED HAM OR BACON.—Choose some very fine bacon streaked with a good deal of lean ; cut this into very thin slices, and afterwards into small square pieces ; throw them into a stewpan and set it over a gentle fire, that they may lose some of their fat. When as much as will freely come is thus melted from them, lay them on a warm dish. Put into a stewpan a ladleful of melted bacon or lard; set it on a stove ; put in about a dozen of the small pieces of bacon, then incline the stewpan and break in an egg. Manage this carefully, and the egg will presently be done : it will be very round, and the little dice of bacon will stick to it all over, so that it will make a very pretty appearance. Take care the yolks do not harden. When the egg is thus done, lay it carefully on a warm dish, and do the others.

1098. TASTY BEEF SAUSAGES. —Take a pound of lean beef, and half-a-pound of suet, remove the skin, chop it fine as for mince collop, then beat it well with a roller, or in a marble mortar, till it is all well mixed and will stick together ; season highly, and make into flat round cakes, about an inch thick, and shaped with a cup or saucer, and fry of a light brown. The sausages should be served up on boiled rice, as for curry ; if for company, you may do them with eggs and bread-crumbs ; but they are quite as good without. Or they may be rolled in puff or pie paste, and baked.

1099. POTATO PUFFS.—Take cold roast meat, either beef, or mutton, or veal and ham, clear it from the gristle, cut it small, and season with pepper, salt, and pickles, finely minced. Boil and mash some potatoes, and make them into a paste with one or two eggs ; roll out the paste, with a dust of flour, cut it round with a saucer, put some of your seasoned meat on one half, and fold the other half over it like a puff ; pinch or nick it neatly round, and fry of a light brown. This is a good method of preparing meat that has been dressed before.

1100. SCRAMBLED EGGS.—Beat up two eggs (without the whites) in a tablespoonful of milk. Put a small piece of butter into a clean saucepan. When the butter becomes hot (not boiled) put the eggs in quickly and scramble them about for two minutes with a fork without leaving them. Spread some anchovy on a slice of toast, and then put the egg over it.

1101. LOBSTER SCALLOPS.—Take some tinned lobster and strain the liquor off. Then put into a basin a teaspoonful of anchovy sauce, the same of vinegar, some pepper, salt, and half-a-teaspoonful of salad oil. Mix all these together, and then cut the lobster into small pieces and mix them up with the other ingredients. Sift some bread crumbs through a colander, and mix them with a little melted bacon dripping. Fill some patty-pans with the mixed lobster, place the bread crumbs on top, and bake in a hot oven till the crumbs are browned, that is to say about twenty minutes.

1102. OYSTER FRITTERS.—Make a batter of flour, milk, and eggs ; season with a very little nutmeg. Beard the oysters, and put as many as you think proper in each fritter.

1103. OYSTER PIE.—Take a large dish, butter it, and spread a rich paste over the sides and round the edge, but not at the bottom. The oysters should be fresh, and as large and fine as possible. Drain off part of the liquor from the oysters. Put them into a pan, and season them with pepper, salt, and spice. Stir them well with the seasoning. Have ready the yolks of some hard-boiled eggs, chopped fine, and the grated bread. Pour the oysters (with as much of their liquor as you please) into the dish that has the paste in it. Strew over them the chopped egg and grated bread. Roll out the lid of the pie, and put it on, crimping the edges handsomely. Take a small sheet of paste, cut it into a square, and roll it up. Cut it with a sharp knife into the form of a double tulip. Make a slit in the centre of the upper crust, and stick the tulip in it. Cut out eight large leaves of paste, and lay on the lid. Bake in a quick oven.

1104. MARBLED GOOSE.—The following is suitable for larger supper parties, or as a stock dish for families where visitors are frequent ; it is also excellent for breakfasts, or for picnics :—Take a fine mellow ox-tongue out of pickle, cut off the root and horny part at the tip, wipe dry, and boil till it is quite tender. Then peel it, cut a deep slit in its whole length, and lay a fair proportion of the following mixture within it :—Mace half-an-ounce, nutmeg half-an-ounce, cloves half-an-ounce, salt two tablespoonfuls, and twelve Spanish olives. The olives should be stoned, and all the ingredients well pounded and mixed together. Next take a barn-door fowl and a good large goose, and bone them. Put the tongue inside the fowl, rub the latter outside with the seasoning, and having ready some slices of ham divested of the rind, wrap them tightly round the fowl. Put the fowl and its wrapping of ham inside the goose, with the remainder of the seasoning, sew it up, and make all secure and of natural shape with a piece of new linen and tape. Put it in an earthen pan or jar just large enough to hold it, with plenty of clarified butter, and bake it for two hours and a half in a slow oven ; then take it out, and when cold take out the goose and set it in a sieve ; take off the butter and hard fat, which put by the fire to melt, adding, if required, more clarified butter. Wash and wipe out the pan, put the bird again into it, and take care that it is well covered with the warm butter ; then tie the jar down with bladder and leather. It will keep thus for a long time. When wanted for the table the jar should be placed in a tub of hot water, so as to melt the butter, the goose then can be taken out, and sent to table cold.

1105. SALADS, TO MIX.—This requires care. The salad should be very fresh, carefully washed, picked, and dried in a clean cloth, cut up separately, well mixed, and put into a bowl just before using. The dressing or sauce for which we give a recipe in next paragraph should be poured down the side of the salad bowl, but do not stir up the salad till wanted to be eaten, for if mixed, the vegetables lose that crispness which is so delicious. Garnish the top of the salad with the white of the eggs, and beet, or boiled potatoes, cut in slices ; these may be arranged in such manner as to be ornamental on the table.

1106. SALAD SAUCE OR DRESS-ING.—Boil two eggs for ten or twelve minutes, and then put them in cold water for a few minutes, so that the yolks may become quite cold and hard. Rub them through a coarse sieve with a wooden spoon, and mix them with a tablespoonful of water or cream, and then add two tablespoonfuls of fine flask oil, or melted butter ; mix, and add by degrees a teaspoonful of salt,

and the same quantity of mustard ; mix till smooth, and then incorporate with the other ingredients about three tablespoonfuls of vinegar.

1107. SALAD MIXTURE IN VERSE.

Two large potatoes, passed through kitchen sieve,
Unwonted softness to the salad give ;
Of mordant mustard add a single spoon—
Distrust the condiment which bites so soon ;
But deem it not, thou man of herbs, a fault
To add a double quantity of salt ;
Three times the spoon with oil of Lucca crown,
And once with vinegar procured from town.
True flavour needs it, and your poet begs
The pounded yellow of two well-boiled eggs ;
Let onion atoms lurk within the bowl,
And, scarce suspected, animate the whole ;
And lastly, on the favoured compound toss
A magic teaspoon of anchovy sauce ;
Then, though green turtle fail, though veni-son's tough,
And ham and turkey be not boiled enough,
Serenely full, the epicure may say,—
"Fate cannot harm me—I have dined to-day."

1108. FRENCH MODE OF DRESSING SALAD.—Fill the salad bowl with lettuce and small salading, taking care not to cut up the lettuce into too small strips. Sprinkle with salt and pepper, and, if liked, drop some mustard, mixed thin, over the salad, and strew a little moist sugar over it. Then pour over the whole three tablespoonfuls of good salad oil and one of Orleans vinegar, and turn over the lettuce lightly with a salad spoon and fork, that every portion of it may be brought into contact with the mixture. This mode of preparing a salad is far more expeditious than the ordinary way.

1109. PIES AND PUDDINGS.—When much pastry is made in a house, a quantity of fine flour should be kept on hand, in dry jars, and quite secured from the air, as it makes lighter pastry and bread when kept a short time, than when fresh ground.

1110. PASTRY FOR TARTS, &c. —Take of flour one pound ; baking powder, three teaspoonfuls ; butter, six ounces ; water, enough to bring it to the consistence required.

1111. PUFF PASTE.—To a pound and a quarter of sifted flour, rub gently in with the hand half-a-pound of fresh butter, mix up with half-a-pint of spring water, knead it well, and set it by for a quarter of an hour ; then roll it out thin, lay on it in small pieces a quarter of a pound more butter, throw on it a little flour, double it up in folds, and roll it out thin three times, and set it by for about an hour *in a cold place.* Or, if a more substantial and savoury paste be desired, use the following :—

1112. PASTE FOR MEAT, OR SAVOURY PIES.—Sift two pounds of fine flour to a pound and a half of good salt butter broken up into small pieces, and washed well in cold water ; rub gently together the butter and flour, and mix it up with the yolks of three eggs, beat together with a spoon, and nearly a pint of spring water ; roll it out, and double it in folds three times, and it is ready.

1113. AN EXCELLENT PASTE for fruit or meat pies may be made with two-thirds of wheat flour, one-third of the flour of boiled potatoes, and some butter or dripping ; the whole being brought to a proper consistence with warm water, and a small quantity of yeast or baking powder added when lightness is desired. This will also make very pleasant cakes for breakfast, and may be made with or without spices, fruits, &c.

1114. APPLE PIE.—Pare, core, and quarter the apples ; boil the cores and parings in sugar and water ; strain off the liquor, adding more sugar ; grate the rind of a lemon over the apples, and squeeze the juice into the syrup ; mix half-a-dozen cloves with the fruit, put in a piece of butter the size of a walnut ; cover with puff paste.

1115. Use of Cup in a Fruit Pie.— The principal use is to hold the *crust* up, and prevent it from sinking when the cooked fruit gives way under it Some persons imagine that the cup will prevent the juice from boiling over ; but it rather tends to *make* it boil over as there is less room in the dish. When the pie is put into the oven, the air in the cup begins to *expand* and drives every particle of juice from under it, in consequence of which, the pie-dish has a cupful *less room* to hold its fruit in, than if the cup were taken out. When the pie is taken out of the oven, the air in the cup *contracts* again and occupies a smaller space, and as the cup is no longer full of air, juice rushes in to occupy the void. The juice rushing into the cup prevents it from being *spilt over the crust* when the pie is carried about ; but it does not prevent the fruit from boiling over.

1116. APPLE PUDDING.—One pound of flour, six ounces of very finely minced beef suet ; roll thin, and line a buttered basin, then fill with one pound and a quarter of boiling apples ; add the grated rind and strained juice of a small lemon, cover it with a thin paste and tie a cloth over ; boil for one hour and twenty minutes, or longer. A small slice of fresh butter stirred into it when it is sweetened will be an acceptable addition ; grated nutmeg, or cinnamon in fine powder, may be substituted for lemon rind. For a richer pudding use half-a-pound of butter for the crust, and add to the apples a spoonful or two of orange or quince marmalade.

1117. APPLE DUMPLINGS.— Paste the same as for apple pudding, divide into as many pieces as dumplings are required ; peel and core the apples ; roll out your paste large enough ; put in the apples ; close the dumplings, tie each in a cloth very tightly. Boil them one hour. When you take them up dip them quickly in cold water, and put them in a cup while you untie them ; they will turn out without breaking.

1118. APPLE AND RICE DUMP-LINGS.—Pick and wash a pound of rice, and boil it gently in two quarts of water till it becomes dry—keeping the pot well covered, and not stirring it. Then take it off the fire, and spread it out to cool on the bottom of an inverted sieve, loosening the grains lightly with a fork, that all the moisture may evaporate. Pare a dozen pippins, or some large juicy apples, and scoop out the core ; then fill up the cavity with marmalade, or with lemon and sugar. Cover every apple all over with a thick coating of the boiled rice. Tie up each in a separate cloth, and put them into a pot of cold water. They will require about an hour and a quarter after they begin to boil, perhaps longer.

1119. BOSTON APPLE PUDDING.—Peel and core one dozen and a half of good apples ; cut them small ; put them into a stewpan with a little water, cinnamon, two cloves, and the peel of a lemon ; stew over a slow fire till soft ; sweeten with moist sugar, and pass it through a hair sieve ; add the yolks of four eggs and one white, a quarter of a pound of good butter, half a nutmeg, the peel of a lemon grated, and the juice of one lemon ; beat well together ; line the inside of a pie-dish with good puff paste ; put in the pudding, and bake half-an-hour.

1120. ALBERT PUDDING.—Beat half-a-pound of butter to cream, add half-a-pound of crushed lump sugar, half-a-pound of flour, half-a-pound of chopped raisins, some lemon juice, and some candied peel chopped small. Mix together, beat six eggs, mix and put into a mould. Boil three and a half hours, and serve with wine sauce.

1121. BREAD PUDDING.—Unfermented brown bread, two ounces ; milk, half-a-pint ; one egg ; sugar, quarter of an ounce. Cut the bread into slices, and pour the milk over it boiling hot ; let it stand till well soaked, and stir in the egg and sugar, well beaten, with a little grated nutmeg ; and bake or steam for one hour.

1122. BREAD AND JAM PUD-DING.—Take light white bread, and cut it in thin slices. Put into a pudding shape a layer of any sort of preserve, then a slice of bread, and repeat until the mould is almost full. Pour over all a pint of warm milk, in which four beaten eggs have been mixed ; cover the mould with a piece of linen, place it in a saucepan with a little boiling water, let it boil twenty minutes, and serve with pudding sauce.

1123. CABINET PUDDING.—Cut three or four muffins in two, pour over them boiling milk sufficient to cover them, cover them up until they are tender. Make a rich custard with the yolks of eight eggs and the whites of four, a pint of cream, a quarter of a pound of loaf sugar, an ounce of almonds, blanched and cut, lemon- peel and nutmeg grated, and a glass of ratafia or brandy, and add to the soaked muffins. Butter a tin mould for boiling—for baking, a dish. Put a layer of dried cherries, greengages, apricots, or French plums ; cover with the mixture, adding fruit and mixture alternately, until the mould or dish is quite full. Boil an hour, and serve with wine sauce. In boiling this pudding it should be placed in a stewpan with only water enough to reach half-way up the mould. If for baking, it will not take so long. Lay a puff paste round the edges of the dish.

1124. HALF-PAY PUDDING.—Four ounces of each of the following ingredients, viz. suet, flour, currants, raisins, and bread-crumbs ; two table-spoonfuls of treacle, half-a-pint of milk—all of which must be well mixed together, and boiled in a mould, for four hours.

1125. POTATO PUDDING.—Bruise with a wooden spoon, through a colander, six large or twelve middle-sized boiled potatoes ; beat four eggs, mix with a pint of good milk, stir in the potatoes ; sugar and seasoning to taste ; butter the dish ; bake half-an-hour. A little Scotch marmalade makes a delicious accompaniment.

1126. BATTER PUDDING.—Take of flour, four ounces ; a teaspoonful of baking powder ; a little sugar, and one egg. Mix with milk to a thin batter, and bake in a well-buttered tin, in a brisk oven, half-an-hour. A few currants may be strewed in the bottom of the tin if preferred.

1127. BATTER PUDDING, BAKED OR BOILED.—Six ounces of fine flour, a little salt, and three eggs ; beat well with a little milk, added by degrees until it is the thickness of cream ; put into a buttered dish ; bake three-quarters of an hour ; or if boiled put it into a buttered and floured basin, tied over with a cloth ; boil one hour and a half or more.

1128. PLUM PUDDING.—Take of flour, one pound ; baking powder, three teaspoonfuls ; beef suet, eight ounces ; currants and raisins four ounces each ; nutmeg and orange peel, grated fine, a quarter of an ounce ; three eggs. Boil or steam four hours.

1129. FIG PUDDING.—Three-quarters of a pound of grated bread, half-a-pound of best figs, six ounces of suet, six ounces of moist sugar, a teacupful of milk, and a little nutmeg. The figs and suet must be chopped very fine. Mix the bread and suet first, then the figs, sugar, and nutmegs, one egg beaten well, and lastly the milk. Boil in a mould four hours. To be eaten with sweet sauce.

1130. PLAIN SUET PUDDING.—Take of flour, one pound and a half ; bicarbonate of soda, three drachms ; or two teaspoonfuls of baking powder ; beef suet, four ounces ; powdered ginger, half-a-drachm ; water or milk, one pint. Boil or steam for two hours.

1131. CARROT PUDDING.—Grate a raw red carrot ; mix with double the weight of bread-crumbs or biscuit,

or with the same weight of each : to a pound and a half of this mixture, put a pint of new milk or cream, or half-a-pint of each, four or six ounces of clarified butter, three or four eggs well beaten, sugar to taste, a little nutmeg, and a glass of brandy ; line or edge a dish with puff paste ; pour in the mixture ; put slices of candied lemon or orange peel on the top, and bake in a moderately hot oven.

1132. ALMOND PUDDING.—A large cupful of finely-minced beef suet, a teacupful of milk, four ounces of bread-crumbs, four ounces of well-cleaned currants, two ounces of almonds, half-a-pound of stoned raisins, three well-beaten eggs, and the whites of other two ; sugar, nutmeg, and cinnamon, and a small glass of rum. Butter a shape, and place part of the raisins neatly in rows. Blanch the almonds ; reserve the half of them to be placed in rows between the raisins just before serving. Mix all the remaining ingredients well together, put into the shape, and boil three hours.

1133. SAUCE FOR ALMOND PUDDING.—One teaspoonful of milk, and two yolks of eggs well beaten, and some sugar. Place on the fire and stir till it *just comes to the boil* : then let it cool. When lukewarm, stir into it a glass of sherry or currant wine, and serve in a sauce tureen. This sauce is a great improvement to raisin pudding.

1134. BARLEY PUDDING.—Take a quarter of a pound of Scotch or pearl barley. Wash and simmer it in a small quantity of water ; pour off the water, and add milk and flavouring as for rice pudding. Beat up with sugar and nutmeg, and mix the milk and barley in the same way. It may be more or less rich of eggs, and with or without the addition of butter, cream, or marrow. Put it into a buttered deep dish, leaving room for six or eight ounces of currants, and an ounce of candied peel, cut up fine, with a few apples cut in small pieces. An hour will bake it.

1135. BAKED CUSTARD PUDDING.—Boil in a pint of milk a few coriander seeds, a little cinnamon and lemon peel ; sweeten with four ounces of loaf sugar, mix with it a pint of cold milk ; beat eight eggs for ten minutes ; add the other ingredients ; pour it from one pan into another six or eight times, strain through a sieve ; let it stand ; skim the froth from the top, pour it into earthen cups, and bake immediately in a hot oven till they are of a good colour ; ten minutes will be sufficient.

1136. BOILED CUSTARD.—Boil half-a-pint of new milk, with a piece of lemon peel, two peach leaves, half a stick of cassia, a few whole allspice, from four to six ounces of white sugar. Cream may be used instead of milk ; beat the yolks and white of four eggs, strain the milk through coarse muslin, or a hair sieve ; then mix the eggs and milk very gradually together, and stir it well from the bottom, on the fire, till it thickens.

1137. MOTHER EVE'S PUDDING.

If you want a good pudding, to teach you I'm willing ;

Take two pennyworth of eggs, when twelve for a shilling ;

And of the same fruit that Eve had once chosen,

Well pared and well chopped, at least half-a-dozen ;

Six ounces of bread (let your maid eat the crust),

The crumb must be grated as small as the dust ;

Six ounces of currants from the stones you must sort,

Lest they break out your teeth, and spoil all your sport ;

Six ounces of sugar won't make it too sweet ;

Some salt and some nutmeg will make it complete ;

Three hours let it boil, without hurry or flutter,

And then serve it up, without sugar or butter.

1138. A GOOD RICE PUDDING.

—Wash a couple of handfuls of rice thoroughly, and cook it in about one quart of milk sweetened to liking, the rind of a lemon, and a small piece of cinnamon. Let the rice simmer until it has taken up all the milk. Turn out into a basin and take out the cinnamon and lemon. Stir into it the yolks of three eggs, add some candied citron, and mix. Butter a plain mould, put the pudding in and bake for half-an-hour or so in a quick oven.

1139. YELLOW RICE.—Take one pound of rice, wash it clean, and put it into a saucepan which will hold three quarts ; add to it half-a-pound of currants picked and washed, one quarter of an ounce of the best turmeric powder, previously dissolved in a cupful of water, and a stick of cinnamon ; pour over them two quarts of cold water, place the saucepan uncovered on a moderate fire, and allow it to boil till the rice is dry, then stir in a quarter of a pound of sugar, and two ounces of butter : cover up, and place the pan near the fire for a few minutes, then mix it well and dish up. This is a favourite dish with the Japanese, and will be found excellent as a vegetable with roast meat, poultry, &c. It also forms a capital pudding, which may be improved by the addition of raisins, and a few blanched almonds.

1140. LEMON RICE.—Boil sufficient rice in milk, with white sugar to taste, till it is soft ; put it into a pint basin or an earthenware blanc-mange mould, and leave it till cold. Peel a lemon very thick, cut the peel into shreds about half or three-quarters of an inch in length, put them into a little water, boil them up, and throw the water away, lest it should be bitter, then pour about a teacupful of fresh water upon them ; squeeze and strain the juice of the lemon, add it with white sugar to the water and shreds, and let it stew gently at the fire for two hours. (When cold it will be a syrup.) Having turned out the jellied rice into a cut-glass dish, or one of common delf, pour the syrup gradually over the rice, taking care the little shreds of the peel are equally distributed over the whole.

1141. BOILED RICE FOR CURRY.—Put the rice on in *cold* water, and let it come to a boil for a minute or so : strain it quite dry, and lay it on the hob in a stewpan without a cover to let the steam evaporate, then shake it into the dish while very hot. A squeeze of lemon juice after it boils will make it separate better.

1142. A BLACK MAN'S RECIPE TO DRESS RICE.—Wash him well, much wash in cold water, the rice flour make him stick. Water boil all ready very fast. Throw him in, rice can't burn, water shake him too much. Boil quarter of an hour or little more ; rub one rice in thumb and finger ; if all rub away him quite done. Put rice in colander, hot water run away ; pour cup of cold water on him, put back rice in saucepan, keep him covered near the fire, then rice all ready. Eat him up !

1143. TAPIOCA PUDDING.— Boil a quarter of a pound of tapioca, with one pint of milk, sweetened to taste, and flavoured with lemon peel or vanilla. Pour into a buttered pie-dish and bake for half-an-hour.

1144. MACARONI CHEESE.— Fill a dish or tin with some boiled macaroni ; butter it and pile it up with layers of macaroni and grated cheese (a high-flavoured one, such as Gruyère or Parmesan). Add sufficient butter and mustard, cayenne, salt and pepper. Cover with grated cheese, bake, and serve hot.

1145. REMAINS OF COLD SWEET DISHES.

i. **Rice Pudding.**—Over the cold rice pudding pour a custard, and add a few lumps of jelly or preserved fruit. Remember to remove the baked coating of the pudding before the custard is poured over it.

ii. **Apple Tart.**—Cut into triangular pieces the remains of a cold apple tart : arrange the pieces around the sides of a glass or china bowl, and leave space in the centre for a custard to be poured in.

iii. **Plum Pudding.**—Cut into thin round slices cold plum pudding, and fry them in butter. Fry also fritters, and place them high in the centre of the dish, and the fried pudding all round the heaped-up fritters. Powder all with lump sugar, and serve them with wine sauce in a tureen.

1145a. FRENCH BATTER.—Two ounces of butter cut into bits, pour on it less than a quarter of a pint of boiling water ; when dissolved, add three-quarters of a pint of cold water, so that it shall not be quite milk warm ; mix by degrees smoothly with twelve ounces of fine dry flour and a small pinch of salt, if the batter be for fruit fritters, but with more if for meat or vegetables. Before used, stir into it the whites of two eggs beaten to solid froth ; previously to this, add a little water if too thick. This is excellent for frying vegetables, and for fruit fritters.

1146. FRITTERS.—Make them of any of the batters directed for pancakes, by dropping a small quantity into the pan ; or make the plainer sort, and dip pared apples, sliced and cored, into the batter, and fry them in plenty of hot lard. Currants, or sliced lemon as thin as paper, make an agreeable change. Fritters for company should be served on a folded napkin in the dish. Any sort of sweetmeat, or ripe fruit, may be made into fritters.

1147. APPLE FRITTERS.—Peel and core some fine pippins, and cut into slices. Soak them in wine, sugar, and nutmeg, for a few hours. Make a batter of four eggs to a tablespoonful of rose water, a tablespoonful of wine, and a tablespoonful of milk, thickened with enough flour, stirred in by degrees ; mix two or three hours before wanted. Heat some batter in a frying-pan ; dip each slice of apple separately in the batter, and fry brown ; sift pounded sugar, and grate a nutmeg over them.

1148. POTATO FRITTERS.—Boil two large potatoes, bruise them fine, and beat four yolks and three whites of eggs, and add to the above one large spoonful of cream, another of sweet wine, a squeeze of lemon, and a little nutmeg. Beat this batter well half-an-hour. It will be extremely light. Put a good quantity of fine lard into a stewpan, and drop a spoonful at a time of the batter into it. Fry the fritters ; and serve as a sauce, a glass of white wine, the juice of a lemon, one dessertspoonful of peach-leaf or almond water, and some white sugar, warmed together ; not to be served in a dish.

1149. PANCAKES.—Make a light batter of eggs, flour, and milk ; a little salt, nutmeg, and ginger may be added; fry in a small pan, in hot dripping or lard. Sugar and lemon should be served to eat with them. Or, when eggs are scarce, make the batter with small beer, ginger, and so forth ; or water, with flour, and a very little milk, will serve, but not so well as eggs and all milk. They should be fried thin.

1150. CREAM PANCAKES.—Mix two eggs, well beaten, with a pint of cream, two ounces of sifted sugar, six of flour, a little nutmeg, cinnamon, and mace. Fry the pancakes thin, with a bit of butter.

1151. RICE PANCAKES.—Boil half-a-pound of ground rice to a jelly in a pint of water or milk, and keep it well stirred from the bottom to prevent its being burnt ; if too thick add a little more milk ; take it off the fire ; stir in six or eight ounces of butter, a pint of cream, six or eight eggs well beaten, a pinch of salt, sugar, or nutmeg, with as much flour as will make the batter thick enough. Fry with lard or dripping.

1152. ORDINARY OMELETTE.—Take four eggs, beat the yolks and whites together with a tablespoonful of milk, and a little salt and pepper ; put two ounces of butter into a frying-pan to boil, and let it remain until it begins to brown ; pour the batter into it, and let it remain quiet for a minute ; turn up the edges of the omelette gently from the bottom of the pan with a fork ; shake it to keep it from burning at the bottom, and fry it till of a bright brown. It will not take more than five minutes' frying.

1153. FRIAR'S OMELETTE.—Boil a dozen apples, as for sauce ; stir in a quarter of a pound of butter, and the same of white sugar ; when cold, add four eggs, well beaten ; put it into a baking dish thickly strewed over with crumbs of bread, so as to stick to the bottom and sides ; then put in the apple mixture ; strew crumbs of bread over the top ; when baked, turn it out and grate loaf sugar over it.

1154. Miss Acton's Observations on Omelettes, Pancakes, Fritters, &c.—"There is no difficulty in making good omelettes, pancakes or fritters ; and, as they may be expeditiously prepared and served, they are often a very convenient resource when, on short notice, an addition is required to a dinner. The eggs for all of them should be well and lightly whisked ; the lard for frying batter should be extremely pure in flavour, and quite hot when the fritters are dropped in ; the batter itself should be smooth as cream, and it should be briskly beaten the instant before it is used. All fried pastes should be perfectly drained from the fat before they are served, and sent to table promptly when they are ready. Eggs may be dressed in a multiplicity of ways, but are seldom more relished in any form than in a well-made and expeditiously served omelette. This may be plain or seasoned with minced herbs and a very little shallot, when the last is liked, and is then called *Omelette* *aux fines herbes* ; or it may be mixed with minced ham or grated cheese ; in any case it should be light, thick, full-tasted, and *fried only on one side* ; if turned in the pan, as it frequently is in England, it will at once be flattened and rendered tough. Should the slight rawness, which is sometimes found in the middle of the inside when the omelette is made in the French way, be objected to, a heated shovel, or a salamander, may be held over it for an instant, before it is folded on the dish. The pan for frying it should be quite small ; for if it be composed of four or five eggs only, and then put into a large one, it will necessarily spread over it and be thin, which would render it more like a pancake than an omelette ; the only partial remedy for this, when a pan of proper size cannot be had, is to raise the handle of it high, and to keep the opposite side close down to the fire, which will confine the eggs in to a smaller space. No gravy should be poured into the dish with it, and, indeed, if properly made, it will require none. Lard is preferable to butter for frying batter, as it renders it lighter ; but it must not be used for omelettes. Filled with preserves of any kind, it is called a *sweet* omelette."

1155. CAKES AND BISCUITS.

1156. PLUM CAKE.—One pound of flour, quarter of a pound of butter, quarter of a pound of sugar, quarter of a pound of currants, three eggs, half-a-pint of milk, and a small teaspoonful of carbonate of soda or baking powder. It is a very good plan to bake these cakes in a common earthen *flower-pot saucer*.

1157. NICE PLUM CAKE.—Take of flour one pound ; baking powder, three teaspoonfuls ; butter, six ounces ; loaf sugar, six ounces ; currants, six ounces ; three eggs ; milk, about four ounces ; bake for one hour and a half in a tin or pan.

1158. CHEAP PLUM CAKE.— Two pounds and a half of flour, three-quarters of a pound of sugar, three-quarters of a pound of butter, half-a-pound of currants or quarter of a pound of raisins, quarter of a pound of orange peel, two ounces of caraway seeds, half-an-ounce of ground cinnamon or ginger, four teaspoonfuls of carbonate of soda or some baking powder ; mixed well, with rather more than a pint of new milk. The butter must be well melted before being mixed with the ingredients.

1159. LUNCHEON CAKE.—Take of flour one pound ; baking powder, three teaspoonfuls ; sugar, three ounces ; butter, three ounces ; currants, four ounces ; milk, one pint, or twenty ounces : bake one hour in a quick oven.

1160. SODA CAKE.—Take of flour half-a-pound ; bicarbonate of soda, two drachms ; tartaric acid, two drachms ; butter, four ounces ; white sugar, two ounces ; currants, four ounces ; two eggs ; warm milk, half-a-tea- cupful.

1161. DROP CAKES.—One pint of flour, half-a-pound of butter, quarter of a pound of pounded lump sugar, half a nutmeg grated, a handful of currants, two eggs, and a large pinch of carbonate of soda, or a little baking powder. To be baked in a slack oven for ten minutes or a quarter of an hour. The above quantity will make about thirty excellent cakes.

1162. SEED CAKE (Plain).—A quarter of a peck of flour ; half-a-pound of sugar ; quarter of an ounce of all spice, half-a-pound of melted butter ; half-a-pint of milk ; quarter of a pint of yeast ; a little ginger. Add seeds and bake for an hour and a half.

1163. GINGERBREAD CAKE.— Take one pound and a half of treacle ; one and a half ounces of ground ginger ; half-an-ounce of caraway seeds ; two ounces of allspice ; four ounces of orange peel, shred fine ; half-a-pound of sweet butter ; six ounces of blanched almonds ; one pound of honey ; one and a half ounces of carbonate of soda ; and five pounds of fine flour. Make a pit in the flour ; then pour in the treacle, and all the other ingredients, creaming the butter ; mix them altogether into a dough ; work it well ; then put in three-quarters of an ounce of tartaric acid, and put the dough into a buttered pan, and bake for two hours in a cool oven. To know when it is ready, plunge a skewer into it, and if it comes out sticky, put the cake in the oven again ; if not it is ready. This is a good and simple test, which may be resorted to in baking bread and all kinds of cakes.

1164. SPONGE CAKE.—Take five eggs, half their weight of flour and half-a-pound of loaf sugar, sifted ; break the eggs upon the sugar, and beat with a steel fork for half-an-hour. After you have beaten the egg and sugar the time specified, grate in the rind of a lemon (the juice may be added at pleasure), stir in the flour, and immediately pour it into a tin lined with buttered paper, and let it be instantly put into rather a cool oven.

1165. ALMOND SPONGE CAKE is made by adding blanched almonds to the above.

1166. YULE CAKE.—Take one pound of fresh butter ; one pound of sugar ; one pound and a half of flour ; two pounds of currants ; a glass of brandy ; one pound of sweetmeats ; two ounces of sweet almonds : ten eggs ; a quarter of an ounce of allspice ; and a quarter of an ounce of cinnamon. Melt the butter to a cream, and put in the sugar. Stir it till quite light, adding the allspice and pounded cinnamon ; in a quarter of an hour, take the yolks of the eggs, and work them two or three at a time ; and the whites of the same must by this time be beaten into a strong snow, quite ready to work in. As the paste must not stand to chill the butter, or it will be heavy, work in the whites gradually,

then add the orange peel, lemon, and citron, cut in fine strips, and the currants, which must be mixed in well, with the sweet almonds ; then add the sifted flour and glass of brandy. Bake this cake in a tin hoop, in a hot oven, for three hours, and put twelve sheets of paper under it to keep it from burning.

1167. CAKE OF MIXED FRUITS. —Extract the juice from red currants by simmering them very gently for a few minutes over a slow fire ; strain it through folded muslin, and to one pound of the juice add a pound and a half of freshly-gathered cooking apples, pared, and rather deeply cored, that the fibrous part may be avoided. Boil these quite slowly until the mixture is perfectly smooth ; then, to evaporate part of the moisture, let the boiling be quickened. In from twenty-five to thirty minutes, draw the pan from the fire, and throw in gradually a pound and a quarter of sugar in fine powder ; mix it well with the fruit, and when it is dissolved, continue the boiling rapidly for twenty minutes longer, keeping the mixture constantly stirred ; put it into a mould, and store it, when cold, for winter use, or serve it for dessert, or as a pudding, in which case decorate it with spikes of almonds, blanched, and heap solid whipped cream round it, or pour a custard into the dish. For dessert, it may be garnished with dice of the palest apple jelly.

1168. WEDDING CAKES.—Four pounds of fine flour, well dried ; four pounds of fresh butter ; two pounds of loaf sugar ; a quarter of a pound of mace, pounded and sifted fine ; the same of nutmegs. To every pound of flour add eight eggs ; wash four pounds of currants, let them be well picked and dried before the fire ; blanch a pound of sweet almonds, and cut them lengthwise very thin ; a pound of citron ; one pound of candied orange ; the same of candied lemon ; half-a-pint of brandy. When these are made ready, work the butter with your hand to a cream ; then beat in the sugar a quarter of an hour ; beat the whites of the eggs to a very strong froth ; mix them with the sugar and butter ; beat the yolks half-an-hour at least, and mix them with the cake ; then put in the flour, mace, and nutmeg ; keep beating it well till your oven is ready—pour in the brandy, and beat the currants and almonds lightly in. Tie three sheets of white paper round the bottom of your hoop to keep it from running out ; rub it well with butter, put in your cake ; lay the sweetmeats in layers ; with cake between each layer ; and after it is risen and coloured cover it with paper before your oven is stopped up. It will require three hours to bake properly.

1169. ALMOND ICING FOR WEDDING CAKE.—Beat the whites of three eggs to a strong froth, pulp a pound of Jordan almonds very fine with rose water, mix them, with the eggs, lightly together ; put in by degrees a pound of common loaf sugar in powder. When the cake is baked enough, take it out, and lay on the icing ; then put it in to brown.

1170. SUGAR ICING FOR WEDDING CAKE.—Beat two pounds of double refined sugar with two ounces of fine starch, sift the whole through a gauze sieve, then beat the whites of five eggs with a knife upon a pewter dish for half-an-hour ; beat in the sugar a little at a time, or it will make the eggs fall, and injure the colour ; when all the sugar is put in, beat it half-an-hour longer, and then lay it on your almond icing, spreading it even with a knife. If put on as soon as the cake comes out of the oven, it will harden by the time the cake is cold.

1171. TEA CAKES.—Take of flour one pound ; sugar, one ounce ; butter, one ounce ; baking powder, three tea-spoonfuls ; milk, six ounces ; water, six ounces. Rub the butter and baking powder into the flour ; dissolve the sugar in the water, and then add the milk. Pour this mixture gradually over the flour, and mix well together ; divide the mass into three portions, and bake twenty-five minutes. Flat round tins or earthen pans are the best to bake the cakes in. Buttermilk may be used instead of milk and water if preferred.

1172. BELVIDERE CAKE FOR BREAKFAST OR TEA.—Take a quart of flour ; four eggs ; a piece of butter the size of an egg ; a piece of lard the same size ; mix the butter and lard well in the flour ; beat the eggs light in a pint bowl, and fill it up with cold milk ; then pour it gradually into the flour ; add a teaspoonful of salt ; work it for eight or ten minutes only ; cut the dough with a knife to the size you wish it ; roll them into cakes about the size of a breakfast plate, and bake in a quick oven.

1173. SCONES.—Flour, two pounds ; bicarbonate of soda, quarter of an ounce ; salt, quarter of an ounce ; sour buttermilk, one pint, more or less. Mix to the consistence of light dough, roll out about half-an-inch thick, and cut them out to any shape you please, and bake on a *griddle* over a clear fire about ten or fifteen minutes ; turning them to brown on both sides—or they may be done on a hot plate, or ironing stove. A griddle is a thin plate of cast-iron about twelve or fourteen inches in diameter, with a handle attached, to hang it up by.—These scones are excellent for tea, and may be eaten either cold or hot, buttered, or with cheese.

1174. MUFFINS.—Add a pint and a half of good ale yeast (from pale malt, if possible) to a bushel of the very best white flour ; let the yeast lie all night in water, then pour off the water quite clear ; heat two gallons of water just milk-warm, and mix the water, yeast, and two ounces of salt well together for about a quarter of an hour. Strain the whole, and mix up your dough as light as possible, letting it lie in the trough an hour to rise ; next roll it with your hand, pulling it into little pieces about the size of a large walnut. These must be rolled out thin with a rolling-pin, in a good deal of flour, and if covered immediately with a piece of flannel, they will rise to a proper thickness ; but if too large or small, dough must be added accordingly, or taken away ; meanwhile, the dough must be also covered with flannel. Next begin baking ; and when laid on the iron, watch carefully, and when one side changes colour, turn the other, taking care that they do not burn or become discoloured. Be careful also that the iron does not get too hot. In order to bake muffins properly, you ought to have a place built as if a copper were to be set ; but instead of copper a piece of iron must be put over the top, fixed in form like the bottom of an iron pot, underneath which a coal fire is kindled when required. Toast the muffins crisp on both sides with a fork ; pull them open *with your hand*, and they will be like a honeycomb ; lay in as much butter as you intend ; then clap them together, and set by the fire : turn them once, that both sides may be buttered alike. When quite done, cut them across with a knife ; but if you use a knife either to spread or divide them, they will be as heavy as lead. Some kinds of flour will soak up more water than others ; when this occurs, add water ; or if too moist, add flour : for the dough must be as light as possible.

1175. CRUMPETS.—To one pound of best flour, put a tablespoonful of yeast, and two eggs, make into a batter with a quart of warm water or milk—pour the batter into tin rings of the size and thickness required, previously placed on a hot greased *griddle* (*see* par. 1173) ; turn them quickly.

1176. "JERSEY WONDERS"— The oddity of these "wonders" consists solely in the manner of cooking, and the consequent shape. Take two pounds of flour, six ounces of butter, six ounces of white sugar, a little nutmeg, ground ginger, and lemon peel ; beat eight eggs, and knead them all well together ; a taste of brandy will be an improvement. Roll the paste into a long mass about the thickness of your wrist ; cut off a slice and roll it into an oval, about four inches long and three inches wide, not too thin ; cut two slits in it, but not through either end ; there will then be three bands. Pass the left one through the aperture to the right, and throw it into a *brass* or *bell-metal* skillet of BOILING lard or beef or mutton dripping. You may cook three or four at a time. In about two minutes turn them with a fork, and you will find them browned, and swollen or risen in two or three minutes more. Remove them from the pan to a dish, when they will dry and cool.

1177. BANBURY CAKES.—Roll out a rich puff paste about half-an-inch thick, and cut it into pieces ; then roll again till each piece becomes twice the size ; put some Banbury meat in the middle of one side ; fold the other over it, and pinch it up into a somewhat oval shape ; flatten it with your hand at the top, letting the seam be quite at the bottom ; rub the tops over with the white of an egg, laid on with a brush, and dust loaf sugar over them : bake in a moderate oven.

1178. MEAT FOR BANBURY CAKES.—Beat up a quarter of a pound of butter until it becomes in the state of cream ; then mix with it half-a-pound of candied orange and lemon peel, cut fine ; one pound of currants, a quarter of an ounce of ground cinnamon ; and a quarter of an ounce of allspice : mix all well together, and keep in a jar till wanted for use.

1179. SHREWSBURY CAKES.— Take half-a-pound of flour ; a quarter of a pound of sugar ; the same of butter and enough eggs well beaten to mix it—grate in some nutmeg, mix well, roll thin, cut with a pastry cutter or wineglass, and bake on buttered paper.

1180. CHEESE CAKES.—Beat a quarter of a pound of butter with the hand in a warm pan until it becomes creamy. Add a quarter of a pound of powdered sugar and beat thoroughly ; then add the yolks of two eggs, and beat again. After this add a little milk and beat all together ; add a quarter of a pound of currants and mix together. Put puff paste in patty-pans, fill them half full, sprinkle some sugar over, and bake in a quick oven.

1181. Mixture for Lemon Cheese Cakes.—Half-a-pound of butter, two pounds of lump sugar, yolks of a dozen eggs and the whites of eight, rind of four lemons (peeled thin and minced fine), juice of six lemons. Place them all into a saucepan, and boil till the sugar is melted and quite thick, stirring it well whilst on the fire. Then pour into a jar, with a wineglassful of brandy or whisky. It will keep for months. When required for use add four tablespoonfuls of fine-grated bread.

1182. BATH BUNS.—A quarter of a pound of flour ; four yolks and three whites of eggs, with four spoonfuls of solid fresh yeast. Beat in a bowl, and set before the fire to rise ; then rub into one pound of flour ten ounces of butter ; put in half-a-pound of sugar, and caraway comfits ; when the eggs and yeast are pretty light, mix by degrees altogether ; throw a cloth over it, and set before the fire to rise. Make the buns, and when on the tins, brush over with the yolk of egg and milk ; strew them with caraway comfits ; bake in a quick oven. If baking powder is used instead of yeast, use two teaspoonfuls, and proceed as directed, omitting to set the dough before the fire to rise, which is useless as regards all articles made with baking powder.

1183. PLAIN BUNS.—Flour, two pounds ; sugar, five ounces ; butter, eight ounces ; some salt, ginger and caraway, according to taste. Make a paste with warm milk and four teaspoonfuls of yeast, and bake in a hot oven.

1184. CURRANT BUNS.—The same as the preceding, but adding half-a-pound of currants, and a little water stained with saffron.

1185. CROSS BUNS.—Take of flour two pounds and a half ; sifted sugar, half-a-pound ; some mace, cassia, and coriander seeds ; then form a paste consisting of half-a-pound of butter dissolved in half-a-pint of hot milk. Work it with three tablespoonfuls of yeast and place it before the fire for about an hour. Make into buns and set them on a tin in front of the fire for half-an-hour, brush them over with warm milk, and bake in a fairly hot oven.

1186. LEMON BUNS.—Take of flour one pound ; baking powder, three teaspoonfuls ; butter, six ounces ; loaf sugar, four ounces ; one egg ; essence of lemon, six or eight drop : make into twenty buns, and bake in a quick oven for fifteen minutes.

1187. EXCELLENT BISCUITS.—Take of flour two pounds ; carbonate of ammonia, three drachms, in fine powder ; white sugar, four ounces ; arrowroot one ounce ; butter, four ounces ; one egg ; mix into a stiff paste with new milk, and beat them well with a rolling-pin for half-an-hour ; roll out thin, cut them out with a docker, and bake in a quick oven for fifteen minutes.

1188. ARROWROOT BISCUITS are made with equal parts of arrowroot and flour.

1189. GINGER BISCUITS AND CAKES.—Work into small crumbs three ounces of butter, two pounds of flour, and three ounces of powdered sugar and two of ginger, in fine powder ; knead into a stiff paste, with new milk ; roll thin, cut out with a cutter ; bake in a slow oven until crisp through ;

keep of a pale colour. Additional sugar may be used when a sweeter biscuit is desired. For good ginger cakes, butter six ounces, sugar eight, for each pound of flour ; wet the ingredients into a paste with eggs : a little lemon peel grated will give an agreeable flavour.

1190. GINGER CAKES.—To two pounds of flour add three-quarters of a pound of good moist sugar, one ounce best Jamaica ginger well mixed in the flour ; have ready three-quarters of a pound of lard, melted, and four eggs well beaten : mix the lard and eggs together, and stir into the flour, which will form a paste ; roll out in thin cakes, and bake in a moderately heated oven. Lemon biscuits may be made in a similar way, by substituting essence of lemon for ginger.

1191. PICNIC BISCUITS.—Take two ounces of fresh butter, and well work it with a pound of flour. Mix thoroughly with it half-a-saltspoonful of pure carbonate of soda, two ounces of sugar ; mingle thoroughly with the flour, make up the paste with spoonfuls of milk ; it will require scarcely a quarter of a pint. Knead smooth, roll a quarter or an inch thick, cut in rounds about the size of the top of a small wineglass ; roll these out thin, prick them well, lay them on lightly floured tins, and bake in a gentle oven until crisp. When cold put into dry canisters. Thin cream used instead of milk, in the paste, will enrich the biscuits. To obtain variety caraway seeds or ginger can be added at pleasure.

1192. WINE BISCUITS.—Take of flour half-a-pound ; butter, four ounces ; sugar, four ounces ; two eggs ; carbonate of ammonia, one drachm ; white wine, enough to mix to a proper consistence. Cut out with a glass.

1193. ALMOND CUSTARDS.—Blanch and pound fine, with half-a-gill of rose water, six ounces of sweet and half-an-ounce of bitter almonds ; boil a pint of milk, with a few coriander seeds, a little cinnamon, and some lemon-peel ; sweeten it with two ounces and a half of sugar, rub the almonds through a fine sieve, with a pint of cream ; strain the milk to the yolks of eight eggs, and the whites of three well beaten ; stir it over a fire till it is of a good thickness, take it off the fire, and stir it till nearly cold, to prevent its curdling.

1194. BLANCMANGE.—Take one pint of milk and half a handful of picked isinglass ; boil it till all the isinglass is melted ; strain it through a sieve ; pound fine four ounces of sweet and six or seven bitter almonds, mix with the milk adding a little spice ; sweeten with loaf sugar, boil it up, pass it again through a sieve, then put it in moulds and let it stand till cold.

1195. ARROWROOT BLANC-MANGE.—A teacupful of arrowroot to a pint of milk ; boil the milk with twelve sweet and six bitter almonds, blanched and beaten ; sweeten with loaf sugar, and strain it ; mix the arrowroot with a little of the milk as smooth as possible ; pour the boiling milk upon it by degrees, stirring the while ; put it back into the pan and boil a few minutes, still stirring : then pour it into the shape, which should be previously dipped in cold water, and turn it out when cold.

1196. LEMON SPONGE.—For a quart mould—dissolve two ounces of isinglass in a pint and three-quarters of water ; strain it, and add three-quarters of a pound of sifted loaf sugar, the juice of six lemons and the rind of one ; boil the whole for a few minutes, strain it again, and let it stand till quite cold and just beginning to stiffen ; then beat the whites of two eggs, and put them to it, and whisk till it is quite white ; put it into a mould, which must be first wetted with cold water. Salad oil is much better than water for preparing the mould for turning out jelly, blancmange, &c., but great care must be taken not to pour the jelly into the mould till *quite cool*, or the oil will float on the top, and after it is turned out it must be carefully wiped over with a clean cloth. This plan only requires to be tried once to be invariably adopted.

1197. CALF'S FOOT JELLY.— Slit it in two, and take every particle of fat from the claws ; wash well in warm water, put it in a large stewpan, and cover with water ; skim well, and let it boil gently for six or seven hours, then strain and skim off any oily substance on the surface. It is best to boil the foot the day before making the jelly, as, when the liquor is cold, the oily part being at the top, and the other being firm, with pieces of blotting paper applied to it, you may remove every particle of the oily substance without wasting the liquor. Put the liquor in a stewpan to melt, with a pound of lump sugar, the peel of two lemons, and the juice of six, six whites and shells of eggs beaten together, and a bottle of sherry or Madeira ; whisk the whole together until it is on the boil, then put it by the side of the stove, and let it simmer a quarter of an hour ; strain it through a jelly-bag : what is strained first must be poured into the bag again, until it is as bright and clear as distilled water ; then put the jelly in moulds, to get cold and firm ; if the weather is too warm, it requires some ice or some of Nelson's gelatine. If required to be very *stiff*, half-an-ounce of isinglass may be added when the wine is put in. It may be flavoured by the juice of various fruits and spices, &c., and coloured with saffron, cochineal, the juice of beetroot, spinach juice, claret, &c. It is sometimes made with cherry brandy, red noyeau, curaçoa, or essence of punch.

1198. JELLY FOR INVALIDS. —Take rice, sago, pearl-barley, hartshorn shavings, each one ounce ; simmer in three pints of water till reduced to one pint and strain it. When cold, it will be a jelly, which give, dissolved in wine, milk, or broth, in change with the other nourishment.

1199. ARROWROOT JELLY.—A tablespoonful of arrowroot, and cold water to form a paste ; add a pint of boiling water ; stir briskly, boil for a few minutes. A little sherry and sugar may be added. For infants, a drop or two of the essence of caraway seed or cinnamon is preferable to the sherry.

1200. APPLE JELLY.—Take some apples with red skins and cut them into quarters, but do not peel them. For each pound of apples take three pints of cold water, bring it to the boiling point, and then boil fast for half-an-hour. Then strain, and allow one pound of lump sugar for each pint of juice, replace in pan, and again boil quickly for half-an-hour.

1201. ORANGE JELLY.—Take six oranges and one lemon, and peel them very thin. Pour some hot water on the peel and let it soak. Then scoop out the insides of the oranges and lemon into a basin ; pour an ounce of melted gelatine over the pulp ; boil for a short time, and add some lump sugar to taste. Then pour it whilst hot over the peel and strain it through muslin.

1202. APRICOT JELLY.—Divide two dozen ripe apricots into halves, peel and stone them, pound half of the kernels in a gill of water, and a teaspoonful of lemon juice ; reduce the fruit to a pulp, and mix the kernels with it ; put the whole into a stewpan with a pound of sugar, boil thoroughly, skim till clear, and put into small pots.

1203. RED CURRANT JELLY.— With three parts of fine ripe red currants mix one of white currants ; put them into a clean preserving pan, and stir them gently over a clear fire until the juice flows from them freely ; then turn them in a fine hair sieve, and let them drain well, but without pressure. Pass the juice through a folded muslin, or a jelly bag ; weigh it, and then boil it *fast* for a quarter of an hour ; add for each pound, eight ounces of sugar coarsely powdered, stir this to it off the fire until it is dissolved, give the jelly eight minutes more of quick boiling, and pour it out. It will be firm, and of excellent colour and flavour. Be sure to clean off the scum as it rises, both before and after the sugar is put in, or the preserve will not be clear. Juice of red currants, three pounds ; juice of white currants, one pound : fifteen minutes. Sugar, two pounds : eight minutes. An excellent jelly may be made with equal parts of the juice of red and of white currants, and of raspberries, with the same proportion of sugar and degree of boiling as mentioned in the foregoing recipe.

1204. WHITE CURRANT JELLY. —White currant jelly is made in the same way as red currant jelly, only double refined sugar should be used, and it should not be boiled above ten minutes. White currant jelly should be put through a lawn sieve.

1205. Another Recipe for White Currant Jelly.—After the fruit is stripped from the stalks, put it into the pan, and when it boils, run it quickly through a sieve : take a pound of sugar to each pint of juice, and let it boil twenty minutes.

1206. BLACK CURRANT JELLY. —To each pound of picked fruit allow one gill of water ; set them on the fire in the preserving-pan to scald, but do not let them boil ; bruise them well with a silver fork, or wooden beater ; take them off and squeeze them through a hair sieve, and to every pint of juice allow a pound of loaf or raw sugar ; boil it ten minutes.

1207. ALMOND FLAVOUR (Essence of Peach Kernels—Quintessence of Noyeau).—Dissolve one ounce of essential oil of bitter almonds in one pint of spirit of wine. Use it as flavouring for cordials and pastry.

In large quantities it is exceedingly poisonous. A few drops only should be used to several pounds of syrups, pastry, &c. This and other flavourings may be bought in small bottles, ready for use, of grocers or oilmen.

1208. BLANCHED ALMONDS.— Put the almonds into cold water, and heat them slowly to scalding ; then take them out and peel them quickly, throwing them into cold water as they are done. Dry them in a cloth before serving.

1209. POUNDED ALMONDS.— The almonds should be dried for a few days after being blanched. Set them in a warm place, strewn singly over a dish or tin. A little pounded lump sugar will assist the pounding. They may be first chopped small, and rolled with a rolling pin.—Almond Paste may be made in the same manner.

1210. ORANGE MARMALADE. Select the largest Seville oranges, as they usually contain the greatest quantity of juice, and take those that have clear skins, as the skins form the largest part of the marmalade. Weigh the oranges, and weigh also an equal quantity of loaf sugar. Peel the oranges, dividing the peel of each into quarters, and put them into a preserving-pan ; cover them well with water, and set them on the fire to boil. In the meantime prepare your oranges ; divide them into gores, then scrape with a teaspoon all the pulp from the white skin ; or, instead of peeling the oranges, cut a hole in the orange and scoop out the pulp ; remove carefully all the pips, of which there are innumerable small ones in the Seville orange, which will escape observation unless they are very minutely examined. Have a large basin near you with some cold water in it, to throw the pips and peels into—a pint is sufficient for a dozen oranges. Boil these in the water, and having strained off the glutinous matter which comes from them, add it to the other parts.

When the peels have boiled till they are sufficiently tender to admit of a fork being stuck into them, scrape away all the pith from the inside of them ; lay them in folds, and cut them into thin slices of about an inch long. Clarify the sugar ; then throw the peels and pulp into it, stir it well, and let it boil for half-an-hour. Then remove it from the fire, and when it becomes cool, put it by in air-tight pots. Marmalade should be made at the end of March, or at the beginning of April, as Seville oranges are then in their best state.

1211. APPLE MARMALADE.— Peel and core two pounds of sub-acid apples—Wellingtons are excellent for the purpose—and put them in an enamelled saucepan with one pint of sweet cider, or half-a-pint of pure wine, and one pound of crushed sugar. Cook them by a gentle heat three hours, or longer, until the fruit is very soft, then squeeze it first through a colander and then through a sieve. If not sufficiently sweet, add powdered sugar to taste, and put away in jars made air-tight by covering them with a piece of wet bladder.

1212. MINCEMEAT.— Take three and a half pounds of currants well picked and cleaned ; one and three-quarter pounds each of finely chopped beef suet, and finely chopped apples (Kentish or golden pippins), four ounces each of citron, lemon peel, and orange peel cut small ; one pound of fine moist sugar ; mixed spice, half-an-ounce ; the rind of two lemons and two Seville oranges ; mix well, and put in a deep pan. Mix half a bottle of brandy, and half a bottle of ginger wine, and the juice of the lemons and oranges that have been grated, together in a basin ; pour half over and press down tight with the hand, then add the other half and cover closely. This may be made one year so as to be used the next.

Half the above weight of currants with the same quantity of stoned and well chopped raisins is sometimes preferred.

1213. TO MAKE A SYRUP.— Dissolve one pound of sugar in about a gill of water, boil for a few minutes, skimming it till quite clear. To every two pounds of sugar add the white of one egg well beaten. Boil very quickly, and skim carefully while boiling.

1214. INDIAN SYRUP (*a delicious summer drink*).—Five pounds of lump sugar, two ounces of citric acid, a gallon of boiling water ; when cold add half-a-drachm of essence of lemon and half-a-drachm of spirit of wine ; stir it well and bottle it. About two tablespoonfuls to a glass of cold water.

1215. APRICOTS STEWED IN SYRUP.— Wipe the down from young apricots, and stew them as gently as possible in a syrup made of four ounces of sugar to half-a-pint of water, boiled the usual time.

1216. SYRUP OF ORANGE OR LEMON PEEL.— Of fresh outer rind of Seville orange or lemon peel, three ounces, apothecaries' weight ; boiling water, a pint and a half ; infuse the peel for a night in a close vessel ; then strain the liquor ; let it stand to settle ; and having poured it off clear from the sediment, dissolve in it two pounds of double refined loaf sugar, and make it into a syrup with a gentle heat.

1217. APPLES IN SYRUP (for Immediate Use).— Pare and core some hard round apples, throwing them into a basin of water as each is peeled. Clarify as much loaf sugar as will cover them ; put the apples in water with the juice and rind of a lemon, and let them simmer till they are quite clear. Great care must he taken not to break them. Place them on the dish they are to appear upon at table, and pour the syrup over them.

1218. APPLES WITH CUSTARD. —Pare and core apples ; cut them in pieces ; bake or stew them with as little water as possible ; when they have become pulpy, sweeten and put them in a pie-dish, and, when cold, pour over them in unboiled custard, and put back into the oven till the custard is fixed. Equally good eaten hot or cold.

1219. BAKED PEARS.—Take twelve large baking pears ; pare and cut them into halves, leaving on about half-an-inch of the stem. Take out the core with the point of a knife, and place the pears thus prepared close together in a block-tin saucepan, the inside of which is quite bright, and whose cover fits quite close. Put to them the rind of a lemon cut thin, with half its juice, a small stick of cinnamon, and twenty grains of allspice ; cover them with spring water, and allow one pound of loaf sugar to a pint and a half of water : cover up close, and bake for six hours in a very slow oven ;—they will be quite tender, and of a good colour. Prepared cochineal is sometimes used for colouring the pears.

1220. HINTS ON MAKING JAM. —It is not generally known that boiling fruit a long time, *without sugar, without a cover* to the preserving-pan, and *skimming it well* is a very economical and excellent way— economical, because the bulk of the scum rises from the *fruit*, and not from the *sugar*. Boiling it without a *cover* allows the evaporation of all the watery particles therefrom, and renders the preserves firm and well flavoured. The sugar should be added after the skimming is completed. The proportions are, three-quarters of a pound of sugar to a pound of fruit. Jam made in this way of currants, strawberries, raspberries, or gooseberries is excellent.

1221. COVERINGS FOR JAM.— White paper cut to a suitable size, dipped in brandy, or glazed over with the white of egg should be put over the jam when cold. The pots should then stand a night before they are covered. Thin paper immersed in milk or gum-water and pressed while wet over and round the edge of the pot forms a good covering, as it dries firm and air-tight.

"Lightning Jam Pots."—An American dealer advertised "Lightning Fruit Jars" ; but for *lightening* fruit jars a small boy and solitude want a lot of beating—especially the boy sometimes.

1222. PLUM, GREENGAGE, OR APRICOT JAM.—After taking away the stones from the fruit, and cutting out any blemishes, put them over a slow fire, in a clean stewpan, with half-a-pint of water, and when scalded, rub them through a hair sieve. To every pound of pulp put one pound of sifted loaf sugar, put it into a preserving-pan over a brisk fire, and when it boils skim it well, and throw in the kernels of the apricots and half-an-ounce of bitter almonds, blanched. Then boil it fast for a quarter of an hour longer, stirring it all the time. Store away in pots in the usual manner.

1223. RHUBARB JAM.—This preserve should be made in the spring. Peel one pound of the finest rhubarb, and cut it into pieces of two inches in length ; add three-quarters of a pound of white sugar, and the rind and juice of one lemon—the rind to be cut into narrow strips. Put all into a preserving kettle, and simmer gently until the rhubarb is quite soft ; take it out carefully with a silver spoon, and put it into jars ; then boil the syrup a sufficient time to make it keep well,— say one hour,—and pour it over the fruit. When cold cover down in the usual manner.

1224. TO BOTTLE FRUITS.— Let the fruit to be preserved be quite dry, and without blemish. Take a wide-mouth bottle that is perfectly clean and dry within, and put in the fruit in layers, sprinkling sugar between each layer, put in the bung, and tie a bladder over, setting the bottles, bung downwards, in a large stewpan of cold water, with hay between to prevent breaking. Simmer over the fire until the skin is just cracking, then take the bottles out, remove the bungs, and place a piece of paper dipped in sweet oil over the top of the fruit ; prepare thin paper, immersed in gum water, and while wet, press it over and around the top of the jar : and as it dries, it will become quite firm and tight

1224a. TOMATO JAM.—Some tomatoes not quite ripe. Take off the stems ; put into the preserving kettle with water and sugar enough to make a syrup. Allow half-a-pound of white sugar to one pound of fruit. Cook till done and the syrup appears thick.

1225. ON PRESERVING FRUIT. The grand secret of preserving is to deprive the fruit of its water of vegetation in the shortest time possible ; for which purpose the fruit ought to be gathered just at the point of proper maturity. An ingenious French writer considers fruit of all kinds as having four distinct periods of maturity— the maturity of vegetation, of honeyfication, of expectation, and of coction.

i. The First Period he considers to be that when, having gone through the vegetable processes up to the ripening, it appears ready to drop spontaneously. This however is a period which arrives sooner in the warm climate of France than in the colder orchards of England ; but its absolute presence may be ascertained by the general filling out of the rind, by the bloom, by the smell, and by the facility with which it may be plucked from the branch. But even in France, as generally practised in England, this period may be hastened, either by cutting circularly through the outer rind at the foot of the branch, so as to prevent the return of the sap, or by bending the branch to a horizontal position on an espalier, which answers the same purpose.

ii. The Second Period, or that of Honeyfication, consists in the ripeness and flavour which fruits of all kinds acquire if plucked a few days before arriving at their first maturity, and preserved under a proper degree of temperature. Apples may acquire or arrive at this second degree of maturity upon the tree, but it too often happens that the flavour of the fruit is thus lost, for fruit over-ripe is always found to have parted with a portion of its flavour.

iii. The Third Stage, or of Expectation, as the theorist quaintly terms it, is that which is acquired by pulpy fruits, which, though sufficiently ripe to drop off the tree, are even then hard and sour. This is the case with several kinds both of apples and pears, not to mention other fruits, which always improve after keeping in the confectionery,—but with respect to the medlar and the quince, this maturity of expectation is absolutely necessary.

iv. The Fourth Degree of maturity, or of Coction, is completely artificial, and is nothing more nor less than the change produced upon fruit by the aid of culinary heat.

1226. TO STORE APPLES.— They should be laid out on a *dry* floor for three weeks. They may then be packed away in layers with dry straw between them. Each apple should be rubbed with a dry cloth as it is put away. They should be put in a cool place, but should be sufficiently covered with straw to protect them from frost. They should be plucked on a dry day.

1227. DRIED APPLES are produced by taking fine apples of good quality, and placing them in a very slow oven for several hours. Take them out occasionally, rub and press them flat. Continue until they are done. If they look dry, rub over them a little clarified sugar.

1228. CANDIED APRICOTS.— Gather before ripe, scald in a jar put into boiling water, pare and stone them ; put into a syrup of half their weight of sugar, in the proportion of half-a-pint of water to two pounds of sugar ; scald, and then boil until they are clear. Stand for two days in the syrup, then put into a thin candy, and scald them in it. Keep two days longer in the candy, heating them each day, and then lay them on glasses to dry.

1229. PRESERVED PEACHES. —Wipe and pick the fruit, and have ready a quarter of the weight of fine sugar in powder. Put the fruit into an ice-pot that shuts very close ; throw the sugar over it, and then cover the fruit with brandy. Between the top and cover of the pot put a double piece of grey paper. Set the pot in a saucepan of water till the brandy is as hot as you can bear to put your finger into, but do not let it boil. Put the fruit into a jar, and pour on the brandy. Cover in same manner as preserves.

1230. BRANDY PEACHES.— Drop them into a weak boiling lye, until the skin can be wiped off. Make a thin syrup to cover them, boil until they are soft to the finger-nail ; make a rich syrup, and add, after they come from the fire, and while hot, the same quantity of brandy as syrup. The fruit must be covered.

1231. CHERRY BRANDY.—Take of brandy and crushed cherries one gallon of each ; let them remain together for three days, then draw off the liquor, and add two pounds of lump sugar. Bottle off the clear portion in a week or ten days.

1232. PRESERVED PLUMS.— Cut your plums in halves (they must not be quite ripe), and take out the stones. Weigh the plums, and allow a pound of loaf sugar to a pound of fruit. Crack the stones, take out the kernels, and break them in pieces. Boil the plums and kernels very slowly for about fifteen minutes, in as little water as possible. Then spread them on a large dish to cool, and strain

the liquor. Next day add your syrup, and boil for fifteen minutes. Put into jars, pour the juice over when warm, and tie up with bladder when cold, with paper dipped in brandy over the preserve.

1233. PRESERVED PLUMS (Another Method).—Plums for common use are very good done in treacle. Put your plums into an earthen vessel that holds a gallon, having first slit each plum with a knife. To three quarts of plums put a pint of treacle. Cover them over, and set them on hot coals in the chimney corner. Let them stew for twelve hours or more, occasionally stirring, and next day put them up in jars. Done in this manner, they will keep till the next spring.

1234. TO PRESERVE LEMONS WHOLE, FOR DESSERT.—Take six fine, fresh, well-shaped lemons, cut a hole just round the stalk, and with a marrow-spoon scoop out the pips, and press out the juice, but leave the pulp in the lemons. Put them into a bowl with two or three quarts of spring water, to steep out the bitterness. Leave them three days, changing the water each day ; or only two days if you wish them to be very bitter. Strain the juice as soon as squeezed out, boil it with one pound of loaf sugar (setting the jar into which it was strained in a pan of boiling water fifteen or twenty minutes) ; tie it up, *quite hot*, with bladder, and set by till wanted. Taste the water the lemons are lying in at the end of the third day ; if not bitter, lift the lemons out into a china-lined pan, pour the water through a strainer upon them, boil gently one or two hours ; set by in a pan. Boil again next day, until so tender that the head of a large needle will easily pierce the rind. Put in one pound of loaf sugar, make it just boil and leave to cool. Next day boil the syrup, and pour it on the lemons ; add one pound of sugar, and hot water to supply what was boiled away. Lift out the lemons, and boil the syrup and pour on them again every day for a fortnight, then every three or four days, adding gradually three pounds of sugar. When the lemons look clear and bright, boil the syrup pretty hard, add the lemon juice which had been set by, just boil, skim ; put the lemons into jars, pour the syrup upon them, and tie up the jars *instantly* with bladder.

1235. PRESERVED CHERRIES. —Take equal weights of cherries and sugar, cut stalks of cherries, and wipe them clean ; strew a little powdered sugar over them ; boil the sugar in a pint of water to each three pounds of sugar ; clarify it with whites of eggs, strain, and boil it Next day boil up the cherries with the syrup for five or six minutes, and let them stay in the syrup for twenty-four hours. Strain off the syrup, boil it again, a degree higher, and pour it over the cherries. The following day boil again (yet a degree more), dip each cherry in the syrup, and put them on a sieve to dry in a warm place.

1236. PRESERVED GINGER.— Scald the young roots till they become tender, peel them, and place in cold water, frequently changing the water ; then put into a thin syrup, and, in a few days, put into jars and pour rich syrup over them.

1237. TO PRESERVE EGGS.—It has been long known to housewives, that the great secret of preserving eggs fresh is to place the small end downwards, and keep it in that position—other requisites not being neglected, such as to have the eggs perfectly fresh when deposited for keeping, not allowing them to become wet, keeping them cool in warm weather, and avoiding freezing in winter. Take an inch board of convenient size, say a foot wide, and two and a half feet long, and bore it full of holes, each about an inch and a half in diameter ; a board of this size may have five dozen holes bored in it, for as many

eggs. Then nail strips of thin board two inches wide round the edges to serve as a ledge. Boards such as this may now be made to constitute the shelves of a cupboard in a cool cellar. The only precaution necessary is to place the eggs as fast as they are laid in these holes, with the small end downwards, and they will keep perfectly fresh for a considerable time. [The great advantage of this plan is the perfect ease with which the fresh eggs are packed away, and again obtained when wanted. A carpenter would make such a board for a trifling charge.]

1238. TO PRESERVE EGGS (Another Method).—Apply with a brush a solution of gum arabic to the shells, and afterwards pack them in dry charcoal dust.

1239. PRESERVING EGGS (Mixture for).—The following mixture for preserving eggs was devised several years ago by Mr. Jayne, of Sheffield, who alleged that by means of it he could keep eggs for two years. A part of his composition is often made use of—perhaps the whole of it would be better. Put into a tub or vessel one bushel of quicklime, two pounds of salt, half-a-pound of cream of tartar, and mix the same together, with as much water as will reduce the composition, or mixture, to that consistence that it will cause an egg put into it to swim with its top just above the liquid ; then place the eggs therein.

1240. TO PRESERVE BUTTER. —Dry some salt thoroughly before the fire, pound it as fine as possible. Spread a layer of it at the bottom of a jar, then press and beat the butter down on it with a wooden rammer, cover the top with a thick layer of salt, so that when converted into brine it will completely protect the butter.

1241. SALT BUTTTER may be freshened by churning it with new milk, in the proportion of a pound of butter to a quart of milk. Treat the butter in all respects in churning as fresh. Cheap earthenware churns for domestic use may be had at any hardware shop.

1242. BAD BUTTER may be improved greatly by dissolving it in thoroughly hot water ; let it cool, then skim it off, and churn again, adding a little good salt and sugar. A small portion can be tried and approved before doing a larger quantity. The water should be merely hot enough to melt the butter, or it will become oily.

1243. TO PRESERVE MILK.—Provide bottles, which must be perfectly clean, sweet, and dry ; draw the milk from the cow into the bottles, and as they are filled, immediately cork them well up, and fasten the corks with pack-thread or wire. Then spread a little straw at the bottom of a boiler, on which place the bottles, with straw between them, until the boiler contains a sufficient quantity. Fill it up with cold water ; heat the water, and as soon as it begins to boil, rake out the fire, and let the whole gradually cool. When quite cold, take out the bottles, and pack them in sawdust, in hampers, and stow them in the coolest part of the house. Milk preserved in this manner, and allowed to remain even eighteen months in bottles, will be as sweet as when first milked from the cow.

1244. "Morning's Milk," says an eminent German philosopher, "commonly yields some hundredths more cream than the evening's at the same temperature. That milked at noon furnishes the least ; it would therefore be of advantage, in making butter, &c., to employ the morning's milk, and keep the evening's for domestic use."

1245. TO PRESERVE MEAT.—Joints may be kept several days in the height of summer, sweet and good, by lightly covering them with bran or powdered borax and hanging them in some high or windy room, or in a passage where there is a current of air.

1246. TO CURE BACON AND HAMS.—The most simple method is to use one ounce and a half of common soda and the same quantity of salt-petre, to fourteen pounds of ham or bacon, using the usual quantity of salt. The soda prevents that hardness in the lean of the bacon which is so often found, and keeps it quite mellow all through, besides being a preventive of rust.

1246a. Another Method of Curing Hams.—Choose the short thick legs of well-fed hogs. To each large ham allow half-a-pound of bay salt, an ounce of saltpetre, half-a-pound of coarse sugar, half-a-pound of common salt, a quarter of a pound of pepper, and an ounce of coriander seeds. Pound the ingredients, and beat and mix them well ; but first rub in about six ounces of the salt and the saltpetre, and after two days drain and rub in the remainder of the salt and the spices. Rub for half-an-hour ; lay the hams in a trough, keep them carefully covered, and baste them with the brine every day ; turn them occasionally, and rub the brine well in. When this is done, hang the ham in a cool dry place, where there is a thorough current of air, and let it remain there until it is perfectly dry ; then remove it into the store closet and lay it by in clean straw.

1247. GLAZING FOR HAMS, TONGUES, &c.—Boil a shin of beef twelve hours in eight or ten quarts of water ; draw the gravy from a knuckle of veal in the same manner ; put the same herbs and spices as if for soup, and add the whole to the shin of beef. It must be boiled till reduced to a quart. It will keep good for a year ; and when wanted for use, warm a little, and spread over the ham, tongue, &c., with a feather.

1248. TO PRESERVE MACK-EREL.—Mackerel are at certain times exceedingly plentiful, especially to those who live near the coast. They may be preserved so as to make an excellent and well-flavoured dish, weeks or months after the season is past, by the following means. Having chosen some fine fish, cleanse them perfectly, and either boil them or lightly fry them in oil. The fish should be divided, and the bones, heads, and skins removed ; they should then be well rubbed over with the following seasoning :—For every dozen good-sized fish use three tablespoonfuls of salt (heaped), one ounce and a half of common black pepper, six or eight cloves, and a little mace, finely powdered, and as much nutmeg, grated, as the operator chooses to afford,—not, however, exceeding one nutmeg. Let the whole surface be well covered with the seasoning ; then lay the fish in layers packed into a stone jar (not a glazed one) ; cover the whole with good vinegar, and if they be intended to be long kept, pour salad oil or melted fat over the top. *Caution.*— The glazing on earthen jars is made from lead or arsenic, which poisons vinegar draws forth.

1249. TO PRESERVE POTATOES.—The preservation of potatoes by dipping them in boiling water is a valuable and useful discovery. Large quantities may be cured at once, by putting them into a basket as large as the vessel containing the boiling water will admit, and then just dipping them a minute or two, at the utmost. The germ, which is so near the skin, is thus destroyed without injury to the potato. In this way several tons might be cured in a few hours. They should then be dried in a warm oven, and laid up in sacks, secure from the frost, in a dry place.

1250. TO PRESERVE FLOWERS. —Dip them, whilst fresh gathered, in gum water. Let them drain for a few minutes and place them in a vase. The gum will then produce a thin coating on the stems and leaves, thus preserving their shape and colour.

Faded flowers may be restored by dipping them in very hot water half-way up the stems, then lay them by until the water cools. The portions of the stems which have been immersed must then be cut off and the flowers placed in clean cold water.

1251. PICKLING, first Method.— This, the most simple one, is merely to put the article into cold vinegar. The strongest pickling vinegar of white wine should always be used for pickles ; and for white pickles, use distilled vinegar. This method may be recommended for all such vegetables as, being hot themselves, do not require the addition of spice, and such as do not require to be softened by heat, as capsicum, chilli, nasturtiums, button onions, radish-pods, horseradish, garlic, and shallots. Half fill the jars with best vinegar, fill them up with the vegetables, and tie down immediately with bladder and leather. One advantage of this plan is that those who grow nasturtiums, radish-pods, and so forth, in their own gardens, may gather them from day to day, when they are exactly of the proper growth. They are very much better if pickled quite fresh, and all of a size, which can scarcely be obtained if they be pickled all at the same time. The onions should be dropped in the vinegar as fast as peeled ; this secures their colour. The horseradish should be scraped a little outside, and cut up in rounds half an inch deep.

1252. PICKLING, second Method, is that of heating vinegar and spice, and pouring them hot over the vegetables to be pickled, which are previously prepared by sprinkling with salt, or immersing in brine. Do not boil the vinegar, for if so its strength will evaporate. Put the vinegar and spice into a jar, bung it down tightly, tie a bladder over, and let it stand on the hob or on a trivet by the side of the fire for three or four days ; shake it well three or four times a day. This method may be applied to gherkins, French beans, cabbage, broccoli, cauliflowers, onions, and so forth.

1253. PICKLING, third Method, is when the vegetables are in a greater or less degree done over the fire. Walnuts, artichokes, artichoke bottoms and beetroots are done thus, and sometimes onions and cauliflowers.

1254. HINTS ON PICKLING.

i. Do not keep pickles in common earthenware, as the glazing contains lead, and other poisons which combine with the vinegar.

ii. Keep pickles only in wood, glass, or stone ware. Anything that has held grease will spoil pickles.

iii. If you use copper, bell-metal, or brass vessels for pickling, never allow the vinegar to cool in them, as it is then poisonous.

iv. Vinegar for pickling should be sharp, though not the sharpest kind, as it injures the pickles.

v. Vinegar may be prepared ready for use for any kind of pickling by adding a teaspoonful of alum and a teacupful of salt to three gallons of vinegar, with a bag containing pepper, ginger root, and all the different spices that are used in pickling.

vi. Stir pickles occasionally, and if they are soft ones take them out, and scald the vinegar, and pour it hot over the pickles.

vii. Keep enough vinegar in every jar to cover the pickles completely ; if it is weak, take fresh vinegar and pour on hot.

viii. Copper in pickles may be detected by immersing a piece of thick bright iron wire in the vinegar for some hours. If there is the least quantity of copper, it will become deposited on the wire.

ix. Most pickle vinegar, after the vegetables have been used, may be again utilized, walnut pickle in particular ; boil it up, allowing to each quart four or six anchovies chopped small, and a large tablespoonful of shallots, also chopped. Let it stand a few days, till it is quite clear, then pour off and bottle. It is an excellent store sauce for hashes, fish, and various other purposes.

1255. TOMATOES, to Pickle.— Take five pounds of the ripe fruit, remove the stalks, and wipe with a soft cloth or piece of flannel ; put the tomatoes in a jar, with a breakfast-cupful of salt and the same quantity of vinegar. Close the jar with a paste of flour and water round the lid ; put the jar into a pan of boiling water, and let the fruit simmer for six hours, then pulp through a colander so as to get rid of the cores and skins ; now shred two ounces of red chillies, two ounces of garlic, make a syrup of two pints of vinegar and two pounds of lump sugar, cut two ounces of ginger up small, mix all these with the tomatoes, and simmer gently on a slow fire till it comes to the boil. Bottle when cold, and keep it (tightly corked) in a warm place.

1256. FRENCH BEANS, to Pickle. —The best sort for this purpose are white runners. They are very large, long beans, but should be gathered quite young, before they are half-grown ; they may be done in the same way as described in par. 1251.

1257. ONIONS, to Pickle.— Onions should be chosen about the size of marbles ; the silver-skinned sort are the best. Prepare a brine, and put them into it hot ; let them remain one or two days, then drain them, and when quite dry, put them into clean dry jars, and cover them with hot pickle, in every quart of which has been steeped one ounce each of horseradish sliced, black pepper, allspice, and salt, with or without mustard seed.

1258. GARLIC AND SHALLOTS. —These may be pickled in the same way as onions.

1259. RED CABBAGE, to Pickle. —Choose fine firm cabbages—the largest are not the best ; trim off the outside leaves ; quarter the cabbage, take out the large stalk, slice the quarters into a colander, and sprinkle a little salt between the layers ; put but a little salt—too much will spoil the colour ; let it remain in the colander till next day, shake it well, that all the brine may ran off ; put it in jars, cover it with a hot pickle composed of black pepper and allspice, of each an ounce, ginger pounded, horseradish sliced, and salt, of each half-an-ounce to every quart of vinegar (steep as directed in par. 1252) ; two capsicums may be added to a quart, or one drachm of cayenne.

1260. BROCCOLI OR CAULI-FLOWERS, to Pickle.—Choose such as are firm, and of full size ; cut away all the leaves, and pare the stalk ; pull away the flowers by bunches, steep in brine two days, then drain them, wipe them dry, and put them into hot pickle.

1261. MELONS, MANGOES AND LONG CUCUMBERS may all be pickled in the following manner. Melons should not be much more than half-grown ; cucumbers full-grown, but not overgrown. Cut off the top, but leave it hanging by a bit of rind, which is to serve as a hinge to a box-lid ; with a marrow-spoon scoop out all the seeds, and fill the fruit with equal parts of mustard seed, ground pepper, and ginger, or flour of mustard instead of the seed, and two or three cloves of garlic. The lid which encloses the spice may be sewn down or tied, by running a white thread through the cucumber and through the lid, and tying them together. A pickle may be prepared which bears a resemblance to the Indian method :—To each quart of vinegar put salt, flour of mustard, curry powder, bruised ginger, turmeric, half-an-ounce of each, cayenne pepper one drachm, all rubbed together with a large glassful of salad oil ; shallots two ounces, and garlic half-an-ounce, sliced ; steep the spice in the vinegar as before directed, and put the vegetables into it hot.

1262. GHERKINS, to Pickle.—Pat about two hundred and fifty in strong brine, and let them remain in it three hours. Put them in a sieve to drain, wipe them, and place then in a jar. For a pickle, beat vinegar, one gallon ; common salt, six ounces ; allspice, one ounce ; mustard seed, one ounce ; cloves, half-an-ounce ; mace, half-an-ounce ; one nutmeg, sliced ; a stick of horseradish, sliced ; boil fifteen minutes ; skim it well. When cold, pour it over them, and let stand twenty-four hours, covered up ; put them into a pan over the fire, and let them simmer only until they attain a green colour. Tie the jars down closely with bladder and leather.

1263. BEETROOTS, to Pickle.—Boil or bake them gently until they are nearly done ; according to the size of the root they will require from an hour and a half to two hours ; drain them, and when they begin to cool, peel and cut in slices half-an-inch thick, then put them into a pickle composed of black pepper and allspice, of each one ounce ; ginger pounded, horseradish sliced, and salt, of each half-an-ounce to every quart of vinegar, steeped. Two capsicums may be added to a quart, or one drachm of cayenne.

1264. ARTICHOKES, to Pickle.—Gather young artichokes as soon as formed ; throw them into boiling brine, and let them boil two minutes ; drain them ; when cold and dry, put them in jars, and cover with vinegar, prepared as in par. 1253, but the only spices employed should be ginger, mace, and nutmeg.

1264a. ARTICHOKE BOTTOMS, to Pickle.—Select full-grown artichokes and boil them ; not so much as for eating, but just until the leaves can be pulled ; remove them and the choke ; in taking off the stalk, be careful not to break it off so as to bring away any of the bottom ; it would be better to pare them with a silver knife, and leave half-an-inch of tender stalk coming to a point ; cold, add vinegar and space, the same as for artichokes.

1265. MUSHROOMS, to Pickle.— Choose small white mushrooms ; they should be of but one night's growth. Cut off the roots, and rub the mushrooms clean with a bit of flannel and salt ; put them in a jar, allowing to every quart of mushrooms one ounce of salt, one ounce of ginger, half-an-ounce of whole pepper, eight blades of mace, a bay-leaf, a strip of lemon rind, and a wineglassful of sherry ; cover the jar close, and let it stand on the hob or on a stove, so as to be thoroughly heated, and on the point of boiling. Let it remain thus a day or two, till the liquor is absorbed by the mushrooms and spices ; then cover them with hot vinegar, close them again, and stand till it just comes to a boil ; then take them away from the fire. When they are quite cold, divide the mushrooms and spice into wide-mouthed bottles, fill them up with the vinegar, and tie them over. In a week's time, if the vinegar has shrunk so as not entirely to cover the mushrooms, add cold vinegar, and at the top of each bottle put a teaspoonful of salad or almond oil ; cork close, and dip in bottle resin.

1266. WALNUTS, to Pickle.— Be particular in obtaining them exactly at the proper season ; if they go beyond the middle of July, there is danger of their becoming hard and woody. Steep them a week in brine. If they are wanted to be soon ready for use, prick them with a pin, or run a larding-pin several times through them ; but if they are not wanted in haste, this method had better be left alone. Put them into a kettle of brine, and give them a gentle simmer, then drain them on a sieve, and lay them on fish drainers (or what is equally good, the cover of a wicker hamper), in an airy place, until they become black ; then make a pickle of vinegar, adding to every quart, black pepper one ounce,

ginger, shallots, salt, and mustard seed, one ounce each.

1267. NASTURTIUMS, to Pickle.— A week or ten days after the blossoms have fallen off, gather a gallon of the nasturtiums and put them in a pail of salt and water (changing the water occasionally) for three or four days ; put them in a sieve to drain, and dry them with cloths until perfectly dry. Boil one gallon white vinegar, four sliced shallots, four ounces of salt, one ounce of nutmeg, one ounce of mace, two ounces of white peppercorns, for a quarter of an hour ; skim, and when almost cold pour it all over the fruit previously placed in jars and tie up tightly.

1268. GRAPES, to Pickle.— Cut the grapes off before they are ripe, taking care not to bruise them. Boil a gallon of vinegar with one ounce of peppercorns, two dozen cloves, and two ounces of ginger. When it is cold pour over the grapes, cover them well, and let them stay for three or four days. Then boil the vinegar again and pour it (when cold) over the grapes. Bottle, and cork tightly.

1269. SAMPHIRE, to Pickle.— On the sea-coast this is merely preserved in water, or equal parts of sea-water and vinegar ; but as it is sometimes sent fresh as a present to inland parts, the best way of managing it under such circumstances is to steep it two days in brine, then drain and put it in a stone jar covered with vinegar, and having a lid, over which put a thick paste of flour and water, and set it in a very cool oven all night, or in a warmer oven till it nearly but not quite boils. Then let it stand on a warm hob for half-an-hour, and allow it to become quite cold before the paste is removed ; then add cold vinegar, if any more is required, and secure as other pickles.

1270. PICKLED EGGS.— If the following pickle were generally known, it would be more generally used. It is an excellent pickle to be eaten with cold meat, &c. The eggs should be boiled hard (say ten minutes), and then divested of their shells ; when *quite cold* put them in jars, and pour over them vinegar (sufficient to quite *cover* them), in which has been previously boiled the usual spices for pickling ; tie the jars down tight with bladder, and keep them till they begin to change colour.

1271. INDIAN PICKLE.—The vegetables to be employed for this favourite pickle are small hard knots of white cabbage, sliced ; cauliflowers or broccoli in flakes ; long carrots, not larger than a finger, or large carrots sliced (the former are far preferable), gherkins, French beans, small button onions, white turnip radishes half-grown, radish-pods, shallots, young hard apples ; green peaches, before the stones begin to form ; vegetable marrow, not larger than a hen's egg ; small green melons, celery, shoots of green elder, horseradish, nasturtiums, capsicums, and garlic. As all these vegetables do not come in season together, the best method is to prepare a large jar of pickle at such time of the year as most of the things may be obtained, and add the others as they come in season. Thus the pickle will be nearly a year in making, and ought to stand another year before using, when, if properly managed, it will be excellent, but it will keep and continue to improve for years. For preparing the several vegetables, the same directions may be observed as for pickling them separately, only following this general rule—that, if possible, boiling is to be avoided, and soaking in brine to be preferred. Be very particular that every ingredient is perfectly dry before it is put into the jar, and that the jar is very closely tied down every time that it is opened for the addition of fresh vegetables. *Neither mushrooms, walnuts, nor red cabbage are to be admitted.* FOR THE PICKLE :—To a gallon

of the best white wine vinegar add salt three ounces, flower of mustard half-a-pound, turmeric two ounces, white ginger sliced three ounces, cloves one ounce, mace, black pepper, long pepper, white pepper, half-an-ounce each, cayenne two drachms, shallots, peeled, four ounces, garlic, peeled, two ounces ; steep the spice in vinegar for two or three days. The mustard and turmeric must be rubbed smooth with a little cold vinegar, and stirred into the rest when as near boiling as possible. Such vegetables as are ready may be put in ; when cayenne, nasturtiums, or any other vegetables mentioned in the first method of pickling (par. 1251) come in season, put them in pickle as they are ; for the preparation of vegetables mentioned in the second method (par. 1252), use a small quantity of hot vinegar without spice : when cold, pour it off, and put the vegetables into the general jar. If the vegetables are greened in vinegar, as French beans and gherkins, this will not be necessary, but the adoption of this process will tend to improve all. Onions had better not be wetted at all ; but if it be desirous not to have the full flavour, both onions, shallots, and garlic may be sprinkled with salt in a colander, to draw off all the strong juice ; let them lie two or three hours. The elder, apples, peaches, and so forth, should be greened as gherkins. The roots, radishes, carrots, celery, are only soaked in brine and dried. Half-a-pint of salad oil is sometimes added. It should be rubbed up in a bowl with the flower of mustard and turmeric.—It is not essential to Indian pickle to have every variety of vegetable here mentioned ; but all these are admissible, and the greater the variety the more the pickle will be approved.

1272. TO MAKE BRITISH ANCHOVIES.—Procure a quantity of sprats, as fresh as possible ; do not wash or wipe them, but just take them as caught, and for every peck of the fish take two pounds of common salt, a quarter of a pound of bay salt, four pounds of saltpetre, two ounces of salprunella, and two pennyworth of cochineal. Pound all these ingredients in a mortar, mixing them well together. Then take stone jars or small kegs, according to your quantity of sprats, and place a layer of the fish and a layer of the mixed ingredients alternately, until the pot is full ; then press hard down, and cover close for six months, when they will be fit for use.

1273. ORNAMENTAL STAINING. General Observations.—When *Alabaster*, *Marble*, and other *Stones* are coloured, and the stain is required to be deep, it should be poured on boiling hot, and brushed equally over every part, if made with water ; if with spirit, it should be applied cold, otherwise the evaporation, being too rapid, would leave the colouring matter on the surface, without any, or very little, being able to penetrate. In greyish or brownish stones, the stain will be wanting in brightness, because the natural colour combines with the stain ; therefore, if the stone be a pure colour, the result will be a combination of the colour and stain. In staining *Bone* or *Ivory*, the colours will take better before than after polishing ; and if any dark spots appear, they should be rubbed with chalk, and the article dyed again, to produce uniformity of shade. On removal from the boiling hot dye-bath, the bone should be immediately plunged into cold water, to prevent cracks from the heat. If *Paper* or *Parchment* is stained, a broad varnish brush should be employed, to lay the colouring on evenly. When the stains for *wood* are required to be very strong, it is better to soak and *not* brush them ; therefore, if for inlaying or fine work, the wood should be previously split or sawn into proper thicknesses ; and when it is necessary to brush the wood several times over with the stains, it should be

allowed to dry between each coating. When it is wished to render any of the stains more durable and beautiful, the work should be well rubbed with Dutch or common rushes after it is coloured, and then varnished with seed-lac varnish, or if a better appearance is desired, with three coats of the same, or shellac varnish. Common work only requires frequent rubbing with linseed oil and woollen rags.

1274. TO STAIN ALABASTER, MARBLE, AND STONE.—These may be stained yellow, red, green, blue, purple, black, or any of the compound colours, by the stains used for wood.

1275. TO STAIN BONE AND IVORY.

i. Black.—After being well cleansed from grease and dirt, lay the article for several hours in a strong solution of nitrate of silver, and exposed to the light or dried, and then dipped in a solution of sulphide of ammonium. Or boil the article for some time in a strained decoction of logwood, and then steep it in a solution of persulphate or acetate of iron.

ii. Blue. Immerse for some time in a dilute solution of sulphate of indigo—partly saturated with potash—and it will be fully stained. Or steep in a strong solution of sulphate of copper, or in a solution of soluble Prussian blue.

iii. Brown.—The same as for Black, but with a weaker solution of silver.

iv. Green.—Dip blue-stained articles for a short time in nitro-hydrochlorate of tin, and then in a hot decoction of fustic. Or boil in a solution of verdigris in vinegar until the desired colour is obtained ; a glass or stone-ware utensil should be used.

v. Red.—Dip the articles first in the tin mordant used in dyeing, and then plunge into a hot decoction of Brazil wood—half-a-pound to a gallon of water—or cochineal. Or steep in red ink until sufficiently stained.

vi. Scarlet.—Use lac dye instead of the preceding.

vii. Purple.—Immerse the pieces in a weak solution of terchloride of gold, and then expose to the light.

viii. Violet.—Dip in the tin mordant, and then immerse in a decoction of logwood.

ix. Yellow.—Impregnate with nitro-hydrochlorate of tin, and then digest with heat in a strained decoction of fustic. Or steep for twenty-four hours in a strong solution of the neutral chromate of potash, and then plunge for some time in a boiling solution of acetate of lead. Or boil the articles in a solution of alum—a pound to half-a-gallon—and then immerse for half-an-hour in the following mixture :—Take half-a-pound of turmeric, and a quarter of a pound of pearlash ; boil in a gallon of water. When taken from this, the bone must be again dipped in the alum solution.

1276. TO STAIN HORN.—This must be treated in the same manner as bone and ivory for the various colours given under that heading.

1277. TO IMITATE TORTOISE-SHELL.—First steam and then press the horn into proper shapes, and afterwards lay the following mixture on with a small brush, in imitation of the mottle of tortoiseshell :—Take equal parts of quicklime and litharge, and mix with strong soap-lees ; let this remain until it is thoroughly dry, brush off and repeat two or three times, if necessary. Such parts as are required to be of a reddish-brown should be covered with a mixture of whitening and the stain.

1278. TO POLISH TORTOISE-SHELL.—Take some rouge powder, and with a piece of soft rag or leather rub the shell, and then finish with the hand.

1279. TO STAIN IRON. Black.—To one gallon of vinegar add a quarter of a pound of iron rusk, let it stand for a week ; then add a pound

of dry lampblack, and three-quarters of a pound of copperas : stir it up at intervals for a couple of days. Lay five or six coats on the article with a sponge, allowing it to dry well between each. Polish with linseed oil and soft woollen rag, and it will look like ebony.

1280. TO STAIN PAPER OR PARCHMENT.

i. Blue.—Stain the materiel green with the verdigris stain given in No. 1281 (iii), and brush over with a solution of pearlash—two ounces to the pint—till it becomes blue. Or use the blue stain for wood.

ii. Green or Red.—The same as for wood.

iii. Orange.—Brush over with a tincture of turmeric, formed by infusing an ounce of the root in a pint of spirit of wine ; let this dry, and give another coat of pearlash solution, made by dissolving two ounces of the salt in a quart of water.

iv. Purple.—Brush over with the expressed juice of ripe privet berries. Or use the same as for wood.

v. Yellow.—Brush over with tincture of turmeric. Or add anatto or dragon's-blood to the tincture of turmeric, and brush over as usual.

1281. TO STAIN WOOD.

i. Black.—1. Drop a little sulphuric acid into a small quantity of water, brush over the wood and hold to the fire ; it will turn a fine black, and take a good polish.

2. Take half-a-gallon of vinegar, an ounce of braised nutgalls, of logwood chips and copperas each half-a-pound—boil well ; add half-an-ounce of the tincture of sesquichloride of iron, formerly called the muriated tincture, and brush on hot.

3. Use the stain given for iron, par. 1279.

4. Take half-a-gallon of vinegar, half-a-pound of dry lampblack, and three pounds of iron rust, sifted. Mix and let stand for a week. Lay three

coats of this on hot, and then rub with linseed oil, and you will have a fine deep black.

5. Add to the above stain an ounce of nutgalls, half-a-pound of logwood chips, and a quarter of a pound of copperas ; lay on three coats, oil well, and you will have a black stain that will stand any kind of weather.

6. Take a pound of logwood chips, a quarter of a pound of Brazil wood, and boil for an hour and a half in a gallon of water. Brush the wood several times with this decoction while hot. Make a decoction of nutgalls by simmering gently, for three or four days, a quarter of a pound of the galls in two quarts of water ; give the wood three coats of this, and, while wet, lay on a solution of sulphate of iron (two ounces to a quart), and when dry, oil or varnish.

7. Give three coats with a solution of copper filings in aquafortis, and repeatedly brush over with the log-wood decoction, until the greenness of the copper is destroyed.

8. Boil half-a-pound of logwood chips in two quarts of water, add an ounce of pearlash, and apply hot with a brush. Then take two quarts of the logwood decoction, and half-an-ounce of verdigris, and the same of copperas ; strain, and throw in half-a-pound of iron rust. Brush the work well with this, and oil.

ii. **Blue.**—Dissolve copper filings in aquafortis, brush the wood with it, and then go over the work with a hot solution of pearlash (two ounces to a pint of water) till it assumes a perfectly blue colour. Or boil a pound of indigo, two pounds of woad, and three ounces of alum in a gallon of water ; brush well over until thoroughly stained.

iii. **Green.**—Dissolve verdigris in vinegar, and brush over with the hot solution until of a proper colour.

iv. **Dark Mahogany Colour.**—Boil half-a-pound of madder and two ounces of logwood chips in a gallon of water, and brush well over while hot ; when dry go over the whole with pearlash

solution, two drachms to the quart. Or put two ounces of dragon's-blood, bruised, into a quart of oil of turpentine ; let the bottle stand in a warm place, shake frequently, and when dissolved, steep the work in the mixture.

v. **Light Red Brown.**—Boil half-a-pound of madder and a quarter of a pound of fustic in a gallon of water ; brush over the work when boiling hot, until properly stained ; or the surface of the work being quite smooth, brush over with a weak solution of aquafortis, half-an-ounce to the pint, and them finish with the following :—Put four ounces and a half of dragon's-blood and an ounce of soda, both well bruised, to three pints of spirits of wine ; let it stand in a warm place, shake frequently, strain, and lay on with a soft brush, repeating till of a proper colour ; polish with linseed oil or varnish.

vi. **Purple.**—Brush the work several times with the logwood decoction used for No. 6 *black* (*see* par. 1281), and when perfectly dry give a coat of pearlash solution—one drachm to a quart—taking care to lay it on evenly.

vii. **Red.**—Boil a pound of Brazil wood and an ounce of pearlash in a gallon of water, and while hot brush over the work until of a proper colour. Dissolve two ounces of alum in a quart of water, and brush the solution over the work before it dries ; or use a cold infusion of archil, and brush over with a pearlash solution of two drachms to the quart.

viii. **Yellow.**—Brush over with the tincture of turmeric ; or warm the work and brush over with weak aquafortis, then hold to the fire. Varnish or oil as usual.

ix. **Imitation of Botany Bay Wood.**—Boil half-a-pound of French Berries (the unripe berries of the *rhamnus infectorius*) in two quarts of water till of a deep yellow, and while boiling hot give two or three coats to the work. If a deeper colour is desired, give a coat of logwood decoction over the yellow. When nearly dry form the grain with

No. 8 *black stain* (*see* par. 1281) used hot; and when dry, dust varnish.

 x. Imitation of Rose Wood.—Boil half-a-pound of logwood in three pints of water till it is of a very dark red, add half-an-ounce of salt of tartar ; stain the work with the liquor while boiling hot, giving three coats ; then with a painter's graining brush, form streaks with No. 8 *black stain* (*see* par. 1281) ; let the work dry, and varnish ; or brush over with the logwood decoction used for No. 6 *black*, three or four times ; put half-a-pound of iron filings into two quarts of vinegar ; then with a graining brush, or cane bruised at the end, apply the iron filing solution in the form required, and when dry polish with bees'-wax and turpentine or varnish.

 1282. DYEING. General Observations.—The filaments from which stuffs of all kinds are fabricated are derived either from the animal or vegetable kingdom. We recognize the former by the property they possess of liberating ammonia on being treated with potash ; while the latter afford a liquor having an acid reaction under the same treatment. The animal kingdom furnishes three varieties—silk, wool, and the furs, &c. of various animals ; the vegetable kingdom also three—flax, hemp, and cotton.

 The Various Shades produced by colouring matters may be classed in one or other of the following groups :—

  1. Blues.
  2. Reds.   *Simple.*
  3. Yellows
  4. Violets.
  5. Orange colours *Binary.*
  6. Greens.
  7. Compound colours. *Ternary.*
  8. Black

 Some colours adhere at once to the stuff, and are called *substantial colours* ; while others require that the material to be dyed should undergo some previous preparation in order to render it permanent. The substances used to fix the colouring matters are called *Mordants*, which should possess four qualifications :—

 i. An equal affinity for the fibre of the material and the colouring matter.

 ii. They should be incapable of injuring or destroying either by prolonged action.

 iii. They should form, with the colour, a compound capable of resisting the action of air and water.

 iv. They should be capable of readily conforming to the various operations of the dyer.

 1282a. MORDANTS FOR DYEING.—For the reasons above given, the acetate or tartrate of iron is preferable to the sulphate ; and the acetate or tartrate of alumina to alum. For *reds*, *yellows*, *greens*, and *pinks*, aluminous mordants are to be used. For *blacks*, *browns*, *puces*, and *violets*, the acetate or tartrate of iron must be employed. For *scarlets* use a tin mordant, made by dissolving in strong nitric acid one-eighth of its weight of sal-ammoniac, then adding by degrees one-eighth of its weight of tin, and diluting the solution with one-fourth of its weight of water.

 1283. TO DYE CALICO, LINEN, AND MUSLIN.

 i. **Blue.**—Wash well to remove dressing, and dry ; then dip in a strong solution of sulphate of indigo—partly saturated with potash—and hang up. Dry a piece to see if the colour is deep enough ; if not dip again.

 ii. **Saxon Blue.**—Boil the article in alum, and then dip in a strong solution of chemical blue.

 iii. **Buff.**—Boil an ounce of anatto in three quarts of water, add two ounces of potash, stir well, and put in the calico while boiling, and stir well for five minutes ; remove and plunge into cold pump water, hang up the articles without wringing, and when almost dry, fold.

 iv. **Pink.**—Immerse in the acetate of alumina mordant, and then in the colouring of a pink saucer.

v. **Green.**—Boil the article in an alum mordant, and then in a solution of indigo mixed with any of the yellow dyes until the proper colour is obtained.

vi. **Yellow.**—Cut potato tops when in flower, and express the juice ; steep articles in this for forty-eight hours ; or dip in a strong solution of weld after boiling in an aluminous mordant. Turmeric, fustic, anatto, &c., will answer the same as weld.

1284. TO DYE CLOTH.

i. **Black.**—Impregnate the material with the acetate of iron mordant, and then boil in a decoction of madder and logwood.

ii. **Madder Red.**—Boil the cloth in a weak solution of pearlash—an ounce to a gallon of water,—wash, dry, and then steep in a decoction of bruised nutgalls. After drying it is to be steeped twice in dry alum water, then dried, and boiled in a decoction made of three-quarters of a pound of madder to every pound of the article. It should then be taken out and dried, and steeped in a second bath in the same manner. When dyed, the articles should be washed in warm soap and water, to remove a dun-coloured matter given out by the madder.

iii. **Scarlet.**—Three-quarters of a pint of a tin mordant, made by dissolving three pounds of tin in sixty pounds of hydrochloric acid, is added to every pound of lac dye, and digested for six hours. To dye twenty-five pounds of cloth, a tin boiler of seventy-five gallons capacity should be filled nearly full with water, and a fire kindled under it When the heat is 150° Fahr., half a handful of bran and two ounces of tin mordant are to be thrown into it. The froth which rises is skimmed off, the liquor is made to boil, and two pounds and three-quarters of lac dye, previously mixed with a pound and three-quarters of the solvent, and fourteen ounces of the tin solvent are added. Immediately afterwards two pounds and three-quarters of tartar, and a pound of ground sumach, both tied up in a linen bag, are to be added, and suspended in the bath for five minutes. The fire being withdrawn, five gallons of cold water and two pints and three-quarters of tin mordant being poured into the bath, the cloth is immersed in it. The fire is then replaced, and the liquid made to boil rapidly for an hour, when the cloth is removed and washed in pure water.

iv. **Yellow.**—Quercitron and weld produce a solid yellow ; fustic a very brilliant tint ; while turmeric yields a less solid yellow.

1285. TO DYE FEATHERS.—

The feathers must be put into hot water, and allowed to drain before they are put into the dye. After they are taken out of the dye, rinse them two or three times, in clear cold water (except the red, which most only be done once), then lay them on a tray, over which a cloth has been spread, before a good fire ; when they begin to dry and unfold, draw each feather gently between your thumb and finger, until it regains its proper shape.

i. **Black.**—Use the same as for cloth.

ii. **Blue.**—Every shade may be given by indigo,—or dip in silk dye.

iii. **Crimson.**—Dip in acetate of alumina mordant, then in a boiling-hot decoction of Brazil wood—and, last of all, pass through a bath of cudbear.

iv. **Pink or Rose-colour** is given by safflower and lemon juice.

v. **Deep Red.**—Proceed as for crimson, omitting the cudbear bath.

vi. **Yellow.**—Mordant with acetate of alumina, and dip in a bath of turmeric or weld. More or less of the turmeric will give them different shades and a very small quantity of soda will yield an orange hue.

vii. **Green.**—Mix the indigo liquid with turmeric, and pour boiling water over it ; let the feathers simmer in the dye until they have acquired the shade you want them.

viii. Lilac.—About two teaspoonfuls of cudbear in about a quart of boiling water ; let it simmer a few minutes before you put in the feathers. A small quantity of cream of tartar turns the colour from lilac to amethyst.

1286. TO DYE GLOVES.

i. Yellow, Brown or Tan Colour.—Steep saffron in boiling-hot soft water for about twelve hours ; sew up the tops of the gloves to prevent the dye staining the insides, wet the outsides over with a sponge dipped in the liquid. A teacupful of dye will do a pair of gloves. The quantity of saffron used must depend on the depth of colour required.

ii. Purple.—Boil four ounces of logwood and two ounces of roche alum in three pints of soft water till half wasted ; strain, and let it cool. Sew up the tops, go over the outsides with a brush or sponge twice ; then rub off the loose dye with a coarse cloth. Beat up the white of an egg, and rub it over the leather with a sponge. Vinegar will remove the stain from the hands.

1287. TO DYE LEATHER.—
Black.—Use No. 4 *black stain* (*see* par. 1281), and polish with oil.

1288. TO DYE SILK.

i. Black.—The same as for cloth (par. 1284), but black dyeing is difficult.

ii. Blue.—Wash quite clean, rinse well, and then dip in a hot solution of sulphate of iron : after a short time take it out and rinse again. Have ready in another vessel a hot solution of prussiate of potash, to which a small quantity of sulphuric acid has been added. Dip the silk in this liquid ; on removal rinse in clean water, and expose to the air to dry ; or wash well, rinse, wring out, and then dip in the following :—Boil a pound of indigo, two pounds of woad, and three ounces of alum, in a gallon of water. When the silk is of a proper colour, remove, rinse, and dry.

iii. Carnation.—Boil two gallons of wheat and an ounce of alum in four gallons of water ; strain through a fine sieve ; dissolve half-a-pound more of alum and white tartar ; add three pounds of madder, then put in the silk at a moderate heat.

iv. Crimson.—Take about a spoonful of cudbear, put it into a small pan, pour boiling water upon it ; stir and let it stand a few minutes, then put in the silk, and turn it over in a short time, and when the colour is full enough, take it out ; but if it should require more violet or crimson, add a spoonful or two of purple archil to some warm water ; steep, and dry it within doors. It must be mangled, and ought to be pressed.

v. Lilac.—For every pound of silk take one and a half pounds of archil, mix it well with the liquor ; make it boil for a quarter of an hour, dip the silk quickly, then let it cool, and wash it in river water, and a fine half-violet, or lilac, more or less full, will be obtained.

vi. Madder Red.—Use the dye for cloth (No. ii par. 1284).

vii. Yellow.—Take clear wheat bran liquor fifteen pounds, in which dissolve three quarters of a pound of alum ; boil the silk in this for two hours, and afterwards take half-a-pound of weld, and boil it till the colour is good. Nitre used with alum and water in the first boiling fixes the colour.

1289. TO DYE WOOL.

i. Blue.—Boil in a decoction of logwood and sulphate or acetate of copper.

ii. Brown.—Steep in an infusion of green walnut peels.

iii. Drab.—Impregnate with brown oxide of iron, and then dip in a bath of quercitron bark. If sumach is added, it will make the colour a dark brown.

iv. Green.—First imbue with the blue, then with the yellow dye.

v. Orange.—Dye first with the red dye for cloth, and then with a yellow.

vi. Red.—Take four and a half pounds of cream of tartar, four and a quarter pounds of alum ; boil the wool gently for two hours ; let it cool, and wash it on the following day in pure water. Infuse twelve pounds of madder for half-an-hour with a pound of chloride of tin, in lukewarm water ; filter through canvas, remove the dye from the canvas, and put it in the bath, which is to be heated to 100° Fahr. ; add two ounces of aluminous mordant, put the wool in and raise to boiling heat. Remove the wool, wash, and soak for a quarter of an hour in a solution of white soap in water.

vii. Yellow.—Dye with that used for calico, &c. (No. vi par. 1283).

1290. TO DYE BONNETS.

Chip and straw bonnets or hats may be dyed black by boiling them three or four hours in a strong liquor of logwood, adding a little green copperas occasionally. Let the bonnets remain in the liquor all night, then take out to dry in the air. If the black is not satisfactory, dye again after drying. Rub inside and out with a sponge moistened in fine oil. Then block.

1291. TO CLEAN WHITE SATIN AND FLOWERED SILKS.—Mix

sifted stale bread-crumbs with powder blue, and rub it thoroughly all over the article ; then shake it well, and dust it with clean soft cloths. Afterwards, where there are any gold or silver flowers, take a piece of crimson ingrain velvet, rub the flowers with it, which will restore them to their original lustre.

Another Method.—Pass them through a solution of fine hard soap of a moderate heat, drawing them through the hand ; rinse in lukewarm water, dry and finish by pinning out. Brush the flossy or bright side with a clean clothes-brush, the way of the nap. Finish them by dipping a sponge into a size made by boiling isinglass in water, and rub the wrong side. Rinse

out a second time, and brush, and dry near a fire in a warm room.—Silk may be treated in the same way, but not brushed.

1292. TO CLEAN COLOURED SILK, SATINS, WOOLLEN DRESSES, &c.—Four ounces of soft

soap, four ounces of honey, the white of an egg, and a wineglassful of gin ; mix well together, and scour the article with a rather hard brush thoroughly ; afterwards rinse it in cold water, leave to drain, and iron whilst quite damp.

1293. TO CLEAN BLACK CLOTH CLOTHES.—Beat and brush the

garments well, then boil four ounces of logwood in a boiler or copper containing two or three gallons of water for half-an-hour ; dip the clothes in warm water and squeeze dry, then put them into the copper and boil for half-an-hour. Take them out, and add three drachms of sulphate of iron ; boil for half-an-hour, then take them out and hang them up for an hour or two ; take them down, rinse them thrice in cold water, dry well, and rub with a soft brush which has had a few drops of olive oil applied to its surface. If the clothes are threadbare about the elbows, cuffs, &c., raise the nap with a teasel or half-worn hatter's card, filled with flocks, and when sufficiently raised, lay the nap the right way with a hard brush.

1294. TO CLEAN FURS.—Strip

the fur articles of their stuffing and binding, and lay them as nearly as possible in a flat position. They must then be subjected to a very brisk brushing, with a stiff clothes-brush ; after this any moth-eaten parts must be cut out, and neatly replaced by new bits of fur to match. *Sable, Chinchilla, Squirrel, Polecat,* &c., should be treated as follows :—Warm a quantity of new bran in a pan, taking care that it does not burn, to prevent which it must be actively stirred. When well warmed, rub it thoroughly into the fur with the hand. Repeat this two or three times : then shake the fur, and give it another sharp brushing until free from dust. *White furs, Ermine,* &c., may be cleaned as follows :—Lay the fur on a table, and rub it well with bran made moist with warm water ; rub until quite dry, and afterwards with dry bran. The wet bran should be put on with flannel, and the dry with a piece of book muslin. They should also be well rubbed with magnesia, or a piece of book muslin, after the bran process. Furs are usually much improved by stretching, which may be managed as follows :—In a pint of soft water dissolve three ounces of salt ; with this solution, sponge the inside of the skin (taking care not to wet the fur, until it becomes thoroughly saturated) ; then lay it carefully on a board with the fur side downwards, then stretch as much as it will bear, and to the required shape, and fasten with small tacks. The drying may be accelerated by placing the skin a little distance from the fire or stove.

1295. TO CLEANSE FEATHERS OF THEIR ANIMAL OIL.—The following recipe gained a premium from the Society of Arts :—Take for every gallon of clean water one pound of quicklime, mix them well together, and when the undissolved lime is precipitated in fine powder, pour off the clean lime water for use. Put the feathers to be cleaned in another tub, and add to them a quantity of the clean lime water, sufficient to cover them about three inches when well immersed and stirred about therein. The feathers, when thoroughly moistened, will sink, and should remain in the lime water three or four days ; after which the foul liquor should be separated from them, by laying them in a sieve. The feathers should be afterwards well washed in clean water, and dried upon nets, the meshes of which may be about the fineness of cabbage nets. The feathers must be from time to time shaken on the nets, and, as they get dry, they will fall through the meshes, and must be collected for use. The admission of air will be serviceable in drying. The process will be completed in three weeks. When thus prepared, the feathers need only be beaten to get rid of the dust.

1296. TO CLEAN WHITE OSTRICH FEATHERS.—Four ounces of white soap, cut small, dissolved in four pints of water, rather hot, in a large basin ; make the solution into a lather, by beating it with birch rods, or wires. Introduce the feathers, and rub well with the hands for five or six minutes. After this soaping, wash in clean water, as hot as the hand can bear. Shake until dry.

1297. TO CLEAN GREBE FEATHERS.—First remove the lining, then wash with warm water and soap, as described for ostrich feathers. Do not shake the feathers until perfectly dry, and before re-making the skin mend any tears, &c., in it.

1298. TO CLEAN STRAW HATS AND BONNETS.—They may be washed with soap and water, rinsed in clear water, and dried in the air. Then wash them over with white of egg well beaten. Remove the wire before washing.

1299. TO BLEACH STRAW HATS, &c.—Wash them in pure water, scrubbing them with a brush. Then put them into a box in which has been set a saucer of burning sulphur. Cover them up, so that the fumes may bleach them.

1300. BALLS FOR CLEANING CLOTHES.—Take some fuller's earth, dried till it crumbles to powder ; moisten it with the juice of lemon, add a small quantity of pearlash, work and knead carefully together till it forms a thick paste ; make into balls, and dry them in the sun. Moisten the spot on clothes with water, then rub it with the ball. Wash out the spot with clean water.

1301. TO CLEAN VELLUM AND PARCHMENT.—A sponge dipped in a little benzine will remove all stains without injuring the material.

1302. TO REMOVE STAINS FROM WALL-PAPERS.—Marks or oil stains may be removed by mixing pipeclay and water together to the thickness of cream and placing it on the spot. Let it stay there for twelve hours and then remove it with a brush or penknife.

1303. TO BLEACH A FADED DRESS.—Wash it well in hot suds, and boil it until the colour seems to be gone, then wash, and rinse, and dry it in the sun ; if still not quite white, repeat the boiling.

1304. TO BLEACH DISCOL-OURED LINEN.—Let it lie on the grass exposed to the sun, air, and dews day and night, as long as may be necessary.

1305. HINTS ON WASHING.—If the water is hard owing to its being impregnated with lime, it may be much softened by boiling it before use. Even exposure to the atmosphere will produce this effect in a great degree upon spring water so impregnated, leaving it much fitter for lavatory purposes. In both cases the water ought to be carefully poured off from the sediment, as the neutralized lime, when freed from its extra quantity of carbonic acid, falls to the bottom by its own gravity. Preparations for softening water, and facilitating the process, exist in the Extract of Soap, and the various washing powders now to be purchased of most grocers and oil and colourmen. Cold-water soap, too, has achieved considerable popularity, for by its use a lather can be quickly produced, even in the hardest water.

1306. WASHING MACHINES.—By the introduction of these machines, the labour of washing-day, formerly so severe, has been much abridged. Suitable machines for washing, wring-ing, and mangling may be purchased at comparatively low prices of any of the makers of what is termed "labour-saving machinery."

1307. TO WASH HOUSE LINEN.—To save your linen and your labour,—pour on half-a-pound of soda two quarts of boiling water, in an earthenware pan ; take half-a-pound of soap, shred fine ; put it into a saucepan with two quarts of cold water ; stand it on a fire till it boils ; and when perfectly dissolved and boiling, add it to the former. Mix it well, and let it stand till cold, when it will have the appearance of a strong jelly. Let your linen be soaked in water, the seams and any other soiled part rubbed well with soap the night before. Get your copper ready, and add to the water about a pint basin full of the above soap jelly ; when *lukewarm* put in your linen, and allow it to boil for twenty minutes. Rinse it in the usual way, and that is all which is necessary to get it clean, and to keep it in good colour. Housekeepers will find the above recipe invaluable.

1308. TO WASH MUSLINS AND CHINTZES.—Soap may be almost dispensed with in getting up these articles, which may be treated in the Oriental manner ; that is, to wash them in plain water, and then boil them in rice water ; after which chintzes should be calendered, an operation much more satisfactory than ironing.

1309. TO WASH FLANNELS.—These should always be washed with a lather of white soap, and in hot but not boiling water ; do not use soda, as it changes the colour. They should be washed and dried very quickly to prevent shrinking. In washing squeeze and knead them, but *do not rub* them.

1309a. TO SHRINK FLANNELS.—Before they are made up they should be well soaked, first in cold, then in hot water.

1310. TO WASH BLANKETS.— First shake them well and soak for a quarter of an hour in warm soap lather in which a small lump of ammonia has been dissolved, then wash in the same way as flannels, afterwards rinsing well in several waters, the last of which should be nearly cold. They should be dried in the open air, being taken down occasionally and well shaken to raise the nap.

1311. TO WASH BED FURNI-TURE, &c.— Before putting into the water, see that you shake off as much dust as possible, or you will greatly increase your labour. Use no soda, or pearlash, or the articles will lose their colour. Use soft water, not hot, but warm : have plenty of it. Rub with mottled soap. On wringing out the second liquor, dip each piece into cold hard water for finishing. Shake out well, and dry quickly. If starch is desired, it may be stirred into the rinsing water.

1312. TO WASH A WHITE LACE VEIL.— Put the veil into a strong lather of white soap and very clear water, and let it simmer slowly for a quarter of an hour ; take it out and squeeze it well, but be sure not to rub it : rinse it twice in cold water, the second time with a drop or two of liquid blue. Have ready some very clear weak gum arabic water, or some thin starch, or rice water ; pass the veil through it, and clear it by clapping ; then stretch it out evenly, and pin it to dry on a linen cloth, making the edge as straight as possible, opening out all the scallops, and fastening each with pins. When dry, lay a piece of thin muslin smoothly over it, and iron it on the wrong side.

1313. TO WASH CHINA CRAPE SCARVES, &c.— If the fabric be good, these articles of dress can be washed as frequently as may be required, and no diminution of their beauty will be discoverable, even when the various shades of green have been employed among other colours in the patterns. In cleaning them, make a strong lather in boiling water ; suffer it to cool ; when cold or nearly so, wash the scarf quickly and thoroughly, dip it immediately in cold hard water in which a little salt has been thrown (to preserve the colours), rinse, squeeze, and hang it out to dry in the open air ; pin it at its extreme edge to the line, so that it may not in any part be folded together ; the more rapidly it dries the clearer it will be.

1314. TO RENDER LINEN, &c. INCOMBUSTIBLE.— All linen, cotton, muslins, &c., &c., when dipped in a solution of tungstate of soda or common alum, will become incombustible. A little alum should therefore be added to the rinsing water, especially for children's clothes, and curtains.

1315. CARE OF WASHING TUBS. —If made of wood those should have a little water left in them to prevent shrinking when not in use. Zinc tube should be well dried and turned upside down.

1316. GUM ARABIC STARCH.— Procure two ounces of fine white gum arabic and pound it to powder. Next put it into a pitcher, and pour on it a pint or more of boiling water, according to the degree of strength you desire, and then, having covered it, let it set all night. In the morning, pour it carefully from the dregs into a clean bottle, cork it, and keep it for use. A tablespoonful of gum water stirred into a pint of starch that has been made in the usual manner will give to lawns (either white or printed) a look of newness to which nothing else can restore them after washing. It is also good (much diluted) for thin white muslin.

1317. LAVENDER WATER.— Essence of musk, four drachms ; essence of ambergris, four drachms ; oil of cinnamon, ten drops ; English lavender, six drachms ; oil of geranium, two drachms : spirit of wine, twenty ounces. To be all mixed together.

1318. LAVENDER SCENT BAG.—Take of lavender flowers, free from stalk, half-a-pound ; dried thyme and mint, of each half-an-ounce ; ground cloves and caraways, of each a quarter of an ounce ; common salt, dried, one ounce ; mix the whole well together, and put the product into silk or cambric bags. In this way it will perfume the drawers and linen very nicely.

1319. PERFUME FOR CLOTHES. —A very pleasant perfume, and also preventive against moths, may be made of the following ingredients : Take of cloves, caraway seeds, nutmeg, mace, cinnamon, and Tonquin beans, one ounce each ; then add as much Florentine orris root as will equal the other ingredients put together. Grind the whole well to powder ; and then put it in little bags among your clothes, &c.

1320. HONEY WATER.—Rectified spirit, eight ounces ; oil of cloves, oil of bergamot, oil of lavender, of each half-a-drachm ; musk, three grains ; yellow sanders shavings, four drachms. Let it stand for eight days, then add two ounces each of orange-flower water and rose water.

1321. HONEY SOAP.—Cut thin two pounds of yellow soap into a double saucepan, occasionally stirring it till it is melted, which will be in a few minutes if the water is kept boiling around it, then add a quarter of a pound of palm oil, a quarter of a pound of honey, threepennyworth of true oil of cinnamon ; let all boil together another six or eight minutes ; pour out and let it stand till next day, it is then fit for immediate use.

1322. A GOOD TOILET SOAP.— Palm-oil soap and olive-oil soap, one part of each ; curd soap, three parts. Melt them together and then scent With oil of verbena, ginger-grass, or rose geranium.

1323. TO WHITEN THE HANDS. —Take a wine-glassful of Eau-de-Cologne, and another of lemon juice ; then scrape two cakes of brown Windsor soap to a powder, and mix well in a mould. When hard, it will be an excellent soap for whitening the hands.

1324. STAINS ON THE HANDS may be removed by washing them in a small quantity of oil of vitriol and cold water without soap. Salts of lemon is also efficacious in removing ink-stains from the hands as well as from linen.

1325. TO WHITEN THE NAILS. —Diluted sulphuric acid, two drachms ; tincture of myrrh, one drachm ; spring water, four ounces : mix. First cleanse with white soap, and then dip the fingers into the mixture. A delicate hand is one of the chief points of beauty, and these applications are really effective.

1326. WHEN TO PARE THE NAILS.—The old formula was as follows—

Cut them on Monday, cut them for health.
Cut them on Tuesday, cut them for wealth.
Cut them on Wednesday, cut for a letter.
Cut them on Thursday, for something better.
Cut them on Friday, you cut for a wife.
Cut them on Saturday, cut for long life.
Cut them on Sunday, you cut them for evil,
For all of that week you'll be ruled by the devil

(or, according to another version)

A man had better ne'er be born
Than have his nails on Sunday shorn.

Josh Billings said, "Yu kant alwus tell a gentleman by hiz clothes, but yu kan by his finger nails."

1327. COLD CREAM.—i. Oil of almonds, one pound ; white wax, four ounces. Melt together gently in an earthen vessel, and when nearly cold stir in gradually twelve ounces of rose-water.— ii. White wax and spermaceti, of each half-an-ounce ; oil of almonds, four ounces ; orange-flower water, two ounces. Mix as directed for No. 1.

1328. TO SOFTEN THE SKIN and Improve the Complexion.—If flowers of sulphur be mixed in a little milk, and after standing an hour or two the milk (without disturbing the sulphur) be rubbed into the skin, it will keep it soft and make the complexion clear. It is to be used before washing. The mixture, it must be borne in mind, will not keep. A little should be prepared over night with evening milk, and used the next morning, but not afterwards. About a wine-glassful made for each occasion will suffice.

1329. WASH FOR THE TEETH.—Dissolve two ounces of borax in three pints of water ; before quite cold, add thereto one teaspoonful of tincture of myrrh, and one tablespoonful of spirits of camphor : bottle the mixture for use. One wine-glassful of the solution, added to half-a-pint of tepid water, is sufficient for each application. This solution, applied daily, preserves and beautifies the teeth, removes tartar, produces a pearl-like whiteness, arrests decay, and induces a healthy action in the gums.

1330. CAMPHORATED DENTIFRICE.—Prepared chalk, one pound ; camphor, one or two drachms. The camphor must be finely powdered, moisten it with a little spirit of wine, and then intimately mix it with the chalk.

1331. MYRRH DENTIFRICE.—Mix powdered cuttlefish, one pound ; powdered myrrh, two ounces.

1332. QUININE TOOTH POWDER.—Rose pink, two drachms ; precipitated chalk, twelve drachms ; carbonate of magnesia, one drachm ; quinine (sulphate), six grains. All to be well mixed together.

1333. THE CARE OF TOOTH-BRUSHES.—Do not shut them up closely in a brush tray, or dressing-bag, as it will cause the bristles to acquire an unpleasant smell. After use shake the water out and place them so that they may drain.

1334. EYELASHES.—To increase the length and strength of the eyelashes, simply clip the ends with a pair of scissors about once a month. In eastern countries mothers perform the operation on their children, both male and female, when they are mere infants, watching the opportunity whilst they sleep.

1335. HAIR DYE.—To make good hair dye some lime must be first obtained, and reduced to powder by throwing a little water upon it. The lime must then be mixed with litharge in the proportion of three parts of lime to one of litharge. This mixture, when sifted through a fine hair sieve, forms the most effectual hair dye that has yet been discovered.

1336. How to use the Dye.—Put a quantity of the mixture in a saucer, pour boiling water upon it, and mix it up with a knife like thick mustard ; having cleansed the hair thoroughly from grease divide it into thin layers with a comb, and plaster the mixture thickly into the layers to the roots, and all over the hair. When it is completely covered with it, lay over it a covering of damp blue or brown paper, then bind over it, closely, a handkerchief, then put on a night-cap, over all, and go to bed ; in the morning brush out the powder, wash thoroughly with soap and warm water, then dry, curl, oil, &c. Hair thus treated will be dyed a beautiful black. Should brown be desired use milk instead of water with mixture.

1337. Care necessary in Application of Hair Dye.—The efficacy of hair dyes depends as much upon their proper application as upon their chemical composition. If not evenly and patiently applied, they give rise to a mottled and dirty condition of the hair. A lady, for instance, attempted to use the lime and litharge dye, and was horrified on the following morning to find her hair spotted red and black, almost like the skin of a leopard. The mixture had not been properly applied.

1338. TO TEST HAIR DYE.— To try the effect of hair dye upon hair of any colour, cut off a lock and apply the dye thoroughly as directed above. This will be a guarantee of success, or will at least guard against failure.

1339. EXCELLENT HAIR WASH.—Take one ounce of borax, half-an-ounce of camphor ; powder these ingredients fine, and dissolve them in one quart of boiling water ; when cool, the solution will be ready for use ; damp the hair frequently. This wash effectually cleanses, beautifies, and strengthens the hair, preserves the colour, and prevents early baldness. The camphor will form into lumps after being dissolved, but the water will be sufficiently impregnated.

1340. BAY RUM is an American wash for the head, and is very cooling and pleasant to use, promoting the growth of the hair. It is made by distilling rum from the leaves of the bayberry tree ; sometimes called the wax myrtle.

1341. POMADE AGAINST BALDNESS.—Beef marrow, soaked in several waters, melted and strained, half-a-pound ; tincture of cantharides (made by soaking for a week one drachm of powdered cantharides in one ounce of proof spirit), one ounce ; oil of bergamot, twelve drops.

1342. ERASMUS WILSON'S LOTION AGAINST BALDNESS.—Eau-de-Cologne, two ounces ; tincture of cantharides, two drachms ; oil of lavender or rosemary, of either ten drops. These applications must be used once or twice a day for a considerable time ; but if the scalp become sore, they must be discontinued for a time, or used at longer intervals.

1343. BANDOLINE OR FIXATURE.

i. Mucilage of clean picked Irish moss, made by boiling a quarter of an ounce of the moss in one quart of water, until sufficiently thick ; add a teaspoonful or so of rectified spirit to prevent its being mildewed. The quantity of spirit varies according to the time it requires to be kept.

ii. Gum tragacanth, one drachm and a half ; water, half-a-pint ; proof spirit (made by mixing equal parts of rectified spirit and water), three ounces ; otto of roses, ten drops ; soak for twenty-four hours and strain. Bergamot may be substituted for the otto of roses.

1344. COSMETIC.—For *black*, take five parts of lard, two parts of wax, melt and stir in finely powdered ivory black two parts. Then pour into small moulds. For *brown*, the same as the preceding, but using finely powdered umber, or terra di Siena. For *white*, no colouring matter is used.

1345. ROSE HAIR OIL.—Olive oil, one pint ; otto of roses, five to sixteen drops. Essence of bergamot, being much cheaper, is commonly used instead of the more expensive otto of roses. The oil can be coloured red before scenting, by steeping in it one drachm of alkanet root, with a gentle heat, until the desired tint is produced.

1346. TO MAKE POMATUMS.— The lard, fat, suet, or marrow used must be carefully prepared by being melted with as gentle a heat as possible, skimmed, strained, and cleared from the dregs which are deposited on standing.

i. **Ordinary Pomatum.—**Mutton suet, prepared as above, one pound ; lard, three pounds ; carefully melted together, and stirred constantly as it cools, two ounces of bergamot being added.

ii. **Hard Pomatum.—**Lard and mutton suet carefully prepared, of each one pound ; white wax, four ounces ; essence of bergamot, one ounce.

1347. CASTOR OIL POMADE.—
Castor oil, four ounces ; prepared lard, two ounces ; white wax, two drachms ; bergamot, two drachms ; oil of lavender, twenty drops. Melt the fat together, and on cooling add the scents, and stir till cold.

1348. SUPERFLUOUS HAIR.—
Any remedy is doubtful ; many of those commonly used are dangerous. The safest plan is as follows :—The hairs should be perseveringly plucked up by the roots, and the skin, having been washed twice a day with warm soft water, without soap, should be treated with the following wash, commonly called MILK OF ROSES :—Beat four ounces of sweet almonds in a mortar, and add half-an-ounce of white sugar during the process ; reduce the whole to a paste by pounding ; then add, in small quantities at a time, eight ounces of rose water. The emulsion thus formed should be strained through a fine cloth, and the residue again pounded, while the strained fluid should be bottled in a large stoppered phial. To the pasty mass in the mortar add half-an-ounce of sugar, and eight ounces of rose water, and strain again. This process must be repeated three times. To the thirty-two ounces of fluid, add twenty grains of the bichloride of mercury, dissolved in two ounces of alcohol, and shake the mixture for five minutes. The fluid should be applied with a towel, immediately after washing, and the skin gently rubbed with a dry cloth, till *perfectly* dry. Wilson, in his work on *Healthy Skin*, writes as follows :—"Substances are sold by the perfumers called depilatories, which are represented as having the power of removing hair. But the hair is not destroyed by these means, the root and that part of the shaft implanted within the skin still remain, and are ready to shoot up with increased vigour as soon as the depilatory is withdrawn. The effect of the depilatory is the same,

in this respect, as that of a razor, and the latter is, unquestionably, the better remedy. It must also be remembered that depilatories are violent irritants, and require to be used with the utmost caution."

1349. TO CLEAN HAIR BRUSHES.—
As hot water and soap very soon soften the bristles, and rubbing completes their destruction, use soda, dissolved in cold water, instead ; soda having an affinity for grease, cleanses the brush with little friction. Do not set them near the fire, nor in the sun, to dry, but after shaking well, set them on the point of the handle in a shady place.

1350. TO CLEAN SPONGE.—
Take two or three ounces of carbonate of soda and dissolve it in a couple of pints of water. After having soaked the sponge in this for a day, wash it thoroughly in clean water ; after which immerse it for a couple of hours in three pints of water, and a wineglassful of muriatic acid. Then rinse it in cold water and let it dry. Sponges after being used should always if possible be dried in the sun.

1351. THE YOUNG LADY'S TOILET REQUISITES.

The Enchanted Mirror—*Self-Knowledge.*
This curious glass will bring your faults to light,
And make your virtues shine both strong and bright.

Wash to Smooth Wrinkles—*Contentment.*
A daily portion of this essence use,
'Twill smooth the brow, and tranquillity infuse.

Fine Lipsalve—*Truth.*
Use daily for your lips this precious dye,
They'll redden, and breathe sweet melody.

Mixture for the Voice—*Prayer.*
At morning, noon, and night this mixture take.
Your tones, improved, will richer music make.

Best Eye-water—*Compassion.*
These drops will add great lustre to the eye ;
When more you need, the poor will you
supply.

Solution to prevent Eruptions—*Wisdom.*
It calms the temper, beautifies the face,
And gives to woman dignity and grace.

Matchless Pair of Ear-rings—*Attention
and Obedience.*
With these clear drops appended to the ear,
Attentive lessons you will gladly hear.

Indispensible Pair of Bracelets—*Neatness
and Industry.*
Clasp them on carefully each day you live,
To good designs they efficacy give.

An Elastic Girdle—*Patience.*
The more you use the brighter it will grow,
Though its least merit is external show.

Ring of Tried Gold—*Principle.*
Yield not this golden bracelet while you live,
'Twill sin restrain, and peace of conscience
give.

Necklace of Purest Pearl—*Resignation.*
This ornament embellishes the lair.
And teaches all the ills of life to bear.

Diamond Breast-pin—*Love.*
Adorn your bosom with this precious pin,
It shines without, and warms the heart
within.

A Graceful Bandeau—*Politeness.*
The forehead neatly circled with this band.
Will admiration and respect command.

A Precious Diadem—*Piety.*
Whoe'er this precious diadem shall own.
Secures herself an everlasting crown.

Universal Beautifier—*Good Temper.*
With this choice liquid gently touch the
mouth,
It spreads o'er all the face the charms of
youth.

1352. VASELINE.

This indispensable household
requisite is a product of petroleum,
from which it is obtained by an
elaborate system of filtration,
without the addition or aid of any
chemical whatever. The substance
thus produced, to which the name
of "Vaseline" has been given, is in
the form of a lemon-coloured jelly,
completely devoid of either smell or
taste, and of exquisite softness and
smoothness to the touch. It may be
procured from any chemist.

1353. VASELINE FOR THE TOILET.

—The toilet soap and tar
soap made from vaseline are superior
in emollient and healing properties, to
similar preparations from glycerine.
For the hair an excellent hair tonic
and pomade are supplied, which have
the effect not only of strengthening,
but of promoting its growth. For the
complexion, vaseline cold cream should
be used, and for the lips, when sore and
chapped by cold winds or any other
cause, vaseline camphor ice.

1354. VASELINE FOR MEDICINAL USE.

—The pure jelly itself,
without any addition, is an invaluable
family remedy for burns, chilblains,
chapped hands, and skin roughened
by exposure to wind and water in
cold weather ; as well as for sunburns,
wounds, sprains, and all diseases of
the skin ; for inflamed eyelids, and
for preventing pitting in small-pox,
when used externally as an ointment.
When taken internally, in doses of
half-a-teaspoonful, or in smaller quantities, it forms a cure for diseases of
the throat, chest, and stomach, and
gives speedy relief in cases of diphtheria, croup, &c. For convenience in
using it, a confection is prepared from
it for complaints of the throat and
lungs.

1355. VASELINE FOR THE HOUSEHOLD.

—As time progresses
there can be no doubt that this valuable preparation will be turned to
good account for many domestic uses.
It has already been found an excellent
anticorrosive, being an efficient protection against rust, when smeared
over guns, bicycles, arms, knives, tools,
and steel goods of any kind in general
household use. An excellent boot and
shoe paste is prepared from it, which

renders boots and shoes absolutely waterproof, and over which any ordinary blacking may be used to produce a polish.

1356. VASELINE IN THE STABLE.—When mixed with graphite, vaseline affords a valuable lubricant for application to the axles of light and heavy carriages of every description and for all bearings in machinery of any kind, especially where great speed is required. A paste is also prepared from it which renders leather harness soft, pliable, impervious to wet, and free from any tendency to crack, thus increasing its durability. Another preparation is found most useful for the cure of injuries and diseases of cattle and domestic animals. This, which is supplied under the name of Veterinary Vaseline, has been found to promote the growth of the hair, unchanged in colour, in the case of broken knees. Its use will also improve the condition of the coat on horses, and will keep off the flies, and cure the mange, and all skin disease commonly met with in the stable, including injuries to the frogs, hoofs, and fetlocks,

1357. CLEANLINESS.

Nothing can be more agreeable to the senses, more to the honour of the inhabitants, or conducive to their health, than a clean town ; nor does anything impress a stranger sooner with a disrespectful idea of any people than its opposite. It were well if the lower classes of the inhabitants of Great Britain would imitate their neighbours the Dutch in their assiduity in cleansing their streets, houses, &c. Water, indeed, is easily obtained in Holland ; but the situation of most towns of Great Britain is more favourable to cleanliness.

It is well known that infectious diseases are caused by tainted air. Everything, therefore, which tends to pollute the air or spread the infection ought with the utmost care to be avoided. For this reason, in great towns, no filth of any kind should be permitted to lie upon the streets. We are sorry to say that the importance of general cleanliness in this respect does by no means seem to be sufficiently understood.

One common cause of putrid and malignant fevers is the want of cleanliness. Those fevers commonly begin among the inhabitants of close, dirty houses, who breathe bad air, take little exercise, eat unwholesome food, and wear dirty clothes. There infection is generally hatched, which spreads far and wide, to the destruction of many. Hence cleanliness may be considered as an object of public attention. It is not sufficient that I be clean myself, while the want of it in my neighbour affects my health as well as his own.

If dirty people cannot be removed as a common nuisance, they ought at least to be avoided as infectious. All who regard their health should keep at a safe distance, even from their habitations.

In hospitals and other places where great numbers of sick people are kept, cleanliness ought most religiously to be observed. The very smell in such places is often sufficient to make one sick. It is easy to imagine what effect that is likely to have upon the diseased. A person in health has a greater chance to become sick than a sick person has to get well, in a hospital or infirmary where cleanliness is neglected.

1358. PERSONAL CLEANLINESS.

The want of cleanliness is a fault which admits of no excuse. Where water can be had for nothing, it is surely in the power of every person to be clean.

Frequent washing not only removes the filth which adheres to the skin, but likewise promotes the perspiration, braces the body, and enlivens the spirits. Even washing the feet tends greatly to preserve health. The persspiration and dirt with which these parts are frequently covered cannot fail to obstruct their pores. This piece of cleanliness would often prevent colds and fevers. Were people to bathe their feet and hands in warm water at night, after being exposed to cold or wet through the day, they would seldom experience any of the effects from these causes which often prove fatal.

Change of apparel greatly promotes the secretion from the skin, so necessary to health. When that matter which ought to be carried off by perspiration is either retained in the body or re-absorbed in dirty clothes, it is apt to occasion fevers and other diseases.

Most diseases of the skin proceed from want of cleanliness. These indeed may be caught by infection, but they will seldom continue long where cleanliness prevails. To the same cause must we impute the various kinds of vermin that infest the human body, houses, &c. These may generally be banished by cleanliness alone. Perhaps the intention of Nature, in permitting such vermin to annoy mankind, is to induce them to the practice of this virtue.

The brutes themselves set us an example of cleanliness. Most of them seem uneasy, and thrive ill, if they be not kept clean. A horse that is kept thoroughly clean will thrive better on a smaller quantity of food than with a greater where cleanliness is neglected. Even our own feelings are a sufficient proof of the necessity of cleanliness. How refreshed, how cheerful and agreeable does one feel on being washed and dressed ; especially when these have been long neglected.

Superior cleanliness sooner attracts our regard than even finery itself, and often gains esteem where the other fails.

1359. **Mahomedan Cleanliness.** It is remarkable that in most eastern countries, cleanliness makes a great part of their religion. The Mahomedan, as well as the Jewish religion, enjoins various bathings, washings, and purifications. No doubt these were designed to represent inward purity ; but they are at the same time calculated for the preservation of health. However whimsical these washings may appear to some, few things would seem more to prevent diseases than a proper attention to many of them. Were every person, for example, after handling a dead body, visiting the sick, &c., to wash before he went into company or sat down to meat, he would run less hazard either of catching the infection himself or communicating it to others.

1360. **The Doctor's Bet.**—A certain doctor at a dinner party placed his hand on the table. One of the guests said to another, "What a dirty hand Dr. —— has." The doctor, who had overheard the remark, said, "I'll bet you a bottle of wine there is a dirtier in company." "Done," said the other ; upon which the doctor produced his other hand, winning the bet.

1361. THE BATH.

If to preserve health be to save medical expenses, without even reckoning upon time and comfort, there is no part of the household arrangement so important as convenience for personal ablution. Most modern dwelling-houses are now fitted with pipes conveying both cold and hot water to the various floors, and few of them are without a fitted bath-room ; but in houses not so furnished, though temporary or zinc baths may be extremely useful upon pressing occasions, it will be found to be finally as cheap, and much more readily convenient, to have a permanent bath constructed, which may be done in any dwelling-house of moderate size, without interfering with other general purposes. Many baths are now procurable at very reasonable prices furnished with apparatus for heating water in a few minutes. Some of these however, fitted with burners for coal-gas and atmospheric air combined, give out poisonous fumes, and should therefore have a flue to carry them out from the bath-room.

1361a. VAPOUR BATHS may be contrived by putting boiling water in a pan, and placing a cane-bottom chair in the pan, the patient sitting upon it, enveloped from head to foot in a blanket covering the bath. Sulphur, spirit, medicinal, herbal, and other baths may be obtained in the same manner. They should not be taken except under medical advice. Another equally easy method of procuring a vapour bath at home is to attach one end of a piece of flexible tubing to the spout of the kettle on the fire, and to introduce the other end below the chair, on which the person who requires the bath is sitting enveloped in a blanket as described above.

1362. EXERCISE.—Exercise in the open air is of the first importance to the human frame, yet how many are in a manner deprived of it by their own want of management of their time ! Females with slender means are for the most part destined to indoor occupations, and have but little time allotted them for taking the air, and that little time is generally sadly encroached upon by the ceremony of dressing to go out. It may appear a simple suggestion, but experience only will show how much time might be redeemed by habits of regularity : such as putting the shawls, cloaks, gloves, shoes, &c., &c., or whatever is intended to be worn, in readiness, instead of having to search one drawer, then another, for possibly a glove or collar—wait for shoes being cleaned, &c. Whereas, if all were in readiness, the preparations might be accomplished in a few minutes, the walk not being curtailed by unnecessary delays.

1363. Three Points to be Observed in the manner of taking exercise are :—

i. The kind of exercise.
ii. The proper time for exercise.
iii. The duration of it.

With respect to the kinds of exercise the various species of it may be divided into Active and Passive.

1364. Active Exercises are more beneficial to youth, to the middle-aged, to the robust in general, and particularly to the corpulent and the plethoric. Among these which admit of being considerably diversified, may be enumerated walking, running, leaping, swimming, riding, cycling, fencing, different sorts of athletic games, &c.

1365. Passive Exercises which comprise riding in a carriage, sailing, friction, swinging, &c., are better calculated for children ; old, thin, and emaciated persons of a delicate and debilitated constitution ; and particularly for the asthmatic and consumptive.

1366. The Time at which exercise should be taken and the duration of exercise depend on such a variety of concurrent circumstances, that they cannot be regulated by any general rules, and must therefore be decided from observations made on the effects of air, food, &c., and the state of the mind and body, bearing in mind the following—

1367. Hints on Exercise.

i. That Exercise is to be preferred which, with a view to brace and strengthen the body, we are most accustomed to. Any unusual one may be attended with a contrary effect.

ii. Exercise should be begun and finished gradually, never abruptly.

iii. Exercise in the open air has many advantages over that used within doors.

iv. To continue exercise until a profuse perspiration or a great degree of weariness takes place, is far from being wholesome.

v. In the forenoon when the stomach is not too much distended, muscular motion is both agreeable and healthful ; it strengthens digestion, and a good appetite after it is a proof that it has not been carried to excess.

vi. It is not advisable to take violent exercise immediately before a meal, as digestion might thereby be retarded.

vii. Do not sit down to a substantial dinner or supper immediately on returning from a fatiguing walk, at the time when the blood is heated, and the body in a state of perspiration from previous exertion, as the worst consequences may arise, especially when the meal is commenced with cooling dishes, salad, or a glass of cold drink.

viii. Exercise is always hurtful immediately after meals, from its impeding digestion, by propelling those fluids too much towards the surface of the body which are designed for the solution of the food in the stomach.

1368. Walking.—To walk gracefully, the body must be erect, but not stiff, and the head held up in such a posture that the eyes are directed forward. The tendency of untaught walkers is to look towards the ground near the feet ; and some persons appear always as if admiring their shoe-laces. The eyes should not thus be cast downward, neither should the chest bend forward to throw out the back, making what are termed round shoulders : on the contrary, the body should be held erect, as if the person to whom it belongs were not afraid to look the world in the face, and the chest by all means be allowed to expand. At the same time, everything like strutting or pomposity must be carefully avoided. An easy, firm, and erect posture is alone desirable. In walking, it is necessary to bear in mind that the locomotion is to be performed entirely by the legs. Awkward persons rock from side to side,

helping forward each leg alternately by advancing the haunches. This is not only ungraceful but fatiguing. Let the legs alone advance, bearing up the body.

1369. TO AVOID CATCHING COLD.—Accustom yourself to the use of sponging with cold water every morning on first getting out of bed. It should be followed by a good deal of rubbing with a wet towel. It has considerable effect in giving tone to the skin, and maintaining a proper action in it, and thus proves a safeguard to the injurious influence of cold and sudden changes of temperature. Sir Astley Cooper said, "The methods by which I have preserved my own health are—temperance, early rising, and sponging the body every morning with cold water, immediately after getting out of bed,—a practice which I have adopted for thirty years without ever catching cold."

1370. UTILITY OF SINGING.—It has been asserted, and we believe with some truth, that singing is a corrective of the too common tendency to pulmonic complaints. Dr. Rush, an eminent physician, observes on this subject :—"The Germans are seldom afflicted with consumption ; and this, I believe, is in part occasioned by the strength which their lungs acquire by exercising them in vocal music, for this constitutes an essential branch of their education. The music master of an academy has furnished me with a remark still more in favour of this opinion. He informed me that he had known several instances of persons who were strongly disposed to consumption, who were restored to health by the exercise of their lungs in singing."

1371. TO TEST THE STATE OF THE LUNGS.—Persons desirous of ascertaining the true state of their lungs should draw in as much breath as they conveniently can ; they are then to count as far as they are able, in a slow and audible voice, without drawing in more breath. The number of seconds they can continue counting must be carefully observed ; in cases of consumption the time does not exceed ten, and is frequently less than six seconds ; in pleurisy and pneumonia it ranges from nine to four seconds. When the lungs are in a sound condition, the time will range as high as from twenty to thirty-five seconds.

1372. SLEEPLESSNESS.

How to get sleep is to many persons a matter of high importance. Nervous persons who are troubled with wakefulness and excitability usually have a strong tendency of blood on the brain, with cold extremities. The pressure of the blood on the brain keeps it in a stimulated or wakeful state, and the pulsations in the head are often painful. Let such rise and chafe the body and extremities with a brush or towel, or rub smartly with the hands, to promote circulation and withdraw the excessive amount of blood from the brain, and they will fall asleep in a few moments. A cold bath, or a sponge bath and rubbing, or a good run, or a rapid walk in the open air, or going up and down stairs a few times just before retiring, will aid in equalizing circulation and promoting sleep. These rules are simple and easy of application in all cases. Many people derive benefit from taking a tumbler of hot milk on getting into bed.

1373. VENTILATING BED-ROOMS.—A sheet of finely perforated zinc, substituted for a pane of glass in one of the upper squares of a chamber window, is the cheapest and best form of ventilator ; there should not be a bedroom without it.

1374. A SIMPLE METHOD OF VENTILATION.—Get a piece of deal two inches wide and one inch thick, and exactly as long as the width of the sashes of the window in

which it is to be used. Raise the lower sash—drop in the piece of wood, so that it rests on the bottom part of the window frame, the ends being within the stops on either side, and then close the sash upon it. If properly planed up, no draught can enter between the wood and the bottom of the sash ; but the air can enter the room in an upward direction, through the opening between the top of the lower sash and the bottom of the upper sash, any direct draught into the interior of the room being prevented by the position of the lower sash.

1375. NIGHT CLOTHES.—The perfection of dress, for day or night, where warmth is the purpose, is that which confines around the body sufficient of its own warmth, while it allows escape to the exhalations of the skin. Flannel best fulfils these conditions. Where the body is allowed to bathe protractedly in its own vapours we must expect an unhealthy effect upon the skin. Where there is too little allowance for ventilation, insensible perspiration is checked, and something analogous to fever supervenes ; foul tongue, ill taste, and lack of morning appetite betray the evil.

1376. DAMP SHEETS.—Few things are attended with more serious consequences than sleeping in damp linen. Persons are frequently assured that the sheets have been at a fire for many hours, but the question is what sort of fire, and whether they have been turned, so that every part has been exposed to the fire. The fear of creasing the linen, we know, prevents many from unfolding it, so as to be what we consider sufficiently aired ; but health is of more importance than appearances. With gentleness there need be no fear of want of neatness.

1377. EARLY RISING.—Dr. Wilson Philip in his *Treatise on Indigestion* says :—"Although it is of consequence to the debilitated to go early to bed, there are few things more

hurtful to them than remaining in it too long. Getting up an hour or two earlier often gives a degree of vigour which nothing else can procure. For those who are not much debilitated, and sleep well, the best rule is to get out of bed soon after waking in the morning. This at first may appear too early, for the debilitated require more sleep than the healthy ; but rising early will gradually prolong the sleep on the succeeding night, till the quantity the patient enjoys is equal to his demand for it. Lying late is not only hurtful, by the relaxation it occasions, but also by occupying that part of the day at which exercise is most beneficial."

1378. APPETITE.—This is frequently lost through excessive use of stimulants, food taken too hot, sedentary occupation, costiveness, liver disorder, and want of change of air. The first endeavour should be to ascertain and remove the cause. Change of diet and change of air will frequently be found more beneficial than medicines.

1379. HANDEL'S APPETITE.—The great Handel was apparently blessed with a fairly good appetite, for, intending one day to dine at a certain inn, he ordered a dinner sufficient for three ordinary people. Returning at the time he had appointed for dinner, he was surprised to find that it was not served up, and complained to the landlord. The latter replied, "It shall come up, sir, directly the company arrive." "Den pring up der tinner *brestissimo*," replied Handel ; "*I am der gompany !*"

1380. TEMPERANCE.—"If," observes a writer, "men lived uniformly in a healthy climate, were possessed of strong and vigorous frames, were descended from healthy parents, were educated in a hardy and active manner, were possessed of excellent natural dispositions, were placed in comfortable situations in life, were engaged only in healthy occupations, were happily connected in marriage, and kept their passions in due subjection, there would be little occasion for medical rules."

All this is very excellent and desirable ; but, unfortunately for mankind, unattainable. Man must be something more than man to be able to connect the different links of this harmonious chain—to consolidate this *summum bonum* of earthly felicity into one uninterrupted whole ; for, independent of all regularity or irregularity of diet, passions, and other sublunary circumstances, thousands are visited by diseases and precipitated into the grave, independent of accident, to whom no particular vice could attach, and with whom the appetite never overstepped the boundaries of temperance. Do we not hear almost daily of instances of men living near to and even upwards of a century ? We cannot account for this either ; because of such men we know but few who have lived otherwise than the world around them ; and we have known many who have lived in habitual intemperance for forty or fifty years, without interruption and with little apparent inconvenience.

The assertion has been made by those who have attained a great age (Parr, and Henry Jenkins, for instance), that they adopted no particular arts for the preservation of their health ; consequently, it might be inferred that the duration of life has no dependence on manners or customs, or the qualities of particular food. This, however, is an error of no common magnitude.

Peasants, labourers, and other hard-working people, more especially those whose occupations require them to be much in the open air, may be considered as following a regulated system of moderation ; and hence the higher degree of health which prevails among them and their families. Some also observe rules ; and those which it is said were recommended by Old Parr are remarkable for good sense ; namely, "Keep your head cool by temperance, your feet warm by exercise ; rise early, and go soon to bed ; and if you are inclined to get fat, keep your eyes open and your mouth shut,"—in other words sleep moderately and be abstemious in diet ;—excellent admonitions, more especially to those inclined to corpulency.

1381. John Brown and Temperance.

John Brown was a man without houses or lands,

But happy while making good use of his hands ;

He kept a good home by the sweat of his brow,

And when asked to drink would firmly say No !

John Brown had a wife who was fond of her home,

So John was unwilling to wander or roam ;

She could bake, she could make, she could trim, she could sew ;

And find time to teach her three boys to say No !

On John as a workman you could always depend,

Till one cold winter's night he met an old friend,

Who asked him to drink— it would keep out the snow ;

John refused, then consented, ashamed to say No !

John Brown had a home, but a change is now seen,

Tho' his wife did her best to keep the boys clean :

The savings are spent, the best chairs had to go,

John saw the sad change, but could not say No !

John Brown had a heart ; he saw his wife's tears ;

He thought of his home, the home of past years ;

He thought of his boys, so ill-clad in the snow,

He thought what they suffered through his not saying No !

John Brown took the pledge, and asked help from above,

That he still might provide for those he should love ;

He went back to his work, determined to show

That John Brown was a man when he learned to say No !

1382. Galen's Advice for a Regular Mode of Living.—Galen, who is said to have reached the great age of 140 years without having ever experienced disease, advises the readers of his *Treatise on Health* as follows :—"I beseech all persons who shall read this work not to degrade themselves to a level with the brutes, or the rabble, by gratifying their sloth, or by eating and drinking promiscuously whatever pleases their palates, or by indulging their appetites of every kind. But whether they understand physic or not, let them consult their reason, and observe what agrees and what does not agree with them, that, like wise men, they may adhere to the use of such things as conduce to their health, and forbear everything which, by their own experience, they find to do them hurt ; and let them be assured that, by a diligent observation and practice of this rule, they may enjoy a good share of health, and seldom stand in need of physic at physicians."

1383. YOUTHFUL IRREGULAR-ITIES.—Late hours, irregular habits and want of attention to diet, are common errors with most young men, and these gradually, but at first imperceptibly, undermine the health, and lay the foundation for various forms of disease in later life. It is a very difficult thing to make young persons comprehend this. They frequently sit up as late as twelve, one, or two o'clock, without experiencing any ill effects ; they go without a meal to-day, and to-morrow eat to repletion, with only temporary inconvenience. One night they will sleep three or four hours, and the next nine or ten ; or one night, in their eagerness to get away into some agreeable company, they will take no food at all, and the next, perhaps, will

eat a hearty supper, and go to bed upon it. These, with various other irregularities, are common to the majority of young men, and are, as just stated, the cause of much bad health in mature life. Indeed, nearly all the shattered constitutions with which too many are cursed, are the result of a disregard to the plainest precepts of health in early life.

1384. CORPULENCE.—The late Mr. William Banting, author of a *Letter on Corpulence*, gives the following excellent advice, with a dietary for use in cases of obesity (corpulence) :—

i. **Medicine.**—None, save a mining cordial, as a corrective.

ii. **Dietary.**

Breakfast.—Four or five ounces of beef, mutton, kidneys, broiled fish, bacon, or any kind of cold meat except pork, a large cup (or two) of tea without milk or sugar, a little biscuit, or dry toast.

Dinner.—Five or six ounces of any fish except salmon, any meat except pork, any vegetables except potatoes ; one ounce of dry toast ; fruit out of a pudding ; any kind of poultry or game, and two or three glasses of claret or sherry. Port, champagne, and beer forbidden.

Tea.—Two or three ounces of fruit ; a rusk or two, and a cup or two of tea, without milk or sugar.

Supper.—Three or four ounces of meat or fish as at dinner, with a glass or two of claret.

Nightcap (if required).—A glass or two of grog,—whisky, gin, or brandy,—without sugar ; or a glass or two of sherry. Mr. Banting adds : "Dietary is the principal point in the treatment of corpulence (also in rheumatic diseases, and even in incipient paralysis). If properly regulated, it becomes in a certain sense a medicine. It purifies the blood, strengthens the muscles and viscera, and sweetens life if it does not prolong it."

1385. WEIGHT OF MEN AND WOMEN.

The Weight of a Man, if in health, should be as follows :—

Height	ft.	in.	Weight	st.	lbs.
Height	5	1	Weight	8	8
„	5	2	„	9	0
„	5	3	„	9	7
„	5	4	„	9	10
„	5	5	„	10	2
„	5	6	„	10	3
„	5	7	„	10	6
„	5	8	„	11	1
„	5	9	„	11	7
„	5	10	„	12	1
„	5	11	„	12	6
„	6	0	„	12	10

The Weight of a Woman: —

Height	ft.	in.	Weight	st.	lbs.
Height	5	0	Weight	7	0
„	5	2	„	7	12
„	5	4	„	9	0
„	5	5	„	9	10
„	5	6	„	10	0
„	5	7	„	10	7
„	5	8	„	10	12
„	5	9	„	11	6

1386. DIET IN HOT WEATHEB.

In dry, sultry weather the heat ought to be counteracted by means of a cooling diet. To this purpose cucumbers, melons, and juicy fruits are subservient. We ought to give the preference to such alimentary substances as lead to contract the juices which are too much expanded by the heat, and this property is possessed by all acid food and drink. To this class belong all sorts of salad, lemons, oranges, pomegranates sliced and sprinkled with sugar, for the acid of this fruit is not so apt to derange the stomach as that of lemons ; also cherries and strawberries, curds turned with lemon acid or cream of tartar ; cream of tartar dissolved in water ; lemonade, and Rhenish or Moselle wine mixed with water.

1387. BEVERAGE FOR HOT WEATHER.—The yolk of eggs beaten

up, lump sugar (to taste), Rhenish wine or not, citric acid powdered, or tartaric acid (small quantity, exact quantity soon found) ; one or two drops of essence of lemon on a lump of sugar, to make it mix readily with the water ; one quart of water. This is really an excellent, agreeable, and, without the wine, an inexpensive beverage.

1388. DAMP SITUATIONS, Remedy for.—People who live in damp localities, particularly near undrained land, are apt to think that there is no help for them save in removal. They are mistaken. Successful experiments have shown that it is possible to materially improve the atmosphere in such neighbourhoods by the planting of the laurel and the sunflower. The laurel gives off an abundance of ozone, whilst the sunflower is potent in destroying the malarial condition. These two, if planted on the most restricted scale in a garden or any ground close to the house, will be found to speedily increase the dryness and salubrity of the atmosphere.

1389. CHARCOAL as a Disinfectant.—The great efficacy of wood and animal charcoal in absorbing effluvia, and the greater number of gases and vapours, has long been known. Charcoal powder has also, during many centuries, been advantageously employed as a filter for putrid water, the object in view being to deprive the water of numerous organic impurities diffused through it, which exert injurious effects on the animal economy. The best form of charcoal, however, for filters is the animal charcoal. Charcoal removes the alkaloids, resins, metallic salts, &c. It does not however retain its powers for any great length of time, and therefore the charcoal of a filter requires renewing occasionally. Charcoal not only absorbs effluvia and gaseous bodies, but especially, when in contact with atmospheric air, oxidizes

and destroys many of the easily alterable ones, by resolving them into the simplest combinations they are capable of forming, which are chiefly water and carbonic acid. It is on this oxidizing property of charcoal, as well as on its absorbent power, that its efficacy as a deodorising and disinfecting agent chiefly depends.

1390. CHARCOAL AS AN ANTISEPTIC.—Charcoal is an antiseptic, that is to say, a substance which arrests the decay and decomposition of animal substances. Meat, poultry, game or fish, &c. may be preserved for a longer period in hot weather by sprinkling it with powdered charcoal, which should be washed off in clean cold water before the article is cooked.

1391. CHARCOAL VENTILATORS.—It has been proposed to employ charcoal ventilators, consisting of a thin layer of charcoal enclosed between two thin sheets of wire gauze, to purify the foul air which is apt to accumulate in water-closets, in the close wards of hospitals, and in the impure atmospheres of many of the back courts and mews-lanes of large cities, all the impurities being absorbed and retained by the charcoal, while a current of pure air alone is admitted into the neighbouring apartments. In this way pure air may be obtained from exceedingly impure sources. The proper amount of air required by houses in such situations might be admitted through sheets of wire gauze or coarse canvas, containing a thin layer of coarse charcoal powder. A tolerably thick charcoal ventilator, as described above, could be very advantageously applied to the gully-holes or common sewers, and to the sinks in private dwellings, the foul water in both cases being carried into the drain by means of tolerably wide syphon pipes, retaining always about a couple of inches of water. Such an arrangement would effectually prevent the escape of any effluvia, would be easy of construction, and not likely to get soon out of order.

1392. CHARCOAL RESPIRATORS.—In respirators for the mouth the air is made to pass through a quarter of an inch of coarsely powdered charcoal, retained in its place by two sheets of silvered wire gauze, covered over with thin woollen cloth, by which means its temperature is greatly increased. The charcoal respirator possesses a decided advantage over respirators of the ordinary construction, in that all disagreeable effluvia are absorbed by the charcoal, so that comparatively pure air is alone inhaled. Adaptations may be made to cover the nostrils as well as the mouth, for protecting the wearer against fevers and other infectious diseases, and chiefly for use in chemical works, common sewers, &c., to protect the workmen from the noxious effects of the deleterious gases to which they are frequently exposed.

1393. CHARCOAL APPLIED TO SORES, &c.—Charcoal powder has been most successfully employed at hospitals, to arrest the progress of gangrene and other putrid sores. The charcoal does not require to be put immediately in contact with the sores, but is placed above the dressings, not unfrequently quilted loosely in a little cotton wool. In many cases patients who were rapidly sinking have been restored to health.

1394.—BORAX AND ITS USES. —The utility of borax for medicinal purposes, such as relieving soreness of the throat, and for the cure of thrush in young children, has long been known, but it is only in the present day that its good qualities as an antiseptic have become known, and its use in every kind of domestic work, in the laundry, in the garden, vinery, and greenhouse, and even for the toilet, under various forms specially prepared for all personal and domestic purposes, has been promoted by its production in small packets, varying

in price from 1*d.* to 6*d.*, which may be purchased of almost any chemist, oilman, grocer, or dealer, throughout the world.

1395. BORAX AS AN ANTISEPTIC.—The Patent Borax, which consists of a combination of boron and sodium, acts in a marvellous manner as an arrester of decay, and as such is useful for the preservation of meat, milk, butter, and all articles of animal food liable to taint and decay, especially in hot weather. When infused in small quantities in water, it preserves and softens it for drinking, cooking, washing, and all household purposes ; it whitens linen and cleanses it far better than soda ; it kills harmful insect life, though perfectly harmless to human beings and domestic animals ; it cleanses and heals ulcers, festering wounds, sore throat, &c. ; is useful in the nursery for washing the heads of children, cleans sponges, destroys unpleasant and unwholesome smells, and is beneficial to teeth and gums when used as a tooth-powder, or put in water used for washing the teeth.

1396. BORAX FOR CLEANSING.—A solution in hot water, allowed to cool, is useful for washing any kind of glass or china, imparting a lustre and brightness to them that they never exhibit when washed in the ordinary way. When it is put into water used for washing floors it destroys all vermin with which the solution comes in contact.

1397. BORAX FOR KILLING INSECTS.—When sprinkled in the form of powder on places infested with insects, black beetles, &c., these troublesome pests will soon disappear.

1398. BORAX IN COOKERY.—A few grains added to the tea before the water is poured on it greatly improves the flavour of the infusion. When used instead of soda, or carbonate of soda, in cooking vegetables, such as greens, peas, beans, &c., it improves their flavour, preserves their colour, and renders them tender. Vegetables eaten in an uncooked state, as salad, are rendered more crisp and of better flavour, by steeping them for a short time before they are brought to table in a solution of borax.

1399. BORAX AS A PRESERVATIVE OF MEAT, &c.—Meat may be preserved, and taint removed by soaking it for a short time in a solution of borax, or by sprinkling it with the dry powder. Game, poultry, hams, bacon, and all kinds of meat may be thus preserved. Milk cans should be washed with the solution, and milk itself may be preserved and kept sweet for some time by adding to each quart about half-a-thimbleful of this prepared borax dissolved in a tablespoonful of hot water. Butter may also be preserved by washing it in a solution of borax, or sprinkling the powder over it, or the cloths in which it is wrapped.

1400. BORAX IN THE LAUNDRY.—For washing add a half-pound packet to every ten gallons of hot water used ; let the clothes soak all night, in the solution ; in the morning give them a slight boil, adding a little more borax, if they be very greasy or dirty. By this means the clothes are rendered whiter, soap is saved, and the hands are uninjured. It acts, moreover, as a disinfectant, if the clothes have been taken from the bed or person of any one who is suffering from any infectious disorder. Flannels are rendered softer, and the appearance of lace, fine articles, coloured prints, soiled ribbons, &c., greatly improved by washing them in this solution. A teaspoonful to each pint of starch, when hot, will add to the stiffness and gloss of linen when ironed.

1401. BORAX IN THE TOILET.—As a wash for the mouth add half-a-teaspoonful of spirits of camphor, and a teaspoonful of tincture of myrrh to a pint of hot water, in which a penny packet of borax has been dissolved, and use a wineglassful of this mixture in half-a-tumbler of water, when brushing the teeth. When the mouth is washed out with this solution, it removes the smell of tobacco and any unpleasant odour arising from decayed teeth. Camphorated chalk dentrifice is improved as a tooth powder by the addition of a little powdered borax. For washing hair-brushes, sponges, &c., a solution of a small packet in a pint of hot water should be used.

1402. BORAX IN THE NURSERY.—A little borax added to water for bathing infants and children has a beneficial effect on the skin. For cleansing the hair and removing scurf or dandriff wash the head with a solution of a small packet of borax in a pint of hot water, after which the head should be rinsed with cold water, and carefully dried. This wash may be improved by the addition of half-an-ounce of rosemary spirit sold by any chemist.

1403. BORAX IN THE GARDEN.—A solution made by dissolving borax in hot water in the proportion of a penny packet of the former to a pint of the latter, will kill the green fly on roses and other plants. A weaker solution may be used for syringing the plants. When applied to the stems of fruit trees, and other trees, it destroys all insects in and about the bark, and clears the blight on apple trees. For these purposes the solution should be applied with a brush. For washing the shelves, boards, and woodwork of greenhouses, the solution is especially valuable, and when used for syringing vines in the proportion of a pint of the solution to ten gallons of water, and half-a-pound of borax dry soap, as soon as the grapes have been thinned, it will keep them free from red spider and other insects.

1404. DOMESTIC WHYS AND WHEREFORES.

The following paragraphs are from *The Housewife's Reason Why*, containing upwards of 1,500 reasons upon every kind of domestic subject. (2s. 6d. Houlston and Sons.)

1405. *Why is the flesh of sheep that are fed near the sea more nutritious than that of others ?*—Because the saline particles (sea salt) which they find with their green food give purity to their blood and flesh.

1406. *Why does the marbled appearance of fat in meat indicate that it is young and tender ?*—Because in young animals fat is dispersed through the muscles, but in old animals it is laid in masses on the outside of the flesh.

1407. *Why is some flesh white and other flesh red ?*—White flesh contains a larger proportion of albumen (similar to the white of egg) than that which is red. The amount of blood retained in the flesh also influences its colour.

1408. *Why are raw oysters more wholesome than those that are cooked ?* —When cooked they are partly deprived of salt water, which promotes their digestion ; their albumen also becomes hard (like hard-boiled eggs).

1409. *Why have some oysters a green tinge ?*—This has been erroneously attributed to the effects of copper ; but it arises from the oyster feeding upon small green sea-weeds, which grow where such oysters are found.

1410. *Why is cabbage rendered more wholesome by being boiled in two waters ?* —Because cabbages contain an oil, which is apt to produce bad effects, and prevents some persons from eating "green" vegetables. When boiled in two waters, the first boiling carries off the greater part of this oil.

1411. *Why are salt and soda used in cooking greens ?*—Because salt makes the water hotter and gives a better taste to the greens, and the soda, by extracting the oil from the greens, gives them a good colour.

1412. *Why should horseradish be scraped for the table only just before it is required ?*—Because the peculiar oil of horseradish is very volatile ; it quickly evaporates, and leaves the vegetable substance dry and insipid.

1413. *Why is mint eaten with pea soup ?*—The properties of mint are stomachic and antispasmodic. It is therefore useful to prevent the flatulence that might arise, especially from soups made of green or dried peas.

1414. *Why is apple sauce eaten with pork and goose ?*—Because it is slightly laxative, and therefore tends to counteract the effects of rich and stimulating meats. The acid of the apples also neutralizes the oily nature of the fat, and prevents biliousness.

1415. *Why does milk turn sour during thunderstorms ?*—Because in an electric condition of the atmosphere ozone is generated. Ozone is oxygen in a state of great intensity ; and oxygen is a general acidifier of many organic substances. Milk may be prevented from becoming sour by boiling it, or bringing it nearly to boiling point, for, as the old proverb says, "Milk boiled is milk spoiled." Heating the milk expels the oxygen.

1416. *Why does the churning of cream or milk produce butter ?*—Because the action of stirring, together with a moderate degree of warmth, causes the cells in which the butter is confined to burst ; the disengaged fat collects in flakes, and ultimately coheres in large masses.

1417. *What is the blue mould which appears sometimes upon cheese ?*—It is a species of fungus, or minute vegetable, which may be distinctly seen when examined by a magnifying glass.

1418. *Why are some of the limbs of birds more tender than others ?*—The tenderness or toughness of flesh is determined by the amount of exercise the muscles have undergone. Hence the wing of a bird that chiefly walks, and the leg of a bird that chiefly flies, are the most tender.

1419. *Why does tea frequently cure headache ?*—Because, by its stimulant action on the general circulation, in which the brain participates, the nervous congestions are overcome.

1420. *Why are clothes of smooth and shining surfaces best adapted for hot weather ?*—Because they reflect or turn back the rays of the sun, which are thus prevented from penetrating them.

1421. *Why is loose clothing warmer than tight articles of dress ?*—Because the loose dress encloses a stratum of warm air which the tight dress shuts out ; for the same reason, woollen articles, though not warmer in themselves, appear so, by keeping warm air near to the body.

1422. *Why should the water poured upon tea be at the boiling point ?*—Because it requires the temperature of boiling water to dissolve and extract the tea oil and tannic acid.

1423. *Why does the first infusion of tea possess more aroma than the second ?*—Because the first infusion, if the water used is at the boiling temperature, takes up the essential oil of the tea, while the second water receives only the bitter extract supplied by the tannic acid of tea.

1424. *Why does a head-dress of sky-blue become a fair person ?*—Because light blue is the complementary colour of pale orange, which is the foundation of the blonde complexion and hair.

1425. *Why are yellow, orange, or red colours suitable to a person of dark hair amd complexion ?*—Because those colours, by contrast with the dark skin and hair, show to the greater advantage themselves, while they enrich the hue of black.

1426. *Why is a delicate green favourable to pale blonde complexions ?*—Because it imparts a rosiness to such complexions—red, its complementary colour, being reflected upon green.

1427. *Why is light green unfavourable to ruddy complexions ?*—Because it increases the redness, and has the effect of producing an overheated appearance.

1428. *Why are violet draperies unfavourable to every kind of complexion?*—Because reflecting yellow, they augment that tint when it is present in the skin or hair, change blue into green, and give to an olive complexion a jaundiced look.

1429. *Why is blue unsuitable to brunettes ?*—Because it reflects orange, and adds to the darkness of the complexion.

1430. *Why do blue veils preserve the complexion ?*—Because they diminish the effect of the scorching rays of light, just as the blue glass over photographic studios diminishes the effect of certain rays that would injure the delicate processes of photography.

1431. FEMALE DRESS.—It is well known that a loose and easy dress contributes much to give the sex the fine proportions of body that are observable in the Grecian statues, and which serve as models to our present artists, nature being too much disfigured among us to afford any such. The Greeks knew nothing of those ligatures and bandages with which our bodies are compressed. Their women were ignorant of the use of stays, by which ours distort their shape instead of displaying it. This practice, carried to excess as it is in England, is in bad taste. To behold a woman cut in two in the middle, as if she were like a wasp, is as shocking to the eye as it is painful to the imagination. Such a deformity would be shocking in a naked figure ; wherefore, then, should it be esteemed a beauty in one that is dressed ? The effect of tight-lacing is to prevent the natural motion of the ribs, thus impeding respiration, and the inspiration of air being insufficient, the system requires quicker respiration, which disturbs the lungs and excites the heart. Everything that confines and lays nature under restraint is an instance of bad taste. This is as true in regard to the ornaments of the body as to the embellishments of the mind. Life, health, reason, and convenience ought to be taken first into consideration. Gracefulness cannot subsist without ease. High heeled boots and shoes also are very injurious, as the whole weight of the body is thrown forward on the toes, and the strain on the instep and contraction of the muscles at the back of the heel are very great.

1432. HINTS ON THE CARE OF CLOTHES.

(See also pars. 342 to 350.)

1433. CARE OF MEN'S HATS.

i. Should you get caught in a shower, always remember to brush your hat while wet. When dry, brush the glaze out, and gently iron it over with a smooth flat iron.

ii. If your hat is VERY wet, or stained with *sea* water, get a basin of clean cold water, and a good stiff brush ; wash it well all over, but be careful to keep the nap straight ; brush it as dry as you can, then put it on a peg to dry. When dry, brush the glaze out, and gently iron it over as above.

iii. Should you get a spot of grease on your hat, just drop one drop of benzine or sapine on the place, and then rub it briskly with a piece of cloth until out.

iv. Should you be travelling, always tie your hat up in a handkerchief before putting it into your case ; this will save it from getting rubbed or damaged through the friction of the rail or steamboat.

v. Never put your hat flat on the brim, as it will spoil its shape ; but always hang it up on a peg.

vi. Never put your hat, wet or dry,

in front of the fire, as it will soften it, and throw it all out of shape.

vii. Before putting your hat down, be careful to see if the place is free from spot of grease, beer, sugar, &c., as these things often spoil a good hat more than a twelvemonth's wear, and are often very difficult to remove. These simple rules will save a good hat for a very long time.

1434. CARE OF GLOVES.— Nothing looks worse than shabby gloves ; and, as they are expensive articles in dress, they require a little management. A good glove will, with care, out-last three cheap ones. Do not wear your best gloves at night ; the heat of the gas, &c., gives a moisture to the hands that spoils the gloves ; do not wear them in very wet weather, as carrying umbrellas, and drops of rain, spoil them.

1435. TO CLEAN KID GLOVES. —Make a strong lather with curd soap and warm water, in which steep a small piece of new flannel. Place the glove on a flat, clean, and unyielding surface—such as the bottom of a dish, and having thoroughly soaped the flannel (when squeezed from the lather), rub the kid till all dirt be removed, cleaning and re-soaping the flannel from time to time. Care must be taken to omit no part of the glove, by turning the fingers, &c. The glove must be dried in the sun, or before a moderate fire, and will present the appearance of old parchment. When quite dry, they must be gradually "pulled out," and will look new.

1435a. Another way.—Have ready a little new milk in one saucer, and a piece of brown soap in another, and a clean cloth or towel folded three or four times. On the cloth, spread out the glove smooth and neat. Take a piece of flannel, dip it in the milk, then rub off a good quantity of soap to the wetted flannel, and commence to rub the glove downwards towards the fingers, holding it firmly with the left hand. Continue this process until the glove, if white, looks of a dingy yellow, though clean ; if coloured, till it looks dark and spoiled. Lay it to dry ; and old gloves will soon look nearly new. They will be soft, glossy, smooth, well-shaped, and elastic.

1436. TO CLEAN WASH-LEATHER GLOVES.—Rub the grease spots out with magnesia, or cream of tartar. Then wash with soap dissolved in water, afterwards rinsing in warm water and then with cold. Dry in the sun, or before the fire.

1437. TO CLEAN BUCKSKIN GLOVES.—Mix together four ounces of Paris white, four ounces scraped pipe-clay, and three ounces of isinglass. Boil them down, stirring well. Put the substance on thick, and when dry beat it out by clipping your hands. Finally iron the gloves with a hot smoothing iron.

1438. TO PRESERVE THE COLOUR OF DRESSES WHEN WASHING THEM.—We need scarcely say that no coloured articles should ever be *boiled* or *scalded.* The colours of merinos, mousseline-de-laines, ginghams, chintzes, printed lawns, &c., may be preserved by using water that is only milk-warm ; making a lather with white soap *before* you put in the dress, instead of rubbing it on the material ; and stirring into a first and second tub of water a large tablespoonful of ox-gall. The gall can be obtained from the butcher, and a bottle of it should always be kept in every house. No coloured articles should be allowed to remain long in the water. They must be washed fast, and then rinsed through two cold waters. In each rinsing water stir a teaspoonful of vinegar, which will help to brighten the colours ; and after rinsing, hang them out immediately. When *ironing-dry* (or still a little damp), bring them in ; have irons ready heated, and iron them at once—as it injures the

colours to allow them to remain damp too long—or sprinkle and roll them up in a cover for ironing next day. If they cannot be conveniently ironed immediately, let them hang till they are quite dry, and then damp and fold them on the *following day*, a quarter of an hour before ironing. It is better not to do coloured dresses on the day of the general wash, but to give them a morning by themselves. They should only be undertaken in clear bright weather. If allowed to freeze, the colours will be irreparably injured. If you get from a shop a slip for testing the durability of colours, give it a fair trial by washing it as above ; afterwards pinning it to the edge of a towel, and hanging it to dry. Some colours (especially pinks and light greens), though they may stand perfectly well in washing, will change as soon as a warm iron is applied to them ; the pink turning purplish, and the green bluish. No coloured article should be smoothed with a *hot* iron.

1439. TO RENOVATE SILKS.—Sponge faded silks with warm water and soap, then rub them with a dry cloth on a flat board ; afterwards iron them on the *inside* with a smoothing iron. Old black silks may be improved by sponging with spirits ; in this case, the ironing may be done on the right side, thin paper being spread over to prevent glazing.

1440. BLACK SILK REVIVER.—Boil logwood in water for half-an-hour ; then simmer the silk half-an-hour ; take it out, and put into the dye a little blue vitriol, or green copperas ; cool it, and simmer the silk for half-an-hour. Or use the decoction of fig-leaves described in par. 1443.

1441. GREASE SPOTS FROM SILK.—Upon a deal table lay a piece of woollen cloth or baize, upon which lay smoothly the part stained, with the right side downwards. Having spread a piece of brown paper on the top, apply a flat iron just hot enough to scorch the paper. About fire or eight seconds is usually sufficient. Then rub the stained part briskly with a piece of whitey-brown paper.

1441a. RESTORING COLOUR TO SILK.—When the colour has been taken from silk by acids, it may be restored by applying to the spot a little hartshorn, or sal volatile.

1442. TO REMOVE WATER STAINS FROM BLACK CRAPE.—When a drop of water falls on a black crape veil or collar, it leaves a conspicuous white mark. To obliterate this, spread the crape on a table (laying on it a large book or a paperweight to keep it steady), and place underneath the stain a piece of old black silk. With a large camel's-hair brush dipped in common ink go over the stain, and then wipe off the ink with a small piece of old soft silk. It will dry at once, and the white mark will be seen no more.

1442a. TO CLEAN CRAPE.—Rinse it in ox-gall and water to take out the dirt, and then in clean water ; finally in gum-water to stiffen it, then beat it between the hands until it is dry.

1443. TO REMOVE STAINS FROM MOURNING DRESSES.—Boil a handful of fig-leaves in two quarts of water until reduced to a pint. Bombazines, crape, cloth, &c., need only be rubbed with a sponge dipped in this liquor, and the stains will be instantly removed.

1444. TO RESTORE VELVET.—When velvet gets crushed from pressure, hold the parts over a basin of *hot* water, with the lining of the article next the water ; the pile will soon rise, and assume its original beauty.

1444a. TO EXTRACT WAX OR GREASE SPOTS FROM CLOTH.—Hold a red-hot iron within an inch or two of the marks, and afterwards rub them with a soft clean rag.

1445. TO BANISH MOTHS.—

i. Procure shavings of cedar wood, and enclose in muslin bags, which can be distributed freely among the clothes.

ii. Procure shavings of camphor wood, and enclose in bags.

iii. Sprinkle pimento (allspice) berries among the clothes.

iv. Sprinkle the clothes with the seeds of the musk plant.

v. To destroy the eggs when deposited in woollen cloths, &c., use a solution of acetate of potash in spirits of rosemary, fifteen grains to the pint.

1445a. TO PROTECT FUR FROM MOTH.—Warm water, one pint ; corrosive sublimate, twelve grains. If washed with this, and afterwards dried, furs are safe from moth. Care should be taken to label the liquid—*Poison.*

1446. CARE OF FURS.—In the month of April or May, beat your fur garments well with a small cane or elastic stick, then wrap them up in linen, without pressing the fur too hard, and put betwixt the folds some camphor in small lumps ; then put your furs in this state in boxes well closed. When the furs are wanted for use, beat them well as before, and expose them for twenty-four hours to the air, which will take away the smell of the camphor. If the fur has long hair, as bear or fox, add to the camphor an equal quantity of black pepper in powder.

1447. CARE OF BOOTS AND SHOES.—These should be cleaned frequently, whether they are worn or not, and should never be left in a damp place, nor be put too near to the fire to dry. In cleaning them, be careful to *brush* the dirt from the seams, and not to scrape it off with a knife, or you may cut the leather. Let the hard brush do its work thoroughly well, and the polish will be all the brighter.

1448. LIQUID BLACKING.—Ivory black and treacle, of each one pound : sweet oil and oil of vitriol, of each a quarter of a pound. Put the first three together until the oil is perfectly mixed or *"killed"* ; then add the oil of vitriol, diluted with three times its weight of water, and after standing three hours add one quart of water or sour beer. The ivory black must be very finely ground for liquid blacking, otherwise it settles rapidly. The oil of vitriol is powerfully corrosive when undiluted, but uniting with the lime of the ivory black, it is partly neutralized, and does not injure the leather, whilst it much improves the quality of the blacking.

1448a. PASTE BLACKING.—Ivory black, two pounds ; treacle, one pound ; olive oil and oil of vitriol, of each, a quarter of a pound. Mix as before, adding only sufficient water to form into a paste.

1449. French Polish for Boots and Shoes.—Mix together two pints of the best vinegar and one pint of soft water ; stir into it a quarter of a pound of glue, broken up, half-a-pound of logwood chips, a quarter of an ounce of finely powdered indigo, a quarter of an ounce of the best soft soap, and a quarter of an ounce of isinglass. Put the mixture over the fire, and let it boil for ten minutes or more. Then strain the liquid, and bottle and cork it : when cold it is fit for use. Apply it with a clean sponge.

1449a. To Polish Enamelled Leather.—Two pints of the best cream, one pint of linseed oil ; make them each lukewarm, and then mix them well together. Having previously cleaned the shoe, &c., from dirt, rub it over with a sponge dipped in the mixture : then rub it with a soft dry cloth until a brilliant polish is produced.

1450. BOOT-TOP LIQUID.—Oxalic acid and white vitriol, of each one ounce ; water, one pint and a half.

To be applied with a sponge to the leather, previously washed, and then wiped off again. *This preparation is poisonous.*

1451. To Waterproof Boots and Shoes.—Linseed oil, one pint ; oil of turpentine, or camphine, a quarter of a pint ; yellow wax, a quarter of a pound ; Burgundy pitch, a quarter of a pound. Melt together with a gentle heat, and when required for use, warm and well rub into the leather before a fire, or in the hot sun. The composition should be poured, when melted, into small gallipots, or tin boxes. Or—warm a little bees'-wax and mutton suet until it is a liquid, and rub some of it slightly over the edges of the sole, where the stitches are.

1451a. To Stop Boots Creaking.—Drive a small peg into the middle of the sole.

1452. TO CLEAN GOLD AND SILVER LACE.—Grate the crumb part of a small loaf into fine crumbs and mix them with a quarter of a pound of powder-blue, sift some of the mixture over the lace, and then rub with a piece of flannel. Brush away the crumbs, and finally rub with a piece of red velvet.

1453. FINGER RINGS which have precious stones in them should always be taken off the finger when the hands are washed, or they will become discoloured.

1454. TO REMOVE TIGHT FINGER RINGS.—Pass the end of a piece of fine string under the ring, and wind it evenly round the finger *upward* as far the middle joint. Then take the lower end of the string under the ring, and slowly unwind it upward. The ring will then gradually move along the string and come off.

1455. HINTS ON ETIQUETTE.

Whatever objections may be raised to the teachings of works on etiquette, there can be no sound argument against a series of simple and brief hints, which shall operate as precautions against mistakes in personal conduct.

1456. LETTERS OF INTRO-DUCTION.

i. When giving a letter to introduce a friend leave it unsealed, as he may wish to see what you have said before he makes use of it.

ii. In availing yourself of a letter of this kind intended as a *friendly* introduction, send it in an envelope with your card and address, but do not call until the friends to whom you are introduced have called upon you.

iii. If the letter is a *business* introduction deliver it without delay.

iv. On receiving a letter of introduction be sure to acknowledge it at once, and call on the person introduced as soon as possible.

1457. CALLS AND VISITS.

i. It is now usual for ladies to have an "at home day" once or twice a month, when they make a point of being at liberty to receive any friends who wish to call on them. It is customary to have the intimation of your at home day printed on your visiting card, such as ("1st and 3rd Thursday") ("2nd Monday").

ii. A formal visit should never be made before noon. If a second visitor arrives it is advisable not to remain long, unless you are very intimate both with the host and the visitor ; or the host expresses a wish for you to stay.

iii. A gentleman should hold his hat in his hand, unless requested to put it down, but should leave his umbrella in the hall.

iv. Visits after balls or parties should be made within a month.

v. Visits of condolence should be paid within a week or fortnight *after* the event and require a grave style of dress.

vi. When you introduce a person, pronounce the name distinctly, and say whatever you can to make the introduction agreeable. Such as "an old

and valued friend," "a school-fellow of mine," "an old acquaintance of our family."

vii. A gentleman should be introduced to the lady, not the lady to the gentleman.

viii. Be hearty in your reception of guests ; and where you see much diffidence, assist the stranger to throw it off.

ix. Request the servant, during the visits of guests, to attend to the door the moment the bell rings.

x. When your visitor retires, ring the bell for the servant. You may then accompany your guest as far towards the door as the circumstances of your friendship seem to demand.

xi. If visiting for a few days at a friend's house, give as little trouble as possible and endeavour to conform to the habits of the family. Ascertain the usual times for meals, and make a point of being punctual.

1458. DINNER PARTIES.

i. Invitations should be sent out at least a week beforehand.

ii. Accept or decline an invitation by return of post.

iii. Strictly keep to your engagements and make a point of punctuality.

iv. For gentlemen black coats and trousers are indispensable for either a dinner or a ball.

v. The host and hostess should be in the drawing-room to receive their guests.

vi. When dinner is announced the host offers his arm to the principal lady guest and conducts her to the dining-room, the rest of the company follow in couples as arranged by either the master or mistress of the house—the latter with her attendant gentleman always entering the dining-room last.

vii. The places of the various guests at the table are usually indicated by cards bearing their names.

viii. Each gentleman during dinner should attend to the wants of the lady placed under his care, and choose subjects of conversation likely to prove agreeable to her.

1459. BALLS AND EVENING PARTIES.

i. An invitation to a ball should be given *at least* a fortnight beforehand.

ii. Upon entering the reception-room first address the lady of the house ; and after her, the nearest acquaintances you may recognize in the room.

iii. If you introduce a friend, make him acquainted with the names of the chief persons present. But first present him to the lady of the house, and to the host.

iv.. Appear in full dress.

v. Always wear gloves, and put them on previous to entering the room.

vi. Avoid an excess of jewellery, and do not wear rings on the outside of your gloves.

vii. Gentlemen should not select the same partner fluently, but distribute their attentions as much as possible.

viii. If there are more dancers than the room will accommodate, do not join in every dance.

ix. Do not remain to the close, and in leaving a large party it is unnecessary to bid farewell, and improper to do so before the guests.

x. The host and hostess should look after all their guests, and not confine their attentions. They should, in fact, attend chiefly to those who are the least known in the room.

xi. The hostess may introduce any gentleman to a lady without first asking the lady's consent, after ascertaining that the lady is willing to dance.

xii. After dancing, conduct your partner to a seat, or resign her as soon as her next partner advances.

xiii. An introduction to a lady at a ball does not entitle the gentleman to bow to her on a future occasion, unless she first recognizes him.

(*For the Figures of Dances, see pars.* 141 to 163.)

1460. MARRIAGE ARRANGEMENTS.

1461. Special Licences.—Special licences are dispensations from the ordinary rule, under which marriages can only take place canonically in the parish church, or other places duly licensed for that purpose. They can only be obtained from the Metropolitan or Archbishop of the province, and often with no small difficulty, not being readily granted, and when obtained the fees are about £30.

1462. Common Licences enable persons of full age, or minors with consent of parents or guardians, to be married in the church of the parish in which one of them has resided for three weeks. They are procured from The Faculty Office, Doctors' Commons, or from any Surrogate, at a cost of from £2 to £8.

1463. Banns must be published *three times* in the parish church, in *each place* where the persons con- cerned reside. The clerk is applied to on such occasions ; his fee varies from 1s. 6d. upwards. When the marriage ceremony is over, the parties repair to the vestry, and enter their names in the parish registry. The registry is signed by the clergyman and the witnesses present, and a certificate of the registry is given to the bridegroom if desired. The charge for a certificate of marriage is 2s. 7d., including the penny stamp on the documents, as by law required, and the clergyman's fee varies according to circumstances. The clerk will at all times give information thereupon ; and it is best for a friend of the bridegroom to attend to the pecuniary arrangements.

1464. Marriages of Dissenters may be solemnized at any place of worship duly licensed, and in accordance with the forms of their worship. In some cases the service of the Church of England is read, with slight additions or modifications. The clerk of the place of worship should be applied to for information.

1465. Marriage by Registration.—An Act was passed in the reign of William the Fourth, by which it was rendered legal for persons wishing to be married by a civil ceremony, to give notice of their intention to the Registrar of Marriages in their district or districts. Three weeks' notice is necessary, to give which the parties call, separately or together, at the office of the registrar, who enters the names in a book. When the time of notice has expired, it is only necessary to give the registrar an intimation, on the previous day, of your intention to attend at his office on the next day, and complete the registration. The ceremony consists in merely answering a few questions, and making the declaration that you take each other to live as husband and wife. The fee amounts only to a few shillings, and in this form no wedding-ring is required, though it is usually placed on the ring-finger of the bride's left hand, in the presence of the persons assembled. The married couple receive a certificate of marriage, which is in every respect lawful.

1466. Wedding Rings.—The custom of wearing wedding rings appears to have taken its rise among the Romans. Before the celebration of their nuptials, there was a meeting of friends at the house of the lady's father, to settle articles of the marriage contract, when it was agreed that the dowry should be paid down on the wedding day or soon after. On this occasion there was commonly a feast, at the conclusion of which the man gave to the woman, as a pledge, a ring, which she put on the fourth finger of her left hand, *because it was believed that a nerve reached thence to the heart*, and a day was then named for the marriage.

1467. Why the Wedding Ring is placed on the Fourth Finger.—"We have remarked on the vulgar error

which supposes that an artery runs from the fourth finger of the left hand to the heart. It is said by Swinburn and others, that therefore it became the wedding finger. The priesthood kept up this idea by still retaining it as the wedding finger, but the custom is really associated with the doctrine of the Trinity ; for, in the ancient ritual of English marriages, the ring was placed by the husband on the top of the thumb of the left hand, with the words, 'In the name of the Father ;' he then removed it to the forefinger, saying, 'In the name of the Son ;' then to the middle finger, adding, 'And of the Holy Ghost ;' finally, he left it as now, on the fourth finger, with the closing word, 'Amen.' "—*The History and Poetry of Finger Rings.*

1468. Wedding Dress.—It is impossible to lay down specific rules for dress, as fashions change and tastes differ. The great art consists in selecting the style of dress most becoming to the person. A stout person should adopt a different style from a thin person ; a tall one from a short one. Peculiarities of complexion, and form of face and figure, should be duly regarded ; and in these matters there is no better course than to call in the aid of any respectable milliner and dressmaker, who will be found ready and able to give the best advice. The bridegroom should simply appear in morning dress, and should avoid everything eccentric and conspicuous in style. The bridesmaids should always be made aware of the bride's dress before they choose their own, which should be determined by a proper harmony with the former.

1469. The Order of Going to Church is as follows :—

i. **The Bride,** accompanied by her *father*, occupies the *last carriage*. The father hands out the bride, and leads her direct to the altar, round which those who have been invited have already grouped themselves, leaving room for the father, the bride, and the bridesmaids, who usually await the bride's coming at the entrance to the church, or at the bottom of the chancel, and follow her to the communion rails.

ii. **The Bridegroom,** who has made his way to the church, accompanied by his "best man," or principal groomsman—an intimate friend or brother—should be waiting at the communion rails to receive his future wife on her arrival. He and she then stand facing the altar, he being on the right of the bride, and the father or the gentleman who is to "give away" the bride, on the left.

iii. **The Chief Bridesmaid** occupies a place immediately behind the *bride*, to hold her gloves, handkerchief, and flowers ; her companions range themselves close to, and slightly in the rear of the principal bridesmaid.

1470. When the Ceremony is concluded, the Bride, taking the Bridegroom's arm, goes into the vestry, the others following ; signatures are then affixed, and a registration made, after which the married pair enter their carriage, and proceed to the reception, every one else following.

1471. The "Best Man" should be careful that the Bridegroom does not forget to take the licence and ring with him to the church. He should also see to the payment of the fees and to the arrangement of the carriages and comfort of the guests on the return from the church. The fee to the clergyman is according to the rank and fortune of the bridegroom ; the clerk if there be one, expects *five shillings*, and a trifle should be given to the pew opener, and other officials of the church. There is a fixed scale of fees at every church, to which the parties married can add if they please.

1472. The Order of Returning from Church differs from the above only in the fact that the Bride and Bridegroom now ride together in the first carriage, the bride being on his left. The bridesmaids and other guests follow in the remaining carriages under the direction of the "best man" to the house of the Bride's parents, or other place where the wedding reception is held.

1473. The Wedding Breakfast having been already prepared, the wedding party return thereto. If a large party, the bride and bridegroom occupy seats in the centre of the long table, and the two extremities should be presided over by the father and mother of the bride, or, failing these, by elderly relatives, if possible one from each family. Every one should endeavour to make the occasion as happy as possible. One of the senior members of either the bride or bridegroom's family should, some time before the breakfast has terminated, rise, and in a brief but graceful manner, propose the "Health and happiness of the wedded pair." It is much better to drink their healths together than separately ; and, after a brief interval, the bridegroom should return thanks, which he may do without hesitation, since no one looks for a speech upon such an occasion. A few words, feelingly expressed, are all that is required. The breakfast generally concludes with the departure of the happy pair upon their wedding tour.

1474. Wedding Receptions.— Since it has been made legal for marriages to be solemnized after noon, the wedding breakfast has been very generally superseded by a reception held by the bride's parents, either at their own house or at a hall or rooms engaged for the purpose. Liberal refreshments are provided, but there is no formal sit-down meal. Friends, although not invited to the church, may be asked to the reception. They are expected to offer their congratulations to the newly-married couple and their families, and after partaking of refreshments, and in some cases viewing the presents, take their leave. This arrangement enables many more friends to be invited, and is more easily managed and less expensivse than the regular wedding breakfast.

1475. Wedding Cards.—A newly married couple usually, on the day of the ceremony, have their new address-cards sent out to their friends and acquaintances with the intimation of the date of their first "at home." Recently, the custom of sending cards has been in a great measure discontinued, and instead of this, the words "No cards" are appended to the ordinary newspaper advertisement, and the announcement of the marriage, with this addition, is considered all-sufficient.

1476. The Wedding Tour must depend upon the tastes and circumstances of the married couple. Home-loving Englishmen and women may find much to admire and enjoy without ranging abroad. Those whose time is somewhat restricted should visit some spot which may be reached without difficulty. Cornwall and Devonshire, the Isle of Wight, &c., are each delightful to the tourist. The scenery of the North of Devon, and of both coasts of Cornwall is especially beautiful. North Wales offers a delightful excursion ; the lakes of Westmoreland and Cumberland ; the lakes of Killarney, in Ireland ; also the magnificent scenery of the Scottish lakes and mountains. To those who wish for a wider range, France, Germany, Switzerland, and the Rhine offer charms which cannot be surpassed.

1477. The Bride's First "At Home."—When the married pair have returned, and the day of reception arrives, the bride should have her mother, sister, or other female friend with her when she receives her guests, even though her husband be present. Wedding cake, wine, or tea and coffee are handed round, of which every one partakes, and each expresses some kindly wish for the newly-married couple.

1478. REGISTRATION OF BIRTHS.

The law of registration requires the parents, or occupiers of houses in which the births happen, or any person present at the birth, and the person having the charge of the child, to register such birth within *six weeks* after the date thereof. For registration, within the time specified, *no charge is made*. But after the expiration of the forty-second day from the birth, a fee of *seven shillings and sixpence* must be paid. After the expiration of six months from the date of the birth, no registration is allowed. It is therefore most important, as soon as possible after the birth of a child to go to the office of the registrar of the district, and communicate the following particulars :—

1. Date when born.
2. Name of the child.
3. Boy or girl.
4. Name of the father.
5. Name and maiden name of the mother.
6. Bank or profession of the father.
7. Signature, description, and residence of the person giving the information.
8. Date of the registration.

1479. Registration of Births at Sea.—If any child of an English parent shall be born at sea on board a British vessel, the captain or commanding officer shall make a minute of the particulars touching the birth of the child, and shall, on the arrival of the vessel at any port of the kingdom, or sooner, by any other opportunity, send a certificate of the birth through the post-office (*for which no postage will be charged*) to the Registrar General, London.

1480. CHRISTENINGS may be performed either in accordance with the rites of the Established Church, or of dissenting congregations ; the time of birth, and the name of every child, must also be registered. The fees paid for christening vary with a variety of circumstances. Particulars should in each case be obtained of the clerk of the place of worship. It is usual to make a christening the occasion of festivity ; but not in such a manner as to require special remark. The parents and god-parents of the child appear at church at the appointed hour. The child is carried by the nurse. The dress of the parties attending a christening should be what may be termed demi-costume, or half-costume ; but the infant should be robed in the choicest manner that the circumstances will allow. It is usual for the sponsors to present the child with a gift to be preserved for its future years. Silver spoons, a silver knife and fork, a clasp-Bible, a silver cup, and other such articles, are usually chosen. It is usual, also, to give a trifling present to the nurse.

1481. CHOICE OF NAMES.—To choose names for children, parents should consult the list of names in pars. 806 and 807.

1482. Baptismal Name.—If any child born in England, whose birth has been registered, shall, within six months of such registration, have any name given to it in baptism other than that originally registered, such baptismal name may be added to the previous registration, if, within seven days of such baptism, application be made to the registrar by whom the child was originally registered. For this purpose a certificate of the baptism must be procured of the clergyman, for which a fee of 2s. 7d. (including stamp) must be paid. This certificate must be taken to the registrar, who will charge another fee of *one shilling* for adding the baptismal name to the original registration.

1483. REGISTRATION OF DEATHS.—The father or mother of any child that dies, or the occupier of a house in which any person may die, must, within *five days* after such death, give notice to the registrar of the district. Some person present at the death should at the same time attend and give to the registrar an account of the circumstances or cause of the death, to the best of his or her knowledge or belief. Such person must sign his or her name, and give the place of abode at which he or she resides. The following are the particulars required :—.

1. Date of Death.
2. Name in full.
3. Sex and age.
4. Rank or profession.
5. Cause of death.
6. Signature, description, and residence of the person giving the information
7. Date of the registration.

A certificate of the cause of death must be obtained from the medical man in attendance, who is required to state when he last saw the patient.

1483a. Householder's Responsibility for Burial.—It is not generally known that by common law a person in whose house a death takes place is bound to bury the corpse. He must not send it away, or take it uncovered to the grave ; but must provide decent burial for it.

1484. Registration of Deaths at Sea.—The commander of any British vessel, on board of which a death occurs at sea, must act the same as in a case of birth. (*See* par. 1479.)

1485. CERTIFICATES OF DEATH.—Every registrar must deliver to the undertaker, *without fee*, a certificate of the death, which certificate shall be given up at the funeral to the officiating minister. No dead body can be buried without such certificate, under a penalty of £10.

1486. INTIMATIONS OF DEATHS AND FUNERALS.—It is usual, when a death takes place, to communicate it immediately, upon mourning note-paper, to the principal members of the family, and to request them to notify the same to the more remote relatives in their circle. A subsequent note should state the day and hour at which the funeral is fixed to take place. Special Invitations to funerals are not considered requisite to be sent to near relatives ; but to friends and acquaintances such invitations should be sent.

1487. FUNERALS.

It is always best to place the direction of a funeral under a respectable undertaker, with the precaution of obtaining his estimate for the expenses, and limiting him to them. He can best advise upon the observances to be attended to, since the style of funerals differs with the station of the deceased's family, and is further modified by the customs of particular localities, and even by religious views. He will also make the necessary arrangements at the cemetery or place of interment.

1488. Gloves.—Most persons who attend funerals will provide themselves with gloves ; but it is well to have a dozen pairs, of assorted sizes, provided in case of accident. An arrangement can be made for those not used to be returned.

1489. Hatbands and Cloaks are now rarely, if ever, worn at funerals.

1490. Mourning.—The dressmaker will advise upon the "degree" of mourning to be worn, which must be modified according to the age of the deceased, and the relationship of the mourner. The undertaker will advise respecting the degree of mourning to be displayed upon the carriages, horses, &c.

1491. In the Funeral Cortège the nearest relatives of the deceased occupy the carriages nearest the hearse. The same order prevails in returning. Only the relatives and most intimate friends of the family should return to the house after the funeral ; and their visit should be as short as possible.

1492. In Walking Funerals it is considered a mark of respect for friends to become pall-bearers. In the funerals of young persons, the pall should be borne by their companions, wearing white gloves. It is a pretty and an affecting sight to see the pall over the coffin of a young lady borne by six of her female friends. Flowers may be placed upon the coffin, and strewed in and over the grave.

1493. CREMATION is the process of reducing the human remains to ashes by means of fire, and is a very ancient usage. Danger to the health of those persons who live in the vicinity of cemeteries and graveyards, by reason of the noxious gases given forth and pollution of water, is very great ; but by burning the body it is quickly reduced to its component elements without creating any nuisance or danger, and without any want of reverence or respect. The process has been in vogue for some years abroad, being first made legal in Italy in the year 1877 ; but in England the first public crematorium was erected at Woking cemetery in 1885. There are now crematories in various parts of the country. The apparatus used nearly everywhere is the Gorini furnace, consisting of a furnace, receiver, and chimney. The receiver is a chamber with open ends, one of these ends is in contact with the furnace and the other with the chimney. The furnace is supplied with wood fuel, or coke ; and the time occupied in the process of cremating a body is from an hour and a quarter to an hour and three-quarters. After cremation the ashes of a grown-up person weigh from five to seven pounds.

1494. FUNERAL EXPENSES.— As funerals in England, when conducted in the ordinary way, with the usual display of hearse, mourning carriages, and costly mourning, are attended with considerable expense, societies have been formed in many parishes with the view of reducing the outlay resorted to on these occasions, and at a time perhaps when it would be better in many cases to observe the strictest economy. The members of these societies agree among themselves to do all that is possible to reduce expenditure at funerals, and to render the accompaniments of the sad ceremony as inexpensive as possible. Instead of going into mourning, many now content themselves with wearing a simple band of cloth round the left arm. This is done by women as well as by men.

1495. VISITS OF CONDOLENCE after funerals should be paid by relatives within from a week to a fortnight ; by friends within the second week of the fortnight ; friends of less intimacy should make enquiries and leave cards.

1496. CARE OF INFANTS.

1497. INFANTS' FOOD.

i. Happy indeed is the child who, during the first period of its existence, is fed upon no other aliment than the milk of its mother or that of a healthy nurse. If other food become necessary before the child has acquired teeth, it ought to be of a liquid form ; for instance, biscuits or stale bread boiled in an equal mixture of milk and water, to the consistence of a thick soup ; but by no means even this in the first few weeks of its life. Children who are brought up by hand, that is to say, who are not nursed by mother or wet nurse, require an occasional change of diet, and thin gruel affords a wholesome alternation to milk. When cows' milk is used it should be obtained, if possible, from one and the same cow, and be freely diluted with boiled water. Swiss milk is recommended by some medical men. Several dairy companies furnish a specially prepared milk for young children, which is often useful.

ii. After the first six months weak veal or chicken broth may be given, and also, progressively, vegetables that are not very flatulent, and occasionally a little stewed fruit, such as apples, pears, or rhubarb.

iii. When the infant is weaned, and has acquired its proper teeth, it is advisable to let it have small portions of meat finely minced, and other vegetables, as well as milk puddings, made of sago, semolina, rice, &c., so that it may gradually become accustomed to every kind of strong and wholesome food. Care, however, should be taken not upon any account to allow a child pastry, confectionery, cheese, onions, horseradish, mustard, smoked and salted meat, especially pork, and all compound dishes ; for the most simple food is the most wholesome. Potatoes should be given only in moderation, and not to be eaten with butter, but rather with other vegetables, either mashed up or in broth.

iv. The time for giving food is a matter of importance ; very young infants may be fed more frequently, as their consumption of vital power is more rapid. It is, however, advisable to accustom even them to a certain regularity, for children fed indiscriminately through the whole day, are subject to debility and disease. The stomach should be allowed to recover its tone, and to collect the juices necessary for digestion, before it is supplied with a new portion of food.

v. The following order of giving food to children will be found conducive to their health :—After rising in the morning, suppose about seven o'clock, a moderate portion of lukewarm milk, with well baked stale bread ; at nine o'clock, bread with some fruit, or, if fruit be scarce, a small quantity of fresh butter, or bacon liquor ; about twelve o'clock, the dinner, of a sufficient quantity of wholesome food (*see* pars. 1506 to 1526). Between four and five, some bread with fruit, or, in winter, some preserve as a substitute for fruit ; at this meal children should be allowed to eat till they are satisfied, without surfeiting themselves, so that they will only need a light supper, about seven o'clock ; they ought then to eat but little, and not be put to sleep for at least an hour after it.

vi. It has often been contended that bread is hurtful to children ; but this applies only to new bread, or such as is not sufficiently baked ; for instance, nothing can be more hurtful or oppressive than rolls, muffins, and crumpets. Good wheaten bread, especially that baked by the aerated bread process, is extremely proper during the first years of infancy ; but that made of whole wheat meal, or wheat flour from which the bran has not been eliminated is, perhaps, more conducive to health after the age of childhood.

1498. CHILDREN'S DRINK.

i. Doctors are decidedly against giving drink to children in large quantities and at irregular periods, whether it consists of the mother's milk, or any other equally mild liquid. In the latter part of the first year, pure water, milk-and-water, or toast-and-water may occasionally be given. On no account should a young child be permitted to taste beer or wine, unless specially ordered by a medical man.

ii. Many children acquire a habit of drinking during their meals ; it would be more conducive to digestion if they were accustomed to drink only after having made a meal ; this salutary rule is too often neglected.

1499. CRYING OF INFANTS.

i. It is a mistake to consider every noise of an infant as a claim upon our assistance, and to give either food or drink, with a view to satisfy its supposed wants. By such injudicious conduct, children readily acquire the injurious habit of demanding nutriment at improper times, and without necessity.

ii. In the first year of infancy, many expressions of the tender organs are to be considered only as efforts of manifestations of power, in many instances, these vociferating sounds imply the effort which children necessarily make to display the strength of their lungs and exercise their organs of respiration. You will observe, for instance, that a child, as soon as it is undressed, or disencumbered from swaddling clothes, moves its arms and legs, and often makes a variety of strong exertions. Nature has wisely ordained that by these very efforts the power and utility of functions so essential to life should be developed, and rendered more perfect with every inspiration.

iii. Hence it follows, that those over-anxious parents or nurses, who continually endeavour to prevent infants crying do them a material injury ; for, by such imprudent management, their children seldom or never acquire a perfect form of chest, while the foundation is laid in the pectoral vessels for obstructions and other diseases. Independently of any particular causes, the cries of children, with regard to their general effects, are highly beneficial and necessary.

iv. In the first Period of Life such exertions are almost the only exercises of the infant ; thus the circulation of the blood, and all the other fluids, is rendered more uniform ; digestion, nutrition, and the growth of the body are thereby promoted ; and the different secretions, together with the very important office of the skin, or insensible perspiration, are duly performed. Sometimes, however, the mother or nurse removes the child from its couch, carries it about frequently in the middle of the night, and thus exposes it to repeated colds, which are in their effects infinitely more dangerous than the most violent cries.

v. There are frequently instances in which the loud complaints of infants demand our attention. Thus, if their cries be unusually violent and long continued, we may conclude that they are troubled with colic pains ; if, on such occasions, they move their arms and hands repeatedly towards the face, painful teething may account for the cause; and if other morbid phenomena accompany their cries, or if these expressions be repeated at certain periods of the day, we ought not to alight them, but endeavour to discover the cause.

1500. THE VACCINATION OF INFANTS.

Parents or guardians are obliged by law to have every child born in the United Kingdom vaccinated within four months of its birth, either by a registered private medical practitioner, or by the public vaccinator for the district in which they reside. If the child should be in such a state of health as to be unfit for the operation and a postponement is advisable, a medical certificate to that effect must be procured. We regret to say that an Act of Parliament was passed in 1898, which provides that any parent who can satisfy two justices or magistrates that he conscientiously believes that vaccination would be prejudicial to the health of his child, and can obtain their certificates to that effect, is exempt from any penalties incurred by failing to comply with the first-mentioned most salutary law. It is, however, to be fervently hoped that this recent Act will be speedily repealed, as vaccination has proved itself a wonderful preventive and safeguard from the ravages of that fearful disease—small-pox.

1501. CHILDREN'S SLEEP.

i. Infants cannot sleep too long ; and it is a favourable symptom when they enjoy a calm and long-continued rest, of which they should by no means be deprived, as this is the greatest support granted to them by nature.

ii. A child lives comparatively much faster than an adult ; its blood flows more rapidly ; every stimulus operates more powerfully ; and not only its constituent parts, but its vital resources also, are more speedily consumed. Sleep promotes a more calm and uniform circulation of the blood ; it facilitates the assimilation of the nutriment received, and contributes towards a more copious and regular deposition of alimentary matter, while the horizontal posture is the most favourable to the growth and development of the child.

iii. Sleep ought to be in proportion to the age of the infant. After the age of six months, the periods of sleep, as well as all other animal functions, may in some degree be regulated ; yet, even then, a child should be suffered to sleep the whole night, and several hours both in the morning and in the afternoon. Mothers and nurses should endeavour to accustom infants, from the time of their birth, to sleep in the night preferably to the day, and for this purpose they ought to remove all external impressions which may disturb their rest, such as noise, light, &c., and especially not to obey every call for taking them up, and giving food at improper times.

iv. After the second year of their age, children will not instinctively require to sleep in the forenoon, though after dinner it may be continued to the third and fourth year of life, if the child shows a particular inclination to repose ; because, till that age, the full half of life may safely be allotted to sleep. From that period, however, sleep ought to be shortened for the space of one hour with every succeeding year, so that a child of seven years old may sleep about eight, and not exceeding nine hours ; this proportion may be continued to the age of adolescence, and even manhood.

v. To awaken children from their sleep with a noise, or in an impetuous manner, is extremely injudicious and hurtful ; nor is it wise to carry them from a dark room immediately into a glaring light, or against a dazzling wall ; for the sudden impression of light debilitates the organs of vision, and lays the foundation of weak eyes.

vi. Children should never be frightened or threatened by references to ghost stories, or goblins, &c. They have such a small amount of reasoning power, and are so susceptible to fear and fright, that if such stories are told to them they suffer acutely during the hours of darkness and quiet.

1502. NIGHT NURSERIES.

i. A bedroom or night nursery ought to be spacious and lofty, dry, airy, and not inhabited through the day. The windows should never be opened at night, but may be left open the whole day in fine clear weather.

ii. If possible, no servant should be suffered to sleep in the same room, and no linen or washed clothes should ever be hung there to dry, as they contaminate the air in which so considerable a portion of infantile life must be spent, as the consequences attending a vitiated atmosphere in such rooms are serious, and often fatal.

iii. Feather-beds should be banished from nurseries, as they are unnatural and debilitating contrivances. The horsehair mattress is now generally preferred ; being cooler, more healthy, and more comfortable. Chaff beds also may be highly recommended, as they are warm, cheap, and easy to refill.

iv. Spring and wire-woven beds are very largely used now, instead of laths or sacking. They are by no means expensive, can be easily cleaned, and save the use of mattresses.

v. Lastly, the bedstead must not be placed too low on the floor ; nor is it proper to let children sleep on a couch which is made without any elevation from the ground ; because the most pernicious air in an apartment is that within one or two feet from the floor, while the most wholesome, or atmospheric air is in the middle of the room.

1503. WASHING CHILDREN.

A child should never go to bed dirty, the whole body should be washed every day. Young children should be washed after breakfast, and older ones before that meal. Care should be taken lest the child catches a chill whilst being dried. A sponge is generally used for washing children ; but some persons prefer a piece of flannel. Special care should be taken to use only the best and purest soap.

1504. TEETHING.

Young children whilst cutting their first set of teeth, often suffer severe constitutional disturbance. At first there is restlessness and peevishness, with slight fever, and not unfrequently these are followed by convulsive fits, which are caused by the brain becoming irritated, and sometimes under this condition the child either dies suddenly, or the foundation of serious mischief to the brain is laid. The remedy, or rather the safeguard against these frightful consequences, is trifling, safe, and almost certain, and consists merely in lancing the gum covering the tooth which is making its way through. When teething is about it may be known by the saliva constantly drivelling from the mouth and wetting the frock. The child has its fingers often in its mouth, and bites hard any substance it can get hold of. If the gums be carefully looked at, the part where the tooth is pressing up is swollen and redder than usual ; and if the finger be pressed on it the child shrinks and cries, showing that the gum is tender. When these symptoms occur, the gum should be lanced, and sometimes the tooth comes through the next day, if near the surface ; but if not so far advanced the cut heals and a scar forms, which is thought by some objectionable, as rendering the passage of the tooth more difficult. This, however, is not so, for the scar will give way much more easily than the uncut gum. If the tooth do not come through after two or three days, the lancing may be repeated ; and this is more especially needed if the child be very fractious, and seems in much pain. Lancing the gums is further advantageous, because it removes the blood from the inflamed part, and so relieves the pain and inflammation. The relief children experience in the course of two or three hours from the operation is often very remarkable, as they almost immediately become lively and cheerful. A small grey powder, say one grain, given at night affords relief.

1505. THE DISCIPLINE OF CHILDREN.

i. Children should not be allowed to ask for the same thing twice. This may be accomplished by parents, teacher, or whoever may happen to have the management of them, paying attention to their little wants, if proper, at once, when possible. Children should be made to understand that when they are not answered immediately, it is because it is not convenient. Let them learn patience by waiting.

ii. We learn from daily experience, that children who have been the least indulged, thrive much better, unfold all their faculties quicker, and acquire more muscular strength and vigour of mind, than those who have been constantly favoured, and treated by their parents with the most solicitous attention: bodily weakness and want of self-reliance are the frequent attributes of the latter.

iii. The greatest art in educating children consists in a continued vigilance over all their actions, without letting them discover that they are being watched and guided.

1506. COOKING FOR CHILDREN.

1507. Food for Infants.—Take of fresh cow's milk, one tablespoonful, and mix with two tablespoonfuls of hot water ; sweeten with loaf sugar, as much as may be agreeable. This quantity is sufficient for once feeding a new-born infant ; and the same quantity may be given every two or three hours,—not oftener,—till the mother's breast affords natural nourishment.

1508. Milk for Infants Six Months Old.—Take one pint of milk, one pint of water, boil it, and add one tablespoonful of flour. Dissolve the flour first in half-a-teacupful of water ; it must be strained in gradually, and boiled hard twenty minutes. As the child grows older, one-third water. If properly made, it is the most nutritious, at the same time the most delicate food that can be given to young children.

1509. Nursery Biscuits soaked in boiling water or milk and beaten up well with a fork are very beneficial to some infants, while others thrive best on one or other of the many infants' foods which are now manufactured.

1510. Broth, made of mutton, veal, or chicken, with stale bread toasted, and broken in, is safe and wholesome for the dinners of children when first weaned.

1511. New Milk, with a very little loaf sugar, is good and safe food for young children. From three years old to seven, pure milk, into which stale bread is crumbled, is the best breakfast and supper for a child.

1512. Milk Porridge.—Stir four tablespoonfuls of oatmeal, smoothly, into a quart of milk, then stir it quickly into a quart of boiling water, and boil it up a few minutes till it is thickened: sweeten with sugar. Oatmeal, where it is found to agree with the stomach, is much better for children, being a mild aperient as well as cleanser ; fine flour in every shape is the reverse. Where biscuit-powder is in use, let it be made at home ; this, at all events, will prevent them getting the sweepings of the baker's counters, boxes, and baskets. All the waste bread in the nursery, hard ends of stale loaves, &c., ought to be dried in the oven or screen, and reduced to powder in the mortar.

1513. For a Child's Luncheon.— Good sweet butter, with stale bread, is one of the most nutritious, at the same time the most wholesome articles of food that can be given children after they are weaned.

1514. Meats for Children.— Mutton and poultry are the best. Birds and the white meat of fowls are the most delicate food of this kind that can be given. These meats should be slowly cooked, and no gravy, if made rich with butter, should be eaten by a young child. Never give children hard, tough, half-cooked meats, of any kind.

1515. Eggs for Children should be boiled slowly and soft.

1516. Vegetables for Children.— For children rice ought to be cooked in no more water than is necessary to swell it ; Apples roasted, or stewed with no more water than is necessary to steam them ; Vegetables should be thoroughly well cooked. Potatoes, particularly some kinds, are not easily digested by children ; but this may be remedied by mashing them very fine, and seasoning them with salt and a little milk. Peas should be seasoned with mint and salt, which will take off the flatulency. If they are old, let them be pulped, as the skins cannot be digested by children's stomachs. Never give them vegetables less stewed than would pulp through a colander. Should the children be flatulent or bilious, a very little curry powder may be given with vegetables with good effect. Turmeric and the warm seeds (not hot peppers) are also particularly useful in such cases.

1517. Fruits for Children.—That fruits are naturally healthy in their season, if rightly taken, no one who believes that the Creator is a kind and beneficent Being can doubt. And yet the use of summer fruits appears often to cause most fatal diseases, especially in children. Why is this ? Because we do not conform to the natural laws in using this kind of diet These laws are very simple, and easy to understand. Let the fruit be ripe when you eat it ; and eat when you require *food*. Fruits that have *seeds* are much more wholesome than the *stone* fruits. But all fruits are better, for very young children, if baked or cooked in some manner, and eaten with bread. The French always eat bread with raw fruit. Apples and winter pears are very excellent food for children,—indeed, for almost any person in health,—but best when eaten for breakfast or dinner. If taken late in the evening, fruit often proves injurious. The old saying, that apples are *gold in the morning, silver at noon, and lead at night*, is pretty near the truth. Both apples and pears are often good and nutritious when baked or stewed, and when prepared in this way are especially suitable for those delicate constitutions that cannot bear raw fruit. Much of the fruit gathered when unripe might be rendered fit for food by preserving in sugar.

1518. To prepare Fruit for Children.—A far more wholesome way than in pies or puddings, is to put apples sliced, or plums, currants, gooseberries, &c., into a stone jar, and sprinkle among them as much sugar as necessary. Set the jar in the oven, with a teacupful of water to prevent the fruit from burning ; or put the jar into a saucepan of water till its contents be perfectly done. Slices of bread or some rice may be put into the jar to eat with the fruit.

1519. Rice Pudding with Fruit. —Into a pint of new milk put two large spoonfuls of rice, well washed ; then add two apples, pared and quartered, or a few currants or raisins. Simmer slowly till the rice is very soft, then add one egg beaten to bind it : serve with cream and sugar.

1520. Rice and Apples.—Core as many nice apples as will fill the dish ; boil them in light syrup ; prepare a quarter of a pound of rice in milk with sugar and salt ; put some of the rice in the dish, put in the apples, and fill up the intervals with rice : bake it in the oven till it is a fine colour.

1521. A nice Apple Cake for Children.—Grate some stale bread, and slice about double the quantity of apples ; butter a mould, and line it with sugar paste, and strew in some crumbs, mixed with a little sugar ; then lay in apples, with a few bits of butter over them, and so continue till the dish is full ; cover it with crumbs, or prepared rice ; season with cinnamon and sugar. Bake it well.

1522. Ripe Currants are excellent food for children. Mash the fruit, sprinkle with sugar, and let them eat freely, taking some good bread with the fruit.

1523. Blackberry Pudding or Pie.—A pudding or pie made of blackberries only, or of blackberries and apples mixed in equal proportions is excellent. For suitable suet crust *see* par. 1116, and for puff paste see par. 1110.

1524. Blackberry Jam.—Gather the fruit in dry weather ; allow half-a-pound of good brown sugar to every pound of fruit ; boil the whole together gently for an hour, or till the blackberries are soft, stirring and mashing them well. Preserve it like any other jam, and it will be found very useful in families, particularly for children, regulating their bowels, and enabling you to dispense with cathartics. It may be used in the ordinary way in roll-over puddings, and for tarts, or spread on bread instead of butter ; and even when the blackberries are bought, it is cheaper than butter. In the country every family should preserve at least half-a-peck of blackberries.

1525. To make Senna and Manna Palatable.—Take of senna leaves and manna a quarter of an ounce of each, and pour over them a pint of boiling water ; when the strength is abstracted, pour the infusion over from a quarter to half-a-pound of prunes and two large tablespoonfuls of West India molasses. Stew the whole slowly until the liquid is nearly absorbed. When cold it can be eaten with bread and butter, without detecting the senna, and is excellent for children when costive.

1526. Milk a disseminator of Disease.—Cows' milk very readily absorbs infectious germs, and by its agency many diseases such as diphtheria, typhoid, and other fevers, &c., have been widely spread. It is, therefore, a wise precaution, which should be adopted in all families, especially those resident in cities and towns, to *boil all milk before it is used by the household.* By this simple measure the danger is very considerably lessened.

1527. HINTS ON CONDUCT AND MANNERS.

1528. Ceremonies.—These are in themselves superficial things ; yet a man of the world should know them. They are the outworks of manners and decency, which would be too often broken in upon, if it were not for that defence which keeps the enemy at a proper distance. It is for that reason we always treat fools and coxcombs with great ceremony, true good-breeding not being a sufficient barrier against them. Books on etiquette are useful, inasmuch as they expound the laws of polite society. Experience alone, however, can give effect to the *precise* manner in which those laws are required to be observed.

1529. Choice of Friends.—Dr. Blair has said : "We should ever have it fixed in our memories, that *by the character of those whom we choose for our friends our own character is likely to be formed*, and will certainly be judged of by the world. We ought, therefore, to be slow and cautious in contracting intimacy ; but when a virtuous friendship is once established, we must ever consider it as a sacred engagement."

1530. Rules of Conduct.—The following rules of conduct were drawn up by the celebrated Quakeress, Mrs. Fry, who combined in her character and conduct all that is truly excellent in woman :

i. Never lose any time.—I do not think that time lost which is spent in amusement or recreation some part of each day ; but always be in the habit of being employed.

ii. Never err the least in truth.

iii. Never say an ill thing of a person when thou canst say a good thing of him ; not only speak charitably, but feel so.

iv. Never be irritable or unkind to anybody.

v. Never indulge thyself in luxuries that are not necessary.

vi. Do all things with consideration ; and when thy path to act right is most difficult, feel confidence in that Power alone which is able to assist thee, and exert thy own powers as far as they go.

1531. The Art of being Agreeable.—The true art of being agreeable is to appear well pleased with all the company, and rather to seem well entertained with them than to bring entertainment to them. A man thus disposed, perhaps, may not have much learning, nor any wit ; but if he has common sense and something friendly in his behaviour, it conciliates men's minds more than the brightest parts without this disposition ; and when a man of such a turn comes up to old age, he is almost sure to be treated with respect. It is true, indeed, that we should not dissemble and flatter in company ; but a man may be very agreeable, strictly consistent with truth and sincerity, by a prudent silence where he cannot concur, and a pleasing assent where he can. Now

and then you meet a person so exactly formed to please, that he will gain upon every one that hears or beholds him : this disposition is not merely the gift of nature, but frequently the effect of much knowledge of the world, and a command over the passions.

1532. Personal Manners.—Artificial manners, and such as spring from good taste and refinement, can never be mistaken, and differ as widely as tinsel and gold. How captivating is gentleness of manner derived from true humility, and how faint is every imitation ! That suavity of manner which renders a real gentlewoman courteous to all, and careful to avoid giving offence, is often copied by those who merely subject themselves to certain rules of etiquette : but very awkward is the copy. Warm professions of regard are bestowed on those who do not expect them, and the esteem which is due to merit appears to be lavished on every one alike. And as true humility, blended with a right appreciation of self-respect, gives a pleasing cast to the countenance, so from a sincere and open disposition springs that artlessness of manner which disarms all prejudice. Feeling, on the contrary, is ridiculous when affected, and even when real, should not be too openly manifested. Let the manners arise from the mind, and let there be no disguise for the genuine emotions of the heart.

1533. Avoid Intermeddling with the Affairs of Others.—This is a most common fault. A number of people seldom meet but they begin discussing the affairs of some one who is absent. This is not only uncharitable, but positively unjust. It is equivalent to trying a *cause in the absence of the person implicated.* In our criminal code a prisoner is presumed to be innocent until he is found guilty. Society, however, is less just, and passes judgment without hearing the defence. Depend upon it, as a certain rule, *that the people who unite with you* *in discussing the affairs of others will proceed to your affairs and conduct in your absence.*

1534. Be consistent in the Avowal of Principles.—Do not deny to-day that which you asserted yesterday. If you do, you will stultify yourself, and your opinions will soon be found to have no weight. You may fancy that you gain favour by subserviency ; but so far from gaining favour, you lose respect.

1535. Avoid Falsehood.—There can be found no higher virtue than the love of truth. The man who deceives others must himself become the victim of morbid distrust. Knowing the deceit of his own heart, and the falsehood of his own tongue, his eyes must be always filled with suspicion, and he must lose the greatest of all happiness—confidence in those who surround him.

1536. Avoid Manifestations of Ill-temper.—Reason is given for man's guidance. Passion is the tempest by which reason is overthrown. Under the effects of passion, man's mind becomes disordered, his face disfigured, his body deformed. A moment's passion has frequently cut off a life's friendship, destroyed a life's hope, embittered a life's peace, and brought unending sorrow and disgrace. It is scarcely worth while to enter into a comparative analysis of ill-temper and passion ; they are alike discreditable, alike injurious, and should stand equally condemned.

1537. Avoid Pride.—If you are handsome, God made you so ; if you are learned, some one instructed you ; if you are rich, God gave you what you own. It is for others to perceive your goodness ; but you should be blind to your own merits. There can be no comfort in deeming yourself better than you really are ; that is self-deception. The best men throughout all history have been the most humble.

1538. Affectation a Form of Pride.—It is, in fact, pride made ridiculous and contemptible. Some one writing upon affectation has remarked as follows :

"If anything will sicken and disgust a man it is the affected, mincing way in which some people choose to talk. It is perfectly nauseous. If these young jackanapes, who screw their words into all manner of diabolical shapes, could only feel how perfectly disgusting they were, it might induce them to drop it. With many, it soon becomes such a confirmed habit that they cannot again be taught to talk in a plain, straightforward, manly way. In the lower order of ladies' boarding-schools, and indeed, too much everywhere, the same sickening, mincing tone is too often found. Do, pray, good people, do talk in your natural tone, if you don't wish to be utterly ridiculous and contemptible."

1539. Avoid Vulgarity in manner, in speech, and in correspondence. To conduct yourself vulgarly is to offer offence to those who are around you ; to bring upon yourself the condemnation of persons of good taste ; and to incur the penalty of exclusion from good society. Thus, cast among the vulgar, you become the victim of your own error.

1540. Avoid Swearing.—An oath is but the wrath of a perturbed spirit. It is *mean*. A man of high moral standing would rather treat an offence with contempt than show his indignation by an oath. It is *vulgar*, altogether too low for a decent man. It is *cowardly*, implying a fear either of not being believed or obeyed. It is *ungentlemanly*. A gentleman, according to Webster, is a *genteel man*—well-bred, refined. It is *indecent*, offensive to delicacy, and extremely unfit for human ears. It is *foolish*. "Want of decency is want of sense." It is *abusive*—to the mind which conceives the oath, to the tongue which utters it, and to the person at whom it is aimed. It is *contemptible*, forfeiting the respect of all the wise and good. It is *wicked*, violating the Divine law, and provoking the displeasure of Him who will not hold him guiltless who takes His name in vain.

1541. Be a Gentleman.—Moderation, decorum, and neatness distinguish the gentleman ; he is at all times affable, diffident, and studious to please. Intelligent and polite, his behaviour is pleasant and graceful. When he enters the dwelling of an inferior, he endeavours to hide, if possible, the difference between their ranks of life ; ever willing to assist those around him, he is neither unkind, haughty, nor overbearing. In the mansions of the rich, the correctness of his mind induces him to bend to etiquette, but not to stoop to adulation ; correct principle cautions him to avoid the gaming-table, inebriety, or any other foible that could occasion him self-reproach. Gratified with the pleasures of reflection, he rejoices to see the gaieties of society, and is fastidious upon no point of little import. Appear only to be a gentleman, and its shadows will bring upon you contempt ; be a gentleman, and its honours will remain even after you are dead.

1542. The Happy Man or True Gentleman.

How happy is he born or taught,
   That serveth not another's will,
Whose armour is his honest thought,
   And simple truth his only skill :

Whose passions not his masters are,
   Whose soul is still prepared for death,
Not tied unto the world with care
   Of prince's ear, or vulgar breath :

Who hath his life from rumours freed,
   Whose conscience is his strong retreat,
Whose state can neither flatterers feed.
   Nor ruin make oppressors great :

Who God doth late and early pray
   More of His grace than gifts to lend.
And entertains the harmless day
   With a well chosen book or friend ?

This man is freed from servile bands.
   Of hope to rise or fear to fall ;
Lord of himself, though not of lands.
   And having nothing, yet hath all.
           Sir Henry Wotton, 1530.

1543. Be Honest.—Not only because "honesty is the best policy," but because it is a duty to God and to man. The heart that can be gratified by dishonest gains ; the ambition that can be satisfied by dishonest means ; the mind that can be devoted to dishonest purposes, must be of the worst order.

1544. Avoid Idleness.—it is the parent of many evils. Can you pray, "Give us this day our daily bread," and not hear the reply, "Do thou this day thy daily duty" !

1545. Avoid Telling Idle Tales, which is like shooting arrows in the dark : you know not into whose heart they may fall.

1546. Avoid Self-praise, extolling your own works, and proclaiming your own deeds. If they are good they will proclaim themselves, if bad, the less you say of them the better.

1547. Avoid Envy ; for it cannot benefit you, nor can it injure those against whom it is cherished.

1548. Avoid Disputation for the mere sake of argument. The man who disputes obstinately, and in a bigoted spirit, is like the man who would stop the fountain from which he should drink. Earnest discussion is commendable ; but factious argument never yet produced a good result.

1549. Be Kind in Little Things.—The true generosity of the heart is more displayed by deeds of minor kindness, than by acts which may partake of ostentation.

1550. Be Polite.—Politeness is the poetry of conduct—and like poetry, it has many qualities. Let not your politeness be too florid, but of that gentle kind which indicates a refined nature.

1551. Be Sociable—avoid reserve in society. Remember that the social elements, like the air we breathe, are purified by motion. Thought illumines thought, and smiles win smiles.

1552. Be Punctual.—One minute too late has lost many a golden opportunity. Besides which, the want of punctuality is an affront offered to the person to whom your presence is due.

1553. Be hearty in your salutations, discreet and sincere in your friendships.

1554. Behave, even in the presence of your relations, as though you felt respect to be due to them.

1555. In society never forget that you are but one of many. Prefer to listen rather than talk.

1556. Pry not into letters that are not your own.

1557. Pay unmistakable respect to ladies everywhere, carefully avoiding foppery, and silly flirtation.

1558. In public places be not too pertinacious of your own rights, but find pleasure in making concessions.

1559. Speak distinctly, look at the person to whom you speak, and when you have spoken, give him an opportunity to reply.

1560. Avoid drunkenness as you would a curse ; and modify all appetites, especially those that are acquired.

1561. Dress well, but not superfluously ; be neither like a sloven, nor like a stuffed model.

1562. Study personal cleanliness. Let the nails, the teeth, and, in fact, the whole system receive *salutary* and careful attention at the toilet—not elsewhere.

1563. Avoid displaying excess of jewellery. Nothing looks more effeminate upon a man.

1564. Every one of these suggestions may be regarded as the centre of many others, which the earnest mind cannot fail to discover. (See Hints on Etiquette, par. 1455.)

1565. A Few Words on Words.—Soft words soften the soul. Angry words are fuel to the flame of wrath, and make it blaze more freely. Kind words make other people good-natured. Cold words freeze people, and Hot words scorch them, and Bitter words make them bitter, and Wrathful words make them wrathful. There is such a rush of all other kinds of words in our days, that it seems desirable to give kind words a chance among them. There are Vain words, and Idle words, and Hasty words, and Spiteful words, and Silly words, and Empty words, and Profane words, and Boisterous words, and Warlike words. Kind words also produce their own image on men's souls, and a beautiful image it is. They smooth, and quiet, and comfort the hearer. They shame him out of his sour, and morose, and unkind feelings. We have not yet begun to use kind words in such abundance as they ought to be used.

1566. Gossiping.—If you wish to cultivate a gossiping, meddling, censorious spirit in your children, be sure when they come home from church, a visit, or any other place where you do not accompany them, to ply them with questions concerning what everybody wore, how everybody looked, and what everybody said and did ; and if you find anything in this to censure, always do it in their hearing. You may rest assured, if you pursue a course of this kind, they will not return to you unladen with intelligence ; and rather than it should be uninteresting, they will by degrees learn to embellish, in such a manner as shall not fail to call forth remarks and expressions of wonder from you. You will, by this course, render the spirit of curiosity, which is so early visible in children, and which, if rightly directed, may be made the instrument of enriching and enlarging their minds, a *vehicle of* *mischief which will serve only to narrow them.*

1567. Counsels for the Young.

i. Never be cast down by trifles. If a spider break his thread twenty times, he will mend it again as often.

ii. Make up your mind to do a thing, and you will do it.

iii. Fear not if a trouble comes upon you ; keep up your spirits, though the day be a dark one. If the sun is going down, look up to the stars. If the earth is dark, keep your eye on heaven. With God's promises, a man or a child may be cheerful.

iv. Mind what you run after. Never be content with a bubble that will burst—firewood that will end in smoke and darkness. Get that which you can keep, and which is worth keeping.

v. Fight hard against a hasty temper. Anger will come, but resist it strongly. A fit of passion may give you cause to mourn all the days of your life.

vi. Never revenge an injury. If you have an enemy, act kindly to him, and make him your friend. You may not win him over at once, but try again. Let one kindness be followed by another, till you have compassed your end. By little and little, great things are completed ; and repeated kindnesses will soften the heart of stone.

vii. Whatever you do, do it willingly. A boy that is whipped to school never learns his lessons well. A man who is compelled to work cares not how badly it is performed. He that pulls off his coat cheerfully, turns up his sleeves in earnest, and sings while he works, is the man of action.

1568. Advice to Young Ladies.

i. If you have blue eyes you need not languish : if black eyes, you need not stare.

ii. If you have pretty feet there is no occasion to wear short petticoats : if

you are doubtful as to that point, there can be no harm in letting the petticoats be long.

iii. If you have good teeth, do not laugh in order to show them : if bad teeth do not laugh less than the occasion may warrant.

iv. If you have a bad voice, speak in a subdued tone : if you have the finest voice in the world, never speak in a high tone.

v. If you dance well, dance but seldom ; if ill, never dance at all.

vi. If you sing or play well, make no foolish excuses : if only moderately, do not hesitate when you are asked but do your best, as every one appreciates a desire to please.

vii. To preserve beauty, rise early.

viii. To preserve esteem, be gentle.

ix. To live happily, try to promote the happiness of others.

1569. On Training Daughters.—
Mothers who wish not only to discharge well their own duties in the domestic circle, but to train up their daughters for a later day to make happy and comfortable firesides for their families, should watch well, and guard well, the notions which they imbibe and with which they grow up. There will be many persons ready to fill their young heads with false and vain fancies, and there is so much always afloat in society opposed to duty and common sense, that if mothers do not watch well, their children may contract ideas very fatal to their future happiness and usefulness, and hold them till they grow into habits of thought or feeling. A wise mother will have her eyes open, and be ready for every emergency. A few words of common, downright practical sense, timely uttered by her, may be enough to counteract some foolish idea or belief put into her daughter's head by others, whilst if it be left unchecked, it may take such possession of the mind that it cannot be corrected at a later time. One false

notion rife in the present age is the idea that women, unless compelled to it by absolute poverty, are out of place when engaged in domestic affairs. Now mothers should have a care lest their daughters get hold of this conviction as regard themselves—there is danger of it ; the fashion of the day engenders it, and even the care that an affectionate family take to keep a girl, during the time of her education, free from other occupations than those of her tasks, or her recreations, may lead her to infer that the matters with which she is never asked to concern herself are, in fact, no concern to her, and that any attention she may ever bestow on them is not a matter of simple duty, but of grace, or concession, or stooping, on her part. Let mothers bring up their daughters from the *first* with the idea that in this world it is required to give as well as to receive, to minister as well as to enjoy ; that every person is bound to be useful in his own sphere, and that a woman's first sphere is the house, and its concerns and demands. Once really imbued with this belief, a young girl will usually be anxious to learn all that her mother is disposed to teach, and will be proud and happy to aid in any domestic occupations assigned to her. These need never be made so heavy as to interfere with the peculiar duties or enjoyments of her age. If a mother wishes to see her daughter become a good, happy, and rational woman, never let there be contempt for domestic occupations, or suffer them to be deemed secondary.

1570. Treatment of Servants.— There are frequent complaints in these days, that servants and assistants generally are unsatisfactory and deteriorating. If so what is the inference ? Domestic servants, and assistants in business and trade, come closely and continually into contact with their employers ; and they are about them from morning till night, and see them in every phase of character, in every style of humour, in every act of life. How powerful is the force of example ! Rectitude is promoted, not only by precept but by example, and, so to speak, by contact it is increased more widely. Kindness is communicated in the same way. Virtue of every kind acts with magnetic power ; those who come under its influence imbibe its principles. The same with qualities and tempers that do no honour to our nature. If servants come to you bad, you may at least improve them ; possibly almost change their nature. Here follows, then, a recipe to that effect:—*Recipe for obtaining good servants.*—Let them observe in your conduct to others just the qualties and virtues that you would desire they should possess and practise as respects you. Be uniformly kind and gentle. If you reprove, do so with reason and with good temper. Be respectable, and you will be respected by them. Be kind, and you will meet kindness from them. Consider their interests, and they will consider yours. A friend in a servant is no contemptible thing. Be to every servant a friend ; and heartless, indeed, will be the servant who does not warm in love to you.

1571. A Wife's Power.— The power of a wife for good or evil is irresistible. Home must be the seat of happiness, or it must be for ever unknown. A good wife is to a man wisdom, and courage, and strength, and endurance. A bad wife is confusion, weakness, discomfiture, and despair. No condition is hopeless where the wife possesses firmness, decision, and economy. There is no outward prosperity which can counteract indolence, extravagance, and folly at home. No spirit can long endure bad domestic influence. Man is strong, but his heart is not adamant. He delights in enterprise and action ; but to sustain him he needs a tranquil mind, and a whole heart. He needs his moral force in the conflicts of the world. To recover his equanimity and composure, home must be to him a place of repose, of peace, of cheerfulness, of comfort ; and his soul renews its strength again, and goes forth with fresh vigour to encounter the labour and troubles of life. But if at home he find no rest, and is there met with bad temper, sullenness, or gloom, or is assailed by discontent or complaint, hope vanishes, and he sinks into despair.

1572. The Wife's Temper.—No trait of character is more agreeable in a female than the possession of a sweet temper. Home can never be happy without it. It is like the flowers that spring up in our pathway, reviving and cheering us. Let a man go home at night, wearied and worn by the toils of the day, and how soothing is a word dictated by a good disposition ! It is sunshine falling on his heart. He is happy, and the cares of life are forgotten. A sweet temper has a soothing influence over the minds of a whole family. Where it is found in the wife and mother, you observe a kindness and love predominating over the natural feelings of a bad heart. Smiles, kind words and looks, characterize the children, and peace and love have their dwelling there. Study, then, to acquire and maintain a sweet temper.

1573. Three Wifely Virtues.—There are three things which a good wife should resemble, and yet those three things she should not resemble. She should be like a town clock—keep time and regularity. She should *not*, however, like a town clock—speak so loudly that all the town may hear her. She should be like a snail—prudent, and keep within her own house. She should *not* be like a snail—carry all she has upon her back. She should be like an echo—speak when spoken to. But she should not be like an echo—determined always to have the last word.

1574. Counsels for Husbands.—You can hardly imagine how refreshing it is to occasionally call up the recollection of your courting days. How tediously the hours rolled away prior to the appointed time of meeting ; how swiftly they seemed to fly when you had met ; how fond was the first greeting ; how vivid your dreams of future happiness, when, returning to your home, you felt yourself secure in the confessed love of the object of your warm affections ! Is your dream realized ?—are you as happy as you expected ? Consider whether, as a husband, you are as fervent and constant as you were when a lover. Remember that the wife's claims to your unremitting regard, great before marriage, are now exalted to a much higher degree. She has left the world for you—the home of her childhood, the fireside of her parents, their watchful care and sweet intercourse have all been yielded up for you. Look, then, most jealously upon all that may tend to attract you from home, and to weaken that union upon which your temporal happiness mainly depends ; and believe that in the solemn relationship of husband is to be found one of the best guarantees for man's honour and happiness.

If your wife complain that young ladies of the present day are very forward, don't accuse her of jealousy. A little concern on her part only proves her love for you, and you may enjoy your triumph without saying a word. Don't evince your weakness either, by complaining of every trifling neglect. What though her knitting and crochet seem to absorb too large a share of her attention ; depend upon it, that as her eyes watch the intertwinings of the threads, and the manoeuvres of the needles, she is thinking of the events of bygone times, which entangled your two hearts in the network of love, whose meshes you can neither of you unravel or escape.

Summer is the season of love and

innocent enjoyment. What shall the husband do when summer returns to gladden the earth, and all who live upon it ? Must he still pore over the calculations of the counting-house, or ceaselessly pursue the toils of the work-room—sparing no moment to taste the joys which Heaven measures out so liberally ? No ! Let him ask his wife once more to breathe with him the fresh air of heaven, and look upon the beauties of earth. The summers are few that they may dwell together ; so let him not give them all to mammon, but seek invigorating and health-renewing recreation abroad, which shall make the hearts of each glow with emotions of renewed love.

1575. Counsels for Wives.—Perchance you think that your husband's disposition is much changed ; that he is no longer the sweet-tempered, ardent lover he used to be. This may be a mistake. Consider his struggles with the world—his everlasting race with the busy competition of trade. What is it makes him so eager in the pursuit of gain—so energetic by day, so sleepless by night—but his love of home, wife, and children, and a dread that their respectability, according to the light in which he has conceived it, may be encroached upon by the strife of existence ? This is the true secret of that silent care which preys upon the hearts of many men ; and true it is, that when love is least apparent, it is nevertheless the active principle which animates the heart, though fears and disappointments make up a cloud which obscures the warmer element. As above the clouds there is glorious sunshine, while below are showers and gloom, so with the conduct of man—behind the gloom of anxiety is a bright fountain of high and noble feeling. Think of this in those moments when clouds seem to lower upon your domestic peace, and, by tempering your conduct accordingly, the gloom will soon pass away, and warmth and brightness take its place.

If your husband occasionally looks a little troubled when he comes home, do not say to him, with an alarmed countenance, "What ails you, my dear ?" Don't bother him ; he will tell you of his own accord, if need be. Be observant and quiet. Let him alone until he is inclined to talk ; take up your book or your needlework pleasantly and cheerfully; and wait until he is inclined to be sociable. Don't let him ever find a shirt-button missing. A shirt-button being off a collar or wristband has frequently produced the first impatient word in married life.

Never complain that your husband pores too much over the newspaper, to the exclusion of that pleasing converse which you formerly enjoyed with him.—Don't hide the paper, but when the boy leaves it at the door take it in pleasantly, and lay it down before him. Think what man would be without a newspaper, and how much good newspapers have done by exposing bad husbands and bad wives, by giving their errors to the eye of the public. When your husband is absent, instead of gossiping or looking into shop windows, sit down quietly, and look over that paper ; run your eye over its home and foreign news ; glance rapidly at the accidents and casualties ; carefully scan the leading articles ; and at tea-time, when your husband again takes up the paper, make some brief remarks on what you have read, and depend upon it, he will put it down again. If he has not read the information, he will hear it all from your lips, and when you have read, he will ask questions in his turn, and, gradually, you will get into as cosy a chat as you ever enjoyed ; and you will soon discover that, rightly used, the newspaper is the wife's real friend, for it keeps the husband at home, and supplies capital topics for every-day table-talk.

"It was !" "It was not !" "It *was !*" "It was *not !*" "Ah !" " Ha ! "—

Now who's the wiser or the better for this contention for the last word ? Does obstinacy establish superiority or elicit truth ? Decidedly not ! Woman has always been described as clamouring for the last word, and men, generally, have agreed in attributing this trait to her, and in censuring her for it. This being so, it remains for some one of the sex, by an exhibition of noble example, to aid in sweeping away the unpleasant imputation. The wife who will establish the rule of allowing her husband to have the last word, will achieve for herself and her sex a great moral victory! Is he *right* ?—it were a great error to oppose him. Is he *wrong* ?—he will soon discover it, and applaud the self-command which bore unvexed his pertinacity. And gradually there will spring up such a happy fusion of feelings and ideas, that there will be no "last word" to contend about, but a steady and unruffled flow of generous sentiment.

1576. EARLY RISING.

The difference between rising every morning at six o'clock or eight, in the course of forty years, amounts to 29,200 hours, or three years one hundred and twenty-one days and sixteen hours, which are equal to eight hours a day for exactly ten years. So that rising at six will be the same as if ten years of life (a weighty consideration) were added, wherein we may command eight hours every day for the cultivation of our minds and the despatch of business.

1577. DR. FRANKLIN ON FRUGALITY.

We quote some of this great philosopher's proverbial truisms on this subject.

i. "A man may, if he knows not how to save as he gets, keep his nose all his life to the grindstone, and die not worth a groat at last. A fat kitchen makes a lean will."

" Many estates are spent in the getting,
Since women for tea forsook spinning and knitting.
And men for punch forsook hewing and splitting."

ii. "If you would be wealthy, think of saving as well as of getting. The Indies have not made Spain rich, because her out-goes are greater than her in-comes."

iii. "Away with your expensive follies, and you will not have so much cause to complain of hard times, heavy taxes, and chargeable families."

iv. "What maintains one vice would bring up two children."

v. "You may think, perhaps, that a little tea, or superfluities now and then, diet a little more costly, clothes a little finer, and a little entertainment now and then, can be no great matter ; but remember, 'Many a little makes a mickle.'"

vi. "Beware of little expenses ;" "A small leak will sink a great ship;" "Who dainties love, shall beggars prove ;" "Fools make feasts and wise men eat them."

vii. "Here you are all got together to this sale of fineries and nick-nacks. You call them goods ; but if you do not take care they will prove evils to some of you. You expect they will be sold cheap, and perhaps they may, for less than they cost ; but if you have no occasion for them they must be dear to you."

viii. "Buy what thou hast no need of, and ere long thou shalt sell thy necessaries."

1578. CASH VERSUS CREDIT.

If you would get rich, don't deal in bill books. Credit is the "Tempter in a new shape." Buy goods on trust, and you will purchase a thousand articles that Cash would never have dreamed of. A shilling in the hand looks larger than ten shillings seen through the perspective of a three months' bill. Cash is practical, while Credit takes horribly to taste and romance. Let Cash buy a dinner, and you will have a beef-steak flanked with onions. Send Credit to market, and he will return with eight pairs of woodcocks and a peck of mushrooms. Credit believes in diamond pins and champagne suppers. Cash is more easily satisfied. Give him three meals a day, and he doesn't care much if two of them are made up of roasted potatoes and a little salt. Cash is a good adviser, while Credit is a good fellow to be on visiting terms with. If you want double chins and contentment, do business with Cash.

1579. DON'T RUN INTO DEBT.

"Don't run into debt ;"—never mind, never mind
  If your clothes are faded and torn ;
Mend them up, make them do ; it is better by far
  Than to have the heart weary and worn.

Who'll love you the more for the shape of your hat,
  Or your ruff, or the tie of your shoe,
The cut of your vest, or your boots, or cravat,
  If they know you're in debt for the new ?

There's no comfort, I tell you, in walking the street
  In fine clothes, if you know you're in debt,
And feel that, perchance, you some trades-man may meet,
  Who will sneer— "They're not paid for yet."

Good friends, let me beg of you, don't run in debt ;
  If the chairs and the sofas are old
They will fit your back better than any new set.
  Unless they are paid for—with gold ;

If the house is too small, draw the closer together.
  Keep it warm with a hearty good-will ;
A big one unpaid for, in all kinds of weather,
  Will send to your warm heart a chill.

Don't run in debt—now, dear girls, take a hint.
  If the fashions have changed since last season,
Old Nature is out in the very same tint.
  And old Nature, we think, has some reason;

But just say to your friend, that you cannot afford
  To spend time to keep up with the fashion ;
That your purse is too light and your honour too bright.
  To be tarnished with such silly passion.

Men, don't run in debt—let your friends, if they can,
  Have fine houses, and feathers, and flowers ;
But, unless they are paid for, be more of a man
  Than to envy their sunshiny hours.

If you've money to spare, I have nothing to say—
  Spend your silver and gold as you please :
But mind you, the man who his bill has to pay
  Is the man who is never at ease.

Kind husbands, don't run into debt any more ;
  'Twill fill your wives' cup full of sorrow,
To know that a neighbour may call at your door,
  With a claim you must settle to-morrow.

Oh ! take my advice— it is good, it is true !
  But, lest you may some of you doubt it,
I'll whisper a secret now, seeing 'tis you—
  I have tried it, and know all about it.

The chain of a debtor is heavy and cold,
  Its links all corrosion and rust ;
Gild it o'er as you will, it is never of gold,
  Then spurn it aside with disgust.

    1580. Josh Billing said, "Never run into debt, not if you can find ennything else to run into."

1581. HINTS UPON MONEY MATTERS.

    i. Have a supply of change in hand-shillings, sixpences, halfpence. This will obviate the various inconveni-ences of keeping people at the door, sending out at unreasonable times, and running or calling after any in-mate in the house, supposed to be better provided with "the needful." The tradespeople with whom you regularly deal will always give you extra change, *when* you are making purchases or paying bills ; while those to whom you apply for it, on a sudden emergency, may neither be willing nor able to do so. Some housekeepers object to this arrangement, that, "as soon as five-pound notes or sovereigns are changed, they always seem to go, without their understanding how ;" but to such persons I would humbly intimate, that this is rather the fault of their *not getting understanding*, than any inevitable consequence of *getting change*. The fact is, that it is the necessity of parting with your money which obliges you to get the larger pieces changed, and not the circumstance of having smaller coin that *necessitates* your parting with your money, though it certainly facilitates your doing so when the necessity arrives. However, as it is easier to count a few sovereigns than many shillings, and loose money is most objectionable, it is well to put up reserve change in small collective packets, and to replenish the house-keeping purse from these daily or weekly, as may be most convenient.

ii. if money for daily expenses has to pass through the hands of a servant, it is a time-and-trouble-saving plan to settle with her *every* night, and to make up her cash in hand to a certain *similar* sum. This will prevent such puzzling calculations as the following : "Let me see: I gave you 10s. on Saturday, and 9d. the day before. Was it 9d. ? No, it must have been 11d., for I gave you 1 s., and you gave me 1d. out for the beggar ; then there was 6s. 6d. on Monday, and 8d. you owed me from last money ; and then the 1s. 6d. your master gave you for a parcel—you brought him 2d. back, and 3½d. out of the butcher's bill ; no—*you* had to give 3½d. to the butcher, but you came to me for the ½d. and I had no coppers, so we still owe him the ½d. ; by the way, don't forget to pay him the next time you go. Then there's the baker—no, I paid the baker myself, and I *think* the housemaid paid the butterman ; but you got in the cheese the day before, and I have a sort of recollection that I may possibly owe you for *that*, all but a few pence you must have had left of mine, that I told you to take from off the chimney-piece. Well, cook, I think that's *nearly* all ! Now how do your accounts stand ?" This the poor cook, who *is* a cook, and *not* a conjuror, finds it no easy matter to discover ; all that she is quite certain of is, that her disbursements have somewhat exceeded her receipts, and being an honest woman, though a poor one, she wishes to cheat neither her mistress nor herself ; but what with her memory and her want of it, her involved payments, and different receipts ; what she owed her mistress, and what her mistress owes her ; what she got from her master, and what was partly settled by the house-maid ; the balance from the butcher's bill, and the intricacies of the cheese account, the poor woman is perfectly bewildered. She counts again and again ; recapitulates her mistress's data and her own ; sums upwards, backwards, and forwards, and endeavours to explain the differences between them ; then, if she can read and write, she brings her slate to "explain the explanation," and the united calculations of maid and mistress, which are after all entirely unavailing to produce a more correct account, probably consume more time, and are expressed in more words, than would suffice to fill another volume like the present. Two minutes' daily reckoning from a *regular* sum in hand would do the business effectually, and prevent either party from being out of pocket or out of temper. Thus, for instance, the maid has her usual sum of 5s. to account for ; she pays during the day, for—

	s.	d.
Bread	1	9
Beer	0	6
Vegetables and fruit	0	10
Milk	0	4
Matches	0	1
Parcel	1	0
Total	4	6

This is easily reckoned, even by the unlearned ; the mistress enters the items in her day-book, takes the remaining sixpence, and again gives her servant 5s. , in convenient change, to be as readily accounted for on the succeeding day.—*"Home Truths for Home Peace; or, Muddle Defeated."*

1582. HABITS OF A MAN OF BUSINESS.—A sacred regard to the principles of justice forms the basis of every transaction, and regulates the conduct of the upright man of business. The following statements afford a bird's-eye view, as it were, of his habits, practice, and mode of procedure :—

i. He is strict in keeping his engagements.

ii. He does nothing carelessly or in a hurry.

iii. He employs nobody to do what he can easily do himself.

iv. He keeps everything in its proper place.

v. He leaves nothing undone that ought to be done, and which circumstances permit him to do.

vi. He keeps his designs and business from the view of others.

vii. He is prompt and decisive with his customers, and does not over-trade his capital.

viii. He prefers short credits to long ones ; and cash to credit at all times, either in buying or selling ; and small profits in credit cases with little risk, to the chance of better gains with more hazard.

ix. He is clear and explicit in all his bargains.

x. He leaves nothing of consequence to memory which he can and ought to commit to writing.

xi. He keeps copies of all his important letters which he sends away, and has every letter, invoice, &c., belonging to his business, titled, classed, and put away.

xii. He never suffers his desk to be confused by many papers lying upon it, but has a place for everything, and everything in its place.

xiii. He is always at the head of his business, well knowing that if he leaves it, it will leave him.

xiv. He holds it as a maxim that he whose credit is suspected is not one to be trusted.

xv. He is constantly examining his books, and sees through all his affairs as far as care and attention will enable him.

xvi. He balances regularly at stated times, and then makes out and transmits all his accounts current to his customers, both at home and abroad.

xvii. He avoids as much as possible all sorts of accommodation in money matters, and lawsuits where there is the least hazard.

xviii. He is economical in his expenditure, always living within his income.

xix. He keeps a memorandum-book in his pocket, in which he notes every particular relative to appointments, addresses, and petty cash matters.

xx. He is cautious how he becomes security for any person ; and is generous when urged by motives of humanity.

xxi. He makes his business known in few words without loss of time.

xxii. He treats all with respect, confides in few, and wrongs no one.

xxiii. He attends to his own business, and not to his neighbour's.

Let a man act strictly to these habits—ever remembering that he hath no profits by his pains whom Providence doth not prosper—and success will attend his efforts.

1583. HINTS TO SHOPKEEPERS.

If you are about to take a place of business, you will do well to consider the following remarks :—

i. **Small Capitalists.**—Let us take the case of a person who has no intimate knowledge of any particular trade, but having a very small capital, is about to embark it in the exchange of commodities for cash, in order to obtain an honest livelihood thereby. It is clear that unless such a person starts with proper precaution and judgment, the capital will be expended without adequate results ; rent and taxes will accumulate, the stock will lie dead, or become deteriorated, and loss and ruin must follow. For the fast absorption acting upon a small capital will soon dry up its source ; and we need not picture the trouble that will arise when the mainspring of a tradesman's success abides by him no more.

ii. Larger Capitalists.—The case of the larger capitalist can scarcely be considered an exception to the same rule. For it is probable that the larger capitalist, upon commencing a business, would sink more of his funds in a larger stock—would incur liability to a heavier rent ; and the attendant taxes, the wages of assistants and servants would be greater, and, therefore, if the return came not speedily, similar consequences must sooner or later ensue.

iii. Localities.—Large or small capitalists should, therefore, upon entering on a shopkeeping speculation, consider well the nature of the locality in which they propose to carry on trade, the number of the population, the habits and wants of the people, and the extent to which they are already supplied with the goods which the new adventurer proposes to offer them.

iv. New neighbourhoods.—There is a tendency among small capitalists to rush into new neighbourhoods with the expectation of making an early connection. Low rents also serve as an attraction to these localities. General experience, however, tends to show that the early suburban shops seldom succeed. They are generally entered upon at the very earliest moment that the state of the locality will permit—often before the house is finished the shop is tenanted, and goods exposed for sale—even while the streets are unpaved, and while the roads are as rough and uneven as

country lanes. The consequence is, that as the few inhabitants of these localities have frequent commnnication with adjacent centres of business, they, as a matter of habit or of choice, supply their chief wants thereat ; and the newly-arrived shopkeeper has to depend principally for support upon the accidental forgetfulness of his neighbour, who omits to bring something from the cheaper and better market ; or upon the changes of the weather, which may sometimes favour him by rendering a "trip to town" exceedingly undesirable.

v. Failures.—"While the grass is growing the horse is starving ;" and thus, while the new district is becoming peopled the funds of the small shopkeeper are gradually eaten up, and he puts up his shutters just at the time when a more cautious speculator steps in to profit by the connection already formed, and to take advantage of the now improved condition of the locality. It seems, therefore, desirable for the small capitalists rather to run the risk of a more expensive rent, in a well-peopled district, than to resort to places of slow and uncertain demand ; for the welfare of the small shopkeeper depends entirely upon the frequency with which his limited stock is cleared out and replaced by fresh supplies.

vi. Precautions.—But should the small capitalist still prefer opening in a suburban district, where competition is less severe, and rents and rates less burdensome, there are certain precautions which he will do well to observe. He should particularly guard against opening a shop to supply what may be termed the superfluities of life ; for the inhabitants of most new suburban districts are those who, like himself, have resorted to a cheap residence for the sake of economy. Or if this be not the case—if they are people of independent means, who prefer the "detached villa" to the town house, squeezed up on both sides, they have the means of riding and driving to town, and will prefer choosing articles of taste and luxury from the best marts, enriched by the finest display.

vii. **Necessaries of Luxuries.**— The suburban shopkeeper should, therefore, confine himself to supplying the *necessaries* of life. Hungry people dislike to fetch their bread from five miles off ; and to bring vegetables from a long distance would evidently be a matter of considerable inconveni- ence. The baker, the butcher, the greengrocer, the beer retailer, &c., are those who find their trade first established in suburban localities. And not until these are doing well should the tailor, the shoemaker, the hatter, the draper, the hosier, and others, expect to find a return for their capital, and reward for their labour.

viii. **Civility.**—In larger localities, where competition abounds, the small shopkeeper frequently outstrips his more power rival by one element of success, which may be added to any stock without cost, but cannot be withheld without loss. That element is *civility*. It has already been spoken of elsewhere, but must be enforced here, as aiding the little means of the small shopkeeper to a wonderful degree. A kind and obliging manner carries with it an indescribable charm. It must not be a manner which indicates a mean, grovelling, time-serving spirit, but a plain, open, and agreeable demeanour, which seems to desire to oblige for the pleasure of doing so, and not for the sake of squeezing an extra penny out of a customer's pocket.

ix. **Integrity.**—The main reliance of the shopkeeper should be in the integrity of his transactions, and in the civility of his demeanour. He should make it the interest and the pleasure of the customer to come to his shop. If he does this, he will form the very best "connections," and so long as he continues this system of business, they will never desert him.

x. **Duties of a Shopkeeper.**— He should cheerfully render his best labour and knowledge to serve those who approach his counter, and place confidence in his transactions ; make himself alike to rich and poor, but never resort to mean subterfuge and deception to gain approbation and support. He should be frugal in his expenditure, that in deriving profits from trade, he may not trespass unduly upon the interest of others ; he should so hold the balance between man and man that he should feel nothing to trouble his conscience when the day comes for him to repose from his labours and live upon the fruits of his industry. Let the public discover such a man, and they will flock round him for their own sakes.

xi. A very useful book, *The Handy Book of Shopkeeping, Shopkeeper's Guide* (published at one shilling, by Houlston and Sons), enlarges upon these subjects in a very able manner, and gives most useful hints to people in every department of trade.

1584. ADULTERATIONS.

A series of papere were published in the *Lancet* and elsewhere a few years back on the subject of Adulteration. These brought about a parliamentary inquiry ; the inquiry ended in demon- strating that nearly everything we ate and drank was adulterated—in many cases with ingredients very prejudicial to human health. The result of the inquiry was the passing of an Act of Parliament for the purpose of putting a stop to this wholesale adulteration by making it a criminal offence. The Act is called the "Sale of Foods and Drugs Act," and the following are the most important clauses it contains:—

"No person shall mix, colour, stain, or powder any article of food with any ingredient or material, so as to render the article injurious to health, with the intent that the same may be sold in that state, and no person shall sell such article under a penalty not exceeding £50."

"No person shall sell to the prejudice of the purchaser any article of food, or any drug which is not of the nature, substance, and quality of the article demanded under a penalty not exceeding £20."

The Act also provides for the appointment of public analysts for counties and boroughs. A later Act provides that all substances or compounds made to imitate butter shall be sold as *Margarine*, and all wrappers, &c., used in its sale must be plainly marked. These Acts are intended for the protection of the public ; but we give below the names of a few of the chief articles of consumption that are liable to be adulterated, and, when possible, how to detect the adulteration, or the best mode of avoiding it.

1585. Bread.—The chief adulteration of *bread* is alum. This is added to give the bread a pure white colour, which is supposed to be an advantage, thus enabling the baker to use inferior or damaged flour. The presence of alum can be detected by soaking a piece of the bread in an ammoniacal tincture of logwood. If alum be present the bread will be turned *blue*, whereas pure bread will remain *pink*. Recent investigations have proved that the presence of alum is extremely injurious, especially to children, affecting the coats of the stomach and impairing the digestion. Other substances stated to be used in adulterating bread are borax, sulphate of copper, sulphate of zinc, carbonate of magnesia, chalk, flour of rice, and bran, and potatoes.

1586. Butter is made heavy by water being beaten up with it. Cheap samples are sometimes adulterated with other fats and grease, which however require an experienced analyst to detect.

1587. Butterine and Margarine are made of animal fat melted, the top layer being taken off and mixed with oil. This is washed in milk, salted, and made up to imitate butter.

1588. Cayenne Pepper.—The cayenne of commerce is adulterated with brickdust, red wood dust, cochineal, vermilion, and red lead. The last two are highly injurious. These can be detected by any one possessing a good microscope. The best way to avoid the impurities is to purchase the capsicums or chillies, pounding them with a pestle and mortar, and rubbing through a sieve, in small quantities as required. The pepper is far better flavoured when fresh ground.

1589. Chocolate and Cocoa.—Those who prefer the pure cocoa can obtain the "nibs," or more properly "beans," and grind them. But many prefer the soluble cocoa, which is simply cocoa modified by admixture with less stimulating substances, such as sugar, arrowroot, and other starchy matters.

1590. Coffee is adulterated with roasted beans, peas, and acorns ; but chiefly with chicory. Have your own mill, buy the roasted beans from a respectable grocer, ascertain his roasting-day, *and always buy from a fresh roast.* If you like the flavour of chicory, purchase it separately, and add to taste. Chicory in small quantities is not injurious, but you need not pay the coffee price for it. Grind your coffee, and mix it with chicory for yourself.

1591. Honey.—A great portion of so-called honey is merely starch (sugar or glucose) mixed with a little real honey.

1592.—Milk is "adulterated" by skimming off part of the cream, also by the addition of water.

1593. Mustard is largely adulterated with flour and turmeric ; as, however, mustard is usually sold in tins it is easy to obtain it pure, as under the Sale of Foods and Drugs Act, all that is mixed with flour and other flavourings has to be labelled as such on the outside of the package. Many prefer this mixture to the pure article.

1594. Oatmeal is usually adulterated with barley-flour, to give it a whiter appearance.

1595. Pepper is adulterated with inferior grain, husks of seeds, sand, rice-flour, sago, linseed, and even dust of a variety of descriptions. Have your own pepper-mill, purchase the seed whole, and grind for yourself. You will then obtain the pure article at a moderate cost.

1596. Sausages.—The most offensive of all adulterations are found in these savoury morsels. Horseflesh, diseased animals, and odds and ends of every description appear in the tempting guise of "sausages." To escape this evil, make your own sausages by the aid of the sausage-machine, which will enable you to add many savoury morsels to the attractions of your table. The same machine may be used for *chopping vegetables*, which it will do to such perfection that they will perfectly dissolve in soups and stews, and afford most delicious made-dishes. And in this you will soon save the cost of the machine.

1597. Tea now undergoes examination by the Customs authorities before "duty" is allowed to be paid upon it ; it is, therefore, practically pure. Almost the only form which adulteration now takes is in the "faced tea." This is black tea, to which an improved appearance has been imparted by means of indigo, French chalk, plumbago, &c.

1598. Vinegar is principally adulterated with water, or sulphuric acid.

1599. Water.—This perhaps is more often adulterated than any other article of consumption. As a rule the water supplied by the companies to the large towns is exceedingly pure, that supplied by the London companies

being analyzed every month by a Government official ; but the adulteration chiefly rests with the consumer or householder, in not keeping the cistern clean ; dust, soot, and even dead mice, cockroaches, &c., being allowed to contaminate the water ; also by permitting the overflow pipe to be connected with the soil pipe, or drain, whence the water absorbs poisonous gases. The overflow pipe should in all cases be entirely disconnected with all drains. The cisterns should, if possible, have a cover, and be cleaned out thoroughly at least every three months. In places where the water is drawn from wells great care should be taken that the well cannot be contaminated by any drain or cesspool leaking into it. Many cases of serious illness, notably diphtheria, have been traced to this cause. When there is the least reason to doubt the purity of the well all the water for drinking purposes should be boiled before using, and no time should be lost in having it examined by an experienced analyst. All water that is used for drinking should be first filtered through a *reliable* filter. Small glass filters for the table can now be obtained in every town for two or three shillings.

1600. OTHER EVILS BESIDES "ADULTERATIONS."

The butcher cannot adulterate the beef and the mutton, but he can send home *short weight* ; and in casting up a bill, he can make mistakes in reckoning the odd ounces ; and the baker, besides putting alum into the bread, to make it white and retain water, can send home deficient weight ; the same with the grocer, and the greengrocer, and the coal merchant ; the publican can give short measure, and froth up the porter to fill the jug and disguise the shortness of quantity ; and the draper can slip his scissors on the wrong side of his finger, and make a yard contain only thirty-three inches. We don't mean to say that they *do* this, nor do we mean to say that they *don't*. We argue, *that people ought to possess the means of ascertaining who among shopkeepers are honest and who are not* ; then the just would meet with justice, and the unjust would suffer for their own sins.

1601. NUTRIMENT CONTAINED IN VARIOUS FOODS.

Bread contains eighty nutritious parts in 100 ; meal, thirty-four in 100 ; French beans, ninety-two in 100 ; common beans, eighty-nine in 100 ; peas, ninety-three in 100 ; lentils, ninety-four in 100 ; cabbages and turnips, the most aqueous of all the vegetables compared, produce only eight pounds of solid matter in 100 pounds ; carrots and spinach produce fourteen in the same quantity ; whilst 100 pounds of potatoes contain twenty-five pounds of dry substance. From a general estimate it results, that one pound of good bread is equal to two and a half or three pounds of potatoes ; that seventy-five pounds of bread and thirty of meat may be substituted for 300 pounds of potatoes. The other substances bear the following proportions : four parts of cabbage to one of potatoes ; three parts of turnips to one of potatoes ; two parts of carrots and spinach to one of potatoes ; and about three parts and a half of potatoes to one of rice, lentils, beans, French beans, and dry peas.

1602. UTILITY OF FRUIT.

Instead of standing in any fear of a generous consumption of ripe fruits, we regard them as conducive to health. No one ever lived longer or freer from disease by discarding the fruits of the land in which he finds a home. On the contrary, they are necessary to the preservation of health, and are therefore designed to make their appearance at the very time when the condition of the body, operated upon by deteriorating causes not always understood, requires their renovative influences.

1603. Blackberries are very beneficial in cases of dysentery. The berries are healthful eating. Tea made of the roots and leaves is good ; and syrup made from the berries excellent.

1604. Sloe Wine is useful in cases of diarrhœa, the astringent properties of this fruit tending to counteract relaxation of the bowels. It is made by steeping sloes in water, and letting them stand therein until a thick coating of mildew is formed on the surface. This is removed, and the liquor is then strained and bottled, and tightly corked down. Not more than from half a wine-glassful to a wine-glassful should be taken when required.

1604a. Sloe Gin.—Get a two-gallon jar, and put into it one gallon of gin, three quarts of sloes, 2½ lbs. of lump sugar, ½ oz. of bitter almonds. Lay it by for three months, taking care to shake it two or three times a week. Then strain it and bottle it, sealing the bottles carefully.

1605. OBSERVANCES OF THE DINNER TABLE.

i. A dinner table should be well laid, well lighted, and always afford a little spare room. It is better to invite one friend less in number, than to destroy the comfort of the whole party. The room should be warmed to the right heat ; before bringing in the cloth or other articles for the table, have the grate swept, and the sideboard and mantelpiece dusted.

ii. The laying out of a table must greatly depend upon the nature of the dinner or supper, the taste of the host, the description of the company, and the appliances possessed. It would be useless, therefore, to lay down specific rules. The whiteness of the table-cloth, the clearness of glass, the polish of plate, and the judicious distribution of ornamental groups of fruits and flowers, are matters deserving the utmost attention.

iii. A sideboard will greatly relieve

a crowded table, as many things incidental to the successive courses may be placed upon it until they are required.

iv. A Bill of Fare or *Menu* at large dinner parties, where there are several courses, should be provided, neatly inscribed upon small tablets, and distributed about the table, so that the diners may know what there is to come.

v. Napkins should be folded neatly. The French method, which is very easy, of folding the napkin like a fan, placing it in a glass, and spreading out the upper part, is very pleasing. But the English method of folding it like a slipper or a mitre and placing the bread inside its folds is convenient as well as neat.

vi. Bread should be cut into thick squares, the last thing after the table is laid. If cut too early it becomes dry. Small dinner rolls are very convenient. A tray should be provided, in which there should be a further supply of bread, new, stale, and brown. For cheese, pulled bread should be provided.

vii. Carving-knives should be sharpened before the dinner commences, for nothing irritates a good carver, or perplexes a bad one, more than a knife which refuses to perform its office and there is nothing more annoying to the company than to see the carving-knife gliding to and fro over the steel while the dinner is getting cold, and their appetites are being exhausted by delay.

viii. At large dinner parties the carving is usually done at a side table by a professional carver, but when this plan is not adopted joints that require carving should be set upon dishes sufficiently large. The space of the table may be economized by setting upon small dishes those things that do not require carving.

ix. The vegetables should be placed upon the sideboard, and handed round by those who wait upon the guests.

x. Geese, turkeys, poultry, sucking-pigs, &c., should be CARVED BEFORE BEING SET ON TABLE ; especially in those cases where the whole or the principal part of such dishes is likely to be consumed.

xi. Ladies should be helped before gentlemen, and the waiters should present dishes on the left hand ; so that the diner may help himself with his right.

xii. Wine should be taken after the first course ; and it will be found more convenient to let the waiter serve it, than to hand the decanters round, or to allow the guests to fill for themselves.

xiii. Waiters should be instructed to remove whatever articles upon the table are thrown into disuse by the progress of the dinner, as soon as they are at liberty.

xiv. Finger-glasses, or glass bowls, filled with water, slightly scented or not, as may be preferred, and slightly warm in winter, and iced in summer, should be placed before each guest with the dessert plate.

xv. When the dessert is served, the wine should be set upon the table, and the decanters passed round by the company.

1606. A COUNTRY DINNER PARTY.

Sydney Smith thus describes the delights of a dinner party in the country :—

"Did you ever dine out in the country ? What misery human beings inflict on each other under the name of pleasure ! We went to dine last Thursday with Mr. ——, a neighbouring clergyman, a haunch of venison being the stimulus to the invitation. We set out at five o'clock, drove in a broiling sun, on dusty roads, three miles, in our best gowns ; found squire and parsons assembled in a small hot room, the whole house redolent of frying ; talked, as is our wont, of roads, weather, and turnips ; that done, began to grow hungry, then serious, then impatient. At last a stripling, evidently caught up for the occasion, opened the door and beckoned our host out of the room. After some minutes of awful suspense, he returned to us with a face of much distress, saying, 'The woman assisting in the kitchen had mistaken the soup for dirty water and had thrown it away, so we most do without it ; we all agreed perhaps it was as well we should, under the circumstances ; at last, to our joy, dinner was announced ; but oh, 'Ye gods,' as we entered the dining-room what a gale met our nose! the venison was high—the venison was uneatable, and was obliged to follow the soup with all speed. Dinner proceeded, but our spirits flagged under these accumulated misfortunes. There was an ominous pause between the first and second course ; we looked each other in the face—what new disaster awaited us ? The pause became fearful. At last the door burst open, and the boy rushed in, calling out aloud, 'Please, sir, has Betty any right to leather I?' What human gravity could stand this ? We roared with laughter ; all took part against Betty, obtained the second course with some difficulty, bored each other the usual time, ordered our carriages, expecting our postboys to be drunk, and were grateful to Providence for not permitting them to deposit us in a wet ditch."

1607. HINTS ON CARVING.

Sufficient general instructions are here given to enable the carver, by observation and practice, to acquit himself well. The art of carving does not consist merely in dissecting the joints sent to table, but in the judicious and economical distribution of them, and the grace and neatness with which this distribution is effected. Every dish should be sent to table properly garnished (where needed), and the carver should preserve the neatness of the arrangement as much as possible.

1608. Fried Fish should be divided into suitable slices, before the fire, as soon as it leaves the frying-pan.

1609. Cod's Head and Shoulders. —The thick part of the back is best. It should be carved in unbroken slices, and each solid slice should be accompanied by a bit of the sound, from under the back-bone, or from the cheek, jaws, tongue, &c., of the head.

1610. Hake, if sent to table, simply boiled, is served as cod. The better way of dressing hake is to cut it transversely to the length into slices about one inch in thickness. These should be fried and sent to table garnished with parsley.

1611. Turbot—Strike the fish-slice along the back-bone, which runs from head to tail, and then serve square slices from the thick part, accompanying each slice with some of the gelatinous skin of the fins and thin part, which may be raised by laying the fish-slice flat.

1612. Brill is served in the same manner.

1613. John Dory is also served in the same way. This fish has a favourite piece on the cheek, and the fin is a delicacy, like that of the turbot.

Epicure Quin used to say, "Of all the banns of marriage I ever heard, none gave me half such pleasure as the union of delicate *Ann-chovy* with good *John Dory*."—*Kitchiner.*

1614. Plaice and Flat-fish generally are served in the same manner.

1615. Soles, when large, may be served as turbot; but when small they should be sliced across.

1616. Red Mullet—Divide them lengthwise into two parts, if the fish is too large for one. The liver is a great delicacy, and must be fairly apportioned, while there is delicious picking in the head and brain.

1617. Salmon.—Serve a slice of the thick with a *smaller* slice of the thin part. Keep the flakes of the thick part as unbroken as possible.

1618. Mackerel should be served in pieces cut through the side when they are large. If small, they may be divided through the back-bone, and served in halves. The shoulder part is considered the best. A *boiled* mackerel should never be divided through ; but a *broiled* mackerel, being split, should be cut through, bones and all.

1619. Haddock and Gurnet are served as directed for mackerel.

1620. Whiting are usually fried and curled ; they should be cut in halves across the back, and served. The shoulder-part is best.

1621. Eels are usually cut into several pieces, either for stewing or frying. The thick parts are considered best.

1622. Trout, if small, are served whole ; if large, they may be divided through the back-bone and served in halves. The same applies to perch and other smaller fresh-water fish.

1623. Pike and Jack should be served in thick unbroken pieces taken from the side or shoulder of the fish accompanied by a piece of the stuffing with which these fish are usually filled.

1624. Remarks.—In carving fish, a fish-slice should always be used, not a steel knife. The *roes* of mackerel, the *sound* of cod, the *head* of carp, the *cheek* of John Dory, the *liver* of cod, &c., are severally considered delicacies, though not by all persons.

1625. Saddle of Mutton.—Cut thin slices parallel with the back-bone ; or slice it obliquely from the bone to the edge, and serve with each portion, a piece of fat from the region of the kidneys.

1626. Haunch of Mutton or Venison.—Make an incision across the knuckle-end, right into the bone, and set free the gravy. Then cut thin slices the whole length of the haunch. Serve pieces of fat with slices of lean. The incision along the haunch is called "Alderman's Walk."

1627. Rump or Sirloin of Beef.—The undercut, called the "fillet," is exceedingly tender, and some carvers will turn the joint and serve the fillet first, reserving the meat on the upper part to be eaten cold. The fillet should be cut transversely into thick slices like a tongue ; as also should the fat at the thin end, a portion being served with each slice of lean. From the upper part, whether hot or cold, the slices should be cut lengthways from top to bottom, so that the fat and lean may be distributed in fair proportions.

1628. Ribs of Beef are carved in the same way as the sirloin ; but there is no fillet.

1629. Round of Beef.—First cut away the irregular outside pieces, to obtain a good surface and then serve thin and broad slices. Serve bits of the udder fat with the lean.

1630. Brisket of Beef.—Cut off the outside, and then serve long slices, cut the whole length of the bones.

1631. Shoulder of Mutton.—Make a cross incision on the fore-part of the shoulder, and serve slices from both sides of the incision ; then cut slices lengthways along the shoulder-blade. Cut fat slices from the round corner. Another and more economical way is to cut slices from the under first when first brought to table. The joint then presents a better appearance when cold.

1632. Leg of Mutton.—Make an incision across the centre, and serve from the knuckle-side, or the opposite, according to choice. The knuckle-side will be generally found well done, and the opposite side underdone, for those who prefer it.

1634. Loin of Mutton.—Cut down between the bones, into chops.

1635. Quarter of Lamb.—Lay the knife flat, and cut off the shoulder. The proper point for incision will be indicated by the position of the shoulder. A little lemon juice may be squeezed over the divided part, and a little cayenne pepper, and the shoulder transferred to another dish, for the opposite end of the table. Next separate the *brisket*, or short bones, by cutting lengthways along the breast. Then serve from either part as desired.

1636. Loin of Veal may be cut across through the thick part ; or slices may be taken in the direction of the bones. Serve pieces of kidney and fat with each plate.

1637. Fillet of Veal is carved as a round of beef. The browned bits of the outside are esteemed, and should be shared among the company, with bits of fat, and of forcemeat from the centre.

1638. Breast of Veal should be divided by cutting the brisket, or soft bones, the same as the brisket of lamb. When the sweetbread comes to table with the breast, a small piece should be served on each plate.

1639. Sucking Pig should be sent to table in two halves, the head divided, and one half laid at each end of the dish.—The shoulders and legs should be taken off by the obvious method of laying the knife under them, and lifting the joint out. They may be served whole, or divided. The ribs are easily divided, and are considered choice.

1640. Tongues are cut across in tolerably thick slices.

1641. Calves' Heads are carved across the cheek, and pieces taken from any part that is come-at-able. The tongue and brain sauce are served separately.

1642. Knuckle of Veal is carved by cutting off the outside pieces, and then obtaining good slices, and apportioning the fat to the lean, adding bits of the sinew that lie around the joint.

1643. Leg of Pork is carved as a ham, but in thicker slices ; when stuffed, the stuffing must be sought for under the skin at the large end.

1644. Loin of Pork is carved the same as a loin of mutton.

1645. Spare-rib of Pork is carved by separating the chops, which should previously have been jointed. Cut as far as the joint, then return the knife to the point of the bones, and press over, to disclose the joint, which may then be divided with the point of the knife.

1646. Hams are cut in very thin slices from the knuckle to the blade.

1647. Pheasants.—Carve the breast in slices. Then take off the legs and wings.

1648. Fowls.—Fix the fork firmly into the breast, then slip the knife under the legs, and lay it over and disjoint ; detach the wings in the same manner. Do the same on both sides. The smaller bones require a little practice, and it would be well to watch the operations of a good carver. When the merry-thought has been removed (which it may be by slipping the knife through at the point of the breast), and the neck-bones drawn out, the trunk may be turned over, and the knife thrust through the back-bone.

1649. Partridges ars best carved by cutting off the breast, and then dividing it. But for more economical carving, the wings may be cut with a small breast slice attached.

1650. Woodcooks and Snipes may be cut right through the centre, from head to tail. Serve with each portion a piece of the toast upon which they come to table.

1651. Pigeons may be carved as woodcocks, or as partridges.

1652. Turkey.—Cut slices from each side of the breast down to the ribs ; the legs may then be removed, and the thighs divided from the drumsticks, which are generally tough ; but the pinions of the wing are very good, and the white part of the wing is preferred by many to the breast. The stuffing is usually put in the breast ; but when truffles, mushrooms, or oysters are put into the body, an opening must be made into it by cutting through the apron.

1653. Goose.—The apron must be cut off in a circular direction, when a glass of port wine, mixed with a teaspoonful of mustard, may be poured into the body or not. Some of the stuffing should then be drawn out, and, the neck of the goose being turned a little towards the carver, the flesh of the breast should be sliced on each side of the bone. The wings may then be taken off, then the legs. The other parts are carved the same as a fowl.

1654. Ducks may be carved, when large, the same as geese ; but when young, like chickens. The thigh joints, however, lie much closer into the trunk than those of fowls.

1655. Hares should be placed with their heads to the left of the carver. Slices may be taken down the whole length of the back ; the legs, which, next to the back, are considered the best eating, may then be taken off, and the flesh divided from or served upon them, after the small bones have been parted from the thighs. The shoulders, which are not much esteemed, though sometimes liked by sportsmen, may be taken off by passing the knife between the joint and the trunk. When a hare is young, the back is sometimes divided at the joints into three or four parts, after being freed from the ribs and underskin.

1656. TO MAKE DESSERT ICES. —Directions for freezing are given in pars. 1663-1667.

1657. Strawberry Cream Ice.— Take one pint of strawberries, one pint of cream, nearly half-a-pound of powdered white sugar, the juice of a lemon ; mash the fruit through a sieve, and take out the seeds : mix with the other articles, and freeze. A little new milk added makes the whole freeze more quickly.

1658. Raspberry Cream Ice.— The same as strawberry. These ices are often coloured by cochineal, but the addition is not advantageous to the flavour. Strawberry or raspberry jam may be used instead of the fresh fruit, or equal quantities of jam and fruit employed. Of course the quantity of sugar must be proportionately diminished.

1659. Strawberry-Water Ice.— One pound of strawberries, the juice of a lemon, a pound of sugar, or one pint of strong syrup, half-a-pint of water. Mix, first rubbing the fruit through a sieve,—and freeze.

1660. Raspberry-Water Ice is made in precisely the same manner as Strawberry-water ice.

1661. Lemon-Water Ice.—Lemon juice and water, each half-a-pint ; strong syrup, one pint: the rind of the lemons should be rasped off, before squeezing, with lump sugar, which is to be added to the juice ; mix the whole ; strain after standing an hour, and freeze. Beat up with a little sugar the whites of two or three eggs, and as the ice is beginning to set, work this in with the spatula, which will be found to much improve the consistence and taste.

1662. Orange-Water Ice is made in the same way as lemon-water ice.

1663. FREEZING WITH ICE.

The use of ice in cooling depends upon the fact of its requiring a vast quantity of heat to convert it from a solid into a liquid state, or in other words to melt it ; and the heat so required is obtained from those objects with which it may be in contact. A pound of ice requires nearly as much heat to melt it as would be sufficient to make a pound of cold water boiling hot; hence its cooling power is extremely great. But ice does not begin to melt until the temperature is above the freezing point, and therefore it cannot be employed in freezing liquids, &c., but only in cooling them. If, however, any substance is mixed with ice which is capable of causing it to melt more rapidly, and at a lower temperature, a still more intense cooling effect is the result ; such a substance is common salt, and the degree of cold produced by the mixture of one part of salt with two parts of snow or pounded ice is greater than thirty degrees below freezing.

In making ice-creams and dessert ices, the following articles are required :— Pewter ice-pots with tightly-fitting lids, furnished with handles ; wooden ice-pails, to hold the rough ice and salt—the pails should be stoutly made, about the same depth as the ice-pots, and nine or ten inches more in diameter, with a hole in the side, fitted with a good cork, in order that the water from the melted ice may be drawn off as required. In addition, a broad spatula, about four inches long, rounded at the end, and furnished with a long wooden handle, is necessary to scrape the frozen cream from the sides of the ice-pot, and for mixing the whole smoothly together.

When making ices, place the mixture of cream and fruit to be frozen in the ice-pot, cover it with the lid, and put the pot in the ice-pail, which proceed to fill up with coarsely-pounded ice and salt, in the proportion of about one part of salt to three of ice ; let the whole remain a few minutes (if covered by a blanket so much the better), then whirl the pot briskly by the handle for a few minutes, take off the lid, and with the spatula scrape the iced cream from the sides, mixing the whole smoothly ; put on the lid, and whirl again, repeating all the operations every few minutes until the whole of the cream is well frozen. Great care and considerable labour are required in stirring, so that the whole cream may be smoothly frozen, and not in hard lumps. When finished, if it is required to be kept any time, the melted ice and salt should be allowed to escape, by removing the cork, and the pail filled up with fresh materials. It is scarcely necessary to add, that if any of the melted ice and salt is allowed to mix with the cream, the latter is spoiled.

1664. FREEZING WITHOUT ICE.

From the difficulty of obtaining ice in places distant from large towns, and in hot countries, and from the impracticability of keeping it any length of time, or, in fact, of keeping small quantities more than a few hours, its use is much limited, and many have been the attempts to obtain an efficient substitute. For this purpose various salts have been employed, which, when dissolved in water, or in acids, absorb a sufficient amount of heat to freeze substances with which they may be placed in contact.

Many of the freezing mixtures which are to be found described in books are incorrectly so named, for although they themselves are below the freezing point, yet they are not sufficiently powerful to freeze any quantity of water, or other substances, when placed in a vessel within them. In order to be efficient as a freezing mixture, as distinguished from a cooling one, the materials used ought to be capable of producing by themselves an amount of cold more than thirty degrees below the freezing point of water, and this the ordinary mixtures will not do.

Much more efficient and really freezing mixtures may be made by using acids to dissolve the salts. The cheapest, and perhaps the best, of these for ordinary use, is one which is frequently employed in France, both for making dessert ices, and cooling wines, &c. It consists of coarsely-powdered Glauber salt (sulphate of sodium), on which is poured about two-thirds its weight of spirit of salts (hydrochloric acid). The mixture should be made in a wooden vessel, as that is preferable to one made of metal, which conducts the external heat to the materials with great rapidity ; and when the substance to be cooled is placed in the mixture, the whole should be covered with a blanket, a piece of old woollen carpet doubled, or some other non-conducting material, to prevent the access of the external warmth ; the vessel used for icing wines should not be too large, that there may be no waste of the freezing mixture. This combination produces a degree of cold thirty degrees below freezing ; and if the materials are bought of any of the wholesale druggists or drysalters, it is exceedingly economical. It is open, however, to the very great objection, that the spirit of salt is an exceedingly corrosive liquid, and of a pungent, disagreeable odour : this almost precludes its use for any purpose except that of icing wines.

1665. Nitrate of Ammonium as a Freezing Mixture.—Another substance, which is free from any corrosive action or unpleasant odour, is nitrate of ammonium, which, if simply dissolved in rather less than its own weight of water, reduces the temperature about twenty-five degrees below freezing. The objections to its use are that its frigorific power is not sufficiently great to freeze readily ; and if it be required to form dessert ices, it is requisite to renew the process, at the expiration of a quarter of an hour, a second time, and, if the weather is very hot, and the water used is rather warm, even a third or fourth time. Again, nitrate of ammonium is a very expensive salt. One great recommendation, however, attends its use, namely, that it may be recovered again, and used any number of times, by simply boiling away the water

in which it is dissolved, by a gentle fire, until a small portion, on being removed, crystallizes on cooling.

1666. Washing Soda as a Freezing Mixture.—If, however, nitrate of ammonium in coarse powder is put into the cooler, and there is then added twice its weight of freshly-crushed washing soda, and an equal quantity of the coldest water that can be obtained, an intensely powerful frigorific mixture is the result, the cold often falling to forty degrees below freezing. This is by far the most efficacious freezing mixture that can be made without the use of ice or acids. But, unfortunately, it has an almost insuperable objection, that the nitrate of ammonium is decom- posed by the soda, and cannot be recovered by evaporation ; this raises the expense to so great a height, that the plan is practically useless.

1667. Sal Ammoniac as a Freezing Mixture.—If the ordinary sal ammoniac of the shops is used, it will be found both difficult to powder, and expensive ; in fact, it is so exceedingly tough, that the only way in which it can be easily divided, except in a drug mill, is by putting as large a quantity of the salt into water, which is actually boiling, as the latter will dissolve ; as the solution cools, the salt crystallizes out in the solid form, and if stirred as it cools, it separates in a state of fine division. As this process is troublesome, and as the sal ammoniac is expensive, it is better to use the crude muriate of ammonium, which is the same substance as sal ammoniac, but before it has been purified by sublimation. This is not usually kept by druggists, but may be readily obtained of any of the artificial manure merchants, at a very moderate rate ; and its purity may be readily tested by placing a portion of it on a red-hot iron, when it should fly off in a vapour, leaving scarcely any residue.

1668. BEVERAGES.

1669. CIDER is a pleasant and refreshing beverage made from the juice of the apple, and with persons in good health is not unwholesome when drunk in moderation. By persons who suffer from rheumatism or indigestion, however, it should be carefully avoided, nor should it be drunk by persons when they are over-heated, as it is apt to cause colic and other disagreeable symptoms.

1670. To Make Cider.—The process of making cider varies in different localities, but in every case essentially consists of the collection of the fruit, and the expression and fermentation of the juice. The *collection of the fruit* should not be commenced before it has become sufficiently mature. The apples, after being gathered, are usually left for fourteen or fifteen days in a barn or loft to mellow, during which time the mucilage is decomposed, and alcohol and carbonic acid developed. *The expression of the juice* is the next step in cider-making. The apples are ground to a pulp in a mill, consisting of two fluted cylinders of hard wood or cast iron working against each other. The pulp is afterwards put into coarse, strong bags, and pressed with a heavy weight so as to squeeze out all the juice. This is then placed in large open tubs, and kept at a heat of about sixty degrees. After two or three days for weak cider, and eight or ten days for strong cider, or as soon as the sediment has subsided, the liquor is drawn off into clean casks. The casks are then stored in a cellar, shaded barn, or other cool place, where a low and regular temperature can be insured, and are left to mature and ripen until the following spring. The refuse pulp may be given to pigs and store cattle.

1671. To Bottle Cider.—Preparatory to bottling, it should always be examined, to see whether it is clear and sparkling. If not so, it should be clarified, and left for a fortnight. The night previous to bottling, the bung should be taken out of the cask, and the filled bottles should not be corked down until the day after ; as, if this is done at once, many of the bottles will burst by keeping. The best corks should be used. Champagne bottles are the best for cider. When the cider is wanted for immediate use, or for consumption during the cooler seaaon of the year, a small piece of lump sugar may be put into each bottle before corking it. When intended for keeping, it should be stored in a cool cellar, when the quality will be greatly improved by age.

1672. Cider Champagne.—Cider, eighteen gallons ; spirit, three pints ; sugar, five pounds. Mix and let them rest for a fortnight, then fine with one pint of skimmed milk. Bottle in champagne bottles : when opened, it will be found to approach very nearly to genuine champagne.

1673. Cider Cup.—Mix one bottle of cider, one bottle of soda water, two glasses of sherry, a little powdered sugar according to taste, and a sprig of borage.

1674. PERRY.—A beverage made from pears. The fruit used for this purpose should contain a large proportion of sugar, and be likewise astringent, or the liquor from it will be acetous when it ceases to be saccharine. In making perry, the pears are pressed and ground in precisely the same manner as apples are in the making of cider. The method of fermenting perry is nearly the same as that for cider ; but the former does not afford the same indications as the latter by which the proper period of racking off may be known. The thick scum that collects on the surface of cider rarely appears in the juice of the pear, and during the time of the suspension of its fermentation, the excesssive brightness of the former liquor is seldom seen in the latter ; but when the fruit has been regularly ripe, its produce will generally become moderately clear and quiet in a few days after it is made, and it should then be drawn off from its grosser lees. In the after management of perry the process is the same as that of cider ; but it does not so well bear situations where it is much exposed to change of temperature. If it remain sound and perfect at the conclusion of the first succeeding summer it is advisable to bottle it, as it retains its good qualities best when in bottle.

1675. HOME-MADE WINES from Rhubarb, Unripe Grapes, Currants, Gooseberries, &c.—The whole art of wine-making consists in the proper management of the fermenting process ; the same quantity of fruit, whether it be rhubarb, currants, gooseberries, unripe grapes, leaves, tops, and tendrils, water, and sugar, will produce two different kinds of wine, by varying the process of fermentation only—that is, a dry wine like sherry, or a brisk beverage like champagne. The following directions will do for rhubarb, or any of the above-mentioned fruits.

1676. English Champagne.—Take fifty pounds of rhubarb and thirty-seven pounds of fine moist sugar. Provide a tub that will hold from fifteen to twenty gallons, taking care that it has a hole for a tap near the bottom. In this tub bruise the rhubarb ; when done, add four gallons of water ; let the whole be well stirred together ; cover the tub with a cloth or blanket, and let the materials stand for twenty-four hours ; then draw off the liquor through the tap ; add one or two more gallons of water to the pulp, let it be well stirred, and then allowed to remain an hour or two to settle, then draw off ; mix the two liquors together, and in it dissolve the sugar. Let the tub be made clean, and return the liquor to it, cover it with a blanket, and place it in a room the temperature of which is not below 60° Fahr. ; here it is to remain for twenty-four, forty-

eight, or more hours, until there is an appearance of fermentation having begun, when it should be drawn off into the ten-gallon cask, as fine as possible, which cask must be filled up to the bung-hole with water if there is not liquor enough ; let it lean to one side a little, that it may discharge itself ; if there is any liquor left in the tub not quite fine, pass it through flannel, and fill up with that instead of water. As the fermentation proceeds and the liquor diminishes, it must be filled up daily, to encourage the fermentation, for ten or twelve days ; it then becomes more moderate, when the bung should be put in, and a gimlet-hole made at the side of it, fitted with a spile ; this spile should be taken out every two or three days, according to the state of the fermentation to allow some of the carbonic acid gas to escape. When this state is passed, the cask may be kept full by pouring a little liquor in at the vent-hole once a week or ten days, for three or four weeks. This operation is performed at long intervals, of a month or more, till the end of December, when on a fine frosty day it should be drawn off from the lees as fine as possible, and the turbid part passed through flannel. Make the cask clean, return the liquor to it, with one drachm of isinglass (pure) dissolved in a little water ; stir the whole together, and put the bung in firmly.

Choose a clear dry day in March for bottling. The bottles should be champagne bottles—common wine bottles are not strong enough ; secure the corks in a proper manner with wire, &c. The liquor is generally made up to two or three pints over the ten gallons, which is bottled for the purpose of filling the cask as it is wanted. The wine contains spirit enough without the addition of brandy, which spoils all wines ; a proper fermentation producing spirit enough.

The way to obtain a dry wine from these materials is to keep the cask constantly filled up to the bung-hole, daily or every other day, as long as any fermentation is perceptible by applying the ear near to the hole ; the bung may then be put in lightly for a time, before finally fixing it ; it may be racked off on a fine day in December, and fined with isinglass as above directed, and bottled in March.

1677.   Parsnip   Wine.—Take fifteen pounds of sliced parsnips, and boil until quite soft in five gallons of water ; squeeze the liquor well out of them, run it through a sieve, and add three pounds of coarse lump sugar to every gallon of liquor. Boil the whole for three-quarters of an hour. When it is nearly cold, add a little yeast on toast. Let it remain in a tub for ten days, stirring it from the bottom every day ; then put it into a cask, in which it should remain for a year. As it works over, fill it up every day.

1678. Turnip Wine.—Take a large number of turnips, pare and slice them ; then place in a cider-press, and obtain all the juice you can. To every gallon of juice add three pounds of lump sugar, and half-a-pint of brandy. Pour the liquor into a cask, and when it has done working, bung it close for three months, and draw off into another cask. When it is fine, bottle, and cork well.

1679. Blackberry Wine.—Gather the fruit when ripe, on a dry day. Put into a vessel, with the head out, and a tap fitted near the bottom ; pour on boiling water to cover it. Mash the berries with your hands, and let them stand covered till the pulp rises to the top and forms a crust, in three or four days. Then draw off the fluid into another vessel, and to every gallon add one pound of sugar ; mix well, and put into a cask, to work for a week or ten days, and throw off any remaining lees, keeping the cask well filled, particularly at the commencement. When the working has ceased, bung

down ; after six to twelve months it may be bottled.

1680. Elderberry Wine.—Gather the berries ripe and dry, pick them, bruise them with your hands, and strain them. Set the liquor by in glazed earthen vessels for twelve hours, to settle ; put to every pint of juice a pint and a half of water, and to every gallon of this liquor three pounds of good moist sugar ; set it in a kettle over the fire, and when it is ready to boil, clarify it with the white of four eggs ; let it boil one hour, and when it is almost cold, work it with strong ale yeast, and tun it, filling up the vessel from time to time with the same liquor, saved on purpose, as it sinks by working. In a month's time, if the vessel holds about eight gallons, it will be fine and fit to bottle, and after bottling, will be fit to drink in twelve months.

1681.   ARRACK   (Imitation).— Take one quart of good rum and one quart of water, one drachm flowers of benzoin, and quarter ounce of sliced pine-apple (or half-a-teaspoonful of essence of pine-apple). Digest this for a fortnight, with occasional stirrings, and then add a wineglassful of skimmed milk. Shake well for a quarter of an hour, and in a day or two decant the clear portion.

1682.   SCOTCH   PUNCH,   or Whisky Toddy.—Pour about a wine-glassful of *boiling* water into a half-pint tumbler, and sweeten according to taste. Stir well up, then put in a wineglassful of whisky, and add a wineglassful and a half more boiling water. *Be sure the water* is boiling. Never put lemon into toddy. The two in combination, in almost every instance, produce acidity in the stomach. If possible, store your whisky *in the wood* ; not in bottles, as keeping it in the cask mellows it, and dissipates the coarser particles.

1683. Athol Brose.—Put a wine-glassful of whisky into a half-pint tumbler ; sweeten with a large tea-spoonful of honey, and fill up with milk that has been *nearly* brought to boiling over a clear fire. Remember that "milk boiled is milk spoiled."

1684. Buttered Rum.—Put a wineglassful of good rum into a half-pint tumbler, with a lump or two of sugar and a piece of butter the size of a filbert. Fill up with *boiling* water. This is excellent for hoarseness and husky condition of the throat.

1685. Ginger Brandy.—Half-a-pound of bruised Jamaica ginger should be steeped in a gallon of brandy for a fortnight. Strain and make a decoction of the ginger with one gallon of boiling water. Dissolve ten pounds of sugar in the decoction, and then add the brandy and some finings to clear.

1686. Claret Cup.—Required, one bottle of sound claret, one bottle of soda water, four tablespoonfuls of powdered sugar, half-a-pound of crushed ice, half-a-teaspoonful of grated nutmeg, a liqueur-glassful of maraschino, and a sprig of borage.

1687. Summer Champagne.—To four parts of seltzer water add one of Moselle wine (or hock), and put a teaspoonful of powdered sugar into a wineglassful of this mixture ; an effervescence takes place, and the result is a sort of champagne, which is more wholesome in hot weather than the genuine wine known by that name.

1688.—Champagne Lemonade, composed of two bottles of champagne, one bottle of seltzer water, three pomegranates, three lemons, and of sugar sufficient, is a *princely beverage* in hot weather ; only care must be taken that perspiration is not hereby too much encouraged.

1689. Raspberry Vinegar.—Put a pound of very fine ripe raspberries in a bowl, *bruise them well*, and pour upon them a quart of the best white wine vinegar ; next day strain the liquor on a pound of fresh ripe raspberries ; bruise *them* also, and the following day do the same, *but do not squeeze the fruit, or it will make it ferment* ; only drain the liquor as dry as you can from it. Finally, pass it through a canvas bag, previously wet with the vinegar, to prevent waste. Put the juice into a stone jar, with a *pound of sugar*, broken into lumps, to *every pint of juice* ; stir, and when melted, put the jar into a pan of water ; let it simmer, and skim it ; let it cool, then bottle it. When cold it will be fine, and thick, like strained honey, newly prepared.

1690. Ginger Beer. —The follow, ing recipe is taken from the celebrated treatise of Dr. Pereira on Diet. The honey gives the beverage a peculiar softness, and from not being fermented with yeast, it is less violent in its action when opened, but requires to be kept a somewhat longer time before use. White sugar, five pounds ; lemon juice, one quarter of a pint ; honey, one quarter of a pound ; ginger, bruised, five ounces ; water, four gallons and a half. Boil the ginger in three quarts of water, for half-an-hour, then add the sugar, lemon juice and honey, with the remainder of the water, and strain through a cloth ; when cold add a quarter of the white of an egg, and a small teaspoonful of essence of lemon ; let the whole stand four days, and bottle ; it will keep for many months. This quantity will make 100 bottles.

1691. Ginger-beer Powders.—*Blue paper :* Carbonate of soda, thirty grains ; powdered ginger, five grains ; ground white sugar, one drachm to one drachm and a half ; essence of lemon, one drop. Add the essence to the sugar, then the other ingredients. A quantity should be mixed and divided, as recommended for Seidlitz powders.—*White paper:* Tartaric acid, thirty grains. *Directions.*—Dissolve the contents of the blue paper in water ; stir in the contents of the white paper, and drink during effervescence. Ginger-beer powders do not meet with such general acceptation as lemon and kali, the powdered ginger rendering the liquid slightly turbid.

1962. Lemon and Kali, or Sherbet.—Large quantities of this wholesome and refreshing preparation are manufactured and consumed every summer ; it is sold in bottles, and also as a beverage, made by dissolving a large teaspoonful in a tumbler two-thirds filled with water. The ingredients are—ground white sugar, half-a-pound ; tartaric acid and carbonate of soda of each a quarter of a pound ; essence of lemon, forty drops. All the powders should be well dried ; add the essence to the sugar, then the other powders ; stir all together, and mix by passing through a hair sieve. Must be kept in tightly-corked bottles, into which a damp spoon must not be inserted. The sugar must be very finely pulverized.

1693. Soda Powders furnish a saline beverage which is very slightly laxative, and well calculated to allay the thirst in hot weather. Half-a-pound of carbonate of soda, and six and three-quarters ounces of tartaric acid, supply the materials for 128 powders of each sort. Put into blue papers thirty grains of carbonate of soda, and into white papers twenty-five grains of tartaric acid. *Directions.*— Dissolve the contents of the blue paper in half-a-tumbler of water, stir in the other powder, and drink during effervescence.

1694. Seidlitz Powders make a cooling aperient draught and are usually put up in two papers. The larger blue paper contains tartarized soda (also called Rochelle salt) two drachms, and carbonate of soda two scruples ; in practice it will be found more convenient to mix the two materials in larger quantity by passing them twice through a sieve, and then divide the mixture either by weight or measure, than to make each powder separately. One pound of tartarized soda, and five

ounces and a half of carbonate of soda, will make sixty powders. The smaller powder, usually placed in white paper, consists of tartaric acid, half-a-drachm. *Directions for use.*—Dissolve the contents of blue paper in half-a-tumbler of cold water, stir in the other powder, and drink during effervescence.

1695.   Lemonade.—Powdered sugar, four pounds ; citric or tartaric acid, one ounce ; essence of lemon, two drachms : mix well. Two or three teaspoonfuls make a very sweet and agreeable glass of lemonade.

1696. Milk lemonade.—Dissolve three-quarters of a pound of loaf sugar in one pint of boiling water, and mix with them one gill of lemon juice, and one gill of sherry, then add three gills of cold milk. Stir the whole well together, and strain it.

1697. NATURAL MINERAL WATERS WITH THEIR PROPERTIES

Apollinaris	Table Water
Biebrach	„ „
Gerolstein	„ „
Reginaris	„ „
Johannis	Gaseous Water
Rosbach	„ „
St. Galmier	„ „
Taunus	„ „
Æsculap	Saline Aperient
Friedrichshall . . .	„ „
Franz Josef	„ „
Hunyadi-Janos . . .	„ „
Leamington Spa . .	„ „
Pullna.	„ „
Rabinat	„ „
Oberbrunnen	Saline Lithiated
Woodhall	Bromo-iodized
Kronenquelle	Sodio-lithiated
Royat	Arsenicated
Homburg	Chalybeate
Carlsbad	Alkaline Lithiated
Contrexeville	„ „
Selters	Acidulated
Vals	„ „
Vichy	„ „
Bonnes	Sulphurous
Bourboule	Arsenical Iron
Schwalbach	Chalybeate

1698. TO MAKE TEA.—Scald the teapot and empty it, then put the tea in, allowing one teaspoonful for each person with an extra one "for the pot." Pour over it as much boiling water as will be required ; let it stand for a few minutes before using. Soft water is the best, and should be *freshly* boiled, as water that has been boiled several times will not draw the strength of the tea properly. Some teapots are now fitted with a perforated cup to contain the tea leaves and enable them to be removed after infusion.

1699. Another Method.—Put in the teapot as much water as necessary for the first cups ; put the tea on it as in brewing, and close the lid as quickly as possible. Let it stand three minutes and a half, or, if the quantity be large, four minutes, then fill the cups. By this method, the aroma is preserved instead of escaping with the steam, as it does when the water is poured on the tea.

1700. Substitute for Cream in Tea or Coffee.—Beat the white of an egg to a froth, put to it a very small lump of butter, and mix well. Then stir it in gradually, so that it may not curdle. If perfectly mixed, it will be an excellent substitute for cream.

1701. TO MAKE COFFEE.—Warm your coffee-pot and put in two teaspoonfuls of freshly-ground coffee for each half-pint required ; pour in the boiling water. Then pour out a tea-cupful and put it back in the coffee-pot. Repeat this, and then stand the pot on the hob, *but do not allow it to boil.* The broader the bottom and the smaller the top of the vessel, the better the coffee will be.

1702. Turkish Mode of Making Coffee.—The Turkish way of making coffee produces a very different result from that to which we are accustomed. A small conical saucepan something like our beer-warmer, with a long handle, and calculated to hold about two tablespoonfuls of water, is the vessel used. The fresh roasted berry is pounded, not ground, and about a dessertspoonful is put into the minute boiler ; it is then nearly filled with water, and thrust among the embers. A few seconds suffice to make it boil, and the decoction, grounds and all, is poured out into a small cup, which fits into a brass socket, much like the cup of an acorn, and holding the china cup as that does the acorn itself. The Turks seem to drink this decoction boiling, and swallow the grounds with the liquid. We allow it to remain a minute, in order to leave the sediment at the bottom. It is always taken plain ; sugar or cream would be thought to spoil it, and Europeans, after a little practice, are said to prefer it to the clear infusion drunk in France. In every hut these coffee boilers may be seen suspended, and the means for pounding the roasted berry are always at hand.

1703. To Detect Chicory in Ground Coffee.—Put a little of the coffee into a wineglass with some cold water, shake it up, and the coffee will float but the chicory will sink.

1704. Coffee Milk (FOR THE SICK-ROOM).—Boil a dessertspoonful of ground coffee in nearly a pint of milk a quarter of an hour, then put into it a shaving or two of isinglass, and clear it ; let it boil a few minutes, and set it by the side of the fire to clarify. This is a very fine breakfast beverage ; but it should be sweetened with sugar of a good quality.

1705. Iceland Moss Chocolate (FOR THE SICK-ROOM).—Iceland moss has been in the highest repute on the Continent as the most efficacious remedy in incipient pulmonary complaints ; combined with chocolate, it will be found a nutritious article of diet, and may be taken as a morning and evening beverage mixed with boiling water or milk.

1706. COCOA.—For many persons cocoa forms a better beverage than either tea or coffee, and is considered more nutritious and easy of digestion. Many excellent preparations are manufactured and directions for mixing are given with each tin or packet.

1707. Alum Whey.—A pint of cow's milk boiled with two drachms of alum, until a curd is formed. Then strain off the liquor, and add spirit of nutmeg, two ounces ; syrup of cloves, an ounce. It is useful in diabetes, and in uterine fluxes, &c.

1708. Barley Water.—Pearl barley, two ounces ; wash till freed from dust, in cold water. Boil in a quart of water a few minutes, strain off the liquor, and throw it away. Then boil the barley in four pints and a half of water, until it is reduced one half. If made with Robinson's Patent Barley less preparation is required. Lemon flavouring renders it more palatable.

1709. Agreeable Effervescent Drink for Heartburn, &c.—Orange juice (of one orange), water, and lump sugar to flavour, and in proportion to acidity of orange, bicarbonate of soda about half-a-teaspoonful. Mix orange juice, water, and sugar together in a tumbler, then put in the soda, stir, and the effervescence ensues.

1710. Apple Water.—A tart apple well baked and mashed, on which pour a pint of boiling water. Beat up, cool, and strain. Add sugar if desired. Cooling drink for sick persons.

1711. Tincture of Lemon Peel.— A very easy and economical way of obtaining and preserving the flavour of lemon peel, is to fill a wide-mouthed pint bottle half full of brandy, or proof spirit ; and when you use a lemon pare the rind off very thin, and put it into the brandy, &c. ; in a fortnight it will impregnate the spirit with the flavour very strongly.

1712. Camomile Tea.—One ounce of the flowers to a quart of water boiling. Simmer for fifteen minutes and strain. Emetic when taken warm ; tonic when cold. *Dose*, from a wineglassful to a breakfast cup. Dried orange peel added to camomile flowers, in the proportion of half the quantity of the flowers, improves the tonic.

1713. HINTS ON BREWING.

The best time of the year for brewing is the autumn. The spring is also suitable, but less so. It is a great object to secure a moderate temperature for the cooling of the worts, and to insure gradual fermentation. To those who wish to enter upon the practice, without any previous knowledge, we would advise their calling in the aid of some one practically acquainted with the process for the first operation. By so doing they will save a great deal of trouble, disappointment, and expense. In all places, town or country, there are persons who have worked in brewing establishments, or in gentlemen's families where they have superintended the operations of the brew-house, and the aid of such persons would be valuable. With such assistance, the following recipes will be of importance, since many who are able to go through the manipulations of brewing are unaware of the proper proportions to employ :—

1714. Ale.—Take three bushels of malt, three pounds of hops, fifty-two gallons of water, for two workings. Or,—malt, two bushels and a half ; sugar, three pounds ; hops, three pounds ; coriander seeds, one ounce ; capsicum, a drachm. Thirty-six gallons. This gives a pleasant ale, with a good body.

1715. Amber Ale.—Three bushels of amber malt, three quarters of a bushel of pale amber malt, two pounds of hops, a tablespoonful of salt. Three mashes, forty to fifty gallons. Skim, and fine with isinglass.

1716. Burton Ale.—One quarter of pale malt, eight pounds and a half pale hops ; mash three times. Work the first mash at 170°, second at 176°, third at 150°. Boil the first wort by itself ; when boiling add three pounds of honey, a pound and a half coriander seeds, one ounce of salt. Mix the worts when boiled, cool to 61°, set to work with a pint and a half of yeast. As soon as the liquor gets yeasty, skim the head half off ; rouse the rest with another pint and a half of yeast, three-quarters of an ounce of bay salt, and a quarter of a pound of malt or bean flour. This makes a hogshead.

1717. Edinburgh Ale. —Mash two barrels per quarter, at 183° ; mash for three-quarters of an hour ; let it stand one hour, and allow half-an-hour to run off. Or, mash one barrel per quarter, at 190° ; mash three-quarters of an hour, let it stand three-quarters of an hour, and tap.

1718. Porter.—Brown amber and pale malt, in equal quantities ; turn them into the mash-tub. Turn on the first liquor at 165° ; mash one hour, then coat the whole with dry malt. In one hour set the tap. Mix ten pounds of brown hops to a quarter of malt, half old, half new ; boil the first wort briskly with the hops for three-quarters of an hour, after putting into the copper one pound and a half of sugar, and one pound and a half of extract of liquorice to the barrel ; turn it into coolers, rousing the wort the while. Turn on the second liquor at 174°, set tap again in an hour. The second wort having run off, turn on again at 145° : mash an hour, and stand an hour ; boil the second wort with the same hops for one hour. Turn into the coolers, and let into the tub at 64°, mixing the yeast as it comes down. Cleanse the second day at 80°, previously adding a mixture of flour and salt, and rousing well.

1719. Spruce Beer.—Take one pound of sugar, half-an-ounce of essence of spruce, and one gallon of boiling water. Mix these thoroughly, and when cool add half-a-wineglassful of yeast. Let it stand for a day and then bottle it. When made with lump sugar it is called "white spruce ;" when moist sugar or treacle is used, "brown spruce." A pleasant summer drink, and anti-scorbutic.

1720. Finings for Beer.—Take some sole skins and boil them in a little beer. Let them cool down into a jelly. When required for use take a tablespoonful or two of this jelly (according to the size of your cask) and dissolve it in a pint of beer ; stir it into the cask, and if there is reason to expect that the beer will work leave the bung out for a day or so.

1721. Bottling Beer.—See that the bottles are clean and dry and the corks sound. The bottles should be filled, but not corked till the following day : then pack them *upright*.

1722. CHEAP AND GOOD VINE-GAR.—To eight gallons of clear rain water, add three quarts of molasses ; turn the mixture into a clean, tight cask, shake it well two or three times, and add three spoonfuls of good yeast ; place the cask in a warm place, and in ten or fifteen days add a sheet of common wrapping paper, smeared with molasses, and torn into narrow strips, and you will have good vinegar. The paper is necessary to form the "mother," or life of the vinegar.

1723. HORSERADISH VINEGAR. —Pour a quart of best vinegar on three ounces of scraped horseradish, an ounce of minced shallot, and one drachm of cayenne ; let it stand a week, and you will have an excellent relish for cold beef, salads, &c., costing but little. Horseradish is in the highest perfection about November.

1724. MINT VINEGAR.—Place into a wide-mouthed bottle, fresh, nice, clean mint leaves enough to fill it loosely ; then fill up the bottle with good vinegar ; and after it has been corked close for two or three weeks, pour it off clear into another bottle, and keep well corked for use. Serve with lamb when mint cannot be obtained.

1725. CRESS VINEGAR.—Dry and pound half-an-ounce of *cress seed* (such as is sown in the garden with mustard), pour upon it a quart of the best vinegar, let it steep for ten days, shaking it up every day. This is very strongly flavoured with cress, and is useful for salads, and as a sauce for cold meats, &c. Celery vinegar may be made in the same manner.

1726. ESSENCE OF MUSH-ROOMS.—This delicate relish is made by sprinkling a little salt over either flap or button mushrooms : three hours after, mash them,—next day, strain off the liquor that will flow from them, put it into a stewpan, and boil it till it is reduced one half. It will not keep long, but is preferable to any of the ketchups containing spice, &c., to preserve them, which overpowers the flavour of the mushrooms. An artificial mushroom bed will supply these all the year round.

1727. MUSHROOM KETCHUP.—Mix some moderate-sized mushrooms with common salt, stirring them for a day or two. Then press out the juice, and put in half-an-ounce of bruised cloves and half-an-ounce of mustard seeds to each gallon : also bruised ginger, black pepper, and allspice, one ounce of each. Heat them until they come to the boil, steep them for about a fortnight, decant or strain.

1728. TOMATO KETCHUP.—This is made from tomatoes in the same way as the preceding, adding a small quantity of very strong chili vinegar.

1729. OYSTER KETCHUP.—Take some fresh oysters ; wash them in their own liquor, strain it, pound them in a marble mortar ; to a pint of oysters add a pint of sherry ; boil them up, and add an ounce of salt, two drachms of pounded mace, and one of cayenne ; let it just boil up again, skim it, and rub it through a sieve ; when cold, bottle it, cork well, and seal it down.

1730. WALNUT KETCHUP.—Take two sieves of green walnut shells, put them into a tub, mix them up well with from two to three pounds of common salt, let them stand for six days, frequently beating and mashing them. By this time the shells become soft and pulpy, then by banking the mass up on one side of the tub, and at the same time raising the tub on that side, the liquor will drain clear off to the other : then take that liquor out : the mashing and banking-up may be repeated as often as liquor is found. The quantity obtained will be about six quarts. When done, let it be simmered in an iron boiler as long as any scum arises ; then bruise a quarter of a pound of ginger, a quarter of a pound of allspice, two ounces of long pepper, and two ounces of cloves. Let it slowly boil for half-an-hour with the above ingredients ; when bottled, let an equal quantity of the spice go into each bottle. Before corking, let the bottles be filled quite up : cork them tight, seal them over, and put them into a cool and dry place for one year before they are used.

1731. ESSENCE OF CELERY.—This is prepared by soaking for a fortnight half-an-ounce of the seeds of celery in a quarter of a pint of brandy. A few drops will flavour a pint of soup or broth equal to a head of celery.

1732. TINCTURE OF ALLSPICE.—Bruised allspice, one ounce and a half ; brandy, a pint. Steep for a fortnight, occasionally shaking, then pour off the clear liquor. This is excellent for many of the uses of allspice, such as making bishop, mulling wine, flavouring gravies, potted meats, &c.

1733. FLAVOURING POWDER FOR SOUPS.—Pound in a marble mortar half-an-ounce each of dried mint and sage, a drachm of celery seed, and a quarter of a drachm of cayenne pepper ; rub them together through a fine sieve. This gives a very savoury relish to pea soup and even to gruel. A drachm of allspice, or black pepper, may be pounded with the above as an addition, or instead of the cayenne.

1734. HORSERADISH POWDER. —The time to make this is during November and December: slice the radish the thickness of a shilling, and lay it to dry very gradually in a Dutch oven (a strong heat soon evaporates its flavour) ; when dry enough, pound it and bottle it.

1735. CURRY POWDER.—Take two ounces of turmeric, six ounces of coriander seed, half-an-ounce of powdered ginger, two drachms of cinnamon, six drachms of cayenne pepper, four drachms of black pepper, one drachm of mace and cloves, powdered fine, two drachms of pimento, four drachms of nutmeg, and an ounce and a half of fennel seed ; powder finely, mix, dry, and bottle for use.

1736. Another Curry Powder.— Take of coriander seed and turmeric, each six drachms ; black pepper, four drachms ; fennel seed and powdered ginger, each two drachms ; cayenne pepper, half-a-drachm ; powder finely, mix, dry, and bottle for use.

1737. Indian Curry Powder.— Turmeric, four ounces ; coriander seeds, eleven ounces ; cayenne, half-an-ounce ; black pepper, five ounces ; pimento, two ounces ; cloves, half-an-ounce ; cinnamon, three ounces ; ginger, two ounces ; cummin seed, three ounces ; shallots, one ounce. All these ingredients should be of a fine quality, and recently ground or powdered.

1738. CHUTNEY.—One pound of salt, one pound of mustard seed, one pound of stoned raisins, one pound of brown sugar, twelve ounces of garlic, six ounces of cayenne pepper, two quarts of unripe gooseberries, two quarts of best vinegar. The mustard seed gently dried and braised ; the sugar made into a syrup with a pint of the vinegar ; the gooseberries dried and boiled in a quart of the vinegar ; the garlic to be well bruised in a mortar. When cold, gradually mix the whole in a large mortar, and with the remaining vinegar thoroughly amalgamate them. To be tied down close. The longer it is kept the better it will become.

1739. Wow Wow Sauce.—This is excellent for stewed or boiled beef. Chop parsley fine ; take two or three pickled cucumbers, or walnuts, and divide into small squares, and set them by in readiness ; put into a saucepan a piece of butter as big as an egg ; when it is melted, stir into it a tablespoonful of fine flour, and half-a-pint of the broth of the beef ; add a tablespoonful of vinegar, one of mushroom ketchup, or port wine, or both, and a tablespoonful of made mustard ; simmer together till it is as thick as you wish, put in the parsley and pickles to get warm, and pour it over the beef, or send it up in a sauce-tureen.

1740. ANCHOVY SAUCE (*à la minute*).—Take a few anchovies and cut them up small, two tablespoonfuls of vinegar, three ounces of butter, half-a-tumblerful of water, and a tablespoonful of flour. Stir over the fire until it thickens, and then pass it through a sieve.

1741. ANCHOVY BUTTER.— Scrape the skin from a dozen fine anchovies, take the flesh from the bones, pound it smooth in a mortar ; rub through a hair sieve, put the anchovies into the mortar with three-quarters of a pound of fresh butter, a small quantity of cayenne, and a saltspoonful of grated nutmeg and mace ; beat together until thoroughly blended. If to serve cold, mould the butter in small shapes, and turn it out. For preservation, press the butter into jars, and keep cool.

1742. LOBSTER BUTTER is made in the same manner as anchovy butter. A mixture of anchovy butter and lobster butter is considered excellent.

1743. WHITE SAUCE, or Melted Butter.—Put a dessertspoonful of flour and a little salt in a basin, mix gradually with a quarter of a pint of cold water, turn it into a small clean saucepan, boil for two minutes, stirring well, then add an ounce and a half of butter cut small and stir till it is quite melted. In mixing water and flour to form melted butter, a small hole should be made in the middle and the water then poured into this hole. Then stir round *from the centre* instead of from the side of the basin, and the butter will by this means be free from lumps.

1744. EGG SAUCE.—Put the eggs on the fire in cold water, and after they have come to the boil, let them continue boiling for five minutes. Then take them out of the saucepan, pour cold water over them, crack the shells, and put them into fresh cold water until they are wanted ; then chop them finely and add them to melted butter made as above.

1745. LIVER SAUCE FOR FISH.—Boil the liver of the fish, and pound it in a mortar with a little flour, stir it into some broth, or some of the liquor the fish was boiled in, or melted butter, with some chopped parsley, a few grains of cayenne, and a little essence of anchovy, soy, or ketchup ; give the whole a boil up, and rub it through a sieve ; a little lemon juice, or lemon cut in dice, may be added, if liked.

1746. SAUCE FOR FISH—Twenty-four anchovies, chopped ; ten shallots ; two ounces of horseradish, scraped ; four blades of mace ; one lemon, sliced ; twelve cloves ; one quarter of an ounce of black pepper, whole ; one gill of the anchovy liquor ; one quart of best vinegar ; one quart of water. Let the whole simmer on the fire, in a covered saucepan, until reduced to one quart, strain, and bottle for use. If required for long keeping, add a quarter of an ounce of cayenne pepper.

1747. APPLE SAUCE.—Pare and core three good-sized baking apples, put them into a well-tinned pint saucepan, with two tablespoonfuls of cold water ; cover the saucepan close, and set it on a trivet over a slow fire a couple of hours before dinner,—some apples will take a long time stewing, others will be ready in a quarter of an hour. When the apples are done enough pour off the water, let them stand a few minutes to get dry ; then beat them up with a fork, with a bit of butter about as big as a nutmeg, and a teaspoonful of powdered sugar ; some persons add lemon peel, grates or minced fine,—or boil a small piece with the apples. Many persons are fond of apple sauce with cold pork, goose, and ducks.

1748. GRILL SAUCE.—To a quarter of a pint of gravy add half-an-ounce of butter and a dessertspoonful of flour, well rubbed together ; the same of mushroom or walnut ketchup ; a teaspoonful of lemon juice ; half-a-teaspoonful of made mustard, and of minced capers ; a small quantity of black pepper ; a little lemon peel grated very thin ; a saltspoonful of essence of anchovies ; a very small piece of minced shallot, and a little chili vinegar, or a few grains of cayenne ; simmer together for a few minutes ; pour a portion of it over the grill, and send up the remainder in a sauce-tureen.

1749. TOMATO SAUCE.—Twelve tomatoes, ripe and red ; take off the stalk ; cut in halves ; put them in a stewpan with a capsicum, and two or three tablespoonfuls of beef gravy ; set on a slow stove till properly melted ; rub them through a sieve into a clean stewpan ; add a little white pepper and salt, and let them simmer a few minutes.—French cooks add an onion or shallot, a clove or two, or a little tarragon vinegar.

1750. BEEF GRAVY SAUCE, Or Brown Sauce for Ragout, Game, Poultry, Fish, &c.—If you want gravy, put in a thick and well-tinned stewpan a thin slice of fat ham or bacon, or an ounce of butter, and a middling-sized onion ; on this lay a pound of nice juicy gravy-beef well beaten and scored ; cover the stewpan, set it on a slow fire ; when the meat begins to brown, turn it about, and let it get slightly browned (*but take care it is not at all burnt*) : then pour in a pint and a half of boiling water, set the pan on the fire. When it boils, carefully catch the scum, and then put in a crust of bread toasted brown (don't burn it), a sprig of winter savoury, or lemon thyme and parsley, a roll of thin-cut lemon peel, a dozen berries of allspice, and a dozen of black pepper ; cover the stewpan close, let it *stew very gently* for about two hours, then strain it through a sieve into a basin. If you wish to thicken it, set a clean stewpan over a slow fire, with about an ounce of butter in it ; when it is melted, dredge into it (by degrees) as much flour as will dry it up, stirring them intimately ; when thoroughly mixed, pour in a little of the gravy,—stir it well together, and add the remainder by degrees ; set it over the fire, let it simmer gently for fifteen or twenty minutes longer, and skim off the fat, &c., as it rises. When it is about as thick as cream, squeeze it through a tamis or fine sieve, and you will have a fine rich brown sauce, at a very moderate expense, and without much trouble. *Observe*—If you wish *to make it still more relishing*—for poultry, you may pound the liver with a piece of butter, rub it through a sieve, and stir it into the sauce when you put in the thickening.

1751. RELISH FOR CHOPS, &c. —Pound fine an ounce of black pepper, and half-an-ounce of allspice, with an ounce of salt, and half-an-ounce of scraped horseradish, and the same of shallots, peeled and quartered ; put these ingredients into a pint of mushroom ketchup, or walnut pickle, and let them steep for a fortnight, and then strain it. *Observe*—A teaspoonful

or two of this is generally an acceptable addition, mixed with the gravy usually sent up for chops and steaks ; or added to thick melted butter.

1752. CAPER SAUCE.—Put into a saucepan two ounces of butter and a tablespoonful of flour, and stir them over the fire until brown : then add about a pint of stock, first skimming the fat off, and add pepper, salt, and a little Worcester sauce. Directly the sauce boils, put sufficient capers in, and boil once more, when it is ready for use.

1753.   SAGE-AND-ONION SAUCE.—Chop very fine an ounce of onion and half-an-ounce of green sage leaves, put them into a stewpan with four spoonfuls of water, simmer gently for ten minutes, then put in a teaspoonful of pepper and salt, and one ounce of fine bread-crumbs ; mix well together ; then pour to it a quarter of a pint at broth, or gravy, or melted butter ; stir well together, and simmer it a few minutes longer. This is an excellent relish for roast pork, poultry, geese or ducks, or green peas.

1754. MOCK CRAB.—Take any required quantity of good fat mellow cheese, pound it well in a mortar, incorporating made mustard, salad oil, vinegar, pepper (cayenne is the best), and salt sufficient to season and render it about the consistence of the cream of a crab. Add and mix well half-a-pint or more of pickled shrimps, and serve in a crab-shell, or on a dish, garnished with slices of lemon.

1755. GARNISHES.

i. Parsley is the most universal garnish for all kinds of cold meat, poultry, fish, butter, cheese, and so forth. Horseradish is the garnish for roast beef, and for fish in general ; for the latter, slices of lemon are sometimes laid alternately with the horseradish.

ii. Slices of lemon for boiled fowl,

turkey, and fish, and for roast veal and calf's head.

iii. Carrot in slices for boiled beef, hot or cold.

iv. Barberries, fresh or preserved, for game.

v. Red beetroot sliced for cold meat, boiled beef, and salt fish.

vi. Fried smelts as garnish for turbot.

vii. Fried sausages, forcemeat balls are placed round turkey, capon, or fowl.

viii. Lobster coral and parsley round boiled fish.

ix. Fennel for mackerel and salmon, either fresh or pickled.

x. Currant jelly for game, also for custard or bread pudding.

xi. Seville orange or lemon in slices for wild ducks, widgeons, teal, and so forth.

xii. Mint, either with or without parsley, for roast lamb, either hot or cold.

xiii. Pickled gherkins, capers, or onions, for some kinds of boiled meat and stews.

1756. CREAM WHIPPED.—Take the whites of a dozen eggs, one quart of cream, half-a-pint of sherry, ten drops of essence of musk, three drops of essence of orange peel. Whisk into froth and put it in a sieve. Fill glasses with the cream, the froth being poured on top.

1757. Coffee Custard.—Take half-a-pint of hot milk, and the same quantity of strong coffee, also two ounces of sugar. Having dissolved the sugar in the hot milk and coffee, add the same slowly to four eggs previously well beaten up.

1758. DEVONSHIRE JUNKET.—Put warm milk into a bowl, turn it with a little rennet, then add some scalded cream, sugar, and cinnamon on the top, without breaking the curd.

1759. LEGAL INFORMATION.

The following particulars have been very carefully compiled by experienced legal practitioners ; great pains have been taken to ensure correctness, but the publishers do not hold themselves responsible for any possible inaccuracies that may arise from the passing of new acts, &c.

1760. Requisites for a Successful Law Suit.—A lady asked an attorney what were the requisites for going to law. He replied, "First, you must have a good cause ; secondly, a good attorney ; thirdly, a good counsel ; fourthly, good evidence ; fifthly, a good jury ; sixthly, a good judge ; and lastly, good luck."

1761. LAWS OF EMPLOYER AND EMPLOYED.

1762. Hiring and Dismissal.—A general hiring of domestic servants is construed as a hiring for a year, but the hiring may be put an end to by either party giving to the other one month's notice, or in the case of the employer one month's wages in lieu of notice. As regards governesses and clerks the general hiring is the same, but in the absence of special arrangement made at the time of hiring a three months' warning is required. The terms on which clerks and superior servants are employed being very various, it is desirable to have a specific agreement.

1763. Agreements with Menial Servants need not be stamped ; but contracts of a higher and special character should be.

1764. Agreements should bear Evidence of Mutuality of Interest.—If one party agrees to stay with another, and give gratuitous services, with the view of acquiring knowledge of a business, and the other party does not agree to employ and to *teach*, the agreement is void, as being without consideration.

1765. An Employer must Contract to Employ, as well as a servant to *serve*, otherwise the employer may put an end to the contract at his own pleasure. In such a case a servant may be dismissed without notice. But where a servant agrees to serve a master in a certain capacity for a definite time, it must not be implied, from this circumstance alone, that the master agrees to retain the servant in his employ until the expiration of that time.

1766. Agreements to give Permanent Employment are received as extending only to a substantial and reasonable period of time, and that there shall be no immediate and peremptory dismissal without cause.

1767. Breakages.—When no stipulation is made at the time of the hiring, or in the agreement, that a servant shall be liable for breakages, injuries from negligence, &c., the employer can only recover from the servant by due process of law. The effect of recent decisions is to permit deductions to be made from the servant's wages for breakages ; and if the master is sued for the full amount of the wages, he may counterclaim for the damage.

1768. It is Advisable to Stipulate that, if a servant quit his employ before the specified time, or without due notice, a certain amount of wages shall be forfeited ; otherwise the employer can only recover by action for damages.

1769. Liveries.—It should be agreed that servants deliver these up on quitting service.

1770. Illnesses.—If a servant, retained for a year, happen within the period of his service to fall sick, or to be hurt or lamed, or otherwise to become of infirm body by the act of God, while doing his master's business, the master cannot put such servant away, nor abate any part of his wages for such time, unless the servant agrees that he may do so.

1771. Medical Attendance.—A master is not bound to provide medical attendance for his menial servants, but if he calls in his own medical attendant and instructs him to attend the servant he is liable for his fees.

1772. Upon the Death of a Servant, his personal representative may claim arrears of wages due, unless the contract of employment specified and required the completion of any particular period.

1773. Dismissals.—When the hiring of a superior servant is for a year, if the servant, prior to the expiration of the year, commits any act by which he may be lawfully discharged, he cannot claim wages for the part of the year which he may have served. But a menial servant may claim up to the date of his dismissal, unless his discharge be for embezzlement or other felonious acts.

1774. When a Master becomes Bankrupt or Insolvent, the wages or salary of any clerk or servant in his employ, not exceeding four months' wages or salary, and not more than £50, is payable on an equality "with twelve months' rates and taxes in priority to any other debts." So also the wages of any labourer or workman not exceeding £25. For any further sums due to him, the clerk, servant, or workman must prove against the bankrupt's estate the same as other creditors.

1775. Receipts should be taken for Wages paid.—Where servants have been under age, it has been held that moneys advanced for fineries and extravagances unbecoming to a servant did not constitute payment of wages, and the employer has been compelled to pay again.

1776. Moneys paid to a Married Woman.—The receipt of a married woman is a good discharge for any wages or earnings acquired or gained by her in any employment or occupation in which she is engaged separately from her husband.

1777. When a Servant Reserves to Himself Special Privileges, such as particular portions of his time, the hiring becomes special, and cannot be governed by the terms of general engagements. So, also, where a servant stipulates to be exempted from particular duties that usually belong to his situation.

1778. Should a Servant Refuse to Perform any duty required from him, his right so to refuse will generally be determined by the usages prevailing among servants of a similar class.

1779. Purchase of Goods by Servants for Employer.—A servant cannot by buying goods for his employer's use pledge his master's credit, unless his master authorized him to do so, or unless the master has previously paid for goods bought by the servant in like manner on a former occasion. If a master contracts with a servant to provide certain things and pays him for so doing, a tradesman supplying the things can only sue the servant and not the master for his money.

1780. Responsibility for Acts of Servant.—It is an established maxim in law, that whoever does an act by the hands of another shall be deemed to have done it himself. And hence, in many matters, masters are responsible for the acts of their servants. But if a servant does an unlawful act, not arising out of the discharge of his duties to his master, then the employer is not responsible.

1781. A Servant being Seduced from the Employment of a master, the latter has a right of action against the seducer for losses sustained.

1782. Giving Characters Optional. —An employer is not bound to give a servant a character, but if he does, he must give what he believes to be a true one. If he give a false character from motives of malice he will render himself liable for an action for libel or slander ; but the representations must be proved to be false as well as malicious.

1783. Employers' Liability to Workmen for Injuries.—By the "Employers' Liability Act," 1880, a workman may recover from his employer damages for personal injuries sustained by him in the course of his employment, if the accident happen through any one of the following causes: —

i. A defect in the way, works, machinery, or plant used in the employer's business, and which defect the employer negligently allows to remain unremedied.

ii. The negligence of some superintendent or overlooker in the service of the employer.

iii. The negligence of the foreman or other person in the service of the employer, whose orders or directions the workman was bound to obey and did obey.

iv. The act or omission of any person in the service of the employer, done or made in obedience to the rules, byelaws, or instructions of the employer.

v. The negligence of any person in the service of the employer, who has the charge or control of any signal, points, locomotive engine, or train upon a railway.

1784. Notice to Employer.— Notice in writing of the injury must be given to the employer, or sent by registered post, within six weeks of the injury, giving the name and address of the person injured, the date of the accident, and stating in ordinary language the cause of the injury.

1785. Actions for Compensation to be brought in County Court—All actions for compensation under the above Act must be brought in the County Court, and commenced within *six* months of the accident, or, in case the workman die and the action is brought by his representatives, then within *twelve* months from his death.

1786. The Workmen's Compensation Act, 1897 (60 and 61 Vic. c. 37), is another Act which enables workmen engaged in certain trades therein specified to recover damages for injuries sustained in the course of their employment, and in the event of the death of such workmen through such injury enables the dependents of such workmen to recover—

(1) If wholly dependent on his earnings, a sum equal to his earnings in the employment of the same employer during the three years preceding the injury, or £150, whichever sum be the larger, but not exceeding in any case £300.

(2) If partially dependent, such sum, not exceeding in any case the amount payable under the foregoing provision, as may be agreed upon, or in default of agreement, as may be determined by arbitration under the Act.

(3) If no dependents, the reasonable expenses of medical attendance and burial, not exceeding £10.

Proceedings for recovery of damages under this Act shall not be maintainable unless notice of the accident has been given as soon as practicable after the happening thereof, and before the workman has voluntarily left the employment in which he was injured, and unless the claim has been made within six months from the accident, or in the case of death within six months from the time of death.

N.B.—It is impossible in a work of this description to allude to all the provisions of this Act. Our readers should therefore refer to the Act itself, or in case of accident should consult some respectable solicitor as to their rights under the Act

1787. LAWS OF LANDLORD AND TENANT.

1788. Leases.—A lease is a conveyance from the lessor to the lessee of premises or lands for a specified term of years, at a yearly rent, with definite conditions as to alterations, repairs, payment of rent, forfeiture, &c. Being an instrument of much importance, it should always be drawn by a respectable solicitor, who will see that all the conditions, in the interest of the lessee, are fulfilled.

1789. Precautions.—In taking a lease, the tenant's solicitor should carefully examine the covenants, or if he take an under-lease, he should ascertain the covenants of the original lease, otherwise, when too late, he may find himself so restricted in his occupation that the premises may be wholly useless for his purpose, or he may be involved in perpetual difficulties and annoyances ; for instance, he may find himself restricted from making alterations convenient or necessary for his trade ; he may find himself compelled to rebuild or pay rent in case of fire ; he may find himself subject to forfeiture of his lease, or other penalty, if he should underlet or assign his interest, carry on some particular trade, &c.

1790. Covenants.—The covenants on the landlord's part are usually for the quiet enjoyment of the premises by the lessee. On the tenant's part, they are usually to pay the rent and taxes, to insure against fire, to keep the premises in suitable repair ; and to deliver up possession when the term has expired.

1791. Rent and Taxes. —The lessee covenants to pay the rent and all taxes, except the land and property taxes and tithe rent charge, which may be deducted from the rent.

1792. Assignments.—Unless there be a covenant against assignment, a lease may be assigned, that is, the whole interest of the lessee may be conveyed to another, or it may be under-let ; if, therefore, it is intended that it should not, it is proper to insert a covenant to restrain the lessee from assigning or under-letting. Tenants for terms of years may assign or under-let, but tenants at will cannot.

1793. Repairs.—A tenant who covenants to keep a house in repair is not answerable for its natural decay, but is bound to keep it wind and water tight, so that it does not decay for want of cover. A lessee who covenants to pay rent and keep the premises in repair, is liable to pay the rent although the premises may be burned down ; unless a stipulation to the contrary be inserted in the lease.

1794. Insurance.—When insuring the premises against damage by fire the lessee should also insure for one year's rent.

1795. Neglect of Repairs by Landlord.—If a landlord covenant to repair, and neglect to do so, the tenant may do it, and withhold so much of the rent. But it is advisable that notice thereof should be given by the tenant to the landlord, in the presence of a witness, prior to commencing the repairs.

1796. Right of Landlord to Enter Premises.—A landlord may enter upon the premises (having given previous notice, although not expressed in the lease), for the purpose of viewing the state of the property.

1797. Termination of Leases.—A tenant must deliver up posession at the expiration of the term (the lease being sufficient notice), or he will continue liable to the rent as tenant by sufferance without any new contract ; but if the landlord recognizes such tenancy by accepting a payment of rent after the lease has expired, such acceptance will constitute a yearly tenancy ; but previous to accepting rent, the landlord may bring his ejectment without notice ; for, the lease having expired, the tenant is a trespasser. A lease covenanted to be void if the rent be not paid upon the day appointed, is good, unless the landlord make an entry.

1798. Dilapidations.—Under the ordinary tenants' covenants to keep and give up the premises in repair, the following appears to be the general rule:—"If repairs can be effected they can be so made: but if the damage is so great as to render repairs impossible, the parts must be made good. A tenant is bound to replace all broken and loose tiles in the roof ; to restore all pointing and filleting ; to make good (that is *renew*, not repair) all defective brickwork in chimneys, walls, parapets, &c. ; and to replace broken chimney-pots. "

1799. Compensation on Termination of Lease.—Under the "*Allotments and Cottage Gardens Act*, 1887" (50 & 51 Vict. c. 26), on the termina- tion of a holding the tenant can, notwithstanding any agreement to the contrary, obtain compensation in money from the landlord in respect of:—

(*a*) Crops, including fruit, growing on the holding, and fruit trees and bushes which the tenant has planted with the previous written consent of the landlord.

(*b*) Labour and manure bestowed on the holding since the last crop in anticipation of another crop ; and

(*c*) Drains and structural improvements made with the written consent of the landlord.

If they cannot agree upon the amount and time of payment, the question is to be settled by arbitration.

1800. Married Women, with the concurrence of their husbands, may grant leases by deed for any term. Husbands, seised in right of their wives, may grant leases for twenty-one years. If a wife is executrix, the husband and wife have the power of leasing, as in the ordinary case of husband and wife. A married woman living separate from her husband may by taking a lease bind her separate estate for payment of the rent and performance of the covenants.

1801. Copyholders may not grant a lease for longer than one year, unless by custom, or permission of the lord : and the lease of a steward of a manor is not good, unless he is duly invested with a power for that purpose.

1802. Yearly Tenancies.—Houses are considered as let for the year, and the tenants are subject to the laws affecting annual tenancies, unless there be an agreement in writing to the contrary.

1803. *Agreement for taking a House on an Annual Tenancy.*—Memorandum of Agreement, entered into this ———— day of 18 , between R. A., of ————, and L. O., of ————, as follows—

The said R. A. doth hereby let unto the said L. O. the dwelling-house, situate in ————, in the parish of ————, for the term of one year certain, and so on from year to year, until half-a-year's notice expiring at the end of the current year of the tenancy to quit be given by or to either party, at the yearly rent of ———— pounds, payable quarterly ; the tenancy to commence at ———— day next.

And the said R A. doth undertake to pay the land-tax, the property-tax, and the sewer-rate, and to keep the said house in all necessary repairs, so long as the said L. O. shall continue therein. And the said L. O. doth undertake to take the said house of R. A. for the before-mentioned term and rent, and pay all rent, rates and taxes, except as aforesaid. The said R. A. to be at liberty to re-enter if any rent shall be in arrear for 31 days, whether such rent has been demanded or not.

Witness our hands, the day and year aforesaid.   R A.

Witness, G. C.   L. O.

1804. Payment of Taxes by Landlord.—If the landlord agree to pay all the rates and taxes, then a different wording of the agreement should take place, as thus :—

And the said R A. doth undertake to pay all rates and taxes, of whatever nature or kind, chargeable on the said house and premises, and to keep the said house in all necessary repairs, so long as the said L. O. shall continue therein.

1805. Indemnity from arrears.— If the landlord agree to secure the incoming tenant from all arrears (and the tenant should see to this) due on account of rent, rates, and taxes, the indemnification should be written on a separate paper, and in something like the following terms :—

1806. *Indemnification against Rents, Rates, and Taxes in Arrear.*—I, R. A., landlord of a certain house and premises now about to be taken and occupied by L. O., do hereby agree to indemnify the said L. O. from the payment of any rent, taxes, or rates, in arrear, prior to the date of the day at which his said tenancy commences. As witness my hand this ———— day of ———— 18

R.A.,
Landlord of the above premises.

Witness, G. C.

1807. *Agreement for taking a House for Three Years.*— Memorandum of an agreement made the ———— day of ————, 18 , between R. A., of ————, and L. O. of ————, as follows :—

The said R A. doth let unto the said L. O. a house and garden (if any) with appurtenances, situate in ————, in the parish of ————, for three years certain. The rent to commence from ———— day next, at and under the yearly rent of ————, payable quarterly on the usual quarter days, the first payment to be at day next.

The said L. O. doth agree to take the said house (and garden) of the said R. A., for the term and rent payable in manner aforesaid, and will also pay all rates, taxes, and assessments payable in respect of the said premises ; and that he will, at the expiration of the term, leave the house in as good repair as he found it [reasonable wear and tear excepted]. The said R. A. to be at liberty to re-enter, if any rent shall be in arrear for 21 days, whether such rent has been demanded or not. Witness our hands.

R. A.

Witness, G. C.   L. O.

1808. Payment of Rent.—Rent is usually payable at the regular quarter-days, namely, Lady-day, or March 25th ; Midsummer-day, or June 24th ; Michaelmas-day, September 29th ; and Christmas-day, December 25th. It is due at mid-day ; but no proceedings for non-payment, where the tenant remains upon the premises, can be taken till the next day.

1809. Payment of Rent Imperative.—No consideration will waive the payment of the rent, should the land-lord insist on demanding it. Even should the house be burnt, blown, or fall down, the tenant is still liable for rent ; and the tenancy can only be voided by the proper notice to quit, the same as if the house remained in the most perfect condition.

1810. Demanding Rent.—The landlord himself is the person most proper to demand rent ; he may employ another person, but if he does, he must authorize him by letter, or by power of attorney ; or the demand may be objected to.

1811. Receipt for Rent.—When an agent has been duly authorized, a receipt from him for any subsequent rent is a legal acquittance to the tenant, notwithstanding the landlord may have revoked the authority under which the agent acted, unless the landlord should have given the tenant due and proper notice thereof.

1812. Legal Tender.—A tender of rent should be in the current coin of the kingdom. But a tender of Bank of England notes is good, even in cases of distress, and though the tender be made on a Sunday, it will be a legal one. If the landlord take a distress after the rent has been tendered it will be illegal, and he will be liable to an action.

1813. *Form of a Receipt for Rent.*—Received of Mr. L. O. the sum of ten pounds ten shillings, for a quarter's rent due at Lady-day last, for the house, No. , ——— street.

£10 10s.   [Stamp]   R. A.
           [Date]

If the receipt be given by an agent, it should be signed—

G. C.

Agent for R. A., landlord of the above premises.

1814. Care of Receipts for Rent.—Be careful of your last quarter's receipt for rent, for the production of that document bars all prior claim. Even when arrears have been due on former quarters, the receipt, if given for the last quarter, precludes the landlord from recovery thereof.

1815. Notices.—All notices of whatever description, relating to tenancies, should be in writing, and the person serving the said notice should write on the back thereof a memorandum of the date on which it was served, and should keep a copy of the said notice, with a similar memorandum attached.

1816. Notices to Quit—When either the landlord or tenant intends to terminate a tenancy, the way to proceed is by a notice to quit, which is drawn up in the following ways :—

1817. *Form of a Notice to Quit from a Tenant to his Landlord.*— Sir,—I hereby give you notice, that on or before the ———day of ——— next, I shall quit and deliver up possession of the house and premises I now hold of you, situate at ———, in the parish of ———, in the county of ———.

Dated the ——— day of ———, 18
Witness, G. C.   L. O.
To Mr. R. A.

1818. *Notice from Landlord to his Tenant.*—Sir,—I hereby give you notice to quit and deliver up possession to me of the house and appurtenances, situate No. ———, which you now hold of me, on or before ——— next.

Dated , 18 .
(Signed)   R. A. (landlord).
To Mr. L. O.

1819. *Form of Notice from a Landlord to his Tenant to Quit or Pay an incresed Rent.*—To Mr. R. A.— Sir,—I hereby give you notice to deliver up possession, and quit on or before ———, the [*here state the house or apartment*] and appurtenances which you now hold of me in [*insert the name of the street, &c.*] and in default at your compliance therewith, I do and will insist on your paying me for the same, the [*annual or monthly*] rent of ———, being an additional rental of ——— pounds per annum [*over and above the present annual rental*] rent, for such time as you shall detain the key and keep possession over the said notice.

Witness my hand, this —— day of ——, 18

Witness, G. C.   L. O.

1820. Length of Notice required. —An opinion is very generally entertained, that a quarter's warning to quit, where the house is of small rental, is sufficient notice ; but where the rent is payable quarterly, or at longer intervals, this is a mistake, for unless a special agreement is made defining the time to be given as a warning, six months' notice to quit must be given, to expire on the same day of the year upon which the tenancy commenced. Where the rent is payable weekly or monthly, the notice to quit will be good if given for the week or month, provided care be taken that it expires upon the day of the week or month of the beginning of the tenancy.

1821. Refusal to Give up Possession.—If a tenant holds over, after receiving a sufficient notice to quit, *in writing*, he becomes liable to pay double the yearly value ; if he holds over after having himself given even parole notice to quit, he is liable to pay double rent. If he refuses to quit, the landlord is not justified in putting him out by force, but must take proceedings by ejectment. If, however, the tenant be gone away, and the house deserted (no one being in possession), the landlord may be justified in breaking into it and obtaining possession.

1822. LODGINGS AND LODGERS.

1823. Distraint on Furniture, &c. of Lodger.—The goods of a lodger are not liable to distress for rent due to the superior landlord. If any furniture, goods, or chattels of a lodger are distrained for rent due to the superior landlord, the lodger should immediately serve the superior landlord or his bailiff or person distraining with a declaration in writing, setting forth that the immediate tenant ot the house has no interest in the things distrained, and that the same are the property, or in the lawful possession, of such lodger, and also setting forth whether any and what rent is due, and for what period, from the lodger to his immediate landlord ; and the lodger should pay to the superior landlord, or his bailiff, or person distraining, the rent so due from him, or so much as shall be sufficient to discharge the claim of the superior landlord. The lodger should make out and sign an inventory of the things claimed by him, and annex it to his declaration.

1824. Application to Magistrate. —If, after taking these steps, the superior landlord, or his bailiff, should proceed with a distress upon the lodger's goods, the lodger should apply to a stipendiary magistrate or to two justices of the peace, who will order his goods to be restored to him, and the superior landlord will also be liable to an action at the suit of the lodger.

1825. Broker Entering Apartments.—A broker having obtained possession through the outer door, may break open any of the private doors of the lodgers, if necessary, for the purpose of distraining the goods of the tenant.

1826. Renting for a specific Term. —If lodgings are taken for a certain and specified time, no notice to quit is necessary. If the lodger, however, continue after the expiration of the term, he becomes a regular lodger, unless there is an agreement to the contrary. If he owe rent, the housekeeper can detain his goods whilst on the premises, or distrain, as a landlord may distrain the goods of a tenant.

1827. Lodgers and Householders bound by the same Law.—No distinction exists between lodgers and other tenants as to the payment of their rent, or the turning them out of possession ; they are also similarly circumstanced with regard to distress for rent, as householders, except that (as above mentioned) the goods of lodgers cannot be distrained for rent due to the superior landlord.

1828. Weekly Tenants.—In case of weekly tenants, the rent should be paid weekly, for if it is once let to run a quarter, and the landlord accept it as a quarter, the tenant cannot be forced to quit without a quarter's notice.

1829. Yearly Lodgers.—Lodgings by the year should only be taken from a person who is either proprietor of the house, or holds possession for an unexpired term of years.

1830. Furnished Lodgings.—Furnished lodgings are usually let by the week, on payment of a fixed sum, part of which is considered as rent for the apartment, and part for the use of the furniture. In some instances an agreement is made for so much per week rent, and so much for the use of the furniture, and to place all moneys received to the account of the furniture, until that part of the demand shall be satisfied, as the landlord cannot distrain for the use of his furniture.

1831. Lodgers Leaving without Notice.—Persons renting furnished apartments frequently absent themselves without apprising the householder, perhaps with the rent in arrear. If there is probable reason to believe that the lodger has left, on the second week of such absence the householder may send for a policeman, and in his presence enter the lodger's apartment and take out the latter's property, and secure it until application is made for it.

1832. Verbal Agreements.—If a person make a verbal agreement to take lodgings at a future day, and decline to fulfil his agreement, the housekeeper has no remedy, and even the payment of a deposit makes no difference.

1833. Landlord using Lodger's Apartments.—If a landlord enter and use apartments while his tenant is in legal possession, without his consent, he forfeits his right to recover rent.

1834. Lodgings to Immodest Women.—If lodgings are let to an immodest woman, to enable her to receive visitors of the male sex, the landlord cannot recover his rent. But if the landlord did not know the character of the woman when he let the lodgings, he may recover, but not if *after* he knew the fact he permitted her to remain as his tenant. If the woman, however, merely lodges there, and has her visitors elsewhere, her character will not affect his claim for rent.

1835. Rent Recoverable.—If a lodger quit apartments without notice, the landlord can still recover his rent by action, although he has put up a bill in the window to let them.

1836. Removing Goods.—Removing goods from furnished lodgings, with intent to steal, is a felony : unlawful pledging is a misdemeanour.

1837. Liability for Rent.—Where the lodger has removed, and there are no goods whereon to make a levy, the rent becomes a debt, and can only be recovered as such in the County Court of the district.

1838. *Agreement for Letting a Furnished House or Apartment.* Memorandum of an agreement made and entered into this ———— day of ————, 18 , between R. A., of ————, of the one part, and L. O., of ————, of the other part, as follows :— That the said R. A. agrees to let, and the said L. O. to take, all that messuage or tenement (with the gardens and appurtenances thereto) situate at, &c. [*or if an apartment be the subject of demise,* all the entire first floor, *particularly describing the other appurtenances*], together with all the furniture, fixtures, and other things mentioned and comprised in the schedule hereunder written, for the space of —— months, to be computed from the —— day of ——, at the rent of —— pounds per quarter, payable quarterly, the first quarterly payment to be made on the —— day of —— next ensuing the date hereof. And it is further agreed, by and between the said parties, that each party shall be at liberty to determine the said tenancy, on giving to the other a quarter's notice in writing. And the said L. O. agrees, that on the determination of the tenancy, he will deliver up the said dwelling-house (or the entire first floor, &c.), together with all the fixtures and furniture as aforesaid, in as good a condition as the same now are, reasonable wear and tear thereof excepted, and shall and will replace any of the crockery and china or other utensils that shall be broken or otherwise damaged. In witness, &c.—[*Here is to follow the Inventory, or List of Articles referred to above.*]

1839. VOTES OF LODGERS.

The inhabitant occupier of lodgings, of the value of £10 per annum unfur- nished, has a right to vote for the county ; and the inhabitant occupier, as tenant for twelve months ending July 15, of lodgings of the value of £10 per annum unfurnished, has a vote for the borough. Additional rooms may be taken during the year without vitiating the qualification ; but removal from one house to another disqualifies. A lodger who is already on the register in respect of the same lodgings, must send in a claim each year on or before July 25.

1840. REMEDIES TO RECOVER RENT.

Distress is the most efficient remedy to recover rent, but care should be taken that it be done legally ; if the distress be illegal, the party aggrieved has a remedy by action for damages. Excessive distresses are illegal. The distrainer ought only to take sufficient to recover the rent due, and costs ; if, however, the articles sell for a greater sum than is sufficient to pay these, the remainder must be returned to the tenant, who can demand particulars of the sale, and recover the overplus, if any.

1841. Distress, Legal and Illegal.—A distress can be made only for rent that is due, and cannot be made until the day after, nor unless it has been demanded by the landlord or his agent. If a distress be made and the goods sold where no rent is due, the person distraining is liable for double their value. The outer door must not be *broken* open for the purpose of distraining, neither can the distress be made between sun-setting and sun-rising, nor on Sunday, Good Friday, or Christmas-day ; nor after the rent has been tendered to the landlord or his agent. A second distress can be made, if the value of the first is not enough to pay the rent and costs, but not if, at the time of making the first distress, there were sufficient goods upon the premises to satisfy the full amount, if the landlord had then thought proper to take them.

The distrainer may not distrain fixtures, or gas or water fittings let to the tenants by the gas or water companies ; goods of strangers delivered to the tenant to be worked upon or taken care of (in the course of the tenant's business) ; perishable articles (as meat, &c.) ; the instruments of the tenant's trade or profession ; nor things in actual use at the time of the distress.

Wearing apparel and bedding of debtor and his family, and tools or implements of trade to the value of £5 are exempt from seizure, except where a tenant holds possession after term of tenancy or notice to quit has expired.

1842. Days of Grace.

The tenant has five days of grace after the goods have been seized, in which to pay the rent and expenses ; but failing this the bailiff proceeds to call in two appraisers to value the goods, and then to sell them for the best price he can get.

1843. Seizure of Goods removed. —Goods conveyed off the premises to prevent a distress may be seized anywhere within thirty days after the removal, and if force is resorted to by the landlord, it must be in the presence of a constable ; but goods removed before the rent is actually due cannot be followed, but the rent can be recovered by action as a debt in the County Court, The general rule is, that nothing can b. distrained which cannot be returned in the same condition as before the distress was made.

1844. Bankrupt's Rent.—In cases of bankruptcy not more than one year's rent is obtainable by distress ; if more be due, the landlord is only entitled to come in with the rest of the creditors for the further sum due.

1845. Appraisement.—Section 1 of the Act 2 W. and M., cap. 5, requiring appraisement before sale of goods, is repealed, and appraisement is not necessary unless demanded in writing by the tenant, or owner of the goods, who must pay the cost of such appraisement and subsequent removal of goods for sale. Appraisement made by the distraining broker or any interested person is illegal.

1846. Charges for Distraint— By the 51 and 52 Vic. cap. 21 (Law of Distress Amendment Act, 1888), no person distraining for rent shall take other charges than those hereafter scheduled : any party charging more can be sued for treble the amount unlawfully taken.

	£ s.d.
Levying a distress (under £20)	0 3 0
[Over £20 and under £50, 3 p.c. on the amount ; £50 to £200, 2½ p.c. ; above £200, 1 p.c.]	
Man in possession, per day, if rent due be under £20	0 4 6
Ditto, over £20.	0 5 0

(Man to provide his own board in all cases.)

The above charges are payable on account simply of the levy ; if the sum due, with the above charges, be not paid within five days (or fifteen days on written request of debtor), and the goods are removed and sold by auction, all expenses of such removal and sale are deductable from the amount realized.

1847. Broker's Charges.—Brokers must in all cases give written particulars of their charges.

1848. Bailiffs must hold Certificates.—No person may act as a bailiff who does not hold a certificate from a County Court judge (51 and 52 Vict. c. 21, s. 7 ; amended by 58 and 99 Vict. c. 24).

By the Law of Distress Amendment Act, 1895 (58 and 59 Vict. c. 24, s. 2), if any person not holding a certificate levies a distress, he is liable on conviction to a fine not exceeding £10, and liable also in damages.

1849. STAMPED AGREEMENTS. —All Agreements for Tenancies of whatever length of term, require a stamp duty varying with the amount of rent. The proper stamp duty can generally be ascertained at any inland revenue office.

1850. Stamped Documents.—In all cases where the law requires a stamp, whether for an agreement or a receipt, do not omit it. As the stamp laws are liable to frequent alterations, it is best to refer to the tables in the recognized almanacks for the year, or to make enquiries at the stamp offices.

1851. DEBTOR AHD CREDITOR.

1852. BANKRUPTCY.

The former distinction between insolvents and bankrupts is now abolished. All debtors, traders or not, are now subject to the laws of bankruptcy. *Married Women* are now liable to be made bankrupt ; but no person under age, except under certain circumstances, with the sanction of the Receiver. Liquidation by private arrangement is abolished.

1853. Bankruptcy Proceedings commence with a petition, either by the debtor himself or by a creditor or creditors. All petitions go before the High Court (or the district County Court), and no competition or arrangement is sanctioned until after the debtor has been publicly examined. All proceedings are controlled by the Court. For bankruptcy purposes, the County Courts have all the powers and jurisdiction of the High Court of Justice.

1854. "Acts of Bankruptcy" comprise:—Assignment of property for benefit of creditors ; fraudulent transfer of property ; leaving, or remaining out of, England, or absence from dwelling-house to defeat or delay creditors ; having his goods seized under an execution ; filing declaration of insolvency or presenting a bankruptcy petition against self ; failure to comply with a bankruptcy notice to pay a judgment debt ; giving notice to creditors of suspension of payment ; and having a receiving order made against one.

1855. Receiving Order.—If a debtor commit an act of bankruptcy, the Court may, on petition either by creditor or debtor, make a receiving order for the protection of the estate. All receiving orders to be advertised in the *London Gazette* and locally.

1856. Petition.—A creditor (or creditors) cannot present a petition unless the debt (or debts) amount to £50 ; the debt must be a liquidated sum, payable now or at some future time ; the act of bankruptcy on which the petition is grounded must have occurred within *three months* before presentation of petition ; and the debtor must be domiciled in, or within a year before petition have resided in or had a place of business in, England. If the petitioning creditor is a secured creditor, he must in his petition, either state that he is willing to give up his security for the benefit of his creditors, or give an estimate of the value of his security. No petition can, after presentment, be withdrawn without leave of the Court. A creditor's petition most be accompanied by affidavits verifying the statements therein.

1857. Official Receiver.—On a receiving order being made, the debtor's property vests In the Official Receiver, who must summon a first meeting of creditors, giving to each not less than seven days' notice of time and place in the *Gazette* and locally.

1858. The Meeting of Creditors summoned as above shall consider whether a proposal for a composition or scheme of arrangement shall be entertained, or whether the debtor shall be adjudged bankrupt, and the mode of dealing with the debtor's property. The meeting is to be held within fourteen days from the date of the receiving order.

1859. Duties of Debtor.—The debtor must furnish the Official Receiver with a full statement of his affairs in the prescribed form, verified by affidavit, and all such information as the Receiver may require. This statement, if made on a *debtor's petition*, must be submitted to the Receiver within *three days* of the date of the receiving order ; if on a *creditor's petition*, within *seven days* ; or the debtor will be liable to be adjudged bankrupt on application to the Court by Receiver or creditor.

1860. Public Examination.—Before any resolution or composition is approved by creditors, a public examination of the bankrupt, on oath, must be held by the Court, at which the Receiver must be present.

1861. Composition or Scheme of Arrangement.—The creditors may at their first meeting, or any adjournment thereof, by special resolution, entertain a composition or scheme of arrangement, and if the same be accepted by the creditors, application must be made to the Court to approve it, the Official Receiver reporting as to the terms of the composition or arrangement, which the Court will approve or reject according to the circumstances.

1862. Default in Payment of Instalments in composition or scheme, renders the debtor liable to be adjudged bankrupt on application by any creditor to the Court.

1863. Adjudication of Bankruptcy, when a Composition is not accepted.—If after a receiving order has been made the creditors resolve that the debtor be adjudged bankrupt, or pass no resolution, or do not meet, or if a composition or scheme is not accepted and approved within fourteen days after the debtor's public examination, the Court will adjudge the debtor bankrupt, and his property shall become divisible among his creditors, and shall vest in a Trustee. Notice of such adjudication must be advertised in the *London Gazette* and locally.

1864. Appointment of Trustee.— The creditors of a bankrupt may, by ordinary resolution, appoint a Trustee of the debtor's property. If this has not been done prior to adjudication, the Official Receiver shall call a creditors' meeting for that purpose. The creditors may resolve to leave the appointment to the committee of inspection. The person appointed shall give security to the Board of Trade, which shall, if it sees fit, certify the appointment. If no Trustee is appointed by the creditors, the Board may appoint one.

1865. A Committee of Inspection must not exceed five, nor be less than three, in number, and must be creditors qualified to vote, or their authorized representatives.

1866. Bankrupt must Render every Assistance to creditors in realizing his property. He must produce a clear statement of his affairs at the first meeting. He must be present for public examination on the day named by the Court and the adjournment thereof. He must also furnish a list of debts due to or from him. He must attend all meetings of creditors, and wait on the Trustee when required to answer any questions regarding his property, and to execute all documents and to carry out anything that may be ordered by the Trustee or the Court.

1867. The Trustee's Duties are to manage the estate and distribute the proceeds, under regulation of the committee of inspection, or of resolutions arrived at by the creditors at any general meeting. He has to call meetings of committee and creditors when necessary. He can transfer or dispose of the bankrupt's property for the benefit of the creditors as the bankrupt could have done himself prior to his bankruptcy. He can also carry on the bankrupt's business if necessary, compromise or arrange with creditors, and sell bankrupt's property by public auction or private contract.

1868. The Trustee must Render Accounts to the Board of Trade not less than twice a year ; and must pay all money received into the Bankruptcy Estates Account, kept by the Board of Trade at the Bank of England, and not, in any circumstances, into his private banking account.

1869. Certain Debts have Priority, and must be paid in full, or as far as assets will admit. These are—parochial and local rates, due at date of receiving order, or within a year before ; assessed land, property, and income tax, up to April 6th next before date of order, not exceeding one year's assessment ; wages and salaries of clerks, or servants, not exceeding £50, due for four months' service, and of labourers or workmen not exceeding £25 due for two months' service.

1870. Landlord may Distrain for Rent either before or after bankruptcy, but only for six months' rent if *after* bankruptcy. Any balance beyond one year's rent must be proved as in case of an ordinary debt.

1871. Allowance for Maintenance may be made to bankrupt by the Trustee, with consent of committee of inspection, for his support, or for services in winding up the estate. Where the bankrupt is a beneficed clergyman, the Trustee may apply for sequestration of profits, and with concurrence of the bishop, allow a sum equal to a curate's stipend for bankrupt's services in the parish. In the case of officers and civil servants, in receipt of salary, the Court directs what part of bankrupt's income shall be reserved for benefit of creditors.

1872. A Final Dividend may be declared when the Trustee and committee of inspection consider that as much of the estate has been realized as can be done fairly without needlessly protracting the bankruptcy.

1873. Bankruptcy may be Declared Closed, and order to that effect published in the *London Gazette*, when the Court is satisfied that all bankrupt's property has been realized, or a satisfactory arrangement or composition made with the creditors.

1874. Order of Discharge may be granted by the Court on the application of the bankrupt at any time after adjudication. The Court may suspend or withhold order if bankrupt has kept back property or acted fraudulently.

1875. In Cases of Fraud, the bankrupt may be proceeded against and is liable to imprisonment for not exceeding two years with or without hard labour.

1876. Settlement of Property by a Debtor on wife and children will become void if the settler becomes bankrupt within *two* years after date of settlement, and within *ten* years unless it can be proved that the settler was able to pay his debts when settlement was made without aid of property settled. This does not apply to a settlement made before marriage, or after marriage of property accruing in the right of wife, or settlement made in favour of purchaser in good faith for valuable consideration.

1877. Arrest of the Debtor may be ordered by the Court if, after a bankruptcy notice or petition, there is reason to believe he is about to abscond or to remove, conceal, or destroy any of his goods, books, &c., or if, after a receiving order, he removes any goods above the value of £5, or if, without good cause, he fails to attend the Court for examination.

1878. BILLS OF SALE.

The "Bills of Sale Act," which came into operation on November 1, 1882, effects several noteworthy changes of the utmost importance. It repeals part of the Act of 1878, which repealed the Act of 1854.

1879. The term "Bill of Sale" includes in addition to those assignments of personal property which were within its meaning under the Act of 1854, "inventories of goods with receipt thereto attached, and receipts for purchase-moneys of goods," where the goods remain in the possession of the seller, and also an agreement to give a bill of sale.

1880. The term "Personal Chattels" has also a wider meaning than under the old law, as it includes fixtures and growing crops when separately assigned, and trade machinery when assigned, together with an interest in land so as to require registration.

1881. Chief Provisions of the Act.—All bills of sale made or given in consideration of any sum under £30 are void. No bill of sale executed after the Act shall be any protection to the goods comprised therein against distress for poor and other parochial rates.

1882. Instruments giving Powers of Distress.—Certain instruments giving powers of distress are also to be registered under the Act to be of any validity against the trustees in bankruptcy or execution creditors.

1883. Registration of Bills of Sale.—Every bill of sale executed in England must be registered within *seven* days of its making, instead of within *twenty-one* days as under the old law. If executed out of England the Bill must be registered within seven clear days of the time at which it would in the ordinary course of post arrive in England if posted immediately after the execution thereof, and provision is made to prevent the evasion of the Act of 1878 by means of renewed bills of sale in respect of the same debt—a practice much resorted to up to the passing of that Act in order to avoid registration.

1884. Renewal of Registration.—Registration of unsatisfied bills of sale must be renewed every *five* years.

1885. Voidance of Bill of Sale.—A bill of sale executed within seven days after the execution of a prior unregistered bill of sale, if comprising all or part of the same chattels, and if given as a security for the same debt or any part thereof, will be absolutely void.

1886. Execution in presence of Solicitor.—To prevent necessitous persons being inveigled by sharpers into signing bills of sale for sums in excess of advances, or in blank, as has been done in some cases, every bill of sale had to be executed in the presence of a solicitor, but under the Bills of Sale Act, 1882, this is no longer imperative, *the condition only affecting bills drawn under the Act of* 1878.

1887. PROPERTY OF MARRIED WOMEN.

A woman married after January 1, 1883, is entitled to hold all real and personal property which she was entitled to either at or after marriage, for her separate use.

1888. Earnings, &c., of Married Women.—A married woman may carry on business separate from her husband, and is entitled absolutely for her separate use to all wages and earnings acquired by her in any employment, occupation, or trade, in which she is engaged, and which she carries on separately from her husband, and to all money acquired by her through the exercise of any literary, artistic, or scientific skill, and her receipt alone is a good discharge for the amount.

1889. Liability of Husband for Wife's Debts.—A husband is only liable for the debts and liabilities of his wife *contracted before marriage* to the extent of the property which he receives from, or becomes entitled to, through his wife. The wife herself is liable to the extent of her separate property for all debts incurred by her either before or after marriage.

1890. Repayment of Money, &c., borrowed when under Age.—An infant, or person under twenty-one years of age, is not liable to repay money borrowed by him, nor to pay for goods supplied to him, unless they be necessaries. Even if a person after coming of age promise to pay debts contracted during infancy, he is not liable, whether the promise be made in writing or not.

1891. BREACH OF PROMISE OF MARRIAGE.

Oral engagements and promises to marry will sustain an action, unless the marriage is limited to take place upwards of a year from the making of the contract, in which case the agreement to marry must be in writing. No plaintiff can recover a verdict unless his or her testimony shall be corroborated by some other material evidence in support of the promise. Both the plaintiff and the defendant are now competent witnesses. The conduct of the suitor, subsequent to the breaking off the engagement, would weigh with the jury in estimating damages. An action may be commenced although the gentleman is not married. The length of time which must elapse before action must be reasonable. A lapse of three years, or even half that time, without any attempt by the gentleman to renew the acquaintance, would lessen the damages very considerably—perhaps do away with all chance of success, unless the delay could be satisfactorily explained. A promise of marriage is not binding if it be obtained, or the continuation of the engagement procured, by means of a false or fraudulent representation, or wilful concealment from the defendant of the plaintiff's former situation in life, and the circumstances of his or her family.

If a person already married promise to marry another who did not know of the existing marriage, an action may be maintained against such married person for breach of promise. The mode of proceeding is by an action at law. For this a solicitor must be retained, who will manage the whole affair to its termination. The whole costs, to the verdict of the jury, will amount to between £35 and £50, besides the expenses of the lady's witnesses. If the verdict be in her favour, the other side have to pay her costs. If the verdict be against her, the same rule holds good, and she must pay her opponent's costs—probably from £60 to £70.

1892. Preliminary Steps.—Before legal proceedings are commenced, a letter should be written to the gentleman, by the father or brother of the lady, requesting him to fulfil his engagement. A copy of this letter should be kept, and it had better be delivered by some person who can prove that he did so, and that the copy is correct : he should make a memorandum of any remarks or conversation.

1893. DIVORCE AND OTHER MATRIMONIAL CAUSES.—The powers of the Ecclesiastical Court are abolished in these cases, which are now taken in the Probate, Divorce, and Admiralty Division of the High Court.

1894. By Divorce *à mensa et thoro* is meant a separation only ; it does not sever the matrimonial tie, so as to permit the parties to contract another marriage. These are now called *judicial separations*. (*See* pars. 1899—1901.)

1895. By Suits of Jactitation of Marriage is meant suits which are brought when a person maliciously falsely asserts that he or she is already married to another, whereby a belief in their marriage is spread abroad, to the injury of the complaining party.

1896. By Absolute Divorce is meant a dissolution of the marriage, by which the parties are set absolutely free from all marital engagements, and capable of subsequent marriage. In these cases a *decree nisi* is first obtained, which is made absolute after the lapse of six months, unless the decree should be set aside by subsequent appeal.

1897. The Grounds of Divorce are very various, and in most cases fit only for confidential communication to a solicitor. In all cases a highly respectable professional adviser should be employed.

1898. Separation of Husband and Wife.—This may be effected by mutual consent, when a proper Deed of Separation should be prepared by a solicitor, who will see that all proper and adequate provision for the wife's maintenance during separation are inserted. If the husband and wife after the date of the deed should live together again the deed beoomes null and void.

1899. A Sentence of Judicial Separation may be obtained either by the husband or the wife, on the ground of cruelty, or of desertion without cause for two years or upwards. To constitute wilful desertion on the part of the husband, his absence must be against the will of his wife, and she must not have been a consenting party to it.

1900. Persons cannot be judicially separated upon the mere disinclination of one or both to live together. The disinclination must be proved upon reasons that the law recognizes ; and the court must see that those reasons actually exist.

1901. The Amount of Costs of a Judicial separation or a divorce varies from £25 to £500 or more, according to the circumstances of the suit, and the litigation that may ensue. But a person being a pauper may obtain relief from the court by suing *in formâ pauperis*. Any such person must lay a case before counsel, and obtain an opinion from such counsel that he or she has reasonable grounds for appealing to the court for relief, and file an affidavit verifying the facts as true. The case, with opinion thereon, and affidavit, must be sent or delivered to the Registrar of the Probate Division of the High Court, accompanied by an affidavit as to means.

1902. ORDER FOR PROTECTION OF WIFE'S PROPERTY.—When a wife is able to prove that her husband has deserted her without cause and against her will, she may obtain from the Matrimonial Court, or from the judge ordinary, an order to protect her against his creditors, and against any person claiming under him, by way of purchase or otherwise, any property she may acquire by her own lawful industry, or may become possessed of after such desertion. When the wife lives in London the order may be obtained from a police magistrate ; or when she lives in the country, from two magistrates sitting in petty sessions.

1903. The Order does not prevent the Husband returning to his Wife, but only prevents his taking her earnings while the desertion continues.

1904. The Order, when obtained, puts the wife in the same position with regard to ownership of property and the right to sue and be sued upon contracts (that is, all bargains and business transactions), as if she had obtained the decree of judicial separation, placing her, in fact, in the situation of a single woman.

1905. After this Order is made, if the husband, or any creditor of his, or person claiming through him by purchase or otherwise, should seize or continue to hold any property of the wife, after notice of such order, the wife may bring an action against her husband or such other person, and may recover the property itself, and double its value in money.

1906. WILLS.

1907. Hints on making a Will. —When a person has resolved upon making a will, he should select from among his friends persons of trust to become his executors, and should obtain their consent to act. And it is advisable that a duplicate copy of the will should be entrusted to the executor or executors. Or he should otherwise deposit a copy of his will, or the original will, in the office provided by the Probate Division of the High Court for the safe custody of wills.

1908. Simple Form of Will.— This is the last will and testament of J—— B——, of No. 3, King's Road, Chelsea. I hereby give, devise, and bequeath to my wife, Mary B——, her heirs, executors, and administrators, for her and their own use and benefit, absolutely and for ever, all my estate and effects, both real and personal, whatsoever and wheresoever, and of what nature and quality soever ; and I hereby appoint her, the said Mary B——, sole executrix of this my will. In witness whereof I have hereunto set my hand this —— day of ——, one thousand eight hundred and ——.

JOHN B——.

Signed by the said John B—— in the presence of us, present at the same time, who, in his presence, at his request, and in the presence of each other, attest and subscribe our names as witness hereto.

JOHN WILLIAMS, 15, Oxford Street, Westminster.

HENRY JONES, 19, Regent Street, Westminster.

1909. Other Forms of Wills give particular legacies to adults, or to infants, with direction for application of interest during minority ; to infants, to be paid when they reach the age of twenty-one without interest ; specific legacies of Government stock ; general legacies of ditto ; specific legacies or leasehold property or household property ; immediate or deferred annuities ; to daughters or sons for life, and after them their children ; levies with directions for the application of the money ; bequests to wife, with conditions as to future marriage ; define the powers of trustees, provide for and direct the payment of debts, &c. All these more complicated forms of wills require the superintendence of a professional adviser.

1910. Wills, to be Valid, can only be made by persons at or above the age of twenty-one, and in a sound state of mind at the time of making the last will and testament ; not attainted of treason ; nor a felon ; nor an outlaw. As regards the power of married women to make wills, a married woman may make a will, disposing, as she may think fit, of all property to which she is entitled for her separate use.

1911. Wills must be in Writing, signed at the foot or end thereof by the testator, or by some other person in his presence and by his direction. And such signature must be made or acknowledged by the testator, in the presence of two or more witnesses, all of whom must be present at the same time, and such witnesses must attest and subscribe the will in the presence and with the knowledge of the testator.

1912. Alterations in Wills or Codicils require the signature of the testator and of two witnesses to be made upon the margin, or upon some other part of the will, opposite or near to the alteration.

1913. A Will or Codicil cannot be altered or revoked, unless through a similar formal process to that under which it was made ; or by some other writing declaring an intention to revoke the same, and executed in the manner in which an original will is required to be executed ; or by the burning, tearing, or otherwise destroying the same by the testator, or by some person in his presence and by his direction with the intention of revoking the same. Nor can any will or codicil, or any part of either, that has once been revoked by any or all of these acts, be revived again, unless it be executed in the manner that a fresh will or codicil is required to be.

1914. Wills are revoked by Marriage.—Every will is revoked by the subsequent marriage of the testator or testatrix, except a will made in the exercise of a power of appointment, when the property appointed thereby would not, in default of appointment, pass to the heir, executor, or administrator, or next of kin of the testator or testatrix.

1915. A Will so Revoked may be revived by re-execution, or by codicil *after* the marriage, even on the same day.

1916. No Stamp required. — There being no stamp duty, or tax, on a will itself, it should be written on plain parchment or paper. Nor is it necessary, though always advisable where means are sufficient, to employ a professional adviser to draw up and complete the execution of a will.

1917. Legacy to Illegitimate Child.—If it be intended to give a legacy to an illegitimate child, the testator must not class him with the lawful children, or designate him simply as the child of his reputed parent, whether father or mother, but must describe the child by name as the reputed child of —————— or ——————, so as to leave no doubt of identity.

1918. Wearing Apparel, Jewels, &c., belonging to a wife, and suitable to her rank and degree, are considered in law her "paraphernalia"; and though liable for the husband's debts while living, cannot be willed away from her by her husband, unless he wills to her other things in lieu thereof, expressing such intention and desire in the will. The wife may then make her choice whether she will accept the substituted gift, or remain possessed of what the law declares her entitled to.

1919. Where the Property is Considerable, and is to be left to various persons, or in trust for children or for charities, the will should always be drawn up by a qualified legal adviser.

1920. Intestacy or Absence of Will.—The personal property of any person deceased (except a married woman), left undisposed of, is distributed as follows :— (a) If the deceased leave a widow and issue, one-third to the widow and two-thirds equally between the children, any issue of a deceased child taking between them their parent's share. (b) If no widow, but issue, whole to issue divisible as in (a). (c) If widow, but no issue, and estate, *real and personal*, worth not more than £500, whole to widow ; but if worth more than £500, widow has proportionate charge on real and personal estate for £500 and interest at 4% per ann. from death, the residue of personal estate being distributed as follows :—One-half to widow and one-half to next of kin in following order:—i. Father, ii. Mother, brothers and sisters, and nephews and nieces (nephews and nieces taking only share which their parent would have taken, unless no mother, brother or sister are living, when they take

equally between them), iii. Grandfather and grandmother, iv. Uncles and aunts, v. Cousins and great-nephews and nieces. (d) If no widow or issue, then the whole goes to next of kin in same order as above. [N.B.—*The above information does not apply to Scotland.*]

1921. In the case of Intestacy of a Married Woman, the whole of her personal estate passes to her husband.

1922. TO SEARCH FOR WILLS.

If you wish to examine a will, the best course is to go to "The Wills Office," at Somerset House, Strand, have on a slip of paper the name of the testator—this, on entering, give to a clerk whom you will see at a desk on the right. At the same time pay a shilling, and you will then be entitled to search all the heavy Index volumes for the testator's name. The name found, the clerk will hand over the will for perusal, and there is no difficulty whatever, *provided you know about the year of the testator's death.* The Indexes are all arranged and numbered according to their years. Not only the names of those who left wills are given, but also of those intestates to whose effects letters of administration have been granted. There is no charge beyond the shilling paid for entering. If you require a copy of the will, the clerk will calculate the expense, and you can have the copy in a few days. No questions whatever are asked— nor does the length of the will, or the time occupied in reading it, make any difference in the charge. Beyond the shilling paid on entering, there is no other demand whatever, unless for copying the whole or a portion of the will. One is not allowed to personally make copious notes, but merely certain details such as the date, names of testator, executors, &c. If the deceased at the time of his death had a fixed place of abode within the district of any of the District Registries attached to the Court of Probate, the will may now be proved, or letters of administration obtained from the district registrar. There are numerous district registries, viz., at Liverpool, Manchester, Bristol, York, Newcastle, Durham, and other places. If the will has not been proved in London, it will be found in the registry of the district in which the deceased dwelt at the time of his death. The same rules are observed in the country as in London, with regard to examination, &c. The fee—one shilling—is the same in all. Having ascertained that the deceased left a will, and that it has been proved, the next inquiry is, "Where was it proved ?" The above explanation and remarks apply also to the administration granted to the effects of those who died without wills.

1923. BANK CHEQUES.

1924. Crossed Cheques.—If cheques have two parallel lines drawn across them, with or without the addition of the words "*& Co.*," they will only be paid to a banker. If, in addition, the name of any particular banker be written across the cheque, it will only be paid to that banker or his agent.

1925. Meaning of "Not Negotiable" on Cheques.—If the words "*Not Negotiable*" be written across a cheque, the lawful holder of the cheque is not prevented thereby from negotiating it. The effect of these words is to prevent any person receiving a cheque so marked from acquiring a better title to it than the person had from whom he received it. If, therefore, such a cheque has been stolen, the thief cannot, by passing it away for value, vest in the person so acquiring it a good title.

1926. Post-dated Cheques.—Like any other bill of exchange, a *post-dated*, or *ante-dated* cheque is not invalid by reason only of so being post-dated or ante-dated, nor if it bear date on a Sunday. But a post-dated cheque cannot be legally enforced until on or after the date which it bears.

1927. LIMITATION OF RECOVERY OF LAND OR REAL ESTATE.—A person becoming entitled to any land or real estate, must bring an action to recover it within twelve years from the time when his right accrued, otherwise his claim will be barred by the "Statute of Limitations."

1928. BUILDING SOCIETIES.

The object of these societies is to raise, by subscriptions, a fund to assist the members to acquire freehold or other landed property. The law relating to them was consolidated and amended by the Building Societies' Act, 1874 (37 and 38 Vict. c. 42), by the Acts passed in 1875, 1877, and 1884, and by the Building Societies' Act, 1894 (57 and 58 Vict c. 47).

The theory of Building Societies is this:—Money is raised in small amounts from a number of members and lent to others on real security, either to build or trade, or any other purpose. Formerly, the members were only allowed to subscribe fixed amounts and at stated times, but now every opportunity is given to vary the powers of investment and to facilitate entrance and withdrawal.

The repayments are based on a scale allowing of payment of principal and interest in a certain number of years— say fourteen or fifteen ; but advances on private mortgage or repayable at the borrower's convenience are gradually becoming more and more frequent.

Under the Act of 1894 (section 12) a society established after the passing of the Act shall not cause or permit the applicants for advances to ballot for precedence, or in any way make the granting of an advance depend on any chance or lot.

By the same Act it is provided that a society shall not advance money on the security of any freehold, copyhold, or leasehold estate which is subject to a prior mortgage, unless the prior mortgage is in favour of the society making the advance.

The Act further says that no director, secretary, surveyor, solicitor, or other officer of a society shall, in addition to his authorized remuneration, receive from any other person any gift, bonus, commission, or benefit, for or in connection with any loan made by the society. The penalty is £50, and in default six months' imprisonment.

1929. FRIENDLY SOCIETIES.

By an Act of 1896 (59 and 60 Vict. c. 15), which catne into operation on January 1, 1897, the law relating to Friendly Societies was amended and consolidated, the previous Acts having mostly been repealed. Under this Act five classes of societies may be registered, viz. :—

(1) Friendly Societies ; (2) Cattle Insurance Societies ; (3) Benevolent Societies ; (4) Working Men's Clubs ; and (5) Societies specially authorized by the Treasury. No society can be registered unless it consists of at least seven persons.

Further, a member may belong to more societies than one (unless restricted by the rules of a particular society), but he cannot assure to himself more than £200 in all, or an annuity of more than £50. Again, insurances or payments on the death of children are limited to £6 for a child under five years of age, or £10 under ten years.

By another Act of 1896 (59 and 60 Vict. c. 26), the provisions respecting friendly societies and industrial assurance companies which receive contributions and premiums by means of collectors, are consolidated ; and no collector may become a member of the committee of management, or vote or take part in a general meeting, &c.

1930. JURIES.

Unless exempted as stated below, every man between the ages of 21 and 60, having (within the county in which he lives) £10 in lands, or rents out of them in fee or for life—or £20 per annum in leaseholds for twenty-one years and upwards—or who pays rates of £30 in Middlesex (or £20 elsewhere),—or who occupies a house having not less than fifteen windows—is liable to serve on juries in the High Court of Justice ; and in all Courts of Nisi Prius, or Assize, in the county in which he resides.

With regard to the City of London, no man may be summoned to determine issues in the Superior Courts, who is not a householder or occupier of a shop, warehouse, counting-house, chambers, or office, for the purpose of trade within the City, and have lands, tenements, or personal estate of the value of £100.

1931. Special Jurors.—Every man whose name is placed in the Jurors' Book for any county in England or Wales, or for the City of London, and who is an Esquire by law, or of higher degree, or a merchant or banker, or who occupies a private dwelling-house rated at not less than £100 in a town of 20,000 inhabitants and upwards (or rated at not less than £50 elsewhere), or who occupies premises (other than a farm) rated at not less than £100, or a farm rated at not less than £300, is qualified and liable to serve on special juries.

1932. Aliens as Jurors who have been domiciled for ten years, or more, in England or Wales (if duly qualified in other respects) are liable to serve on juries and inquests ; but *no one* is qualified to serve as a juror, who has been convicted of treason, felony, or any infamous crime, unless he has been pardoned. Nor is any one liable to serve on any jury or inquest (except a Grand Jury) more than once in a year, unless all the jurors on the list have already been summoned to serve during the year.

1933. Payment of Jurors.—A *special* juror is legally entitled to such amount as the judge considers reasonable ; but as a rule *special* jurors receive one guinea each for every cause in which they are sworn. In the High Court and County Courts, 1s., and at most Assizes, 8d., may be claimed by a *common* juror for each action in which he is sworn. Where a "view" by jurors is ordered, of "the land or premises affected by the action," a *special* juror is entitled to a guinea a day, and a *common* juror to five shillings a day. *No fee is allowed in criminal cases.*

1934. Persons exempted from serving on Juries.—Peers, M.P.'s, Judges, Clergymen, Roman Catholic Priests, Ministers of any congregation of Protestant Dissenters and of Jews, Barristers, Doctors of Law, Advocates of Civil Law (if actually practising), Solicitors (if actually practising and having taken out their certificates) and their Managing Clerks, Notaries (in actual practice), Officers of Legal Courts, Clerks of the Peace or their Deputies, Coroners, Gaolers and Keepers of Houses of Correction and all subordinate Officers of the same, Keepers in Public Lunatic Asylums, Members and Licentiates of the Royal College of Physicians (if actually practising), Members of the Royal College of Surgeons in London, Edinburgh, and Dublin (if actually practising), Apothecaries, and all registered Medical Practitioners and registered Pharmaceutical Chemists (if actually practising), Officers of the Navy, Army, Militia, or Yeomanry on full pay, Master Wardens and Brethren of the Trinity House, Pilots, Masters of vessels in the buoy and light service of the Trinity House, the Household Servants of Her Majesty, Officers of the Post Office, Commissioners of Customs, and Officers, Clerks, or other persons acting in the management or collection of the Customs, Commissioners of Inland Revenue, and Officers or Persons appointed by the Commissioners of Inland Revenue, or

employed by them, Sheriffs' Officers, Officers of the Rural and Metropolitan Police, Metropolitan Magistrates and their Clerks, Ushers, Doorkeepers and Messengers, Members of the Council of the Municipal Corporation of any Borough, Justices of the Peace, and Officers of the Houses of Lords and Commons.

1935. DOMESTIC PETS.

1936. BLACKBIRDS.—The cock bird is of a deep black, with a yellow bill, and yellow ring round the eye. The female is dark brown. It is difficult to distinguish male from female birds when young ; but the darkest generally are males. The same treatment as given for the thrush (*see* par. 1938) applies to the blackbird.

1937. Food for Blackbirds.—The natural food of the blackbird is berries, worms, insects, shelled snails, cherries, and other similar fruit ; and its artificial food, lean fresh meat, cut very small, and mixed with bread or German paste.

1938. THRUSHES.—A cock may be distinguished from a hen by a darker back, and the more glossy appearance of the feathers. The belly also is white. Their natural food is insects, berries, worms, and snails. In a domesticated state they will eat raw meat, but snails and worms should be procured for them. Young birds are hatched about the middle of April, and should be kept very warm. They should be fed with raw meat, cut small, or bread mixed in milk with hemp seed well bruised ; when they can feed themselves give them lean meat cut small, and mixed with bread or German paste, plenty of clean water, and keep them in a warm, dry, and sunny situation.

1939. CANARIES.—To distinguish a cock bird from a hen, observe the bird when it is singing, and if it be a cock you will perceive the throat heaving with a pulse-like motion, a peculiarity which is scarcely perceptible in the hen. Feed young canaries with white and yolk of hard egg, mixed together with a little bread steeped in water. This should be pressed and placed in one vessel, while in another should be put some boiled rape seed, washed in fresh water. Change the food every day. When they are a month old, put them into separate cases. Cut the claws of cage-birds occasionally, when they become too long, but in doing so be careful not to draw blood.

1940. Treatment of Canaries.—Care must be taken to keep canaries very clean. For this purpose, the cage should be strewed every morning with clean sand, or rather, fine gravel, for small pebbles are *absolutely essential* to life and health in cage-birds : fresh water must be given every day, both for drinking and bathing ; the latter being in a shallow vessel ; and, during the moulting season, a small bit of iron should be put into the water for drinking. The food should consist principally of *summer* rape seed—that is, of those small *brown* rape seeds which are obtained from plants sown in the spring, and which ripen during the summer ; large and *black* rape seeds, on the contrary, are produced by such plants as are sown in autumn and reaped in spring. A little chickweed in spring, lettuce leaves in summer, and endive in autumn, with slices of sweet apple in winter, may be safely given ; but bread and sugar ought to be generally avoided. Occasionally, also, a few poppy or canary seeds, and a small quantity of bruised hemp seed may be added, but the last very sparingly. Cleanliness, simple food, and fresh but not *cold* air, are essential to the well-being of a canary. During the winter, the cage should never be hung in a room without a fire, but even then, when the air is mild, and the sun shines bright, the little prisoner will be refreshed by having the window open. The cage should never be less than eight inches in diameter, and a foot high with perches at different heights.

1941. BULLFINCHES.—Old birds should be fed with German paste (*see* par. 1946), and occasionally rape seed. The Germans sometimes give them a little poppy-seed, and a grain or two of rice, steeped in Canary wine, when teaching them to pipe, as a reward for the progress they make. Bird organs, or flageolets, are used to teach them. They breed three or four times a year.

The young require to be kept very warm, and to be fed every two hours with rape seed, soaked for several hours in cold water, afterwards scalded and strained, bruised, mixed with bread, and moistened with milk. Not more than one, two, or three mouthfuls should be given at a time.

1942. LINNETS.—Cock birds are browner on the back than the hens, and have some of the large feathers of the wings white up to the quills. Canary and hemp seed, with occasionally a little groundsel, water-cress, chickweed, &c., constitute their food.

1943. SKYLARKS.—The cock is recognized by the largeness of his eye, the length of his claws, the mode of erecting his crest, and by marks of white in the tail. It is also a larger bird than the hen. The cage should be of the following proportions: Length, one foot five inchs ; width, nine inches ; height, one foot three inches. There should be a circular protection in front to admit of a fresh turf being placed every two or three days, and the bottom of the case should be plentifully and constantly sprinkled with river sand. All vessels containing food should be placed outside, and the top of the cage should be arched and padded, so that the bird may not injure itself by jumping about. Their food, in a natural state, consists of seeds, insects, and also buds, green herbage, as clover, endive, lettuce, &c., and occasionally berries.

When confined, they are usually

fed with a paste made in the following manner :—Take a piece of stale bread, soak it well in water, then squeeze out the water and pour boiled milk over it, adding two-thirds of the same quantity of barley meal well sifted, or, what is better, wheat meal. This should be made fresh every two days. Occasionally the yolk of a hard-boiled egg should be crumbled small and given to the birds, as well as a little hemp seed, meal worms, and elder-berries when they can be got. The cages of these birds should be kept very clean.

1944. PARROTS may best be taught to talk by covering the cage at night, or rather in the evening, and then repeating to them, slowly and distinctly, the words they are desired to learn. They should not be kept in places where they are liable to hear disagreeable noises, such as street cries, and the whistling and shouts of boys at play, for they will imitate them, and become too noisy to be tolerated. Parrots may be fed upon soaked bread, biscuit, mashed potatoes and rape seed. They are fond of nuts. They should be kept very clean, and allowed a bath frequently. When parrots appear sickly in any way, it is best to keep them warm, change their food for a time, and give them lukewarm water to bathe in.

1945. PIGEONS are most interesting pets for persons residing in country districts, but in breeding and rearing require constant attention and care. There are so many distinct varieties, requiring different treatment, that we cannot afford space for them in this volume.

1946. GERMAN PASTE for cage birds may be made in the following manner :—Boil four eggs until quite hard, then throw them into cold water ; remove the whites and grate or pound the yolks until quite fine, and add a pound of white pea meal and a tablespoonful of olive oil. Mix the whole up together, and press the dough through a tin colander so as to form it

into small grains like shot. Fry these over a gentle fire, gradually stirring them until of a light brown colour, when they are fit for use.

1947. INSECTS IN BIRDCAGES. —Suspend a little bag of sulphur in the cage. This is said to be healthful for birds generally, as well as useful in keeping away insects by which they become infested.

1948. SQUIRRELS.—In a domestic state these little animals are fed with hazel nuts, or indeed any kind of nuts ; and occasionally bread and milk. They should be kept very clean.

1949. RABBITS should be kept dry and warm. Their best food is celery, parsley, and carrots ; but they will eat almost any kind of vegetable, especially the dandelion, milk-thistle, &c. In spring it is recommended to give them tares. A little bran, and any kind of grain occasionally is beneficial, as too much green food is very hurtful. Care should be taken not to over-feed them. When fed upon dry food a little skim milk is good for them. Tea leaves also in small quantities may be given to them.

1950. GUINEA PIGS very much resemble rabbits in their mode of living, and may be treated in much the same manner. They should be kept dry, warm, and very clean.

1951. WHITE MICE are fed upon bread soaked in milk, peas, oats, beans, &c., and any kind of nuts.

1952. SILKWORMS.—The silkworm is a moth which spins its silk in forming its cocoon, when about to pass from the state of the caterpillar unto that of the chrysalis. It comes out of the egg about the latter part of May, and as the worms will confine themselves to those places where food is provided for them, the rapid progress of their growth, their curious changes, and the production of their silk, afford a most interesting study. We recommend our readers to obtain from twenty to thirty silkworms' eggs. They are about the size of a pin's head, and are generally firmly attached to the paper upon which they were laid. A paper tray, about twelve inches long by eight wide, should be made by turning up the edges of a piece of cardboard, or of stiff paper. Into the bottom of this the eggs should be placed, and when the time of hatching arrives, they should be watched from day to day, and some young lettuce leaves be provided for the young caterpillars.

These when first hatched do not exceed a quarter of an inch in length and commence eating food immediately. Their growth is very rapid, and when they are about eight days old, their heads become considerably enlarged, they refuse food, and appear in a lethargic state for about three days. This arises from the pressure of their skins, which become too tight for the increased size of their bodies. As soon as they have cast their skins, they will be re-invigorated, and eat a large amount of leaves. They cast their skins four times in the course of their growth. About the time of the second change of skin, they should be provided with mulberry leaves as well as lettuce leaves, and they will gradually discard the latter.

The worm remains in the caterpillar state about six weeks. When full grown it ceases to feed, and begins to form a loose envelope of silken pipes. It should then be taken from the paper tray, and each worm be placed in a cup of twisted paper, hung against the wall or in a warm aspect ; when it will enclose itself in a ball of silk, called a cocoon, within which it passes into the chrysalis state. In about fifteen days it comes forth in the form of a moth. In escaping from the coooon it destroys a portion of the silk, to prevent which the silk-dealers destroy the chrysalis, or unwind the silk of the cocoon before the chrysalis is broken by the moth.

Each moth will produce a large number of eggs ; and the silk supplied by the cocoons may be wound off and tied into skeins, and these being laid between the leaves of books, may be preserved for many years.

1953. TO FATTEN POULTRY.—Poultry should be fattened in coops, and kept very clean. They should be furnished with gravel, but with no water, except that with which their only food, barley-meal, is mixed. Their thirst makes them eat more than they would, in order to extract the moisture from the food. This should not be put in troughs, but laid upon a board, which should be washed clean every time fresh food is put upon it. Ground rice well scalded with milk, mixed with a little coarse sugar is very fattening. Feed them with this in the daytime, but do not give them too much at once ; let it be rather thick.

1954. EGG-SHELLS FOR POULTRY.—It is a bad thing to give fowls egg-shells. They supply nothing that is not equally well furnished by lime, and especially bricklayers' rubbish, old ceilings, &c. Never do anything that has a tendency to make them eat eggs. They are apt scholars, if they find worms in a natural way they are good food, but it is a bad plan to give them by the handful.

1955. AQUARIUMS.—Full instructions for the stocking and management of fresh or sea water aquariums are given in *The Corner Cupboard*, volume 23 of the Enquire Within Series, price 2s. 6d. Houlston and Sons.

1956. GOLD FISH.—Great care must be taken of gold fish, as they are very sensitive ; and hence a loud noise, strong smell, violent or even slight shaking of the vessel, will sometimes destroy them. Small worms, which are common to the water, suffice for their food in general ; but the Chinese, who bring gold fish to great perfection, throw into the water small balls of paste of which they are very fond. They give them also lean pork, dried in the sun, and reduced to a very fine and delicate powder. Fresh river-water should be given them frequently, if possible. Gold fish seldom deposit spawn when kept in glass vessels. In order to procure a supply, they must be put into reservoirs of a considerable depth, in some part at least, well shaded at intervals with water-lilies, and constantly supplied with fresh water.

1957. DOGS.—The best way to keep dogs healthy is to let them have plenty of exercise, and not to over-feed them. Let them at all times have a plentiful supply of clean water, and encourage them to take to swimming, as it assists their cleanliness. Naldire's soap is recommended as highly efficacious in ridding dogs of fleas. After using any soap rinse it well off with clean water. Properly treated, dogs should be fed only once a day. Meat boiled for dogs, and the liquor in which it is boiled thickened with barley meal, or oatmeal, forms capital food.

1958. Distemper in Dogs.—This disease is liable to attack dogs from four months to four years old. It prevails most in spring and autumn, and is known by dulness of the eye, husky cough, shivering, loss of appetite and spirits, and fits. When fits occur, the dog will most likely die unless a veterinary surgeon he called in. During the distemper, dogs should be allowed to run on the grass ; their diet should be spare ; and a little sulphur be placed in their water. Chemists who dispense cattle medicines can generally advise with sufficient safety upon the diseases of dogs, and it is best for unskilful persons to abstain from doctoring them. In many diseases dogs will be benefited by warm baths.

1959. Hydrophobia in Dogs is the most dreadful of all diseases. The first symptoms are attended by thirst, fever, and languor. The dog starts convulsively in his sleep, and when awake, though restless, is languid. When a dog is suspected, he should be firmly chained in a place where neither children nor dogs nor cats can get near him. Any one going to attend him should wear thick leather gloves, and proceed with great caution. When a dog snaps savagely at an imaginary object, it is almost a certain indication of madness ; and when it exhibits a terror of fluids, it is confirmed hydrophobia. Some dogs exhibit a great dislike of musical sounds, and when this is the case they are too frequently made sport of. But it is a dangerous sport, as dogs have sometimes been driven mad by it.

1960. Mange in Dogs.—This is a contagious disease, which it is difficult to get rid of when once contracted. The best way is to apply to a veterinary chemist for an ointment, and to keep applying it for some time after the disease has disappeared, or it will break out again.

1961. CATS.—It is generally supposed that cats are more attached to places than to individuals, but this is an error. They obstinately cling to certain places, because it is there they expect to see the persons to whom they are attached. A cat will return to an empty house, and remain in it many weeks. But when at last she finds that the family does not return, she strays away, and if she chance then to find the family, she will remain with them. The same rules of feeding which apply to dogs apply also to cats. They should not be over-fed, nor too frequently. Cats are liable to the same diseases as dogs ; though they do not become ill so frequently. A little brimstone in their milk occasionally is a good preventive.

1962. TO STUFF BIRDS, ANIMALS, &c.—Large animals should be carefully skinned, with the horns, skull, tail, hoofs, &c., entire. Then rub the inside of the skin thoroughly with the mixture of salt, pepper, and alum, and hang up to dry. Large birds may be treated in the same way, but should not be put into spirits.

1963. Small Birds may be preserved as follows :—Take out the entrails, open a passage to the brain, which should be scooped out through the mouth ; introduce into the cavities of the skull and the whole body some of the mixture of salt, alum, and pepper, putting some through the gullet and whole length of the neck ; then hang the bird in a cool, airy place—first by the feet, that the body may be impregnated by the salt, and afterwards by a thread through the under mandible of the bill, till it appears to be free from smell ; then hang it in the sun, or near a fire: after it is well dried, clean out what remains loose of the mixture, and fill the cavity of the body with wool, oakum, or any soft substance, and pack it smooth in paper.

1964. To Clean Stuffed Animals. &c.—First brush the specimen well with a clothes-brush. Then put some new bran into a pan and warm it, stirring it well to prevent it burning. Rub the warm bran well into the fur with your hand. Do this three or four times, and then brush the fur until all the bran is out.

1965. BIRDS' EGGS.—In selecting eggs for a cabinet, always choose those which are newly laid ; make a medium-sized hole at the sharp end with a pointed instrument, and one at the blunt end : let this last hole be as small as possible ; this done, apply your mouth to the blunt end, and blow the contents through the sharp end. If the yolk will not come freely, run a pin or wire up into the egg, and stir the yolk well about ; now get a cupful of water, and immersing the sharp end of the shell into it, apply your mouth to the blunt end and suck up some of the water into the empty shell ; then put your finger and thumb upon the two

holes, shake the water well within, and after this, blow it out. The water will clear the egg of any remains of yolk or of white which may stay in after blowing. If the shell is dirty, wash it well in soap and water, and use a nail-brush to get the dirt off. Nothing now remains to be done but to prevent the thin white membrane (which is still inside) from corrupting. Take a wineglass and fill it with a solution of corrosive sublimate in alcohol, then immerse the sharp end of the egg-shell into it, keeping the finger and thumb which hold the egg just clear of the solution. Apply the mouth to the little hole at the blunt end, and suck up some of the solution into the shell, taking care that none enters the mouth. Shake the shell in the same manner as when the water was in it, and then blow the solution back into the glass. The egg-shell will now be beyond the reach of corruption ; the membrane for ever retains its pristine whiteness, and no insect will ever venture to prey upon it. If you wish your egg to appear extremely brilliant, give it a coat of mastic varnish, put on very sparingly with a camel-hair pencil: green or blue eggs must be done with gum arabic, as the mastic varnish is apt to injure the colour.

1966. FISHES.—Large fishes should be opened in the belly, the entrails taken out, and the inside well rubbed with pepper, and stuffed with oakum. Small fishes may be put in spirit, as well as reptiles and worms.

1967. INSECTS, &c.—Insects of fine colours, and also butterflies and moths, should be pinned down in a box prepared for that purpose, with their wings expanded.

1968. TO DRY BOTANICAL SPECIMENS FOR PRESERVATION.—The plants to be preserved should be gathered when the weather is dry. Place the ends in water, and let them remain in a oool place till the next day. When about to be submitted to the process of drying, place each plant between several sheets of blotting paper, and iron it with a large smooth heater, pretty strongly warmed, till all the moisture is dissipated. Colours may thus be fixed, which otherwise become pale, or nearly white. Some plants require more moderate heat than others, and herein consists the nicety of the experiment ; but it is generally found that if the iron be not too hot, and is passed rapidly yet carefully over the surface of the blotting paper, it answers the purpose equally well with plants of almost every variety of hue and thickness. In compound flowers, with those also of a stubborn and solid form, as the Centaurea, some little art is required in cutting away the under part, by which means the profile and forms of the flowers will be more distinctly exhibited. This is especially necessary when the flowers are fixed down with gum upon the paper previous to ironing, by which means they become almost incorporated with the surface. When this very delicate process is attempted, blotting-paper should be laid under every part excepting the blossoms, in order to prevent staining the white paper. Great care must be taken to keep preserved specimens in a dry place.

1969. TO PRESERVE SEA-WEEDS.—First wash the sea-weed in fresh water, then take a plate or dish (the larger the better), cut your paper to the size required, place it in the plate with fresh water, and spread out the plant with a good-sized camel-hair pencil in a natural form (picking out with the pin gives the sea-weed an unnatural appearance, and destroys the characteristic fall of the branches) ; then gently raise the paper with the specimen out of the water, placing it in a slanting position for a few moments, so as to allow the superfluous water to run off ; after which place it in the press. The press is made with either thin pieces of board or pasteboard. Lay on the first board two sheets of blotting-paper ; on that lay your specimens ; place straight and smooth over them a piece of old muslin, fine cambric, or linen ; then some more blotting-paper, and place another board on the top of that, and continue in the same way. The blotting-paper and the muslin should be carefully removed and dried every day, and then replaced ; at the same time, those specimens that are sufficiently dry may be taken away. You can either gum the specimens in a scrap-book, or fix them in, as drawings are often fastened, by making four slits in the page, and inserting each corner. This is by far the best plan, as it admits of their removal without injury to the page at any future period. Some of the large algae will not adhere to the paper, and consequently require gumming. After well cleaning and pressing, brush the coarser kinds over with spirits of turpentine, in which two or three small lumps of gum mastic have been dissolved, by shaking in a warm place : two-thirds of a small phial is the proper proportion, and this will make the specimens retain a fresh appearance.

1970. TO PRESERVE FUNGI.—Recipe of the celebrated botanist, William Withering. "Take two ounces of sulphate of copper, or blue vitriol, and reduce it to powder ; pour upon it a pint of boiling water ; and when cold, add half-a-pint of spirits of wine ; cork it well, and call it 'the pickle.' To eight pints of water add one pint and a half of spirits of wine, and call it 'the liquor.' Be provided with a number of wide-mouthed bottles of different sizes, all well fitted with corks. The fungi should be left on the table as long as possible, to allow the moisture to evaporate ; they should then be placed in the pickle for three hours, or longer if necessary ; then place them in the bottles intended for their reception, and fill with the liquor. They should then be well corked and sealed, and arranged in order, with their names in front of the bottles."

1971. TO MAKE SKELETON LEAVES.—The leaves should be put into an earthen or glass vessel, and a large quantity of rain water poured over them ; after this they must be left in the open air, and to the heat of the sun, without covering the vessel. As the water evaporates and the leaves become dry, more water must be added ; the leaves will by this means putrefy, but the time required for this varies ; some plants will be finished in a month, others will require two months or longer, according to the toughness of their parenchyma. When they have been in a state of putrefaction for some time, the two membranes will begin to separate, and the green part of the leaf to become fluid ; then the operation of clearing is to be performed. The leaf is to be put upon a flat white earthen plate, and covered with clear water ; and being gently squeezed with the finger, the membranes will begin to open, and the green substance will come out at the edges ; the membranes must be carefully taken off with the finger, and great caution must be used in separating them near the middle rib. When once there is an opening towards this separation, the whole membrane follows easily ; when both membranes are taken off, the skeleton is finished, and it has to be washed clean with water, and then dried between the leaves of a book.

1978. TO TAKE IMPRESSIONS OF LEAVES.—Prepare two rubbers by tying up wool or any other soft substance in wash-leather ; then prepare the colours in which you wish to print leaves, by rubbing up with cold-drawn linseed oil the tints that are required, as indigo for blue, chrome for yellow, indigo and chrome for green, &c. Get a number of leaves the size and kind you wish to stamp, then dip the rubbers into the paint, and rub them one over the other, so that you may have but a small quantity of the composition upon the rubbers. Having warmed a leaf between your hands, that it may be pliable, place it upon one rubber and moisten it gently with the other ; take the leaf off and apply it to the substance on which you wish to make the imprint ; upon the leaf place a piece of white paper, press gently, and a beautiful impression of all the veins of the leaf will be obtained.

1979. Another Method Of Taking Leaf Impressions.—Hold oiled paper in the smoke of a lamp or of pitch, until it becomes coated with the smoke ; to this paper apply the leaf of which you wish an impression, having previously warmed it between your hands, that it may be pliable. Place the lower surface of the leaf upon the blackened surface of the oil-paper, that the numerous veins, which are so prominent on this side, may receive from the paper a portion of the smoke. Lay a paper over the leaf, and then press it gently upon the smoked paper with the fingers, or with a small roller covered with woollen cloth, or some similarly soft material, so that every part of the leaf may come in contact with the sooted oil-paper. A coating of the smoke will adhere to the leaf. Then remove the leaf carefully, and place the blackened surface on a sheet of white paper, or in a book prepared for the purpose, covering the leaf with a clean slip of paper, and pressing upon it with the fingers, or roller, as before. With care excellent impressions may be thus obtained.

1980. MODELLING IN CORK, PAPER, PLASTER OF PARIS, WAX, &c.—Modelling, in a general sense, signifies the art of constructing an original pattern, which is to be ultimately carried out on an enlarged scale, or copied exactly. When models are constructed to give a miniature representation of any great work, elevation, or topographical information, they should be con-structed on a scale, which should be appended to them, so that a better idea may be obtained of the proportions and dimensions.

1981. The Materials used in modelling are plaster of Paris, wax, whiting, patty, clay, pipeclay ; common and factory cinders ; sand of various colours ; powdered fluor-spar, oyster-shells, bricks, and slate ; gums, acacia and tragacanth ; starch ; paper, white and brown, cardboard and mill-board ; cork sheets, cork raspings, and old bottle-corks ; gutta-percha ; leather and leather chips ; wood ; paints, oil, water, and varnish ; moss, lichen, ferns, and grass ; talc, window and looking-glass ; muslin and net ; chenille ; carded wool ; tow, wire ; hay and straw ; various varnishes, glue, and cements.

1982. The Tools consist of brushes for paints, varnishes, and cements ; two or three bradawls ; a sharp pen-knife ; a chisel, hammer, and punches ; scissors and pencil.

1983. To Model Caves in Cinders. —Arrange the cinders in such a manner as to resemble the intended design ; then cover in such parts as require it with brown paper soaked in thin glue until quite pulpy. When nearly dry, dust over with sand, powdered brick, slate, and chopped lichen or moss, touch up the various parts with either oil, water, or varnish colours ; and if necessary, form your trees of wire, covered with brown paper and moss, glued on. A cave constructed in the above manner, on a large scale, and the interior sprinkled with powdered fluor-spar, or glass, is very effective by candle-light. To imitate water issuing from the cave, a piece of looking-glass should be glued on the stand, and the edges surrounded by glue, and paper covered with sand.

1984. Stalactites may be repre-sented by rough pieces of wood, which must be smeared with glue, and sprinkled with powdered fluor-spar, or glass.

1985. To Model Caves in Cork.— Construct the framework of wood, and fill up the outline with old bottle-corks. The various projections, recesses, and other minutiæ, must be affixed afterwards with glue, after being formed of cork, or hollowed out in the necessary parts, either by burning with a hot wire and scraping it afterwards, or by means of a sharp-pointed bradawl. Various parts of the model must be touched up with oil, water, or varnish colours ; and powdered brick, slate, and chopped lichen, or moss, dusted on as usual.

1986. Wooden Models are con-structed roughly in deal, according to the proper design, and the various fine parts afterwards affixed with glue or brads. In forming the finer parts, a vast amount of unnecessary labour may be saved, and a better effect obtained, by burning much of the outline, instead of carving it. By this plan, deeper tones of colouring, facility of operating, and saving of time and labour, are the result. In common with other models, those constructed of wood require the aid of lichen, moss, powdered slate, &c., and colours, to complete the effect.

1987. Starch-Paste Models are formed in the usual way, of the fol-lowing composition :—Soak gum tra-gacanth in water, and when soft, mix it with powdered starch till of a proper consistence. It is much improved by adding some double-refined sugar finely powdered. When the model is finished, it must be coloured correctly, and varnished with white varnish, or left plain. This is the composition used by confectioners for modelling the various ornaments on cakes.

1988. Ancient Cities may be modelled in cork or starch-paste, in the same manner as directed above.

1989. Modern Cities are better made of cardboard, starch-paste, or pipeclay ; the houses, public buildings, and other parts being constructed according to scale.

1990. Houses should be cut out of a long, thin strip of cardboard, partially divided by three strokes of a penknife, and glued together ; this must afterwards be marked with a pencil, or pen and ink, to represent the windows, doors, stones, &c. ; and the roof—cut out of a piece of square cardboard, equally and partially divided—is then to be glued on, and the chimney—formed of a piece of lucifer match, or wood notched at one end and flat the other—is to be glued on.

1991. Cathedrals, Churches, and other Public Buildings are made in the same way, but require the addition of small chips of wood, ends of lucifer matches, cork raspings, or small pieces of cardboard, for the various ornaments, if on a large scale, but only a pencil-mark if small. When constructed of starch-paste or pipeclay, the material is rolled flat on a table or marble slab, and the various sides cut out with a sharp penknife ; they are then gummed together, and coloured properly.

1992. The Windows of Houses or of buildings can be made of talc or thin glass, covered with net or muslin. The frames of the windows are made of cardboard, neatly cut out with a sharp penknife.

1993. Paper Composition for Modelling.—Reduce paper to a smooth paste by boiling it in water ; then add an equal weight each of sifted whiting and good size ; boil to a proper consistence, and use.

Or, take equal parts of paper, paste, and size, sufficient finely-powdered plaster of Paris to make into a good paste, and use as soon as possible after it is mixed. This composition may be used to cast architectural ornaments, busts, statues, &c., being very light, and susceptible of a good polish, but it will not stand weather.

1994. Monuments, Ancient or Modern, and Ruins should be constructed of cork, according to the directions given above, and when it is necessary to represent the mouldering walls covered with moss or ivy, a little green baize flock, or moss chippings, should be attached by mucilage to the part ; and oftentimes a brush of raw sienna, combined with varnish, requires to be laid underneath the moss or flock, in order to improve the effect. Prostrate columns and huge blocks are effectively represented in cork, and should be neatly cut out with a sharp knife, and the various parts supposed to be destroyed by age picked away with a pin or blunt knife afterwards.

1995. Rustic-Work Seats, &c., may be constructed of wire twisted to the proper shape and size, and then covered with gutta-percha, rendered soft by being dipped in hot water. The gutta-percha should be twisted round the wire previously warmed, and gently heated over a spirit lamp, or dipped again into hot water, so as to allow the various parts to be covered with it. When the model is finished, it should be touched up here and there with oil colours—green, yellow, sienna, and Venetian red—according to fancy, and the effect produced will be very good.

1996. TO MODEL FLOWERS IN WAX.—There is no art more easily acquired, nor more encouraging in its immediate results, than that of modelling flowers and fruit in wax. The art, however, is attended by this drawback—that the materials required are somewhat expensive.

1997. Materials required will cost from 20s. to 30s., and may be obtained at most fancy repositories in large towns. Persons wishing to commence the art would do well to inquire for particulars, and see specimens of materials ; because in this, as in every other pursuit, there are novelties and improvements being introduced, which no book can give an idea of.

1998. Petals and Leaves are made of sheets of coloured wax, which may be purchased in packets of assorted colours. They are frequently made by thin sheets of wax pressed upon leaves of embossed calico. Leaves of various descriptions are to be obtained of the persons who sell the materials.

1999. The Stems are made of wire of suitable thicknesses, covered with silk, and overlaid with wax.

2000. Copies for Models.—Ladies will often find among their discarded artificial flowers, leaves and buds that will serve as the base of their wax model, but Natural Flowers are the best guides to the construction of a flower, and far better than printed diagrams or patterns. Take a flower, say a *tulip*, a *rose*, or *camellia*. If possible, procure *two* flowers, nearly alike ; and carefully pick one of them to pieces ; lay the petals down in the order in which they are taken from the flower, and then cut paper patterns from them, and number them from the centre of the flower, that you may know their relative positions.

The perfect flower will guide you in getting the wax petals together, and will enable you to give, not only to each petal but to the *contour* of the flower, the characteristics which are natural to it. In most cases, they are merely pressed together and held in their places by the adhesiveness of the wax. They should be cut singly, and the scissors should be frequently dipped in water, to prevent the wax adhering to the blades.

The scraps of wax that fall from the cutting will be found useful for making seed vessels, and other parts of the flowers.

2001. Leaves of Flowers.—Where the manufactured foundations cannot be obtained, patterns of them should be cut in paper ; the venous appear-

ance may be imparted to the wax by pressing the leaf upon it.

2002. Sprigs of Plants.—In the construction of these, it is most important to be guided by sprigs of the natural plant, as various kinds of plants have many different characteristics in the grouping of their flowers, leaves, and branches.

2003. Selection of Wax.—When about to copy a flower, take care in the selection of good sheets of wax, and see that their colours are precisely those of the flower you desire to imitate. For the tints, stripes, and spots of variegated flowers, you will be supplied with colours among the other materials, and the application of them is precisely upon the principle of water-colour painting.

2004. MODELLING FRUIT, &c., IN WAX.—For the imitating of fruit in wax, very different rules are to be observed. The following directions may, however, be generally followed : —The material of which moulds for waxen fruit should be composed is the *best* plaster of Paris, such as is used for plaster casts, &c. If the plaster is faulty, the results of the modelling will of course be more or less faulty also.

The use of an elastic fruit in early experiments often leads to a want of accuracy in the first steps of the operation, which causes very annoying difficulties afterwards ; and therefore a solid, inelastic body—an egg boiled hard—is recommended as the first object to be imitated.

2005. Casting Egg in Wax.—For the first experiments common yellow wax may be used as the material, or the ends of half-burnt wax candles. The materials of the hard (not tallow) composition mould candles will also answer.

2006. Making the Moulds.—*First Half.*—Having filled a small pudding basin about three-quarters full of damp sand (the finer the better), lay the egg lengthways in the sand, so that half of it is above, and half below, the level of the sand, which should be perfectly smooth round it. Then in another basin, which should be half full of water, mix the plaster in quickly till it comes to the consistency of thick cream, then pour the whole upon the egg in the first basin.

While the half mould thus made is hardening thoroughly, carefully remove every particle of plaster from the basin in which it was mixed, and also from the spoon which has been used. This is highly important, since a small quantity of plaster which has set will destroy the quality of a second mixing if it is incorporated therewith. In about five minutes the half mould will be fit to remove, which may be done by turning the basin up with the right hand (taking care not to lose the sand), so that the mould falls into the left hand. The egg should then be gently allowed to fall out of the mould ; if, however, it adheres, lightly scrape the plaster from the edge of the mould, and then shake it out into the hollow of the hand. The mould or casting must be "trimmed" ; that is, the sand must be brushed from the flat surface of the mould with a nail-brush very lightly, without touching the extreme and sharp edges where the hollow of the mould commences. Then upon the broad edge from which the sand has been brushed, make four equidistant hollows (with the round end of a table-knife), like the deep impression of a thimble's end. These are to guide hereafter in the fixing of the second half of the mould. The egg should now be replaced in the casting, the edges of which with the holes should be thoroughly lubricated with sweet oil, laid on with a feather, or, what is better, a large camel-hair brush.

Second Half.—Into the small pudding basin from which the sand has been emptied, place with the egg uppermost the half mould, which, if the operation has been managed properly, should *fit* close at the edges to the side of the vessel ; then prepare some more liquid plaster as before, and pour it upon the egg mud mould.

Completion of Mould.—In due time remove the whole from the basin ; the halves will be found readily separable, and the egg being removed, the mould will be ready to cast in, after it has been set aside for an hour or two, so as to completely harden. This is the simplest form of mould, and all are made upon the same principle.

2007. **Casting in Wax.**—Every large object to be imitated in wax should be cast *hollow* ; and therefore, though the transparent lightness required in the imitation of fruits is not requisite in an artificial egg, the egg may be cast upon the same principle as a piece or fruit, in the following manner.

i. The two pieces of the plaster of Paris mould must be soaked in hot water for ten minutes.

ii. The wax should in the meantime be very slowly melted in a small tin saucepan, with a spout to it, care being taken not to allow it to boil, or it will be discoloured. As to the quantity of wax to be melted, the following is a general rule :—A lump, the size of the object to be imitated, placed in the saucepan, should be sufficient for casting twice, at least.

iii. As soon as the wax is melted thoroughly, place the saucepan on the hob of the grate, and taking the parts of the mould from the hot water, remove the moisture from their surfaces by pressing them gently with a handkerchief or soft cloth. The mould must not be *wiped*, but only *pressed.* If the *weather* has not been hot enough, or if the drying is not performed quickly, the mould will be too cold, and the wax will congeal too rapidly, and settle in ridges and streaks ; on the other hand, if the wax has been made too hot, it will adhere to the mould, and refuse to come out entire.

iv. Having laid the two halves of

the mould so that there can be no mistake in fitting the one in its exact place quickly on the other, pour from the saucepan into *one* of the half moulds as nearly as much wax as will fill the hollow made by the model (egg), quickly fit the other half on the top of it, squeeze the two pieces tightly together in the hand, and, still holding them thus, turn them over in every possible position, so that the wax which is slowly congealing in the internal hollow of the mould may be of equal thickness in all parts. Having continued this process at least two minutes, the hands (still holding and turning the mould) may be immersed in cold water to accelerate the cooling process. The perfect concealment of the wax may be known after a little experience by the absence of the sound of fluid on shaking the mould.

v. As soon as the mould is completely cooled, the halves may be separated carefully, the upper being lifted straight up from the under, and if the operation has been properly managed, a waxen egg will be turned out of the mould.

vi. The egg will only require *trimming*, that is, removing the ridge which marks the line at which the halves of the mould joined, and polishing out the scratches or inequalities left by the knife with a piece of soft rag, wet with spirits of turpentine or spirits of wine.

2008. Colouring the Wax.—While the wax is yet on the hob, and in a fluid state, stir into it a little *flake white*, in powder, and continue to stir the mixture while it is being poured into the half mould. It will be found that unless the fixing and shaking of the moulds is managed quickly, the colouring matter will settle on the side of the half into which the mixture is poured ; a little care in manipulation is therefore again requisite. The colouring of the wax is a matter which comes easily enough by experiment. Oranges, lemons, large gooseberries,

small cucumbers, &c., &c., are excellent objects for practice.

2009. Method of Hardening Objects in Plaster of Paris.—Take two parts of stearine, two parts of Venetian soap, one part of pearlash, and twenty-four to thirty parts of a solution of caustic potash. The stearine and soap are cut into slices, mixed with the cold lye, and boiled for about half-an-hour, being constantly stirred. Whenever the mass rises, a little cold lye is added. The pearlash, previously moistened with a little rain water, is then added, and the whole boiled for a few minutes. The mass is then stirred until cold, when it is mixed with so much cold lye that it becomes perfectly liquid, and runs off the spoon without coagulating and contracting. Previously to using this composition, it should be kept for several days well covered. It may be preserved for years. Before applying it to the objects they should be well dusted, the stains scraped away, and then coated, by means of a thick brush, with the wash, as long as the plaster of Paris absorbs it, and left to dry. The coating is then dusted with a soft brush. If the surface has not become shining, the operation must be repeated.

2010. "Plastiline" for taking Casts.—This is a new compound for taking casts of organic remains found in the earth. Hitherto beeswax, pure or mixed with paraffin and ozokerit, dentists' modelling composition, glue, gelatine, melted sulphur, or plaster of Paris have been used. Plastiline, invented by Professor Luigi Giudico, of Genoa, is of secret composition, but resembles clay or putty, and is made in three varieties, differing in hardness, the medium, No. 2, being fittest for impressions of fossils. It can be softened with vaseline or sweet oil. The modelling tools of sculptors are employed with it ; and otherwise it is very convenient. Plaster casts can be made from it.

2011. IMPRESSIONS FROM COINS.—Melt a little isinglass-glue with brandy, and pour it thinly over the medal, &c., so as to cover its whole surface ; let it remain on for a day or two, till it has thoroughly dried and hardened, and then take it off, when it will be fine, clear, and hard, and will present an excellent impression of the coin. It will also resist the effects of damp air, which occasions other kinds of glue to soften and bend if not prepared in this way.

2012. DIAPHANIE.

This is a beautiful, useful, and inexpensive art, easily acquired, and producing imitations of the richest stained glass, in every variety of colour and design. A peculiar kind of paper is rendered semi-transparent, upon which designs are printed in glass colours (*vitre de couleurs*), which will not change with the light. The paper is applied to the glass with a clear white varnish, and when dry, a preparation is finally applied, which increases the transparency, and adds brilliancy to the effect.

2013. Materials Required.— The printed sheets of designs ready for immediate use are easily procurable at a very moderate price, and comprise a great variety of styles and subjects ; some consist of medallion centres of Watteau figures, &c., and are intended to be surrounded by semi-transparent half-light designs, which add greatly to the effect of the centre pictures. Many thousands of designs are issued, and include borders, corner-pieces, &c. The other articles required are some clear white varnish, some liqueur diaphanie, brushes, a palette knife, and ivory paper-knife.

2014. Practical Instructions.— Choose a fine day for the operation, as the glass should be perfectly dry, and unaffected by the humidity of the atmosphere. If you have a choice, it is more *convenient* to work on your glass before it is fixed in the frame.

If you are working on a piece of unattached glass, lay it on a *flat* table (a marble slab is preferable), over which you must previously lay a piece of baize or cloth to keep the glass steady. The glass being thus fixed, clean and polish the side on which you intend to operate (in windows this is the inner side), then with your brush lay on it very equably a good coat of the prepared varnish ; let this dry for *an hour*, more or less, according to the dryness of the atmosphere and the thickness of the coat of varnish ; meantime cut and trim your designs carefully to fit the glass (if it is one entire transparent sheet you will find little trouble) ; then lay them on a piece of paper, face downwards, and damp the back of them with a sponge, applied several times, to equalize the moisture. In this operation arrange your time so that your designs may now be finally left to dry for fifteen minutes before application to the glass, the varnish on which has now become tacky or sticky, and in a proper state to receive them. Apply the printed side next to the glass without pressure ; endeavour to let your sheet fall perfectly level and smooth on the glass, so that you may avoid leaving creases, which would be fatal. Take now your palette-knife and press out all the air-bubbles, commencing in the centre, and working them out at the sides ; an ivory stick will be found useful in removing creases ; you now leave this to dry, and after twenty-four hours apply a slight coat of the liqueur diaphanie, leaving it another day, when, if dry, apply a second coat of the same kind, which must be left several days ; finally, apply a coat of varnish over all.

If these directions are carefully followed, your glass will never be affected by time or any variations in the weather ; and can be washed the same as ordinary stained glass, to which, in some respects, it is even superior.

2015. Application of Diaphanie.— All kinds of screens, lamp-shades and glasses, lanterns, &c., &c., may be decorated in this way, as heat will produce no effect upon them.

2016. VITREMANIE is a process of imitating painting on glass similar to Diaphanie.

2017. POTICHOMANIE is a process of like nature by which glass plates, vases, &c., are made to resemble porcelain.

2018. DECALCOMANIE.—This recently discovered and beautiful art consists in transferring prepared coloured pictures to glass, porcelain, china, wood, silk, furniture, plaster of Paris, alabaster, ivory, paper, paper-hangings, windows, tea-trays, oilcloth, and all kinds of fancy articles, provided they possess a smooth surface ; the result being an exact resemblance to painting by hand. The art itself is simple and ingenious, and while affording agreeable occupation to ladies, it may be made to serve many useful purposes, on account of the numerous objects which will admit of being thus ornamented.

2019. Materials Required.

i. A bottle of transfer varnish for fixing the drawings.

ii. A bottle of light varnish to pass over the drawings when fixed.

iii. A bottle of spirit to clean the brushes, and to remove those pictures which may not be successful.

iv. A piece of beaver cloth about nine inches square.

v. A paper-knife and roller.

vi. Two or three camel-hair brushes.

vii. A basin of water.

viii. A bottle of opaque varnish.

2020. Instructions.—Thoroughly clean and free from grease the article to be decorated ; then, having cut off the white paper margin of the drawing, give a very light coating of transfer varnish to the parts to be transferred, being especially careful to cover the whole of the coloured portion, but not to allow it to touch the blank paper. When the varnish is first applied it is very liquid, and must remain ten minutes, the best condition for transferring being when the varnish is only just sticky, without being too dry ; then lay the drawing, face downwards, on the object to be ornamented, taking care to place it at once where it is to remain, as it would be spoilt by moving. Moisten the cloth with water, and lay it gently on the drawing, which has been previously laid in its place on the object to be decorated ; then rub it over with the paper-knife or roller, so as to cause the print to adhere in every part ; this done, remove the cloth, well soak the paper with a camel-hair brush dipped in water, and immediately after lift the paper by one corner, and gently draw it off. The picture will be left on the object, while the paper will come off perfectly white. Care must be taken that the piece of cloth, without being too wet, is sufficiently so to saturate the paper completely. The drawing must now be washed with a camel-hair brush, in clean water, to remove the surplus varnish, and then left till quite dry. On the following day, cover the picture with a light coat of the fixing varnish, to give brilliancy to the colours.

2021. To Ornament Dark-coloured Objects, such as the bindings of books, Russia leather, blotting-cases, leather bags, &c., the picture must be previously covered with a mixture of opaque white varnish, taking care not to pass beyond the outline of the design. On the following day, proceed according to the instructions given in the preceding paragraph.

2022. To ornament Silk, Paper, or Articles which will not bear wetting.—Varnish the picture with the transfer varnish, as previously explained, following the outline of the design, then allow it to dry for an hour or two ; when quite dry, pass a damp sponge over the entire surface of the sheet, so as to remove the composition which surrounds the picture, and which may spoil the object. Let the paper dry once more, and varnish the picture again with the transfer varnish ; in about ten minutes, place it face downward on the object to be decorated, and rub it with the paper- knife or roller, over the whole of its surface. Finally, moisten the paper with a wet brush, allow it to remain sufficiently long to become moist, then strip the paper off. *To remove a spoilt picture from any object*, dip a soft rag in the essence, and rub it over the surface.

2023. Designs Appropriate for Decalcomanie.—English flowers of every variety, bouquets, tropical birds, flowers and fruits in imitation of aquatint ; garlands with cupids after Watteau, and garlands with birds ; domestic scenes ; fruit, flowers ; medallions, Gothic initials and monograms, fleur-de-lis ; borders various.

2024. Heraldic Decalcomanie is an extended application of this art, the arms and crests being emblazoned in their proper colours according to the rules of heraldry, and prepared for Decalcomanie. Armorial bearings, thus embellished, serve admirably to ornament and identify the books of a library and pictures of a gallery, to decorate menus for dinners, the invitations to a soirée, &c. By their brilliant colours they give an elegant effect to the table decorations.

2025. TERRA COTTA PAINTING.—Terra Cotta is an Italian term for "burnt earth." Bricks are a coarse kind of terra cotta. The Natural History Museum at Kensington is built entirely of terra cotta slabs. Terra Cotta vases of the early and late Etruscan period, such as those in the British Museum, are priceless. These are painted in various designs, and burnt in. The Doulton Ware is a close, if not exact, representation of those matchless specimens. Terra Cotta painting is simply vases and plates of red terra cotta, painted in Greek designs with ordinary black paint, and then varnished, or plates painted with a similar medium, in flowers of various colours. These last, of course, are no imitations of the antique.

2026.   ANGLO-JAPANESE WORK.—This is an elegant and easy domestic art. Take yellow withered leaves, dissolve gum, black paint, copal varnish, &c. Any articles, such as an old tea-caddy, flower-pots, fire-screens, screens of all descriptions, work-boxes, &c., may be ornamented with these simple materials. Select perfect leaves, dry and press them between the leaves of books ; rub the surface of the article to be ornamented with fine sand-paper, then give it a coat of fine black paint, which should be procured mixed at a colour-shop. When dry rub smooth with pumice-stone, and give two other coats. Dry. Arrange leaves in any manner and varied, according to taste. Gum the leaves on the under side, and press them upon their places. Then dissolve some isinglass in hot water, and brush it over the work. Dry. Give three coats of copal varnish, allowing ample time for each coat to dry. Articles thus ornamented last for years, and are very pleasing.

2027. ORNAMENTAL LEATHER WORK.—An excellent imitation of carved oak, suitable for frames, boxes, vases, and ornaments in endless variety, may be made of a description of leather called basil. The art consists in simply cutting out this material in imitation of natural objects, and in impressing upon it by simple tools, either with or without the aid of heat, such marks and characteristics as are necessary to the imitation. The tools required are ivory or steel points of various sizes, punches, and tin shapes, such as are used for confectionery. The points may be made out of the handles of old tooth-brushes. Begin with a simple object, and proceed by degrees to those that are more complicated. Cut out an ivy or an oak leaf, and impress the veins upon it ; then arrange these in groups, and affix them to frames, or otherwise. Before cutting out the leaves the leather should be well soaked in water, until it is quite pliable. When dry, it will retain the artistic shape. Leaves and stems are fastened together by means of liquid glue, and varnished with any of the drying varnishes, or with sealing-wax dissolved to a suitable consistency in spirits of wine. Wire, cork, gutta-percha, bits of stems of trees, &c., may severally be used to aid in the formation of groups of buds, flowers, seed-vessels, &c.

2028. ETCHING OR ENGRAVING ON IVORY.—The ivory should be covered with wax, and then oil of vitriol used for etching fluid.

2029. TO BLEACH IVORY.—First rub it with finely-ground pumice-stone and water. Then, while it is moist, expose it (under a bell-glass) to the sun, to prevent dryness and cracking. Repeat this until the desired effect is produced ; *or* the ivory may be bleached by dipping it for a little while in water containing a small quantity of sulphurous acid, chlorine, or chloride of lime ; or also, by exposing it, while moist, to fumes of burning sulphur, mixed with air to reduce their strength.

2030. ARTIFICIAL IVORY, TO MAKE.—Make a fine paste of isin-flass, finely-powdered egg-shells, and brandy. Impart the required colour to it, and while it is warm pour it into well-oiled moulds, and leave it until it becomes hard.

2031. PHOTOGRAPHY.

This art has of late years become exceedingly popular among amateurs of both sexes, and it is remarkable how many of one's friends possess cameras, and how soon they acquire the art of using them with success. The camera is a useful and pleasant companion in our rambles, and by its means we can record many pleasant incidents which have occurred during a holiday, many pieces of beautiful scenery, and, more especially, the features of our friends and relatives.

Beginners must not be discouraged by a few early failures ; for since the introduction of the dry-plate process the taking and development of a photograph is a comparatively easy matter, to say nothing of the *cleanliness* of the new process, as compared with the old.

Cameras are generally made in the following three sizes :—whole plate, half plate, and quarter plate ; the most useful being the half plate, as it is sufficiently large for portraits, and is also a very convenient size for landscape views. A really good one should be secured at a cost of about £5, but frequently it may be had for considerably less than that sum.

Of course it is impossible, in the space of an article of this kind, to explain the process of taking and developing a picture, and the only thing is to refer the reader to some of the very cheap and useful hand-books on the subject.

2032. FANCY NEEDLEWORK.

Although there is a continual change in designs and materials for fancy needlework of every description, the fundamental principles on which this kind of work in all its various branches is executed remain the same. These are briefly set forth in the following series of instructions on this subject.

2033. CROCHET EXPLAINED.—Whether as a simple trimming, as an elaborate quilt, or as a fabric, almost rivalling Point Lace, it is popular with every woman who has any time for fancy work, since it is only needful to understand the stitches, and the terms and contractions used in writing the descriptions of the different designs to be enabled to work them without difficulty.

2034. Stitches used in Crochet— These, with their abbreviations, are :— *Chain stitch, Ch. ; Single crochet, S. ; Double crochet, Dc. ; Treble stitch, Tr.,* and *Double and Treble Long.*

i. Chain Stitch, or Ch.—Hook the cotton into a loop, and keep on looping the cotton throogh a previous stitch till a succession of chains are made to form a foundation.

ii. Single Crochet, or S.—This occurs only in working designs ; the hook is inserted in a stitch, and the cotton is pulled through that and the cotton which is on the hook at the same time ; it thus makes a close tie.

iii. Double Crochet, or Dc.—With cotton on the hook insert the latter into a stitch, draw the cotton through ; there are now two loops on the hook, take up the cotton on the hook, and with cotton again upon the hook draw it through two loops.

iv. Treble Stitch, or Tr.—With the loop of last stitch on the hook, twist the cotton over the hook, place the latter through a stitch, draw the cotton through, then put the cotton over the hook, draw the cotton through two loops, and again through two loops.

v. Double and Treble Long.— With the hook in a loop, twist the cotton twice or three times over the hook, and draw the hook successively through either two or three loops.

2035. Square Crochet is also sometimes used. The squares are either open or close. An open square consists of one Tr, two Ch, missing two on the line beneath, before making the next stitch. A close square has three successive Tr's. Thus, any given number of close squares, followed by an open, will have so many times three Tr's ; consequently any foundation for square crochet must have a number that can be divided by three.

2036. To Increase or Decrease.— For the former two stitches may be worked in the same loop ; for the latter, either miss a stitch of the preceding row, or crochet two together.

2037. To Join on a Thread.— Joins should be avoided as much as possible in open work. In joining, finish the stitch by drawing the new thread through, leaving two inches for both ends, which must be held in.

2038. To Use Several Colours.— Hold the threads not in use on the edge of the work, and work them in. Change the colour by beginning the stitch in the old colour, and finishing it with the new, continuing the work with the latter, holding in the old. If only one stitch is wanted in the new colour, finish one stitch, and begin the next with it ; then change.

2039. To Join Leaves, &c.—When one part of a leaf or flower is required to be joined to another, drop the loop from the hook, which insert in the place to be joined ; draw the loop through and continue.

2040. To Work over Cord.—Hold the cord in the left hand with the work, and work round it, as you would over an end of thread, working closely. When beads are used they must be first threaded on silk or thread, and then dropped, according to the pattern, on the *wrong* side of the work. This side looks more even than the other ; therefore, when bead purses are worked from an engraving, they are worked the reverse of the usual way, viz. from right to left.

2041. Oriental Crochet, some-times termed Tricot.—This is worked by just making a chain the length required. Then put the hook through a loop of the chain, pull the wool through without twisting it, and so continue to the end, keeping all the stitches on the hook. *In returning,* twist the wool over the hook, pull it through the first loop, twist the wool again over the hook, pull it through the next, and so continue to the end. There will now be a row of flat loops, but not on the edge. Work exactly as at the first row which was worked with the chain row, but take up the loops instead of the chain stitches.

2042. NETTING EXPLAINED.— The beauty of netting consists in its firmness and regularity. All joins in the thread must be made in a very strong knot ; and, if possible, at an edge, so that it may not be perceived. Stitches in netting are always counted by knots.

2043. Implements used in Netting.—These are a netting needle and a mesh. In filling a netting needle with the material, be careful not to make it so full that there will be a difficulty in passing it through the stitches. The size of the needle must depend on the material to be employed, and the fineness of the work. Steel needles are employed for every kind of netting except the very coarsest. They are marked from 12 to 24, the latter being extremely fine. The fine meshes are usually also of steel ; but, as this material is heavy, it is better to employ bone or wooden meshes when large ones are required. Many meshes are flat ; and in using them the *width* is given.

2044. Diamond Netting.—The first stitch in this work is termed *diamond* netting, the holes being in the form of diamonds. To do the first row, a stout thread, knotted to form a round, is fastened to the knee with a pin, or passed over the foot, or on the hook, sometimes attached to a work cushion for the purpose. The end of the thread on the needle is knotted to this, the mesh being held in the left hand on a line with it. Take the needle in the right hand ; let the thread come over the mesh and the third finger, bring it back under the mesh, and hold it between the thumb and first finger. Slip the needle through the loop over

the third finger, under the mesh and the foundation thread. In doing this a loop will be formed, which must be passed over the fourth finger. Withdraw the third finger from the loop, and draw up the loop over the fourth, gradually, until it is quite tight on the mesh. The thumb should be kept firmly over the mesh while the stitch is being completed. When the necessary number of stitches is made on this foundation, the future rows are to bo worked backwards and forwards. To form a *round*, the first stitch is to be worked into immediately after the last, which closes the netting into a circle.

2045. Round Netting is very nearly the same stitch. The difference is merely in the way of putting the needle through the loop and foundation, or other stitch. After passing the needle through the loop, it must be brought out, and put *downwards* through the stitch. This stitch is particularly suitable for purses.

2046. Square Netting is exactly the same stitch as diamond netting, only it is begun at a corner, on one stitch, and increased (by doing two in one) in the last stitch of every row, until the greatest width required is attained. Then, by netting two stitches together at the end of every row, the piece is decreased to a point again. When stretched out, all the holes in this netting are squares.

2047. Darning on Netting.— Square and diamond netting are the most frequently used, and are ornamented with patterns darned on them, in simple darning or in various point stitches. In the latter case it forms a variety of the sort of work termed *Guipure d'Art*.

2048. TATTING EXPLAINED.

The only necessary implements are a thin shuttle or short netting-needle, and a gilt pin and ring, united by a chain. The cotton used should be strong and soft. There are three available sizes, Nos. 1, 2, and 3.

Attention should be paid to the manner of holding the hands, as on this depends the grace or awkwardness of the movement. Fill the shuttle with the cotton (or silk) required, in the same manner as a netting needle. Hold the shuttle between the thumb and first and second fingers of the right hand, leaving about half-a-yard of cotton unwound. Take up the cotton, about three inches from the end, between the thumb and first finger of the left hand, and let the end fall in the palm of the hand ; pass the cotton round the other fingers of the left hand (keeping them parted a little), and bring it again between the thumb and forefinger, thus making a circle round the extended fingers. There are only two stitches in tatting, called respectively the *English* and the *French* stitch, and they are usually done alternately.

2049. English Stitch.—Let the thread between the right and left hands fall towards you ; slip the shuttle under the thread between the first and second finders ; draw it out rather quickly, keeping it in a horizontal line with the left hand. You will find a slipping loop is formed on this cotton with that which went round the fingers. Hold the shuttle steadily, with the cotton stretched tightly out, and with the second finger of the left hand slip the loop thus made under the thumb.

2050. French Stitch.—Instead of allowing the cotton to fall *towards* you, and passing the shuttle *downwards*, the cotton is thrown in a loop over the left hand, and the shuttle passed under the thread between the first and second fingers *upwards*. The knot must be invariably formed by the thread which passes round the fingers of the *left* hand. If the operation is reversed, and the knot formed by the cotton connected with the shuttle, the loop will not draw up. This is occasioned by letting the cotton from the shuttle

hang loosely instead of drawing it out and holding it tightly stretched. When any given number of these double stitches are done, and drawn closely together, the stitches are held between the first finger and thumb, and the other fingers are withdrawn from the circle of cotton, which is gradually diminished by drawing out the shuttle until the loop of tatting is nearly or entirely closed. The tatted loops should be quite close to each other, unless directions to the contrary are given.

2051. Ornamental Edging.—The pin is used in making an ornamental edge, something like purl edging, thus :—Slip the ring on the left-hand thumb, that the pin attached may be ready for use. After making the required number of double stitches, twist the pin in the circle of cotton, and hold it between the forefinger and thumb, whilst making more double stitches ; repeat. The little loops thus formed are termed *picots*.

2052. Trefoil Tatting.—This is done by drawing three loops up tightly, close together, and then leaving a short space before making more. The trefoil is sewed into shape afterwards with a needle.

2053. To Join Loops.—When two loops are to be connected, a *picot* is made in the *first*, whenever the join is required. When you come to the corresponding part of the second loop, draw the thread which goes round the fingers of the left hand through the *picot* with a needle, pulling through a loop large enough to admit the shuttle. Slip this through, then draw the thread tight again over the fingers, and continue the work. In many patterns a needle is used to work over, in button-hole stitch, the thread which passes from one loop to another. A long needleful of the same cotton or silk used for the tatting is left at the beginning of the work, and a common needle used to buttonhole over bars wherever they occur.

2054. KNITTING EXPLAINED.

We recommend our readers to attain *perfection* in this branch of fancy work, because, above all others, it is a resource to those who, from weak eyes, are precluded from many kinds of industrial amusement, or who, as invalids, cannot bear the fatigue of more elaborate work. The fact is that knitting does not require eyesight at all ; and a very little practice ought to enable any one to knit whilst reading, talking, or studying, quite as well as if the fingers were unemployed.

2055. Implements for Knitting.— These are pins of ivory, bone, or steel. The latter are most commonly used, and should have tapered points, without the least *sharpness* at the extremity. Take care to have needles and cotton or wool that are suitable to each other in size. The work of the best knitter in the world would appear ill done if the needles were too fine or too coarse. In the former case, the work would be close and thick ; in the latter it would be too much like a cobweb.

2056. To "Cast on."—Make a loop, and put it on the left needle, put the right needle through this loop. Twist the cotton or wool over the right needle and draw it through the loop, then transfer this loop just made, from the right needle to the left ; repeat this process till you have made the number required.

To Fasten on.—Twist the two ends of the thread together, and knit a few stitches with both ; or make a strong weaver's knot

2057. Plain Knitting.—Slip the point of the right-hand needle in a loop, bring the thread round it, and with the forefinger push the point of the needle off the loop so that the thread just twisted round forms a new one on the right hand.

2058. Purling.—The right-hand needle is slipped in the loop *in front of*

the left-hand one, and the thread, after passing between the two, is brought round it ; it is then worked as before. The thread is always brought forward before beginning a purled stitch, unless particular directions to the contrary are given.

2059. To Increase.—There are several ways of doing this. If only one stitch is to be increased, bring the thread between the pins and knit the following stitch. This will form an open stitch or hole in the following row. To make a close increase, pick up the loop below the next stitch to be knitted, and knit it. To increase one stitch when the row is being seamed, the thread will be in front of the pin ; pass it quite round the pin to the front again.

2060. To Decrease.—Take one stitch off without knitting ; knit one, then slip the point of the left-hand needle in the unknitted stitch and draw it over the other. It is marked in recipes d. 1. To decrease 2 or more, slip 1, knit 2, 3, or more together, *as one*, and pass the slip stitch over.

2061. To Join a Round.—Four or five needles are used in round work, such as socks, stockings, &c. Cast on any given number of stitches on one needle, then slip another needle in the last stitch, before casting any on it ; repeat for any number. When all are cast on, knit the first 2 stitches off on to the end of the last needle. One needle is always left unused in casting on for a round.

2062. To Cast off:—Knit 2 stitches ; with the left-hand needle draw the first over the second ; knit another ; repeat. Observe that the row before the casting off should never be very tightly knitted.

2063. To Knit Three Stitches together, so that the centre one shall be in front.—Slip 2 off the needle together, knit the third, and draw the others over together.

2064. To Raise a Stitch is to knit the bar of thread between the two stitches as one.

2065. To Pick up a Stitch.—With the left-hand pin pick up the loop below the next stitch to be knitted, knit it and bring to the right pin.

2066. To Slip a Stitch is passing a stitch from the left pin to the right without knitting it.

2067. To Seam a Stitch.—Place the pin in the stitch to be seamed, having the point towards you. Pass the thread quite round the pin, take the pin with the stitch on it out at the back, and repeat.

2068. Abbreviations used in patterns.—K, knit ; P, purl ; D, decrease ; K 2 t, knit two together ; P 2 t, purl two together ; M 1, make one.

2069. MACRAMÉ EXPLAINED.

Macramé work, called also "knotted fringe," and "Mexican lace," consists in knotting, interweaving and tying together threads or strings made for the purpose. This work is strong and durable, and can be used in such a variety of ways that it is well worth the trouble of learning. It is impossible to describe the method of working without the aid of diagrams or patterns ; these, however, may be readily procured.

Materials Required.—A well-stuffed, weighted, oblong cushion, with pegs at the ends, to fix and wind long foundation threads on ; some large glass-headed pins and a crochet needle to pull the thread through when required. Either silk, wool, cotton, gold thread, or cord can be used, but proper Macramé thread, which can be purchased at almost any fancy shop, is most recommended.

2070. FANCY EMBROIDERY AND CANVAS WORK.

Embroidery, properly speaking, includes every sort of ornamental work done with a sewing needle of any kind ; but in its popular acceptation, it applies only to the ornamentation of any article from drawn or marked patterns—whatever may be the material employed. Berlin or canvas work, on the contrary, is the usual designation of all kinds of embroidery or canvas, *done by counting threads*, and frequently by the aid of a painting on checked paper. We will begin by describing some of the former varieties.

2071. Appliqué.—In this, the simplest style of embroidery, the pattern is in one material, laid on another which forms the ground. In this way muslin is worked on net, velvet is laid on cloth, or on another velvet, and cretonne designs cut out and laid on another material, the edges being either sewed over, or ornamented with fancy cord, braid, gold thread, or any other appropriate material.

2072. Braiding.—This is another very easy style of ornamentation : a pattern is first traced on the material and a narrow silk or worsted braid neatly sewn over the lines. Gold and silver braid enter largely into various sorts of decorated needlework, and the Victoria braid, of cotton, which has something of the appearance of satin stitch, is also effective, but considerable care is required to put it on evenly and firmly. The stitches should be taken across the braid. This makes it lie flat.

2073. White Embroidery, or em- broidery on muslin, is used for a great variety of articles of ladies' dress. The pattern is in either satin stitch, or from left to right, formed of holes cut out of the muslin, and sewed over with embroidery cotton. The great art in working is to make the holes all of the same size, and to take the stitches closely and regular.

2074. Satin Stitch is a smooth raised work, used for leaves, flowers, &c. It is done by first tracing the outlines accurately with soft cotton, then taking stitches from point to point of the part to be raised, so as to have the greatest thickness of cotton in the centre, and sewing it over, in stitches taken closely together, but slightly slanting, and completely across the part outlined. The veining of leaves is generally formed by taking the stitches from the vein to the edge, first on one side and then on the other. The borders of embroidered muslin collars, &c., are usually finished with buttonhole stitch, worked either the width of an ordinary buttonhole, or in long stitches, and raised like satin stitch. Eyelet holes are made by piercing round holes with a stiletto, and sewing them round.

2075. Fancy Stitches.—There are many fancy stitches introduced into muslin work, but these require to be practically taught.

2076. Frame for Embroidery.—The kind of frame on which muslin is most easily worked, consists of two hoops of wood, about eight inches in diameter. One is rather smaller than the other. On it the muslin is stretched, and the larger one being slipped over it, and fitting tightly, keeps the muslin in its place.

2077. Patterns may be drawn on cloth, muslin or other materials, with a pen dipped in a liquid made of stone-blue and sugar mixed with water to the consistency required.

2078. Embroidery on Satin, &c.—Satin, velvet, and plush are embroidered in coloured silks, gold and silver bullion, chenille, pearls, &c. A very fashionable style is the work with *ombre* or shaded silks.

2079. Shading in Silks.—It requires considerable care to work well with ombre silks, to avoid incorrect shading. Nature should be followed as closely as possible. Not only must the form be carefully preserved, but the lights and shades must be disposed in an artistic manner. For instance : the point of a leaf is never the darkest

part, nor should the lower leaves and flowers of a group of the same kind be light.

2080. Stem or Crewel Stitch is that used for stems and for ordinary filling-in of flowers and arabesques, and also for outlining. Instead of working from right to left, the stitches are smoother if worked from left to right. In stems a long stitch is made, and then a second, half-way the length of the first, and half-way beyond it, till a stem is formed ; and to complete it work from right to left, placing the needle under a stitch of the stem, not of the material, and so work back upon the top of the previous stitches. In the stem first worked only the tiniest piece of the material is taken up on the needle, so that the wool or silk is all on the surface.

2081. Stem Stitch in Flowers, &c.—In flowers and arabesques the stem stitch is worked straight, but each stitch differing in length from the other, so as to make the wool smooth. Commence the work at the lowest part of the petals, and work upwards to the edge.

2082. Split Stem Stitch.—Having worked one stitch, in making the second, split the first stitch in the centre with the needle. In the stitch, the thread is continued under the material.

2083. Couching is a laying down on the outline of the design, a thick strand of filoselle, or cord or wool or silk of any kind, and then over-stitching it down with a fine silk of the same, or a contrasting colour.

2084. Basket-work and Diaper Stitch.—These are done with gold, silver, or silk cords, stitched on the material in patterns, with silk of another, or of the same colour. The cords are just passed through the back of the work to its surface ; either one, two, or three at a time are held in place by the left hand, the over-stitching being done by the right hand.

2085. Stitches in Canvas Work.
—There are five kinds of stitch used in canvas work—*Cross Stitch*, *Tent Stitch*, *Tapestry Stitch*, *German Stitch*, and *Irish Stitch*.

2086. Cross Stitch is generally known. The needle is brought up in one pole of the canvas and down on another, two threads higher and more to the right. The slanting thread is then crossed in the opposite direction. A cross stitch covers two threads in each direction:

2087. Tent Stitch occupies one-fourth the space of cross stitch. It is taken from one hole to the next above, and on the right hand side of a previous stitch.

2088. Tapestry Stitch crosses two threads of the canvas in the length, and one in the width. It is sometimes called Gobelin stitch, because it resembles somewhat the Gobelin tapestry. It is not suited for coarse canvas, and, in working from a Berlin pattern, *two* straight stitches must be counted as one square cross stitch.

2089. German Stitch is worked diagonally, and consists of the first part of a cross stitch, and a tent stitch alternately worked.

2090. Irish Stitch is worked parallel with the selvedges of the canvas. None of the stitches cross the threads in the *width*. In the first row, take the thread alternately over four and two threads ; in all future rows take the stitches over four threads,—which, as they rise, first from the long and then from the short stitch, will produce the same appearance in others.

2091. Frames for Canvas Work.
—Wooden frames are sometimes used for keeping the canvas in shape while being worked. These should be strong enough to ensure their not warping.

2092. To Frame Canvas.—After herringboning the raw edges of the canvas, sew them, *by* the thread, to the webbing of the frame,—that is, to the top and bottom. Then stretch the ends till the canvas is extended to its utmost length, put in the pegs, and brace the sides with fine twine. If the canvas is too long for the frame, and any part has to be rolled over the end, let the wood be first covered with a few thicknesses of silver paper.

2093. Stretching Work.—Should a piece of work be a little drawn when taken out of the frame, damp the back well with a clean sponge, and stretch it again in the frame in the opposite direction.

2094. Stiffening Work.—Wet the wrong side thoroughly with gum water or gum tragacanth, and dry it before a fire (the wet side nearest the fire), before removing it from the frame.

2095. Canvas Work on Cloth.—Sometimes, to save the trouble of grounding, a design is worked on cloth, over which canvas is laid. In this case, the cloth must be carefully damped, to remove the gloss, before it is put into the frame. Then, as cloth will always stretch much more than canvas, it must be cut a little smaller both ways. The raw edges of the cloth should be turned in, and tacked to the canvas before they are framed. Some people withdraw the threads of canvas after the work is done ; but it has a much richer effect if the threads of canvas are cut close to the outer stitches ; and if there are any small spaces in the pattern, where the ground should be seen, they may be worked in wool of the colour of the ground.

Whenever Berlin-work is done on any solid thick material, as cloth, velvet, &c., a needle should be used with an eye sufficiently large to form a passage for this wool. This prevents the latter from being crushed and impoverished as it passes through.

2096. MATERIALS USED IN EMBROIDERY AND CANVAS WORK.—These may be classed under the names of fancy cotton, wool, silk, chenille, and braid ; beads, and a variety of other fancy materials, are also brought into use. We describe some of the most useful.

2097. Fancy Cottons.—A great variety of coloured cottons for embroidery and crewel work, such as "flourishing thread," "lustrine," &c., are now made which so closely resemble silk that it is difficult to detect the difference, and as they are cheaper, and in many cases clean better, they are naturally much used.

2098. Berlin Wool is a beautiful material for canvas work. It is made only in two sizes, 4-thread and 8-thread, called single and double. Berlin wools are either dyed in one colour, or in shades of the same colour, or (*very rarely*) in shades of several colours. Technically, a silk or wool dyed in shades of the same colour, going gradually from light to dark, and from dark to light again, is termed an *ombre*, or *shaded* wool or silk, whereas *chine* is the term employed when there are several *colours* used. There are, also, what are called *short* and *long* shades ; that is, in the former the entire shades, from the lightest to the lightest again, will occur within a short space, a yard or so ; whereas, in *long* shades the gradation is much more gradually made. We notice these apparently trifling differences that readers may comprehend the importance of obtaining precisely the proper materials for each design. These wools should never be wound, as handling crushes the pile and spoils its appearance.

2099. Fleecy Wool is the sort of wool used for jackets and other large articles. Some of the tints are quite as brilliant as those of Berlin wool. It is made in 3, 4, 6, 8, and 12 threads, and is much cheaper than German wool. It does very well for grounding large pieces of canvas work.

2100. Shetland Wool is very fine and soft, is much used, and prized for shawls and neckties and for veils.

2101. Eis Wool.—A pure German wool of silky brightness, is used for the same purpose as Shetland wool excepting for veils. It is also used instead of silk for embroidering on velvet, for tea cosies, cushions, &c.

2102. Andalusian Wool is less thick than Berlin wool, and is used for cuffs and shawls.

2103. Scotch Fingering Wool is used for knitting stockings and socks, and gentlemen's kilt hose.

2104. Thin Lambs' Wool and Wheeling Yarn.—Scotch yarns, used principally for children's socks and stockings.

2105. Merino Wool is the produce of a Spanish breed of sheep. French Merino is made from this peculiarly soft wool: so also Berlin wool, used for canvas embroidery.

2106. Angola Wool.—The produce of an African breed of sheep ; is a soft hairy wool. Is used for making Angola or Cashmere shawls, and gloves, valued for their extreme softness and warmth. It is also used to make plush ; and in France to produce lace which rivals that of Chantilly and Valenciennes, and at a lesser price.

2107. Camel-hair Wool is the production of the Llama, or Al-Lama, a native of South America.

2108. Alpaca Wool is produced from the Al-Paco, or Peruvian sheep. This creature is also a species of camel, though different in shape.

2109. Other kinds of Wool— There are also other names given to wools by the vendors or manufacturers: for instance, "The Peacock Wool" and "The Coral Wool" are trade marks, and not particular wools.

2110. Embroidery Silk is bright and lustrous, and composed of two rather loosely-twisted large threads. *Sadler's Silk* and *Purse Silk* have three threads. *Sewing Silk* has two. *Tailor's Twist* three threads.

2111. Filoselle Silk as used in needlework, is two-thread silk, or "tram." Eight or ten of these slightly-twisted threads form a strand of silk, so that, according to the purpose required, one, two, or more threads of it can be used for embroidery. This is glossy as satin.

2112. Floss Silk consists of several filaments of untwisted silk sufficient to make a strand of silk. It is used for working on the surface of wool stitches to heighten the effect and give brilliancy.

2113. Chenille is of two kinds. *Chenille à broder* (the finest sort), and *chenille ordinaire*, which is stiff, and about the thickness of a quill: both are round. The extreme richness of the appearance of chenille makes it suitable for any work requiring great brilliancy ; as the plumage of birds, some flowers, and arabesques. It requires very careful handling.

2114. Arrasene is a perfectly flat silk—chenille—and is used for embroidery on all descriptions of material.

2115. Braids are of various kinds. Russian silk braids are generally employed for dresses, slippers, &c. ; but for many of these purposes the Albert braid manufactured in England is much richer and far more effective. Russian silk braid is generally narrow, and the plait is of that kind which is termed Grecian—all the strands going from the edge to the centre. In French braid, on the contrary, the plait of every two strands pass over each other. French braid, in silk, is very little used in this country. Slippers and other small articles worked in braid have the effect greatly improved by laying a gold thread on one or both sides of the braid.

2116. Victoria, Adelaide, or Coronation Braid (for the same article has been called by all these names), is a cotton braid, which, when laid on net or muslin, looks something like satin stitch. It is composed of thick and thin parts alternately, and is made in only two sizes.

2117. Albert Braid is a sort of silk cord, made in many beautiful colours. It is intended for either application, or braiding, and being *raised*, looks extremely well, with very small outlay of time or money.

2118. Gold and Silver Braids are often used in Mosaic work, and for slippers, blotting-cases, &c. The Mosaic braid, which is comparatively cheap, is generally used.

2119. Gold and Silver Embroidery, to Clean.—This work can be cleaned with spirits of wine, either pure or mixed with water. Some persons use gin. Alkaline or acid liquids are, injurious and generally spoil the article.

2120. Beads in Canvas Work have the treble merit of being at once brilliant, durable, and attractive. Transparent, white, or silver beads are usually worked with white silk, but clear glass beads, threaded on cerise silk, produce a peculiarly rich effect by the coloured silk shining through transparent glass. The silk used must be extremely fine, as the beads vary much in size. A change of material, which might appear of no consequence whatever, would completely spoil the effect of the design.

2121. Canvas for Cross-stitch Work.—The Penelope is most generally used. There are different degrees of fineness, determined by the number of double-crossed threads that may fill the space of one inch.

2122. Elephant Penelope Canvas is extremely coarse—fitted for working rugs and eight or twelve-thread wools.

2123. Silk Canvas requires no grounding ; it is made of a cotton thread overcast with silk, and resembles coarse even-threaded cheese cloths, but is silky.

2124. LUSTRA PAINTING is an invention that in appearance much resembles silk embroidery ; the outline of a design is sketched either on Roman satin or any smooth fabric, and then bronze powders of various colours are rubbed in with a preparation which is a trade secret. The leaves and stems are outlined in silk, rendering the imitation more complete.

2125. TAPESTRY PAINTING is an imitation of the famed Gobelin tapestry, which is hand-woven over fine cord. The imitation is painted on a machine-woven rep canvas : the term rep is a corruption of the Saxon terra *wrepp*, or *rape*, a cord, Dutch *roop*, from which we get the word rope. In the Gobelins the shading of the different tints of wool that form a picture, or other designs, are put in by hand work, or shuttles moved by the hand, and on the wrong side of the picture, and the threads of wool, the weft run longitudinally, not horizontally, so that when the design is finished the picture is turned horizontally, and is complete. In Tapestry Painting the *rep* of the canvas is from right to left (horizontal), and this is then painted over and forms a picture in imitation of the Gobelin tapestry. The latter is so named after its French inventor, Giles Gobelin, about 1520. The house in which he lived was purchased by Louis XIV. for a manufactory of tapestry for adorning palaces, the designs for which were drawn by Le Brun, a celebrated French painter, about 1666. Her Majesty Queen Victoria has caused a school to be established at Windsor, where the art of making "Gobelin Tapestry" is successfully taught.

2126. Tapestry of Auxerre.—This town, in the northern part of the province of Burgundy, was once famous for its tapestry of a peculiar make. The design was handwoven in small patches of colour, and then was sewed together at the back to form the picture. Tapestry painting in blocks or masses of a single colour successfully imitates this tapestry.

2127. SEWING MACHINES.

These exceedingly useful modern inventions, which perform the operation of sewing much more expeditiously than can be accomplished by hand, are now almost indispensable requisites in every home. The ordinary Family Machine is usually made so as to be worked by treadle or hand, and is supplied with various appliances for binding, cording, hemming, quilting, tucking, gathering, &c. A really good and serviceable machine, with the usual accessories, and case, can be purchased for from £4 to £6.

2128. CEMENTS.

The term "cement" includes all those substances employed for the purpose of causing the adhesion of two or more bodies, whether originally separate, or divided by an accidental fracture. As the various substances that may require cementing differ very much in texture, &c., a number of cements possessed of very different properties are required, because a cement that answers admirably under one set of circumstances may be perfectly useless in others. The general principles upon which the success or failure of cementing usually depends are :—The different parts of a solid are held together by an attraction between their several particles, which is termed the attraction of cohesion. This attraction acts only when the particles are in the closest possible contact : even air must not be between them. If, after breaking any substance, we could bring the particles into as close a contact as before, and perfectly exclude the air, they would re-unite, and be as strongly connected as ever. But in general this is impossible ; small particles of grit and dust get between them ; the film of interposed air cannot be removed ; and thus, however firmly we press the edges of a broken cup together, it remains cracked china still. The cohesion between the particles of the cement is very much less than the adhesion of the cement to other bodies ; and if torn apart, the connected joint gives way, not by the loosening of the adhesion, but by the layer of cement splitting down the centre. Hence the important rule that the *less* cement in a joint the stronger it is. To unite broken substances with a thick cement is disadvantageous, the object being to bring the surfaces as closely together as possible. The general principles that ought always to be borne in mind having been mentioned, the manufacture and uses of some of the more useful cements may be described.

2129. Mouth Glue.—The very useful preparation sold under this title is merely a thin cake of soluble glue, which, when moistened with the tongue, furnishes a ready means of uniting papers, &c. It is made by dissolving one pound of fine glue or gelatine in water, and adding half-a-pound of brown sugar, boiling the whole until it is sufficiently thick to become solid on cooling ; it is then poured into moulds, or on a slab slightly greased, and cut into the required shape when cool.

2130. Liquid Glue.—The liquid glue of the shops is made by dissolving shellac in water, by boiling it along with borax, which possesses the peculiar property of causing the solution of the resinous lac. This preparation is convenient from its cheapness and freedom from smell ; but it gives way if exposed to long-continued damp, which that made with naphtha resists.

2131. Common Glue.—This is prepared from the chippings of the hides, hoofs, &c., of animals. They are first soaked for two or three weeks in lime water, and afterwards boiled and skimmed ; the solution is then strained through baskets and gently

evaporated to a due consistence, then cooled in wooden moulds, cut into slices, and dried upon nets.

2132. To Melt Glue.—This should always be done in a glue-pot or double vessel, to prevent its being burned, which injures it very materially. It is difficult to heat the glue in the inner vessel to the boiling point ; this, however, can be obviated by employing in the outer vessel some liquid which boils at a higher temperature than pure water, such as a saturated solution of salt (made by adding one-third as much salt as water). This boils at 224° Fahr., or 12° above the heat of boiling water, and enables the glue in the inner vessel to be heated to a much higher temperature than when pure water is employed. If a saturated solution of nitre is used, the temperature rises still higher.

2133. Marine Glue.—In point of strength, all ordinary cements yield the palm to Jeffery's Patent Marine Glue, a compound of India-rubber, shellac, and coal-tar naphtha. Small quantities can be purchased at most of the tool warehouses, at cheaper rates than it can be made. The colour of this glue, however, prevents its being much used.

2134. Diamond Cement.—Soak isinglass in water till it is soft ; then dissolve it in the smallest possible quantity of proof spirit, by the aid of a gentle heat ; in two ounces of this mixture dissolve ten grains of ammoniacum, and whilst still liquid add half-a-drachm of mastic, dissolved in three drachms of rectified spirit ; stir well together, and put into small bottles for sale. *Directions for Use.*—Liquefy the cement by plunging the bottle in hot water, and use it directly. The cement improves the oftener the bottle is thus warmed ; it resists the action of water and moisture perfectly.

2135. Rice Flour Cement—An excellent cement may be made from rice flour, which is at present used for that purpose in China and Japan. It is only necessary to mix the rice flour intimately with cold water, and gently simmer it over a fire, when it readily forms a delicate and durable cement, not only answering all the purposes of common paste, but admirably adapted for joining together paper, cards, &c., in forming the various beautiful and tasteful ornaments which afford much employment and amusement to the ladies. When made of the consistence of plaster-clay, models, busts, bas-relievos, &c., may be formed of it ; and the articles, when dry, are susceptible of high polish, and are very durable.

2136. Lime and Egg Cement.— The white of an egg, well beaten with quicklime, and a small quantity of very old cheese, forms an excellent substitute for cement, when wanted in a hurry, either for broken china or old ornamental glass-ware.

2137. Colourless Cement for China, Glass, &c.—This cement, being nearly colourless, possesses advantages which liquid glue and other cements do not.—Dissolve half-an-ounce of gum acacia in a wineglass of boiling water ; add plaster of Paris sufficient to form a thick paste, and apply it with a brush to the parts required to be cemented together.

2138. White Lead as Cement— Cracked vessels of earthenware and glass may often be usefully, though not ornamentally, repaired by white lead spread on strips of calico, and secured with bands of twine.

2139. Coaguline.—An exceed-ingly strong, and at the same time a transparent and colourless cement is made by Messrs. Kay, Brothers, of Stockport, and is sold by most fancy stationers and chemists under the name of Coaguline. It is easily and quickly applied, and will be found extremely serviceable in repairing glass, china, and stone articles. It is inexpensive.

2140. Red Cement, which is employed by instrument makers for cementing glass to metals, and which is very cheap, and exceedingly useful for a variety of purposes, is made by melting five parts of black resin, one part of yellow wax, and then stirring in gradually one part of red ochre or Venetian red, in fine powder, and previously *well dried.* This cement requires to be melted before use, and it adheres better if the objects to which it is applied are warmed.

2141. Cement for Leather and Cloth.—An adhesive material for uniting the parts of boots and shoes, and for the seams of articles of cloth-ing, may be made thus :—Take one pound of gutta-percha, four ounces of India-rubber, two ounces of pitch, one ounce of shellac, two ounces of oil. The ingredients are to be melted together, and used hot.

2142. Cement for Bicycle Tyres. Take two parts of asphalt and one part of gutta-percha, and melt them together. When quite hot put it on the wheel, which should also be warmed, and then fit on the tyre.

2143. A Soft Cement for Corks, useful for covering the corks of pre-served fruit and other bottles, is made by melting yellow wax with an equal quantity of resin, or of common turpentine (not oil of turpentine, but the resin), using the latter for a very soft cement, and stirring in some dried Venetian red.

2144. Mastic Cement.—This is employed for making a superior coat-ing to inside walls, but must not be confounded with the *resin mastic.* It is made by mixing twenty parts of well-washed and sifted sharp sand with two parts of litharge and one of freshly burned and slaked quicklime, in fine *dry* powder. This is made into a putty, by mixing with linseed oil. It sets in a few hours, having the appearance of light stone ; and we mention it, as it may be frequently employed with advantage in repairing broken stonework (as steps), by filling up the missing parts. The employment of Roman cement, plaster, &c, for masonry work, hardly comes within the scope of this volume.

2145. Paste is usually made by rubbing up flour with cold water, and boiling ; if a little alum is mixed before boiling it is much improved, being less clammy, working more freely in the brush, and thinner, a less quantity is required, and it is therefore stronger. If required in large quantity, as for papering rooms, it may be made by mixing one quartern of flour, one quarter-pound of alum, and a little warm water ; when mixed, the requisite quantity of boiling water should be poured on whilst the mixture is being stirred. Paste is only adapted to cementing paper ; when used it should be spread on one side of the paper, which should then be folded with the pasted side inwards, and allowed to remain a few minutes before being opened and used ; this swells the paper, and permits its being more smoothly and securely attached. If kept for a few days, paste becomes mouldy, and after a short time putrid ; this inconvenience may be obviated by the use of the following—

2146. Permanent Paste is made by adding to each half-pint of flour paste without alum, fifteen grains of corrosive sublimate, previously rubbed to powder in a mortar, the whole to be well mixed ; this, if prevented from drying, by being kept in a covered pot, remains good any length of time, and is therefore convenient ; but unfortunately it is extremely poisonous, though its excessively nauseous taste would prevent its being swallowed accidentally. It possesses the great advantage of not being liable to the attacks of insects.

2147. FRENCH POLISHES.

i. **Naphtha Polish.**—Shellac, three pounds ; wood naphtha, three quarts. Put the shellac in the naphtha and let it dissolve.

ii. **Spirit Polish.**—Shellac, two pounds ; powdered mastic and sandarac, of each one ounce ; copal varnish, half-a-pint ; spirits of wine, one gallon. Digest in the cold till dissolved.

2148. INKS.—There are many recipes published for making ink ; the following is as useful and economical a mode of producing good ink as any of them—

2149. Writing-Ink.—Boil eight ounces of galls in coarse powder, and four ounces of logwood, in thin chips, in twelve pints of rain water for one hour ; strain the liquor, and add four ounces of green copperas, three ounces of powdered gum arabic, one ounce of blue vitriol, and one ounce of coarse sugar ; stir the mixture until the whole be dissolved, then let it subside for twenty-four hours ; strain it off speedily, and put it by in stone bottles for use.

2150. Ink Powder is formed of the dry ingredients for ink, powdered and mixed. Powdered galls, two pounds ; powdered green vitriol, one pound ; powdered gum, eight ounces. Two ounces of this mixture will make one pint of ink.

2151. Red Writing Ink.—Best ground Brazil wood, four ounces ; diluted acetic acid, one pint ; alum, half-an-ounce. Boil the ingredients slowly in an enamelled vessel for one hour, strain, and add an ounce of gum.

2152. Indian Ink.—Take finest lamp-black and make it into a thick paste with thin isinglass ; size it, then mould it, and scent with a little essence of musk.

2153. Marking Ink.—There are several recipes for this ink, but the following is said to be one of the best of its kind :—Dissolve separately, one ounce of nitrate of silver, and one and a half ounce of best washing soda in distilled or rain water. Mix the solutions, and collect and wash the precipitate in a filter ; whilst still moist, rub it up in a marble or Wedgwood mortar with three drachms of tartaric acid ; add two ounces of distilled water, mix six drachms of white sugar, and ten drachms of powdered gum-arabic, half-an-ounce of archil, and water to make up six ounces in measure.

2154. Ink for Zinc Garden-Labels.—Verdigris, one ounce ; sal-ammoniac, one ounce ; lamp-black, half-an-ounce ; water, half-a-pint. Mix in an earthenware mortar, without using a metal spatula. *Directions.*— To be shaken before use, and used with a clean *quill* pen, on bright zinc. *Note.*—Another kind of ink for zinc is also used, made of chloride of platinum, five grains, dissolved in one ounce of distilled or rain water ; but the first, which is much less expensive, answers perfectly, if used as directed, on clean bright zinc.

2155. TRACING PAPER.—Mix together by a gentle heat, one ounce of Canada balsam, and a quarter of a pint of spirits of turpentine ; with a soft brush spread it thinly over one side of good tissue paper. The composition dries quickly, is very transparent, and not greasy, and, therefore, does not stain the paper to which it is applied.

2156. TO DESTROY RATS.

The following recipe originated with Dr. Ure, and is highly recommended as the best known means of getting rid of these most obnoxious and destructive vermin.—Melt hog's-lard in a bottle plunged in water, heated to about 150 degrees Fahrenheit ; introduce into it half-an-ounce of phosphorus for every pound of lard ; then add a pint of proof spirit, or whisky ; cork the bottle firmly after its contents have been heated to 150 degrees, taking it at the same time out of the water, and agitate smartly till the phosphorus becomes uniformly diffused, forming a milky-looking liquid. This liquid, when cooled, will afford a white compound of phosphorus and lard. As the spirit spontaneously separates, it may be poured off and used again for the same purpose. This compound, on being warmed very gently, may be poured out into a mixture of wheat flour and sugar, incorporated therewith, and then flavoured with oil of rhodium, or with oil of aniseed, &c. The dough, being made into pellets, is to be laid into rat holes. Being luminous in the dark it attracts their notice, and being agreeable to their palates it is readily eaten, and proves certainly fatal.

Note.—Chloride of lime is a good preventive, as rats have an extreme aversion to it.

2157. TO KILL BEETLES.

i. Place a few lumps of unslaked lime where they frequent.

ii. Set a dish or trap containing a little beer or syrup at the bottom, and place a few sticks slanting against its sides, so as to form a sort of gangway for the beetles to climb up it, when they will go headlong into the bait set for them.

iii Mix equal weights of red lead, sugar, and flour, and place it nightly near their haunts. This mixture, made into sheets, forms the beetle wafers sold at the oil shops.

2158. To Kill Cockroaches.—A teacupful of well-bruised plaster of Paris, mixed with double the quantity of oatmeal, to which a little sugar may be added. Strew it on the floor, or in the chinks where they frequent.

Speaking of these insects. Josh Billings says:—"The cockroach iz one ov the luxurys of civilizashun. Their food seems to consist not so much ov what they eat az what they kan git into ; and often finding them ded in the soup, at mi boarding house, I have cum tew the painful conclusion that the cockroach kan't swim, but that he kan float for a longtime."

2159. To Destroy Ants.—Drop some quicklime on the mouth of their nest, and wash it in with boiling water ; or dissolve some camphor in spirits of wine, then mix with water, and pour into their haunts ; or tobacco-water has been found effectual. They greatly dislike strong scents. Camphor, or a sponge saturated with creosote, will prevent their infesting a cupboard. To prevent their climbing up trees, place a ring of tar about the trunk, or a circle of rag moistened occasionally with creosote.

Sprigs of winter-green or ground-ivy will drive away red ants ; and wormwood will serve the same purpose for black ants.

2160. TO DESTROY BUGS.—Spirits of naphtha rubbed with a small painters' brush into every part of a bedstead is a certain way of getting rid of bugs. The mattress and binding of the bed should be examined and treated in the same way, as they generally harbour more in those parts than in the bedstead. Three pennyworth of naphtha is sufficient for one bed.

2161. Poison for Bugs. —Mix proof spirit, one pint ; camphor, two ounces ; oil of turpentine, four ounces ; corrosive sublimate, one ounce.

A correspondent says, "I have been for a long time troubled with bugs, and never could get rid of them by any clean and expeditious method, until a friend told me to suspend a small bag of camphor to the bed, just in the centre, overhead. I did so, and the enemy was most effectually repulsed, and has not made his appearance since—not even for a reconnaissance !" This is a simple method of getting rid of these pests, and is worth a trial to see if it be effectual in other cases.

2162. TO KILL FLIES.

i Take half-a-teaspoonful of black pepper in powder, one teaspoonful of sugar, and one tablespoonful of cream ; mix them well together, and place them in the room on a plate, where the flies are troublesome, and they will soon disappear.

ii. Cold green tea, very strong, and sweetened with sugar, will, when set about the room in saucers, attract flies and destroy them.

iii Twenty drops of carbolic acid evaporated on a hot pan or shovel will generally drive flies out of a room.

2163. Blue-bottles may be kept away from a meat-safe by placing a plate containing some water and permanganate of potash near the door of the safe.

2164. Mosquitoes can be driven out of a room by holding over a lamp a piece of camphor gum, about the size of a nutmeg or walnut.

2165. REMEDY FOR BLISTERED FEET.—Rub the feet, on going to bed, with spirits mixed with tallow, dropped from a lighted candle into the palm of the hand.

2166. BUNIONS may be checked in their early development by binding the joint with adhesive plaster, and keeping it on as long as any uneasiness is felt. The bandaging should be perfect, and it might be well to extend it round the foot. An inflamed bunion should be poulticed, and larger shoes be worn. Iodine, twelve grains, and lard or spermaceti ointment, half-an-ounce, make a capital ointment for bunions. It should be rubbed on gently twice or thrice a day.

2167. CORNS.—Any remedy for these painful growths, to be effectual, must include removal of the usual cause—pressure by tight or ill-fitting boots. Strong acetic acid may be used, but great care is necessary in applying it, to avoid burning the adjacent parts. *Soft corns* may be cured by extract of lead.

2168. Celandine is an excellent remedy for corns. It is harmless and easily applied. Any chemist will supply it.

2169. SQUINTING.—This frequently arises from the unequal strength of the eyes, the weaker eye being turned away from the object, to avoid the fatigue of exertion. Cases of squinting of long standing have often been cured by covering the stronger eye, and thereby compelling the weaker one to exertion, or correcting the eyes with properly-selected glasses.

2170. COD-LIVER OIL.—This very beneficial drug, formerly so unpopular on account of its rank odour and nauseous taste, has of late years largely increased in consumption through the skilful manipulations of modern science in its preparation, whereby both the smell and the flavour have been almost entirely removed, rendering it capable of being taken by even the most delicate stomach. It is extremely efficacious in cases of consumption and debility, checking the emaciation, regulating the appetite, and restoring vitality. Coffee, new milk, and orange wine, whichever the patient may fancy, are among the best mediums for taking the oil.

2171. OFFENSIVE BREATH, Remedy for.—From six to ten drops of the concentrated solution of chloride of soda in a wineglassful of pure spring water, taken immediately after completing the morning toilet. In some cases, the odour arising from carious teeth is combined with that of the stomach. If the mouth be well rinsed with a teaspoonful of the solution of the chloride in a tumbler of water, the bad odour of the teeth will be removed.

2172. Breath tainted by Onions.—Leaves of parsley, eaten with vinegar, will prevent the disagreeable consequences of eating onions.

2173. AN IMPROMPTU TRAVELLING-CAP.—Take your pocket handkerchief, and laying it out the full square, double down *one-third* over the other part. Then raise the whole and turn it over, so that the third folded down now shall be underneath. Take hold of one of the folded corners, and draw its point towards the centre ; then do the same with the other, as in making a cocked-hat, or a boat, of paper. Then take hold of the two remaining corners, and twisting the hem of the handkerchief, continue to roll it until it meets the double corners brought to the centre, and catches them up a little. Lift the whole, and you will perceive the form of a cap, which, when applied to the head, will cover the head and ears, and, being tied under the chin, will not come off. Very little practice will enable you to regulate the size of the folds so as to fit the head.

2174. TO PREVENT GALLING IN INVALIDS.—The white of an egg beaten to a strong froth ; then drop in gradually, whilst you are beating, two teaspoonfuls of spirits of wine ; put it into a bottle, and apply occasionally with a feather.

2175. TO CLEAN ARTISTS' BRUSHES.—Artists' brushes used for oil-colours should not be allowed to dry, but the paint should be squeezed out on the palette, and the brush cleaned with turpentine or oil. Some artists clean their brushes with soap, rubbed into a lather.

2176. INDOOR GAMES.—[See also EVENING PASTIMES, pars. 48 to 78, and CARD GAMES, pars. 79 to 137.]

2177. BAGATELLE is played on an oblong board usually from six to ten feet long by a foot and a half to three feet in width. The bed of the table is of slate covered with a fine green cloth ; and at the upper end, which is rounded, there are nine holes or cups, numbered from 1 to 9, thus :—

Into these holes ivory balls are driven by a leather-pointed cue. The player stands at the lower end of the table ; and his object is to hole the balls successively into the several cups. Nine balls are used, eight white and one coloured, or seven white with two coloured balls. The coloured ball is placed on a spot just in front of the 1 hole ; and the game is played as follows.

2178. Rules of Bagatelle.

i. Any number of persons may play, whether singly or on sides.

ii. Each player strings for lead, and he whose ball falls into the highest hole begins.

iii. The winner of the lead plays the nine balls successively up the table from baulk, first striking at the coloured ball on the spot.

iv. The coloured ball must be first struck ; and the rest of the balls are played up to the holes, the sum total of all the holes filled being the striker's score.

v. The coloured ball counts double when holed, and each white ball scores towards game a number corresponding to that marked in the hole (when two coloured balls are used, each counts double).

vi. A ball rebounding beyond the baulk line, or forced off the table, is put aside and not re-used in that round.

vii. Any number of rounds agreed on may be played, and the highest aggregate total by a player or by partners wins the game.

2179. The French Game (*or* **Sans Egal**) is played as follows :—The player who wins the lead takes four balls, leaving the other four for his opponent, and placing the coloured ball on the spot. He plays at it from baulk, and scores all he can. The other player then strikes up one of his balls, and so on alternately ; the maker of the highest number of points winning. The game is 101. While the coloured

ball is on the table, it must be struck, and when it is holed it counts double, in addition to any other score made by the same stroke. If either player hole his adversary's ball he forfeits to him the number scored by the stroke. If he fail to strike the black ball he forfeits five points. The rules as to rebounding balls, foul strokes, &c., are the same as in the ordinary game.

2180. Old Cannon Game, sometimes played on a table without holes or pockets, consists entirely of cannons—two balls struck in succession by the player's ball. The game, 50 or 100 up, each cannon counting two points, is played with three balls only—a white, spot-white, and black (or red) ball. When played on the ordinary bagatelle table, the holes filled after making a cannon score to the player. One point is forfeited for missing the white, five points for missing the red ; and all points made without a cannon. The players go on alternately, the first who scores the stipulated number winning the game.

2181. The Irish Game is played with three balls. It consists of winning hazards and cannons only. The cannon counts two, and the hazard the number of the hole into which a ball is put.

2182. Mississippi, Trou Madame, Cockamaroo, and other toy-games, are sometimes played on the bagatelle table ; but they need no description. To play well at any of the games, however, requires great care and nicety. Much depends on the manner of holding and using the cue, and the slight degree of force employed in making the stroke. Some experts are able to fill all the holes at one essay, placing the coloured balls in the 8 and 7 at the first stroke, and then playing direct at the cups or at the cushion, till all the balls are holed.

2183. BILLIARDS.

This well-known game of skill is played on a rectangular table measuring twelve feet long by six broad, with three ivory balls,—white, spot-white, and red ; the object being to drive one or other of them into either of the six pockets, and to strike one ball against the two others. The first stroke is known as a hazard, and the second as a cannon. The instrument for striking at the ball is a long tapering stick called a cue ; and the game is scored by hazards, cannons, misses, and forfeitures. The ball struck with the cue is known as the player's ball ; the ball played at as the object ball. A ball struck into a pocket is a winning hazard ; the player's ball falling into a pocket after contact with the white or red, is a losing hazard. Three principal games are played on the billiard table—the *English game*, or *Billiards*, *Pyramids*, and *Pool*.

2184. English Billiards—the best of all the games—is usually played 50 or 100 up. The points are thus reckoned—three for each red hazard, two for each white hazard, and two for each cannon. A *coup*—that is, running in a pocket, or off the table without striking a ball—is forfeiture of three points ; a miss gives one point to the adversary. The game commences by striking for lead and choice of balls. The red ball is placed on the spot at the top of the table, and the first player either strikes at it with his own ball, playing from baulk, or gives a miss. Every time the red ball is pocketed, it is replaced on the spot. He who makes a hazard or cannon goes on playing till he fails to score. Then the other goes on, and so they play alternately till one or other completes the required number of points, and wins the game.

2185. Pyramids is a game played by two persons, or by four in sides, two against two. Fifteen coloured balls are placed in the form of a triangle or pyramid, *actually touching one another*, with the apex towards the player thus—

The centre of the apex ball covers the second or pyramid spot. The game consists entirely of winning hazards, and he who succeeds in pocketing the greatest number of balls wins. The first player plays at the pyramid with the white ball from baulk, and if he succeeds in pocketing one of the coloured balls scores one point and proceeds to play with the white ball upon any other ball until he fails to pocket one, when his adversary continues the game until he also fails to score. If a player either pockets the white ball or misses the other balls he forfeits one point and also loses his turn.

2186. Pool.—A game played by several persons, consisting of winning hazards only. Each player subscribes a certain stake to form a pool or gross sum, and at starting has three chances or lives. He then draws haphazard from a bag one of a series of marked or coloured balls, and the game proceeds thus : The white ball is placed on the spot, and the red is played on to it from baulk. If the player pocket the white he receives the price of a life from the owner of that ball ; but if he fail, the next player (yellow) plays on the red ; and so on alternately till all have played, or till a ball is pocketed. When a ball is pocketed the striker plays at the ball nearest his own, and goes on playing as long as he can score. The first player who loses his three lives can *star* : that is, he can purchase as many lives as are held by the lowest number remaining in the pool. The order of play is usually red upon white, yellow upon red, green upon yellow, brown upon green, blue upon brown, black upon blue, spot-white upon black, white upon spot-white ; and this order is retained so long as all the original players remain in the game. When the number of players is reduced to two, they can, if they possess an equality of lives, as two each, or one each, divide the stake ; or they may by agreement play out the game for the entire pool.

2187. Black Pool is ordinary pool with the addition of a black ball, which is placed on the centre spot. When, after pocketing the ball proper to be played on, the black is struck into a pocket, each player pays the price of a life to the striker.

2188. Skittle Pool is pool with three balls and twelve little skittles, placed in order round the table. A stake is determined on, and a price paid out of the pool for every skittle knocked over after striking a ball. An amusing game for a party of ladies and gentlemen.

2189. Single Pool is the game of Pool, but played by two persons, each having one ball and trying to pocket his opponent's for a money stake upon each life.

2190. Shell Out *or* **Penny Pot** is a game of pyramids (*see par.* 2185), played by any number of players, who each pay a penny to the player pocketing a coloured ball, but any player accidentally pocketing the white ball has to pay a penny to each of the other players.

For the scientific principles of Billiards, and the full rules of the several games played on the billiard-table, the reader is referred to the excellent little shilling volume, *Billiards Made Easy,** and to other elaborate treatises.

2191. BOSS ; OR THE FIFTEEN PUZZLE.—Apparently simple, this game is really difficult of solution. Fifteen cubes of wood, severally marked from 1 to 15, are placed indif-

* *Billiards Made Easy.* With the Scientific Principles of the Spot-stroke, and the Side-stroke, famililarly explained. Illustrated by diagrams. With a chapter on Bagatelle. Houlston and Sons. 1s.

ferently in a box made to hold sixteen ; thus—

9	11	3	7
8	14	10	15
6	12	13	2
5	1	4	

1	2	3	4
5	6	7	8
9	10	11	12
13	14	15	

The puzzle consists in sliding the cubes from square to square, without lifting them or removing them from the box, until they are placed in their natural order. It is easy enough to move the squares up to 12 ; but to get the last three into order is often a puzzle indeed. If the figures fall in either of the following positions—13, 15, 14 ; 14, 13, 15 ; or 15, 14, 13— the problem is unsolvable ; it follows, therefore, that the last row must be either 14, 15, 13 ; or 15, 13, 14. If you get the cubes into either of these positions, you can easily bring them right ; but if you cannot, the only way is to begin the game all over again.

2192. THE THIRTY-FOUR PUZZLE.—This is an adaptation of the old magic square, which amused the philosophers of old. A sketch of it appears in Albert Durer's painting of Melancholia. Sixteen discs or squares, numbered from 1 to 16, are placed indifferently on the table—or they may be in the fifteen box ; and the puzzle is to so arrange them as to make the sum of the figures add up to 34, whether counted up, down, across or angularly. Here is the solution :—

1	15	14	4
12	6	7	9
8	10	11	5
13	3	2	16

1	8	13	12
14	11	2	7
4	5	16	9
15	10	3	6

This is the simplest ; but a more elaborate plan is to so arrange the figures that any form of the blocks will form a square sum of 34. See the annexed solution, which the ingenious may still farther complicate:—

16	3	2	13
5	10	11	8
9	6	7	12
4	15	14	1

2193. FOX AND GEESE.—This old-fashioned game is played on a solitaire board. Seventeen geese occupy the upper part of the board lines, with the fox in the middle, thus—

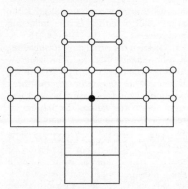

The object of the game is to confine the fox in a corner, so that he cannot move. The geese march forward in straight lines, *not on the diagonals* ; and whenever a goose is on the spot next the fox, the latter can take him, as in draughts, by jumping over to the vacant spot beyond. The fox can move backwards, forwards, or sideways on the straight lines ; but the geese must go forward, and are not allowed to retreat. Properly played, the geese must win ; but when the number of geese is reduced to six, it is impossible for them to confine the fox. There are several ways of playing the game, by placing the fox and geese in other positions, or by insisting on the fox catching all the geese. In the latter case, the fox chooses his own starting place. The game may also be played with eight geese and a fox.

2194. THE ROYAL GAME OF GOOSE.—In the old German game the figure of a goose is printed on a large sheet of paper, and divided into 63 squares or divisions. The object of the players,—any number of whom may join in the game—is to make 63 points by successive throws of two dice. A pool is made by equal contributions by the players, the first of whom gaining the required number wins. The players throw alternately and add each individual throw to that already made. Each player's position is shown on the goose by a counter, a wafer, or any small article. Any number beyond 63 sends the thrower back as many points as he exceeds 63. Thus if he were 58, and by a 6 and 5 he threw eleven he would go forward 5 squares to 63, and back 6 squares from 63. In addition to this, certain numbers on the goose are barred ; and if the player make them he is fined two counters, which are added to the pool. The numbered goose is sold at most toy shops, but a numbered draughtboard will serve as well.

2195. OBSTACLES, OR DINING-ROOM GOLF.

This is played by two or more persons (four or six make the best game) on an ordinary dining-table, covered with a green baize cloth, on which the "obstacles," such as hedges, banks, &c., are placed with a ring between each.

The object of the game is to see who can get round the course first, and is played with large and small counters, the small counters being made to jump forward by drawing the larger counters across them until the pressure on the edge of the small one causes it to be "snicked" away from the player.

Each player on starting places his counter on the starting line, and in his turn snicks it over the fence or other obstacle. Only one try is allowed, until all the other players have had their turns, when it comes round to the first player again.

Only one snick at a time is allowed, except on entering a ring, when the player may have one snick at the next fence.

When the player has cleared a fence, he must snick his counter inside a ring, before attempting to clear another fence from the line adjoining the ring.

The second and third fences are usually larger than the others, and in trying to clear these the counter often becomes lodged on the platform of the fence. In this case the player may (1) try to clear the remainder of the fence from the spot where his counter lies, or (2) he may snick his counter back to a favourable position and from there try a fresh shot.

If the small counter should chance to rest edgeways on a ring, the player may with the counter, held in his right hand, push the small counter over the edge and into the hole, taking the ring in his *left* hand.

Should the small counter fall on the floor, it is to be picked up and placed close to the edge of the table, in line with the spot where it started from and the spot where it fell.

2196. OUT-DOOR PASTIMES.

2197. ARCHERY.

This sport was greatly encouraged in olden days, and it is still a favourite pastime with a good many people.

The Bows are made of Lance-wood. Yew, Hickory, Snake-wood, &c., and one should be selected which is adapted to the player's height and strength. A man's bow may have a pull of fifty or sixty pounds, but a lady, as a rule, will find a pull of thirty to thirty-six pounds quite sufficient. A good weight of pull for general use is forty-two pounds for distances of not more than one hundred yards, and fifty pounds for longer distances. The distance of the string from the centre of the bow when strung should be between five and six inches.

The arrows used should be proportioned in length and weight to the bow for which they are intended. For bows of five feet, twenty-four inch arrows are used ; for five feet nine inches, twenty-seven inch arrows, and for six feet, from twenty-eight to thirty inches. The notches should be lined with horn. The feathers are of goose or turkey, and three in number ; one is of a different colour to the others and is called the "cock" feather ; this is always to be placed uppermost.

The part of the string which receives the arrow is whipped with silk, to prevent the string being rubbed and weakened.

The usual mark is a target some four feet in diameter, placed at distances varying from fifty to one hundred yards or more. The target has a gold centre, surrounded by rings of red, blue, black, and white, with an outside border of green. The gold, when hit, scores nine ; the red, seven ; the blue, five ; black, three ; and white, one ; and the player who scores the greatest value in hits wins the match.

There are over one hundred archery clubs in Great Britain, one of the oldest (except the Honourable Artillery Company) being the Royal Toxophilite Society, which was founded in 1780.

In the act of shooting with the bow the whole muscles of the body are called into play, and it is particularly necessary that the legs should be planted firmly on the ground, otherwise the body will be thrown off its equilibrium and the aim destroyed. In discharging the arrow from the bow the string should be quickly loosed but without a jerk or jar, nor should the hand or elbow be either elevated or depressed, for the slightest derangement in the delivery of the arrow weakens its aim. The archer should study the wind so as to make allowances for the various currents of air.

2198. LAWN BILLIARDS OR TROCO.—This is a game that may be played by any number of persons in a field or open space. The implements are wooden balls and long-handled cues, at the ends of which are spoonlike ovals of iron. In the centre of the ground is fixed a ring of iron, which moves freely on a pivot, the spike of the ring being driven into a piece of wood let into the ground. The wooden ball is lifted from the ground by means of the spoon-ended cue, and thrown towards the ring—the object of the player being to pass the ball through the ring ; and he who succeeds in making any given number of points by fairly ringing his ball, or cannoning against the other balls, wins the game. Cannons are made by the player striking two balls successively with his own ball fairly delivered from his spoon. Considerable skill is required in throwing the ball, as the ring, turning freely on its pivot, twists round on being struck, and to "make the ring," it is necessary that the ball be thrown fairly through its centre. But in order to get nearer to it a judicious player will endeavour to make two or three cannons, if the balls lie within a convenient distance and at a proper angle to each other.

The game is played fifteen, twenty-one, or any other determined number of points. The balls should be perfectly round and smooth. They are generally made of boxwood or lignum vitae, and weigh about three to five lbs. each ; the balls, cues, &c., are sold by most dealers in croquet implements.

2199. Rules of Lawn Billiards.

i. The game may be played by two or more persons, each of whom is provided with a ball and a cue. When more than two play, sides are chosen, and the side which first makes the requisite number of points wins the game.

ii. The players stand in a circle, in the centre of which is set up the pivot ring.

iii. Each player starts from any portion of the circle distant not less than four yards from the ring. The first player lifts his ball with the spoon-cue, and throws it towards the ring ; each of the others taking his turn alternately— the balls remaining on the ground where they stop rolling.

iv. If the first player fail to "make his ring," the next goes on, who may either throw at the ring or at the ball in the circle.

v. Partners may assist each other in getting near the ring ; but no player, at starting, may step within four yards of the ring.

vi. *Two* points are counted for every cannon, and *three* for every fairly-made ring ; and successive points are reckoned for any number of rings or cannons.

vii. Each player goes on till he fails to cannon or ring his ball, when the next plays ; and so on, till the required number of points are made.

viii. One point is taken off the player's score for every foul stroke. Foul strokes are made by touching a ball with hand or person while it is in play ; by playing with a wrong ball ; by playing out of turn ; by overturning the ring ; and by making two or more steps while throwing the ball.

ix. Each player, after the start, must go on from the place at which his ball was left after the previous stroke.

x. All disputed points must be settled by the umpire, whose decision is final.

xi. No ball in play must be removed from its position except by a stroke from another ball, and every ball is considered to be in play while it is within the circle, which may be of any dimensions chosen by the players previous to the commencement of the game.

2200. CROQUET.

This out-door pastime is of comparatively modern creation, and until quite lately was very much in vogue. It may be played by persons of all ages and of either sex ; but it is especially adapted for ladies and young persons, as it demands but slight personal exertion, while it affords delightful and health-giving sport.

The ground is preferably a grass plot of an oblong form ; but an ordinary lawn or expanse of even turf will answer the purpose, so long as it is of sufficient extent for the operations of the game.

The implements are balls, mallets, starting and turning pegs, croquet clips or markers, hoops or arches.

Arrangement of the Hoops.—The starting peg is driven in at one end of the ground, and the turning peg at the other extremity. Between these pegs the hoops are fixed at distances of about eight or ten feet apart, and so arranged as to afford good opportunities for the display of address and skill on the part of the players.

The game consists in striking the balls from the starting peg through the hoops up one side of the ground to the peg at the opposite extremity, and then back again through the hoops on the other side to the starting peg. The game may be played by any number of persons not exceeding eight. A larger number renders the game tedious. The best number is four. If two only play, each player may take two balls, and when as many as eight play, there should be two sides or sets. Each player takes a mallet, ball, and croquet clip of a distinctive colour or number, the clip being used to indicate the hoop at which, in his turn, he aims. The division into sides, choice of balls, mallets, &c., is determined by the players among themselves.

2201. Laws of Croquet.

i. There shall be no restriction to the number, weight, size, shape, or material of the mallets : nor as to the attitude or position of the striker : nor as to the part of the mallet held, provided the ball is not struck with the handle, nor the mace stroke used. The balls used in matches must be 3⅝ inches in diameter.

ii. The players shall toss for choice of lead and of balls : and in a succession of games shall take the lead alternately and keep the same balls.

iii. In commencing, each ball shall be placed at one foot from the first hoop in a direct line between the pegs, and a ball having been struck is at once in play, and can roquet another or be roqueted, whether it shall have made the first hoop or not.

iv. A stroke is considered to have been taken if a ball is moved in the act of striking, but should the player in taking aim have struck it accidentally, and the umpire be satisfied that the stroke was accidental, the ball is replaced and the stroke taken again. If a ball be moved in taking aim, and then struck again without being replaced, the stroke is foul.

v. If the player make a foul stroke he loses his turn and all the points or roquets made therein, and the balls remain where they lie, at the option of the adversary. The following are considered foul strokes :

(*a*) To strike with the mallet another ball instead of, or besides one's own in making the stroke. (*b*) To spoon, that is, to push a ball without an audible knock. (*c*) To strike a ball twice in the same stroke. (*d*) To touch, stop, or divert the course of a ball when in play and rolling, whether this be done by the striker or his partner. (*e*) To allow a ball to touch the mallet (or any part of the player's person) in rebounding from a peg or wire. (*f*) To move a ball which lies close to a peg or wire by striking the peg or wire (*i.e.* to touch with the mallet a wire or peg in making the stroke). (*g*) To press a ball round a peg or wire (crushing stroke). (*h*) To play a stroke after roquet without taxing croquet. (*i*) To fail to move both balls in taking croquet. (*k*) To croquet a ball which the striker is not entitled to croquet.

vi. A player continues to play so long as he makes a point or hits a ball. A point consists in making a hoop or hitting the turning peg in order.

vii. The ball has made its hoop when, having passed through from the playing side and ceased to roll, it cannot be touched by a straight-edge placed across the wires on the side from which it was played.

viii. A player who hits a ball must take croquet : that is, must strike his own ball while in contact with the other, so as perceptibly to stir both. In doing this he is now not allowed to place his foot on his ball. A player, when his turn comes round, may hit and croquet each ball in succession, and can do this again after each point made, but between the points can only take croquet once off each ball.

ix. A playing ball which hits another after making a point is in hand, and the striker can score no point till he has taken croquet. After hitting another a ball may be stopped by any player ; but should it, in rolling, displace any of the other balls, such balls must remain where they are driven.

x. When, at the commencement of a turn, two balls are found touching, roquet is deemed to be made, and croquet must be taken at once.

xi. When a player, in his stroke, hits one or more balls, he must take croquet off the ball that is struck first ; but if he has hit two simultaneously, he may choose from which of them he will take it, and in both cases a second hit is required before he can take it from the other ball.

xii. Should the ball in making its hoop strike another that lies beyond the hoop and then pass through it, the hoop and the hit count to both ; but, should any part of the ball that is hit have been lying beneath the hoop, the croquet must be taken, but the hoop does not count.

xiii. A rover which strikes or is driven by another ball against the winning peg is out of the game, and must be removed from the ground.

xiv. A player who pegs out a rover by a first hit cannot take croquet from it, as the ball is out of the game, and he is not entitled to another stroke.

xv. Should a player play out of his turn, or with a wrong ball, and this be discovered by his antagonist before a second stroke in error has been made, the turn is lost, and all points made after the mistake, and the balls shall remain as they lay at the time the mistake was discovered, or be replaced to the satisfaction of the antagonist. But if he has made a second stroke before the error is discovered, he continues his break, and the next player follows with the ball that is next in rotation to the one with which he has played, and is liable to lose his turn, and all points made therein, if he plays with that which would have been the right ball if no mistake had been made.

xvi. Should a player make the wrong hoop by mistake, or croquet a ball that he is not entitled to croquet, and the mistake be discovered before he has made a second stroke, he loses his turn, and any point so made in error ; but if he has made a second stroke before the discovery, he shall be allowed to continue his break.

xvii. In order to prevent the occurrence of the errors noticed in the above rules (Nos. xv. and xvi), a player is bound, upon being appealed to, to declare truly what is his next hoop or point in order, and is entitled to demand of his antagonist what he had played last, and to insist upon his clip being properly placed.

xviii. When clips are used they should be moved by the umpire, or with his cognizance, at the end of each turn, and their position shall be conclusive as to the position of the balls in the game.

xix. Should a ball in play be accidentally stopped or diverted by the umpire, he places it where he considers that it would have rolled to. Should it be stopped by a player, it will rest with the side opposed to that player to say whether the ball shall remain where it stopped, or be placed by the umpire, or the stroke be taken again.

xx. If a ball lies within a mallet's length of the boundary, and is not the playing ball, it must at once be put out three feet at right angles from the boundary ; but if it is the playing ball, it may, at the discretion of the player, either be put out or played from where it lies.

xxi. If it is found that the height of the boundary interferes with the stroke, the player may, at the umpire's discretion, bring in the balls a longer distance than three feet, so as to allow of a free swing of the mallet. Balls so brought in must be moved in the line of aim.

xxii. Should a player, in trying to make his hoop, knock a wire out of the ground with his ball the hoop does not count. The ball must be replaced, and the stroke taken again ; but if by the same stroke a roquet be made, the striker may elect whether he will claim the roquet or have the balls replaced.

xxiii. Any player may set upright a peg or hoop except the one next in order ; and that, however loose, awry, or slanting it may be, must not be altered except by the umpire.

xxiv. No ball may be moved because of its lying in a hole or on bad ground, except by the umpire or with his permission. The ball must be put back—*i. e.* away from the object aimed at—and so as not to alter the line of aim.

xxv. Where there is no umpire present, permission to move a ball, or to set up a hoop or peg or other indulgence for which an umpire would have been appealed to, must be asked of the other side.

xxvi. The decision of the umpire shall in all cases be final. His duties are : (*a*) To move the clips, or see that they are properly moved ; (*b*) to decide on the application of the laws ; (*c*) to keep the score, and if asked by a player, to disclose the state of it ; (*d*) to replace balls sent off the ground, or to see that they are properly replaced ; (*e*) to adjust hoops or pegs not upright, or to see that they are properly adjusted. But he shall not give his opinion, or notice any error that may be made, unless appealed to by one of the players.

2202. Terms Used in Croquet.

i. *Roquet.*—To strike another ball with your own.

ii. *Croquet.*—When two balls are in contact, the player strikes the other away, either with or without putting the foot on his own ball, as may be previously arranged.

iii. *A loose croquet* is made by striking your opponent's ball without putting your foot on your own ball. In taking "two off" it is, however, necessary that the ball should be seen to move.

iv. *Wired.*—When a ball is in contact with a hoop, so as to prevent it going through.

v. *Bridge Ball.*—One that has passed the first arch.

vi. *Dead Ball.*—One in hand after having roqueted another.

vii *To Peg.*—To play for either of the pegs in regular order.

viii. *The Tour.*—The run given to each player till he fails to strike through a hoop.

ix. *To Dismiss* a ball is to croquet it to a distance.

x. *Rover.*—You become a rover when you have completed the hoops from point to point, and instead of hitting the starting-peg and retiring, you prefer to strike your ball to any part of the ground, croqueting friends or foes.

xi. The terms side stroke, straight stroke, following ball, over-running a bridge, &c., explain themselves.

2203. LAWN BOWLS.

This game is usually played by teams of three or four players on each side, each player having two bowls usually made of lignum vitae, and about four and a half inches in diameter. The game is commenced by the leader bowling a white ball, called the "jack," towards the opposite side of the lawn, and the object of the players is to bowl their bowls so that they may stop as near the white ball as possible. The game consists of any number of points that may be agreed on, and the team having the balls nearest to the white one, count one point for each of such balls.

2204. LAWN TENNIS.

This fashionable and delightful game, suitable for both ladies and gentlemen, is generally played on a lawn or grass plot by two, three, or four players, with balls and racquet-bats. The object of the game is to strike the ball into a part of his opponent's court in such a way that he cannot return it direct or on its first bound. The court or ground may be of any size consistent with the lawn, the base lines being marked out by chalk, or tapes slightly pinned to the turf, which should be frequently mown and rolled. The mode of play may be seen from the following leading rules, which are now generally accepted by all players.

2205. Rules of Lawn Tennis.

i. The *court*, for a single-handed game, should be 78 feet long and 27 feet wide, and for a double-handed game the same length, but 36 feet wide, divided across the centre by a *net* attached to two upright posts. The net should be 3 feet 6 inches high at the posts, and 3 feet at the centre. At each end of the court, parallel with the net, are the *base lines*, whose extremities are connected by the *side lines*. The *half-court line* is half-way between the side lines and parallel with them. The *service lines* are 21 feet from the net and parallel with it.

ii. The *balls* should be 2½ inches in diameter, and 2 ounces in weight.

iii. The choice of sides and the right of serving during the first games are decided by toss.

iv. The players stand on opposite sides of the net. The player who first delivers the ball is called the *server*, the other the *striker-out.*

v. At the end of the first game the striker-out becomes server, and the server striker-out, and so on alternately in the subsequent games of the set.

vi. The server stands with one foot beyond the base line, and delivers the service from the right and left courts alternately, beginning from right.

vii. The balls served must, without touching the net, drop within the service line, half-court line, and side line diagonally opposite to that from which the striker serves it.

viii. If the service be delivered from the wrong court it is a *fault.* It is also a fault if the server does not stand in the manner as stated above, or if the ball served drop in the net or beyond the service line, or if it drop out of court, or go in the wrong court.

ix. A fault may not be taken, that is, played back to the server.

x. After a fault, the server shall serve again from the same court, unless it was a fault because served from the wrong court. A fault may not be claimed after the next service has been delivered. The striker-out may not *volley* the service. Volleying is striking the ball back before it has touched the ground.

xi. The ball, having been returned, must be kept in play either by volleying it, or striking it back after the first bounce. A ball bouncing twice is out of play.

xii. If, in serving, the ball touch the net and go over into the proper court, it is called a *let* and counts to neither server nor striker-out.

xiii. The server scores if the striker-out volley the service, or fail to return the service in such a way that the ball would fall within the opponents' court.

xiv. Two consecutive faults count a stroke against the server.

xv. If the ball when in play touch either player it scores a stroke for his opponent.

xvi. The first stroke won by either player scores 15 to that player ; the second, won by the same player, raises his score to 30 ; his third stroke to 40, and his fourth counts *game*. If, however, the players have both scored 40, it is called *deuce*, and the next stroke won by either is called *advantage* to the winner of it, and if he also win the following stroke he scores *game*. Should he lose it the score returns to *deuce*. The player winning two consecutive strokes directly following a *deuce* scores *game*.

xvii. Whichever player first scores six games is considered to win the *set*, except as follows :

If both players win five games, the score is *games all*, and the next game won by either player is *advantage game* for that player. If the same player win the next game, he wins *the set* ; if he lose the next game the score is again *games all*, and so on until one wins the two games following *games all*, when he wins the *set*.

2206. Three-Handed and Four-Handed Lawn Tennis.

i. The laws as given above apply equally to these games. The difference in the width of the court has been stated.

ii. In Four-handed Tennis the players deliver the service in turns: thus supposing A and B are partners opposed to C and D ; A serves in the first game, C in the second, B serves in the third, and D in the fourth, and so on.

iii. In Three-handed Tennis the single player serves in each alternate game.

iv. No player may return a service that has been delivered to his partner.

2207. BADMINTON.

This game is a somewhat similar one to Lawn Tennis, but is played with shuttlecocks instead of balls, and over a higher net.

2208. BASEBALL.

This, the national game of America, is a modification of the English game of rounders, and (as in the latter game) the players use a bat and ball, and run round bases. A diamond-shaped ground, ninety feet square, is marked out, and bases are set out on or within each angle of this diamond, called *home, first, second,* and *third* bases.

The *ball* weighs from 5 to 5¼ ounces, and it is 9 to 9¼ inches in circumference.

The *bat* is round, and measures about 42 inches in length, and is not more than 2½ inches in diameter at its thickest end.

Each team has nine players, and what is called the home team has the right of first innings, each player taking the bat in regular order. The player taking the bat is called the striker, or batsman, and his team is really the defensive team, the field team being the attacking side.

The *pitcher* stands about the centre of the diamond ; the *catcher* in rear of the home base ; the *first baseman* close to the first base, on the right of the *catcher* ; the *second* and *third basemen*, near the second and third bases ; *short stop,* about half-way between these ; and the *outfielders* at the right, centre, and left fields, about in line with first, second, and third bases respectively.

The field side having taken their proper places, the pitcher delivers the ball, which to constitute a fair ball should pass over the home base, not lower than the batsman's knee, nor higher than his shoulder. The ball is delivered as fast as the pitcher can send it, and is generally an under-hand delivery. A practised player can impart great twist to the ball. A fair ball is counted as a strike, no matter whether the batsman plays at it or not, and after receiving four fair balls the batsman must run, or he can be put out. If, however, five unfair balls have been given the batsman is entitled to a base.

The object of the batsman is to drive the ball out of the fielders' reach, and far enough away to allow him to ran round the bases without being put out. If he can do that he scores a run. The batsman may use each base as a resting place, and is allowed to stay at any base until he can slip to the next one, or a succeeding batsman drives the ball so far as to let him run with safety—for if a runner is touched with the ball by a fielder he is out, except when at a base. All three bases may be occupied at the same time, but when a following batsman becomes a runner, the runner on the first base must proceed to the second base, which must be left for him to take, or else he is put out.

If a striker's ball is caught before it touches the ground, a runner must return and touch the base last occupied. The first batsman is succeeded in rotation by others, until three of the batting side are out, when the field side take the bat. When nine equal innings have been played, the side scoring the most runs wins the match.

A batsman can only run for a fair hit, *i. e.* a ball struck within the lines of the diamond between the home and first and third bases ; but he can be caught out either on a foul hit or a fair one. If after a fair hit or over four strikes the ball is fielded to the first base before he can get there, he is out.

2209. PUSH-BALL.

This game, introduced at Harvard University, America, somewhat resembles football in some of its features. The ball is a large affair, being 6 feet 3 inches in diameter, and weighing 120 lbs. : it is a bladder of india-rubber covered with leather. Notwithstanding its size, however, it can be easily moved. It may only be pushed with the shoulder, no other means being allowed.

A line is drawn across the centre of the field in which the game is played, dividing its length into two parts. At 20 yards distance from this, on each side, is drawn another line. The space between these two lines is the field of play, and the two outside lines may be taken to constitute the goals. The length of the lines may be agreed upon.

The game is played by sixteen players, eight on each side. The game is started by placing the ball in the middle of the centre line, the players standing round it. Then the "centre" of each side stands immediately behind the ball, with two other players, called respectively a "guard" and "tackle," on either side of him.

On the outside of these are two "forwards." The captain, who acts as "full-back," stands a few paces in the rear of the other players, and directs his men from that position.

Cleverness in combination is the principal secret of the game, the object of the players being to find the weak spot in their adversaries' defence, and to force the ball in that direction. Of course, the ball is not upon the ground at all times during the game. It frequently is forced upon the shoulders of the players, and comes down again very often where least expected, necessitating close attention to it.

After two minutes' play, time is called, when the team that has pushed the ball into the other's ground score as follows :—

If they have pushed the ball 5 yards beyond the centre line, they take *one* point ; if 10 yards, *two* points ; if 15 yards, *three* points ; and if 20 yards (by that means crossing the line), *five* points.

2210. FOOTBALL.

2211. THE ASSOCIATION GAME.

The ground from goal to goal should not exceed 200 yards, or be less than 100 yards in length, and the width should be equal to half the length. The boundaries are marked out by the goal lines at each end, and the touch lines at each side, and by flags at each corner. A line is also drawn 6 yards from each goal post, and another 12 yards from the goal lines. The centre of the ground is also indicated, and a circle of 10 yards radius is described round it.

The Goal Posts are placed, on the goal lines, 8 yards apart, with a bar across them 8 feet from the ground.

The Ball has an average circumference of not more than 28 inches, or less than 27 inches, and it weighs from 13 to 15 ounces.

The Game is played with sides of 11 men each ; the players being usually the goal-keeper, 2 backs, 3 half-backs, and 5 forwards. In this game only goals count, and to score a goal the ball must pass between the goal posts *under the bar.*

2212. Mode of Play.

i. The option of kicking off and the choice of goal is decided by tossing, and the game is commenced with a *place kick* from the centre of the ground in the direction of the adversaries' goal line. The other side is not allowed to come within 10 yards of the ball till it has been kicked off, nor may *any* player pass the centre of the field towards his adversaries' goal before the ball is kicked off.

ii. Upon a goal being scored, the losers kick off in the same way ; but upon changing ends at *half-time* the ball is kicked off by the side which did not originally do so.

iii. To obtain a goal the ball must neither be thrown, knocked on, nor carried. Should the ball strike a goal or boundary post, or the goal bar, and rebound into the ground, it is *in play*, but if it crosses goal or touch line, either along the ground or through the air, it is *out of play.*

iv. If the ball be played behind goal line by an opponent, it must be kicked off by one of the players behind whose

line it went, within six yards of the goal post which is nearest the spot where the ball went out. But if played behind by one of the home side it must be kicked off by an opponent from within one yard of the corner flag nearest to which it went out.

v. When the ball is in *touch*, a player who is not on the side that kicked it must throw it in from the spot on the line at which it went out. He must face the ground, having both feet on the line, and throw the ball in over his head, in any direction, using both hands. It is in play as soon as thrown in ; but the thrower must not play it until it has been played by some other player.

vi. A goal cannot be scored from a *free kick* (the penalty for handling the ball, or off-side play), or from a corner kick described above.

vii. Should any player carry, knock on, or handle the ball, under any pretence, a *free kick* is awarded to the opposing side ; the goal-keeper, however, may, within his own half of the ground, use his hands in defence of his goal, either by knocking on or throwing, but not carrying the ball.

viii. The goal-keeper may be changed during the game, after notice to the referee.

ix. No tripping, hacking, or jumping at a player is allowed, nor may a player use his hands to hold or push an opponent, or play in such a way as is likely to cause injury. A player may not charge an adversary from behind, unless such adversary be facing his own goal, and also, in the opinion of the referee, intentionally impeding his adversary.

x. It is not allowable to charge the goal-keeper, except when he is touching the ball, or obstructing an opponent.

xi. If any player wilfully holds, pushes, or trips an opponent, or handles the ball, within 12 yards of his own goal-line, the referee must award a *penalty kick* to the other side.

xii. For a *penalty kick* the ball is placed anywhere the kicker chooses on the 12-yard line, all the players (except the defending goal-keeper) having to stand not less than six yards from the said line on the opposite side from the goal.

2213. Terms used in this Game.

i. A *place-kick* is one made at the ball whilst on the ground, in such position as the kicker may like to place it.

ii. A *free kick* is one made whilst the ball is on the ground, in any direction the player chooses, none of his opponents being allowed to come within 6 yards of the ball, unless they are standing on their own goal line.

iii. *Hacking* is intentionally kicking a player.

iv. *Tripping* is throwing, or trying to throw down an adversary by the use of one's legs, or by stooping in front of him.

v. *Handling* means playing the ball with the hand or arm.

vi. *Holding* is the obstruction of a player by the hand or any part of the arm extended from the body.

vii. *Carrying* is taking more than two steps while holding the ball.

viii. *Touch* is that part of the field on either side of the ground, beyond the line of play.

2214. THE RUGBY GAME is

played by 15 players on each side. The field is 110 yards in length by 75 yards in breadth. The boundaries are the goal lines at the ends, and the touch lines at the sides. The goals are two posts exceeding 11 feet in height, 18 feet 6 inches apart, with a cross-bar 10 feet from the ground.

The Players consist of one full back, three three-quarter backs, two half-backs, and nine forwards. The captain may, however, draw from the forwards for extra strength behind the scrimmage.

The Ball is an oval one of the following measurements :—

Length circumference,		30 to 31 inches.
Width	,,	25½ to 26 ,,
Weight		12 to 13 ounces.

2215. The Mode of Play.

i. The respective captains toss for the kick-off, or choice of goals, and the match is decided by a majority of points. If no point is scored, or the number be equal, the match is drawn. A goal is scored when the ball is kicked *over* the cross-bar ; but it must not go over either of the goal posts.

ii. After choice of goals the ball is kicked off from the centre of the ground in the direction of the opponents' goal, and is then in play, remaining so until stopped either by the ball going into touch, by a fair catch, or some point being scored, or the game being stopped by the referee for some infringement of rule.

iii. The game is divided into two parts or halves, each part usually lasting 35 to 40 minutes. At the expiration of the first half, *half-time* is called by the referee's whistle, and after a brief interval play is started again by the ball being again placed in the centre of the ground, and kicked off by the side losing the toss at the commencement of the game.

iv. Whilst the ball is in play it may be either kicked or picked up and run with according to the discretion of the player, provided always the player is *on side*. A player is not *on side* if he is not behind the ball whilst it is being kicked or run with.

v. The ball may be passed from player to player, provided always it is not passed *forward* to the player receiving it.

vi. A ball is *in touch* when it is kicked or carried across the touch lines. It is then brought again into play as follows: One player on the side other than the one who kicked the ball into touch, but in the case of being carried into touch, on the side of the player carrying it, shall throw out the ball at a right angle to touch line, the opposing sides meantime having formed what is known as a "line out," *i.e.* facing each other in parallel lines ; or the ball may be bounced out, *i.e.* bouncing the ball on the field of play, and then catching it, and then either passing it, running with it, or kicking it, as opportunity serves, or a *scrimmage* may be formed at right angle from point of touch not more than fifteen yards from said point.

vii. A *scrimmage* is when the forwards on either side combine together round the ball and try to push their opponents back towards their own goal, and is broken up immediately the ball comes out of the scrimmage.

viii. It is incumbent in every game to have two *Touch Judges* and a Referee. *Touch Judges* shall carry a flag, shall take opposite sides of the ground, and shall immediately the ball crosses the line into touch hold up their flag at that point. *The Referee* shall carry a whistle, the blowing of which stops the game, and his duty is to see the game fairly played and to stop it on any infringement of rule. He also has power to order any offending player on the ground, and his decision on any point is final.

ix. In addition to the penalties recognized by the Rugby Union, one which is in vogue amongst northern clubs is now generally regarded with approval, *i.e. to penalize touch.* Thus the side other than the one kicking into touch, instead of bringing the ball into play in one of the ways before named, kicks it out from touch in the direction naturally of their opponents' goal, the effect of this being to make the game more open and to do away largely with scrimmages.

x. A *drop kick* is made by dropping the ball to the ground and kicking it immediately it rises.

xi. *A place kick* is effected by kicking the ball after it has been set in a dent in the ground, made to keep it steady.

2216. Method of Scoring.

1. A *Try*, counting three points.

This is gained by the player who first puts his hand on the nail on the ground behind his opponents' goal line within the field of play. The ball may either be carried or kicked across the line.

2. A *Goal* from a try, counting five points.

This is obtained by bringing the ball out in direct line from the place the try was secured, and then kicking it over the opponents' cross-bar, without touching any player in its flight.

3. A *Penalty Goal*, counting four points.

This is obtained by the same process as a goal, the kick being awarded to the side not offending, under the head of penalties, of which the following are the chief:—

i. Picking out the ball from the scrimmage.
ii. Lifting the feet before the ball is in the scrimmage.
iii. Wilfully obstructing his opponents' play by standing offside in a scrimmage, *i.e.* a player not being in the scrimmage standing on his opponents' side of the play, and not behind the ball.
iv. By not immediately placing the ball on the ground and playing it after being held.

4. *Other Goals*, counting four points.

These are obtained by a player kicking a goal from the field of play, no try having been got, and are of two kinds—a dropped goal and a goal from a free kick.

A dropped goal is when a player from the field of play kicks the ball over the cross-bar, the ball having touched the ground first. A free kick is awarded for a fair catch of the ball during the play without its touching the ground after being kicked by an opponent, the player making the catch and at the same moment, without moving, registering it by marking the spot in the ground with his foot.

2217. GOLF.

This is a Scottish game of great antiquity, and is played upon tracts of ground covered with short grass, called "links," "golf course," or "golf green."

A number of small holes are cut in the ground at distances varying from one hundred to five (or even six) hundred yards from one another, according to the extent and character of the course. This is called a circuit, or "round," and a full links usually consists of eighteen holes ; but a course very frequently contains fifteen, twelve, nine, and six holes. The size of the holes as fixed by the laws of golf is 4¼ inches in diameter and at least 4 inches deep.

The game is played either by two persons or four (two against two), the two players in the latter case playing alternately.

At various points along the "round," "teeing-grounds" are marked off, from which the players begin the play to each hole, and at points of 100 to 500 yards from the teeing-grounds, are the "putting-greens" in which the holes are cut into which the ball is to be played.

Flags are set in these holes to indicate their position, and they must be capable of being taken out when the hole is being played for.

There are also various obstructions (either natural or artificial) called "hazards" and "bunkers" ; these are generally between the teeing-grounds and putting-greens, and consist of mounds, sandholes, rushes, &c. They are intended as a punishment for badly-played balls, and sometimes lie right across the line of play, or in some cases on either side of it.

2218. Mode of Play.

Commencing at a few yards in front of the "home hole" on the first teeing-ground, each player drives his ball towards the first hole, his object being to put the ball into the hole in fewer strokes than his opponent.

The ball has to be struck as it happens to lie on the ground, except in playing off from a hole, when it may be *tee'd, i.e.* placed on the top of a little heap of sand called a *tee*. If the two players make an equal number of strokes in holeing the ball, the hole is said to be "halved," and there is no score ; but if one player holes the ball in fewer strokes than the other, he gains that hole, and has the right of making the first stroke for the next hole, or, as it is termed, takes "the honour." So the players continue until the entire round has been traversed, the game being won by the player who has taken most holes. It is often agreed that the match shall consist in completing the round in the fewest strokes. The player who is about to make an equal number of strokes with his opponent is said to play *the like* ; if he plays one more stroke than his opponent, he plays *the odds*, and if two strokes more, *two more*, and so on.

2219. Implements Required.

The balls are made of gutta-percha painted white, in order that they may be easily seen, and they weigh a trifle under two ounces.

The clubs consist of a shaft and head spliced together, made of lance-wood or hickory. The head is weighted with lead, and has a piece of horn fixed to the front of the sole. Sometimes the ball lies in such a position that a club with an iron head has to be used.

The usual number of clubs employed is seven, but some players use ten, or even twelve, and each player has an attendant called a *caddie* to carry his clubs, and *tee* the balls for him.

The principal clubs are the *Driver, Brassy-Niblick, Putter, Cleek, Iron, Mashie* and *Iron Niblick*. The first three are made wholly of wood, and the others have iron heads. Then there are the *Spoons* (long, mid, and short),

Driving Cleek, Driving Mashie, Putting Cleek, Putting Iron, Metal Putter, Driving Putter, Driving Iron, and *Lofting Iron.* These all have iron heads, with the exception of the *Driving Putter* and the *Spoons.*

2220. CYCLING.

This pastime has of recent years become immensely popular, and there is no doubt that, taken in moderation, it is a most health-giving recreation. That it is a great favourite with the ladies there is no possible manner of doubt, as is shown by the great increase of late years in the number of lady riders. Given a modest and well-made costume, a lady's figure is shown to great advantage if she is a graceful rider. We cannot say so much for the so-called "rational" attire.

There are many excellent cycling clubs, one of the best known being the "Cyclists' Touring Club." These greatly facilitate the taking of extended tours throughout the United Kingdom, and also on the Continent, as they make special arrangements, for the benefit of their members, with good hotels in the various principal towns ; they also have caution-posts fixed at the top of hills that are dangerous for cyclists to ride down.

Cycles are liable to a variety of accidents, even the best made machines coming to grief under certain circumstances. Among these may be mentioned one that is caused by want of oil, and is called "firing." The friction makes the bearing hot, and after a time the metal expands, and the bearing is useless. The best thing is to lay some cloths, soaked in boiling water, round the part, and when the bearing is unfixed, give it a good oiling.

If the screw connected with the steering-rod works loose, a hairpin may be placed in the hole and twisted round for temporary use. A broken crank is a very awkward dilemma, and is generally due to a flaw in the metal. The only thing to be done is to tie the crank up with string, and make for the nearest railway station ; or if fortunate enough to find a black-smith, and the crank is a solid one, get him to weld it together.

Loose tyres may be remedied by holding a gas-jet under the rim till the cement oozes out. The tyre should then be pressed home, tied round, and left for a day, to set. Of course, if there is no cement left in the rim, we must make, or buy some. The recipe given in par. 2142 will be found useful.

Punctures in tyres caused by glass, flints, nails, or thorns, are very annoying as they cause delays, but they can usually be remedied by the rider, who should always carry with him a small handy set of tools and requisites which are supplied by the cycle manufacturers in neat leather wallets, which can be strapped on to their machines.

Messrs. Houlston and Sons have brought out a series of HANDY POCKET MAPS, specially intended for Cyclists and Tourists in England and Wales. They are clear, accurate, very convenient in size, and cheap, being only *fourpence* each. A list of these maps will be found in the advertisement pages at the end of this book.

2221. STAMP DUTIES ON BILLS OF EXCHANGE, &c.

	Duty £ s. d.
Bill of Exchange, Draft, or Order for the payment of money on demand at sight, or on presentation, *for any amount.*	0 0 1
Bill of Exchange, and Promissory Notes of any other kind whatsoever (except a Bank Note), drawn, payable, endorsed, or in any manner negotiated in the United Kingdom—	
Not above £5	0 0 1
Above £5 and not above 10	0 0 2
" 10 " 25	0 0 3
" 25 " 50	0 0 6
" 50 " 75	0 0 9
" 75 " 100	0 1 0

And for every additional £100 or fractional part of £100, 1s.

2222. PERCENTAGE OF DISCOUNTS.

Showing the Reduction per £ on Discounts allowed for Cash Purchases, at Rates ranging from 1 to 50 per cent.

		s.	*d.*				*s.*	*d.*	
0½	p.c. is	0	1	per £	11	p.c. is	2	2½	per £
1	"	0	2½	"	12	"	2	5	"
1½	"	0	3½	"	12½	"	2	6	"
2	"	0	5	"	13	"	2	7	"
2½	"	0	6	"	14	"	2	9½	"
3	"	0	7	"	15	"	3	0	"
3½	"	0	8½	"	17½	"	3	6	"
4	"	0	9½	"	20	"	4	0	"
4½	"	0	11	"	22½	"	4	6	"
5	"	1	0	"	25	"	5	0	"
5½	"	1	1	"	27½	"	5	6	"
6	"	1	2½	"	30	"	6	0	"
6½	"	1	3½	"	32½	"	6	6	"
7	"	1	5	"	35	"	7	0	"
7½	"	1	6	"	37½	"	7	6	"
8	"	1	7	"	40	"	8	0	"
8½	"	1	8½	"	42½	"	8	6	"
9	"	1	9½	"	45	"	9	0	"
9½	"	1	11	"	47½	"	9	6	"
10	"	2	0	"	50	"	10	0	"

2223. TABLE OF THE NUMBER OF DAYS, FROM ANY DAY OF ONE MONTH TO THE SAME DAY OF ANY OTHER MONTH.

From	Jan	Feb	Mar	Apr	May	June	July	Aug	Sep	Oct	Nov	Dec
To January	365	334	306	275	245	214	184	153	122	92	61	31
February	31	365	337	306	276	245	215	184	153	123	92	62
March	59	28	365	334	304	273	243	212	181	151	120	90
April	90	59	31	365	335	304	274	243	212	182	151	121
May........................	120	89	61	30	365	334	304	273	242	212	181	151
June........................	151	120	92	61	31	365	335	304	273	243	212	182
July	181	150	122	91	61	30	365	334	303	273	242	212
August........................	212	181	153	122	92	61	31	365	334	304	273	243
September........................	243	212	184	153	123	92	62	31	365	335	304	274
October........................	273	242	214	183	153	122	92	61	30	365	334	304
November	304	273	245	214	184	153	123	92	61	31	365	335
December	334	303	275	244	214	183	153	122	91	61	30	365

USE OF THE ABOVE TABLE.

What is the number of days from 10th October to 10th July?

Look in the upper line for October, let your eye descend down that column till you come opposite to July, and you will find 273 days, the exact number of days required.

Again, required the number of days from 16th of February to 14th of August?

Under February, and opposite to August, is	181 days.
From which subtract the difference between 14 and 16	2 days
The exact number of days required is	179 days.

N.B.— In Leap Year, if the last day of February comes between, add one day for the day over to the number in the Table.

2224. FOR MISTRESSES AND SERVANTS: TABLE OF EXPENSES, INCOME AND WAGES.

Showing at one view what any sum, from £1 to £1,000 per Annum, is per Day, Week, or Month.

Per Year.	Per Month.	Per Week.	Per Day.	Per Year.	Per Month.	Per Week.	Per Day.	Per Year.	Per Month.	Per Week.	Per Day.
£ s.	s. d.	s. d.	d.	£ s.	£ s. d.	s. d.	s. d.	£ s.	£ s. d.	£ s. d.	£ s. d.
1 0	1 8	0 4½	0¾	8 8	0 14 0	3 2¾	0 5½	18 18	1 11 6	0 7 3¼	0 1 0½
1 10	2 6	0 7	1	8 10	0 14 2	3 3¼	0 5½	19 0	1 11 8	0 7 3½	0 1 0½
2 0	3 4	0 9¼	1¼	9 0	0 15 0	3 5½	0 6	20 0	1 13 4	0 7 8¼	0 1 1¼
2 2	3 6	0 9¾	1½	9 9	0 15 9	3 7½	0 6¼	25 0	2 1 8	0 9 7	0 1 4½
2 10	4 2	0 11½	1¾	10 0	0 16 8	3 10¼	0 6½	30 0	2 10 0	0 11 6½	0 1 7¾
3 0	5 0	1 1¾	2	10 10	0 17 6	4 0½	0 7	40 0	3 6 8	0 15 4½	0 2 2¼
3 3	5 3	1 2½	2	11 0	0 18 4	4 3¾	0 7¼	50 0	4 3 4	0 19 2¾	0 2 9
3 10	5 10	1 4¼	2¼	11 11	0 19 3	4 5¼	0 7½	60 0	5 0 0	1 3 1	0 3 3½
4 0	6 8	1 6½	2½	12 0	1 0 0	4 7½	0 8	70 0	5 16 8	1 6 11	0 3 10
4 4	7 0	1 7½	2¾	12 12	1 1 0	4 10¼	0 8¼	80 0	6 13 4	1 10 9¼	0 4 4½
4 10	7 6	1 8¾	3	13 0	1 1 8	5 0	0 8½	90 0	7 10 0	1 14 7½	0 4 11¼
5 0	8 4	1 11	3¼	13 13	1 2 9	5 3	0 9	100 0	8 6 8	1 18 5½	0 5 5¾
5 5	8 9	2 0¼	3½	14 0	1 3 4	5 4½	0 9¼	200 0	16 13 4	3 16 11	0 10 11½
5 10	9 2	2 1½	3¾	14 14	1 4 6	5 7¾	0 9¾	300 0	25 0 0	5 15 4½	0 16 5¼
6 0	10 0	2 3¾	4	15 0	1 5 0	5 9¼	0 9¾	400 0	33 6 8	7 13 10¼	1 1 11
6 6	10 6	2 5	4¼	15 15	1 6 3	6 0¾	0 10¼	500 0	41 13 4	9 12 3¾	1 7 4¾
6 10	10 10	2 6	4¼	16 0	1 6 8	6 1¾	0 10½	600 0	50 0 0	11 10 9¼	1 12 10½
7 0	11 8	2 8¼	4½	16 16	1 8 0	6 5½	0 11	700 0	58 6 8	13 9 2¾	1 18 4¼
7 7	12 3	2 10	4¾	17 0	1 8 4	6 6½	0 11¼	800 0	66 13 4	15 7 8¼	2 3 10
7 10	12 6	2 10½	5	17 17	1 9 0	6 10½	0 11¾	900 0	75 0 0	17 6 1¾	2 9 3¾
8 0	13 4	3 1	5¼	18 0	1 10 0	6 11	0 11¾	1000 0	83 6 8	19 4 7¼	2 14 9½

2225. INTEREST TABLE FOR SAVINGS, INVESTMENTS, &c.

Showing what any sum, from £1 to £500, will produce for a given number of days, which may be, by simple addition, calculated at £5 per cent. for Months or Years, for sums up to £5,000 or any other amount.

	1 day.	2 days.	3 days.	4 days.	5 days.	6 days.	7 days.	8 days.	9 days.	10 days.	20 days.	30 days.
£	s. d.	s. d.	s. d.	s. d.	s. d.	s. d.	s. d.	s. d.	s. d.	s. d.	£ s. d.	£ s. d.
1	0 0	0 0	0 0	0 0	0 0	0 0	0 0	0 0¼	0 0¼	0 0¼	0 0 0½	0 0 0¾
2	0 0	0 0	0 0	0 0¼	0 0¼	0 0¼	0 0¼	0 0½	0 0½	0 0½	0 0 1¼	0 0 1¾
3	0 0	0 0	0 0¼	0 0¼	0 0¼	0 0½	0 0½	0 0¾	0 0¾	0 0¾	0 0 1¾	0 0 2¾
4	0 0	0 0¼	0 0¼	0 0½	0 0½	0 0¾	0 0¾	0 1	0 1	0 1¼	0 0 2½	0 0 3¾
5	0 0	0 0¼	0 0¼	0 0½	0 0¾	0 0¾	0 1	0 1¼	0 1½	0 1½	0 0 3¼	0 0 4¾
6	0 0	0 0¼	0 0½	0 0¾	0 0¾	0 1	0 1¼	0 1½	0 1¾	0 1¾	0 0 3¾	0 0 5¾
7	0 0	0 0¼	0 0½	0 0¾	0 1	0 1¼	0 1½	0 1¾	0 2	0 2¼	0 0 4½	0 0 6¾
8	0 0¼	0 0½	0 0¾	0 1	0 1¼	0 1½	0 1¾	0 2	0 2¼	0 2½	0 0 5¼	0 0 7¾
9	0 0¼	0 0½	0 0¾	0 1	0 1½	0 1¾	0 2	0 2¼	0 2½	0 2¾	0 0 5¾	0 0 8¾
10	0 0¼	0½	0 0¾	0 1¼	0 1½	0 1¾	0 2¼	0 2½	0 2¾	0 3¼	0 0 6½	0 0 9¼
20	0 0½	1¼	0 1¾	0 2½	0 3¼	0 3¾	0 4½	0 5¼	0 5¾	0 6½	0 1 1	0 1 7½
30	0 0¾	0 1¾	0 2¾	0 3¾	0 4¾	0 5¾	0 6¾	0 7¾	0 8¾	0 9¾	0 1 7½	0 2 5½
40	0 1¼	0 2½	0 3¾	0 5¼	0 6½	0 7¾	0 9	0 10½	0 11¾	1 1	0 2 2¼	0 3 3¼
50	0 1½	0 3¼	0 4¾	0 6½	0 8	0 9¾	0 11½	1 1	1 2¾	1 4¼	0 2 8¾	0 4 1¼
60	0 1¾	0 3¾	0 5¾	0 7¾	0 9¾	0 11¾	1 1¾	1 3¾	1 5¾	1 7½	0 3 3¼	0 4 11
70	0 2¼	0 4½	0 6¾	0 9	0 11½	1 1¾	1 4	1 6¼	1 8½	1 11	0 3 10	0 5 9
80	0 2½	0 5¼	0 7¾	0 10½	1 1	1 3¾	1 6¼	1 9	1 11½	2 2¼	0 4 4½	0 6 9¾
90	0 2¾	0 5¾	0 8¾	0 11¾	1 2¾	1 5¾	1 8½	1 11½	2 2½	2 5½	0 4 11	0 7 4¾
100	0 3¼	0 6½	0 9¾	1 1	1 4¾	1 7½	1 11	2 2¼	2 5½	2 8¾	0 5 5¾	0 8 2½
200	0 6½	1 1	1 7½	2 2¼	2 8¾	3 3¼	3 10	4 4½	4 11	5 5¾	0 10 11½	0 16 5¼
300	0 9¾	1 7½	2 5½	3 3¼	4 1¼	4 11	5 9	6 6¾	7 4¾	8 2½	0 16 5¼	1 4 7¾
400	1 1	2 2¼	3 3¼	4 4½	5 5¾	6 6¾	7 8	8 2	9 10¼	10 11½	1 1 11	1 12 10½
500	1 4¼	2 8¾	4 1¼	5 5¾	6 10	8 2½	9 7	10 11½	12 3¾	13 8¼	1 7 4¾	2 1 1

2226. INTEREST TABLE FOR ONE YEAR.

By this Table unlimited calculations may be made. Thus, to find interest on £1,250 per annum, add sums given for £1,000, £200, and £50. 2 per cent is found by taking half of 4 p.c.; 8 p.c., by doubling 4 p.c.; 7½ pc., by adding 5 to 2½ p.c., and so on.

Principal	2½ p.c.	3 p.c.	3½ p.c.	4 p.c.	5 p.c.	Principal	2½ p.c.	3 p.c.	3½ p.c.	4 p.c.	5 p.c.
£	£ s. d.	£ s. d.	£ s. d.	£ s. d.	£ s.	£	£ s. d.	£ s. d.	£ s. d.	£ s. d.	£ s.
1	0 0 6	0 0 7¼	0 0 8½	0 0 9½	0 1	60	1 10 0	1 16 0	2 2 0	2 8 0	3 0
2	0 1 0	0 1 2½	0 1 4¾	0 1 7¼	0 2	70	1 15 0	2 2 0	2 9 0	2 16 0	3 10
3	0 1 6	0 1 9½	0 2 1¼	0 2 4¾	0 3	80	2 0 0	2 8 0	2 16 0	3 4 0	4 0
4	0 2 0	0 2 4¾	0 2 9½	0 3 2½	0 4	90	2 5 0	2 14 0	3 3 0	3 12 0	4 10
5	0 2 6	0 3 0	0 3 6	0 4 0	0 5	100	2 10 0	3 0 0	3 10 0	4 0 0	5 0
6	0 3 0	0 3 7¼	0 4 2½	0 4 9½	0 6	200	5 0 0	6 0 0	7 0 0	8 0 0	10 0
7	0 3 6	0 4 2½	0 4 10¾	0 5 7½	0 7	300	7 10 0	9 0 0	10 10 0	12 0 0	15 0
8	0 4 0	0 4 9½	0 5 7¼	0 6 4¾	0 8	400	10 0 0	12 0 0	14 0 0	16 0 0	20 0
9	0 4 6	0 5 4¾	0 6 3½	0 7 2½	0 9	500	12 10 0	15 0 0	17 10 0	20 0 0	25 0
10	0 5 0	0 6 0	0 7 0	0 8 0	0 10	600	15 0 0	18 0 0	21 0 0	24 0 0	30 0
20	0 10 0	0 12 0	0 14 0	0 16 0	1 0	700	17 10 0	21 0 0	24 10 0	28 0 0	35 0
30	0 15 0	0 18 0	1 1 0	1 4 0	1 10	800	20 0 0	24 0 0	28 0 0	32 0 0	40 0
40	1 0 0	1 4 0	1 8 0	1 12 0	2 0	900	22 10 0	27 0 0	31 10 0	36 0 0	45 0
50	1 5 0	1 10 0	1 15 0	2 0 0	2 10	1000	25 0 0	30 0 0	35 0 0	40 0 0	50 0

2227. READY-RECKONING OR MARKETING TABLE.

No.	2d.	2½d.	3d.	3½d.	4d.	4½d.	5d.	5½d.	6d.	6½d.
	s. d.	s. d.	s. d.	s. d.	s. d.	s. d.	s. d.	s. d.	s. d.	s. d.
2	0 4	0 5	0 6	0 7	0 8	0 9	0 10	0 11	1 0	1 1
3	0 6	0 7½	0 9	0 10½	1 0	1 1½	1 3	1 4½	1 6	1 7½
4	0 8	0 10	1 0	1 2	1 4	1 6	1 8	1 10	2 0	2 2
5	0 10	1 0½	1 3	1 5½	1 8	1 10½	2 1	2 3½	2 6	2 8½
6	1 0	1 3	1 6	1 9	2 0	2 3	2 6	2 9	3 0	3 3
7	1 2	1 5½	1 9	2 0½	2 4	2 7½	2 11	3 2½	3 6	3 9½
8	1 4	1 8	2 0	2 4	2 8	3 0	3 4	3 8	4 0	4 4
9	1 6	1 10½	2 3	2 7½	3 0	3 4½	3 9	4 1½	4 6	4 10½
10	1 8	2 1	2 6	2 11	3 4	3 9	4 2	4 7	5 0	5 5
11	1 10	2 3½	2 9	3 2½	3 8	4 1½	4 7	5 0½	5 6	5 11½
12	2 0	2 6	3 0	3 6	4 0	4 6	5 0	5 6	6 0	6 6
13	2 2	2 8½	3 3	3 9½	4 4	4 10½	5 5	5 11½	6 6	7 0½
14	2 4	2 11	3 6	4 1	4 8	5 3	5 10	6 5	7 0	7 7
28	4 8	5 10	7 0	8 2	9 4	10 6	11 8	12 10	14 0	15 2
56	9 4	11 8	14 0	16 4	18 8	21 0	23 4	25 8	28 0	30 4

No.	7d.	7½d.	8d.	8½d.	9d.	9½d.	10d.	10½d.	11d.	11½d.
	s. d.	s. d.	s. d.	s. d.	s. d.	s. d.	s. d.	s. d.	s. d.	s. d.
2	1 2	1 3	1 4	1 5	1 6	1 7	1 8	1 9	1 10	1 11
3	1 9	1 10½	2 0	2 1½	2 3	2 4½	2 6	2 7½	2 9	2 10½
4	2 4	2 6	2 8	2 10	3 0	3 2	3 4	3 6	3 8	3 10
5	2 11	3 1½	3 4	3 6½	3 9	3 11½	4 2	4 4½	4 7	4 9½
6	3 6	3 9	4 0	4 3	4 6	4 9	5 0	5 3	5 6	5 9
7	4 1	4 4½	4 8	4 11½	5 3	5 6½	5 10	6 1½	6 5	6 8½
8	4 8	5 0	5 4	5 8	6 0	6 4	6 8	7 0	7 4	7 8
9	5 3	5 7½	6 0	6 4½	6 9	7 1½	7 6	7 10½	8 3	8 7½
10	5 10	6 3	6 8	7 1	7 6	7 11	8 4	8 9	9 2	9 7
11	6 5	6 10½	7 4	7 9½	8 3	8 8½	9 2	9 7½	10 1	10 6½
12	7 0	7 6	8 0	8 6	9 0	9 6	10 0	10 6	11 0	11 6
13	7 7	8 1½	8 8	9 2½	9 9	10 3½	10 10	11 4½	11 11	12 5½
14	8 2	8 9	9 4	9 11	10 6	11 1	11 8	12 3	12 10	13 5
28	16 4	17 6	18 8	19 10	21 0	22 2	23 4	24 6	25 8	26 10
56	32 8	35 0	37 4	39 8	42 0	44 4	46 8	49 0	51 4	53 8

2228.—FRENCH WEIGHTS AND MEASURES AND THEIR ENGLISH EQUIVALENTS.

Metres to Yards.		Kilometres to Miles.		Grammes to Grains.		Kilogrammes to Pounds.	
Mtrs.	Yards.	Kilos.	Miles.	Grms.	Grains.	Kilo-grams.	Pounds Avoirdupois.
1	1.093	1	.621	1	15.432	1	2.204
2	2.187	2	1.243	2	30.865	2	4.409
3	3.280	3	1.864	3	46.297	3	6.614
4	4.374	4	2.486	4	61.729	4	8.818
5	5.468	5	3.107	5	77.162	5	11.023
6	6.561	6	3.728	6	92.594	6	13.228
7	7.655	7	4.350	7	108.026	7	15.432
8	8.749	8	4.971	8	123.459	8	17.637
9	9.842	9	5.592	9	138.891	9	19.842
10	10.936	10	6.214	10	154.323	10	22.046
11	12.030	11	6.835	11	169.756	11	24.250
12	13.123	12	7.456	12	185.188	12	26.455
13	14.217	13	8.072	13	200.620	13	28.660
14	15.310	14	8.699	14	216.053	14	30.865
15	16.404	15	9.321	15	231.485	15	33.069
16	17.498	16	9.942	16	246.917	16	35.274
17	18.591	17	10.563	17	262.350	17	37.478
18	19.685	18	11.185	18	277.782	18	39.683
19	20.779	19	11.806	19	293.214	19	41.888
20	21.872	20	12.428	20	308.647	20	44.092
30	32.808	30	18.641	30	462.971	30	66.139
40	43.745	40	24.855	40	617.294	40	88.185
50	54.681	50	31.069	50	771.617	50	110.231

1 Gramme .... = 15.43 grains.	1 Yard .... = 91½ centimetres.
1 Kilogramme .... = 2 lbs. 3¼ ozs.	1 Franc per Kilogramme = 4⅔d. per lb., or
1 Ounce Troy .... = 31.1 grammes.	40 s. 7¾d. per
1 Ounce Avoir. .... = 28¼ grammes.	cwt.
1 Pound .... = 453½ grammes.	1s. per Pound .... = 2 fr. 76 c. per
1 Quarter........... = 12.70 kilogr.	kilogramme.
1 Ton .... = 1016 kilogr.	1 Franc per Metre ..... = 8¾d. per yard.
1 Metre .... = 39½ inches.	1s. per Yard .... = 1 fr. 37 c. per
1 Kilometre .... = 1093 ⅝ yards.	metre.

Although the gramme is the established unit of of weight, the kilogramme is most frequently used.

MEASURES OF LENGTH.

	French	English Equiv.
Millimetre (1000th of a metre)		0.03937 in.
Centimetre (100th of a metre)		0.39371 "
Decimetre (10th of a metre)...		3.93708 "
Metre (the unit of length).....		1.09363 yds.
Decametre (10 metres).......		10.936 "
Hectometre (100 metres)		109.363 "
Kilometre (1000 metres)......		0.621 mile.

The unit is the metre, and is the ten-millionth part of a meridian arc from the pole to the equator.

MEASURES OF SOLIDITY AND WEIGHT.

French	English Equiv.
Décistère (10th of a stère) ...	3.5317 cu. ft.
Stère (cubic metre).........	35.3166 "
Milligramme (1000th of a gr.)	0.0154 grns.
Centigramme (100th of a gr.)	0.1544 "
Décigramme (10th of a grm.)	1.5440 "
Gramme (the unit of weight)	15.4323 "
Décagramme (10 grammes)..	154.3234 "
Hectogramme (100 grammes)	3.5291 oz. av.
Kilogramme (1000 grammes)	2.2057 lbs.

"ENQUIRE WITHIN."

BY THE EDITOR.

(Written on the publication of the Four Hundred and Thirtieth Thousand.)

ONLY a few short years have sped
 Since I this work of love begun ;
By thousands sought, by millions read,
 All their approving smiles I've won.
Now, while reflecting on the past,
 My day of life seems closing in,
Let me, while powers of reason last,
     "Enquire Within."

Oh, ye—who gentle are and fair—
 Who to these modest pages turn,
To raise a smile, to soothe a care,
 Or some moot point of duty learn,—
Forget not this : that whilst you live,
 Your hearts may yield to pride or sin,
Take, then, the warning here I give,—
     "Enquire Within."

Would you acquire the greatest peace—
 The sweetest joy—this world can give?
Bid hatred, pride, and envy cease,
 And learn a Christian's life to live;
Each eve, before your eyelids close,
 And slumbers of the night begin,
That your own heart may find repose,
     "Enquire Within."

INDEX

OF

ENQUIRIES.

⁎ *The Numbers in this Index refer to the* PARAGRAPHS, *not to the Pages.*